Logic of Choice
and
Economic Theory

Logic of Choice
and
Economic Theory

S. N. AFRIAT

CLARENDON PRESS · OXFORD
1987

Oxford University Press, Walton Street, Oxford OX2 6DP
Oxford New York Toronto
Delhi Bombay Calcutta Madras Karachi
Petaling Jaya Singapore Hong Kong Tokyo
Nairobi Dar es Salaam Cape Town
Melbourne Auckland

and associated companies in
Beirut Berlin Ibadan Nicosia

Oxford is a trade mark of Oxford University Press

Published in the United States
by Oxford University Press, New York

British Library Cataloguing in Publication Data
Afriat, S.N.
Logic of choice and economic theory.
1. Consumers' preferences   2. Social choice
I. Title
330   HB801
ISBN 0-19-828461-6

Library of Congress Cataloging in Publication Data
Afriat, S.N., 1925—
Logic of choice and economic theory.
Bibliography: p.
Includes index.
1. Economics. 2. Consumers' preferences.
I. Title.
HB171.5.A334 1987   338.5   85-18726
ISBN 0-19-828461-6

Set by Electronic Village Ltd, Richmond, Surrey
Printed and bound in
Great Britain by Biddles Ltd,
Guildford and Kings Lynn

Oxford University Press, Walton Street, Oxford OX2 6DP
Oxford New York Toronto
Delhi Bombay Calcutta Madras Karachi
Petaling Jaya Singapore Hong Kong Tokyo
Nairobi Dar es Salaam Cape Town
Melbourne Auckland

and associated companies in
Beirut Berlin Ibadan Nicosia

Oxford is a trade mark of Oxford University Press

Published in the United States
by Oxford University Press, New York

British Library Cataloguing in Publication Data
Afriat, S.N.
Logic of choice and economic theory.
1. Consumers' preferences 2. Social choice
I. Title
330   HB801
ISBN 0-19-828461-6

Library of Congress Cataloging in Publication Data
Afriat, S.N., 1925—
Logic of choice and economic theory.
Bibliography: p.
Includes index.
1. Economics. 2. Consumers' preferences.
I. Title.
HB171.5.A334 1987   338.5   85-18726
ISBN 0-19-828461-6

Set by Electronic Village Ltd, Richmond, Surrey
Printed and bound in
Great Britain by Biddles Ltd,
Guildford and Kings Lynn

Logic of Choice
and
Economic Theory

CLARENDON PRESS · OXFORD
1987

Preface

This book approaches various aspects of economics that have to do with choice, and the opportunity for it, such as individual and social choice, production, optimal programming, and the market. The topics belong mostly to microeconomics, but they also have other connections. The object is to state a view about choice and value and to give an account of the logical apparatus. With this there is a wish to present limited matters fairly completely and unproblematically, and where there is some issue about their nature to consider that also.

The work is in six parts, of which Parts I–IV deal with generalities about choice, individual or social, and representative economic topics. The remaining parts have more concern with straightforwardly mathematical subjects, which have an application or interpretation for economics but need not be exclusively connected there. Chapters often are fairly self-contained or belong to sequences that can be taken more or less on their own. The topics are in the main fabric of economic theory, and most students encounter them. A preamble at the start of every chapter tells what it is about; from this and possibly some further scanning, the main ideas should be easily gathered by those who might not be concerned with all details. Expository materials and reworkings of published fragments have been joined with unpublished work from past and recent years. In all, there is a view about choice and 'the optimum' in economics that is surely acceptable to some (and perhaps what they have always thought), but undoubtedly not to everyone.

Though producing the book has occupied two or three years, in another way it goes over more than twenty. I cannot therefore acknowledge all debts very easily; the ones I cite now concern this particular book, even though, perhaps like many, it rests on a debris of others that never were.

I am grateful for an Isaak Walton Killam Memorial Fellowship and for a grant from the Social Sciences and Humanities Research Council of Canada supporting the preparation of this work. An influence in the shape it has taken comes from Amartya Sen. I put aside a condensed treatise on the theory of demand and economic index numbers—done in a manner which, in puzzling over earlier works of which I am the writer, I had grief to approach as the reader. It was after discussions with Sen that I decided to drown the constricted theme in a more cheerful expanse. His generosity overflowed in this undertaking during a year spent as Visiting Fellow at All Souls, Oxford, in 1981–82. My thanks go to him and others there, and to Andrew Schuller of the Oxford

University Press who led me to write the particular book, though I think it was to have been half the length. I also thank Julio Silva, University of Ottawa, whose knowledge and judgement I have often sought and with whom I have constantly been able to discuss the entire work. Further thanks go to Nuri Jazairi of York University, who appeared only after I thought the work was done. Seasoned in index number writings (including mine) from when he was a student of Sir Roy Allen at the London School of Economics, he received a copy of the manuscript during a chance visit. To my surprise he returned many pages covered with notes and corrections, becoming a kind of providential editor. He helped the last stages greatly. For the last stage with the Press, I am greatly indebted to Sue Hughes for her editing, with perceptions quite beyond what I could offer. Before and after these debts is one to Pia-Luisa, my wife, for, beside the many consultations about words, sense, and spelling, I cannot imagine how the work might have been done without her.

As for the shortcomings, I reserve these for myself.

Contents

Part II
Use and Exchange

Part III
The Cost of Living

Part IV
Logic of Price

Part V
Optimal Programming

Part VI
General Mathematics

Introduction

Making choices is important for economics—the only thing that could be more important is having the opportunity for it. But choice is still an unsettled subject, even where the issues touched are quite basic. The offer of anything like formal theory to do with choice seems peculiar to economics, and it started early. Joseph A. Schumpeter (1954) attributes the 'economic principle', that the economic problem is *a maximum problem*, to François Quesnay (1694–1774). It permeates economics as much now as ever, and a question is whether it has overrun its proper course. Possibly it had already done that in the beginning, and the early words have had a remarkable survival.

The accumulation of attention is in good proportion to the duration, and although there has been a fascinated attention to the works of the clock, we are still not always sure of the time. A basic settlement is desirable, where possible. We have been told that 'fools rush in where angels fear to tread', and in having such a settlement there would be better chance of company with the latter. The former might make discoveries, but that is not quite what is wanted, though one could be without any and still be far from the latter. Elaborate structures have been built on precarious drifts of meaning; there might be a desert without them, but then getting used to it would be much more economical.

A cause for some general confusion is ambiguity. What is meant by a choice is ordinarily clear, but it can be less clear how, or where, or why a choice should be perceived in the first place. Then there are problems to do with terms like 'preference', 'optimum', 'efficient', and 'welfare' for an individual, a group, or an economy. Quite often it is possible to wonder whether some offered proposition is true or false, or neither, and then to wonder about the precise value of it. Different organizations and disorganizations of concepts have simultaneous use, and following ordinary usage with key words would be helpful. For example, 'generalized' preferences, which are understood to be without the usual transitivity, are very strange; once it is possible to talk about those an anchor has gone, and anything can be called anything.

A similar case is the Pareto 'optimum'. There can be proper dissatisfaction about a doctrine that has early origins but still prevails and is represented in many textbooks. A reading of the Maximum Doctrine of the physiocrats, which is meaningless when taken literally, has been translated into a misreading of Adam Smith's doctrine of the Invisible Hand, and this now in the hands of mathematical economists using set language and the like has been translated again, but not very well. In the latest version we have the Pareto Optimum.

When that is seen for what it means it is not in any ordinary sense an optimum: it is just called that, but the power it has in economic thinking is as if it *were* that. Pareto fleetingly entertained the idea as having analogy with a maximum, and it has come to have an exaggerated importance. It just filled the vacuum created by the shortage of meaning in the old doctrine.

Even if we are assured that Adam Smith did propose a maximality under government by the Invisible Hand—and it is quite possible that he did—we still should not take it seriously. It could be a quaint residue of earlier thought, and, after all, Newton's mechanics is not vitiated by the importance he gave to number magic and alchemy (perhaps the contrary now—but we can put that aside). It does not matter what views the physiocrats or others had about automatic global economic optimization under various conditions which can be spelt out carefully at length; we still should not believe in them, for we do not, and cannot possibly, know what they mean. To the physiocrats the Maximum Doctrine was not a matter requiring proof but was self-evident. There have been motions to prove it ever since, from piety about the old words mixed with ritual duty to contemporary science, but without knowing quite what it was that should be proved. Words have patterns both with and apart from their meaning—as is recognized in songs. As interesting as the matter itself is the way in which the pathology of it has been preserved intact over generations, and conditions the thinking of many economists even in the present.

Choice has such everyday familiarity that features go without mention, and when stated in arcane terms and notations take on a new appearance. Familiarity with what is said need not diminish a statement: it could be worthy to show what has always been known in some fashion. Efforts in the sphere of artificial intelligence demonstrate it, as they might also in the field of economics, just as one can think of Van Gogh's painting of a pair of old boots. But there could be justifiable reservations about mere translations into such terms and notations, and it may be asked what is served by employing them. For example, that the result of searching a heap of stones for the heaviest does not depend on the order in which they are taken has been known from time immemorial; every computer programmer sorting records knows it, and we all do. It is associated with the transitivity of the relation that stones have when they are held one in each hand and the lighter is rejected. It might be wondered whether that point, which has made a significant entry lately in various places, is a 'discovery' really worth a note, and what kind of treatment it deserves.

From the meaning of it, a voluntary act is a choice; were there no alternative to what was done, all we would have is a constraint. As it is, one can think of all those things that might have been done instead, and that makes the act a *choice* of what was done out of all those things that might have been done.

A choice creates the issue of its 'reason', if that is not known already. It can be wondered what distinction the selected possibility has among all the possibilities that separated it from the rejected ones. That could be why the choice is thought about in the first place and not passed over as a fact simply to be accepted. A cause or motive, or some system that enables the choice to be understood, is sought. Judges and juries, and detectives, are accustomed to such system considerations; so are economists, and perhaps everyone else. A chosen possibility already has one distinction just in being chosen. Having another would make a coincidence, and there ought to be a reason for wanting that. There can be reservations about an argument like 'this was chosen and it alone is red, therefore it was chosen because it is red', though there are arguments in choice theory that go quite like that.

Choice making is a most familiar part of experience. But choice systems, even though they might be in artificially chosen contexts, are not always obvious in matters of choice, or even effectively present. Instead of a formula settling everything outright from the circumstances of the choice, as is usual in theories, in reality there can be complex processes leading to choice, in the midst of which are nebulous features that defy account. Such cases are common, and typical, and getting a hold on them in a theory must be difficult. Reasoning about choice has limited scope if we are to consider every possible encounter with that idea. The general idea of choice is too broad for usefulness, anyway. To the extent that a theory of choice is possible, we must be content to deal with highly restricted ideas. In particular, we will be concerned with a narrow concept of what constitutes a choice system.

With a choice system, when all the circumstances for a choice are the same the resulting choice is the same: from the circumstances one can calculate the result. In real history, the entire circumstances within the broadest horizon are never, so far as we can know or be concerned, ever repeated precisely. That must limit the applicability of the idea of a choice system. But we can always mean a restricted horizon, bringing in only those things that are thought to have a bearing on a particular matter. Some factors of circumstance might be taken to be irrelevant, or constant. In any case, we are not dependent on a repetition of all circumstances to give a choice system meaning.

Among the circumstances for a choice is the range of choice. In many situations the range obviously does not comprise all the important circumstances. For instance, one might want to know whether or not it is raining. That is not a part of choice because one has no control over it, though it could be a significant part of circumstances. It might be crucial in choosing whether or not to take an umbrella. But for the simplest idea of a choice system the range of choice comprises all the important variable circumstances. That gives rise to the idea of a choice function, where the chosen possibility is determined as a function just of the range of possibilities.

An important part of our subject is where preference gives the model for the government of choice. With some usages choice and preference appear to be synonymous. But it is important that they not be taken so, and their confusion sustains paradoxes and myths found in current thought. Semantic devices create problems that make occasion for much discussion, and restoring meanings based on more ordinary usage results in a valuable solution from their evaporation.

Some main terms encountered in the theory of choice and of choice by preference, first are dealt with in a general way, and then their elaborations serving a variety of topics, mostly from economics, are examined. A familiar special example of a choice function is the demand function. Many principles that bear in demand theory have their more essential statement in terms of general choice functions; the peculiar characteristics when demand is dealt with then stand out. Reference to consumer demand will often be used as a means for illustration and exposition of general ideas, beside serving preparations for points to be made in that subject. At the start that will be the main reference, as is convenient and also suitable, since perhaps this is the subject in economics that first occasioned terms and ideas for a theory of choice also having bearings elsewhere.

The first three or four chapters of Part I, and especially the first, are concerned with generalities about choice, and the optimum. The second chapter deals with choice functions and preferences, and with search and elimination processes involved in making a choice. The third has to do with group choice. It is seen that, with group choice determined as a function of individual choices, democratically required neutralities inevitably lead to the ordinary voting method. Then there is an appraisal of the so-called Voting Paradox. The remainder of the chapter concerns the group preference theory originated by K. J. Arrow. In addition to an account of principles involved and certain theorems, there is criticism of the 'welfare' association of this theory, and some consideration of what it could legitimately be about in the first place. The fourth chapter is a comment on conventional consumer theory looked at from the point of view of a simple consumer who does not understand enough of partial differential equations to implement the usual Allocation Rule. The final chapter of Part I is a study of the optimal savings theory of Frank Ramsey (1928), what it represents and the arguments involved.

Parts II and III comprise six chapters about demand and utility cost and another five chapters more intensively about the cost of living problem and price indices. This is a typical area for what is understood as choice theory, because of the hypothetical basis, which has demand governed by efficiencies involving unknown utility. It produces elaborate logical exercises, and developments on the mathematical side that are quite peculiar to the subject. The approach to demand analysis on the basis of a finite collection of demand observations, instead of a demand function, serves especially well for questions in the theory of index numbers. A key feature is the equivalence of demand consistency to a Houthakker 'revealed preference' type of condition, as well as to other conditions, which include the consistency of a certain system of homogeneous linear inequalities. By taking a solution, one can immediately construct utility functions that fit the data.

Economic theory represents consumers or producers as perfectly efficient, according to various criteria. But in experience, inefficiencies of every kind abound. Models should incorporate this phenomenon, and the last chapter of Part II on 'Efficiency and Inefficiency' investigates some ways of doing that, first for consumers and then for producers. There is also a development of questions about efficiency measurement.

The cost of living problem is treated both in a general form and also with the homogeneity restriction that is inseparable from the 'price index' concept. Questions are developed both on the usual basis of demand data for just two periods, the reference periods themselves, and in an extended fashion that involves demand data from any number of periods. The relation between theory and practice with price indices invites the comment that the identification of the CPI (consumer price index) with the Laspeyres index, and along with it an invocation of theoretical properties, is spurious. It is argued that the current practice is most truly related to that of William Fleetwood (1707).

The last three chapters of Part III are an outflow from the finding of S. S. Byushgens (1925) that Irving Fisher's 'Ideal Index' is exact if demand is governed by a homogeneous quadratic utility. The neglected question about admissibility of that assumption is dealt with also where several periods are involved, in which case Fisher's 'chain test' applied to his own index becomes relevant. Dropping the homogeneity, and so abandoning price indices, we arrive at the Four-point Formula. This represents a generalization not only of Byushgens's theorem and Fisher's formula but also of A. Wald's 'New Formula' (1939). The first basis for it was the finding, in 1955, when Robin Marris drew attention to Byushgens's theorem, that demand data for four periods give an essentialy unique determination of utilities and marginal utilities associated with a general quadratic utility. Evolving this finding into the formula with a satisfactory account of complexities encountered on the way led to the other developments found here.

An introduction of the uniquely determined 'critical points' on the expansion lines that are the data for Wald's formula is the key for putting the formula into an extremely simple form, wherein its connection with Fisher's formula is completely transparent, and for seeing the formula as a corollary of Byushgens's theorem about Fisher's formula. It also opens up further considerations about the formula, such as the ranges of incomes to which it can properly apply, which is an essential matter otherwise completely obscured. Most especially, we find a theory of *marginal price indices*, where the data have the form of general expansion lines—instead of single demands, which, from homogeneity with price indices, determine rays through the origin—and where incomes that are equivalent in purchasing power have a general linear relation instead of a homogeneous one. The Paasche and Laspeyres indices have precise 'marginal' counterparts determined from marginal bundles of goods, by the same formulae that usually apply to bundles.

The Four-point Formula is not a freak but a substratum of the others, bringing out the fact that essentially four points are involved also with those, and if that is masked it is because of a special case. Thus, Wald's 'New Formula' has two lines, each determined by two points. We join a pair of points because they are associated with the same prices, so producing an expansion line when expansion loci associated with any prices are hypothetically linear. But if all four points are associated with different prices we cannot do that. In dealing with price indices, the origin is in principle a point on every expansion locus, so when as usual we seem to have just two demand points, we really have four. The remark of Hendrick Houthakker (*c*. 1960) that 'twice two is four' sealed the connection between the Four-point Formula and Wald's 'New Formula'.

Choice presupposes opportunity, and the first chapter of Part IV gives some account of that side of economic models. There follows a review of the characteristics of Leontief's input-output method. The remaining three chapters are concerned with value and price, with questions of consistency, and with general equilibrium and stability. The first of these deals with the phenomenon of the market, and starts with a discourse on the 'logic of price' and a critique of the supply and demand theory. The considerations are taken further with reference to a very simple but none the less adequate linear market model, with an appeal to theorems about distribution matrices known from the theory of Markov processes. A further treatment, without the linearity, involves the KKM lemma. Global stability for a loosely defined *tâtonnement* is demonstrated from a convergence of infinite products of distribution matrices, analogous to the familiar convergence of powers.

'Sraffa's prices' of Chapter IV.4 represent another understanding about 'price' that joins with the centuries-old discourse about 'value' having no obvious connection with market price. But on the surface are issues to do with consistency of the arithmetic involved which can be investigated straightforwardly.

The last chapter of Part IV is concerned with proper microeconomic theory of general equilibrium understood as serving questions raised by Frederic Bastiat (1801–50—'no theorist', Schumpeter said) and illuminating Adam Smith's Invisible Hand, going beyond basic theory of prices and the market. Various conceptually distinct senses of equilibrium happen to be equivalent, among these a certain maximality that might have some mathematical appeal but surely no doctrinal 'welfare' significance.

Part V contains a sequence of three chapters on optimal programming, which is the typical mathematics of economics. This follows a top-down approach, starting with a chapter introducing general ideas in economic terms with reference to the programming problem of a firm. A theorem is proved which is basic to the entire subject, and requires no special assumptions whatsoever about the programming functions. The next chapter introduces convexity conditions, and we can see exactly where they have effect, together with Slater's condition, in assuring the existence of a support to the limit function, so providing 'Lagrange multipliers', or 'shadow prices' of resources, that have part in the 'optimality conditions'. Then for the case of differentiable functions we obtain the Kuhn-Tucker conditions.

Linear programming, as such, might appear to be a special case of convex programming. But it is more substantial, and really is an embodiment of the theory of systems of linear inequalities, as is reflected in our account. The use for practical economics is great and well known, and the theoretical applications are indispensable. The chapter on linear programming initiates the subject with reference to systems of linear inequalities and natural questions about them, and all LP (linear programming) theorems are encountered simply in pursuing those. We also derive theorems about linear inequalities that have uses directly on their own. These are illustrated in many places in this book, apart from the demand theory, which makes yet another addition to the territory. The last two chapters, on Minimum Paths and Distribution Matrices, have a connection also.

The inclusion of chapters on these two subjects might seem at first unsuitable to the declared interests of this book. But the reason for it comes from the part they play in this material. Even if it is in a disguise, the mathematics of minimum paths turns up in the demand theory and then again, in a different disguise, in the theory of price indices. There might be some surprise here; but distribution matrices seem natural to economics, and there could be surprise instead at not having seen more of them. The distributions need not be of probability, but they could, for instance, be of goods in the economy to the economic agents. In that case they would be rectangular, instead of square like the matrix of transition probabilities in a Markov process. Our discussion of 'Sraffa's prices' proceeds in terms of the square distribution matrix of sector outputs to inputs and appeals to standard theorems from the theory of Markov processes. A rather different use is with the linear market theory. Another is for general equilibrium in a Cobb-Douglas world, where two rectangular distribution matrices are involved, describing endowments and wants of the traders. An interesting use is in the approach to proving global stability of a market, under a loose *tâtonnement* with variable reaction coefficients, from the convergence of infinite products of distribution matrices.

Part VI consists of two chapters on propositions, sets and relations, and a further one on fixed point and intersection theorems.

Additional notes in the preambles to many chapters give cross-references to other parts of the book, bibliographical references and descriptions of related material in other works, together with history, acknowledgements, and so forth. Several computer programs have been included which are illustrative of matters in the text. These are in BASICA, the IBM–PC version of Microsoft Standard BASIC, and should be intelligible in terms of other versions in common use.

Some rules of notation are as follows. Prices are represented by a row vector, usually p, and quantities by a column vector, x. Then they have a product $px = \Sigma_k p_k x_k$. A row vector is multiplied on the left by a scalar, and a column vector is multiplied on the right. Transposition is indicated by a prime. A matrix a has elements a_{ij}; $a_{(i}$ denotes row–i, and $a_{j)}$ is column–j. Usually i is reserved as a row index and j as a column index. The use of logical notation is described in Chapter VI.1.

For a scalar function $\phi(x)$ of a vector x the partial derivatives $\partial\phi / \partial x_i$ are elements of the vector ϕ_x, which is a row or column vector depending on x. The transpose is $(\phi_x)' = \phi_{x'}$. With x as a column vector, the gradient is usually represented as a row vector $g = \phi_{x'}$, with elements $g_j = \partial\phi / \partial x_j$. The Hessian is the matrix $h = \phi_{xx'}$ of second derivatives, with elements $h_{ij} = \partial^2\phi / \partial x_i \partial x_j$.

> One of Mr Silk's points ... is that economists go wrong when they put too much strain on their simplifying assumptions. They sure do.
> **Robert M. Solow**, on *Economics in the Real World* by **Leonard Silk**
> (*New York Times*, 30 December 1984)

> It is well known ... that the function of cavalry in battle is to add tone to what would otherwise be an unseemly brawl. The same may be said for the use of mathematics in economic theoretical controversy.
> **Axel Leijonhufvud**, *Keynesian Economics and the Economics of Keynes* (1968)

This seems a winter of discontent for economics. One hears about 'the Crisis in Economic Theory' and a loss of credibility, while the world is taken up with economic problems. Some apology may seem suitable for a book such as this, largely mathematical, that takes no notice whatsoever of events, so that one may wonder what happened in it to the Real World, while its language claims a connection with economics—undoubtedly a part of the Real World. Some offer about the service, and disservice, of mathematical work in economics may fit here.

There is an unsureness about words, wherein we do not completely know what they mean, and still we go on as if we should be understood. For many purposes they are all that can serve, and so impatience about sense is natural. Also, one does not always want to be perfectly clear when what one is offering would then be rejected. Words are tools for many tasks, and are used for effects, like weapons. To avoid bewilderment one might go to the easier part of economics where terms should be free of accidents of language, or to the mathematical parts, which are seemingly less involved in the cross-currents that muddle the use of words and might assist a devious rhetoric. Anything here could be quite interesting in a way—a possible issue is the relevance of it. There is no need to argue the usefulness of mathematics in general, since we are dominated by it; but there is some controversy about the part it has to play in economics.

Reasoning in economics is like any other reasoning, and is valuable in the same way. To the extent that it has value, the standing of economics as a science must be found in the distinctness of its ideas and what is built with them. The same capacities are required as for other sciences. With the present mathematical approach to economics, we cannot develop and test these ideas so well, while words, which are inefficient for mathematical tasks, have so many uses that they lack a precision of meaning, so that correctness is hard to judge. Leijonhufvud's remark says something like this, except that another function of cavalry is to win: were that put aside, what he says may in an unfortunate sense be correct. In any case, from the way it is offered, at least a part of economics is involved in reasoning, though of course not all, and it is in this remaining part that some genuine difficulties may lie. Points of difficulty of an entirely different sort are dealt with in this book, wherein it is possible that 'economists go wrong'. The candour of Professor Solow about 'one of Mr Silk's points' does not touch them, and the effect of it is to cover them over.

If one does not manage well in the clear situations provided in mathematical terms, it may be asked how one should fare in the quicksands of ordinary economic argument. Probably not very well, although in the general confusion one might get away with anything. Inconclusive discourses on matters that should be clear, which have gone on for so long that one might wonder at the intention, are witness. For, taking hold of mathematical types of economic question, a genuine disposition for the ideas and the appropriate mode of thought is helpful. This is not demonstrated by so many pages of calculus: even the opposite. It may be no accident that influential economists had training in mathematics, for example Edgeworth, Marshall, Keynes, Pigou, ... and the list can go on; many of these tended to put the calculus out of the way in an appendix. Mathematics gives no guarantee against failure with ideas and nonsense for economics—it might only make a better servant of the nonsense, give it 'tone' as Professor Leijonhufvud said. There are fair objections to mathematical proliferations that might seem to serve economic thinking, but really do not. Such objections are made often and quite properly, but they do not alter the issue about the nature of matters involved. In any case, in its moderate form mathematical economics has a value for providing experience of definite ideas that have sense for economics. It gives exercise in reasoning with them, as it might give preparedness for situations, whether these be immediately useful or remote theoretical matters. It also serves for dealing with practical problems, formulated as having an importance that is understood and accepted, so that a solution is desirable.

From its nature, economics is an open subject. It does not in itself provide a ready-made structured environment for the mind to operate in comfortably, as with Euclid. One has to be invented, and hence the 'micro', 'macro', etc., of professional economics. A useful structuring for such purposes, it may not hold up under scrutiny—or other testing circumstances, as now. There is a consensus of dissatisfaction with current economics, but still it goes on, for reasons that are understandable. Since the time of Alfred Marshall, economics has become a profession, though the broad matter of economics is really unsuited to make a profession: for that, it would have to be a narrower matter, in which one can appear to know what one is doing. In any case, a social order has its own economics, and so makes a somewhat narrower matter already. With pressing questions, effective answers are expected from professional economists, and if there are none it is a sort of testing time, like now, when there is continual reference to 'the Crisis in Economic Theory'. It is understandable that 'both [President Reagan and Secretary Regan] view with skepticism the advice of professional economists . . .' (*Time Magazine*, 21 January 1985, p. 17).

Keynesian macroeconomics evolved out of a similar time. It gave a fancy dress to the message that it was better to be busy than not to be busy, and the war intervened to support that. With the postwar dynamic, when there were popular books that dealt cheerfully with 'the Affluent Society', the 'Keynesian Revolution' was in high esteem, as if it had had something to do with it. Only the simple-minded were expected to think of the balanced budget, and now everyone is thinking about it (with uncertainty). We heard from Keynes about 'Madmen in authority, who hear voices in the air, . . . distilling their frenzy from some academic scribbler a few years back . . .' and can imagine that those who might stir the rubble of defunct civilizations in the future will think of him again. He was quite an artist in the primitive pre-scientific way of thought that captures forms such as hold savages in thrall. Though there should have been hesitations about it in any classroom, it took over classrooms, and entered rituals of government. In an arbitrary fashion it is in retreat now—there is the disgruntlement from finding it not to 'work' that witch doctors must feel occasionally. But still his offering elicits respect, and doing away with it while relying on what came before is called 'post-Keynesian economics'.

There should be diffidence in such opinions when they may be from a defective mathematician and poor economist. I give mine none the less. The book would be incomplete without them.

Part I

CHOICE AND THE OPTIMUM

I.1

About Choice

When a choice has to be explained, as is often the case, some comparison might be made between the chosen object and the other possibilities. 'Utility' is one term for such comparisons, usual with the consumer; for a firm it might be 'profit'; in cost-benefit analysis there is the cost and the benefit, and the cost-benefit ratio. In most cases the criterion, such as cost, is a matter of calculation from other variables whose values are known. With the consumer there is a difference, in that utility is not calculable in an ordinary way. It is a formal hypothesis, to be known only as such, in relation to whatever data are available to 'reveal' it—as with the 'revealed preference' principle of P. A. Samuelson. Of course, preferences ought to exist before being 'revealed'. They need not be present in any arbitrarily perceived choices; as said, it is a mistake to make choice and preference synonymous. This applies where the economy itself is regarded as an individual, making a choice on the basis of a utility or 'welfare' function. No one knows the function, even those (free!) individuals who are themselves supposed to be governed by it, but it is 'revealed'. It is the same also with a political election and the notion that the result has something to do with 'group preferences'. Groups do not necessarily have preferences in ordinary circumstances, and certainly not if they do not know it. The often entertained—and even ingrained—idea of economic equilibrium as an optimal choice can be subject to such reservations. There could of course be a value associated with equilibrium, and with stability, but it would be in altogether another 'space', not in one having a part in usual models.

Such matters are dealt with more in other chapters, and this one is a preamble for ideas involved. Demand analysis is a major field for choice theory, and is used for general illustration, beside preparation for subsequent material in that area. The importance of choice theory is well recognized, and some emphasis here is on its limitations.

Economic 'optimism' is exposed, at last, by a revelation of roots in the Optimism of Leibniz. I am greatly indebted to Jon Elster, University of Oslo, for discussions with him that tended towards this view, as stated in section 1.8 below, though I will not blame him for it. His works listed in the bibliography, especially *Leibniz et la formation de l'esprit capitaliste* (1975), give expansions on Leibniz in the economic perspective.

1.1 FORMING A CHOICE

Any one thing has a difference from other such things, making it what it is instead of something else, so in recognizing it there must be some allowance for what might have been there instead, and so for a variety of possibilities. Any determination makes sense only in some background of indeterminacy, and that shows a great commonness of the form made up by a set with a distinguished element. There is much concern with the form, such as accounting the—possibly unfathomable—distinction of the distinguished element. A choice has that form. The term applies especially to acts performed by some agent; it is an abstract term for action.

An act that has taken place could be regarded in some fashion as a choice. If it was done voluntarily, then also it might not have been done, since otherwise it would have been a constraint, and that brings forward some idea of all else that might have been done instead. Not being here or doing this, one might have been there or doing that. The problem of any agent is to decide what to do, and that can be represented as making a choice out of a set of possibilities by settling on one of them. What is involved in the decision could be elaborate to consider; but even the mere representation as a choice need not be straightforward. There could be ambiguity about what is perceived to have been done, and also about what is imagined might have been done instead. That is very common, but in our cases usually some fashion stands out as appropriate, and we will be concerned about ambiguity only when making a point about it.

In describing a choice, in many cases one might simply list the possibilities. In others, listing may be unsuitable and the possibilities are indicated by other means. They might be named by elements in some set that is available, or specially constructed for the purpose. With Descartes, first we had the geometrical points that had sense from physical experience. These then were made to correspond to points in a newly invented space, the Cartesian space, constructed from coordinates. In economics, a basket of goods becomes a point in a Cartesian space similar to that used in geometry, giving a means for geometrical thinking. The coordinates, instead of being distances measured along axes, are quantities of various kinds of goods.

Just with the form of description of real things, possibilities might be represented that have no counterpart in reality. For instance, a basket of goods can readily be represented which is so large that it could never be filled by all resources in the world. It is a logical but not a real possibility; the form or method of description creates such possibilities, and only some of these reflect real possibilities. Many possibilities therefore exist only in the sense that they are created with the terms of description, or the manner of picturing the possible. Facts about the world, or just thoughts, might exclude certain of those, leaving a subset of elements that are regarded as the real possibilities. Where actions are concerned, these are the ones that are feasible: possibilities that not only can be described but also can really be performed.

In economics, there is a concern with choice, as there is in many other spheres also. But economics has even been defined as the 'science of choice'. If that says anything it seems both too much and rather too little. System models of economics have hardly more or less to do with choice than many other sciences, yet no such claim is made for those. Perhaps statistics has as good a claim, or logic. After all, if one could know what is going on, making up one's mind might be seen as a process of choice. Certainly it is an important function of the mind, and logic, a part of that, can be offered as the science of Yes and No, giving account of mechanisms and organizations involved at a certain level of the 'making up' process. Some of that, the simpler part, could be described as doing mental Boolean arithmetic with tables learnt by heart. If there is a characteristic of choice in economics, it is the simple framework that could be all that suits thinking about a really intractable reality. Perhaps this is why formal choice theory comes the way it does in economics and nowhere else. The simple terms can be overlaid by formulations that are still simple, though amenable to notations that are not second nature to everyone. Also, structure is added which gives occasion for some sort of mathematical investigation, liable to become self-sustaining without concern for the original roots. Both cases are found here, in the earlier chapters.

Abstractly, a choice is defined by a set S, the opportunity set, together with one of its elements x, the result. It can be denoted $[x; S]$, and so with any use of this notation it is understood that $x \in S$.

Granting that anything might conceivably have been different (or there would have been no sense in the perception of it), and that therefore being as it is appears to be the result of a choice, even though the agent might not be identified, nothing has been accomplished except that now one is in a position to view anything as a choice. The position can be exploited liberally. Someone spends some money: and then what is bought is regarded as a choice out of all those things that might have been bought with it instead. But what about *more* money being spent, or less? There might be a choice there also. Then too, it could be spent cheerfully, or not. Is that a choice? It might well be, and possibly an unimportant one also, at least for economics. But to judge importance one should first know an objective in expressing anything in some way as a choice, or even in thinking about choice at all—that being, on its own, one of the emptiest ideas possible.

The theory of the consumer is concerned with consumer behaviour, and were it raining at the market that fact might not be regarded as part of the consumer's choice, because the consumer did not choose it. The fact that it is raining might then not seem to play a part in consumer behaviour. However, the consumer might buy an umbrella. Then the rain has possible relevance, and what else might not? To be sure of not missing something important, the entire universe would have to be included. But any theory or model must draw a line somewhere at what should be included, and in the theory of the consumer it is drawn early. The recorded act of the consumer is the purchase of a bundle of goods at certain prices. Whether it was raining is not included and so cannot be in the accounts, nor can much else with such limited data. That is just as well, if one is not on the side of the 'millions of equations controversy' where it is thought that if only there were enough equations one could know everything.

The act of the consumer is stated by a vector pair (x, p) defining a *demand*, showing the prices of commodities and the quantities demanded. For practical economic index numbers, and in the traditional theory, using only such a form of data, usually for just a pair of periods, is something like a constitutional edict. One could, unwisely for the ordinary purposes, envisage an enlarged framework where auxiliary data that might be available would be permitted, such as income, occupation, location, and other factors having impact on consumption pattern, and even whether or not it was raining.

1.2   DEMAND AS CHOICE

Given any demand (x, p), there are two standard ways in which it is regarded as a choice, though the difference between them disappears in certain contexts. The expenditure in buying x at the prices p is the cost $M = px$ of x at those prices. Then x certainly belongs to the set $C = [y: py = M]$, which is a locus of constant cost in the commodity space, or a *cost set*. Here we have a cost set associated with the demand. Since now $x \in C$, the pair $[x; C]$ does have the proper form of a choice, showing x as an element chosen out of the set C.

From the model of a market, anyone who bought x when the prices were p was also in a position to buy any bundle $y \in C$ instead, without anything else being altered. In reality, other things might be altered, possibly satisfaction on the part of the buyer, or household, or the goodwill of merchants. But such possible aspects are not represented in the available data. In that way the demand (x, p) is perceived as the choice $[x; C]$ of the demanded bundle of goods x from out of the set of all bundles that have the same cost as x at the price p.

Another set associated with the demand is the *budget set*, $B = [y: py \leq M]$, made up of all these bundles that cost no more than x at the prices. Empirical thinking leads from this set to another. If any quantities x can be bought with a certain amount of money M, then so also can any possibly lesser quantities $y \leq x$ be bought with the same amount. For their cost is $py \leq px = M$, and a fact about money is that it can be given away. Hence the difference $M - py$ can be eliminated, so that in effect any $y \leq x$ can be bought for the same cost M as x. Another way of putting this is that anything bought for a certain amount can also be bought for any greater amount. By this principle, the opportunity set C becomes enlarged to B, since opportunity for choice out of C implies that also out of B.

Here are two usual ways for representing a demand as a choice. It is observed below that, with the same limited data, it is possible to proceed differently, in a way that is just as justifiable, and even requires less justification. That is where the choice is regarded as being of (M, x) from out of the set $[(N, y); N \geq py]$.

The budget and cost sets B and C associated with given prices p and an amount of money M, being the regions of the commodity space specified by the constraints $px \leq M$ and $px = M$, remain unchanged when prices and money are multiplied by any number $t > 0$. The constraints can also be stated as $M^{-1}px \leq 1$, $M^{-1}px = 1$, and so with $u = M^{-1}p$ they are

$$ux \leq 1, \qquad ux = 1.$$

The sets B and C are specified by the constraints in this normalized form by means of the vector u, which can be called a *budget vector*. The sets could be denoted $B(u)$ and $C(u)$ to make the association with u explicit. The correspondence between budget and cost sets B and C and budget vectors u is one-one, in contrast with their relation to vectors (p, M). Hence a function $f(u)$ defined on budget vectors u can also be regarded as a function $f(B)$ defined on budget sets B. This will be exploited, later in this chapter and subsequently, when a demand function is regarded as a choice function.

An alternative notation that will have some use comes from regarding the constraints in the definitions of cost and budget sets as defining relations between commodity bundles and budget vectors. Without confusion with the other use of the letters, binary relations B, C are introduced by the definitions

$$xBu \equiv ux \leq 1, \qquad xCu \equiv ux = 1.$$

If the relation xBu holds, that is if $ux \leq 1$, the bundle x is said to be *within* the budget u. The set of all bundles within the budget u is

$$Bu = [y : yBu] = [y : ux \leq 1],$$

and this is identical with the budget set formerly denoted B, or $B(u)$, though the notation Bu fits the use of binary relations. There is no need to confuse the first considered set B in the budget space with the new set B in the Cartesian product of the commodity and budget spaces that defines a binary relation. A similar remark applies to the relation C. The statement xCu, meaning $ux = 1$, asserts that the bundle x is at the limit of or *on* the budget u. There is a symmetry or exchangeability between roles of commodity bundles and budget vectors in these definitions. This reflects a pattern of duality that has many more substantial manifestations.

The theory of demand commonly deals with a demand function $x = F(p, M)$, which determines quantities x demanded as a function of the prices p and the amount M to be spent on them. Since M is the cost of x at prices p, the function is subject to the *budget identity*

$$pF(p, M) = M. \qquad (\text{i})$$

Money is considered significant only in its ratio to prices, so that if prices are doubled, or multiplied by any factor, then nothing is altered if the money to be spent is doubled or multiplied by the same factor. In other words,

$$F(tp, tM) = F(p, M) \ (t > 0). \qquad (\text{ii})$$

Otherwise there is said to be monetary illusion, so this identity represents the *absence of monetary illusion*.

From (ii), by taking $t = 1/M$ we have

$$F(p, M) = F(M^{-1}p, 1).   \text{(ii$'$)}$$

Let f be the function derived from F by the definition $f(u) = F(u, 1)$, which, by taking $M = 1$ in (i), satisfies the identity

$$uf(u) = 1.   \text{(i$'$)}$$

Then according to (ii), F is recovered from f by the relation

$$F(p, M) = f(M^{-1}p).   \text{(ii$''$)}$$

Hence introducing the *budget vector* $u = M^{-1}p$, determined from any p and M, we have $F(p, M) = f(u)$. Functions F that satisfy (i) and (ii) and the functions f that satisfy (i$'$) are thus in a one-one correspondance. Both are called demand functions, but to distinguish them F is called a *standard demand function* and f, a *normal demand function*.

Any commodity bundle x and budget vector u such that $ux = 1$ form a pair (u, x) that defines a *normal demand*. Any given *standard demand* (x, p) has associated with it an expenditure given by $M = px$ and a budget vector

$$u = M^{-1}p.$$

Then (x, u) is a *normal demand* that is associated with the given standard demand, and defines its *normalization*. The condition for a demand (x, p), with expenditure $M = px$, to belong to a demand function F is that $x = F(p, M)$, that is $x = F(p, px)$. With $u = M^{-1}p$ as the associated budget vector, so that (x, u) is the normalized demand, this condition can be stated $x = f(u)$, where f is the normal demand function that is the normalization of F.

For an instance of *monetary illusion*, we require a case where prices are scaled by a factor t and so is the expenditure M, but where quantities demanded are altered. There is no good reason why we should not have that. Rather, to have monetary illusion in the limited framework of consumers' purchases alone would be sensible and normal. Only the prices and expenditures on consumer goods are scaled, and they are not all the prices and expenditures in the world. You would have to scale every other monetary amount to produce a genuine case of monetary illusion. A possible case is where amounts are stated in pence instead of pounds, or cents instead of dollars, and it makes a difference. With the usual terms affecting economic behaviour, that should alter nothing, and should it do so it would be a case of monetary illusion, though absent-mindedness also would be a description. The condition on a demand function described as the absence of monetary illusion can be related better to a separability condition

$$\psi(M, x) = \theta(M, \phi(x))$$

which applies to the utility of holding money and goods.

A given demand (x, p) now describes the environment in which a choice is to be perceived. Most usually, x is regarded as the chosen object, and the budget set B is the set from which it is chosen. But when a choice is to be perceived, there can be freedom about what is to be regarded as the object chosen, and as the opportunity set. That can be illustrated by the case with the demand, even though the situation in this case is narrow and the point is very general.

Everything that interests an agent can be taken to be gathered in the agent's state. Then it is the state of the agent that concerns the agent in performing an act; the act is identified with a change of state. In a market transaction, goods x are gained and money $M = px$ is lost, and everything included there could be of interest. The change of state is therefore described by the vector (x, M). The presence of the market gives opportunity to choose from the set

$$S = [\,(y, N) : N = py\,].$$

Alternatively, with the liberty of paying more for what is bought than is required by the prices, the set

$$S = [\,(y, N) : N \geq py\,]$$

can be considered instead. In any case, the choice perceived in the the the demand (x, p), with associated expenditure $M = px$, is now the choice of (x, M) out of the set S. That looks different from the first considered choice of x out of the budget set B, or out of the cost set C, and it *is* different. This second version is less restrictive, and more realistic, than the first.

Having adopted a form for the choice, now with (x, M) $(M = px)$ as the object chosen out of the set of possibilities S, one could regard the chosen object as determined by that set. That brings in the idea of a choice function. The result here is to make x a function of p, giving a demand function of the form $x = D(p)$. To justify the earlier and more common choice formulation from this requires the separability that has been mentioned, where some goods have a utility defined for them which is independent of the levels of others. But here we have recognition of an arbitrariness in the way a choice is formulated.

More elaborate formulations that have better capabilities for expressing behaviour could have value for the econometrics of consumer behaviour. But as concerns economic index-numbers, which have a social reference and call for a democratic uniformity in the treatment of individuals, there is a limitation on the individual factors that should enter into the account. In any case, the theoretical understanding of what index numbers should express forces certain neglects. It is required that bundles of goods have two distinct values, in use and in exchange. That already is an imposition, as Veblen has pointed out in his well-known remark. Value in exchange is simply money value as determined by market prices, and value in use, or utility, should be something else, which has nothing to do with prices. The distinction has sense certainly as a formal idea, but how to make more of it than that has been a problem. In Parts II and III there is an approach to dealing with the question in computational terms, based on a scheme of data and an understanding about how this should be viewed.

1.3   CHOICE FUNCTIONS

It has been recognized that the choice form means nothing in itself; everything can be construed as a choice, in limitless ways, moreover. Any significance of using the form must depend on what is built upon it. Often with a choice formulation goes the idea that the object chosen is not just constrained to belong to the opportunity set, but is also determined by it. There should be a function f which, for any choice $[x; S]$ to be considered, has S in its domain of definition and determines a value $x = f(S)$ with $x \in S$.

Such a function f can be called a *choice function*. An example of the idea is familiar from axiomatic set theory. With any set, the assumption of the existence of a function that picks an element out of every subset is called the 'axiom of choice'. Its equivalence to several other axioms that look rather different is well known, but is not important here. The function whose existence is required there is an example of a choice function as now understood. The definition to be used now is broader, in allowing the domain of the function to be not necessarily the entire set of subsets of the given set, but some particular class of subsets. The adaptation fits consumer theory, where any choice in the form usually considered is not out of an arbitrary subset of the commodity space, but out of a set that has the special form of a budget set B, or a cost set C. Also suitable is a further extension of the idea where the value of $f(S)$ is not a single element of S, but a subset of S, that is $f(S) \subset S$. To make the distinction, when that is not understood from context, one could call $[X; S]$ where $X \subset S$ a *partial choice*, and then $[x; S]$ where $x \in S$ would be a complete or *final choice*.

With this enlarged concept, a demand function can be viewed as a choice function. Many arguments about demand functions, especially those to do with revealed preference, depend only on that view and otherwise involve nothing special about demand functions. Such arguments therefore should be given as concerning choice functions, and they come to be interpreted for demand functions when those are considered as choice functions. For a demand function in the normal form $x = f(u)$ ($ux = 1$), the expression as a choice function is immediate. The budget vector u being connected with the budget set $B = [y : uy \leq 1]$, that contains x because $ux \leq 1$, the function can just as well be stated $x = f(B)$ ($x \in B$), making it a choice function with the budget sets as its domain. Anything said about choice functions can now apply to demand functions. The next chapters deal with generalities about choice functions that subsequently have that application.

Nothing is accomplished merely by expressing anything as a choice. The expression should be joined with a further intention. One idea for that comes from the notion that, if someone does something on an occasion when certain other opportunities are available, then that person will do the same thing on similar occasions when the same opportunities are available. That gives rise to the idea of a choice function, and also a use for it. Someone is offered a drink, either bourbon or scotch, and takes bourbon. The assumption is that he will do the same the next time. Wrong that may be, since it happens that this person, out of habit or some sentiment, likes to alternate between bourbon and scotch. But at least, here is an idea for making use of formulating taking a drink as a choice by making it a basis for expectations. It was the wrong formulation in this case, and one might do better next time. The occasions here are not similar, because the drink taken last time was bourbon, and so now it is going to be scotch. Two consecutive drinks should define an occasion in this case, or alternate drinks making two separate streams. In fact, this person likes rum, and when all three drinks are offered rum is always taken. However, when rum and just one of the others is offered, the other is taken since otherwise the other would be lonely in its rejection and rum does not care about that. Obviously, choice can be complicated. Anyway, so long as rum is offered we do have the drink chosen as a function of the opportunity set: $f(R, S, B) = R$, $f(R, S) = S$, $f(R, B) = B$. There is nothing really wrong with that, even though, in a presently popular terminology, to be referred to again, what we have here could be described as 'irrational'. Of course putting aside the habit of alternation between bourbon and scotch, we would have the wanted determinacy unconditionally for all opportunity sets, and a choice function defined on all subsets of drinks. Alternatively, we could have a choice function anyway by making a more elaborate definition of the choice occasions.

A significant simplification in the case considered is that a perfectly systematic behaviour is present, and moreover it is unaffected by outside factors. Instead of always choosing rum on hot days and something else on other days, the kind of day makes no difference. Also, here is a seasoned drinker of settled habits, not doing any experimenting nor are the drinks undergoing quality changes or having different labels, which could be disturbing.

A defence of the choice function is anyway unnecessary in economics. The demand function is undoubtedly a choice function, and it shows wonderful qualities for survival.

1.4 THE OPTIMUM

A choice having the form of a set with a distinguished element, there can be question about the distinction of the element, or what it has got that the other points have not. That the point has been chosen and the others have not is impressive. The other points seem to be losers. Then the point is optimal, in a sense—a sense that makes the best of all possible worlds of Dr Pangloss, or the optimum of general equilibrium, or the paradox of the Voting Paradox, or the revealed preference of the bundle of goods bought over all those that might have been bought instead with the same money. An impression from these cases is of overflowing need for simple purpose, and that the feeling for order does not accept limits; the limits do, however, leave space for such remarks.

Optimal choice has a great part in economics and a definiteness about the sense of the term therefore is important. Here it is taken that optimal means best, for some specific purpose and by a criterion derived from that. It is supposed that there can be no reservations about that and that adherence to common usage should prevent any different meaning being given to the term, even in some special application. Also, where a choice is to be made 'best' means chosen, because weighing alternatives as better or worse is done only in order to make a choice between them. There cannot be a serious objection here, either. It is assumed that there is a way of comparing alternatives, which exists separately or in advance of the matter of making a choice, and then comes to bear in the choice. Consider, for instance, wanting a heavy stone to serve as an anchor, the heavier the better, and looking around for the best, making comparisons. The stones had weight before that need arose and regardless of it, and certainly before the optimal stone was found. A disturbing contrast is in a number of 'optimality' cases of economic teaching, which will be dealt with further. An adjustment must be made somewhere, and here what is judged to be common usage will be adhered to. There might be an error in the judgement, but at least the locus of the error should be clear.

Acting so as to achieve the maximum of something is often offered as the definition of rationality. There can be questions about that. First, it can be asked what is being said. Does it matter what it is that is being made a maximum? If not, then the function that is zero everywhere, and so a maximum everywhere, would serve well. If a strict maximum is wanted, so as to have a full explanation of the uniquely chosen object, then a function that is one somewhere and zero everywhere else will make anywhere that is wanted a strict maximum, and optimal. Obviously such considerations cannot be in the meaning, but still there is no clear guidance in knowing what is wanted.

Take the example of the drinker referred to earlier. We have a solid case of rationality there, certainly according to the maximization model and perhaps by any criterion. Yet the behaviour is a bit unusual, and you may not be able to discover the model without thorough observation and suitable invention. Is rationality, then, just a matter of accidental appearances? One might think from this case that it must be, and also that appearances are a relative matter. Fortunately, the issue about maximality and rationality is without consequences other that giving an elevated tone to a trite and misplaced matter by the verbal linkage with problems that occupy philosophers, as if a clean breakthrough had been made there.

Even putting aside all the problems associated with choice and preference at the individual level, the transfer of the model for an individual to an arbitrary collection of individuals, as found in welfare economics, requires a pause. Such a transfer expresses something like the *volonté générale* of the eighteenth century. That was associated with a collection of individuals being so settled together in some way as to make what amounts to a unified organism representing an individual of a new order, with a will encompassing the individual wills. Now we have the same idea, but it is for an arbitrary collection, an abstract set, since nothing is spelt out about the members of that set, or their relationship to each other, that produces the wonderful result. Modern theories claim to be explicit and to work with models in which everything that is used is always said in advance, if necessary by means of unambiguously stated axioms assisted by a free use of mathematical notations. They never pretended to do that in the rational eighteenth century; with a modern dress we have been taken back earlier.

1.5 OPTIMAL CHOICE FUNCTIONS

Suppose a choice, say $[x; S]$, where S is the opportunity set and $x \in S$ is the chosen object, has been formulated from some observation in order to make a basis for expectation. When the opportunity set S occurs again, so should the element x. The relation of element x to the entire set S is involved, and the occurrence of exactly S is needed for the application. That might suit the illustration about the choice of drinks in the last section. But in other cases, exactly the set S showing up again has small likelihood. That is so with an observed demand (x, p) put in the form of a choice with a budget vector u specifying the opportunity set. One would never expect exactly the budget u to occur again. Continuity in this case might play some part, and with approximately u one might expect to get approximately x. With several demand observations as data, econometricians go further by estimating parameters with some model of a demand function that might then be used for purposes of prediction. However, the immediate concern now is with a bare logic that is not dependent on continuity or other additional structure.

With the arbitrariness about the formulation of choices that has been recognized, observation does not by itself produce an unambiguous choice, but some choice is formulated out of it. The intention is to pick out a stable element that, though found with just one observed occasion, is judged to persist from occasion to occasion and so gives a basis for expectations in others. The rigidity in taking x in relation to exactly the set S leaves small likelihood for usefulness, at least where there is an absence of any further framework in which a usefulness can be developed, as in the demand econometrics illustration. A related but different procedure has greater flexibility and enlarges the opportunity for application if its validity can be granted. But it is more demanding, and its validity correspondingly limited, and in that way the scope is narrower. The procedure consists in judging stability to reside not in the one element provided by the relation of x to S, but in the many elements provided by the relation of x to each one of the elements of S. The stability of the relation (x, S) of x to S, which gives rise to the idea of a choice function, means that, whenever S is the opportunity set the element x will be chosen. The stability of the set of relations $[(x, y): y \epsilon S]$, from which derives also a stability for the relation of x to S, means that, whenever x and any $y \epsilon S$ are together in an opportunity set, y will never be chosen. Consequently if S is again the opportunity set, then x would be chosen.

This is a way of arriving at the special model of choice behaviour where the chosen object from among any that are available is determined by an order, the preference relation. The opportunity sets may vary, but the preferences determining choices in them are, it is hoped, permanent or have some degree of stability. It is the model for an *optimal choice function*, in which the element chosen out of any set is, among the others in it, the one which is top in an order. The function derives from the order; also, subject to the consistency with the model required for it to exist, the order is derivable, or 'revealed', by the function. How to know whether a given demand function, regarded as a choice function, happens to be an optimal choice function is a question that has had much attention in demand theory. Other characterizations of the model shown in the next chapter are by consistency of elimination processes, and invariance in respect to search paths, making the result of search a single-valued function of the opportunity set.

1.6 REVEALED CHOICE AND PREFERENCE

An assertion that something is optimal, though it could be a recommendation, really means nothing without knowing in what respect it is optimal, and perhaps also for whom. There can be disappointments in some instances when all that is found out precisely. In the case of the stones, S is the collection of stones and x is the heaviest, so x is optimal by the criterion of weight, needed for an effective anchor. That is a simple case. The drinker earlier in this chapter is not at first appearances so straightforward. With bourbon chosen between rum and bourbon, and rum between rum, bourbon and scotch, some might consider the drinker already drunk, and 'irrational'. Revealed preferences contradict each other; also the Principle of Independence of Irrelevant Alternatives is contradicted—a bad case. It happens that we know that the drinker is not only settled in habits and quite systematic, but considerate about the feelings of drinks, and how should a revealed preference analyst know that?

Suppose a demand (x, p) is observed, giving quantities x demanded at prices p. This is supposed to show the choice $[x; Bu]$ of x out of the budget set

$$Bu = [y: yBu] = [y: uy \leq 1] = [y: py \leq px],$$

with $u = (px)^{-1} p$ being the budget vector. By the Principle of Revealed Preference, this reveals the preference for x over all other bundles of goods in the budget set, or over all those that cost no more than x at the prices p. With those preferences x is optimal in the set. In fact, *every choice is optimal by the criterion of its own revealed preferences.*

Taken at face value, that is not satisfactory. It is possible to imagine a consumer, in this case rather a non-consumer, who really prefers nothing and goes to the market and buys a few things for no good reason, possibly just to help keep money in circulation. Nothing having been said about not dealing with such a person, the possibility must be allowed. Without some qualification, the principle is certainly wrong. This consumer is so uninterested in goods that he has never even examined them, let alone had any preferences, and a method of revealing preferences that do not exist must be improper. No doubt that is not what should be meant by 'revealed preference'. But the principle is used that way sometimes, within and outside demand analysis. An implicit use of it makes the paradox in the Voting Paradox.

The principle was formulated by P. A. Samuelson for a special use in demand analysis. Two steps can be distinguished in that use, even though they were merged into one. The first is the expression of a demand as a choice, and, as one of the rocks on which to build, it might be called the Revealed Choice Principle. That might be fitting, though again it might not, since it is a device belonging to the demand analysis context without application elsewhere. It has none of the—sometimes unfortunate—universality of the other. The second step applies to the choice and has nothing to do with demand, even though in this case the choice happens to derive from the demand. It is suitable to regard the second step alone as representing the Revealed Preference Principle. But that step produced no significant result on its own, and it is the particular combination initiated by Samuelson in the context of demand analysis that, together with Houthakker, produced the well-known development. Nevertheless, it helps logically and technically to separate these steps.

With a choice $[x; S]$, formed by any set S and an element $x \epsilon S$, the element x is chosen and all other elements $y \epsilon S$ are not. The revealed preference principle applies to any choice, and associates the choice $[x; S]$ with the relation

$$Q = [(x, y): y \epsilon S, y \neq x],$$

that the chosen element has to all the unchosen elements. This is the revealed preference relation belonging to the choice. The ordered couples (x, y) that are elements of it are the revealed preferences of the choice. Certainly Q is a preference system that would make x optimal in S. That is true just from the manner of construction of Q from the choice $[x; S]$.

Though the terminology and the universal applicability suggest otherwise, there need be no involvement in the belief that wherever there is choice there must be preferences. Rather, the principle has use where there is a hypothesis of optimal choice, or choice governed by preferences. It gives basis for a test of the admissability of that hypothesis when it is applied to many choices. In the case of admissability, it enables a construction to be made for the preferences that must, and more broadly could, prevail under that hypothesis. All this is in evidence with the original formulation of Samuelson, and of Houthakker, who added a further component, associated with a preference system being by definition transitive. They were dealing with a single-valued demand function, and so strict preferences which exclude their opposites are required to give a complete explanation of all the unique choices out of the budget sets. We follow that pattern here, so optimal means uniquely optimal, though in Parts II and III there is a departure from it. Also, a demand function is a special infinite collection of demands. Here we consider only two demands, and elsewhere a finite collection, or a completely arbitrary collection.

With two demands (x, p), (y, q), the budget vectors are

$$u = (px)^{-1}p, \quad v = (qy)^{-1}q$$

and the associated choices are $(x; Bu)$, $(y; Bv)$. Under the hypothesis that these are optimal choices, in regard to the same preference system R, the revealed preference of both must belong to R, that is $Q \subset R$. But the preference system R, understood in the strict or exclusive sense of preference, cannot properly contain opposite preferences. Then, because $Q \subset R$, under the hypothesis we cannot have both x revealed preferred to y and y revealed preferred to x. For x to be revealed preferred to y in the one choice we would have $(y \in Bu, y \neq x)$, that is $(py \leq px, y \neq x)$. Then, having that, we cannot also have y revealed preferred to x in the other choice, that is, not $(qx \leq qy, x \neq y)$. Hence we have the condition

$$(py \leq px, y \neq x) \Rightarrow \text{not } (qx \leq qy, x \neq y).$$

But the right is equivalent to $(qx > qy$ or $x = y)$, so, with $y \neq x$ on the left denying $x = y$ now on the right, the condition is equivalent to

$$(py \leq px, y \neq x) \Rightarrow qx > qy,$$

which is exactly the Revealed Preference Axiom as stated by Samuelson. A more symmetrical way of putting it is

$$(py \leq px \text{ and } qx \leq qy) \Rightarrow x = y.$$

Should the condition be violated, that is, should we have

$$py \leq px \text{ and } qx \leq qy \text{ and } x \neq y,$$

then it would be impossible to entertain the hypothesis that both choices are optimal choices in the same preference system.

There is no issue about transitivity of preferences and the 'contradiction of transitivity'. Preferences in the same system are transitive by definition, so if any belong to a system hypothetically, then so do the preferences in their transitive closure. When more than two demands comprise the given data, then, by taking the transitive closure of all revealed preferences and excluding the possibility of contradictions among these, further conditions are derived, as were obtained by Houthakker. If any kind of preference order will do, the conditions so derived are also sufficient for a completely arbitrary collection of demands. That is a completely elementary proposition. The struggle about the Samuelson-Houthakker problem concerning a demand function, involving limiting processes, differential equations, a Lipschitz condition, and so forth, is connected with wanting a numerical utility function. Similar developments especially associated with a finite set of demands are described in Parts II and III.

Returning to a pair, even with a case of violation of the consistency conditions, and with determination to uphold that choices are always 'optimal', it might be argued that both the choices in the example are optimal but with different preference systems. The choices were made in different moments of time, and preferences might have changed in the meanwhile. It is impossible to argue with that one way or the other. The belief can always be entertained but it has no consequences. That does not preclude the possibility of a development that might make the idea useful. Such a development would give some formulation about how preferences are changing. But so far we do not have that kind of development, even though forces whose effect is to change preferences are recognized.

1.7 DINNERS AND BATTLES

Production and consumption are cardinal terms in economics, and consumption has a primacy since supposedly it is the purpose of production. The importance accorded it supports the view that consumption should have a theory. But what type of theory can there be? An economic event, perhaps in this case a dinner, is still an event of history, like a battle. Then reports might be given in much the same way with dinners as with battles, by declarations under the usual classroom headings of cause, course, and results.

But there is a difference between dinners and battles that is significant, especially for econometricians. The former occur with a regularity that is accepted as normal, and to assume they do have that characteristic could be good for an econometric model; while battles rather are unique events happening less predictably. Both have quantitative aspects, and those dedicated to 'cliometrics'—the term, at least, was invented in the Economics Department at Purdue University—can exploit them in both cases. But the difference of character marked by the regularity of consumption and the fitfulness of other historical events has been made much of in economics. The Newtonian influence is present, and with it a belief that some of the usefulness of dealing with mechanisms in physics can extend to economics. The consumer had to be represented as an automaton. More than that, extremality principles, (where something had to be either a maximum or a minimum), which are nice in physics, have become something else in economics. No one would offer, as an understanding of Fermat's principle in optics, the view that the objective of a light ray is to travel the shortest path, as if it contemplated all paths and intelligently picked the shortest because that happened to be what was wanted. The consumer, however, is pictured in quite that way. Faced with all possible bundles of goods that might be bought with a given amount of money, the consumer spends it on buying the 'best'. What is better or worse, and hence what is best, is taken to be settled not on a commonly known basis that can be easily referred to, but by obscure private criteria of the consumer. The criteria are unknown and hypothetical. The entire framework has little or no meaning to actual consumers, those living in time and wandering around a market taking goods off the shelves. When interpreted in time and the changes that go with time, whatever content might be imagined for the theory becomes still less secure.

Fermat's principle has no such obscurity, and we know a content. Any path can be measured, and the path taken by a ray between two points is shorter than any other. The second means nothing without the first and is a proper addition to it. Measuring distances is known about from other connections; there is nothing strange about it and no occasion here for a further examination. The principle can be tested with experience, and its verification gives confidence that it is a safe assumption on which to base considerations about light rays. Anyway, it can be deduced from already established beliefs, such as how they reflect and refract, or Huygens's principle about wave fronts. Unlike Fermat's, these other principles have no explicit dealing with an extremality, but —as with Newton who did not either but had derivatives like Lagrange and Hamilton who did—they do have an implicit one, which then appears to give a nice way of restating how rays behave.

With consumer theory the situation is different. The theory is not deducible from any other that is commonly known and seriously regarded, nor is it based on observation: rather, it is produced out of a hat. The hat is respectable, and perhaps smart, when one thinks of the authorities associated with it, and the product is widely used in economics. The conjuring act is entertaining and does make sense to a great number of economists. The sense belongs to contexts in economic thinking itself and is alien to counterparts in physical science that are based on experiment, even though some affinity there seems to be understood. It is possible to imagine, in the terms ordinarily used for economic description, that consumers are such stable and precise optimal programming automata. Then the tools of economics reasoning ought to be able to deal with the case. They can have a practice on it, even though ordinary experience might be inexpressible by means of it. Any consumer encountered in the supermarket would support that, and even be surprised at the manner of representation.

Physical measurement is an old and common matter that for most purposes can be taken for granted. But the measurement issue with consumer theory is uncommon and relatively new, and it continues to receive attention. If that attention is warranted, it is not from validity of the theory as a statistically useful representation of behaviour. Rather, it is because questions coming unavoidably from the social context and ordinary economic life can be given an intelligibility, not found otherwise, by means of the theory. Giving cost of living questions a sense and an equitable answer based on that sense has been accomplished, at least in principle, by means of the consumer theory. That does not signify the theory is 'true' in an ordinary or typically scientific sense.

1.8 THE MAXIMUM DOCTRINE

Walk ever on the path of truth—with a sneer.

Voltaire to d'Alembert

I have tried to understand what it is that Adam Smith's 'invisible hand' is supposed to be maximizing.

Paul Samuelson, *Maximum Principles in Analytical Economics* (1971)

The pursuit of the optimum, the sorting through of possibilities for some purpose to find the best, is understandable and commonplace. But along with it are doctrines about an 'optimum' with a global reference produced without any intervention from ourselves. It is taught that a General Economic Optimum is associated with Perfect Competition. In another offering—with differences, though they appear not to matter—the Optimum belongs to General Economic Equilibrium, or to a 'competitive equilibrium', though in this case the 'competitive' seems to do no work and to be simply tacked onto the 'equilibrium', keeping up appearances, echoing the old doctrine where the competition is spelt out carefully at length. These matters are not in themselves understandable, but how such thinking ever came to be might still be found out. That would be useful, also because beside these classic cases there is an overflow into choice theory generally.

A promising clue is found in historic simultaneity, and other coincidences, with the 'Optimism' of Leibniz. That was ridiculed by Voltaire, and is now without influence as such. But it seems to have found a niche in economics, where it has been able to survive with better safety from derision. Leibniz, in his *Théodicée* (1710), propounded the doctrine that the actual world is the 'best of all possible worlds', chosen by the Creator out of all the possible worlds which were present in his thoughts by the criterion of being that in which the most good could be obtained at the cost of the least evil. This is the doctrine known as Optimism which in its time had a great deal of attention, and is famous still. Voltaire's *Candide, ou l'Optimisme* (1759), with the well-known character of Dr Pangloss, was 'written to refute the system of optimism, which it has done with brilliant success'. All this and further information is in the Oxford English Dictionary. Leibniz uses 'optimum' as a technical term on the model of maximum, and it first came into a dictionary in 1752. We are told:

The optimism of Leibniz was based on the following trilemma:—If this world be not the best possible, God must either, 1. not have known how to make a better, 2. not have been able, 3. not have chosen. The first proposition contradicts his omniscience, the second his omnipotence, the third his benevolence.

The arguments about the economy are not quite like that. Instead, there is a page of calculus, promising infinitesimal precision. It matters not about what; the results are the same, and here is a parallel to the Maximum Doctrine which came into economics with François Quesnay and the physiocrats and flourishes still. It is impressive to find Quesnay's Economic Principle, 'greatest satisfaction to be attained at the cost of the least labour-pain', perfectly represented in Leibniz's doctrine where it concerns the Creator's choice criterion. The senseless double optimization, found again with the 'greatest happiness of the greatest number' formula, is avoided in the Pareto Optimum. This is not an optimum in the sense intended by Leibniz (even though he abused it), which continues to the present as the understood proper usage. But calling it that gives respectful continuity with the old tradition. For the good and evil of the world in Pareto Optimism, there would be the greatest good attainable with the given evil, and the least evil for the good. Begging the main question by a Cost-Benefit Analysis ritual, suitable to mortals, who have to get on with the job, but contrary to the law of Heaven, Creation would have been delayed by the need to make a choice between points in the good-evil possibility set, as we now say. Leibniz did not suggest a criterion for that. Were there a marginal price to resolve the matter, with the return of good for evil diminishing to a point of equilibrium, the economic analysis of creation could have gone further with a use of the new Calculus. There could also have been discourse about the price, the author of it, and why it was not better, or worse.

By another report, a virus landed on Earth in a meteor and life that we know emerged from the effort to create a hospitable environment. The important question then is whether our proper duty is being performed optimally. Neglect of the Virus Welfare Function only shows the ignorance that prevails about a fundamental matter.

Rather on the side of Pessimism, a worry brought to economists recently, with a formidable display of erudition in scientific formulae, is Entropy. From Steam Engines, it went into Poetry—and now Economics. It is excellent for poetry, where there is no need for Boltzmann's equation. Now it comes bolstered with all possible equations, with a disturbing message: the entropy of the universe is increasing, everything is going downhill, bound to fall apart, final degradation is inevitable, and one is ignorant not to know it. This seems to be the Entropy Law, by an innovation of terminology. It confirms the worst suspicions of ecologists about reality, and gives cheer that truth is revealed at last to properly intimidated economists. There has been a stunned silence in the economics profession proper, but a few words on the subject by Harold Morowitz, a molecular biochemist of Yale University, serve well as a complete comment (*Discover*, January 1981, 83–5).

The 'happiness' formula is known mostly now as a Marxist slogan. But it has an early origin, as does the model for its particular nonsense which came from Leibniz, entered economics with Quesnay, and was accidentally given a new, even though more subdued, life by Pareto, which it still has. J. S. G. Simmons provided the following about the 'happiness' formula. P. P. Wiener (1973) attributes it to Francis Hutcheson (1694–1746), the teacher of Adam Smith; Its classic attribution is to the utilitarians, and Marxists must have borrowed it from them. According to I. Philips (1983),

John Bowring says in his *Deontology* [1834, p. 100] that Jeremy Bentham recalled how on a visit to Oxford in 1768 he had first come across the phrase 'the greatest happiness of the greatest number', in Joseph Priestley's *Essay on the first principles of Government*, published in that year, 1768. 'It was from that pamphlet [Bentham said] ... that I drew the phrase, the words and import of which have been so widely diffused over the civilized world. At the sight of it, I cried out, as it were in an inward ecstasy like Archimedes on the discovery of the fundamental principle of hydrostatics Ευρηχα.

Further to the matter of numbers:

There was a time when numberless races of men wandered the earth . . . Seeing this Zeus took pity and resolved in the wisdom of his heart to relieve the allnourishing earth of men, stirring up the great quarrel of the Trojan War in order to lighten the burden by death. The heros perished in Troy and Zeus' plan succeeded.

> from *The Cypria* (attributed to Stasinos, *c.* seventh to fifth century BC),
> translated by Christopher Ligota

Edgeworth's pleasure machine assumption bore wonderful intellectual fruit . . . it could be shown—with all the irrefutability of the differential calculus—that in a world of perfect competition each pleasure machine would achieve the highest amount of pleasure that could be meted out by society.
Robert Heilbronner, *The Worldly Philosophers* (5th edition), p. 172

Enjoyment of the wonderful fruit should, in this case, be spoilt by a suspicion of worms. What is all the irrefutability of the differential calculus? Is it like irresistible authority of the Chain Rule? Or final truth in the Infinitesimal, unphased by digital diversions? Or the incomprehension, and boredom, of a mass of readers who give a passing glance at the exhibition of machinery and then get on with the text? We should do that first—the outer skin of this fruit is not without blemishes. We are faced once more with the Leibnizian nonsense, with a trip into n dimensions.

That ought to be a relief, since now there should really be no need to go back to the skipped-over calculus, after all. However, belief that there is a complete relief is feeble optimism, a dream of rationality. The particular calculus turns up in countless textbooks — at least, we know now where it started.

Processes of Choice

Market demand has provided a discussion of some aspects of choice, and the demand function is one example of a choice function; also, there was the drinker whose ways received comment, and the search for a stone to serve as an anchor. These cases are illustrative, and other types of situation can be added. Usually a choice does not happen in one stroke but is the result of a process. There might be many ways a process can be realized, and in some cases one would expect the outcome to be independent of the particular way, and in others to be affected by it. The example of the anchor stones illustrates a familiar process: the best stone found so far is in one hand, and is compared with others, which are eliminated in turn until a better one is found to replace it, and so forth to the point where there are no more stones to test. A feature of this example is that, given any heap of stones, the resulting choice (assuming for simplicity that their weights are all different) is independent of the order in which they are taken, or the search path followed. The outcome is stable despite arbitrary variations. Characteristics of such cases will be seen, and also of contrasting ones.

With the path or similar invariance, a choice function is already effectively defined, together with a process for computing its values. For a choice function, as such, a particular process for arriving at the chosen element in any set need not be given in an explicit form. Though there might be some such process in the actual definition of the function, the interest here is not in any possible computational process, but in models that correspond in some way to experience, like the one with the stones already described. For a parallel, the *tâtonnement* of Walras can be regarded as a computational algorithm for equilibrium prices, but it is one carried out by the economy itself, through the automatic mechanism provided by the law of supply and demand. Herbert Scarf (1973) has another algorithm, but the economy is without a built-in mechanism for carrying it out, so Walras's process has a significance not shared by Professor Scarf's.

In the theory of the consumer there is a choice model, and a choice function results from it, namely the demand function. But realism, were that intended, would also require a model for the actual process of arriving at the choice, and we have been without one. There should be one to give better sense to the model provided. The consumer is pictured as an optimal programmer, and when considering the ordinarily familiar consumer one would like to know how the programming is done. The Budget Allocation Rule does not help because the question then is how the consumer would go about implementing it—surely not from a knowledge of partial differential equations and a trip to the computing centre. If there is a gap that should give concern it could be filled by the Purchase Priority Rule of Chapter I.4, by which every next expenditure is concentrated on the most urgent items, or those giving the greatest return in utility. That is rather like what consumers do anyway, and might be supposed to do in the way of a model.

With many, perhaps most, cases of experience in which the mechanisms involved are not already on the surface, as with institutions such as the voting process, they are inaccessibly buried. The drinker already considered could appear to others as a hopeless case. He might be found unpredictable or, with some progress made in getting to know him, to have unaccountable habits. There is not much promise of illumination from theory there. The drinker's concern for the feelings of drinks might never be discovered. Any suggestion that drinks do not have feelings is of course completely immaterial.

There are several candidates for a political office and an election process from which one candidate emerges as the winner. The electors submit their individual choices and the group choice emerges from that. It is worth noting that both the inputs and the outputs in the voting process are choices, and not preferences. This is a type of situation quite different from the anchor stones, where preferences do govern. The difference is important, and to overlook it leads to thinking about such things as group preferences and the social welfare function. The way the election is constituted and organized can affect the outcome, so an unambiguous choice function need not be available, except possibly where the constitutional arrangements leave no ambiguity about the process, and even then one should not see group preferences just because there is a group choice. Such characteristics of group choice procedures are inevitable, and are not the downfall of the democratic process. Alternatively, with sports in which there is a tournament to decide the champion, these take different forms, with 'rounds', or a 'ladder' whereby a contestant challenges the one above, or any place above, and so forth. Comparisons between these, the anchor stone search, the election process and such cases are interesting for their similarities and contrasts.

A case of choice out of a set of elements is a *binary choice*, between a pair. This chapter is especially concerned with choice on the basis of binary choice, choice functions, preference and revealed preference. The more elaborate applications are in demand analysis. The next chapter deals with elections and questions related to democratic choice.

The paper of K. J. Arrow (1959) on 'Rational choice functions and orderings' is an early source for abstract choice discussion of the type shown in this chapter, with elaborations such as are found in Afriat (1956c, 1960a, b, d and 1967c). The last contains the point about path invariance, pursued also by Charles Plott (1973).

2.1 SEARCH AND ELIMINATION

Consider a choice function f with domain D, so that for any set S which is an element of D the value $x = f(S)$ is determined as an element of S. A choice function referred to in this way provides no picture of how the element x is arrived at from the set S. It shows only one step from S to x, instead of a process where there is a series of steps starting at S and coming to a halt at some point yielding the result x. The process need not be fully fixed but can have haphazard elements developing as it goes along. Still there can be a unique outcome, the value of the choice function. Such a process could be masked in the statement that x is determined as a function of S.

In many choice situations, though an element is to be chosen out of a set, all that happens at one time is a choice between a pair of alternatives. An example is in finding the heaviest stone in a heap with one pair of hands, so that only two stones can be held and weighed at a time, one being retained and the other rejected; another is in a sport where contestants oppose each other in pairs. These are models in which binary choice, or choice between two possibilities, is made the basis for choice out of any larger sets. A further phenomenon is where winners in choice out of subsets are retained and losers are eliminated. It should be known if the way that is done can influence the final result.

Suppose the domain D of f is the set of all subsets of a finite set, so any element S of D is a finite set. A search path p describes the elements of S in some order, say $p = (x_0, \ldots, x_k)$, so that $S = [x_0, \ldots, x_k]$. The choice function determines an element $f(S) \in S$ in any set S, and applied to any pair of possibilities it determines an element $f(x_r, x_s) \in [x_r, x_s]$. A choice function is the same as a symmetric function of the elements in a set, since it is a function of the set. A search process, with the given path, consists in formation of a search sequence $y_0, \ldots, y_k$ where

$$y_0 = x_0, y_m = f(y_{m-1}, x_m) \ (m = 1, \ldots, k),$$

and

$$F(x_0, \ldots, x_k) = y_k.$$

Thus, starting with x_0 and proceeding along the path, at any stage there is a current survivor contesting with the next element for survival to the next stage, and so forth until the path is fully described and the search terminated, the final survivor y_k being the result. The search function F is defined by the dependence of the result of search on the search path, so it is given as stated. Unlike f, the function F is not necessarily symmetric, though it could be. The definition can be restated

$$F(x_0, x_1, x_2, \ldots, x_k) = f \ldots f(f(x_0, x_1), x_2), \ldots, x_k). \tag{i}$$

It appears from here that

$$F(x_0, \ldots, x_r, \ldots, x_k) = F(F(x_0, \ldots, x_r), \ldots, x_k), \qquad \text{(ii)}$$

which shows the search as having a progressive nature where the result of an initial stage in the search becomes the starting point for a similar further stage.

A particular question about the choice function f is whether its choice in any set coincides with the result of search along whatever path, that is whether

$$F(x_0, \ldots, x_k) = f(x_0, \ldots, x_k) \qquad \text{(iii)}$$

(search consistency of f, implying symmetry of F).

This is the *search consistency* condition on a choice function. Since f is a function of a set and so a symmetric function of the elements, this condition requires at least that F be symmetric, that is, independent of the path, or unchanged when the elements are permuted. Because the search function F derives from only the binary choice part of the choice function f, the search consistency condition shows the choice function as *reconstructable from its binary part*.

Of interest about any choice processes is whether they have this property or anything similar. While the property is clearly taken for granted in the search for a heavy stone, it cannot be taken for granted in political elections, or in some sport contests; and the drinker of the last chapter, though known to be rational, defeats it completely. Here is no irrationality but a reflection on differences that exist between different contexts of choice.

From (ii), under the consistency (iii), we have

$$f(x_0, \ldots, x_r, \ldots, x_k) = f(f(x_0, \ldots, x_r), \ldots, x_k).$$

For a restatement,

$$f(R \cup S) = f(f(R) \cup S) \qquad \text{(iv)}$$

(elimination consistency of f).

In other words, the choice in any set is the same as the choice in the set obtained from it by eliminating the unchosen elements in any subset. Repeated application of this *elimination consistency* condition gives a return to the search consistency condition from which it was derived, so these two conditions are equivalent. Thus with

$$S = S_0 \cup S_1 \cup S_2 \cup \ldots \cup S_k,$$

we have

$$f(S) = f(\ldots f(f(S_0 \cup S_1) \cup S_2) \cup \ldots \cup S_k). \qquad \text{(v)}$$

In particular, the subsets could be single elements, or singletons, in which case (i) and (v) give (ii).

Two applications of (iv) give

$$f(R \cup S) = f(f(R), f(S)), \qquad \text{(vi)}$$

which might apply to a tournament where the final match is between the winners from two divisions. More generally, there can be a series of rounds between pairs, providing a 'tree' of such matches rooted in the final match, as happens in tennis.

Another form for the elimination consistency condition is given by

$$x = f(S), \; R \subset S, \; x \in R \; \Rightarrow \; x = f(R) \qquad \text{(vii)}$$

$$\text{(contraction consistency)}.$$

That is, if the choice opportunity set is contracted to a subset that retains the original chosen element, then the choice out of the new set is unchanged from the original. Arrow (1959) draws attention to this condition. Another statement is that choice in a set is unaffected by rejection of any rejected elements. For with $y = f(R)$, $z = f(S - R)$, so it is to be shown that $y = x$, we have, by (vi),

$$x = f(S) = f(f(R), f(S - R)) = f(y, z)$$

so $x = y$ or $x = z$. But $x = z$ is impossible, because $S - R$ does not contain x. Conversely, from (vii) we have (iv).

2.2 BINARY CHOICE

It has been seen that binary choice alone can make a basis for choice in larger sets. For dealing with binary choice a particular notation is suitable. Let U be the set of elements between which choices are made, the universe of choice. Let f be a choice function in U, now considered only as a binary choice function, capable of making a choice between any two elements. For any elements x, y of U we have

$$f(x, y) = x \qquad \text{or} \qquad f(x, y) = y. \qquad \text{(i)}$$

A binary relation $P \subset U \times U$, associated with f and stating the relation of the chosen to the unchosen, is defined by

$$xPy \equiv f(x, y) = x. \qquad \text{(ii)}$$

From this definition, with (i), P automatically has the properties

$$xPy \text{ or } yPx \qquad \text{(completeness)}$$
$$xPy, \quad yPx \Rightarrow x = y \qquad \text{(antisymmetry)}. \qquad \text{(iii)}$$

In other words, the relation is complete, holding one way or the other between any pair of elements, and antisymmetric, not holding both ways unless the elements are equal. Reflexivity xPx is implied by completeness. By definition,

$$z = f(x, y) \Leftrightarrow zPx \text{ and } zPy \text{ and } (z = x \text{ or } z = y). \qquad \text{(iv)}$$

Consider now the search function F associated with f, to the extent of being determined by P, which is defined from F by (ii). In restriction to binary choice, or choice in a pair of elements, the choice function f and the search function F are identical, $f(x, y) = F(x, y)$. It has been seen already that search consistency for f implied the symmetry of F.

Suppose now that F is symmetric. Consider any P-cycle of three elements x, y, z; that is, suppose

$$xPy, \quad yPz, \quad zPx; \qquad (v)$$

equivalently, from the definition (ii),

$$f(x, y) = x, \quad f(y, z) = y, \quad f(z, x) = z.$$

Then from this, with the definition of F, in 2.2(i),

$$F(x, y, z) = f(f(x, y), z) = f(x, z) = z,$$
$$F(y, z, x) = f(f(y, z), x) = f(y, x) = x. \qquad (vi)$$

But the symmetry of F requires

$$F(x, y, z) = F(y, z, x). \qquad (vii)$$

Hence, by (vi) and (vii), $z = x$. Similarly $x = y$. Thus we have that, with the symmetry of F, (v) implies $x = y = z$. That is,

$$xPy \text{ and } yPz \text{ and } zPx \Rightarrow x = y = z \text{ (anti-3-cyclic).} \qquad (viii)$$

In other words, P is anti-3-cyclic, or free from cycles of three distinct elements.

This conclusion (viii), together with the reflexivity and completeness of P (iii), now gives

$$xPy \text{ and } yPz \quad \Rightarrow x = z \text{ or } \text{ not } zPx$$
$$\Rightarrow xPz \text{ or } xPz$$
$$\Rightarrow xPz$$

so that $xPyPz \Rightarrow xPz$. That is, P is a transitive relation. Equivalently,

$$xPyP\ldots Pz \Rightarrow xPz \text{ (transitivity).} \qquad (ix)$$

Thus we have:

PROPOSITION 1   If F is symmetric, then P is transitive.

Now, further,

$$xPyP\ldots Px \Rightarrow xPy, \quad yP\ldots Px$$
$$\Rightarrow xPy, \quad yPx$$
$$\Rightarrow x = y.$$

Therefore

$$xPyP\ldots Px \Rightarrow x = y = \ldots \text{ (anticyclic).}$$

That is, P is anticyclic, having no cycles of distinct elements.

With P now reflexive (iii) and transitive (ix), it is an order. By completeness (iii) it is a complete order. By antisymmetry (iii) it is a simple order. As a complete simple order, it is a total order. Hence:

PROPOSITION 2   If P is transitive then it is a total order.

With a search path p extended by a further element y, 2.2(ii) states

$$F(p, y) = F(F(p), y). \tag{x}$$

Let xPp mean x has the relation P to every elements of p,

$$xPp \equiv y \,\epsilon\, p \Rightarrow xPy.$$

With P transitive, we want to show that

$$x = F(p) \Rightarrow xPp. \tag{xi}$$

In other words, the element which is the result of search along a path has the relation P to every element on the path. The proof is by induction on the length of the path p.

From (iv), with the definition (ii), the proposition is true for paths of two elements. Assume it is true for any path p of length n. Suppose $x = F(p)$, so by hypothesis xPp. We want to deduce the proposition for paths of length $n + 1$; that is,

$$z = F(p, y) \Rightarrow zP(p, y).$$

Thus,

$$
\begin{aligned}
&z = F(p, y) \\
\Rightarrow\; &z = F(F(p), y) &&\text{by (x)} \\
\Rightarrow\; &z = F(x, y) &&\text{supposition} \\
\Rightarrow\; &zP(x, y) &&\text{by (iv)} \\
\Rightarrow\; &zPx, \quad zPy &&\text{definition} \\
\Rightarrow\; &zPxPp, \quad zPy &&xPp, \text{ by hypothesis} \\
\Rightarrow\; &zPp, \quad zPy &&\text{transitivity} \\
\Rightarrow\; &zP(p, y) &&\textsc{qed.}
\end{aligned}
$$

That proves:

> PROPOSITION 3   If F is symmetric, then P is a total order and, for any search path p, $F(p)$ is the element on the path which is top in the order.

Because the function F is well defined for all paths p, a consequence of (xi) is that on any path p there exists an element x such that xPp. Only the set formed by the elements of the path p is material in the relation xPp, so if p' is any permutation of p we have

$$xPp \Leftrightarrow xPp'. \tag{xii}$$

There exists at most one element x on any path p such that xPp. For were y another such that yPp, we would have xPy and yPx, which by antisymmetry (iii) implies $x = y$. Thus there exists a unique element x on any path p such that xPp. Because $F(p)$ is such an element, we now have

$$x = F(p) \Leftrightarrow x \,\epsilon\, p, \quad xPp.$$

This with (xii) gives the conclusion

$$F(p) = F(p'),$$

for any permutation p' of p; that is, F is a symmetric function. Here this is a conclusion from the transitivity of P, and before it was a hypothesis for that conclusion. That shows:

PROPOSITION 4 P is transitive if and only if F is symmetric.

We now have:

PROPOSITION 5   The transitivity of a binary choice relation is necessary and sufficient for the result of search along any path to be independent of the path.

Everyone knows that. The idea of choice determined by an order has been arrived at by a roundabout route considering that we knew about it already. Names in a directory, points on a line, numbers and so forth all have order. It is a model for the situation where everything has a place, the opposite of chaos. Given two events x and y, we know (without disrespect for Einstein, who had other views) either that they are simultaneous or that one of them occurred before the other. The decisions are not independent, and with x happening BC and y AD it goes without saying that x happened before y. This is the main point about order, transitivity, and it applies also to a preference order.

2.3   PREFERENCE
For a binary choice relation P, complete and antisymmetric, and the search function F based on it, the symmetry of F is the condition for F to be a choice function choosing a unique element out of any subset, and for P to be transitive and hence a total order. Then the element $x = F(S)$ that F chooses out of any set S is the unique element in S that is top in the order P. This is a special model for a choice function where the function is based on a total order of the possibilities, and for choice where that is determined by preferences. Preferences have effect in a choice when there is an order of the possibilities which determines which one should be chosen, and there simply being a choice does not signify such an effect. The basis for the preferences, or how they should come to be, is a further matter beyond the model.

   The complete choice function that has been considered, which determines a choice out of every subset in a set U, is one case for the preference model, but a basic one. We considered a function f choosing a single element out of every subset of U, and the associated search function F. There was question whether or not $f = F$. The binary choice relation is

$$P = [(x, y) : x = f(z, t), y \epsilon [z, t]].$$

This gives the relation of the selected element in any pair to the elements of the pair. The two elements are included here, making the relation reflexive. If the choices made by the function are based on preferences, this is the set of preferences involved in all the binary choices. Generally any choice $(x; S)$ of an element x out of a set S can be associated with the relation

$$(x, S) = [(x, y) : y \in S].$$ (i)

Again, if the choice is governed by preferences, these are the preferences in the choice. While P is the collection of preferences in just the binary choices of f, the collection for all the choices is given by

$$Q = [(x, y) : x = f(S), y \in S].$$

Because P is complete and antisymmetric and $P \subset Q$, the possibility $Q \neq P$ can arise only when Q contains some preference (x, y) together with the opposite preference (y, x), where $y \neq x$, so making distinct x, y symmetrically connected in Q. Therefore having Q antisymmetric, or not containing any opposite preferences, is necessary and sufficient for $Q = P$. With that and the transitivity of P which is equivalent to the symmetry of F, we have $f = F$, and a choice function f on the model where choice is governed by preferences, P being the preference relation.

This model of a complete choice function is important for simplicity, and for its relation to other cases, which in one way are more general but in another way not so. The difference in the others is put as incompleteness, which could be filled in, or indifference, which can be eliminated by identification of indifferent elements as representatives of the same object—so making a return to this particular model.

The antisymmetry which has been required of a preference relation can be dropped. When preferences holds both ways between a distinct pair of elements, they are equally preferable, or *indifferent*, as concerns choice: in a choice between the pair taken alone, either can taken. When we formally identify indifferent objects as representatives of the same object, we are back where we started, and in that sense what we have is not more general, but still it is more suitable for many applications. For instance, more than one stone in the heap being searched for the heaviest may have the same weight, and we ignored that possibility before. A point about this definition of indifference is that it is not a noncomparison, as sometimes proposed, which later might be taken over by a comparison, but a positive and decisive comparison both ways; it is equal feeling, and not complete apathy. That leads to the matter considered next, after another remark about this definition. With it, *indifference is transitive*, automatically from the transitivity of preference, so this is not an issue as with other definitions.

Another extension is appropriate in other connections, even if not with the stones that can always be weighed. When voters go to vote they might have distinct preference for the candidate they will vote for over all the others. But they might not have given enough attention to those others to have preferences between them. Developing a discrimination between those others which was not going to be expressed by a vote would be a waste of effort, and the apathy is just a matter of economy. Some preferences are needed in order to vote, but not many. Those needed are all expressed by the vote, or 'revealed' by it. This possible economy in preferences is allowed by dropping the requirement that the preference relation be complete. Now it is generally a partial order, but of course it could still be made complete by a voter giving useless attention to those other candidates. Then we would be back with a complete preference order, where we started. Corresponding to this, stating a theorem, any given partial order can be made a part of some complete order.

Denoting a preference relation now by R, it can be any order, that is any reflexive, transitive binary relation, not necessarily antisymmetric or complete. A binary relation R can be partitioned into its symmetric and antisymmetric parts E and P, as we consider in Chapter VI.2. If R is an order, reflexive and transitive, then E is a symmetric order, or an equivalence, reflexive, transitive and symmetric. This is the relation of equivalence in the order. Further, P is a strict order, irreflexive and transitive. If R is a preference order, then E is the *indifference relation* for R, which holds when R holds both ways between a pair of elements, and P is the *strict preference relation*, which holds when R holds one way and not the other.

This modification to allow incompleteness has a counterpart for a choice function f, where the domain of sets to which it applies is only a subset D of the set of all possible subsets of the universe of possibilities U. For example, with a demand function regarded as a choice function, choices are made not out of all possible subsets of the commodity space but only out of the particular subclass consisting of the budget sets.

The allowance of indifference between distinct possibilities has two expressions. We can think of the value of the choice function as representative of an indifference class. Alternatively, the choice function can be a set valued function, in which case the possibly many elements obtained for its value must be indifferent.

A main idea about choice is that there are at first various possibilities, and by it they are reduced to one. However, the process might have stages where the possibilities are reduced progressively. In the final stage one possibility remains, while in any intermediate stage there could be many. For instance, in finding 'A. Smith' in a telephone directory, first find 'S', which makes a reduction to a few pages, then find 'Smith', which leaves a few columns in those, and finally locate (just one) 'A. Smith'. One could choose on every letter, for instance all those names where the third letter is 'i'. All that is needed is a progressive sequence of criteria, making a continual narrowing down of possibilities until just one remains. A description of this process is provided by a series of choice function f, g, ..., k. Any one of these applied to a set S provides a subset, while their product applied to S contains a single element. Thus,

$$x = (k...gf)(S) = k(...(g(f(S))...) \subset ... \subset g(f(S)) \subset f(S) \subset S.$$

A product of choice function is a choice function, and it can be single-valued even though the factors are many-valued or partial choice functions. The lexicographical or dictionary order of words illustrates this.

To put this in terms of preferences, suppose there is a sequence of preference relations where each has priority in decisions over any successor. Though an indifference class of any one relation might contain many elements, an intersection of indifference classes, one of each relation, could contain at most one element always. That means that the indifference classes to which an element belongs provide a set of coordinates identifying the element completely. In that case it is always possible to arrive at a unique choice in any set by applying the preference relations successively. At any stage, the relation then applied leaves a set of elements judged indifferent by the criteria applied so far. But the next preference relation that is applied will make a further reduction to a subset of those that are best in its own terms, and finally there will be only one element left. For instance, with the stones, first the heaviest are chosen, then the most dense among these, then the roundest and so forth, with a series of characteristics each more important than the next. That continues until only one stone remains—the perfect stone, or at least the optimal one among those available.

2.4   REVEALED PREFERENCE

Given an order R, a set S and an element x, the condition for x to be a maximum of R in S is that

$$x \in S, \ y \in S \Rightarrow xRy. \tag{i}$$

That is, x belongs to S and has the relation R every element that belongs to S. If R is a preference system for deciding choice in S, this is the condition that makes x optimal or one of the best possible elements in S, and hence the one chosen out of S. When preferences R are given, finding an optimal choice in a set S consists in finding an x that satisfies (i). If there are several optimal elements, then the relation R must hold from each to any other, making them all have the relation E of equivalence in R, or of indifference, where xEy means xRy and yRx.

That states how, if preferences are given, and if they govern choices, the choices can be determined. Now we must consider the reverse, namely how, if choices are given, and if there is the hypothesis that they are governed by preferences, the preferences can be inferred. In this case the choices are said to reveal the preferences. But it is important that there be some basis for allowing the existence of preferences before there is any thought of having them revealed.

Given a choice $(x; S)$, it is understood that x is in S and so that requires no further indication. Then the condition (i) can be stated $S \subset xR$. That is to say, S lies in the set xR of elements to which x has the relation R, by which x is at least as good as any of them and so optimal in S. With the notation 2.3(i), another restatement is

$$(x, S) \subset R. \tag{ii}$$

With this, if the choice is governed, or permitted by the preferences R, making it an optimal choice, then R must contain the preferences (x, S); R is revealed, so to speak, to the extent of containing those preferences. With that sense the preferences (x, S) are called the revealed preferences of the choice $(x; S)$.

This revealed preference idea, empty as it stands, goes further and becomes more substantial when applied to a collection of choices—that is, when it is proposed to deal with the choices as if they are all governed by preferences, and, moreover, when *the preferences belong to a single system*. Nothing is accomplished without that proviso.

With a choice function f understood, with the possibility of multiple chosen elements, and of incompleteness in that choices are not determined out of all subsets, what we have now is simply an arbitrary collection of choices $(x; S)$, and so it is best stated as a relation, using the notation for that. Then xfS means the element x can be chosen out of the set S, and fS is the set of all such elements. If we have a choice function, fS is always a singleton whenever it is non-empty, and for completeness fS must be non-empty for all subsets S. For the one case fS has at most one element and for the other it has at least one, for all S.

For all the choices of f to be permitted by a preference system R, the condition (i), or (ii), is required for all choices $(x; S)$ that belong to f, that is whenever xfS . Introduce

$$Q = \cup \, [\, (x, S): xfS\,],$$

this being the base collection of preferences in all the choices of f, or the directly revealed preferences. Then the considered condition is equivalent to

$$Q \subset R, \tag{iii}$$

since a union of sets is a subset if and only if they are all subsets. Now introduce

$$R_f = \vec{Q},$$

the transitive closure of Q, so this is transitive and contains Q. Then, because R is an order, and so transitive, (iii) is equivalent to

$$R_f \subset R. \tag{iv}$$

This then is the condition for a choice relation f to be permitted by a preference system R, or to have all its choices represented as optimal by it. Any R that permits f is determined to the extent of being an order that contains the relation R_f.

The relation R_f is itself an order, and it contains itself, so it satisfies (iv), and so it is one such possible relation. It defines the *revealed preference relation* of f, holding between end-points of chains of the basic or directly revealed preferences that form Q. Now we have the empty proposition that all collections of choices are permitted by their own revealed preference relations. If, from an absence of further requirements, it does not matter what preferences are to rule about choices, all choices are permitted. Obviously here there is no test for the possibility of any given collection of choices being governed by some preference system. But if the choices should be so governed then we know something about the preferences.

An additional point is that the symmetric part E_f of the revealed preference relation R_f is an equivalence relation, defining the *revealed indifference relation* of f. Elements that have this relation lie on cycles of the directly revealed preference relation Q, and they must be indifferent in any explanatory preference system for f. For from (iv) we have $E_f \subset E$. While more choices can reveal more preferences, revealed indifferences are not then altered but are preserved.

2.5   REVEALED CONTRADICTIONS

With a choice function f that makes a unique choice x from any set S in its domain D, the uniqueness is a feature that requires explanation, and that cannot be given simply in terms of revealed preferences. To explain the choices together with their uniqueness on the basis of preferences, an element would have to be represented as the unique optimum in a set where it is chosen. While the revealed preferences are preferences that are necessarily involved in any such explanation, there are other revelations now besides. These are the non-preferences which are necessary to make no other element in the set as good as the one chosen, or the *revealed non-preferences*. With these together with the revealed preferences, there is a basis for obtaining contradictions that otherwise would be lacking.

A collection of choices, joined with uniqueness, can reveal a preference and a non-preference opposing each other, in which case we have a *revealed contradiction* and the preference explanation of the choices is impossible. It will be seen that should there be no such contradictions then the revealed preference relation itself always provides one possible explanation. The absence of such contradictions is therefore necessary and sufficient for some such explanation to be possible. Since such devices for interpretation of choices are without any automatic significance, whether it or any other should be entertained is a further matter.

In the context of demand analysis there are other ways of developing non-preferences, without choices being in principle unique. We have the cost side beside the utility, and can join cost effectiveness with cost efficiency as here in Parts II and III. It is not worth pursuing that further subject in an abstract form, and the interest of it is in demand analysis, where additional structure is present for peculiar developments. Now we are dealing with a classic case that applies to a demand function considered as a choice function, and the result obtained corresponds exactly to the revealed preference method used in that context by P. A. Samuelson and elaborated further by H. Houthakker.

Given an order R, a set S and an element x, the condition for x to be a unique maximum of R in S is stated by 2.4 (i) together with the additional requirement

$$y \in S \text{ and } y \neq x \Rightarrow \text{not } yRx.$$

A choice function f has choices $[x; S]$ where $x = f(S)$, and the collection of directly revealed preferences is given by

$$Q = [(x, y) : x = f(S), y \in S]. \tag{i}$$

The condition for all the choices of f to be represented as uniquely optimal by a preference relation R is therefore

$$(a) Q \subset R, (b) Q \cap D \subset P, \tag{ii}$$

where xPy means xRy and not yRx and D is the relation of distinction between elements, so that xDy means $x \neq y$. For the converse complement of R we have $xR'y$, meaning not yRx. With R as an order, reflexive and transitive, its antisymmetric part P is automatically transitive. Antisymmetry for R can be stated $R \cap D \subset P$.

Let R_f and U_f be the transitive closures of Q and $Q \cap D$, as stated by

$$(a) R_f = \vec{Q}, (b) U_f = (Q \overset{\rightarrow}{\cap} D), \tag{iii}$$

so these are the *revealed preference* and *strict revealed preference relations* of f. Then, because R and P are transitive, (ii) is equivalent to

$$(a) R_f \subset R, \quad (b) U_f \subset P. \tag{iv}$$

From the definition of transitive closure, we have $Q \subset R_f$, and so

$$Q \cap D \subset R_f \cap D. \tag{v}$$

In any case, $\vec{Q} \cap D \subset (Q \overset{\rightarrow}{\cap} D)$, and so, from (iii),

$$R_f \cap D \subset U_f. \tag{vi}$$

THEOREM For any choice function, a necessary and sufficient condition for the existence of a preference relation that represents all its choices as uniquely optimal is that the revealed preference relation be antisymmetric, and then the revealed preference relation itself is one such relation.

To prove the necessity, suppose (iv) holds for some R. Then

$$
\begin{aligned}
R_f \cap D &\subset U_f && \text{by (vi)} \\
&\subset P && \text{by hypothesis, (iv-a)} \\
&\subset \bar{R}' && \text{definition of } P \\
&\subset \bar{R}'_f && \text{hypothesis (vi-b) contrapositive}
\end{aligned}
$$

$$\therefore R_f \cap D \subset \bar{R}'_f,$$
$$\therefore R_f \cap D \subset P_f.$$

That shows the necessity of the antisymmetry of R_f, on the given hypothesis. To prove the converse, suppose now that we have the antisymmetry. Then

$$
\begin{aligned}
Q \cap D &\subset R_f \cap D && \text{by (v)} \\
&\subset P_f && \text{by antisymmetry}
\end{aligned}
$$

$$\therefore Q \cap D \subset P_f.$$

So we have (iv-b), with $R = R_f$, and (iv-a) anyway, with that R. That shows

(iv) for some R, proving the sufficiency, and, because of the particular R, the remainder of the theorem also.

From the definitions (i) and (iii-a), with $a = f(A)$ and $b = f(B)$, the antisymmetry requires in particular that

$$b \in A, \quad a \in B \Rightarrow a = b.$$

Equivalently,

$$b \in A, \quad a \neq b \Rightarrow \text{not } a \in B.$$

The last statement has the form of Samuelson's Weak Axiom of Revealed Preference. It becomes that altogether when the demand function is interpreted as a choice function with the budget sets for its domain. There is a similar extended statement of antisymmetry, which with the transitivity is equivalent to an anticyclicity, which has exactly the form of the Strong Axiom of Houthakker, and becomes that when the choice function is made a demand function.

Should the general, and elementary, theorem proved just now seem a complete answer to the question dealt with by Samuelson and Houthakker and others subsequently, it could be wondered why their theory involved so much extra work, with differential equations, problematic limiting processes and so forth, which are absent here. But it is not a complete answer. It could have been a very satisfactory, and most fundamental, first answer. But they still sought a preference relation represented by a numerical utility. There is forgetfulness of the original plea of merit for the revealed preference approach, from its being free of the numerical aspect—that being a 'last vestige' of the obsolete utility of classical economics.

I.3

Democratic Choice

> If we continue the traditional identification of rationality with a
> maximization of some sort, then the problem of achieving a social
> maximum derived from individual desires is precisely the problem
> which has been central to the field of welfare economics.
>
> **Kenneth J. Arrow**, *Social Choice and Individual Values*, 1951

This statement has influenced a generation, and so, even though positions might have changed in the meanwhile, it deserves a comment. For some, possibly everyone, the 'traditional identification' began with it. 'Rational' has diverse uses as a philosophical word, not all to be killed off in the one stroke—it must be about as old as philosophy, and lives on freely there still. Arrow's own use of the word is connected perhaps, if anywhere, with another found in theology, and from carelessess might be taken to be the same. That has to do with the doctrine of free will, where man, being endowed with reason, can and must choose between good and evil; man knows good from evil, but the choice is still a problem. In welfare economics it is rather the other way round; the determination to choose the best or maximum is fully taken for granted; the problem instead is knowing the better from the worse. A fair connection might be found if the choice between good and evil were just as simple as optimization, but apparently it is not, and dispute is possible: Dr Pangloss was hanged—because it was raining (instead of being burnt)—for speaking about the matter, and poor Candide was beaten just for listening.

The brevity of the quoted passage conceals a complexity of which this matter of the use of a word is only a part. The significance of bringing in rationality at all still has to be found out, and we can return to it. Anything going with the name of rationality is usually rated a good thing, though its importance can be greatly exaggerated. In any case, what is brought before us is something social—never mind what—'derived from individual desires'. A sense that can be made out is that the derivation is in some way democratic, with the result for society being decided by its individual members—for instance, by taking a vote, though nothing so commonplace is pursued. One could hold on to this as a possibly clear element in the matter. Rescued—or even not—from the quagmire made by company with rationality, maximality, welfare, and so forth, it has stimulated the great attention now given to democratic decision processes.

But we should revisit the quagmire. One hears about the 'group mind', though it is difficult to be rational about it, and in any case no one ever said it was rational. It is manifested in this very subject, and perhaps that is how the irrational phenomena in it ought to be understood. In the 'traditional' adherence rationality is associated with mind or thought belonging to individuals; however, after maximization has been blessed with the name of 'rationality' by the rhetorical 'if ..., then ...', we find it promptly applied to the group, any group. We had that already in the beginning with the anti-que Maximum Doctrine of the physiocrats, and then with modern welfare economics. Now we should have it still, but with a better modern and at the same time properly traditional conscience, giving complete courage for what follows. That contains mathematics, which is unusual and original in itself so as to give interest regardless of what otherwise it should be about. An accidental effect is to enhance the credibility of ideas offered at the start. The Voting Paradox has prominence, but it is a paradox only if one sees the elected candidate—surely 'derived from individual desires', or votes at least—also as a 'social maximum'. Since the Paradox is not made into a lesson for not seeing elected candidates that way, it becomes the opposite, and reinforces the simplistic optimization way of thinking which is so important for welfare economics.

Though a giver of solutions to problems, the mathematical mode is also a problem itself because of the scientific aura. No 'strategy' is suggested here, but parallels involving the same psychology have been well expressed by Harold Morowitz (1981):

A popular strategy in modern salesmanship is to associate an impressive scientific term with a product. Thus 'protein' has been put into shampoo, 'nucleic acid' into hair rinse—and 'entropy' into economics and sociology.

One should be on proper guard about everything in this book.

A group, as understood in choice theory, should be a model that involves individuals and their connections, and not just an abstract set. The model should be explicit about its features, so that it is known what is being dealt with: there are the individuals, and moreover there is what they have to do together. Here the matter is just terminology, but there can be obscurity in arguments dealing with a group about what it is that makes the individuals into a group.

With a familiar economic model there are individual agents who have nothing to do with each other but trade goods at certain prices. They take notice only of prices, and must have some encounter with each other only because, so we understand, wherever there is a buyer there must be a seller and conversely. These individuals, though a group by virtue of the transaction connections, have no purpose or other government but their own separate ones, by which they voluntarily enter into the transactions, and then the only interface between them is the price. They have no community but prices, no political connection, and no other expression of a common interest in the model. The terms are not even present out of which a definition of group welfare could be made or have a significant function. But still it is talked about. It can be wondered how that is possible, and the matter deserves an enquiry. Having a model where some concept of group welfare could be founded is not ruled out, but it would be a different model.

In microeconomics, an economy is a model where a group of individuals form a system through their transaction relationships. Political theory might take a political body to be made up by a group of individuals bound together by a constitution. For purposes of ideal discussion, economic and political aspects can be isolated from each other, even though in experience they are bound together. The dessicated idealizations are better for purposes of abstract discussion. This chapter deals with characteristics of groups of individuals making group decisions based on individual decisions, as in democratic processes. The interest might belong more to politics; but it has relevance also in economics, where, though there can be doubts that it should, it joins a current of similar interests associated with welfare theory.

Groups of various kinds are found in experience, and they make group decisions, some accountable and others mysterious—a school of dolphins, a flight of geese, a sports team, a military unit, a biological population, a society of cells in an organism, and so forth. Comparisons of a political body or an economic system with such other types for similarities and contrasts is instructive.

The proof of Arrow's theorem in section 3.9 derives from notes given me by Henry Crapo at the University of Waterloo, used for circulation in his combinatorics class. They contain the observation, which I have not come across elsewhere, that the Irrelevance Principle (IP) is implied by positive association (PA). Amartya Sen has told me (September 1973) that PA here is different from the similar condition of Arrow and from another of May, and also from another that he himself has considered; these further conditions are reported in his book (Sen, 1970a). Then what is offered here as Arrow's theorem might be a variant of the original, though the difference need not be important. Sen pointed out that an objectionable feature of our PA is that it permits social indifference to be a gain to some individuals while there is no loss to others. A point we can make is that, if the individuals have total orders, the distinction between all these conditions vanishes, in which case the objection to ours becomes immaterial. In any case with our PA, IP becomes not an extra assumption but one that is already implied. Sen also remarked that the theorem here corresponds to the one in Arrow's first edition of 1951 and not to that in the second edition of 1963, where there is a stronger theorem which does not require PA.

I am much indebted to Franco Romani, University of Rome, for telling me about the theorem of Hansson (1969a). He transmitted a question from Fosco Giovannoni about whether this theorem is correct, and the exposition in section 3.7 is my answer. The Boolean representation idea and the theorem of section 3.8 are in my paper for the Public Economics Seminar in Siena (Afriat, 1973d).

3.1 AXIOMATICS OF VOTING

Frequently a group of individuals, in a situation together, have to make a choice, and it is done by voting. We would like to know the characteristics that underlie this phenomenon. These would concern on the one hand the group, the situation of the group and what they have to do together, and on the other hand the voting process used. Evidences should be found in the combined characteristics compelling the use.

Typically we have an election, the electors being the group of individuals, and there is a set of possibilities, the candidates, from which one has to be selected. The candidates might be for a political office, or they could be courses of action of any kind; in any case, there are many possibilities and just one has to be selected.

Let there be n individuals, labelled 1 to n and forming a set I, and m choice possiblities 1 to m forming a set U. The individuals do not necessarily agree about the choice c they want made, since individually they could make some different choices $c_1, \ldots, c_n$. But as a group they are required to act together and to make a choice, and their possible disagreements are resolved by their agreeing on, or being otherwise bound by, a process by which the choice should be decided.

(I) AUTONOMY OF THE GROUP   The choices of the individuals in the group should decide the choice for the group.

There should be no outside interference and no internal issue about the procedure, as is expressed by there being some function f giving

$$c = f(c_1, \ldots, c_n). \tag{i}$$

(II) ANONYMITY OF THE INDIVIDUALS   The identities of the individuals should not influence the group result.

The individuals are nameless, or at least the process takes no notice of them in connection with the choices. The point is a neutrality of the decision process in regard to the individuals involved and this is guaranteed by anonymity. The group decision function f should give the same value when names are permuted among individuals, unaltering the collection of their choices; that is,

$$f \text{ is a symmetric function.} \tag{ii}$$

In other words, it does not matter who chooses; only the choices are important.

The collection of n choices from the m alternatives is specified by the number of choices that go to each alternative, $v_1, \ldots, v_m$ where

$$v_1 + \ldots + v_m = n.$$

These numbers are just counts of the 'votes' given by the individuals to the alternatives. Now from (ii), with (i), we have a function e such that

$$c = e(v_1, \ldots, v_m). \qquad \text{(iii)}$$

(III) ANONYMITY OF THE ALTERNATIVES The identities of the alternatives should not influence the group result.

This is analogous to (II), and to express it we have:

$$e \text{ is a symmetric function.} \qquad \text{(iv)}$$

Not only is the voter's name not written on the ballot, but when the counting is done it is not known which candidate's votes are being counted, or at least it makes no difference. The following consequence gives a complete expression of these assumptions:

(IV) VOTING PRINCIPLE The alternative chosen by the group is a symmetric function of the counts of votes the individuals give to the alternatives.

The voting principle that familiarly governs elections has been seen as a necessary expression of neutrality ideas that have force in democratic procedures. The way elections are conducted varies a great deal, but this principle is always present.

It is possible to go further and arrive at properties of the function f, or the function e that represents it under the assumptions so far, by bringing in other ideas that bear in the election procedure.

This matter of group choice has arisen because the individuals in the group might not agree directly on the choice to be made, and so they agree to, or are constitutionally bound by, a procedure for arriving at the choice. However, should they be of one mind and agree about the choice, or be unanimous, the result of the procedure should agree with them. For an expression, we have:

(V) UNANIMITY SOVREIGNTY If all the individuals in the group agree on a choice then their agreed choice becomes the choice for the group.

A statement in terms of the group choice function f is that

$$f(c, \ldots, c) = c \qquad \text{(v)}$$

or, equivalently, in terms of the election function e,

$$v_1 = n \Rightarrow e(v) = 1.$$

That is, if all the n votes go to the alternative 1, then 1 is elected. Because of the symmetry of e this holds equally for any alternative.

Where there is unanimity there is no dilemma from differences of opinion and the system is not really needed; its purpose is for individuals committed to act together to be able to do that even when they are not of one mind about the course of action to take. Should they be of one mind, it serves to establish that, and gives a realization to it by making the common choice of the individuals become the choice for the group. In this case there are no dilemmas. The system also serves well when there is near unanimity. This depends on a universally adopted rule, which represents an extension of the case of unanimity, containing it as a special case.

(VI) ELECTION PRINCIPLE   The elected possibility has more votes than any other.

That is,

$$e = i \text{ and } j \neq i \Rightarrow v_i > v_j$$

which is to say that, if i is elected and j not, then i must have more votes than j; equivalently,

$$e = i \Rightarrow v_i > \max_{j \neq i} v_j.$$

This is offered not as a criterion that is always sufficient to produce an election result, but as one that is always required if an election takes place. Were it accepted as also sufficient, we would have

$$e = i \Leftrightarrow v_i > \max_{j \neq i} v_j$$

so an alternative is elected if it has more votes than any other. For the case where i is the unanimous choice and so elected, all n votes go to i and none elsewhere, and the principle is certainly fulfilled.

It is possible to have several possibilities i with the maximum number of votes; that is, $v_i = \max_j v_j$ for several i, giving several top candidates. Usually there is resort to special devices to deal with this unresolved situation. There might be one individual, such as a chairman or president who has the 'casting vote', who does not vote unless this situation arises and then votes for one of the top candidates, thereby making his choice the winner. An alternative procedure is to have a new election between the top candidates, and still other procedures are possible for assuring an election result, based on the same criterion. But the criterion itself could, from background considerations, be unsatisfactory anyway. A more stringent criterion, such as the one stated next, might be more suitable, and even that might not be enough.

Further properties that might be entertained for the group choice function do not have the universality of the foregoing. They would be associated with options in constitutional arrangements suiting special situations, and there can be a proliferation of design possibilities beyond this point.

(VII) MAJORITY RULE   The elected possibility has more votes than all the other possibilities put together.

That is, $v_i > n - v_i$, so necessarily $v_i > n/2$. More than half the total votes are required for election by this often but not always adopted criterion. However, no candidate might achieve that number, and some further elaboration in the constitutional arrangements could be needed to get a result. But now it should be seen why (VI) might be unacceptable and (VII) or even a more demanding condition might be required.

The G(ood)s outnumber the B(ad)s 15 to 10. The Gs are public spirited and have three candidates, eager to do Good. The Bs are mean and see to it that they have just one candidate. In the election the *G* candidates get five votes each, and the one *B* candidate gets 10 and so wins. Next time, if there is one, the Gs will form a party to elect one candidate to represent them and get all their fifteen votes.

This illustrates a familiar feature of the election system, and the formation of parties as an adaption to it. An election is, in a way, a symbolic battle, and any with common interests must keep their forces together if they will win.

A possible view of considerations found later in this chapter is that they are part of an effort to discover a system free of defects that for some reason, possibly no good reason, are found in the ordinary election system. It is true that the particular effort turns out to have inherent infeasibilities. But there might be something wrong with this view of it anyway, and the motive for those considerations is not clear. No system should be blamed for the circumstance that, in going along a road, one might turn left or right, but not both. This is not the impossibility of democracy that some have found even in the Impossibility Theorem, but the cause for it.

3.2 BINARY ELECTIONS

An elections between just two candidates, or a *binary election*, is simpler than one in which there is a greater number. Design possibilities are fewer and unalterable aspects can be taken further. The choice to be made can be represented as between Yes and No. There could be two candidates and Yes means one and No the other, or one candidate to be elected or not, or any decision requiring a Yes or No. With the choice function f in 3.1(i), the individual and group choices now have just two possible values, Yes or No —or, more conveniently, 1 or 0. Then f is a Boolean function, whose arguments and value are all Boolean variables, taking the values 1 or 0. The total number of Yes or 1 votes is now just the sum of the Boolean arguments, so we have

$$v = c_1 + \ldots + c_n \tag{i}$$

and the number of No votes is $n - v$. The election function e in 3.1(iii) becomes $e(v, n - v)$, and this can now be denoted $e(v)$, with value

$$c = e(v) \tag{ii}$$

which is 1 or 0 according as the group choice is Yes or No. Then the symmetry required in 3.1(iv) is stated by $e(n - v) = 1 - e(v)$. From this we have $e(n/2) = 1/2$. But when the function e is defined it can only have the values 0 or 1. Hence with n even, the function cannot be defined for $v = n/2$, in other words no election takes place: *e is undefined for* $v = n/2$.

The unanimity principle (V) in the last section gives

$$e(n) = 1, e(0) = 0. \tag{iii}$$

Thus *e is non-constant*, so the decision to be made is not *imposed*, or settled already by the system, but rather the electors influence the outcome. They decide it in the way stated by (iii) if they happen to agree unanimously one way or the other.

Now we need to consider a counterpart of Arrow's Positive Association principle, to be dealt with later in its original context. It becomes indistinguishable from Arrow's principle after recognition that Arrow's system for electing an order reduces by that principle to a collection of separate binary elections for every pair of possibilities, or every elementary preference. It is immediately plausible that, when the election results are forced by assumption to constitute an order and so to be transitive, all possible preferences are in the result, so producing the 'group indifference' of Hansson's theorem.

We now consider two elections with a change in voting pattern, and conditions before and after:

POSITIVE ASSOCIATION If all who decided Yes before do so again now, then if the group decision was Yes before it will be that again now.

With the c's in 3.1(i) for one election and d's for the other, positive association requires

$$(\text{all } i)\ c_i = 1 \Rightarrow d_i = 1 \ . \ \Rightarrow \ . \ c = 1 \Rightarrow d = 1.$$

These being Boolean variables, we have

$$(c = 1 \Rightarrow d = 1) \Leftrightarrow c \le d,$$

and so this states

$$(\text{all } i)\ c_i \le d_i \Rightarrow c \le d. \tag{iv}$$

Now, with v for the c's from (i) and w similarly for the d's, the representation (ii) of (i) gives $v \le w \Rightarrow c \le d$; that is,

$$e \text{ is a non-decreasing function.} \tag{v}$$

The voting threshold is defined by

$$t = \min\ [v : e(v) = 1] \tag{vi}$$

and by (iii) is such that $0 < t \le n$. Then, by (v) and (vi),

$$e(v) = 1 \Leftrightarrow v \ge t.$$

That is, the group decision is Yes if and only if the number of Yes-votes is at least the threshold t. Impartiality, Unanimity and Positive Association principles have been shown to produce this familiar pattern where group choice is made by voting and decided by the total votes in favour being above a particular threshold. Questions now concern the threshold.

Let N be the next integer above $n/2$, that is $n/2 + 1$ if n is even and $(n + 1)/2$ if n is odd. Suppose, if possible, that $t < N$. Then we could have $v = t$ Yes-votes and $(n - t)$ No-votes, both at least t, so both Yes and No win simultaneously. To prevent the dilemma of this simultaneous Yes and No we must have

$$t \geq N. \qquad (vii)$$

Having that, the possibility arises of there being neither a Yes or a No, that is, of there is no election result and so of the group making no decision at all. This possibility is irremovable in the case where n is even and $v = n/2$. The question now is whether it can be made the only such case. If $t > N$, another such case would be where $v = t - 1$, making both v and $n - v$ less than t, so again there is no result. Hence we must have $t \leq N$, and this with (vii) requires $t = N$. Then for any v we always have either $v \geq t$ or $n - v \geq t$, but not both, except when n is even and $v = n/2$.

With $t = N$ we have the commonly adopted majority rule by which more than half the votes are needed to win. The way it was arrived at consisted in avoiding a simultaneous Yes and No contradiction, and having a Yes or No, that is, some outcome, in all possible cases. Were only the avoidance of contradiction required we would have just (vii). Factors about the group and the decision to be made, such as interests of internal harmony, stability and the like, together with absence of necessity to make a decision immediately, could make a t greater than N suitable, for instance $t = 2n/3$, or even $t = n$ when unanimity is required for a decision.

3.3   THE VOTING PARADOX

Consider three electors A, B, C and three candidates x, y, z. The electors give orders to the candidates, expressing their preferences between them which will determine the votes they cast in elections:

$$
\begin{array}{ll}
A & x\,y\,z \\
B & y\,z\,x \\
C & z\,x\,y
\end{array}
$$

For example, A prefers x to y, so in choice between x and y would choose x, and vote accordingly. Three elections are conducted, running the candidates against each other in pairs:

election candidates	$A\ B\ C$ votes	election results
y, z	$y\ y\ z$	y defeats z
z, x	$x\ z\ z$	z defeats x
x, y	$x\ y\ x$	x defeats y
x, y, z	$x\ y\ z$	none

The added last line is for the inconclusive election in which all candidates run and get one vote each. In the others, the winner defeats the loser with a decisive 2 votes to 1 in each case. This scheme will be looked at in two ways, one perfectly straightforward and the other not so.

Any order is associated with the cyclical order, derived from it by making the first element follow the last. There are two possible cyclical orders of three elements, and each has three orders associated with it, there being six possible orders, associated in two threes with the two cyclical orders. The three orders adopted by the electors happen to be three associated with the same cyclical order. There is a cyclical symmetry in the scheme, so if the elements receive the cyclical permutation where each element goes to its successor, the scheme is reproduced. The orders of the candidates receive a cyclical permutation in their assignment to electors, the three rows of the table being cyclically permuted in their positions. Had the three orders associated with the other cyclical order been picked, cyclical symmetry would have resulted again, and the cyclical order chosen would again be reflected. In the three-way contest, all candidates get one vote each. The result is symmetrical in all respects, being reproduced under any permutation of the candidates.

It is a puzzle to know what else could be said—this matter is now exhausted! None the less, more has been said, and a 'paradox' found. The scheme described is the basis for the well known Voting Paradox.

What is a paradox, and what must been going on in thoughts to see one here?

paradox (*Gr*. doxa, opinion) A statement, view, etc., contrary to received opinion; an assertion seemingly absurd but really correct; a self-contradictory statement or phenomenon.

Cassell's Concise English Dictionary

A list of the three branches will help the enquiry:

P1: A statement, view, etc., contrary to received opinion.

P2: An assertion seemingly absurd but really correct.

P3: A self-contradictory statement or phenomenon.

It might be judged that this matter is not important in itself, or that there is no real paradox, or not one worthy of the name. But it serves the understanding of features in prevailing thought to know why a paradox has been mentioned.

A promising approach to finding a paradox is to work with P1 from the dictionary statement and entertain a notion about received opinion. We do not have to look far for such a notion in prevailing ideas.

(I) Groups have preferences.

Encouragement comes from the welfare function and optimality doctrines about an economy.

(II) Preferences are revealed in choices, and with election choices, where the winner has definitely more votes than the others, they are strict preferences.

That is the much respected Revealed Preference principle, with a bit added —after all how should one know where to stop?

(III) Strict preferences are antisymmetric and transitive.

Preferences of the same system belong to an order and so must be transitive as a matter of meaning, and strict preferences are antisymmetric by definition.

If one goes along with that, we do have a paradox. The elections between x, y and y, z reveal the strict preference of x over y and of y over z. One should conclude then, from the transitivity of strict preferences, that x is strictly preferred to z. However, the election between x and z shows the opposite. The scheme considered is imaginable and so it should certainly be taken seriously. But when the received opinion is brought in a contradiction follows. A possibility is at odds with received opinion, and so, according to P1, we have a paradox.

There is nothing to be done about the first side, and so there must be something wrong with the second, the received opinion. A resolution of the paradox is that groups might make choices, possibly by means of elections, but that does not mean they have preferences, and if they do not have preferences then no preferences can be revealed by any means.

What we have is seemingly absurd if one adheres to the received opinion and is really correct if one does not, so the P2 criteria are met after a fashion. With the adherence we found a preference that must be both present and not present, so giving the self-contradictory phenomenon required by P3. From all sides we do have a paradox, if one believes that wherever there are choices they reveal preferences, and then adds the strictness of preference when one candidate has definitely more votes than another. Without the strictness we would have group indifference between all the alternatives, which is consistent with the indecisiveness of the election when all three candidates run together. If that is an escape, it takes away from the main point, which is simply that the group does not have preferences. Then the elected candidate is not the best candidate, since there is no criterion for the better and worse, but simply the elected candidate; it is the absence of such a criterion that would be cause for having an election in the first place.

A value of settling the well-known paradox is that it has sustaining connections with thought that bears widely in economics, whose shortcomings are undramatized by paradox. Without the received opinion no paradox would have been found here; the paradox rebounds there, after all.

3.4 ELECTING AN ORDER

K. J. Arrow, in his work *Social Choice and Individual Values* (1951, second edition 1963), proposed a procedure that can be compared with an ordinary election. But instead of electing one of the candidates, an order of all the candidates is elected. Rather, the orders are the candidates. The object is to elect one of them, on the usual basis of votes given to them by the electors. That being so, we do have an ordinary election, though the candidates now being orders instead of amorphous entities gives us more to play with.

The proposal is not usually put in that way, but it can be. With m objects there are $m!$ order relations, if we consider total orders, and more if indifference is allowed; in any case, it is some number M, much larger than m. These are the candidates in the election, and every voter chooses, or gives a vote to, one of them. Because there are so many orders, the votes will be spread thinly. The winner of the election, if there is one, becomes the group choice from among the candidates. In this case, being an order chosen by the group, it is called the group order. It is an order of the original objects, which so far as we know are not candidates for anything, at least not immediately.

With any election we have a function

$$R = f(R_1, \ldots, R_n),$$

an election function as in 3.1 (i), which determines the group choice from the individual choices. But here the choices happen to be order relations between the original possibilities. Instead of belonging to the originally considered set U they belong to the set D of all orders of U. The function f, whose arguments and values are orders, we call an *order function*. Following Arrow's work, much attention has been given to mathematics of such a function. First we will consider the motive of it.

The orders R_i are understood to express preferences, and so to govern choices. But the individuals here are not making choices on the basis of those preferences: they are choosing those preferences. Perhaps it is fair to say that they have preferences between those preferences. The group preference order R must be used to make choices for the group; for want of another reason, one must assume so. Then, electing an order does the same work as the old-fashioned election; but though the output is now the same, the input required is much greater. To grant elementary economic efficiency, it must be supposed that there is something more to the output. Ordinary elections decide the group choice out of a set of candidates simply on the basis of individual choices. Here, instead, the individuals have to state all preferences between all candidates to determine the same for the group, and the preferences so determined are applied to making the group choice of a candidate.

Why should anyone think of following such a roundabout procedure, and what could be the possible advantage of it? Originally it was referred to the preoccupation in welfare economics with the idea of a social welfare function; knowledge of this function presented a problem, and it was suggested that here was an approach to that problem. This was the intelligibility and the support proposed for the undertaking. From the terminology adopted, the group order to be arrived at would be the social welfare order.

Reservations have already been expressed about the welfare point of view, and so further comment should come from other sides. This being an election like any other, why should it not be treated like any other? There is no good reason, unless there is something important and special about objects that are orders of objects which is not shared by objects that are not, and unless this uniqueness is relevant here. This cannot be. The ordinary election system in no way depends on the candidates not being orders. On the contrary, the policy priorities of candidates are made much of in political campaign speeches. Candidates in some imaginable election could be distinguishable from each other only by their different political preferences. The candidates become a set of preference orders, from which one is to be chosen. But that is exactly what we have here. Despite the impressive amount of attention given it, there is still a mystery about the intentions of this new approach, and welfare economics with its sublimities gives no guidance. Now we have before us the idea of preferences between preferences. That idea has suffered neglect and it opens a new vista, inviting a caper. If there were a special way to elect an order, it could be applied to orders of orders, and orders of orders of orders, and orders . . . ; instead of that dread of philosophers, the infinite regress, here is infinite progress.

3.5 DEMOCRATIC IMPARTIALITY

Should an election process show evidence of being influenced by the personal identities of the voters or by the particular issues on which votes are being cast, it would give the appearance of being biased and there might be complaints. An essential characteristic of a democratic election process is impartiality on both these sides. The electors have equal standing, and so do the candidates; there is a symmetry between them in their entry into the electoral process so that no one has a different treatment from the others. Also, all concerned bind themselves equally to the process and its results. They do that more willingly because of the equal treatment. They have a commitment to act together, and this is how they do it, even though they have conflicting interests and opinions, and the losers will not like the results. This principle, already applied in section 3.1, is stated again, because of the further application it can have when the candidates are orders of objects.

> IMPARTIALITY PRINCIPLE A democratic election system should show a disregard for the actual identities of both the electors and the candidates.

The test of this impartiality is that both electors and candidates should be represented anonymously by arbitrary tags that do not reveal their identities, and it should make no difference to the result if the tags are rearranged by any permutation. This democratic impartiality principle has already been applied to a function that determines group choice from individual choices, with the conclusion that it is a symmetric function of the vote totals, so showing a main characteristic of ordinary election procedures. But there are some peculiarities when order relations are the alternatives of choice.

Orders as such in the abstract, when the objects being ordered are not named, already have an anonymity. For instance, total orders on m objects without a regard to what they are ordering are indistinguishable from each other and to that extent anonymous. But when the objects they order are identifiable, the orders become identifiable also. When the objects are permuted, one relation gets mapped on to another. Given any binary relation R in the set U, and a permutation π of U, a further binary relation R_π in U is given by the definition:

$$xR_\pi y \equiv (\pi x)R(\pi y).$$

If R is an order of U then so is R_π. It is the modified order obtained from the other when the elements are rearranged by the permutation. Permutations of the elements produce permutations of the relations, though not all possible ones, and that is the main point now.

The structure or type of relations is preserved in the mapping

$$R \to R_\pi;$$

that is, (for instance), complete orders go to complete orders, and so forth. Thus, orders that are indistinguishable in the abstract, having the same structure, are permuted when the elements are permuted. However, there is no exchange between relations that have different structures, and these remain distinguishable. Symmetry or impartiality, and proper invariance of the election result, is therefore not fully tested just by permuting the elements in U if the domain D includes all possible orders of U, partial, with indifference, or whatever. That is because in this case permutations of the elements of U do not produce all possible permutations of D. If D consists of the total orders only, then we still do not have a complete test. In fact, from just one total order and its image, a permutation of the elements of U is determined which determines the image of every other total order. Thus, not all possible permutations of the total orders of the elements arise by permuting the elements.

Now we consider an impartiality about the elements of U, and not, which would be a proper requirement here, an impartiality about orders of those elements, forming the domain D. Were we going to have an ordinary election the latter would be required, and it implies the former. But enough implications for our attention will be found just from the former. For impartiality about the individuals, we just require the order function f of the last section to be a symmetric function, as before with 3.1(i):

f is a symmetric function.

That is, for any permutation p of 1 to n,

$$f(R_{p1}, \ldots, R_{pn}) = f(R_1, \ldots, f_n).$$

Now for the choice possibilities, in this case orders of U forming the domain D, although impartiality about the elements of U does not amount to impartiality for the elements of D, as just remarked, it goes some way there and is all that will be considered now. Let f_π denote the function f with its value transformed by a permutation π of U; and let $R_{i\pi} = (R_i)_\pi$ denote the order R_i similarly transformed. The effect on the value of f of transforming all the arguments of f should be the same as transforming the value directly:

$$f(R_{1p}, \ldots, R_{np}) = f_p(R_1, \ldots, R_n).$$

That is because rearranging the anonymous tags of the elements in the orders chosen by the individuals should have no other effect on the corresponding group order but that occurring from doing the same with the tags there.

3.6 IRRELEVANCE PRINCIPLE

The Irrelevance Principle of Arrow is an immediate consequence of his Positive Association Principle, as will be noted in section 3.8. But it has consequences on its own which will be considered now.

Any binary relation R in a set U determines a binary relation R' in any subset U' of U, its *contraction* in that subset, where

$$xR'y \equiv xRy \text{ and } x, y \in U'.$$

Thus we have $R \subset U \times U$, $U' \subset U$ and

$$R' = R \cap (U' \times U').$$

Now the following can be considered:

> CONTRACTION CONSISTENCY If the individual orders are modified to their contractions on a subset then the group order they determine is modified to its contraction on that subset.

For another statement, in terms of the order function f which determines the group order from individual orders $A, B, \ldots,$:

$$f(A', B', \ldots) = f'(A, B, \ldots) \qquad \text{(i)}$$

where f' is f with its value so contracted. In particular, the contractions could be on to the subset formed by any pair of elements $x, y \in U$. That means:

> The preferences of the group involving a particular pair of elements depends on just those preferences for the individuals, all preferences involving other elements being irrelevant.

For a modification, the contraction of R on any subset $S \subset U \times U$ can be defined by $R' = R \cap S$, and (i) can now be understood with that definition. Then, in contraction on to any single element $(x, y) \in U \times U$, we have:

> IRRELEVANCE PRINCIPLE Whether or not the group has a particular preference depends on just the same for all the individuals, other preferences being irrelevant.

This condition used by Arrow is different from and stricter than the previous one, and its significance should have an examination.

Judging the suitability of a means requires knowledge of the ends, and here the ends are not clear. If the group order produced would have the status of a group convention, or constitution, then so would this principle. There might be nothing more to think about, no other criterion to apply, and the decision of whether or not to use this principle or any other could just as well be made by taking a vote. But knowing the nature of the things being ordered and the use intended for the order might allow a further appraisal.

In considering the relative weights of stones and judging whether a particular one is heavier than another, the relations involving all other stones would ordinarily be irrelevant. Here is a model giving a narrow but specific intelligibility to the Irrelevance Principle. It can be wondered if that represents the entire thought behind it. Validity in the model depends on the means of judging relative weight accurately. Should one directly judge that A is heavier than B, B heavier than C and C heavier than A, one would assume there had been an error somewhere. Without the inaccuracy allowance there would indeed be a paradox, because from the first two direct judgements one would automatically infer that A is heavier than C, contradicting the third.

This model depends for its sense not only on an accuracy of the judgement apparatus but before that on there being something to be accurate about. For all we can know, the voters of the Voting Paradox might be very accurate, but they can be accurate only about their own uncoordinated opinions. There is no opinion-free factor in the story, the way it is told, as an 'objective group welfare', to take the place of the weight of stones about which there can be a convergence of opinion. But all good people should imagine it.

With a conviction about the objectivity of group welfare and the truthful judgement of voters, one could perhaps go the same route about group preferences as we have with the stones. That would depend on some notion of a truth somewhere which everyone perceives accurately. But then, at least about this particular matter of 'objective welfare', there would be less need to have an election or be troubled by the properties of order functions. Taking the advice of a statistician would fit better. Then all the useful 'truth' information that the irrelevance principle would abandon would be put to good use.

At this point, with some relevance to the Irrelevance Principle, and to possible statistical methods without it, but also for a more for a more important reason, it is useful to observe that stones not only have relative weight but also have *weight*, and so do preferences—making some of them definitely more serious than others. There is not a trace of that important attribute of preferences in all this discussion about order relations.

Repeating the statement of the principle,

(I) The Irrelevance Principle reduces the election of a group order to a collection of separate binary elections for each of the possible preferences. For each preference (x, y) the Boolean choice whether or not to include it for the group is a Boolean function f_{xy} of the individual choices.

There is such a function f_{xy} for all x, y in U. If Boolean variables a, b, ..., and e represent the decisions of the individuals and the group about whether or not to prefer x to y then

$$e = f_{xy}(a, b, \dots).$$

These functions f_{xy} provide the *Boolean representation of the order function f*, made possible by the Irrelevance Principle. Now the following can be added.

(II) Anonymity for the electors requires the Boolean functions all to be symmetric.

(III) Anonymity for the elements which are being ordered requires the Boolean functions to be identical with each other.

Thus we have a single symmetric Boolean function f, and $f_{xy} = f$ for all order elements (x, y). Under both these assumptions, the order election function f in section 3.4 is represented by a single symmetric Boolean function, which without ambiguity can also be denoted f, as here. Now for any given x and y we have the relation 3.1 (i) where f appears as an election function, and where the variables are Boolean, and signify decisions on whether or not x is preferred to y. This being a binary election, the considerations made for binary elections can apply, in particular the representation 3.2 (ii) by means of a voting function e. In any case, *the order election is reduced to a collection of separate binary elections, one for each order element.*

The general idea of an order function might be rich in possibilities, but with the Irrelevance and two Anonymity Principles there is a drastic impoverishment of structure. How drastic it is appears from Hansson's theorem in the next section.

3.7   HANSSON'S GROUP INDIFFERENCE THEOREM

Bengt Hansson (1969a) considered an order election function, as in section 3.4, with neutralities for both the electors and the elements being ordered, together with the Irrelevance Principle. He concluded that *such a function can have only one possible value: the order in which all elements are indifferent.*

By *total group indifference* we can mean an order determined for the group with that property. Hansson's theorem is that, under the stated assumptions, total group indifference is the only possible outcome, *whatever the preferences of the individuals*. This is a key theorem, without drama (like the impossibility of democracy) and in a way deflating the mathematical and philosophical fascinations of this subject.

It is understood that all orders involved, for both the individuals and the group, are complete orders. In any such order, for any elements x and y, either x is preferred to y or y is preferred to x, and possibly both. In the latter case x and y are equivalent in the order, or indifferent. We can use the notation

$x \geq y$ for x preferred to y,
$x > y$ for x strictly preferred to y,
$x \sim y$ for x indifferent to y,

where $x \geq y$ is the basic order relation from which the other relations are derived by the definitions

$$x > y \quad \equiv x \geq y \text{ and not } y \geq x,$$
$$x \sim y \quad \equiv x \geq y \text{ and } y \geq x.$$

The basic order being reflexive and transitive, indifference is automatically an equivalence relation, and strict preference is a strict order, irreflexive and transitive (Part VI, Theorem 2.3.II).

In the case of a total order, indifference between different elements is excluded. In that case, between any distinct elements, there will be a strict preference holding from one to the other, or from the other to the one. The impossibility of having strict preference both ways is in the definition of strict preference, which means a preference holding one way and not the other.

The orders provided by the individual electors determine the group order. They could in particular be total orders, so it is permissible in the following argument to take them so restricted. Then for any distinct elements x, y each individual decides either $x < y$ or $y < x$. Note that under this restriction the Irrelevance Principle becomes equivalent to the contraction consistency stated first in the last section.

Total group indifference means that every possible preference is included in the group order. In terms of the voting function e in 3.2(ii), which represents the binary election function f under the neutrality assumptions, this means $e(v) = 1$ for all v. Here, therefore, is an alternative way of stating Hansson's theorem in terms of the voting function e. His argument, which has an exposition here, involves several propositions, which can also be put in those terms:

$$(1)\, n = 2p,\, e(p) = 1,$$
$$(2)\, n = 2p,\, e(0) = e(n) = 1,$$
$$(3)\, n = 2p + 1,\, e(p) = e(p + 1) = 1,$$
$$(4)\, n = 2p + 1,\, e(0) = e(n) = 1,$$
$$(5)\, e(0) = e(n) = 1,$$
$$(6)\, e(v) = 1 \text{ identically.}$$

The argument is assisted by a notation which incorporates the assumptions immediately in its form. The statement that p individuals in the group have the preference $x > y$ is denoted $p\!: x > y$. Also, $G\!: x > y$ asserts that the group has that preference, and similarly with other cases, weak preference or indifference. Then, for instance, the statement

$$p\!: x > y,\, q\!: y > x \rightarrow G\!: x \sim y,$$

where $p + q = n$, asserts a consequence for the group of certain preferences for the individuals. The required immateriality of the identities of the individuals, and of the elements involved in the preferences, is already in the form of that statement. If n is given there is a redundancy in the statement, because if p individuals have $x > y$ and the remaining q do not, the latter, because of completeness, must have $y > x$; otherwise n is implied. The allocation of the total votes, for or against, determines whether or not the group has a preference between any elements, in a way which is independent of the particular elements.

PROPOSITION 1   With $2p$ individuals, if p have $x > y$ then the group has $x \backsim y$:

$$p: x > y, \ p: y > x \rightarrow G: x \backsim y.$$

By completeness, the conclusion here for the group must be $x \geq y$ or $y \geq x$. Suppose it is $x \geq y$, so now it is assumed that

$$p: x > y, \ p: y > x \rightarrow G: x \geq y.$$

Because x, y are arbitrary, the same must be true when they are interchanged. But that does not alter the collection of individual preferences; the left side is symmetrical and unchanged. Therefore the conclusion for the group must be both $x \geq y$ and $x \geq y$, that is, $x \backsim y$. QED

PROPOSITION 2   With $2p$ individuals, if all have $x > y$ then the group has $x \backsim y$:

$$2p: x > y \rightarrow G: x \backsim y.$$

It has to be shown that the result of

$$2p: x > y \tag{i}$$

is $x \backsim y$. With a third element, z, consider

$$p: x > y > z, \ p: z > x > y, \tag{ii}$$

which, since it contracts to (i), is a possibility. Other contractions of (ii) are

$$p: y > z, \ p: z > y \tag{iii}$$

$$p: x > z, \ p: z > x. \tag{iv}$$

By Proposition 1, the results of (iii) and (iv) are $y \backsim z$ and $z \backsim x$, which, by transitivity of indifference, imply $x \backsim y$. QED

PROPOSITION 3   With $2p + 1$ individuals, if $p + 1$ have $x > y$ and p have $y > x$ then the group has $x \backsim y$:

$$p + 1: x > y, \ p: y > x \rightarrow G: x \backsim y.$$

A possible extension of

$$p + 1: x > y, \ p: y > x \tag{i}$$

with a third element z is

$$p: x > y > z, \ p - 1: z > y > x, \ 1: z > x > y, \ 1: y > z > x,$$

and this has contractions

$$p + 1: z > x, p: x > z \tag{ii}$$

$$p + 1: y > z, p: z > y. \tag{iii}$$

The result of (i) is $x \geq y$ or $y \geq x$. Suppose it is $x \geq y$. Then the results of (ii) and (iii) must be $z \geq x$ and $y \geq z$, by transitivity giving $y \geq x$ which, with $x \geq y$, gives $x \backsim y$. The alternative supposition $y \geq x$ gives the same conclusion similarly. Thus in any case the result of (i) is $x \backsim y$. QED

PROPOSITION 4   With $2p + 1$ individuals, if all have $x > y$ then the group has $x \backsim y$:

$$2p + 1: x > y \quad \rightarrow \quad G: x \backsim y.$$

An extension of

$$2p + 1: x > y \tag{i}$$

is

$$p + 1: x > y > z, p: z > x > y,$$

which has contractions

$$p + 1: x > z, p: z > x,$$

$$p + 1: y > z, p: z > y,$$

which by Proposition 3 have results $x \backsim z$, $y \backsim z$, which by transitivity give $x \backsim y$. Thus the result of (i) must be $x \backsim y$. QED

PROPOSITION 5   If all individuals have $x > y$ then the group has $x \backsim y$.

This is the combination of Propositions 2 and 4.

PROPOSITION 6   In any case the group has $x \backsim y$.

Any case for the individual preferences has an extension in which all have $x > z$, $y > z$. This extension has contractions in which all have $x > z$, and all have $y > z$, and the results of these, by Proposition 5, are $x \backsim z$ and $y \backsim z$, which together give $x \backsim y$. QED

3.8   POSITIVE ASSOCIATION

A positive association property of the ordinary election voting system has already been stated in section 3.2, where it applies to binary elections. It is just a counterpart of a property Arrow proposed for order elections. We consider individual orders before and after a change, the group orders they determine, and any particular preference.

POSITIVE ASSOCIATION   If all the individuals who had the preference before have it now, then if the group had it before it will have it now.

With

$$R = f(A, B, \ldots), R' = f(A', B', \ldots),$$

the condition is that

$$(xAy \Rightarrow xA'y, \quad xBy \Rightarrow xB'y, \quad \ldots) \Rightarrow (xRy \Rightarrow xR'y).$$

The idea can be seen as an enlargement on the unanimity principle; the group having a preference is positively influenced by the individuals having it. If the group has a preference it is because of the individuals who have it, and therefore if, after a change, those individuals who had it before still have it, then so will the group. The individuals having a preference are the cause for the group's having it, and so the cause which was present and sufficient before and is present still will be sufficient still.

Then the same holds also the other way:

$$(xAy \Leftarrow xA'y, \quad xBy \Leftarrow xB'y, \quad \ldots) \Rightarrow (xRy \Leftarrow xR'y),$$

and consequently, taking conjunctions on both sides,

$$(xAy \Leftrightarrow xA'y, \quad xBy \Leftrightarrow xB'y, \quad \ldots) \Rightarrow (xRy \Leftrightarrow xR'y).$$

But this is just the Irrelevance Principle. So it is seen that *the Irrelevance Principle is implied by positive association*. Though originally introduced separately (and this relation between them seems largely to have been overlooked), since one is implied by the other, if the second is adopted there is no option at all about the first.

Hansson's theorem involves only the Irrelevance Principle. It does not have the form of a contradiction of basic assumptions; instead, it shows that in a certain combination they imply a striking degeneracy. If the stronger positive association is used instead, a less ingenious argument can be offered to show a contradiction (Afriat 1973d). The method connects with the scheme found in the Voting Paradox.

With positive association, the voting function e must be non-decreasing and non-constant, as in section 3.2. Then there is a voting threshold N that must be exceeded to obtain election,

$$e(v) = 1 \Leftrightarrow v > N. \tag{i}$$

Let g_{xy} be the Boolean variable which is 1 or 0 according as the group does or does not have the preference (x, y). This is a value of the characteristic function of the group order, or an element of the characteristic matrix. Completeness and transitivity are stated by

$$(\mathrm{a})\, g_{xy} + g_{yx} \geq 1 \quad (\mathrm{b})\, g_{xy} g_{yz} \leq g_{xz}. \tag{ii}$$

A consequence of (iia) is that

$$g_{xy} = 0 \Rightarrow g_{yx} = 1.$$

For notational simplicity, let c denote any individual's vote on the preference (x, y) and c' the vote on the opposite preference (y, x). For the individuals to be restricted to have total orders requires $c + c' = 1$. Then summing over the n individuals gives

$$v + v' = n, \qquad\qquad\qquad \text{(iii)}$$

v and v' being total votes on a preference and its opposite. Let g and g' be the corresponding group decisions on those preferences, so by (iia) we have

$$g + g' \geq 1, \qquad\qquad\qquad \text{(iv)}$$

with the consequence that $g' = 1$ if $g = 0$.

Suppose, as is possible since $N < n$, that $v = N$. Then by the election criterion (i) we have $g = 0$. Hence, as a consequence of (iv), $g' = 1$. But then, by the election criterion again, $v' > N$. But $v' = n - v = n - N$ from (iii), so now we have $n - N > N$, that is $2N + M = n$ where $M \geq 1$.

Let the n individuals be partitioned into three subgroups of N, N and M members who give alternatives 1, 2, 3 the orders

$$(1, 2, 3), (2, 3, 1), (3, 1, 2).$$

The characteristic matrices of these orders, representing also how the individuals who have them will vote, are

$$\begin{pmatrix} 1 & 1 & 1 \\ 0 & 1 & 1 \\ 0 & 0 & 1 \end{pmatrix}, \begin{pmatrix} 1 & 0 & 0 \\ 1 & 1 & 1 \\ 1 & 0 & 1 \end{pmatrix}, \begin{pmatrix} 1 & 1 & 0 \\ 0 & 1 & 0 \\ 1 & 1 & 1 \end{pmatrix}.$$

Hence their sum, showing totals of votes, is

$$\begin{pmatrix} n & N+M & N \\ N & n & 2N \\ N+M & M & n \end{pmatrix}.$$

Now for the matrix g_{xy} ($x, y = 1, 2, 3$), obtained from this by the election criterion (i), we have

$$\begin{pmatrix} 1 & 1 & 0 \\ 0 & 1 & 1 \\ 1 & ? & 1 \end{pmatrix}$$

the *?* signifying a result that could be either way. This gives a violation of the transitivity required by (iia). For we have $g_{12} = 1$, $g_{23} = 1$, but $g_{13} = 0$.

Hansson's theorem is that the Impartiality, Unanimity and Irrelevance principles imply total group indifference. Here instead the conclusion is:

> THEOREM The Impartiality, Unanimity and Positive Association Principles together are impossible.

3.9 ARROW'S GROUP DICTATORSHIP THEOREM

A *dictator* is an individual in the group whose preference decisions are imposed on the group. The existence of a dictator is an extreme violation of the symmetry required by democratic impartiality as applied to the individuals. Arrow's theorem is that unanimity and positive association imply the existence of a dictator.

To some, this theorem has appeared to be a demonstration of the impossibility of democracy; as interesting as the theorem, and perhaps more disturbing, is the thought it has provoked.

A subgroup $S \subset I$ of the individuals is *decisive* for a preference $x > y$ if the group has that preference whenever they do:

$$S: x > y \to G: x > y.$$

Thus the Unanimity Principle requires the entire group I to be decisive for every preference:

A *total opposition* to a subgroup having a preference is where the complementary subgroup does not have it and has the opposite preference:

$$S: x > y, I - S: x < y.$$

If, despite such opposition, the group as a whole has the preference, the subgroup has *prevailed over a total opposition*:

$$S: x > y, I - S: x < y, G: x > y.$$

Of course, if the subgroup is decisive for the preference it would prevail over any opposition, by definition, and hence over a total opposition. Morever, from positive association it follows that, if it so prevails over a total opposition, it must prevail over any opposition; that is, it must be be decisive. That gives:

LEMMA 1   A subgroup is decisive for a preference if and only if it prevails over a total opposition.

Moreover:

LEMMA 2   Any individual decisive for some preference must be decisive for all, and so must be a dictator.

Let i be such an individual, with the preference $x > y$; so

$$i: x > y \to G: x > y. \tag{i}$$

Consider the situation, which is a possible extension of this with any third element z,

$$i: x > y > z, I - i: y > z > x.$$

Because $i: x > y$ here, and i is decisive, we have $G: x > y$. But also

$$i: y > z, I - i: y > z$$

and from this, by unanimity, $G: y > z$. Therefore by transitivity, $x > z$. Thus we have

$$i: x > z, I - i: z > x, G: x > z.$$

But this shows that i prevails over a total opposition, and hence, by Lemma 1, is decisive:

$$i: x > z \to G: x > z. \tag{ii}$$

It appears thus that from (i) for any x, y follows also (ii) for any z. By similar argument, also,

$$i: z > y \rightarrow G: z > y.$$

Thus decisiveness for $x > y$, for any x and y, implies decisiveness for $x > z$ and $z > y$, for any z. Now, putting $x > z$ in place of $x > y$ in the first part of the conclusion, and applying this proposition again, using the second part, we have decisiveness for $t > z$, for any t. Thus, decisiveness for $x > y$ implies that for $t > z$, for any t and z, that is for all preferences. QED

THEOREM   Unanimity and Positive Association imply the existence of a dictator.

There exist subgroups decisive for some preference, the entire group I being one, by the unanimity principle. Then, since I is finite, there exists an $S \subset I$ among these for which the number m of elements is a minimum. It will be shown that the supposition $m > 1$ leads to a contradiction, so that $m = 1$, and then by Lemma 2 the theorem is proved.

Suppose, if possible, that $m > 1$, and take any k in S. Then there exist elements i in S different from k. With S decisive for a preference $x > y$,

$$S: x > y \rightarrow G: x > y, \qquad (iii)$$

let z be any third element, and consider the possibility

$$k: x > y > z, S - k: z > x > y, I - S: y > z > x. \qquad (iv)$$

Immediately from this we have $x > y$ for G, because of (iii). Also, we cannot have $z > y$. For otherwise we would have

$$S - k: z > y, k: y > z, I - S: z > y, G: z > y,$$

showing that $S - k$ prevails over a total opposition and is thus, by Lemma 1, decisive for $z > y$, thereby contradicting the hypothesis that S is a smallest subgroup decisive for some preference. Hence we have not $z > y$ for the group, that is $z \leq y$ because of completeness. Now from $x > y$ and $y \geq z$ for the group there follows $x > z$. For otherwise, by completeness, we would have $z \geq x$, which with $y \geq z$ would give $y \geq x$, by transitivity of $\geq$, contradicting $x > y$. Hence, with (ii), we have

$$k: x > z, I - k: z > x, G: x > z,$$

showing that k prevails over a total opposition and is thus decisive for $x > z$, contradicting that $m > 1$. QED

Budget Allocation and Priority

The theory of the behaviour of the individual consumer is concerned with the way the consumer buys goods available on the market at prices which prevail. The intention is to represent the behaviour as systematic, and the demand function provides one form for doing that. The idea that the expenditures on the goods, or the quantities bought of each, are determined by the total money to be spent on them and on the prices of the goods leads to the demand function concept. While the demand function is a model for choices made by the consumer, still there is no model for the process by which the consumer arrives at the choices.

Even when the demand function model is restricted by the hypothesis that a maximum of utility is obtained for the money spent, that situation persists. Adhering to the Budget Allocation Rule makes no alteration: the issue is how the consumer arrives at a budget where it is satisfied.

The same sense that could let the consumer know when that rule is satisfied is applied now to the Purchase Priority Rule. This is a fair model for a process by which consumers could arrive at budgets fulfilling the Allocation Rule. It expresses the idea that, at any stage in making purchases, the next marginal expenditure goes to the currently most urgent items, understood as those giving the greatest return in utility. This rule has an affinity with ordinary consumer behaviour. Also, beside being applicable to the theoretical situation where there are distinct consumption periods in which prices are fixed and complete plans are made, the rule can be interpreted more loosely. It determines a stream of purchases in the less rigid framework where prices change continually and purchase decisions are made independently in every moment, and where the values of stocks as well as flows are taken into account.

An alternative process, related to this but less natural, is the Budget Adjustment Rule. With this, starting with any tentative budget, if the urgencies of goods are then found not all equal then expenditures are transferred from the less to the more urgent, until they become equal. Instead of relying on the Lagrange's method, the Allocation Rule is derived by another argument which gives a direct expression of the Adjustment Rule.

4.1 THE ALLOCATION RULE

A consumer buys quantities x, y of two goods when their prices are $p, q > 0$, so the expenditure on the two goods is $M = px + qy$. The utility obtained, as a differentiable function just of the quantities of these two goods, is $U = U(x, y)$. It is asked if the money M spent on the goods could be redistributed between them so as to get greater utility. This must be by taking away some amount S from the expenditure on one good and spending it instead on the other, so leaving the total expenditure unchanged. Utility is lost from having less of one good, and gained by having more of the other. We need to know if the simultaneous loss and gain in utility can result altogether in a gain.

An expenditure S would buy S/p units of one good or alternatively S/q units of the other. When S is small these quantities are also small, and conversely. For small changes Δx, Δy in the quantities x, y of the goods, the resulting change in utility is

$$\Delta U = U_x \Delta x + U_y \Delta y + E,$$

where U_x, U_y are the rates of change of utility U in respect to the quantities x, y and E is small in absolute value compared with Δx, Δy provided these are small. That is what is meant by the differentiability of the function U.

To shift an amount of expenditure S from being spent on good x to being sent on good y, we set

$$\Delta x = S/p, \ \Delta y = -S/q.$$

The resulting change in utility is

$$\begin{aligned} \Delta U &= U_x S/p - U_y S/q + E \\ &= S(U_x/p - U_y/q) + E \\ &= Sh + E \end{aligned}$$

where E is small compared with S when S is small, and

$$h = U_x/p - U_y/q. \tag{i}$$

Suppose $h > 0$. Then, from the differentiability condition, for sufficiently small $S > 0$ we have $|E| < Sh$ and hence

$$\Delta U = Sh + E \geq Sh - |E| > 0,$$

so there is a gain in utility. Similarly, if $h < 0$ it is possible to gain utility by shifting a sufficiently small expenditure from good y to good x. If utility is at a maximum for the total money spent on the goods, then it is impossible to gain further utility by shifting expenditure from one good to the other either way. In this case, therefore, both $h > 0$ and $h < 0$ are impossible, so we are left just with the possibility $h = 0$. With h given by (i), we have proved the following, which states the Allocation Rule for two goods:

> THEOREM If quantities x, y of two goods are bought at prices p, q so as to get a maximum of utility for the money spent, then necessarily
>
> $$U_x/p = U_y/q,$$
>
> where U_x, U_y are the marginal utilities of the goods.

4.2 MARGINAL UTILITY OF MONEY

Suppose that utility is at the maximum attainable with a given total expenditure M on the two goods, so the allocation is such as to make the Allocation Rule hold, and now there is to be an increase in that total expenditure. Were this increase of expenditure concentrated on good x, the quantity x of this good would be increased at the rate $1/p$ with the expenditure, while the quantity y of the other good would remain fixed. Therefore utility would increase at the rate U_x/p as the expenditure M increases. Similarly, were the increase concentrated on good y, utility would increase at the rate U_y/p. But these two rates are equal by the Allocation Rule, so it makes no difference if the increase of expenditure is concentrated on one good or the other, the rate of increase of utility is the same; and so it is if the increase is distributed between the goods in any way whatsoever. Thus the rate of increase of utility when expenditure increases, which can be denoted U_M, is unambiguous even without specification of how the increase is allocated to the goods. It is given by the rates U_x/p and U_y/p which by hypothesis are equal, so we have:

THEOREM If a consumer spends money to buy quantities x, y of goods at prices p, $q > 0$ always so as to obtain a maximum of utility for the money $M = px+qy$ spent, then as expenditure is increased the marginal utilities of money and the goods are such that $U_M = U_x/p = U_y/q$.

4.3 MANY GOODS

Now suppose a consumer has bought a bundle x of any number of goods when their prices are $p > 0$, and so for an expenditure $M = px$. If the utility $U(x)$ is at a maximum attainable with that expenditure, it is impossible to gain utility by reallocating expenditure between the goods, in particular, between any pair. Therefore, by the Allocation Rule for two goods,

$$U_i/p_i = U_j/p_j \text{ for all } i, j$$

where U_i is the marginal utility of good i, and p_i is the price. But that is equivalent to

$$U_1/p_1 = U_2/p_2 = \ldots = U_n/p_n.$$

This states the Allocation Rule for any number of goods.

The marginal utility of money spent on good i is the ratio U_i/p_i. But under the condition that all these ratios are equal, money has a marginal utility in being spent on the goods regardless of how it is spent. The marginal utility of money U_M has an unambiguous meaning under this condition even though money is understood as being spent on the goods indiscriminately, because the way it is allocated has no effect on the rate of gain of utility. Thus U_M is unambiguously defined, and we have

$$U_M = U_i/p_i \text{ for all } i.$$

4.4 PRIORITY

The marginal utility of money has been defined relative to an efficient allocation of the mony spent so far. It is inapplicable except in the case of that efficiency which gives it an unambiguous value by equalization of the marginal
utilities of expenditures on all the goods. None the less there is a natural way
of extending the definition without dependence on that equalization, giving
a reduction to the original definition in the case where that applies.

With commitment to expenditures having been made so far regardless of
their efficiency, any further expenditure can always be made so as to give the
greatest return in utility gained from it. In other words, utility maximization
will apply to any further expenditures, these to be understood as marginal
increments. The rate of return in utility for money spent on good i is

$$U_{Mi} = U_i/p_i,$$

and so, following this principle, the marginal utility of money has the value

$$U_M = \max_i U_{Mi}.$$

This definition is perfectly general, and free of the Allocation Rule, and it
extends the earlier definition which depended on that rule.

From this definition, the n goods can be partitioned into two classes H and
L, where

$$U_M = U_{Mi} \text{ for } i \in H$$

while

$$U_M > U_{Mj} \text{ for } j \in L.$$

The goods in the classes H and L are the high and low priority goods. The
marginal utility of money is realized in expenditure on the high-priority goods
without regard to how the expenditure is allocated to them. But the return
in utility falls short of that value if any expenditure goes to the low-priority
goods. Therefore the low-priority goods should wait while money is spent on
the top-priority goods first. All the goods can be ranked by the marginal utility
of expenditure on them, that is by the value of U_{Mi}. This provides an order
between them whereby any top good is optimal for receiving the next expenditure. The bottom-priority goods are the class B, giving the lowest rate of
return for expenditure on them;

$$U_{Mk} = \min_i U_{Mi} \text{ for } k \in B.$$

If expenditure is to be withdrawn from any goods in a budget adjustment process, then these are the best candidates.

4.5 LAW OF RETURNS

The law of diminishing returns tells us that the more you have of a thing, while
other things remain the same, the less you get out of having one more unit
of it, that is, its marginal value decreases. There is also a less rigid form of

the law that permits temporary increases but requires the decrease eventually. Most usually, the law applies to factors of production, with output as the return. But utility can be understood as the output of a productive process, the 'making use' of goods, and the thinking that applies to production can apply there also, even though utility might not be directly measurable like a physical amount.

The theory of consumers' budgets is relevant only to the order relation that utility determines between commodity bundles, and so there is emphasis on ordinal utility. But then, if utility is to be thought of at all, aspects of utility are left out that can have significance elsewhere, such as the diminishing returns from consumption that causes expenditure on it to cease at a certain level.

The law of diminishing returns is a tendency rather than a rigid law where a departure should cause surprise. It arises because factors have value from acting in combination, so any one factor loses value when it increases alone and eventually goes out of balance with others. It can seem like a law of nature divorced from accidents to do with economics, but that is an illusion created by selections that take place in the domain of economics; rather, it is a law of economic behaviour. A firm seeking a maximum of profit will operate at a point of diminishing returns, so just from observation of the firm one would always encounter diminishing returns. Similarly, observing a consumer making choices under linear budgets, one can never know about kinks in the indifference surfaces, which none the less might really exist.

To express diminishing returns, it can be supposed that U_i is a decreasing function of x_i, either always or, less restrictively, eventually. A law having a similar basis, subject to qualifications, is that the marginal utility of a good does not decrease as the quantity of another good increases. That might depend on the other good; if the other is a perfect substitute for the first it would not be true. To express it we would have U_i as a non-decreasing function of x_j ($j \neq i$). Less restrictive than either of these assumptions, and consistent with both, is the assumption that, for $j \neq i$,

$$U_i / U_j \to 0 \text{ as } x_i \to \infty .$$

This is an 'ordinal' characteristic of the utility function, invariant when it is replaced by an equivalent one representing the same order. It is a property of the marginal rate of substitution between two goods, or the exchange rate between them, representing the value of one in terms of the other when utility is held constant. A simple example is

$$U = (xy)^{1/2},$$

which gives

$$U_x = (1/2)(y/x)^{1/2}, \; U_y = (1/2)(x/y)^{1/2},$$

and so

$$U_x / U_y = y/x.$$

4.6 ADJUSTMENT AND PRIORITY RULES

A model of the process of choice for a consumer should not involve, for instance, carrying out optimal programming computations, or an ability to solve partial differential equations, in order to implement the Budget Allocation Rule. All that will be required of a consumer here is a sense of the urgency of needs which can guide priorities in making purchases. Different degrees of urgency reflect different returns in utility from expenditure on the various goods. The consumer should have that sense at least to the extent of detecting the most urgent items. The question to be considered is how, with such guidance, a consumer can arrive at an efficient budget, as pictured in the theory, where the allocation of expenditure to goods is such as to obtain a maximum of utility for the money spent.

A possible procedure comes from the proof of the Allocation Rule in section 4.1. Starting with a tentative budget, if any of the marginal utilities of expenditure on the goods are not all equal so that the goods are not all equally urgent, shifting expenditure from the less to the more urgent goods results in an increase in utility without altering the amount of money to be spent. This adjustment process can go on until urgencies become close to equality. Then utility is close to the maximum attainable with the given total expenditure. The process so described can be called the Budget Adjustment Rule. With diminishing returns as expressed by U being a concave function, there is a convergence making it always effective.

The Adjustment Rule represents a process for arriving at an optimal overall consumption plan. But consumers do not proceed quite like that, first thinking of an entire plan and then implementing it. The picture does not correspond to the way consumers buy goods in a sequential fashion, guided by feelings at the moment of purchase. Past purchases are irrevocable, prices change, goods stocked yesterday are consumed today, there is no single definite plan for a definite period in which prices are fixed, and known. In reality, periods and plans, if any, are in a tangle quite unlike the theoretically imagined situation.

A proposal somewhat closer to what consumers do is the Purchase Priority Rule, by which money is always spent first on the items that are most urgent. The effectiveness of this rule depends on the ordinal characteristic of utility stated at the end of section 4.5, which will make the consumer stop buying one good at some point and turn to another. This rule can be favoured because it has applicability even in circumstances more like normal everyday confusion. But still, one should like to know what it means for the unconfused but nevertheless imaginable situation dealt with in theory, where it should have application also. With the Adjustment Rule, any tentative overall plan for the consumption period is taken first. Then it undergoes progressive improvements until it becomes optimal. With the Priority Rule, starting from nothing the consumer makes expenditures in sequence while being guided by it. At any stage, a maximum of utility has been obtained for the money spent so far, and that holds also when all the money budgeted is finally spent. Put in another way, the consumer moves along an expansion path, starting at the origin and stopping when the money is spent.

Since Irving Fisher, consumption expenditure has been identified with 'income'. This is only a manner of speaking and a way of putting aside the determination of expenditure level. Money has other uses that are forgone when it is spent on consumption, so consumption has an opportunity cost. In any case, money spent has to be available, and where it is gained by working there could be a cost of effort and a loss of leisure. Any general assumptions here are bound to be too simple because of ambivalences about work and leisure. The one can meet basic needs for activity and involvement as demonstrated by voluntary work, and the other has confluence with the opposite and shares characteristics with unemployment and alienation. Economic factors do not separate from social factors any more than they do from political ones. In any case, the utility gained by expenditure on consumption has to be weighed against other utilities that would be sacrificed. A limit is reached when U_M, the marginal utility of expenditure on consumption, falls below the marginal utility of not spending on it. Because the marginal utility of spending on consumption decreases as the level increases, expenditure will stop at some level. It would be at the point where the urgency of spending on consumption is balanced by the urgency of not spending there but allocating it elsewhere instead, so again we have the Allocation Rule.

That the old 'cardinal' or classical utility is not needed in demand theory is marked as a discovery, attributed to Pareto. Only the order characteristics, or the preferences represented, are regarded as important. The 'indifference map' (meaning preference map) is all that is essential. The demand theory is really just a theory of the demand function, concerned with the mathematical question of the consistency of such a function with utility maximization under the budget constraint. How the consumer arrived at the constraint is put aside by taking it as settled by income—in throwing away the cardinal aspect to leave only ordinal utility, a really important baby has gone out with the bathwater.

Quesnay's Economic Principle required 'greatest satisfaction to be attained at the cost of the least labour-pain', and there is a tolerance for this kind of formula, which might at first seem to have some sense which then escapes definition. Were the failure to have sense so obvious as to require no comment, one could only find a refusal to be constricted by sense, perhaps for the sake of other effects. That might be the case with the similar 'greatest happiness for the greatest number' formula which Robinson and Eatwell (1973, p. 3) call metaphysics, though it is not really that. With a search for its possible meaning when it has some modification, Quesnay's formula might be regarded as a germ for some ideas, such as the present utility thinking, or for the two criteria of cost-benefit analysis, namely cost effectiveness and efficiency. Common assumptions about utility produce relations between these criteria, but without some additional assumptions they are independent. In any case, the two together fit demand analysis better than either one taken alone, as will be elaborated in Part II.

I.5

Ramsey's Savings Rule

Frank Ramsey (1928) considered how much of an income produced from capital, instead of being spent immediately on consumption, should be saved in order to accumulate capital which would yield more income in the future. At every moment there are competing demands between consumption in the present and consumption in the future, and a choice has to be made. Ramsey made this question specific, and gave it an answer, in his famous Savings Rule. His theory has stimulated much related work, but its first value is that it gives the paradigm for a pervasive form of question, such as the development problem of a developing economy, the deposit-or-withdrawal question concerning a savings account at the bank, and so forth. As to whether or not the theory can serve such questions further, one may allow that it does not, and also that this is not its value; rather, through the instruction it offers, it crystallizes the form of such questions, if that is not crystallized enough already. Other methods are available to deal with the type of question; returning to Ramsey's problem gives these methods some practice, and, reassuringly, they all give the same answer.

In this chapter the terms of Ramsey's theory have been simplified to remove features inessential to his main argument. He introduced labour in addition to capital as an input for the production of income, and also the disutility of labour. But his first step was to eliminate this variable, by constraining it to always have its optimal value with the available capital. In that way, he made a reduction to a simpler problem which embodies the main part of his theory, and which is considered here.

The Savings Rule applies to the case where every future moment is given the same weight as the present. In addition to his own argument, Ramsey cites another of Keynes, given in section 5.5 below together with modifications, which demonstrates the immediacy of the rule. The argument is couched in terms of marginal quantities, to which economists are accustomed. Ramsey suggests that this is of no use for the problem involving a discount rate. It will be seen that the method of argument applies equally to this problem and gives a generalization of Ramsey's rule, though not one with a simple graphical implementation like the original. In addition to Ramsey's method by transformation of the integral, calculus of variations and control theory methods can also be used. The application of these methods produces nothing new, apart from the exercise of their use. Ramsey's was the first economic application of calculus of variations, and it has been followed by others.

5.1 COUNTING AND DISCOUNTING

> One point should perhaps be emphasized more particularly; it is assumed that we do not discount later enjoyments in comparison with earlier ones, a practice which is ethically indefensible and arises merely from the weakness of the imagination. . . .
>
> **Frank Ramsey,** *A mathematical theory of savings*

> Life is not so much an affair of tea-cups as a roaring torrent.
>
> **W. N. P. Barbellion,** *The Journal of a Disappointed Man*

Ramsey is making an excuse for his theorem, which is nice but depends on future moments being given equal weight with the present. Otherwise, the effect of his remark is not clear. One may wish to discount the future not just because one is impatient, but because the future is uncertain. Following Barbellion, there can be a concern that investments might be lost in the torrent. Also, utility, should one ever be able to determine it, cannot be permanently fixed, and what is good today may turn out to be not so good tomorrow. That puts a justifiable limitation on sacrifices for the future. In any case, in order to live tomorrow one has to survive today, and so doing just that has a special claim on resources. Ramsey's and Barbellion's remarks are opposites, and both have influence on behaviour. With regard to Barbellion's, there might be wonder about our concern for preservation of whales, the environment, and so forth, since these things are in the torrent like everything else. The torrent is a good idea, but we are not only in it, we are a part of it—to a significant extent we *are* the torrent, and here are grounds for compromise.

Anything in existence today was programmed to keep going from yesterday; the vast majority of possible entities (so to speak) are not around, and those that are make an elite company. The attention the Egyptians gave to the future is understandable, and so are phrases of Cambridge neo-Platonists — to be admired eternally the way they were locally among themselves.

The compromise between Ramsey and Barbellion is expressed in mathematical economics by a discount rate on future utilities. Ethically, one gathers, this rate should be not too large, and (not from weakness of the imagination but the opposite) not too small. To arrive at such a rate seems a very obscure problem. Then there is the prior matter of the utility which does the counting, to which the discount rate is related. The theory takes this as given, though it never is. If it is given for an individual, free of other authority, then any utility function that is produced claims respect. If it has a social or group reference, then the matter of authority must be more complicated — the sort of thing dealt with in Chapter I.3.

5.2   INCOME DISPOSITION

At any moment t there is a stock of capital K and a rate of income Y, determined as a function

$$Y = f(K). \tag{i}$$

It is assumed that $f'(K) > 0$; that is, a greater flow of income is derived from a greater stock of capital.

An important special form for the production function f which determines income produced from capital is $f(K) = rK$. With this, $f'(K) = r$ is constant and appears as a fixed interest rate on capital. This form can apply, for instance, to a savings deposit at a bank.

It is assumed that only two things can be done with income: it can be consumed or saved. Therefore there is the identity

$$Y = C + S, \tag{ii}$$

showing the partition of income Y into consumption C and saving S, these all being rates in any moment t.

Savings are understood to be additions to the stock of capital, so a rate of saving is the same as a rate of increase of the capital stock. Hence there is the identity

$$dK/dt = S. \tag{iii}$$

Combining (i), (ii) and (iii) we have

$$C = f(K) - dK/dt, \tag{iv}$$

which shows that, if K has a time path, or is given as a function of t, then so does C. The reverse is also true; that is, a time path for C determines a time path for K. For with $C = C(t)$,

$$dK/dt = f(K) - C \tag{v}$$

is an ordinary differential equation for K as a function $K(t)$ of t. Under usual conditions it has a unique solution for any given initial value $K_0 = K(0)$.

5.3   RAMSEY'S PROBLEM

The rate of consumption C in, any moment is supposed to have a rate of utility U determined as a function $U = g(C)$ of C. If C is a function of t then so is U, and the total utility, or satisfaction, associated with a finite time interval from the present $t = 0$ to some $t > 0$ is then the integral

$$P(t) = \int_0^t U\, dt$$

of U over that interval. The larger this value is the better, since having as much utility as possible is the objective.

Instead of a finite interval of time for this objective, Ramsey takes all time from the present throughout the future; that is, $t = \infty$. If U happens to have a positive lower bound, then this integral would always be infinite, so one cannot ask for it to be larger.

However, Ramsey supposes utility U has a finite upper limit U^*, the 'bliss' value. Anyone who enjoys that amount of utility all the time cannot do better, and the objective is to be as near to that state as possible. Though the pleasure integral $P(\infty)$ might be infinite, displeasure, or the distance from the continuous state of bliss, can be measured by the integral of the bliss shortage $U^* - U$ over time. Even if this is not zero, it could be finite, and then the objective can be to make it as small as possible. Therefore the integral

$$D(t) = \int_t^\infty (U^* - U)\,dt$$

is considered, applying to the future from any time t, in particular $t = 0$. With some initial capital K for time t, the object is to make this a minimum, subject to the constraints described in the last section. The minimum V, if it exists, will be a function of $V = V(K, t)$ of the capital K at time t.

Since utility now has a finite upper bound if, unethically, a discount factor $s > 0$ on future utility is allowed, then the discounted sum of utilities is given by the integral

$$\int_0^\infty U e^{-st}\,dt,$$

which now is certainly finite, and it makes sense to maximize this. But the savings rule, which has a simple graphical implementation, is associated with the case $s = 0$.

Should the bliss level U^* of utility be attained with a finite level $C^* < \infty$ of consumption, then we have

$$g(C) < U^* \text{ if } C < C^*,$$
$$g(C) = U^* \text{ if } C \geq C^*.$$

If capital K is already large enough to provide enough income $Y = f(K)$ for bliss in every moment, that is, if $Y \geq C^*$, then $V = 0$. There is not even any need to save, and if surplus income is saved then capital will continue to grow, but uselessly, since one cannot do better than $V = 0$ in the model. This is a problem only for the rich, or for those whose wants are moderate. Others may consult Ramsey's theory to find out what to do—if they can meet his stringent requirements, and the ethics.

5.4   THE RULE

The Savings Rule tells us how to determine the amount of a given income that should be saved, and therefore also how much should be consumed. The first step is to draw the consumption utility curve $U = g(C)$, as in Figure 1. The way it is drawn shows the assumptions made about the curve, or about the utility function g.

As usual, more is better, at least up to the point of satiation, and certainly it is never worse. An issue is whether bliss is attainable with finite consumption, or whether the upper limit U^* of utility is also a maximum. If the utility curve reaches the bliss line at any finite consumption point $C^* < \infty$ it cannot go any higher, and since it also does not go any lower it stays there; the function,

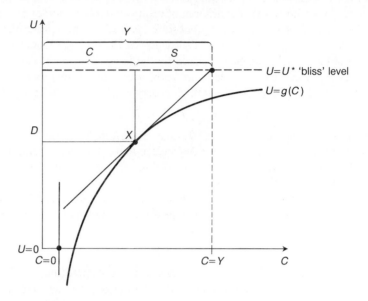

Figure 1   The Savings Rule

having reached its maximum value, remains there. Otherwise the bliss line is asymptotic to the utility curve, approached indefinitely closely but never reached. The curve therefore slopes upwards indefinitely, unless it reaches the bliss line, when it would flatten and remain constant. With $u = U' = g'(C)$ denoting the marginal utility of consumption, we have:

$$u > 0 \text{ if } C < C^*,$$
$$u = 0 \text{ if } C \geq C^*.$$

If $C^* = \infty$, this means $u > 0$ for all C.

Another assumption shown in Figure 1 is that marginal utility of consumption decreases as the level of consumption rises; that is, there are diminishing marginal returns on consumption, expressed by the progressive flattening of the utility curve. Since marginal utility is non-negative and non-increasing, when it reaches the value 0 it stays there, so its derivative then is 0. With $u' = g''(C)$ as the rate of change of marginal utility, therefore

$$u' < 0 \text{ if } C < C^*,$$
$$u' = 0 \text{ if } C > C^*.$$

The assumptions together make the utility function g a non-decreasing concave function. As such, it increases steadily, and if it reaches a maximum it then remains constant.

The way the curve is drawn in the figure, utility becomes $-\infty$ below some positive level of consumption; in other words, there is a positive subsistence level. No amount of utility—or even 'bliss', which here is a finite quantity—in the future can offset the $-\infty$ below this level. The future will never arrive, and there is no solution but a dissolution of the savings problem. With any amount of income above the subsistence level it is possible to save and be better off in the future, and at the end of time to be as well off as anybody else. Social, political and ethical implications of the theory might be imagined here.

With this picture, the Savings Rule is easily stated. Take the point on the bliss line corresponding to the given income Y, and rotate a line about it until it touches the utility curve, say at X. The vertical line through X cuts the bliss line at a point dividing income Y into two parts, with consumption C on the left and savings S on the right.

Displeasure, $D = U^* - U$, with this result is the vertical distance of X from the bliss line, and this decreases as Y increases. The slope of the tangent line is D/S, and since this is the marginal utility of consumption at the level C, we have $u = D/S$. The level of saving is therefore such as to satisfy the condition

$$S = (U^* - U)/u.$$

According to Ramsey's theorem, a requirement for optimality is saving always so as to satify this condition.

5.5 KEYNES'S ARGUMENT

Ramsey attributes to Keynes the following argument for the Savings Rule. Suppose that, in a year when S should have been saved, an extra £1 has been consumed. The effect of the extra unit of consumption is to add the marginal amount u to the utility enjoyed and so to lessen the distance from bliss by that amount. But, by saving only $S - 1$ instead of S, the accumulation of capital which would have been achieved after one year by saving S has been delayed to time T, where $(S - 1)T = S$. Since $T = 1 + 1/S$, to order $1/S$, the delay is $1/S$. The effect of this delay is to add $(U^* - U)/S$ to the distance from bliss. If

$$u > (U^* - U)/S$$

then saving $S - 1$ instead of S is justified, since the resulting gain exceeds the loss. But by hypothesis S is just the amount which should have been saved, so this is impossible. Similarly, the reverse inequality is impossible, leaving the equality as the only possibility and proving the rule.

The argument may be brilliant but it is not completely wholesome. Just one year of escape from the proper savings rate is considered. The consumption benefit is evaluated in it, and so going on saving beyond that at the rate $S - 1$ spoils the evaluation, since there would be additional consumption benefits. A resumption of optimal saving at the end of the year would require a rate above S, not a continuation at the rate $S - 1$. Since the consumption benefit of the rate $S - 1$ was calculated only for that year and not for the longer period of reduced saving, the cost and benefit comparison that was made is problematic.

The argument can be patched up, and it will be done in two ways. The first, where there is a cost-benefit comparison for the longer period, is more like the original. For the second, which goes towards Ramsey's argument dealt with in the next section, there is again the one-year comparison which was offered but not clearly delivered.

Starting with capital K and doing the right thing in that year and for ever after, the distance from bliss is $V(K)$. This can be broken up into enjoyment during the year and after, thus:

$$V(K) = (U^* - U) + V(K + S).$$

If instead of S there is a lower rate of saving $S - 1$ over $S/(S - 1)$ years, so that the period is longer but the capital accumulated in it is again exactly S, and a resumption of good behaviour after that, the total distance becomes

$$V = \{U^* - (U + u)\} S/(S - 1) + V(K + S),$$

and the difference is

$$V - V(K) = \{(U^* - U) - uS\}/(S - 1).$$

If this were positive or negative, S could not have been the optimal rate; therefore it is zero, and we have the Savings Rule.

For the second argument, the effects on the two terms of the year of deviation, consuming an extra £1 and saving $S - 1$ instead of S, are

$$\{U^* - U(C + 1)\} - \{U^* - U(C)\} = -u,$$

as originally offered, and

$$V(K + S - 1) - V(K + S) = -dV(K + S)/dS.$$

For S to be optimal these must be equal. With positive savings, capital continually increases with time, so time can be expressed as a function of capital and we have

$$dt = (dt/dK)dK = dK/S.$$

Therefore, with capital K at $t = 0$ and $K + $ at $t = \infty$, the distance function is
$$V(K) = \int_0^\infty (U^* - U)dt$$
$$= \int_K^{K+} (U^* - U)dK/S,$$

so that

$$dV(K)/dK = -(U^* - U)/S,$$

and therefore

$$dV(K + S))/dS = -(U^* - U)/S.$$

Hence for the effects to be equal, as is required for S to be optimal, the condition is

$$u = (U^* - U)/S,$$

as required.

5.6 RAMSEY'S ARGUMENT

Ramsey transforms the distance integral as in the last section and then goes a step further. Because $S = f(K) - C$, the transformed integral becomes

$$v(K) = \int_K^{K^+} (U^* - U)dK/(f(K) - C).$$

For every K, C can be chosen to make the integrand a minimum, and this will minimize the integral. The C-derivative of the integrand is

$$-u/S + (U^* - U)/S^2,$$

and this vanishes if $S = (U^* - U)/u$, as required.

That shows Ramsey's derivation of the rule, but the second order conditions for a minimum should be verified. The second derivative of the integrand is

$$-u'/S + 2(-u/S + (U^* - U)/S^2)/S,$$

and if the first order conditions are satisfied this reduces to $-u'/S$. With $S > 0$ and $u' < 0$, this value is positive, as required for a strict local minimum.

It is established that, with assumptions that have been made, Ramsey's rule is both necessary and sufficient for a local minimum of the integrand. But from the construction in section 5.4, for any income Y a unique savings rate is determined by the rule. It follows that the minimum is unique and therefore global. A conclusion which can be supplied now is that a minimum does exist for the distance from bliss integral, and moreover it is achieved by saving at the rate determined by Ramsey's rule in every moment. The sufficiency of Ramsey's rule for optimality is therefore proved.

5.7 TIME PATHS

The Savings Rule determines S, and therefore also C, U and u, as a function of Y, and also therefore as functions of K, and monotonicities provide inverses for all these relations. But we are still without references in time.

The savings rule is stated by the relation

$$uS = U^* - U.$$

Differentiating this, using $S = f(K) - C$,

$$(du/dt)S + u(f'(K)dK/dt - dC/dt) = -udC/dt,$$

and this with $S = dK/dt$ gives

$$du/dt = -uf'(K).$$

Regarding K as a function of u, here we have a differential equation for u as a function of t. For the inverse function, it gives

$$t = -\int_{u_0}^u du/uf'(K).$$

Alternatively, one could regard it as a differential equation for the other variables which are monotonically related to u. With $u > 0$ and $f'(K) > 0$ we have $du/dt < 0$, that is, u is decreasing and so also C is increasing with time. Either the bliss value, where $u = 0$, is attained at the start by having enough initial capital, and maintaining it thereafter, or it is approached asymptotically.

Ramsey obtained the time-differential equation directly in the following way. He considered an element of consumption ΔC at time t and the alternative of postponing it for a time Δt, when it would have grown to an amount

$$\{1 + f'(K)\,\Delta t\,\}\Delta\,C.$$

Equalizing the contributions to utility of these alternatives, he obtained

$$u(t)\,\Delta C = u(t + \Delta t\,\{1 + f'(K)\,\Delta t\,\}\Delta C,$$

and then

$$\{u(t) - u(t + \Delta t)\}\,/\,\Delta t = u(t + \Delta t)f'(K).$$

Then, in the limit as $\Delta t \to 0$,

$$du/dt = -\,uf'(K).$$

The rule can also be recovered from the differential equation. For with $Y = f(K)$, so that $dY/dt = f'(K)dK/dt$, and with $dK/dt = Y - C$, the differential equation gives

$$(du/dt)(Y - C) + udY/dt = 0,$$

all variables being functions of t. But since $dU/dt = udC/dt$, in any case

$$(d/dt)\,\{u(Y - C\} = (du/dt)(Y - C) + udY/dt - dU/dt,$$

so now we have

$$(d/dt)\,\{u(Y - C) + U\} = (du/dt)(Y - C) + udY/dt.$$

This shows that the differential equation is equivalent to

$$(d/dt)\,\{u(Y - C) + U\} = 0,$$

which by integration gives

$$u(Y - C) + U = B,$$

B being a constant. Because $S = Y - C$, it remains now to identify the constant of integration B with the bliss value U^*.

It has already been argued that, with the differential equation, we have either $u = 0$ always, or, alternatively, $u > 0$ always, while $u \to 0$. But from the assumptions made, if $u \to 0$ then $U \to U^*$. Hence $U \to U^*$ as $t \to \infty$, and this shows that $B = U^*$.

The same differential equation is obtained by calculus of variations. Thus applied to minimizing the integral

$$\int F(K, H)dt$$

where $H = dK/dt$ and

$$F(K, H) = U^* - U(f(K) - H)$$

so that

$$F_K = -\,uf'(K), \qquad F_H = u,$$

Euler's equation $F_K = dF_H/dt$ gives $du/dt = -\,uf'(K)$.

5.8 A SPECIAL CASE

Consider the case with a production function of the form $f(K) = rK$ where r is constant, touched on in section 5.2. This would apply to a bank savings account with a fixed interest factor r. For this case the differential equation of the last section becomes $du/dt = -ur$, and the solution is

$$u = u_0 e^{-rt},$$

where $u = u_0$ at $t = 0$. The marginal utility u declines to zero exponentially at the rate r, as $t \to \infty$. Correspondingly, utility U rises and converges to the bliss level $U^* < \infty$, and consumption C rises and converges to its satiation value $C^* \le \infty$, as $t \to \infty$.

These conclusions are all independent of the particular utility function g which determines $U = g(C)$. If a particular utility function is given, one can proceed further. For example, consider

$$g(C) = B - 1/C.$$

The utility bliss value is $U^* = B$. The consumption satiation value is $C^* = \infty$, so the bliss value is approached only asymptotically. Marginal utility is $u = 1/C^2$, and Ramsey's rule requires $uS = B - U$, so in this case $S/C^2 = 1/C$, that is, $S = C$. Since $Y = C + S$, therefore,

$$C = Y/2, \ S = Y/2,$$

so in this case the Savings Rule requires that exactly half of any income be saved, and half consumed.

Now further, since $dK/dt = S$ and $Y = f(K)$, we have

$$dK/dt = f(K)/2,$$

and so, with any initial capital K_0 at $t = 0$,

$$t = 2 \int_{K_0}^{K} dK/f(K).$$

For the particular case $f(K) = rK$, therefore,

$$K = K_0 e^{rt/2},$$

and, since C and S are both equal to $f(K)/2 = rK/2$, we have similar relations for them. Moreover

$$U = B - 2e^{-rt/2}/rK_0,$$

showing the distance from bliss declining exponentially at the rate $r/2$.

5.9 DISCOUNTED FUTURE

Suppose now that future utility is discounted at a rate $w > 0$, so the total discounted utility is

$$V = \int_0^\infty U e^{-wt} \, dt.$$

Given that utility U has a finite upper bound U^*, we have

$$V \leq U^* \int_0^\infty e^{-wt} \, dt$$
$$= U^* [-e^{-wt} / w]_0^\infty$$
$$= U^* / w,$$

so that V is finite. In this case maximizing V is the same as minimizing the total discounted distance from bliss given by

$$\int_0^\infty (U^* - U)e^{-wt} \, dt.$$

Proceeding as in section 5.5 suppose S is the optimal savings rate for the first year, and consider saving $S - 1$ for

$$S/(S - 1) = 1 + 1/(S - 1)$$

years instead, and then resuming optimal savings. For the two cases we have

$$V(K) = U^* - U + e^{-w} V(K + S)$$

and

$$V = \{U^* - (U + u)\} \, S/(S - 1) + e^{-w\{1 + S/(S - 1)\}} V(K + S).$$

Since

$$e^{-w(1 + \epsilon)} = (1 - w\epsilon)e^{-w},$$

to the first order, the difference is

$$V - V(K) = \{ (U^* - U) - uS \}/(S - 1) + wV(K + S)/(S - 1).$$

For this to be zero,

$$(U^* - U) - uS + wV(K + S) = 0,$$

so, with 'year' indefinitely small making S negligible compared with K,

$$(U^* - U) - uS + wV(K) = 0.$$

If $w = 0$ we have Ramsey's rule; otherwise this replaces it.

For a restatement,

$$uS + U = U^* + w \int_0^\infty (U^* - U)e^{-wt} \, dt.$$

Equivalently,

$$uS + U = w \int_0^\infty U e^{-wt} \, dt.$$

We will now show this is equivalent to

$$du/dt = -u \{f'(K) - w\}.$$

Thus, multiply this relation by

$$dK/dt = S = Y - C,$$

where $Y = f(K)$, and we have

$$S \, du/dt + u \, dY/dt = wuS.$$

But, from section 5.7,

$$(d/dt)(uS + U) = S \, du/dt + u \, dY/dt,$$

so this is

$$(d/dt)(uS + U) = wuS.$$

Equivalently,

$$(d/dt)\{e^{-wt}(uS + U)\} = -we^{-wt}U.$$

Then, by integration,

$$[e^{-wt}(uS + U)]_0^\infty = -w\int_0^\infty e^{-wt}U dt.$$

On the left with $t =$ we have zero, and with the value for $t = 0$ we obtain the generalized rule, as required. These steps can be reversed and so the wanted equivalence is shown.

Ramsey's argument in section 5.6 can be modified to obtain the same differential equation. The element of consumption ΔC which there had a growth factor $1 + f'(K)\Delta t$ now also has a discount factor $1 - w\Delta t$, making a resultant factor

$$1 + \{f'(K) - w\}\Delta t.$$

Then, continuing the argument as before gives the result

$$du/dt = -u\{f'(K) - w\}.$$

We have the same result by calculus of variations, applying Euler's equation to the maximum of

$$\int_0^\infty F(K, dK/dt, t)dt,$$

where

$$F = g(f(K) - dK/dt)e^{-wt}.$$

Part II

USE AND EXCHANGE

II.1

Utility Hypothesis

The word VALUE, it is to be observed, has two different meanings, and sometimes expresses the utility of some particular object,
and sometimes the power of purchasing other goods which the
possession of that object conveys. The one may be called 'value
in use'; the other, 'value in exchange'

Adam Smith, *The Wealth of Nations*, Volume I

[Henry Sidgwick] ate his dinner not because he had toted up the
satisfactions to be gained therefrom, but because he was hungry.

told by **Robert Heilbroner,** *The Worldly Philosophers*,
(5th edition), p. 173

The distinction offered by Adam Smith is easily appreciated in some fashion,
and his terms for it are still in use. But what altogether should be made of
it has remained uncertain. In whatever form it takes, the 'theory of value' has
been the subject of endless pursuit. His reference must be to things that are
subject to choice and, when they are wanted, can become objects of trade.
These need not always be commodities, or bear a market price, or even be of
a material kind at all. There is trade in liberty, justice, simplicity, and in favours;
it takes place also with nature, or technology, or wherever there are allowances
under a constraint. Talk about certain values being 'absolute' (or not) relates
to their availability for trade.

Value has a bearing in decisions, distinguishing and comparing issues in an
attempt to arrive at a conclusion. The mathematical usage where a function
has 'values', and so gives things numbers or other labels, is somewhat different, though even that might be related to the economic sense, since perhaps
it comes from analogy with the ordinary experience of things having numbers
in the market. Otherwise, value is related mostly to use in some purpose. Use
and value have common meanings, and often are synonyms. In that way 'value
in use' is something of a pleonasm. Objects have many uses, the individual
uses are all part of their general, overall use, and by the optimizing principle
the best application is chosen for the occasion, as the example of beating swords
into ploughshares illustrates. One can keep a thing or, with the opportunities
provided by the market or by 'technology', exchange it for (or beat it into)
another thing. The thing, and any of the other things by which it could be

replaced, are alternatives which embody different uses of the same thing. In any case, a thing has value only because it is wanted by someone, and that is the cause of any exchange, because it is impossible to exchange a thing which no one wants.

With things that have a price on the market, their exchange value is simply that price—and if you are going to sell them, that is also their use value. But, in its original intention, the idea of use value had nothing to do with price. Goods are supposed to be useful in themselves, quite apart from accidental exchange value. This value is original, but it is also the basis for exchange value. As can be submitted, it is an achievement of general equilibrium theory that it can show how this might be possible; also, this may be all there is in 'theory of value' that is relevant to economics.

A producer exchanges inputs for outputs, and in maximizing profit the technical exchange rates coincide with market exchange rates. For the consumer, Gossen's Law requires use exchange rates to coincide with market exchange rates. The interesting distinction becomes obliterated in the end. It arises from putting market exchanges in a category of their own instead of seeing them as just one sector of exchange opportunity among others, all of which are exploited to the point of equalization required by optimality. The special characteristic of the socially created market is that it offers exchanges governed uniformly by prices. In the general equilibrium picture, exchanges take place modifying individual possessions, and also prices, with the final effect being the coincidence of individual exchange rates with the general market exchange rates, whatever they are finally. In equilibrium there is a global equalization of exchange rates, whether they be associated with consumers' utilities, producers' technologies, or market exchange.

Phyllis Deane (1978, p. 23) describes various 'interrelated difficulties involved in devising an acceptable theory of value'. One of them 'lies in actually measuring value in operational terms—for if value is not measurable the theory is not testable'. Over these difficulties there is a puzzling ambiguity about what is meant by 'theory of value'. Theories which claim consideration under the same general heading seem to have no relation to each other at all.

The theory of general economic equilibrium goes towards other interests also, but it does contain something of a theory of value. That might have been the thought of Gerard Debreu (1959) in calling his book *Theory of Value : An Axiomatic Analysis of Economic Equilibrium*. But he does not dwell on the idea, and so one must gather that value here simply means price. With his and other models, the utility functions of individuals are given, and they determine individual exchange rates, which generally are different from each other in any economic position, but in the final position are all equal, their common value being the equilibrium prices, or exchange rates.

This is a theory of value to the extent of showing how diverse individual utilities, or value functions, can be a basis for the socially uniform exchange rates required in the idea of market prices. An important point is that these exchange rates are still for the individual, each one separately, despite their coincidence. On the other hand, one should not see them as exchange rates for an overall social welfare. There is no social value in this model, at least not one that has reference to the commodity space or the utility space. One could see social value in the theoretical coordinating effectiveness of the market mechanism and the stability—but that would be in another 'space' altogether, not one recognized in this model. Despite that, there are persistent visions of social optimality, as we well know. The problem there is not mathematical, but comes from inertia of conventionality and piety about old words, preserving them as part of current thought instead of as curious items from a primitive past.

Sraffa's prices are associated with another approach to theory of value altogether, and make a play with forms and consistencies that might be required were the 'labour theory of value' applied in some fashion. Regardless of inherent inconsistencies that can be found, and formal steps taken to evade them of the kind dealt with in Chapter IV.4, the entire approach shares in mysteries coming from the early beginnings in the subject—or from Ricardo, for whom theory of value was the final goal of economic thought—that are still not clarified. With the 'labour-pain' recognized by Quesnay, and by everyone else, one can think that here might be a quest for a justice where reward equals pain instead of product. The measurement of pains and rewards creates a problem, and how 'Love's Labour Lost' should come into the settlement creates another. Anyway, the words bring those who labour to the centre of the picture, and Marx cleverly picked them up.

In contrast, the general equilibrium theory of value is perfectly clear. The consumers' utility functions are taken formally to be given, and there is no concern with how they could be known. The 'difficulties' described by Phyllis Deane might seem to have a bearing, but not much, considering the objective of the theory. It is a theory of consistency, which involves the elements in the economy to the extent of their described general nature, and not beyond that.

A notable point about the individuals of the new models is that they are working individuals—not just consumers, but visibly producers as well. Their utility depends on production output as well as consumption input. This is in contrast with the textbook consumer, who has an income, from an unknown source, to spend and whose utility has nothing to do with labour or its pain, the only possible pain being a shortage of consumption. The utility curves are drawn boxed in as in Edgeworth's box, never crossing the commodity space boundary to give evidence of production. These would be pure capitalist consumers of the ownership class, living in bounty from the toil of workers and knowing nothing of work themselves—from the shape of their curves, it is clear they have not even thought about it. But now they have changed their character, though textbooks take no notice, not even of the need for a change. Also, utility has become 'ordinal' beside being confined to the consumption space; throwing out everything not ordinal, credited to Pareto, eliminates the only possible tie between consumption and productive work.

The textbook consumer can be redeemed to an extent by granting that the operative utility is really a function $U(x, y)$ of consumption x and production y, increasing in the one and decreasing in the other, and that it enters into the overall problem

$$\max U(x, y) : px = py + a(p),$$

$a(p)$ being a profit function representing unearned income, if any, as formulated in Chapter IV.5. The general activity z of the consumer is here resolved into a difference $z = y - x$ of non-negative parts, so the problem in effect has the form

$$\max W(z) : pz = a(p).$$

The assumption made now, for a reconciliation with the textbook account, is that the utility has the separable form

$$U(x, y) = F(g(x), y).$$

When the overall problem is solved, with the solution (x, y), we can take the income $M = py + a(p)$, and then x is also a solution of the problem

$$\max g(x) : px = M.$$

Of course, M is not known until the overall problem is solved. However, here the picture is that the individual works to earn, or otherwise obtains, the income M; but since consumption utility is separable in the overall utility, we need not talk about that aspect—that is, again, once we know M. It is completely usual in economics to represent a dependence between input and output. A defect of this picture is that the consumer's consumption needs are independent of what the consumer is doing, which is not realistic unless the consumer is doing nothing.

A comment on Quesnay's 'greatest satisfaction attained with the least labour-pain' fits here. It is impossible to understand this plainly as received, and it invites experiment in modification. The satisfaction is localized in x and the pain in y. For pain to have a distinct measure which can be minimized, Quesnay requires the further separability in overall utility which gives it the form

$$U(x, y) = F(g(x), h(y)).$$

With the usually understood monoticities, and with all variables taking all non-negative values, if satisfaction $g(x)$ is maximized under the budget constraint $px = py + a(p)$, it will be infinite, but so will be the pain. If, instead, the pain $g(y)$ is minimized it will be zero, but satisfaction will depend on the unearned income $a(p)$, if there is any. Possibly Quesnay has been incorrectly received and his principle should apply to a different model. Such a model would not be hard to discover; it is in evidence with anyone who has a tenured position and minimizes the pain of work consistent with preserving the tenure while spending the income for the greatest satisfaction. The tenure provides ready-made budget and work constraints and two separate optimization problems. Those in more precarious circumstances strike a delicate balance between satisfaction and pain by maximizing the function $F(g(x), h(y))$, or, if they are not to be forced into this separability, by a function $U(x, y)$.

Contrary arguments of the sort given above do not destroy the distinction between use and exchange value in detachment from equilibrium. Whether or not this has been neglected as one of the main achievements, the theory of general equilibrium pictures a remarkable global coincidence that abolishes the distinction, as concerns general equilibrium. But you still need the distinction in order to enjoy the coincidence that gives a relief from the responsibility of having to pursue it—except in artificial circumstances like when we have 'indexation'. Use value represents the relation that goods have to an individual and varies between individuals; it is easy to talk about it without knowing what it is. Exchange value is understandable unproblematically as market value determined by prices. If they are actual prices, then, with a belief in them as general equilibrium prices, they reveal use value also, for everyone. But in the imagination they could be any prices, such as last year's. In that case we do have the awkward distinction—and the 'index number problem'.

A bundle of goods x is bought when the prices are p and so a demand (x, p) has been observed. The bundle has exchange value $E = px$, and any other bundle y with the same exchange value, or smaller, could have been bought instead, but was not. There is nothing here that is not in principle a matter of direct observation. But then it is offered that the goods have another value, independent of their exchange value; their use value. It is that which causes them to be bought and justifies the sacrifice involved. The reason why x is bought instead of any y which could have taken its place for the same or even a lesser expenditure is because it has higher use value to the buyer and so is preferable by that criterion. The choice between possibilities is supposed to be made on the basis of a system of preferences applied to the goods by the buyer which has nothing to do with their prices or the money needed to possess them, all of which are observable. The preferences are part of the nature of the possessor, about which nothing further is known since the demand (x, p) is the only observation. It is not easy to know what to make of this story. If it has a truth, it is not of the kind that requires a demonstration. Any truth to do with it is not so much *in* it, but *about* it. It is that this represents a common way of thinking in economics, and one that is imposed with the popular 'cost of living' question.

1.1 NEEDS OF MEASUREMENT

The interests of theory are different from those coming from everyday needs. One should not have to think of 'measuring' utility just because it is talked about in theory, especially the kind of theory, so well represented in economics, in which form is everything. The separability of consumption utility might be unacceptable as a description of the real consumer; but real consumers insist on it in demands for protection of their purchasing power. When prices change they do not wish to change their work, but their pay should be adjusted to ensure them a constant level of utility for their constant level of work. In any case, there is the social need for a yardstick of purchasing power, understood in terms of consumption utility.

Utility applies to the individual, and so there is the question of what utility, and what individual. There would be no problem if that were settled, but in the simplest circumstances knowing about utility presents a problem. It can be understood to depend on general activity, on the work done, and on all kinds of factors. But in this public matter there cannot be a separate treatment for every individual, or even for every kind of work or similar factor, on the assumption that all individuals in similar circumstances are similar. Then, consumption has already been separated from everything else in the initial thought.

The utility being considered, therefore, applies to consumption alone. There is to be no separate treatment for individuals with their different utilities; in any case, that is practically impossible. Then the democratic impartiality which is a force in this matter requires that we take all individuals to be similar as concerns utility. They face the same prices, and the only recognized differences between them are their incomes. The data, and the method to produce from them a resolution of the puchasing power question, should embody that impartiality. There is an analogy here with the questions about the individual and the group dealt with in Chapter I.3, with which the investigations of K. J. Arrow are associated. The measurement problem is not the one described by Phyllis Deane, since there is no theory to test. There is a kind of 'measurement' involved, not quite like taking a temperature but influenced by thought and general social acceptability, based on a use of expenditure data, which is rather like taking a vote. A model is used that could be, and very frequently is, construed as a behaviour description of the individual consumer. Here we have no obligation to accept it as such. For all one need care, it could be another of those idealizations conjured up in economic thinking and, from being taught again and again on countless blackboards, come to be regarded as knowledge. But it happens to give an intelligibility to this socially originated income adjustment problem that is hard to find otherwise.

The question is popularly imposed, without a popular concern for its possible logic. That matter is taken up by the theory of index numbers, which may not always be conditioned by the simplicity required in the social use or by immediate statistical practicality, but which affects thinking none the less. It has some value in itself and for historical reasons derived from the long attention that has been given to its questions, and also for its part in making more explicit the sense that some terms used in economics may or may not have. Questions seemingly similar to the present one but much less tractable arise in other connections where there is a 'price level'. There are many prices and so many levels, and it may be asked in what sense they should have a single level. If just having a word for it is enough, it might also be allowed that, in games with words, it is sufficient for the matter of understanding, just to join in the play. The question has a perfectly good resolution here, involving highly restrictive conditions, but this is not the only place where 'price level' is encountered.

A reason has been given for wanting to measure consumers' utility and for doing it in a particular way. It must be as if the consumers do nothing but consume, and are in similar circumstances with similar wants, their differences being only in their incomes. The result then is applicable to all individuals separately and equally. It is not an aggregate, but rather an unbiased democratic average of individuals. The dissociation that comes from separation in time destroys the comparison dealt with, but it is wanted, and so the yardstick for it—the utility that persists through time and its changes, including the price changes—must be statistically determined across time as if time did not matter. With the change, and its neglect, the homogenization of individuals, which also is embodied in the principle of this matter, is easy to accept. A further homogenization occurs in the practice of representing the entire structure sought by a single number, the price index. Even that has acceptability, considering the nature of the original question and the compromises in giving it a practical answer.

The approach to be followed has a perspective with traditional demand analysis, next to which it is seen as a finite variation. The main concern has usually been with the mathematics of demand functions, and with the estimation of models from econometric data. The 'integrability' problem, concerning the determination of utility from demand functions, has been dealt with familiarly by the differential calculus approach of Antonelli and Slutsky and the relational approach of Samuelson and Houthakker. But a basic observation on the consumer consists in a demand observation of the form (x, p), giving quantities demanded and the prices. A finite collection of such observations could in principle be available. The theory of index numbers has dealt mostly with just two, and in any case with a finite number; in contrast, a demand function represents an infinite collection. But any econometric demand function has been estimated from a finite collection, and has a highly restricted form, imposed only by requirements of statistical workability. It is unsuitable to apply questions to the demand function which can also apply directly to the original demand observations from which it has been artificially constructed. This is true of index number questions which refer to two demand observations, and also when they involve more.

The approach to demand analysis based on a finite collection of demand observations, instead of a demand function, is appropriate for dealing with index numbers; also, it stands apart from that subject as parallel to the theory which has applied usually to demand functions. The questions dealt with are similar, but now we have indeterminacies, important for index numbers, and one of the interests is to characterize them completely. The mathematics of the subject is quite different. It belongs more to combinatorial linear algebra than to the differential calculus, and is finitely constructive everywhere. It is anyway quite peculiar to this work. There is a connection with the theory of minimum paths in networks, which from the surface of the matters dealt with may seem unlikely. This chapter and the next deal with concept and method while other chapters take further the index number and other related interests.

A motivation arising from index number questions has been offered for dealing statistically with utility. There seem no other grounds, since no additional power for predicting behaviour is obtained from it; rather the contrary. At the same time, statistical practice with price indices, directed to the same matter, has a remoteness from the theory based on utility. That should deserve a comment.

The next section, like the somewhat different account of 'Fleetwood's Student' in *The Price Index* (see Afriat, 1978b), gives a way of looking at the practice by reference to William Fleetwood (1707), which helps to clarify a view of the relationship, and perhaps explains why practice has been unperturbed by the centuries of theory that followed. There then follows an outline of the theory about demand functions associated especially with Antonelli (1886) and Slutsky (1915) and with Samuelson (1948) and Houthakker (1950), and its finite counterpart.

1.2   COMMON PRACTICE, AND FLEETWOOD

> . . . money is of no other use, than it is the thing with which we purchase the necessities and conveniences of life. . . .
>
> **William Fleetwood** *Chronicon Preciosum,* 1707

When prices change, the same amount of money might not be able to buy the same things as before, and certainly not if all prices have increased. If prices change from p_0 to p_1 and x is the bundle of goods being bought, then, instead of the original amount of money $M_0 = p_0 x$, the new amount $M_1 = p_1 x$ is needed. Much more is said about the purchasing power question, but for the arithmetic involved this is the foundation of current statistical practice, as it was also for the calculation of William Fleetwood in 1707.

With prices p_0, p_1 given for two periods 0 and 1, to be distinguished as the *base* and *current periods*, any bundle x determines a point with coordinates M_0, M_1. This we call the *Fleetwood point*, $F(x) = (M_0, M_1)$, associated with x in the *income space*. If x has a locus C in the commodity space, then $F(x)$ has a corresponding locus in the income space, the *Fleetwood locus*, $F(C)$, corresponding to the *consumption locus*, C. In particular, if C is a line in the commodity space, then $F(C)$ is a line in the income space, and if one goes through the origin of its space, then so does the other.

The amounts of expenditure on the various goods in period $t = 0$ or 1 are

$p_{ti} x_i$ for $i = 1, \ldots, n$ and so the *expenditure shares* which express each as a fraction of the total,

$$M_t = p_t x = \Sigma_i p_{ti} x_i,$$

are $w_{ti} = p_{ti} x_i / p_t x$, such that

$$w_{ti} \geq 0, \ \Sigma_i w_{ti} = 1.$$

The *cost ratio* $R = M_1 / M_0$ has the expression

$$R = \Sigma_i p_{1i} x_i / M_0 = \Sigma_i (p_{1i}/p_{0i}) p_{0i} x_i / M_0 = \Sigma_i (p_{1i}/p_{0i}) w_{0i}$$

as an average of the price ratios p_{1i}/p_{0i}, with *weights* given by the expenditure shares w_{0i} of period 0. This is the slope of the line from the origin in the income space going through the Fleetwood point, $F(x)$. As x varies, on any locus, so does the slope $R = R(x)$ of this line, or ray. It will *not* vary only if the Fleetwood points $F(x)$ all lie together on the same ray in the income space, as would be the case if the consumption points x all lay on the same ray in the commodity space.

The cost ratio $R(x)$ associated with any bundle of goods x has no general significance, and it had none at all for Fleetwood. It has importance for current practice only because a varied population is dealt with instead of one typical individual with a life-style represented by a single bundle of goods x; and at the same time, practical simplicity requires a single number to state the individual cost ratio for everyone. Conceptually, the *consumer price index* (CPI) is an estimate of the cost ratio for a bundle or goods representative of the entire community. Whether this be an average or an aggregate of consumption makes no difference to the ratio, provided the individuals are identified in the same way, as wage earners, households, or a subgroup of those, or whatever. An ambiguity when individuals have to be identified is avoided when x is approached as a comprehensive aggregate. Corresponding to its ordinary use, $R(x)$ is then uniformly applicable to all money allocated to consumption.

We can understand the described procedure with the CPI and the compromises involved in it by returning to the original procedure of Fleetwood and putting the one in terms of the other. Defects in both are brought out by examining their consistency with the thinking that derives from the utility theory. Whether or not any shortcomings seen in this way or on other grounds deserve a remedy may then better be determined. In any case, this must depend on factors specific to circumstances of the use. There is a rejection not of the conventional procedure but of its textbook association with the Laspeyres and Paasche formulae of price index theory, and a connection instead with Fleetwood's elementary procedure.

Bishop William Fleetwood found it unjust that a theft of £1 or over should be a capital offence. The law had been made 'in H.VI's Days' four hundred years earlier, and prices had increased in the meanwhile. This early case was for the indexation of crime. He argued similarly about a statute that required the resignation of any Fellow of a certain College who had an annual income of £5. As he said, the value of money resides just in the things it can buy, and in this sense had deteriorated. There is ambiguity in the fact that money can buy many things. The price of a particular good is of no importance to someone who never buys it. According to the utility theory, money buys utility through intermediate goods that have it. Standard of living is measured by utility, and cost of living is the minimum cost of attaining a standard at the prevailing prices of the goods. If costs of goods all increase, then so does the cost of any living standard. There is no limitation to the talk about utility until there is a need to know what it is, or how to measure it. It takes place freely, except that it ceases when one gets to the Statistical Office.

This chapter is concerned with the peculiar measurement problem, and what can be made of it in a particular way. It would not have been useful for Fleetwood to have brought in utility, if he had thought of it, any more that it is useful now to bring it in with the CPI. Standard of living was for him, as it is in current practice, a concrete bundle of goods representing a particular lifestyle. Fleetwood's argument occurs is in a letter to a student, and he took the student life as the model for his illustration, involving '4 Hogsheads of Beer, 6 Yards of Cloth, 5 Quarters of Wheat, . . .'. He found that '£5 in H.VI's Days' would make him 'full as rich a man as he who has now £20'. He might have taken any other representative type and, instead of the figures 5 and 20, obtained some others, say 25 and 50, for a civil servant.

Should every individual in the population perform this calculation, perhaps not over an interval of four hundred years but from one year to another, there would be a consumption point x representing each individual in the commodity space and as many Fleetwood points $F(x)$ in the income space. Instead of all individuals, in practice there is a statistical sample providing a set S in the commodity space. Then the prices for any two years determine a corresponding set $F(S)$ in the income space. If a is the average point of S, then $F(a)$ is the average point of $F(S)$, and the ratio of the coordinates of $F(a)$ is the cost ratio $P = R(a)$, which conceptually is the CPI. This therefore is the slope of the ray in the income space which passes through the average of the Fleetwood points of all the consumptions, which is also the Fleetwood point $F(a)$ of the average consumption a. It is used as if $R(x) = P$ for all x in the sample S, and in the population. If, following this practice, any income M_0 found in one period is adjusted to $M_1 = PM_0$ in the other, then the total of the M_1 would be correct, on Fleetwood's principle, but the distribution of income in the population might be wrong. It would be right in every individual case, at least for the sample, only if all the points of $F(S)$ lay on the same ray in the income space, as would occur, generally, only if all points of S lay on a ray in the commodity space.

The model required in order that the use of the CPI be correct for all individuals in the population is now apparent. It is that the quantities of goods consumed by individuals are in proportion to their incomes; twice the income buys twice as much of everything, and t times buys t times as much. If one individual consumes the bundle x with an income M, then any individual with an income Mt will consume the bundle xt ($t \geq 0$). This tells us that the consumption expansion path is a ray. The condition is highly restrictive and does not allow for the proportions of goods consumed by rich and poor, or their *consumption patterns*, to be very different. Even requiring the expansion path to be a line, not necessarily a ray through the origin, is unacceptable. It tells us that an extra £1 of income given to rich or poor is spent in the same way, that is, that their *marginal consumption patterns* are identical, which is absurd. The poor might spend it all on food, while the rich are already overfed. Expansion paths are definitely curved, turning away from basic necessities and going towards luxuries as income increases. The terminology of *pattern* and *marginal pattern* has been received from W. M. Gorman.

All this, concerning consumption patterns being independent of income, holds whatever the prices. An additional point is that consumption patterns do not change when prices change at different rates; there is no 'substitution' in reaction to a change in relative prices. There is no inherent conflict here with the utility theory, since it is as if every individual in the population has the Leontief-type function

$$f(x) = \max [t : at \leq x]$$

as a utility function. One can only think that the type of function is overlimiting. The earlier objections apply to the CPI, with its bearing on many individuals simultaneously, and Fleetwood is invulnerable to it with his separate treatment of a single individual, or individual type. But this further objection applies to him as well. The practicality of it is another issue, but the utility theory of purchasing power measurement, already seen to be an extension of what we have with the CPI and Fleetwood, is free of these conceptual and statistical limitations. A consideration is whether compromises inherent in any treatment of the measurement question, from the nature of the question, and the data for it, are such as to overwhelm these others, especially when practical constraints coming from the social use are brought in. There are many different issues here, but enough has been described for our immediate interests.

1.3   PARALLELS IN THEORY

The approach to utility construction has commonly dealt with a demand function $x = F(p, M)$. This determines the quantities x of goods demanded as a function of the prices p of the goods and the money M spent on them, M usually being identified with 'income'. The starting point here will be with an arbitrary finite collection of demands (x_t, p_t), $t = 1, 2, \ldots, T$. Any demand (x, p) belongs to a demand function F if $x = F(p, M)$ for $M = px$. One could consider a demand function and the infinite collection of demands belonging to it, or more generally an arbitrary collection, in particular an arbitrary finite collection as here. Now I shall give an outline of theory based on the demand function or, what is in effect the same, the infinite collection of demands associated with one.

Because M is the money spent, and is equal to the cost px of x at the prices p, we have the *budget identity* $px = M$ for $x = F(p, M)$; that is,

$$pF(p, M) = M \text{ for all } p, M.$$

The function F is supposed to describe the behaviour of a consumer. At the same time, there is the theory that the consumer measures utility by some function $U(x)$ putting an order on all possible consumption bundles x, and acts so as to attain the maximum of utility with the money spent. If this is true of the consumer whose behaviour is represented by the demand function F, it can be asked what condition is implied on F, beyond the budget identity which is part of the definition of F. A further question is how, and to what extent, the utility function U is constructible from any F subject to this condition. Put that way, the questions are not well formulated. A constant utility function which makes every point a maximum is always available to be associated with any demand function. For proper questions an elaboration is needed which makes the demand function determined by a utility function.

A utility function $U(x)$ which has a unique maximum x under the constraint $px \le M$ such that $px = M$ is said to be *decisive* for that constraint, and to *decide* the point x on it. If U is decisive for every budget constraint, the point it decides for any constraint is a single-valued function $x = F(p, M)$ of the constraint and so of the p and M which specify it, and satisfies the budget identity. The function F therefore is a demand function, *derived* from the utility function. Since the constraint depends only on the ratio of prices p to the expenditure M, it must satisfy the condition

$$F(pt, Mt) = F(p, M).$$

In words, it must be homogeneous of degree zero in its arguments. This condition is commonly described as the *absence of monetary illusion* and is incorporated into the definition of a demand function. It has been seen here to be a first requirement for a demand function which is derived from some utility function.

Now the originally proposed question about a demand function can be replaced. It is asked, by what criteria can it be known if a given demand function is derivable from some utility function, and if it is, then how can a utility function from which it is derived be constructed from it? Before describing approaches to this question, there is an observation which is of importance again later. With a utility function U and a demand (x, p), the condition for x to give a maximum of utility under the associated budget constraint is stated by

$$H' \equiv py \le px \Rightarrow U(y) \le U(x)$$

for all y; that is, no greater utility is attainable if there is no greater expenditure. Any constant function satisfies this condition, with any demand, and so with any demand function, as already remarked. We do not yet have a proper requirement. But this condition could be joined with the further condition

$$py < px \Rightarrow U(y) < U(x).$$

That is, the expenditure is essential for attaining the utility, or any less expenditure results in less utility. The equivalent, contrapositive form is that

$$H'' \equiv U(y) \geq U(x) \Rightarrow py \geq px.$$

That is, at least as much utility costs at least as much, or the utility has been obtained at minimum cost. In the terms of cost-benefit analysis, with U as the benefit criterion, the first condition is for the demand (x, p) to be *cost-effective* and the second is for it to be *cost-efficient*. The conditions H' and H'' are generally independent. However, properties of the function U can produce relations between them. In particular if U is given to be continuous and semi-increasing then they become equivalent.

The relation between demand and utility functions could have been based on the conjunction H of H' and H'' . That will be more suitable in dealing later with arbitrary collections of demands, instead of with a demand function, and with arbitrary utility orders, instead of a utility function with any special properties. Instead, the relation has been based on the condition

$$H^* \equiv py \leq px, y \neq x \Rightarrow U(y) < U(x)$$

for x to give more utility than any other not exceeding the cost. This implies H, and so is more stringent. But it is the usual condition that plays a part in dealing with a demand function. It is suitable because a demand function is a single-valued function, and so, in order to explain the single value fully on the basis of utility, it would have to be a unique maximum under the budget constraint. It happens that, if the demand function is subject to further conditions, such as the differentiability often assumed, or something less, the resulting conditions become equivalent, so in the particular application there is no mathematical difference between using H or H^*, though there is still a difference of idea and H is the more basic principle. With a demand function which is not single-valued, and so also with arbitrary collections of demands, there is a proper difference.

The condition H^* defines a relation between a utility function U and a demand (x, p), which can also be stated $UH^*(x, p)$. Then a relation between U and a demand function F, which can also be denoted H^*, is defined by its having this relation to every demand of F; thus,

$$UH^*F \equiv x = F(x, px) \Rightarrow xH^*(x, p).$$

The considered question about a given demand function F is whether there exists a utility function having this relation to it, that is, whether $H^*F \neq 0$. With the affirmative, which can be stated $H^*(F)$, the demand function F is *consistent*, in the sense of the hypothesis concerning utility; and any utility function having the relation H^* to F, so demonstrating that consistency, is *compatible* with F. It is clear that only the order in the commodity space represented by a utility function is essential to this relation with a demand function, and all utility functions which represent the same order are equivalent, as concerns the relation. Such equivalent functions are of the form $w(U)$ where w is an arbitrary monotonic increasing function.

For a continuously differentiable demand function $x = F(p, M)$ the question can be settled in terms of the coefficients formed from the derivatives introduced by Slutsky (1915). These are

$$s_{ij} = \partial x_i / \partial p_j + (\partial x_i / \partial M) x_j,$$

forming the matrix $s = x_p + x_M x'$. For the consistency of F, it is necessary and sufficient that the Slutsky matrix s be symmetric and nonpositive definite. What is involved in arriving at this easily stated result is enough to fill a volume—for a proof, see *Demand Functions and the Slutsky Matrix* (Afriat, 1980d). We do well to leave it, and it does not have bearing on anything dealt with now. Instead, the quite different approach to the same question initiated by P. A. Samuelson (1948) and H. S. Houthakker (1950) will have a useful, unprecedented, elaboration.

1.4   REVEALED PREFERENCE

Compatibility of a utility function U with a pair of demands (x, p), (y, q) requires in particular that

$$py \le px, \ y \ne x \Rightarrow U(x) > U(y),$$
$$qx \le qy, \ x \ne y \Rightarrow U(y) > U(x),$$

and since the right-hand sides in conjunction are impossible, so are the left. The impossibility of the left is equivalent to

$$py \le px, \ qx \le qy \Rightarrow x = y,$$

and to

$$py \le px, \ y \ne x \Rightarrow qx > qy.$$

If the utility is compatible with a demand function F, this condition must hold for all pairs of demands belonging to it. With the last statement of the condition thus applied to a demand function, we have the so-called Strong Axiom of Revealed Preference of Samuelson, in the form in which he stated it originally. This has been seen to be a necessary condition for the existence of a compatible utility, or for the consistency of F.

Instead of a pair, any finite number of demands can be considered just as well, as by Houthakker. The compatibility of U with (x, p), (y, q), ..., (z, r) requires in particular that

$$py \le px, \ y \ne x \Rightarrow U(x) > U(y)$$

$$\cdot \quad \cdot \quad \cdot \quad \cdot \quad \cdot$$
$$\cdot \quad \cdot \quad \cdot \quad \cdot \quad \cdot$$
$$\cdot \quad \cdot \quad \cdot \quad \cdot \quad \cdot$$

$$rx \le rz, \quad x \ne z \Rightarrow U(z) > U(x).$$

From conjuction of the right, we have

$$U(x) > U(y) > \ldots > U(z) > U(x),$$

which implies the impossibility $U(x) > U(x)$, so it is impossible. Hence also the conjunction of the left is impossible; equivalently,

$$py \leq px, \ldots, rx \leq rz \Rightarrow x = \ldots = z = x.$$

For another statement,

$$py \leq px, y \neq x, \ldots \Rightarrow rx > rz.$$

This condition, applied to all finite collections of demands belonging to a demand function, taken cyclically in a sequence where the first follows the last, is known as the Strong Axiom of Revealed Preference of Houthakker. It includes Samuelson's condition, and it also is necessary for the consistency of the demand function.

The demand function here has been related to the hypothesis about it involving utility, and we have derived a necessary condition for the hypothesis to be admissible. For sufficiency, some utility function would have to be constructed which realizes the hypothesis. That issue also comes into the work of Samuelson and Houthakker, and we shall return to it later. The sense of 'revealed preference' is that any demand (x, p) reveals the preference for x over any other bundle y which, being such that $py \leq px$, costs no more.

Utility has such an extensive presence in economic theory that not actually measuring it might seem a shortcoming. If models depending on it are to be more than purely formal and have a test, utility would have to be measured. The 'difficulties' described by Phyllis Deane are encountered. A release from some of the measurement obligations came with the abolition of 'cardinal' utility, or recognition that it is not essential to some models, ordinal utility being all that mattered. But utility functions persist with their arbitrary cardinal aspect—a senseless residue from the earlier era. Here, it was offered, is a method making utility operational since it deals directly with observations, and 'purged of the last vestiges' of the obsolete cardinality since it deals directly with a preference relation instead of with numbers whose relation determines the preference. Going to the base of a fundamental matter, 'revealed preference' has become established in economic terminology, and has a wider currency also.

The theory, as offered, is simply about a demand function, like the Slutsky theory (hence the title *Demand Functions and the Slutsky Matrix* for that work in demand theory). Its standing as an operational theory therefore is limited by such standing as first concerns the demand function. Applied to a single demand observation, revealed preference is operational, and finitely so, but the consistency test becomes vacuous in this case, since an arbitrary single demand observation is compatible with some utility. Because a finite collection of demands is contained in the statement of the consistency test, first of Samuelson, and then just as well of Houthakker, it was regarded originally as a finite test. But all finite collections belonging to the demand function have to enter, and the number of these is not finite, so with this promise there must be a disappointment.

A merit seen in the revealed preference approach is associated with the determination to do away with cardinal utility, and so with utility functions. But the utility function was promptly resurrected in the first approach to sufficiency of the consistency test, or 'axiom'. If one is truly content with any utility order, then the Houthakker Strong Axiom, or condition, is both necessary and sufficient for the existence of an order that is compatible with the demand function. The proof of sufficiency is elementary, like the proof of necessity. It involves no extra assumptions about the demand function at all, and in fact applies just as well to a completely arbitrary collection of demands. The labour of the Samuelson proof, and its extension by Houthakker, arises entirely from wanting a utility order that is representable by a continuous utility function. Auxiliary assumptions about the demand function are involved, Samuelson requiring differentiability and Houthakker something less. Samuelson dealt with the case of just two goods, for which his Weak Axiom is adequate, and Houthakker extended the treatment to n goods. The method of proof has difficulties, and overcoming them has been an issue, several proofs following the same method having been offered since by different writers; in my opinion, the issue has remained. The method gained interest from the effort given to it, and its intricacies; another much simpler proof was offered early but not noticed, possibly because, when given in outline to make it simple, it was quite simple (Afriat 1960b; a full account is in 1973a; preparations for following the original method are in 1972g). Here we can mention a modification of the Samuelson–Houthakker theorem, stated in terms of a normalized demand function, with a weaker hypothesis than the original and some sacrifice in the conclusion: *for any demand function f to have a lower-semicontinuous utility, it is necessary and sufficient that Houthakker's condition holds, and the sets* $[v : f(v) = f(u)]$ *be closed* (Afriat, 1973b).

The next section presents a treatment of the same questions with reference to an arbitrary finite collection of demands, instead of a demand function. For this case the consistency test, having the form of Houthakker's Axiom, becomes truly finite, the utility order which demonstrates consistency is finitely constructed, and so is the continuous utility function representing it, should one want one. The same consistency test is valid regardless of whether consistency is defined with reference to an arbitrary utility order, or a complete one, or a utility function with all the properties usually associated with a utility function—continuity, monotonicity and convexity of the indifference surfaces — and which, moreover, is a concave function. This has a significance affecting the empirical status of such properties. Chapter II.3 goes further with this finite approach and the additional questions that are associated with it.

1.5   CLASSICAL CASE

Any collection F of demands (x, p) can be considered as a relation, and can be taken to define a *demand correspondence F*, where xFp means $(x, p) \in F$. It should be assumed that $xFp \Rightarrow px > 0$, so making a positive cost associated with each demand. A *demand function* is then the special case of a correspondence F which determines a single consumption bundle under every budget constraint, so for all p and M there is a unique $x \in Fp$ for which $px = M$.

The demand collection, or correspondence, can also be represented as an indexed set (x_t, p_t) $(t \in T)$. It is finite if the index set T is finite, in which case, if m is the number of members, it can be taken that $T = [1, \ldots, m]$. Then the demands are described by (x_t, p_t) for $t = 1, \ldots, m$. For now, the collection is completely arbitrary, apart from the positive cost proviso. Later it will be required to be finite.

Utility is represented by a strict order P in the commodity space, irreflexive and transitive and otherwise completely arbitrary. Should P be representable by a utility function U, we would have $xPy \Leftrightarrow U(x) > U(y)$, but no such assumption is made, nor any other. The question dealt with is the classical one of the Slutsky and the Samuelson-Houthakker theories, where compatibility between demand and utility, involving a unique maximum of utility, is defined by the condition H^* instead of H as in the next chapter.

For a given demand correspondence F, the first question is whether there exists a strict order P compatible with it, or such that PH^*F, making F consistent. Immediately, the Houthakker condition is necessary for the consistency. Two relations are constructed from F, one irreflexive and the other transitive, and neither necessarily both. If they coincide, it must be in a relation P_0, which is both irreflexive and transitive, and so a strict order. Then from its construction P_0 must be compatible with F, so F is consistent. The Houthakker condition implies this coincidence, and so the consistency. Thus, *on its own*, it is *both necessary and sufficient* for the consistency of F. Under it, P_0 is always one compatible strict order which demonstrates the consistency, and any P is another if and only if it is a strict order such that $P_0 \subset P$, so P_0 is the smallest and gives a characterization of all the others.

When consistency of F is made more stringent by requiring the compatible utility to have special properties, in general the test for it should be more stringent also. For instance, when the utility is required to be homogeneous, so defining the *homogeneous consistency* which is of importance in the consideration of price indices, the test is definitely stronger than the general consistency test provided by the Houthakker condition. For any special properties to have empirical significance, they must require a test of the demand data which is stronger than the general test applicable when they are not required; otherwise there would be no way of knowing whether or not they may be present.

The first special properties which ought to be considered are those usually assumed about utility: that it be representable by a utility function, with continuity and monotonicity, and convexity of the indifference surfaces. If it is added that the utility function is a concave function we have the *classical utility function*, and *classical consistency* is the compatibility of F with some such function. However, it will appear that, *for a finite demand correspondence F, general consistency is equivalent to classical consistency*. This result has implications of the kind just stated concerning the empirical status of the classical properties. Subject to the general test, a consumer can always be represented as being governed by a classical utility. There may, in 'reality', be very real kinks in the indifference surfaces of individuals, but in the poor language of choice under linear budgets the consumer is unable—too dumb —to express it.

The finiteness limitation allows a proof by finite induction. The Houthakker condition is stated in terms of numbers D_{rs} determined by the demands, and is shown to be necessary and sufficient for the existence of numbers w_r, $U_r > 0$ such that

$$w_r D_{rs} > U_s - U_r \ (r \neq s).$$

With any such numbers, let

$$U_r(x) = U_r + w_r(p_r x / p_r x_r - 1),$$

and

$$U(x) = \min_r U_r(x).$$

Then $U(x)$ is an example of a classical utility function which is compatible with F, so demonstrating the classical consistency of F.

The demands (x_t, p_t) $(t \in T)$ determine coefficients

$$D_{rs} = p_r x_s / p_r x_r - 1,$$

such that $D_{rr} = 0$. In terms of these, $D_{rs} \leq 0$ and $x_s \neq x_r$ 'reveals' that x_r is preferred over x_s. Let P be a strict preference order, any irreflexive transitive relation in the commodity space. For simplicity, $x_r P x_s$ can be stated rPs, and similarly with other relations when they are applied to the observed bundles x_r. Any sequence $r, i, j, \ldots, k, s$ determines a vector

$$D_{rij\ldots ks} = (D_{ri}, D_{ij}, \ldots, D_{ks}).$$

A statement of Houthakker's condition is that

$$D_{r\ldots s\ldots r} \leq 0 \Rightarrow r = \ldots = s = \ldots.$$

The revealed preference relation Q_r of a single demand (x_r, p_r) is given by

$$xQ_r y \equiv x = x_r, \quad p_r y \leq p_r x_r,$$

and the *revealed preference relation* of the collection F is the transitive closure QT of the union Q of these. In particular,

$$rQs \Leftrightarrow D_{rs} \leq 0,$$

and

$$rQTs \Rightarrow (\vee \; i \ldots) \, D_{ri \ldots s} \leq 0.$$

The irreflexive part QI of Q is the same as the union of the irreflexive parts of the Q_r, and is given by

$$xQIy \equiv xQy, \; x \neq y.$$

Then the condition for the compatibility of F with P can be stated $QI \subset P$, and because P is transitive this is equivalent to $QIT \subset P$, where QIT, the *revealed strict preference relation* of F, is the transitive closure of QI. Since P is irreflexive, this implies that QIT is irreflexive. The consistency of F which requires the existence of such P therefore implies that QIT is irreflexive. Thus, *the irreflexivity of the revealed strict preference relation is a necessary condition for the consistency of F*. Since QIT is transitive by construction, reflexivity makes it a strict order, and since $QI \subset QIT$, it satisfies the condition for compatibility with F. Hence *the irreflexivity is also sufficient for the consistency*. Then also, the P, which are compatible with F, are refinements of the strict order provided by QIT under this condition.

The irreflexive part QTI of the revealed preference relation QT is the *strict revealed preference relation*. Since this by its construction is irreflexive, it is a strict order if it is transitive. Houthakker's condition is equivalent to the irreflexivity of QIT, to the transitivity of QTI, and to the identity of QIT and QTI. These and related points are dealt with at greater length in the next chapter, together with the theorem about the equivalence of general and classical consistency.

Algebra of Revealed Preference

Prices and quantities are elementary economic variables whose values are determined from collected statistical data; they are not problematic conceptually and are treated as simple observables. In any period there are some n goods, and their prices and the quantities demanded can be given by a vector pair (x, p) representing the *demand observation* for that period. This is accepted in principle, though the practice with such data cannot be simple. Distinguishable goods are so numerous that similar ones must be grouped together and regarded as the same good, and at the same time apparently identical goods are found with different prices. When any (x_t, p_t) is given as the demand observation in a period t, an ideal model has already been imposed on the more ragged reality. But for this observation, there will be no concern with such questions about the origin of the data. It is just supposed that demand observations are already given for some m periods $t = 1, \ldots, m$.

The scheme of data can be analysed with reference to hypotheses about it. The basic hypothesis is ordinarily that demand is governed by a valuation of the utility of goods which is independent of time, together with efficiency criteria, bearing on exchange cost and use benefit, familiar from cost-benefit analysis. It is one thing to have some determination of utility; to apply it efficiently, with perfect knowledge of the possibilities, is another matter (Schumpeter, 1954, makes a remark like this). A modification in which perfect efficiency is relaxed to allow partial efficiency in some degree is dealt with in Chapter II.6, in connection with production as well as consumption. In this chapter efficiency will be dealt with only in a strict sense. The basic hypothesis then has possible variations depending on special assumptions that can be made about the utility involved.

At first, no special assumptions are made at all. The utility of goods is represented by an arbitrary order in the commodity space, and so is any reflexive and transitive relation R. The first question is about the existence of a utility which fits the given data scheme, or is *compatible* with it, in that the efficiency criteria are represented as being met. The *consistency* of the data with the considered hypothesis requires that existence. Then there are many possible utilities, and an object is to characterize all of them, and to evaluate indeterminacies which arise because there are many. When special properties are imposed on R, such as homogeneity, or a special separability structure, usually consistency of the data becomes a more restrictive condition, and indeterminacies are reduced also. However, it is found that the imposition of a certain group of properties, the *classical properties*, has no such effects, and there are theorems about that.

The cost of the bundle of goods found in one period at the prices found in another defines the *cross-cost* from the second period to the first. From these, taken between all periods, a matrix of *cross-coefficients* is derived. They are the coefficients

$$D_{rs} = p_r x_s / p_r x_r - 1,$$

introduced in the last chapter. There are a several theorems concerning the equivalence of conditions applied to these, and their equivalence to consistency of the demand data. Some such conditions are analogous to the type Houthakker familiarly applied to a demand function, or are closely related. Others require the existence of a solution to some system of simultaneous homogeneous linear inequalities, formed on the basis of the cross-coefficients. By means of such solutions, it is possible to construct compatible utility functions, in a finitely constructive way. The main theorems about inequalities are unfamiliar in any other context and a peculiarity of this subject. There is an involvement with theorems, (see Afriat, 1960c, and Chapter V.4 below) that also have an interpretation for minimum paths in networks, and have given an accidental anticipation of some features of that subject.

Since utility is ordinal — or rather, since the cardinal aspect, that may in reality exist, is indeterminate here—it can be given no absolute measure. However, utility can be given a cost measure, using any prices for the goods which produce it. Adam Smith's use and exchange value distinction, lost in a situation of general equilibrium, now has an expression, since any use value can be given a definite exchange value. The *utility cost function* $c(p, x)$ associated with a utility relation R determines the minimum cost at the prices p of attaining the use value of the bundle of goods x;

$$c(p, x) = \min [py : yRx].$$

The set Rx is where the *standard of living*, or utility, represented by the bundle x is attained, and when the prices are p we have $c(p, x)$ as the *cost of living* at the standard. In particular, there are the numbers $c_{rs} = c(p_r, x_s)$ determined between all pairs of periods, which give the cost, at the prices of one period, of living at the standard of another. The range of these numbers can be determined, as the utility R describes all possible utilities under the constraint of compatibility with the data. In that way, we have an approach to the general cost of living problem and the indeterminacies involved in it. Wald's 'New Formula' described in Chapter III.5 deals with the same problem, but with retrictions on the form of data and on the utility, which have the effect of removing particular indeterminacies, and under which the utility cost function must have the special form

$$c(p, x) = c(p)f(x) + d(p).$$

The price index idea corresponds to the further specialization where $d(p) = 0$. This chapter contains results for the general problem, and others are concerned with these two specializations.

2.1 DEMAND AND UTILITY

The given demands (x_t, p_t) $(t = 1, \ldots, m)$, form a finite demand corre-spondence F, so xFp means $x_t F p_t$ for some t. At first the finiteness of F is immaterial, and the demands can be understood to be indexed in an arbitrary set. Later, where proofs by finite induction occur, the finiteness is essential. In any case, it is assumed that $xFp \Rightarrow px > 0$, so that a positive cost is associated with every demand. Then the demands determine costs $M_t = p_t x_t$, and budget vectors

$$u_t = M_t^{-1} p_t = (p_t x_t)^{-1} p_t,$$

these being such that $u_t x_t = 1$. The pair (x_t, u_t) is the *normal demand* obtained from the demand (x_t, p_t) by *normalization*. The demands also determine the cross-costs $p_r x_s$ and then the cross-coefficients

$$D_{rs} = u_r x_s - 1 = p_r x_s / p_r x_r - 1,$$

which are such that

$$D_{rr} = u_r x_r - 1 = 0.$$

Many conditions important in the consideration of the demands can be put simply in terms of the cross-coefficients D_{rs}. The normal demands (x_t, u_t) which are normalizations of the demands (x_t, p_t) of F are the elements of a *normal demand correspondence f*. Many discussions of F effectively con-cern only f, and are put more simply in terms of it. In particular, the numbers D_{rs} derived from F depend only on the normalization f.

Any sequence $r, i, j, \ldots, k, s$ determines the vector

$$D_{rij\ldots ks} = (D_{ri}, D_{ij}, \ldots, D_{ks}).$$

In terms of this, Houthakker's condition applied to the given collection of demands F can be stated

$$K_F^* \equiv D_{rs\ldots r} \leq 0 \Rightarrow x_r = x_s = \ldots$$

Because

$$x_r = x_s \Rightarrow D_{rs} = u_r x_s - 1 = u_r x_r - 1 = 0,$$

this implies the condition

$$K_F \equiv D_{rs\ldots r} \leq 0 \Rightarrow D_{rs\ldots r} = 0$$

which will have a similar role as a consistency condition, though it is somewhat less restrictive. It has been noted that

$$K_F^* \Rightarrow K_F$$

This relation between conditions shows the relaxation in the definition of compatibility between demand and utility which is mainly adopted now.

A general utility relation will be considered. This is any order R in the commodity space, and as such it is reflexive and transitive;

$$xRx, \ xRyRz \ \Rightarrow \ xRz.$$

For the transitivity condition there is the equivalent extended statement

$$xRyR\ldots Rz \ \Rightarrow \ xRz.$$

The transitive closure of R is identified with its *chain-extension* $\vec{R}$, the relation between the end-points of R-chains (see Chapter VI.2), with the definition

$$x\vec{R}y \ \equiv \ (\vee \ a, b, \ \ldots, c) \ x = a, \ y = c, \ aRbR\ldots Rc.$$

Transitivity therefore means identity between R and its transitive closure. No further properties need be assumed for R, but for the relation it will be required to have to the demand data.

Relations H' and H'' between a utility R and a demand (x, p) are defined by

$$RH'(x, p) \ \equiv \ px \geq py \ \Rightarrow \ xRy$$

and

$$RH''(x, p) \ \equiv \ yRx \ \Rightarrow \ py \geq px.$$

The conjuction, or intersection,

$$H = H' \cap H''$$

of these will now define *compatibility* between a utility and a demand. It is implied by the formerly considered compatibility relation H^*, defined by

$$RH^*(x, p) \ \equiv \ px \geq py, \ y \neq x \ \Rightarrow \ xPy,$$

where P is the antisymmetric part of R, for which

$$xPy \ \Leftrightarrow \ xRy, \ \sim yRx.$$

This relation will be referred to now as *strict compatibility*, and evidently it implies H:

$$H^* \subset H.$$

With benefit decided by utility, and cost by the cost of the goods that produce the utility, the conditions H' and H'' correspond to the *cost effectiveness* and *cost efficiency* criteria familiar in cost-benefit analysis. The relation H between a utility and a demand requires the demand to be represented as fulfilling these criteria. With the demand given, this relation becomes a constraint on the utility.

The efficiency criteria have simpler statements in terms of normalized demands where budget vectors replace prices. Thus with a normal demand (x, u), for which $ux = 1$, we have

$$RH'(x, u) \ \equiv \ uy \leq 1 \ \Rightarrow \ xRy$$

and

$$RH''(x, u) \equiv yRx \Rightarrow uy \geq 1.$$

The allowable utilities will be those that are simultaneously compatible with all the given demands forming the correspondence F, or its normalization f. Such utilities R therefore must satisfy have the relation H to the demand correspondence F defined by

$$RHF \equiv (\wedge\ t)\ RH(x_t, p_t).$$

The assertion is conveniently denoted also by $H_F(R)$, and we can let H_F assert the existence of such R, or the *consistency* of the given demands,

$$H_F \equiv (\vee\ R)\ H_F(R).$$

Similarly, H_F^* can assert the *strict consistency* of the data as defined by the strict compatibility relation treated earlier.

The entire role of the demand observations is in putting a constraint on allowable utilities by the requirement of compatibility with them. Where there are more observations, there are more constraints and fewer utilities, and indeterminacies are correspondingly reduced. With some demand observations the constraints could be inconsistent, or unsatisfiable by any utility. We will be able to connect the consistency H_F of a collection of demands with the condition K_F, and also with the consistency of certain systems of homogeneous linear inequalities. To make the connection, we also require the idea of a *canonical order* of the demands, and the existence of one. The demands would be already in such an order were it the case that

$$D_{rs} \leq 0 \Rightarrow r \leq s.$$

The existence of such an order is yet another condition equivalent to consistency. Arguments by finite induction on the number of demand observations, used to show that consistency is equivalent to the solubility of certain simultaneous linear inequalities, will depend on taking the demands in such an order.

2.2   CONSISTENCY CONDITIONS

Though the finiteness of the given demand correspondence F will be important for the continuation, in this section it is not. We can suppose the index t to be in an arbitrary set, not necessarily finite.

The condition $H_F(R)$ for a utility R to be compatible with the given demand correspondence F requires

$$(H')\quad u_t x \leq 1 \Rightarrow x_t R x$$

and

$$(H'')\quad x R x_t \Rightarrow u_t x \geq 1,$$

for all t. The revealed preference relation of the single demand (x_t, p_t) is

$$R_t = [(x_t, x) : u_t x \leq 1],$$

and the union of these is

$$Q_F = \cup_t R_t.$$

This is the set of *directly revealed preferences* for F. Now (H') is equivalent to $R_t \subset R$ for all t, and so to

$$Q_F \subset R.$$

But since R is transitive, this is equivalent to

$$R_F \subset R,$$

where R_F, the *revealed preference relation* for the demand correspondence F, is the transitive closure of the union Q_F of the individual revealed preference relations R_t. It follows that $H_F(R)$ implies

$$R_F \subset R \quad \text{and} \quad xRx_t \Rightarrow u_t x \geq 1,$$

and consequently,

$$xR_F x_t \Rightarrow xRx_t \Rightarrow u_t x \geq 1,$$

showing that R_F satisfies (H''). But in any case R_F must satisfy (H'), just because $R_F \subset R_F$, and here we have that is satisfies (H''). So now we have $H_F(R_F)$ as a consequence of $H_F(R)$ for some R, that is, of the consistency H_F of F. It is immediate that if R_F satisfies (H'') then, since it in any case satisfies (H'), it must satisfy (H), and so we have the following:

THEOREM I For any demand correspondence F,

$$H_F \Leftrightarrow H_F(R_F).$$

That is, *there exists a compatible utility for F if and only if R_F is one such utility*. We also have a characterization of all such utilities as being those that contain the revealed preference relation R_F and satisfy (H'').

From the construction of R_F, with xRx_s it is required that $x = x_r$ for some r. Also

$$x_r Rx_s \Leftrightarrow rDs,$$

where D is the relation between the demands of F defined by

$$rDs \equiv (\vee\ i\ \dots)D_{ri\dots s} \leq 0.$$

Thus the condition (H') applied to R_F is equivalent to

$$D_{ri\dots s} \leq 0 \Rightarrow D_{sr} \geq 0,$$

and so to

$$D_{ri\dots s} \leq 0 \Rightarrow D_{sr} = 0.$$

But this, from the cyclical symmetry, is equivalent to

$$D_{ri\dots r} \leq 0 \Rightarrow D_{ri\dots r} = 0,$$

which is the formerly defined condition K_F, so we have:

THEOREM II   For any demand correspondence F,

$$H_F(R_F) \Leftrightarrow K_F.$$

As a consequence of Theorems I and II, we have:

THEOREM III   For any demand correspondence F,

$$H_F \Leftrightarrow K_F.$$

The condition K_F is now established as the general consistency condition for any demand correspondence F, finite or otherwise, since we have nowhere made use of the finiteness which will be of importance later.

2.3   ORDER LOGIC

An order in the commodity space produces an order between the commodity bundles of the demand correspondence F, and so between the demands which are elements of F. That in turn produces an order between the budget vectors of F, which can be extended to an order in the budget space. Here is a pattern of duality, or symmetry, between representations in the budget and commodity spaces B and C. One aspect of this duality is developed in Chapter II.5 on 'Direct and Indirect Utility', and it will have further elaboration as concerns demand correspondences. It is enough now to recognize that, standing between orderings in the commodity and budget spaces, with a neutral symmetry as concerns the duality — from bearing equally on both sides simultaneously — is an ordering of the elements of F. Such orderings of the demands which are elements of F, which are expressed by orderings of the set in which they are indexed, are to be dealt with now. The index set is $[1, \ldots, m]$ in the finite case treated later; otherwise, as now, it is quite arbitrary. Generalities about orders which are needed, and have a fuller account in Chapter VI.2, will be stated first.

Any binary relation R has *symmetric* and *antisymmetric parts*.

$$E = R \cap R', P = R \cap \bar{R}'.$$

For these,

$$xEy \Leftrightarrow xRy \wedge yRx, \quad xPy \Leftrightarrow xRy \wedge \sim yRx,$$

and they partition R:

$$E \cap P = O, E \cup P = R.$$

Evidently then also $P = R \cap \bar{E}$ and $E = R \cap \bar{P}$.

If R is an order, reflexive and transitive, then E is an equivalence relation, reflexive, transitive and symmetric, defining *equivalence in the order*; and P is a strict order, irreflexive and transitive, the *strict part of the order*. Beale and Drazin (1956) drew my attention to the implied transitivity of P, dealt with in Chapter VI.2, which lies at the basis of this formulation.

The relation $\geq$ between numbers, being reflexive and transitive, is a particular model for an order R. With this model the relation E of equivalence reduces to the identity relation I = ' = ', making it a *simple order*. The co-incidence betweeen equivalence in the order and the relation of identity, characteristic of a simple order, is stated E = I. The relation $\geq$ is also such that xRy or yRx for all x and y, making it a *complete order*. The characteristic of a complete order is that $\bar{R}' \subset P$, and since in any case $P \subset \bar{R}'$ this is equivalent to $P = \bar{R}'$, and so also to $R = \bar{P}'$. But orders R which are to be considered need not be simple or complete.

A *refinement* of a strict order P is any other strict order T for which $P \subset T$. If T is also such that

$$x \neq y \Rightarrow xTy \vee yTx,$$

it is a *total order*. Any strict order P either is a total order already or it has a total order refinement T. In the latter case there would be many possibilities for T.

There is no important distinction between a simple complete order R and a total order. For in this case the strict part P of R is a total order, derivable from it also as its irreflexive part, and from which R is recoverable simply as the reflexive closure,

$$P = R \cap \bar{I}, R = P \cup I.$$

The simple complete orders and total orders are in a one-to-one correspondence with the distinction that one is represented in a reflexive form and the other not, and which representation is used is unimportant.

The stated order refinement theorem of E. Szpilrajn (1930) is dealt with in Chapter VI.2. For arbitrary sets this 'theorem' or axiom is equivalent to the 'axiom of choice' of set theory, and similarly to other axioms. For finite sets the theorem is proved by finite induction; this matter therefore is elementary for finite sets, though the sets dealt with now can still be allowed to be arbitrary. But the real interest is in the finite case, and in preparing for proofs by finite induction, which depend on the possibility of taking the demands in an order with a special property, about to be described. Such a special order will define a *canonical order* for F. It will appear that the possibility of finding one is equivalent to the consistency of the demand correspondence F as expressed by the condition H_F, and also by the condition K_F, which has been seen to be equivalent to consistency.

The order refinement theorem can be put in the following more general form, in which it will be used:

THEOREM Any order is contained in some complete order which has the same equivalence relation.

We have this because any order is representable as a simple order of its equivalence classes, which by the order refinement theorem is contained in some simple complete order, representing a complete order with the same equivalence relation as the original.

2.4   REVEALED PREFERENCE REVEALED

A *canonical order* is any complete order W of F such that

$$sWr \Rightarrow D_{rs} \geq 0, \quad sVr \Rightarrow D_{sr} > 0,$$

V being the strict part of W, given by $V = \overline{W}'$ since W is complete. Let $G_F(W)$ assert that W is such an order and G_F that such a W exists. Because W is complete, the conditions are equivalent to

$$D_{rs} \leq 0 \Rightarrow rWs, \quad D_{rs} < 0 \Rightarrow rVs.$$

The issue therefore is about the existence of a complete order W satisfying these conditions.

From Theorem 2.2.II, it is known that K_F is equivalent to the compatibility of the revealed preference relation R_F with F, and so to the conditions

$$u_r x \leq 1 \Rightarrow x_r R_F x, \quad x R_F x_r \Rightarrow u_r x > 1.$$

Therefore, by taking $x = x_s$, K_F implies in particular that

$$D_{rs} \leq 0 \Rightarrow rDs, \quad sDr \Rightarrow D_{rs} \geq 0,$$

because $x_r R_F x_s \Leftrightarrow rDs$. Let W_F and V_F denote D and its antisymmetric part. Then the first of these conditions implies the equivalence of the second to

$$D_{rs} < 0 \Rightarrow rDs \lor {\sim} sDr,$$

and so to

$$D_{rs} < 0 \Rightarrow rV_F s.$$

Therefore the two are equivalent to

$$D_{rs} \leq 0 \Rightarrow rW_F s, \quad D_{rs} < 0 \Rightarrow rV_F s.$$

But given W_F satisfying these conditions, we can appeal to the order refinement theorem in the extended form stated for having a complete order W such such that

$$W_F \subset W, \quad V_F \subset V$$

and this satisfies the conditions for being a canonical order.

The condition K_F therefore is sufficient for the existence of a canonical order. It is necessary. For if W is a canonical order, from

$$D_{rs} \leq 0 \Rightarrow rWs$$

we have $W_F \subset W$. Then from this, with

$$D_{rs} < 0 \Rightarrow rVs,$$

we have

$$rW_F s \Rightarrow rWs \Rightarrow D_{rs} > 0,$$

and hence

$$rW_F s \Rightarrow D_{rs} \geq 0.$$

But it has already been seen that this last condition is equivalent to K_F, so the following has been shown.

THEOREM I The consistency of a demand correspondence is necessary and sufficient for the existence of a canonical order of its elements.

This theorem is needed for the inductive proof of the next section to do with the construction of multipliers and levels.

The 'revealed' here is not quite that of Samuelson and Houthakker, since the model is different; soothsayers have a model, also somewhat different — there is choice about what should be revealed.

The revealed preference method is made up not by the revealed preferences alone, but by those taken together with the less well noted revealed non-preferences. If the fact that X is chosen over Y means that X is as good as Y, according to the assumed model, then the revealed preference principle is in the sure proposition that, if X is as good as Y, because of the model, then X is as good as Y, by assumption. But it is critical for Samuelson and Houthakker that then also Y is definitely not as good as X: here are their revealed non-preferences, which can be forgotten about, especially when the revealed preference idea runs its wider course into vacuity. Without them the model could never be rejected — revealed preference would have no 'axiom'. The ground has been shifted here to the extent of having fewer revealed non-preferences while keeping the same revealed preferences: if X is chosen over Y and Y costs less, then Y is not as good as X. Further 'revealed' definitions give an expansion on this. We have

$$rRs \equiv (\text{v } i \ldots) \, D_{ri \ldots s} \leq 0,$$

defining the *revealed preference relation R*, in any case reflexive and transitive and so an order. The *revealed indifference relation* is the relation E of equivalence in R, given by the symmetric part, for which

$$rEs \Leftrightarrow (\text{v } i \ldots j \ldots) \, D_{ri \ldots sj \ldots r} \leq 0.$$

The *strict revealed preference relation* is the strict or antisymmetric part $P \subset R$. With any addition to the data, the revealed indifference may only be enlarged, but a strict revealed preference could be eliminated by being turned into a revealed indifference. More significant than the strict revealed preference is the *revealed strict preference* relation $S \subset R$ given by

$$rSs \equiv (\text{v } i \ldots) \, D_{ri \ldots s} \lesssim 0.$$

The *non-revealed preferences* are given by $\overline{R}'$ and the *revealed non-preferences* by S'. A simultaneously revealed preference and non-preference makes a *revealed contradiction*. This is a case where $R \cap S' \neq O$, and *revealed consistency* is the absence of revealed contradictions as stated by $R \cap S' = 0$, equivalently by $S \subset \overline{R}'$; and since in any case $S \subset R$, this is equivalent to $S \subset P$; that is, every revealed strict preference should be a strict revealed preference. Most simply, revealed consistency is equivalent to the irreflexivity of S, and to the already considered consistency condition K given by

$$K \equiv D_{rs\ldots r} \le 0 \Rightarrow D_{rs\ldots r} = 0.$$

These definitions have to be modified in order to have a correspondence with the Samuelson-Houthakker revealed preference theory. We can define R^* and S^* by

$$rR^*s \equiv (\vee\, r \ne i\ldots \ne s)\, D_{ri\ldots s} \le 0$$

and

$$rS^*s \equiv (\vee\, i\, \ldots)\, D_{ri\ldots s} \le 0 \text{ and } r \ne s.$$

From these definitions, immediately $S^* \subset R^*$, R^* is transitive, S^* is irreflex-ive and neither is necessarily both, and with the formerly defined R and S, $S \subset R^*$ and $S^* \subset R$. Houthakker's condition

$$K^* \equiv D_{rs\ldots r} \le 0 \Rightarrow r = s = \ldots$$

is equivalent to the irreflexivity of R^*, to the transitivity of S^*, and to the iden-tity $S^* = R^*$. It is also equivalent to the existence of a strict order P^*, simultaneously identical with both R^* and S^*, having the property

$$D_{rs} \le 0 \text{ and } r \ne s \Rightarrow rP^*s.$$

By the order refinement theorem this has a total order refinement T, which then has the property

$$D_{rs} \le 0 \text{ and } r \ne s \Rightarrow rTs,$$

or, from the contrapositive form, because T is a total order,

$$sTr \Rightarrow D_{rs} > 0.$$

Conversely the existence of such T implies K^* and so also all the other men-tioned conditions equivalent to this, in particular the existence of the relation P^*, and then necessarily $P^* \subset T$.

A total order with this property will be called a *strict canonical order* for the given demand correspondence F. It has been seen that the condition K^*, already seen equivalent to the strict consistency of F, is necessary and suffi-cient for the existence of one, and so we have the following.

> THEOREM II The strict consistency of a demand correspondence is necessary and sufficient for the existence of a strict canonical order of its elements.

This theorem is useful in developing the finitely constructive approach to the Samuelson-Houthakker problem.

There have been two lines of theory going round the conditions (H^*) and (H). The first, distinguished as the 'strict' theory, is the one usually applied to a single valued demand function where there is not only a choice to be explained but also the uniqueness. Applied to a demand correspondence, it would be rejected if the correspondence happened not to be single valued. The uniqueness expresses no generally significant economic criterion. Instead the less stringent H-model is based only on ordinary economic criteria of efficiency. Its relation to the other is that it provides fewer revealed non-preferences. In Chapter II.6, on 'Efficiency and Inefficiency', there is a further relaxation by recognizing still fewer revealed non-preferences, and so still less opportunity for contradictions with the revealed preferences which are the same with all the models. This is done in order to bring a tolerance into the model and to admit efficiency in a partial degree given by a parameter e. The same idea is then applied to production.

2.5   FINITE HOUTHAKKER TEST

THEOREM I For any numbers

$$D_{rs}(r, s = 1, \ldots, m)$$

such that

$$r > s \Rightarrow D_{rs} > 0$$

there exist numbers

$$L_r > 0 \text{ and } U_r(r = 1, \ldots, m)$$

such that

$$r > s \Rightarrow U_r < U_s$$

and

$$r \neq s \Rightarrow L_r D_{rs} > U_s - U_r.$$

The proof is by induction on m. Let T_m assert the theorem for any m. The case T_1 is verified, vacuously. Now T_m ($m > 1$) will be deduced on the hypothesis T_{m-1}, and the proof by induction will be complete.

By hypothesis, there exist numbers L_r, U_r ($r < m$) that give the required conclusion as concerns $r, s < m$. It suffices now to show that there exist further numbers L_m, U_m which together with these give the required conclusion, that is, which satisfy

$$L_m > 0, \ U_m < U_r(r < m),$$

and also

$$L_r D_{rm} > U_m - U_r(r < m), \ L_m D_{ms} > U_s - U_m(s < m).$$

The last conditions are equivalent to

$$U_r + L_r D_{rm} > U_m > U_s - L_m D_{ms}(r, s < m),$$

and so, because $D_{ms} > 0$ ($s < m$), it is possible to satify all these conditions with any sufficiently large and positive L_m, giving the conclusion T_m. QED

This theorem combines with the foregoing discussion and last theorem to give the following, the significance of which in the matter of utility construction appears in the next section.

THEOREM II For any finite demand correspondence with elements (x_t, p_t) and coefficients

$$D_{rs} = p_r x_s / p_r x_r - 1$$

forming vectors

$$D_{rij\ldots ks} = (D_{ri}, D_{ij}, \ldots, D_{ks}),$$

the condition

$$K^* \equiv D_{rs\ldots r} \leq 0 \Rightarrow r = s = \ldots$$

is necessary and sufficient for the transitive relation P^* given by

$$rP^*s \equiv (\vee\, r \neq i \neq \ldots s)\, D_{ri\ldots s} \leq 0$$

to be irreflexive, and thereby a strict order, and for the existence of numbers $L_r > 0$ and U_r such that

$$L_r D_{rs} > U_s - U_r (r \neq s),$$

and

$$rTs \Rightarrow U_r > U_s$$

where T is any refinement of P^*.

Any of numbers L_r, U_r such that

$$(S^*)\quad L_r > 0,\ L_r D_{rs} > U_s - U_r (r \neq s)$$

defined a *strict multiplier-level solution* for the given demand correspondence F. Let S^* assert that such a solution exists, this condition defining *strict multiplier-level consistency* of F. *A* part of the theorem is that $K^* \leftrightarrow S^*$, and all that remains to be proved is that

$$S^* \Rightarrow K^*.$$

Call any L_r a *strict multiplier solution* if

$$(L^*)\quad L_r D_{ri} + L_i D_{ij} + \ldots + L_k D_{kr} > 0\ (r \neq i \neq \ldots)$$

and let L^* assert that one exists, this defining *multiplier consistency* for F. Immediately, if L_r, U_r is any multiplier-level solution, then, for any cyclical sequence $r \neq i \ldots r$, by addition of the S^*-inequalities, we have

$$L_r D_{ri} + \ldots + L_k D_{kr} > U_i - U_r + \ldots + U_r - U_k = 0,$$

and so L_r is a multiplier solution. Hence $S^* \Rightarrow L^*$. Also, any case of reflexivity rP^*r would, for any $L_r > 0$, give

$$L_r D_{ri} + \ldots + L_k D_{kr} \leq 0,$$

and so contradict L^*, so L^* implies the irreflexivity of P^*, and therefore the condition K^*. Thus we have

$$K^* \Rightarrow S^* \Rightarrow L^* \Rightarrow K^*$$

and hence the equivalence. QED

That Houthakker's condition K^* should be a test for the consistency of a system of simultaneous linear inequalities, (S^*), and similarly the system (L^*), is a striking result, which permits a further development in the subject. Stating this consequence:

> COROLLARY Houthakker's revealed preference condition K^* applied to a finite demand correspondence F is necessary and sufficient for the existence of a positive solution to the system of simultaneous strict homogeneous linear inequalities (S^*).

It will be found in the next section that, by taking any solution of the system (S^*), it is possible to construct a utility function U of the classical type which fits the data, in the required strict compatibility sense. With this function we will have $U(x_r) = U_r$, so the levels U_r in any multiplier-level solution are *utility levels*, and in the same connection the multipliers L_r are *marginal utilities* of money, and, what amounts to the same, *Lagrange multipliers* in Kuhn-Tucker optimality conditions.

That any solution L_r, U_r of the system (S^*) provides a solution L_r of the system (L^*) has already been remarked; in other words, *the multipliers in multiplier-level solutions are all multiplier solutions*. Its is also true that *the multiplier solutions exhaust all multipliers obtainable from the multiplier-level solutions*. This is seen from the theory in Chapter V.4, on 'Minimum Paths'. Thus, with $a_{rs} = L_r D_{rs}$, because $D_{rr} = 0$ and L_r is a multiplier solution, we have

$$a_{rr} = 0,\ a_{ri} + a_{ij} + \ldots + a_{kr} > 0\ (r \neq i \ldots \neq r),$$

so assuring the existence of U_r for which

$$a_{rs} > U_s - U_r\ (r \neq s),$$

as required for the following.

> THEOREM III The multiplier solutions are identical with the multipliers in the multiplier-level solutions.

Just as, in the proof of Theorem I, the L_r, U_r for a multiplier-level solution has been constructed sequentially by taking the demands in a canonical order, the existence of which requires Houthakker's condition, so also can the L_r alone be so constructed for a multiplier solution. That will be dealt with further later in the consideration of extreme solutions.

It should be observed that *Houthakker's test applied to a finite demand correspondence*, which though it is not already given as a finite test, *is equivalent to a finite test*. For it concerns a cyclic series $r, i, \ldots, r$ and requires

$$D_{ri\ldots r} \leq 0 \Rightarrow r = s = \ldots$$

The set of cycles of elements taken from a finite set is not finite; however, the set of simple cycles, without repeated elements, is finite. Moreover, where there are repeated elements, by repeating the decomposition

$$D_{ri...sj...sk...r} = D_{ri...sk...r} + D_{sj...s},$$

we eventually have the D-value on a cycle expressed as a sum of D-values on simple cycles. It follows that the test restricted to simple cycles, which is finite, implies the general test on all cycles.

2.6 CONSTRUCTIVE SOLUTION

This chapter ends with a demonstration of how the multiplier-level solution concept provides an immediate construction of utility functions that fit the data in the required fashion, and have all the monotonicity and convexity properties most usually attributed to utility. The existence of such solutions for a finite demand correspondence is equivalent to Houthakker's condition, and so we have a counterpart of the Samuelson-Houthakker problem with demand functions, and a constructive solution. Demand functions are a main subject in demand theory, and here is a parallel in finite terms. In the continuation in the next chapter we change from using the strict condition (H^*) as basis and instead have the condition (H), which has as much or more economic sense, and also is simpler.

Two utility functions $\phi^o(x)$, $\phi^i(x)$ will be associated with the given demand data together with any multipliers and levels λ_r and ϕ_r. They have the monotonicity and convexity properties required for them to be classical utility functions. One has the polyhedral form, specified by a finite set of linear support functions. The other has the polytope form and is given by a linear programming formula.

The significance of these functions for the utility construction problems is that ϕ^i is strictly compatible with the demand data, in the sense of (H^*), and so is a solution of the construction problem, if and only if the multipliers and levels form a strict multiplier-level solution, satisfying the system (S^*). The strict consistency of demand correspondence F, or the existence of a solution given by any strictly compatible utility, is equivalent to the existence of a strict multiplier-level solution, or the consistency of the system (S^*), and is equivalent also to Houthakker's condition K^*. Thus if there exists any utility which solves the construction problem, then it can be found in this way, by taking any strict multiplier-level solution and forming the function ϕ^i.

The other function ϕ^o is not compatible with F in the strict sense (H^*), but it is in the sense (H) under the same conditions that make ϕ^i strictly compatible. Then both these functions have values at the demand points x_r, given by the levels ϕ_r. All utility functions having these values at these points, and which are strictly compatible with F, are exactly those which lie between ϕ^o and ϕ^i. While ϕ^o is included among these, ϕ^i is not, but is a limiting case, there being such functions arbitrarily close to it. Also, all functions lying between any such function and ϕ^i are included. Thus ϕ^o and ϕ^i provide a complete description of all such functions, or almost all. The only reason why ϕ^o fails to be strictly compatible with F is that it is flat, or locally linear, at the points x_r. While x_r is represented as giving a unique maximum of utility under the associated budget constraint, it is not a unique maximum. A suitable function has to be curved at x_r, however slightly. The other function ϕ^i is at the other extreme, being sharply pointed at the points x_r.

The function ϕ^i and ϕ^o will be distinguished as the *inner* and *outer envelope functions* for this class of strictly compatible utility function associated with any strict multiplier-level solution. Their construction is as follows.

The multiplier λ_r with the budget vector u_r determines the vector $g_r = \lambda_r u_r$ and then, with the level ϕ_r, determines the linear function

$$\phi_r(x) = \phi_r + g_r(x - x_r) = \phi_r + \lambda_r(u_r x - 1)$$

with gradient g_r, and the value

$$\phi_r(x_s) = \phi_r + \lambda_r(u_r x_s - 1) = \phi_r + \lambda_r D_{rs}$$

at any demand point x_s, in particular

$$\phi_r(x_r) = \phi_r.$$

Therefore from the condition

$$\lambda_r D_{rs} > \phi_s - \phi_r \, (r \neq s),$$

for a strict multiplier-level solution, we have

$$\phi_r(x_s) > \phi_s(x_s) \, (r \neq s).$$

Consequently the monotonic concave polyhedral function

$$\phi^o(x) = \min_r \phi_r(x)$$

has values

$$\phi^o(x_s) = \phi_s(x_s) = \phi_s.$$

Moreover, because of the strict inequalities, we have

$$\phi^o(x) = \phi_s(x) \text{ near } x_s,$$

so ϕ^o is locally linear, and therefore differentiable, at x_s, with gradient g^o at x_s identical with the gradient g_s of the function $\phi_s(x)$. Thus

$$g^o(x_s) = g_s.$$

But $g_s = \lambda_s u_s$, so now we have

$$g^o(x_s) = \lambda_s u_s.$$

Since the function ϕ^o is concave, from its definition, with this relation the Kuhn-Tucker conditions are satisfied for x_s to be a maximum of $\phi^o(x)$ subject to $u_s x \leq 1$, $x \geq 0$, λ_s being the Lagrange multiplier. Thus,

$$(H') \, u_s x \leq 1 \Rightarrow \phi^o(x) \leq \phi^o(x_s).$$

Also, because $\lambda_s > 0$, the maximum value is sensitive to the cost, and we have

$$(H'') \, u_s x < 1 \Rightarrow \phi^o(x) < \phi^o(x_s).$$

From the conjunction of (H') and (H'') we have the condition (H), showing that *the utility function ϕ^o is compatible with the given demand data.*

However, we do not have the wanted strict compatibility, which requires

$$(H^*)\ u_s x \leq 1 \text{ and } x \neq x_s \Rightarrow \phi^o(x) < \phi^o(x_s).$$

We will have that instead with the monotone concave polytope function

$$\phi^i(x) = \max[\Sigma \, \phi_r t_r : \Sigma x_r t_r \leq x, \, \Sigma t_r = 1, \, t_r \geq 0].$$

Because $t_s = 1$, $t_r = 0$ $(r \neq s)$ is feasible with $x = x_s$, this function is immediately such that

$$\phi^i(x_s) \geq \phi_s.$$

Introduce

$$w_r = \phi_r - g_r x_r,$$

so that

$$\phi_r(x) = \phi_r + g_r(x - x_r) = w_r + g_r x.$$

Then we have

$$\phi^o(x) = \min_r w_r + g_r x.$$

By linear programming duality, $\phi^i(x)$ has the equivalent formula

$$\phi^i(x) = \min\,[\,w + gx : w + gx_r \geq \phi_r, \, g \geq 0\,].$$

Again, from the multiplier-level inequalities, we have that $w = w_s$, $g = g_s$ is feasible, and so, for all x,

$$\phi^i(x) \leq w_r + g_r x \quad \text{for all } r.$$

Equivalently,

$$\phi^i(x) \leq \phi^o(x) \quad \text{for all } x.$$

We now have

$$\phi_s \leq \phi^i(x_s) \leq \phi^o(x_s) = \phi_s$$

and consequently $\phi^i(x_s) = \phi_s$.

Any monotone concave function $\phi(x)$ satisfies the condition

$$\Sigma x_r t_r \leq x, \, \Sigma t_r = 1, \, t_r \geq 0 \Rightarrow \Sigma \phi(x_r)t_r \leq \phi(x).$$

It follows that if $\phi(x)$ is any such function, for which moreover

$$\phi(x_r) = \phi_r \quad \text{for all } r,$$

then

$$\phi^i(x) \leq \phi(x) \quad \text{for all } x.$$

Now, from the strict multiplier inequalities again,

$$w_s + g_s x_r > \phi_r(r \neq s), \, w_s + g_s x_s = \phi_s.$$

Therefore, for any s and any $\Sigma t_r = 1$, $t_r \geq 0$, by multiplying by the t_r and summing, it follows that

$$w_s + \Sigma x_r t_r \geq \Sigma \phi_r t_r \quad \text{for all } s,$$

where the equality holds if and only if $t_r = 0 \, (r \neq s)$, $t_s = 1$. Since $\lambda_s > 0$, so that $g_s \geq 0$, this holding for all s and all such t is equivalent to

$$\phi^o(x) \geq \phi^i(x) \quad \text{for all } x,$$

with equality if and only if $x = x_s$ for some s.

For a restatement of the budget constraint $u_r x \leq 1$, we have

$$w_r + g_r x \leq \phi_r,$$

and from the strict multiplier-level conditions the equality here holds for some $x = x_s$ if and only if $s = r$. Therefore the budget constraint has the consequence

$$\phi_r(x) = w_r + g_r x \leq \phi_r,$$

and hence

$$\phi^o(x) \leq \phi_r = \phi^i(x_r);$$

and subject to $x \neq x_r$ we have also

$$\phi^i(x) < \phi^o(x).$$

Thus

$$u_r x \leq 1 \quad \text{and} \quad x \neq x_r \Rightarrow \phi^i(x) < \phi^i(x_r),$$

showing that *the utility function $\phi^i(x)$ is strictly compatible with the given demand data*.

A main part of our conclusions is in the following.

THEOREM If there exists any utility order or function which is strictly compatible with the given demands (x_r, p_s), then the inequalities

$$\lambda_r > 0, \quad \lambda_r D_{rs} > \phi_s - \phi_r (r \neq s)$$

formed with the cross-coefficients

$$D_{rs} = P_r x_s - 1$$

have a solution λ_r, ϕ_r, and one such function is given by

$$\phi(x) = \max \, [\Sigma_r t_r : \Sigma \, x_r t_r \leq x, \, \Sigma t_r = 1, \, t_r \geq 0].$$

Because $\phi(x)$ is monotone concave immediately from the form of its definition, and so has the classical properties for a utility function, the following can be added:

COROLLARY The strict consistency of any finite collection of demands, for which Houthakker's condition provides a finite test, is sufficient for their strict classical consistency.

2.7 MULTIPLIERS AND LEVELS

Now there are two utility functions ϕ^o and ϕ^i, both with the classical properties, one compatible and the other strictly compatible with the given demand data. Any utility function ϕ which lies between them, being such that

$$\phi^i(x) \leq \phi(x) \leq \phi^o(x) \quad \text{for all } x,$$

is compatible also, and arbitrarily close to another which is strictly compatible, obtained for instance by averaging it with ϕ^i. The threshold distinction between compatibility and strict compatibility was brought in for maintaining continuity with demand theory where the strict form is customary, but it will now be abandoned. Then it will be enough simply that ϕ^o and ϕ^i are compatible and so are all the functions in between.

Our original definition of consistency of the demands, (H) or (H^*), was by simultaneous compatibility with a completely arbitrary utility order. Houthakker's condition was found to be necessary and sufficient for that, in the strict sense (H^*). But now it has been found necessary and sufficient also for *strict classical consistency* C^*, where the utility order is not arbitrary but is required to be representable by a classical utility function, monotone and concave. It follows that *strict consistency is equivalent to strict classical consistency*, $H^* \Leftrightarrow C^*$.

The utility functions ϕ^o and ϕ^i have been constructed from strictly consistent data on the basis of any strict multiplier-level solution (λ_r, ϕ_r), the λ_r being called *mutipliers* and the ϕ_r *levels*. Houthakker's condition was proved necessary and sufficient for the existence of such a solution. Moreover, when such a solution exists, it can be chosen to make the order of the given demands produced by the ϕ_r coincide with any total order which is a refinement of a partial order constructed on the basis of 'revealed preference', so *the orders produced by the ϕ_r exhaust all such refinements*. Both these functions, and so also all functions lying between them, have values ϕ_r at the data points x_r, and so *the levels ϕ_r in any strict multiplier-level solution are interpreted as utility levels* at the data points for this class of functions. We will now consider the significance of the multipliers λ_r as Lagrange multipliers, and so also as marginal utilities.

With any utility function ϕ, we can introduce

$$V_r(M) = \max [\phi(x) : p_r x \leq M].$$

This function is in any case non-decreasing, and increasing if ϕ is semi-increasing, and concave if ϕ is concave. Then, by the concave function support theorem (see Chapter V.2), there exists l_r such that

$$V_r(M) - V_r(M_r) \leq l_r(M - M_r),$$

for all M. There is just one such l_r in the case where $V_r(M)$ is differentiable at $M = M_r$, in which case it is simply the derivative. If ϕ is compatible with the demand (x_r, p_r), we have $V_r(M_r) = \phi_r$, and some $l_r > 0$. Also l_r is identified with the 'Lagrange multiplier' in the optimality conditions of Slater's theorem, or of the Kuhn-Tucker theorem in the case where ϕ is differentiable, where we have $\phi(x) - l_r p_r x$ is maximum at $x = x_r$, or $g(x_r) = l_r p_r$ when

ϕ has a gradient $g(x)$ (Chapter V.2 deals with these theorems). In any case $l_r p_r$ is required to be a support gradient of ϕ at $x = x_r$, for some $l_r > 0$. We have dealt with the demands in the normalized form where the budget vector $u_r = M_r^{-1} p_r$ replaces the prices p_r, and so $\lambda_r = M_r l_r$ replaces l_r as Lagrangian multiplier. Then for a compatible utility ϕ we have

$$V_r(M) - \phi_r \le \lambda_r(M/M_r - 1),$$

where in the differentiable case λ_r is unique and

$$M_r \, \partial V_r(M)/\partial M|_{M = M_r} = \lambda_r.$$

Everything here applies in particular to the pair of functions ϕ^o and ϕ^i and the functions lying between them. These are selected from among other compatible classical utilities simply by identifying the multipliers and levels they determine at the data points x_r with the ϕ_r and λ_r. The multiplier-level inequalities for which these are a solution describe exactly all the mutipliers and levels which can so occur.

THEOREM For any classical utility function $\phi(x)$ with values $\phi_r = \phi(x_r)$ and

$$V_r(M) = \max [\phi(x) : p_r x \le M]$$

a necessary and sufficient condition for it to be compatible with the given demands is that $V_r(M_r) = \phi_r$ and

$$V_r(M) - \phi_r \le \lambda_r(M/M_r - 1) \text{ for all } M,$$

for some $\lambda_r > 0$. Then the numbers λ_r, ϕ_r satisfy

$$\lambda_r D_{rs} > \phi_s - \phi_r (r \ne s)$$

and the function ϕ lies between the inner and outer functions ϕ^o and ϕ^i constructed from the demands and based on these numbers, and conversely.

Combinatorics of Demand

The 'integrability problem' refers in economics to the use of a demand function for arriving at a utility function, and to the question of possibility. It came to be so called because Vito Volterra (1906), reviewing a work of Vilfredo Pareto that dealt with the idea, pointed out that using a demand function to arrive at a utility function required the integrability of a certain linear differential form, in the sense of a theorem of Frobenius which gave necessary conditions in terms of the coefficients and their derivatives. Antonelli (1886) had applied such conditions before, and Slutsky put them in another form, joining them with further conditions which demonstrated that more than just integrability is involved. P. A. Samuelson (1948) and H. S. Houthakker (1950) approached the same matter in a way that was not dependent from the start on numerical utility, but dealt first with preference relations implied or 'revealed' by the basic hypothesis. However, their objective was still to construct a numerical utility function, and with that they were involved in limiting processes, defeating the hope of a finitely operational, purely ordinal approach to utility construction.

The promise of the finite consistency test is not realizable without data that permit it. But from the earlier approach, with the Slutsky coefficients, once the derivatives are known, as they are with certain examples, we do have a finite test—if one does not mind that derivatives are limits. The elementary result of the section II.1.5, or I.2.5 where it is put more abstractly, free of the numerical aspect and close to hand, might have given satisfaction, but, notwithstanding declared motives, the goal was a numerically represented utility.

It has already been seen that, when the same question is applied to a finite collection of demands, instead of a demand function, the intentions of Samuelson in proposing the revealed preference approach are realized. Moreover, for that possibility, it makes no difference at all whether the quest is for a completely arbitrary utility order, or for one represented by a numerical utility function, or for one represented by a utility function with all the properties ever assumed or desired for a utility function—continuous and differentiable, and then monotone and concave, so as to express non-satiation and diminishing returns. This raised questions about the empirical significance, or status, of these assumptions. The possibility of consumption satiation may be well represented in reality, as one might hope, but it would not be in the area of observations, simply because people do not buy things when they are satiated and the observations are of purchases and purchasers. As concerns possible kinks in indifference surfaces of individuals, violating diminishing returns, these also may be a proper part of reality, but not a part that can ever be 'revealed' in choice under linear budgets.

The idea of utility has had persistent attention in such a highly abstract way that it is possible to question its usefulness. But the drive of economic activity is understood to come, ultimately, from the utility of goods produced. The idea of utility would therefore seem to be compelled if not from all sides, as this might suggest, then from many. There is some escape from having to follow the causal chain to the end because goods have prices and economic questions can, and usually do, refer to these. An ample escape is offered by the theory of general economic equilibrium, which proposes a global coincidence of exchange rates in the sense of both use and exchange. But from experience, that is not always quite enough. Occasion for the entry of utility as distinct from prices is made by the question of the purchasing power of incomes; seized upon in theory, it evaporates in the Statistical Office.

Utility is a function or a relation in the form usually given to it. But settlement of the form in which utility is stated, or in which it is proposed to approach learning about utility, does not carry with it any knowledge. For content, an observational basis is required. If utility is understood to be the ultimate governor of economic activity, that basis should be everywhere, but without a limiting form we do not know how to look for it. We have such a limitation, by assumption, when consumption has been separated from everything else and utility for it alone is the recognized governor of consumer demand. The logic of that separation and hypothesis has been pursued, and we will go further now with the construction of utility costs and an evaluation of their indeterminacies, and also with the imposition of special strucures on utility, such as homogeneity, or separability. The mathematics of the approach is peculiar to it and a part of the interest in it, and there are expansions on that side also.

3.1 GENERAL CONSISTENCY

Let R be any utility order, (x, p) $(px > 0)$ any demand and (x, u) $(ux = 1)$ the corresponding normal demand, its *normalization*, obtained by replacing the prices p by the budget vector $u = (px)^{-1}p$. The relation H of *compatibility* between the utility and the demand is defined by conditions

$$py \le px \Rightarrow xRy, \qquad yRx \Rightarrow py \ge px,$$

and equivalently, in terms of the normalized demand,

$$uy \le 1 \Rightarrow xRy, \qquad yRx \Rightarrow uy \ge 1.$$

Dealing with normal demands is most convenient and should be understood now unless the contrary is stated.

The elements of the normal demand relation f_R *derived* from R are all the normal demands (x, u) compatible with it. Any demand relation f is compatible with R if all its elements are simultaneously compatible with R, so the condition, which is stated $H_f(R)$, requires that $f \subset f_R$. The *consistency* of f, stated H_f, requires this for some R. A commodity bundle x and budget vector u are *conjugates* with respect to R if (x, u) is compatible, that is if $xf_R u$.

A demand relation f is now supposed given. As before, when suitable we can take its elements to be an indexed set (x_t, u_t) where t ranges in some set. In the finite case where there are m elements, the index set is just $[1, \ldots, m]$. The cross-coefficients for f are $D_{rs} = u_r x_s - 1$, and determine vectors

$$D_{rij\ldots ks} = (D_{ri}, D_{ij}, \ldots, D_{ks}).$$

Then f determines a relation R_f between its own elements given by

$$rR_f s \equiv (\vee \, i \ldots) \, D_{ri\ldots s} \leq 0.$$

It is immediate from the definition that R_f is transitive, and because $D_{rr} = 0$ it is also reflexive. Therefore it is an order, the *revealed preference order* of the elements of the demand relation f.

Though R_f is defined originally here between the elements of f, it determines an order in the commodity space which without confusion can also be denoted R_f and is given by

$$xR_f y \equiv (\vee \, rR_f s) \, x = x_r \text{ and } u_s y \leq 1.$$

In a dual fashion it determines an order in the budget space given by

$$uR_f v \equiv (\vee \, rR_f s) \, ux_r \leq 1 \text{ and } v = u_s.$$

With these definitions, the statements $x_r R_f x_s$, $rR_f s$, and $u_r R_f u_s$ all mean the same.

The revealed preference idea usually concerns preferences in the commodity space. But there is an equally good dual principle which applies to the budget space, so this is only one half of the complete matter. By the relation W between points in the commodity and budget spaces given by

$$xWu \equiv ux \leq 1,$$

we say x is *within* u, and can just as well say u is within x. The utility of a budget is the maximum utility of the bundles attainable within it. Therefore this relation reveals that u has at least the utility of x. This applies in particular to a normal demand (x, u), for which $ux = 1$. But compatibility with the utility by definition requires that x have at least the utility of any bundle within u, and therefore at least the utility of u, and so now the same utility as u. Just as the demand (x, u) reveals the preference of x to every y within u, so also it reveals the preference to u of every v within x. This duality between the commodity and budget space is developed further in the next chapter, on 'Direct and Indirect Utility'. But it can be noted that the revealed preference principle has a proper, less well-known, dual: with every statement where the primary reference is to the commodity space, there is a similar statement for the budget space in which commodity bundles and budget vectors have exchanged their roles. (This is like the classic duality of projective geometry.)

This duality is spoilt when compatibility between demand and utility is based on the condition (H^*), usual in demand analysis instead of on the here adopted (H). The complete symmetry and therefore true duality obtained with (H) undergoes an awkward unsymmetrical modification for (H^*). Here are good grounds besides the already described economic grounds for working with (H), which makes other simplifications also.

For R_f as an order in the commodity space to be compatible with f, in other words for the condition $H_f(R_f)$ to hold, it is required that

$$u_r x \leq 1 \Rightarrow x_r R_f x, \qquad x R_f x_r \Rightarrow u_r x \geq 1.$$

From the way R_f is defined, this is equivalent to

$$D_{rs} \leq 0 \Rightarrow r R_f s, \qquad s R_f s \Rightarrow D_{rs} \geq 0.$$

The first condition here is satisfied automatically, again from the definition of R_f. Therefore $H_f(R_f)$ is equivalent to the second, which obviously is equivalent to the condition K_f given by

$$K_f \equiv D_{rs\ldots r} \leq 0 \Rightarrow D_{ri\ldots r} = 0.$$

Hence we have

THEOREM I The condition K_f is necessary and sufficient for the demand relation f to be compatible with its own revealed preference relation R_f,

$$K_f \Leftrightarrow H_f(R_f).$$

It will be seen now that, for any order R,

$$H_f(R) \Rightarrow H_f(R_f).$$

It is immediate that $H_f(R_f) \Rightarrow H_f$, and so it will follow that

$$H_f \Leftrightarrow H_f(R_f) \Leftrightarrow K_f.$$

Thus, the compatibility $H_f(R)$ of R with f requires

$$u_r x \leq 1 \Rightarrow x_r R x, \qquad x R x_r \Rightarrow u_r x \geq 1.$$

Taking $x = x_s$, the first part of this condition requires in particular that

$$D_{rs} \leq 0 \Rightarrow x_r R x_s,$$

and because R is transitive this is equivalent to $R_f \subset R$. With this and the second part we have that

$$x R_f x_r \Rightarrow x R x_r \Rightarrow u_r x \geq 1$$

and so, taking $x = x_s$,

$$s R_f r \Rightarrow D_{rs} \geq 0,$$

which is the condition K_f, equivalent to $H_f(R_f)$.

THEOREM II There exists a utility order compatible with the demand relation f if and only if its own revealed preference relation R_f is one such relation;

$$H_f \Leftrightarrow H_f(R_f).$$

As a consequence of Theorems I and II we have:

THEOREM III $H_f \Leftrightarrow H_f(R_f) \Leftrightarrow K_f.$

To characterize all orders R which are compatible with f, or such that $H_f(R)$, it is useful to introduce the *revealed strict preference* relation $S_f \subset R_f$ for f by

$$rS_f s \equiv (\vee \ i \ldots) \ D_{ri \ldots s} \lessgtr 0$$

as applied to elements of f, and by

$$xS_f y \equiv (\vee \ x = x_r, s) \, (rS_f s, \quad u_s y \leq 1) \vee (rR_f s, \quad u_s < 1)$$

as a relation in the commodity space. Evidently

$$K_f \Leftrightarrow R_f \subset \bar{S}'_f$$

and, with P as the strict part of R,

$$H_f(R) \Leftrightarrow R_f \subset R, \quad S_f \subset P \Leftrightarrow R_f \subset R \subset \bar{S}'_f.$$

It being true that

$$R_f \subset \bar{S}'_f \Leftrightarrow R_f \subset R_f \subset \bar{S}'_f,$$

from here in one stroke we also have the earlier results. For the additional conclusion, we have:

THEOREM IV The condition $H_f(R)$ for any utility order R with antisymmetric part P to be compatible with the demand relation f with revealed preference and strict preference relations R_f and S_f is equivalent to

$$R_f \subset R, \quad S_f \subset P$$

and to

$$R_f \subset R \subset \bar{S}'_f.$$

Nothing so far requires f to be finite, and the propositions apply to a completely arbitrary demand correspondence f, and just as well to a completely arbitrary order R in the commodity space. But f is required to be finite in further developments of these results.

3.2 CROSS-COSTS

The given demands (x_t, p_t), elements of a demand relation F with normalization f, determine *cross-costs* $p_r x_s$, which, if the demands are associated with different periods, give the cost of a bundle found in one period at the prices of another. The collection of all these has a role quite apart from the further content in the data. For normalization, the cross-costs are compared with the direct costs $p_r x_r$, determining the *relative cross-costs* which are the ratios $p_r x_s / p_r x_r = u_r x_s$ where the $u_r = (p_r x_r)^{-1} p_r$ are the derived budget vectors. These ratios look like Laspeyres price indices, but should not be regarded as such because they are not price indices. The price index is a restricted idea depending on a homogeneity which has no part in present assumptions. When the required homogeneity is brought in later, these ratios will become bounds of possible price indices, as usually understood with the Laspeyres formula. But at the same time there is a generalization which, with the additional data, improves on the bounds and possibly excludes them as price indices that fit the data, as spelled in Chapter III.2 on 'the True Index'.

The cross-costs are dealt with through the cross-coefficients

$$D_{rs} = u_r x_s - 1.$$

Certain constructions involving these are unchanged by the dualization in which there is an exchange of role between the commodity and budget spaces, that is, they are self-dual. Developments are going to depend on the equivalence of various conditions on the demand data which are formulated in terms of these numbers alone. The first such condition is provided by the condition K, similar to the Houthakker condition K^*, which can be stated in various equivalent forms which have been noted.

Two important constructions based entirely on the numbers D_{rs} are the *revealed preference* and *revealed strict preference relations* R_f, S_f. In terms of the vectors

$$D_{rij...ks} = (D_{ri}, D_{ij}, \ldots, D_{ks}),$$

these are given by

$$rR_f s \equiv (\vee\ i \ldots)\, D_{ri...s} \leq 0,$$

and

$$rS_f s \equiv (\vee\ i \ldots)\, D_{ri...s} \leq 0.$$

Evidently from these definitions both are transitive, and R_f is also reflexive because the $D_{rr} = 0$. Also

$$S_f \subset R_f, \qquad S_f R_f \subset S_f, \qquad R_f S_f \subset S_f.$$

The symmetric and antisymmetric parts of R_f are denoted E_f and P_f. Then E_f is an equivalence relation which defines the *revealed indifference relation*, and P_f is a strict order, the *strict revealed preference relation*, to be distinguished from the revealed strict preference relation S_f, though with this again there are the same absorption properties with P_f,

$$P_f \subset R_f, \qquad P_f R_f \subset P_f, \qquad R_f P_f \subset P_f.$$

The condition K_f has the obviously equivalent statements

$$D_{rs...r} \leq 0 \Rightarrow D_{rs...r} = 0$$

and

$$rR_f s \Rightarrow D_{sr} \geq 0,$$

and also

$$rR_f s \;\Rightarrow\; \sim s S_f r.$$

The last, which is that $R_f \subset \bar{S}'_f$, shows the equivalence to $S_f \subset P_f$, so one way of putting the condition is that under it *the revealed strict preferences are strict revealed preferences*. The condition implies that S_f is irreflexive, but we do not have the converse.

It has been shown already that K_f is equivalent to

(O_f):   there exists a complete order R of f, with antisymmetric part P, such that

$$sRr \;\Rightarrow\; D_{rs} \geq 0, \qquad sPr \;\Rightarrow\; D_{rs} > 0.$$

Such an order was called a canonical order for f, and it was seen that when one exists it can be chosen to be any complete order which contains R_f and has the same equivalence relation. This is the most important equivalence with K_f; it does not depend on f being finite, but for when f is finite it gives the means for proving the others by finite induction. Another condition to be considered is

(L_f):   there exist numbers $\lambda_r > 0$ such that

$$\lambda_r D_{rs} + \lambda_s D_{st} + \ldots + \lambda_q D_{qr} \geq 0$$

for all (distinct) r, s, t, $\ldots$, q.

This condition involves values on cycles of elements. But since these are all expressible as sums of values on simple cyles, without repeated elements, it is equivalent to the same condition with restriction to those. Therefore it makes no difference to the condition whether the elements are restricted to be distinct, but when they are we have a finite system of inequalities. The method of solving it is simpler than might be supposed and consists in determining classes of the λ_r in succession according to any canonical order with its total order of equivalence classes.

The equivalence of this condition to the next is seen from a theorem that has a bearing also on the theory of minimum paths in networks:

(M_f):   there exist numbers $\lambda_r > 0$ and ϕ_r such that

$$\lambda_r D_{rs} \geq \phi_s - \phi_r.$$

Given any such numbers, by summing over a cycle we have

$$\lambda_r D_{rs} + \lambda_s D_{st} + \ldots + \lambda_q D_{qr} \geq (\phi_s - \phi_r) + (\phi_t - \phi_s) + \ldots + (\phi_q - \phi_r) = 0$$

Thus for any λ_r, ϕ_r which satisfy M_f, the λ_r satisfy λ_f. Also conversely, for any such λ_r there exist ϕ_r to satisfy the first condition, as follows from the theorem proved in Chapter V.4, where it is also shown how to compute the ϕ_r. Thus, in addition to the equivalence of these two conditions, there is also the identity between the λ_r which occur in them.

We will briefly consider yet another condition with equivalence to the foregoing:

(T_f): there exist numbers $t_{rs} \geq 0$ such that

$$t_{rs} \geq 0, \; \Sigma_s t_{rs} = \Sigma_s t_{sr}, \; \Sigma_s D_{rs} t_{rs} \leq 0 \quad \text{for all } r,$$

and

$$\Sigma_s D_{rs} t_{rs} < 0 \quad \text{for some } r.$$

From the first line the matrix of these numbers is sum-symmetric and so, interpreted for a flow network, can be regarded as a flow matrix corresponding to the case of a closed flow, without sources or sinks, or with conservation at the nodes so that total flow into any node equals total flow out. There is the theorem that any closed flow is decomposable into a non-negative combination of elementary closed flows, where there is a unit flow through a cycle of nodes. By using this or otherwise the equivalence of conditions S_f and K_f can be shown (see Afriat, 1974a).

3.3 CLASSICAL CONSISTENCY

We now consider *classical consistency* of the given demands f, the existence of a utility function which is compatible with them and has the classical properties. Let $C_f(\phi)$ mean that ϕ is such a utility function, and C_f that one exists. It will be seen eventually that $H_f \Leftrightarrow C_f$; that is, *general consistency is equivalent to classical consistency*. This equivalence means that, whenever it is possible to find any compatible utility at all, it is also possible to find one which is representable by a utility function with all the classical properties.

First it will be shown that classical consistency C_f is equivalent to the multiplier-level consistency condition M_f, and there will be elaborations around that. Afterwards we show that M_f is equivalent to the condition K_f, already seen equivalent to general consistency. The development goes parallel to that provided already on the basis of the stricter condition (H^*).

Let $\phi(x)$ be a classical utility function, with $G(x)$ as the set of support gradients at any point. Because ϕ is concave $G(x)$ is always non-empty, and because ϕ is semi-increasing also $g \geq 0$ for all $g \in G(x)$. Then, in particular,

$$\phi(x) \leq \phi(x_r) + g_r(x - x_r) \quad \text{for all } x,$$

for all r, and $g_r \in G(x_r)$; and so also

$$\phi_s \leq \phi_r + g_r(x_s - x_r),$$

where $\phi_r = \phi(x_r)$.

Consider the convex programming problem

$$\max \phi(x) : u_r x \leq 1, x \geq 0.$$

Since $u_r x_r = 1$, we have $u_r x < 1$ for some $x \geq 0$, so that Slater's condition is satisfied. Therefore, by the convex programming optimality theorem, the conditions for $x = x_r$ to be an optimal solution are that

$$\lambda_r \geq 0, \quad u_r x_r \leq 1, \quad \lambda_r u_r x_r = \lambda_r$$

together with

$$\phi(x) - \lambda_r u_r x \leq \phi(x_r) - \lambda_r u_r x_r \quad \text{for all } x,$$

for some λ_r. The compatibility of ϕ with the demand (x_r, u_r) therefore requires this.

The last condition shows that $g_r = \lambda_r u_r$ is a support gradient of ϕ at the point x_r, so $g_r \epsilon G(x_r)$, therefore $g_r \geq 0$, and hence $\lambda_r > 0$. The other conditions being now automatic, we have the following:

THEOREM I   For any classical utility function $\phi(x)$ with support gradient set $G(x)$ at any point, a necessary and sufficient condition for it to be compatible with the demand correspondence f is that

$$\lambda_r > 0, \lambda_r D_{rs} \geq \phi_s - \phi_r$$

where $\phi_r = \phi(x_r)$ and $\lambda_r u_r \epsilon G(x_r)$.

As a consequence,

COROLLARY   Classical consistency implies multiplier-level consistency, that there exist numbers $\lambda_r > 0$ and ϕ_r such that

$$\lambda_r > 0, \quad \lambda_r D_{rs} \geq \phi_s - \phi_r,$$

that is,

$$C_f \Rightarrow M_f.$$

Now we show the converse together with an elaboration which gives a characterization of all compatible classical utilities.

For any numbers λ_r and ϕ_r consider the classical functions

$$\phi^o(x) = \min_r \phi_r + \lambda_r u_r (x - x_r)$$

and

$$\phi^i(x) = \max [\Sigma \phi_r t_r : \Sigma x_r t_r \leq x, \Sigma t_r = 1, t_r \geq 0].$$

These are the functions ϕ^i and ϕ^o considered before, and similar arguments apply again. Now we can add that, with $g_r = \lambda_r u_r$, the four conditions, each holding for all r,

$$g_r \epsilon G^o(x_r), \quad g_r \epsilon G^i(x_r),$$
$$\phi_r = \phi^o(x_r), \quad \phi_r = \phi^i(x_r),$$

and also

$$\phi^i(x) \leq \phi^o(x) \quad \text{for all } x,$$

are all equivalent to each other. They are equivalent also to λ_r, ϕ_r satisfying the inequalities stated in the Corollary, and to one, and equivalently the other, of these functions being compatible with f. In that case every classical function ϕ which lies between them is also compatible, and moreover such that

$\phi_r = \phi(x_r)$ and $g_r \epsilon G(x_r)$. Moreover, any compatible classical function satisfying these last two conditions, and therefore in the *multiplier-level class* identified by the λ_r and ϕ_r, must lie between them, or be such that

$$\phi^i(x) \le \phi(x) \le \phi^o(x) \quad \text{for all } x.$$

We can call the pair of functions ϕ^i and ϕ^o *multiplier-level bracket functions*, distinguished as *inner* and *outer*. The class of classical functions bracketed by them in this way is exactly the multiplier-level class just described.

THEOREM II For every multiplier-level solution there is a multiplier-level class of compatible classical utilties.

From this,

COROLLARY Multiplier-level consistency implies classical consistency,
$$M_f \Rightarrow C_f.$$

With the corollary to the last theorem, we now have the required equivalence.

3.4 MULTIPLIER-LEVEL SOLUTIONS

The existence of multiplier-level solutions implies classical consistency and so general consistency, for which the condition K_f provides a test. Now it will be shown how, subject to K_f, multiplier-level solutions can be constructed step by step by taking the elements together in classes in a certain order. *A conse-quence of the construction is that the general consistency test implies the existence of multiplier-level solutions.*

By taking any complete order R which contains the revealed preference order R_f and has the same equivalence classes, the condition K_f assures that this is a canonical order, so with P as the antisymmetric part we have

$$rRs \Rightarrow D_{sr} \ge 0, \quad rPs \Rightarrow D_{sr} > 0.$$

Let E_i ($i = 1$ to h) enumerate the equivalence classes of R in corresponding order and let

$$F_i = \cup_{j \le i} E_j = F_{i-1} \cup E_i,$$

so that

$$r, s \epsilon E_i \Rightarrow D_{rs} \ge 0, \quad s \epsilon F_{i-1} \text{ and } t \epsilon E_i \Rightarrow D_{ts} > 0.$$

Suppose now that numbers λ_r, ϕ_r for $r \epsilon F_{i-1}$ have been found as required, and we can make the additional requirement that

$$rRs \Leftrightarrow \phi_r \ge \phi_s.$$

It will be seen that now further numbers for $r \epsilon E_i$ can be determined so that all these numbers together are as required.

The requirement for the further numbers, beside $\lambda_r > 0$, is first that

$$\lambda_r D_{rs} \ge \phi_s - \phi_r \quad (r, s \epsilon E_i)$$

and also that

$$\lambda_r D_{rt} \geq \phi_t - \phi_r \quad (r \in F_{i-1}, t \in E_i),$$
$$\lambda_t D_{ts} \geq \phi_s - \phi_t \quad (s \in F_{i-1}, t \in E_i),$$

which can be stated

$$\phi_r + \lambda_r D_{rt} \geq \phi_t \geq \phi_s - \lambda_t D_{ts} \quad (r, s \in F_{i-1}, t \in E_i),$$

and finally

$$\phi_r > \phi_t \quad (r \in F_{i-1}, t \in E_i).$$

Because

$$r, s \in E_i \Rightarrow D_{rs}, D_{sr} \geq 0,$$

the first requirement is that $\phi_r = \phi_s$ $(r, s \in E_i)$, say $\phi_r = V_i$ $(r \in \phi_i)$. The problem now is to determine V_i and the $\lambda_t > 0$ $(t \in E_i)$ to meet the second, that is

$$\phi_r + \lambda_r D_{rt} \geq V_i \geq \phi_s - \lambda_t D_{ts} \quad (r, s \in F_{i-1}, t \in E_i),$$

and also

$$\phi_r > V_i \quad (r \in F_{i-1}).$$

First, V_i can be chosen within the stated upper bounds. Then, because all the $D_{ts} > 0$, the λ_t can be made large enough to satisfy the remaining conditions, and so we have the wanted conclusion.

The initial case with E_1 is satisfied by taking $\lambda_r > 0$ $(r \in E_1)$ and $\phi_r = \phi_s$ $(r, s \in E_1)$ arbitrarily. It follows that the required construction can be carried through to $i = h$.

THEOREM The general consistency test K_f implies the existence of numbers λ_r and ϕ_t such that $\lambda_r > 0$, $\lambda_r D_{rs} \geq \phi_s - \phi_r$ and moreover

$$rRs \leftrightarrow \phi_r \geq \phi_s$$

where R is any complete order which contains the revealed preference order R_f and has the same equivalence classes.

With this construction method to hand, there should be no thought of using a linear programming approach, such as the Simplex Algorithm to solve the inequalities in the textbook way. From Chapter II.6 it appears equally unsuitable to solve them by such methods in cases where they are inconsistent, since the above construction method is applicable there also. Such suggestions have been offered, either by way of a contribution to this subject, or as a reason for calling this a 'linear programming approach' to demand analysis. Instead, it can be noted that all proofs here are constructive, and embody efficient algorithms, such as have been brought out by Hal Varian (1981, 1982). I thank him for discussions, communications, and acknowledgements.

COROLLARY General consistency implies multiplier-level consistency,

$$K_f \Rightarrow M_f.$$

3.5 UTILITY COST

The cost of living question asks for a determination of the cost, at the prices found in one period, of attaining a standard of living found in another. The question is understood in terms of utility, R, and if p are the prices and x consumption bundle representative of the standard of living, then

$$c(p, x) = \min [py : yRx]$$

is the cost required.

There would be no 'cost of living problem' were the utility R, which in principle provides the yardstick for the question, given. The problem arises because it is not given. But we already have a view of how demand data can put a constraint on utility by the requirement of their being compatible with it. That leads to the well defined problem of determining the set of possible values of $c(p, x)$ when R is restricted to compatibility with a collection of demands (x_t, p_t), the elements of a finite demand correspondence f. Additional constraints on R, so long as consistency is maintained, produce additional constraints on utility costs based on it, reducing their indeterminacy. The constraints could involve requiring compatibility with further demand observations, or alternatively imposing a special form on R.

A limited treatment of this problem consists in determining the possible values of $c_{rs} = c(p_r, x_s)$ when R is restricted by compatibility with f. We will find that the range of c_{rs} is an interval and obtain formulae for the endpoints, so giving a complete description of the possible values, but for the issue of inclusion of the end-points.

When any further restriction is put on R, the values of c_{rs} should become restricted to a subset. An effective method, which we will use, is to calculate the range when R is restricted by the classical properties, and then establish that the unrestricted range must be some subset of this, and so identical with it.

From the definition of $c(p, x)$, because R is reflexive,

$$c(p, x) \leq px \quad \text{for all } p, x.$$

That states again the by far most commonly stated relation of the theory of index numbers—that a minimum is indeed a lower bound—a point at which the subject is frequently abandoned. It occupies several pages of the much cited paper of Könus (1924)—what followed having being corrected by Schultz (1939).

The compatibility of R with the demand (x, p) requires

$$c(p, x) = px.$$

For this asserts that the cost px of x at the prices p is also the minimum cost of attaining the utility of x, or that the demand (x, p) is cost-efficient when utility is the benefit criterion.

Since $c(p, x)$ from its definition is a conical, or linearly homogeneous, function of p, we have

$$c(p, x)/px = c((px)^{-1}p, x) = c(u, x)$$

where $u = (px)^{-1}p$ is the budget vector for the demand (x, p), and so (x, u) is the normalized demand. Compatibility can therefore be stated equivalently in terms of the normalized demand. If R is restricted to compatibility with the given demands, we therefore have

$$c(u_r, x_r) = u_r x_r = 1,$$

while in any case

$$c(u_r, x_s) \leq u_r x_s.$$

Rather than utility costs $c_{rs} = c(p_r, x_s)$, it is more convenient to deal instead with the relative utility costs

$$c_{rs} = c(u_r, x_s) = c(p_r, x_s)/p_r x_r,$$

where, subject to compatibility, we also have

$$c(p_r, x_r) = p_r x_r \text{ and equivalently } c(u_r, x_r) = 1.$$

The problem now is to describe the values of these c_{rs} for all utility orders R compatible with f.

From the characterization of compatible utilities in Theorem IV of section 3.1 as being orders R such that

$$R_f \subset R \subset \bar{S}'$$

certain bounds for the numbers c_{rs} can be found immediately. For

$$c_{rs} = \min [u_r x : xRx_s],$$

and introducing the *critical cost functions*

$$\hat{c}_{rs} = \inf [u_r x : xR_f x_s], \quad \check{c}_{rs} = \inf [u_r x : \sim x_s S_f x],$$

we have immediately that

$$\check{c}_{rs} \leq c_{rs} \leq \hat{c}_{rs},$$

showing that c_{rs} lies in the *critical cost interval* with end-points determined by these functions.

From the definition of the revealed preference relation R_f, first as a relation between the elements of f and then as a relation determined from this in the commodity space, $xR_f x_s$ requires $x = x_t$ for some t, and $x_t R_f x_s$ means the same as $tR_f s$. Thus, more explicitly,

$$\hat{c}_{rs} = \min [u_r x_t : tR_f s].$$

Because $x_s S_f x$ means that, for some t,

$$(sS_f t, \quad u_t x \leq 1) \qquad \text{or} \qquad (sR_f t, \quad u_t x < 1),$$

the denial therefore is that, for all t,

$$sS_f t \Rightarrow u_t x > 1, \quad sR_f t \Rightarrow u_t x \geq 1.$$

Now because anyway $S_f \subset R_f$, the only possible effect of the first condition in this conjunction is to exclude parts of the boundary of the region in the commodity space defined by the second, not altering the required lower limit. Therefore

$$\check{c}_{rs} = \min \, [\, u_r x : sR_f t \Rightarrow u_t x \geq 1 \,].$$

This is a linear programming formula where the constraints include $u_t x \geq 1$ for all $t \, \epsilon \, sR_f$, and where $x \geq 0$ is understood.

We now have bounds for c_{rs} when R is restricted to compatibility with f. We need not make an issue about whether min $[\, py : yRx \,]$ exists. It does for some compatible R, for instance the classical R which we know must exists whenever any compatible R exist. A proper issue now is whether these bounds are the best possible, and therefore are limits. A further issue is whether the range of values of c_r is connected, and therefore is an interval. Whether it is closed at each end is yet another issue, though less compelling. All these issues will be resolved when the range of c_{rs} corresponding to all classical compatible utilities is found. This should be a subset of the general range, and is found to be identical with it. At this point we have the following:

THEOREM I   For the utility cost function
$$c(p, x) = \min \, [\, py : yRx \,]$$
and the values $c_{rs} = c(\, u_r, x_s \,)$, if the utility order R is restricted to be compatible with the demand relation f then

$$\check{c}_{rs} \, \leq \, c_{rs} \, \leq \, \hat{c}_{rs} \, ,$$

where

$$\hat{c}_{rs} = \min \, [\, u_r x_t \, : \, tR_f s \,].$$

and

$$\check{c}_{rs} = \min \, [\, u_r x : sR_f t \Rightarrow u_t x \geq 1 \,],$$

where R_f is the revealed preference order of the elements of f.

From this theorem it appears that the existence of compatible R, meaning the consistency of f, implies that $\check{c}_{rs} \leq \hat{c}_{rs}$ for all r, s. The converse also is true. For $\check{c}_{rs} > \hat{c}_{rs}$ implies that there exist t and q such that

$$tR_f s, \; sR_f q, \; u_q x_t < 1$$

and this violates the general consistency test K_f.

THEOREM II   The consistency of the demand relation f is necessary and sufficient for the critical cost intervals $[\, \check{c}_{rs}, \hat{c}_{rs} \,]$ all to be non–empty.

3.6   CLASSICAL LIMITS

Whenever any compatible utilities exist, we know that among them are classical utilities, and these have been characterized as belonging to multiplier–level classes, described by means of the bracket functions ϕ^i, ϕ^o. Now we will find the range of values of c_{rs} corresponding to a multiplier–level class of utilities and see how this range varies for all classes.

The outer function

$$\phi^o(x) = \min_t \phi_t + \lambda_t(u_t x - 1)$$

determines the value

$$c_{rs}^o = \min [u_r x : \phi^o(x) \geq \phi^o(x_s)]$$
$$= \min [u_r x : u_t x \geq 1 + (\phi_s - \phi_t)/\lambda_t].$$

and the function

$$\phi^i(x) = \max [\Sigma \phi_t w_t : \Sigma x_t w_t \leq x, \Sigma w_t = 1, w_t \geq 0]$$

determines

$$c_{rs}^i = \min [u_r x : \phi^i(x) \geq \phi^i(x_s)]$$
$$= \min [\Sigma u_r x_t w_t : \Sigma \phi_t w_t \geq \phi_s, \Sigma w_t = 1, w_t \geq 0].$$

For any multiplier-level solution the bracket functions are compatible utilities, and so is any average of them; so these are possible values of c_{rs}, and so is any point between them. Therefore when it is shown that, by varying the multiplier-level solution, c_{rs}^i can approach arbitrarily close to c_{rs} and similarly that c_{rs}^o can approach c_{rs}, it will have been shown that the possible values of c_{rs}, which in any case lie in the critical cost interval $[c_{rs}, c_{rs}]$, also exhaust all its interior points.

To see this, we have to refer to the method of constructing multiplier-level solutions described in section 3.4 and used there in proof of the theorem.

The elements of f were taken in revealed indifference classes E_i and these classes were in a total order that refined their descending revealed preference partial order. It was made a part of the theorem proved that this total order was an arbitrary such refinement. Now in addition to using this we must go further with the manner of construction. When it came to the point of determining multipliers and levels for the class E_i, the utility level $\Phi_i (= \Phi_r$ for $r \epsilon E_i)$, assigned equally to all elements in it, was chosen arbitrarily subject to certain upper bounds, which included all previously determined levels; and then all the various multipliers λ_r ($r \epsilon E_i$) just had to be positive and sufficiently large to meet remaining conditions depending on the adopted Φ_i: the lower the Φ_i, the higher they had to be. Our argument will depend on the choice of canonical order, and on lowering a Φ_i indefinitely, and so at the same time forcing the associated λ_r to $+\infty$. With this, the indefinite lowering of all subsequently determined levels and raising of their associated multipliers would be forced at the same time.

To see that c_{rs}^i can be made to approach $\hat{c}_{rs}$, take a canonical order where all elements not revealed above s are placed below, and when it comes to determining Φ_i for the class E_i to which s belongs, make Φ_i approach $-\infty$. This will force all subsequently determined levels to approach $-\infty$ also, and make c_{rs}^i approach $\hat{c}_{rs}$. QED

Now instead take a canonical order in which all elements not revealed below s are placed above, and again make the level Φ_i for the class of s approach. We have to note now that all current and subsequent multipliers in the process are forced to $+\infty$, while as before all subsequent levels are forced to $-\infty$. It is evident then that c_{rs}^o approaches c_{rs}. QED

The set of multiplier-level solutions is linearly connected, since convex, and therefore connected. The bracket functions associated with any solution depend continuously on it, and so the values of c_{rs} determined from them depend continuously on the solution. Also, they are end-points of closed intervals of possible values of c_{rs}, corresponding to the multiplier-level class of compatible classical utilities. It follows that the classical range of c_{rs}, the set of values corresponding to classical compatible utilities, is connected. Since the only connected sets of numbers are the intervals, this shows that the set is an interval. It must in any case have the critical costs $\check{c}_{rs}$, $\hat{c}_{rs}$ as bounds. But it has been shown to have these as limit points. It follows that these are its limits.

Now we can append to Theorem I of the last section that the bounds there offered for the possible values of c_{rs} are the best possible, and therefore are limits, and moreover that the values exhaust at least all interior points of the interval between these limits.

THEOREM The set of possible values for the utility cost c_{rs} determined with respect to all compatible utilities is an interval with the numbers $\check{c}_{rs}$ and $\hat{c}_{rs}$ as limits.

II.4

Separable Utility

The universe cannot be dealt with all in one stroke, and so a bit has to be broken off and treated as if the rest did not matter. Statements are offered as true on the condition of 'other things being equal'—as if one should know when they are. Ricardo is supposed to have pioneered that way of arguing in economics. Another escape from the influence of other things is 'separability', where things do not have to be equal because they do not matter. When it is not stated explicitly this assumption is often implicitly understood, and then regarded as being not worth mentioning.

Everything in utility theory depends on separability, either explicitly or implicitly. It is made explicit with the idea of a subgroup of goods producing a separate utility on their own which is unaffected by other goods—and by all else besides. Then it becomes a matter of the internal structure of utility. W. W. Leontief (1957) approached this for differentiable utility functions, obtaining the conditions in terms of the derivatives, and further developments not dependent on differentiability have been shown by W. M. Gorman (1968). The interest now is to consider the same matter with reference to a scheme of demand data and compatible utilities, by the finite methods.

4.1 MODELS OF SEPARABILITY

Quantity and price vectors have partitions

$$x = \begin{pmatrix} x_0 \\ x_1 \end{pmatrix}, p = (p_0 \ p_1),$$

corresponding to a partition $n = n_0 + n_1$ of the goods, so with any demand (x_t, p_t),

$$x_t = \begin{pmatrix} x_{0t} \\ x_{1t} \end{pmatrix}, p_t = (p_{0t} \ p_{1t})$$

and for the budget vector, $u_t = (u_{0t}, u_{1t})$. Then the expenditure shares for the component demands (x_{it}, p_{it}) ($i = 0, 1$) are $w_{it} = u_{it} x_{it}$, and the budget vectors are $w_{it}^{-1} u_{it}$. The normalized component demands therefore are

$$(x_{0t}, w_{0t}^{-1} u_{0t}) \ (i = 0, 1),$$

with cross-coefficients $D_{irs} = u_{ir} x_{is} / w_{ir}$, so that

$$D_{rs} = w_{0r} D_{0rs} + w_{1r} D_{1rs}.$$

We consider the consistency of the data required by compatibility with utility functions having a separability on the models

(0)1 $\phi(x) = \Phi(\phi_0(x_0), x_1)$,
(0)(1) $\phi(x) = \Phi(\phi_0(x_0), \phi_1(x_1))$,
(0)+(1) $\phi(x) = \phi_0(x_0) + \phi_1(x_1)$,

all functions involved being classical.

The classical consistency condition C, for the existence of a compatible classical utility without other qualification, was found equivalent to general consistency H, to multiplier-level consistency M, and also to the general consistency test K. Let C^* be the consistency condition for the utility model $*$, required when the form $*$ is imposed on the utility beside its compatibility with the data. Since this is more restrictive than classical consistency without a further qualification, we have $C^* \Rightarrow C$, for each model $*$. The three models are in a sequence of increasing restriction, each being a specialization of its predecessor, and so moreover

$$C_{(0)+(1)} \Rightarrow C_{(0)(1)} \Rightarrow C_{(0)1} \Rightarrow C.$$

Any test obtained for these various consistencies should reflect these relations between them.

4.2   SEPARABILITY TESTS

We already have a test for classical consistency C which is related also to its constructive realization by means of specific functions, the multiplier-level consistency test M. It should be restated now for comparison with such tests for the other consistencies which will be obtained. The suffix f showing reference to the given demand data, which forms the finite demand relation f, can be dropped since that reference is understood.

(M):   there exist numbers λ_r, ϕ_r such that $\lambda_r > 0$ and

$$D_{rs} - (\phi_s - \phi_r)/\lambda_r \geq 0.$$

For the more restrictive *classical separable consistency* ($C_{(0)1}$), based on the utility model (0)1, we will find the following test. Just as with condition M, the numbers involved are the multipliers and levels associated with the functions that the consistency requires, and permit the immediate construction of examples.

$(M_{(0)1})$: there exist numbers λ_{0r}, ϕ_{0r} and λ_r, ϕ_r such that $\lambda_{0r}, \lambda_r > 0$ and

$$D_{rs} - (\phi_s - \phi_r)/\lambda_r \geq w_{0r}\{D_{0rs} - (\phi_{0s} - \phi_{0r})/\lambda_{0r}\} \geq 0.$$

This condition requires condition M as applied simultaneously to the demands (x_t, p_t) and the partial component demands (x_{0r}, p_{0r}) with a further restriction. In any case, as anticipated, $M_{(0)1} \Rightarrow M$.

$(M_{(0)(1)})$:   there exist numbers λ_{ir}, ϕ_{ir} ($i = 0, 1$) and λ_r, ϕ_r

such that $\lambda_{ir}, \lambda_r > 0$,

$$D_{0rs} \geq (\phi_{0s} - \phi_{0r}) / \lambda_{0r}, \quad D_{1rs} \geq (\phi_{1s} - \phi_{1r}) / \lambda_{1r},$$

and

$$w_{0r}(\phi_{0s} - \phi_{0r}) / \lambda_{0r} + w_{1r}(\phi_{1s} - \phi_{1r}) / \lambda_{1r} \geq (\phi_s - \phi_r) / \lambda_r.$$

This requires the condition M as applied to each of the component demands separately, together with a further restriction. Because of the relation

$$D_{rs} = w_{0r} D_{0rs} + w_{1r} D_{1rs},$$

connecting cross-coefficients of the demands and component demands, the condition implies

$$D_{rs} - (\phi_s - \phi_r) / \lambda_r \geq 0$$

and therefore the main condition M, so we have $M_{(0)(1)} \Rightarrow M$. Also it implies

$$D_{rs} - (\phi_s - \phi_r) / \lambda_r \geq$$
$$w_{0r}\{D_{0rs} - (\phi_{0s} - \phi_{0r}) / \lambda_{0r}\} + w_{1r}\{D_{1rs} - (\phi_{1s} - \phi_{1r}) / \lambda_{1r}\},$$

where the two terms in the sum on the right are non-negative. The inequality therefore remains true when 1 is replaced by 0, showing the condition $M_{(0)1}$, and just as well $M_{0(1)}$. Thus, $M_{(0)(1)} \Rightarrow M_{(0)1}$.

$(M_{(0)+(1)})$: there exist numbers λ_r and ϕ_{ir} $(i = 0, 1)$ such that $\lambda_r > 0$ and

$$\lambda_r w_{ir} D_{irs} \geq \phi_{is} - \phi_{ir}.$$

By this the condition M must apply simultaneously to the component demands with the additional constraint that the multipliers be proportional to the expenditure shares w_{ir}. From these conditions,

$$\lambda_r D_{rs} \geq \phi_s - \phi_r,$$

where

$$\phi_r = \phi_{0r} + \phi_{1r},$$

showing that the condition M is satisfied, so certainly this condition implies M. That it implies $M_{(0)(1)}$ follows from the further inequality required in order to establish that it has been satisfied as an equality.

It has been verified that all these conditions have the relations

$$M_{(0)+(1)} \Rightarrow M_{(0)(1)} \Rightarrow M_{(0)1} \Rightarrow M,$$

to be expected from the promise of their equivalence to the existence of compatible utilities with correspondingly restricted forms.

4.3 CONSTRUCTIONS

Now there will be a definition of functions that can be constructed on the basis of solutions of these conditions, the solubility of which will be established as tests of the demand data for admissibility of the various separability models. They have the forms the models require and, as to be shown, they are compatible with the data.

(C): $\qquad\qquad \phi(x) = \min_r \phi_r + \lambda_r u_r(x - x_r).$

This is the polyhedral function used before to demonstrate classical consistency. It is one of the bracket functions used to characterize a multiplier-level class of compatible classical utilities. Now we consider its separable counterparts. The other bracket function with polytope form also has separable counterparts, with a similar role, but we will not pursue that.

$(C_{(0)1})$: $\qquad\qquad \phi(x) = \Phi(\phi_0(x_0), x_1),$

where

$$\phi_0(x_0) = \min_r \phi_{0r} + \lambda_{0r} u_{0r}(x_0 - x_{0r})/w_{0r}$$

and

$$\Phi(\phi_0, x_1) = \min_r \phi_r + \lambda_r(\phi_0 - \phi_{0t})/\lambda_{0r} + \lambda_r u_{1r}(x_1 - x_{1r})$$

$(C_{(0)(1)})$: $\qquad \phi(x) = \Phi(\phi_0(x_0), \phi_1(x_1)),$

where

$$\phi_i(x_i) = \min_r \phi_{ir} + \lambda_{ir} u_{ir}(x_i - x_{ir})/w_{ir} \quad (i = 0, 1)$$

and

$$\Phi(\phi_0, \phi_1) = \min_r \phi_r + \lambda_r \Sigma_i w_{ir}(\phi_i - \phi_{ir})/\lambda_{ir}.$$

$C_{(0)+(1)}$: $\qquad\qquad \phi(x) = \Sigma_i \phi_i(x_i)$

where

$$\phi_i(x_i) = \min_r \phi_{ir} + \lambda_r u_{ir}(x_i - x_{ir}).$$

Proofs of the necessity and sufficiency of M^* for C^* in each of the three $*$ cases, will be given at the end of this chapter, using these functions to demonstrate the sufficiencies.

4.4 UTILITY DIMENSION

Separability concerns the structure of utility, and there are various standard models for it. But the structure can be understood in other ways also and dealt with similarly, as will be illustrated. We shall deal with the matter in a way that has some bearing on the so called 'New' approach to demand analysis in terms of attributes of goods. Utility itself is one attribute, the one of ultimate importance, and the quantities of goods are basic attributes, from which, by knowing the goods, all others must be derivable. The *utility dimension* of a group of goods could be defined as the smallest number of attributes, functions of the quantities, from which their utility can be determined. This is at most their number, and with their separability from the others in the usual sense it is 1.

With separability on the basic model $(0)1$, the n_0 goods x_0 have their own separate utility ϕ_0, which they alone determine and which enters the master utility function Φ as a single variable. They determine, so to speak, a single 'attribute' of the bundle x, so it has $1 + n_1$ attributes instead of $n_0 + n_1 = n$. The basic attributes of a bundle of goods are the quantities of the various goods in it, which tell everything about the bundle. Any other attribute must be determined from them, or from some subset. One could just as well propose that ϕ_0 has m_0 dimensions, representing that number of attributes, instead of just one. That is all there is to the 'New' approach to demand analysis in terms of attributes, as concerns its form. In this more general case of separability we could say the n_0 goods are separable in dimension m_0, so dimension 1 corresponds to the usually understood sense. Separability representation in any dimension implies that in any higher dimension, and separability in dimension n_0, the number of goods, is automatic. The issue, as concerns just the possibility of representation, is the smallest possible dimension, permitted by the data.

Alternatively, there may be a prior hypothesis about the attribute function ϕ_0 which should be tested. That would make better sense, since to deal with attributes in general, without any identification of specific attributes that are in view and can be determined for any bundles, makes no sense. W. M. Gorman made an econometric study of the fish market on the attribute model before it was 'New'. The Second World War army diet problem, where foods produce nutrients in varying amounts, and a minimum-cost diet meeting certain requirements in these nutrients is sought, is another case of the attribute model. In this case the attribute function ϕ_0 is linear, having the form $\phi_0 = ax_0$ where the matrix a is known in advance and determined by an analysis of foods. Nutrient contents are not the only attributes of foods that are of possible relevance to demand behaviour, so this might make a poor model for demand analysis; what we have with the diet problem is more like demand planning.

The separability model (0) 1 with dimension m_0 can be treated just like the others. Now the function ϕ_0 is a vector with m_0 elements. The original condition $M_{(0)1}$ becomes the following, where g_{00r} is a matrix whose rows are to be identified with support gradients of the elements of the attribute function $\phi_0(x_0)$ at the point x_{0r}, a Hessian in the case of differentiability, known already in advance or to be determined, and G_r is to be identified with a support gradient of the master function Φ at a point (ϕ_{0r}, x_{1r}). Were ϕ_0 to be a linear function with coefficient matrix a, as with the diet problem, then we would have $g_{00r} = a$, for all r, and a should be substituted for g_{00r} in the following.

($M_{(0)1}$): there exist numbers λ_r, ϕ_r and ϕ_r, vectors G_{0r} and matrices g_{00r}
such that

$$\lambda_r > 0, \ \lambda_r u_{0r} = G_{0r} g_{00r},$$
$$g_{00r}(x_{0s} - x_{0r}) \geq \phi_{0s} - \phi_{0r},$$

and

$$D_{rs} - (\phi_s - \phi_r)/\lambda_r \geq w_{0r} D_{0rs} - G_{0r}(\phi_{0s} - \phi_{0r}).$$

For the case $m_0 = 1$, taking $\lambda_{0r} = g_{00r} x_{0r}$, so that $\lambda_r w_{0r} = G_{0r} \lambda_{0r}$, this condition reduces immediately to the earlier $M_{(0)1}$ for dimension 1.

4.5 BUDGET SEPARABILITY

The utility separability of a group of goods is associated with their *budget separability*, by which the expenditures on each of them are fully determined, by their own separate utility function, when the total expenditure on all in the group is determined (Afriat, 1954b). Of course, that total expenditure cannot be determined without solving the master problem involving all the goods. That problem is

$$\max \phi(x) : px = M,$$

and when this is solved we can determine $M_0 = p_0 x_0$. Assuming differentiability, the solution is characterized by the Lagrange conditions $\phi_x = \lambda p$ and $px = M$, which are

$$\phi_{x_0} = \lambda p_0, \quad \phi_{x_1} = \lambda p_1, \quad p_0 x_0 + p_1 x_1 = M$$

in partitioned form. With the separability $\phi = \Phi(\phi_0, x_1)$, so that $\phi_{x_0} = \Phi_{\phi_0} \phi_{0x_0}$, we have from these that

$$\phi_{x_0} = \lambda_0 p_0, \quad p_0 x_0 = M_0,$$

where $\lambda_0 = \lambda / \Phi_{\phi_0}$ and M_0 is as stated. But these are the Lagrange conditions for the separate problem

$$\max \phi_0(x_0) : p_0 x_0 = M_0,$$

so we have the required conclusion. Without differentiability, but with classical functions, this argument can be given just as well in terms of support gradients and the optimality conditions of convex programming. The arguments for the equivalences $C* \Leftrightarrow M*$ in the next section proceed that way, and there can be preparations now.

The relation H of compatibility between a utility and a demand requires two conditions, which have been designated H' and H''. Dealing with a normalized demand (x_t, u_t), where $u_t x_t = 1$, H' requires $x = x_t$ to be an optimal solution of the convex problem

$$\max \phi(x) : u_t x \leq 1,$$

$x \geq 0$ now being understood. Slater's condition $u_t x < 1$ for some $x \geq 0$ is satisfied, and so the convex programming optimality conditions apply, which require that, for some λ_t,

$$\lambda_t \geq 0, \quad u_t x_t \leq 1, \quad \lambda_t u_t x_t = 1$$

and

$$\phi(x) - \phi(x_t) \leq \lambda_t u_t (x - x_t) \quad \text{for all } x.$$

These conditions express the condition H', and for H'' we just have to add to these the further requirement $\lambda_t > 0$. With this, since anyway $u_t x_t = 1$, the first line is satisfied automatically. The second line tells us that $g_t = \lambda_t u_t$ is a support gradient of ϕ at the point $x = x_t$. Thus, *compatibility between the utility ϕ and the demand (x_t, u_t) requires $g_t = \lambda_t u_t$ to be a support* *gradient of ϕ at the point $x = x_t$ for some* $\lambda_t > 0$. Should ϕ be differentiable at x_t, and so with a unique support gradient g_t, identical with the differential gradient, this would imply $g_t = \lambda_t u_t$ and $\lambda_t > 0$ becomes equivalent to $g_t \geq 0$. Were ϕ given to be semi-increasing and so with non-vanishing gradient, $\lambda_t > 0$ would be implied; for such functions $H' \Rightarrow H''$.

With a function of the form

$$\phi(x_0, x_1) = \Phi(\phi_0(x_0), x_1),$$

if g_{00} is a support gradient of ϕ_0 at x_0, and (h_0, h_1) is a support gradient of Φ at (ϕ_0, x_1), then we have that $g = (g_0, g_1)$, where $g_0 = h_0 g_{00}$, is a support gradient of ϕ at $x = (x_0, x_1)$. Moreover, all support gradients of ϕ have this form. The further suffix t will indicate values associated with the point $x_t = (x_{0t}, x_{1t})$.

From the condition

$$g_t = \lambda_t u_t, \quad \lambda_t > 0$$

for compatibility between ϕ and (x_t, u_t) we now have $g_{0t} = \lambda_t u_{0t}$, and so $h_{0t} g_{00t} = \lambda_t$. From this, with

$$\lambda_{0t} = h_{0t}^{-1} \lambda_t w_{0t},$$

we have

$$g_{00t} = \lambda_{0t} w_{0t}^{-1} u_{0t}, \quad \lambda_{0t} > 0.$$

But this, for some λ_{0t}, is the condition for the compatibility of the utility function ϕ_0 with the normalized component demand $(x_{0t}, w_{0t}^{-1} u_{0t})$. The budget separation principle is thus demonstrated again. It will be taken for granted now, and appealing to it directly simplifies arguments.

The foregoing discussion can be continued to show that $C_{(0)1} \Rightarrow M_{(0)1}$. Let ϕ_{0t} be the value of ϕ_0 at x_{0t} and ϕ_t the value of ϕ at x_t, so this is also the value of Φ at (ϕ_{0t}, x_{1t}).

With the compatibility of ϕ with (x_t, u_t) we had (h_{0t}, h_{1t}) is a support gradient of Φ at (ϕ_{0t}, x_{1t}) where

$$h_{0t} = \lambda_t w_{0t} / \lambda_{0t}, \quad h_{1t} = \lambda_t u_{1t},$$

so that, for all t, and all ϕ_0 and x_1,

$$\Phi(\phi_0, x_1) \leq \Phi(\phi_{0t}, x_{1t}) + h_{0t}(\phi_0 - \phi_{0t}) + h_{1t}(x_1 - x_{1t}).$$

It follows that, for s and t,

$$\phi_s \leq \phi_t + \lambda_t w_{0t}(\phi_{0s} - \phi_{0t}) / \lambda_{0t} + \lambda_t u_{1t}(x_{1s} - x_{1t}).$$

But the last term is

$$\lambda_t w_{0t} D_{0ts} = \lambda_t(D_{ts} - w_{1t} D_{1ts}),$$

and so, joining this with the condition M applied to the 0-component demand, as follows by budget separation, we have the conclusion $M_{(0)1}$, as required.

For the converse, consider the polyhedral function defined in section 4.3 associated the present case. By argument similar to that used in the last chapter for showing that $M \Rightarrow C$, with such a function, it can be established that ϕ has $\lambda_t u_t$ as a support gradient at x_t, and since $\lambda_t > 0$ this shows the required compatibility. The arguments for the other cases are similar.

II.5

Direct and Indirect Utility

According to William Fleetwood (1707), 'money is of no other use, than it is the thing with which we purchase the necessities and conveniences of life ...'. Veblen has said the opposite, but this is a normal understanding. Others would go further and give money both a quantitative utility and a marginal utility. Fleetwood describes a function for money, and the others want also to measure the extent to which money fulfils that function. A difficulty with the value of money being simply what it can buy is that it can buy many things, so its value is not completely decided. In the utility theory, money really buys utility, by buying goods which have it, and so it has the utility of the goods with highest utility that it can buy. That resolves the difficulty, even though goods are more visible than utility and there can be misgivings here about this otherwise satisfactory resolution.

A bundle of goods x that an amount M of money can buy is any whose cost px at the prices does not exceed M. Therefore it must satisfy the *budget constraint* $px \leq M$, that is, $ux \leq 1$ where $u = M^{-1}p$ is the *budget vector* which specifies the constraint. This vector, which is dependent also on the prices, determines all that the money can buy, and so the value of the money, related to what it can buy, must be related to this vector.

While the commodity bundles x are in the *commodity space* C of non-negative vectors with n elements, the budget vectors u are in a space B like it, the *budget space*, except that we represent points of B by row vectors and those of C by column vectors. Then any $u \in B$ and $x \in C$ have a product ux which is a non-negative number. Utility is attributed first to commodity bundles and so this is the primary or *direct utility* in the commodity space. From this we have the derived or *indirect utility* in the budget space, which applies instead to budget vectors. The utility of a budget vector u is the utility of a bundle of goods x of highest utility attainable under the budget constraint $ux \leq 1$. If the direct utility is represented by a function ϕ then the indirect utility is the *adjoint function* $\psi = \phi^*$ given by

$$\psi(u) = \max[\phi(x) : ux \leq 1].$$

If instead we have a direct utility relation $R \subset C \times C$, then the indirect utility $S \subset B \times B$ is the *adjoint relation* $S = R^*$ given by

$$uSv \equiv (\vee\ ux \leq 1)(\wedge\ vy \leq 1)\ xRy.$$

Should the function ϕ *represent* the relation R, that is, should

$$xRy \Leftrightarrow \phi(x) \geq \phi(y),$$

then the function ψ represents the relation S,

$$uSv \Leftrightarrow \psi(u) \geq \psi(v).$$

But the relation has an adjoint even when it is not representable by a function. When the adjoint function or relation is not defined one can consider the *limit adjoints*

$$\dot{\psi}(u) = \sup [\, \phi(x) : ux \leq 1\,],$$

and

$$u\dot{S}v \equiv (\wedge\ vy \leq 1)\ (\vee\ ux \leq 1)\ xRy,$$

which are always defined and coincide with them when they are defined. The properties of adjoint functions and relations, including duality properties by which direct and indirect utilities are derivable from each other, will have an account.

A symmetry, or duality, holds between the commodity and budget spaces, in that each is the space of non-negative homogeneous linear functions defined on the other. Symmetry between commodity bundles and budget vectors is also, in the relation between them, defined by the condition $ux \leq 1$, by which the bundle x is *within* the budget u; in view of the exchange of roles the symmetry permits, it could also be said that u is within x. The same symmetry is present with a normal demand, any $(x, u) \in C \times B$ for which $ux = 1$. The duality between B and C, at the start with these simple examples, goes further in many aspects of demand and utility and their relationship.

5.1 PURCHASING POWER

The *cost of living problem* concerns the relation between incomes which, at different prices, have the same purchasing power, and this is decided by indirect utility. If the prices are p_0, p_1, then for the purchasing power equivalence of incomes M_0, M_1 at these prices, the budget vectors $u_0 = M_0^{-1}p_0$, $u_1 = M_1^{-1}p_1$ that they determine with these prices are required to have the same indirect utility, $\psi(u_0) = \psi(u_1)$, so the relation is

$$\psi(M_0^{-1}p_0) = \psi(M_1^{-1}p_1).$$

With ψ semi-increasing, ψ is semi-decreasing and so $\psi(M^{-1}p)$ is increasing in M. Therefore this relation can be solved to give M_1 as an increasing function

$$M_1 = F_{10}(M_0)$$

of M_0, depending on p_0, p_1. In general this could be any increasing function. In the homogeneous or conical case, where the relation admits representation by a single number, the 'price index', the relation reduces to one with the simple form

$$M_1 = P_{10} M_0$$

where P_{10}, the *price index*, is independent of the incomes and depends only on the prices. This is the case where ψ has the form

$$\psi(M^{-1}p) = M/\sigma(p).$$

The utility the money M can purchase at the prices p is $X = \psi(M^{-1}p)$ and is the utility $X = \phi(x)$ of the bundle of goods x of highest utility attainable with it at the prices. Therefore we have both $px = M$ and $PX = M$, where $P = \psi(p)$ and $X = \phi(x)$, and consequently $PX = px$. It is as if utility has a price P depending only on the prices of the goods, so that to buy utility X the cost is PX. Since the utility is bought by buying the goods x that have it, we also have the usual market cost px, identical with this cost PX, determined as if there were a single good with a single price P, in an imaginary Utility Market where a single good is sold. This is a remarkable arrangement, and the idea of a price index requires it. We have $P_0 = \sigma(p_0)$, $P_1 = \sigma(p_1)$ as price levels giving $P_{10} = P_1/P_0$ as the price index in the relation $M_1 = P_{10} M_0$. Generally, since $M/\sigma(p)$ is the maximum of $\phi(x)$ subject to $px \leq M$, we have the functional inequality

$$\sigma(p)\phi(y) \leq py \text{ for all } p, y.$$

satified by the *conjugate price and quantity functions* σ and ϕ. E. R. Lorch (1951), dealing with 'differentiable inequalities and the theory of convex bodies', considers such pairs of functions.

5.2   THE INDIRECT 'INTEGRABILITY' PROBLEM

Another use of indirect utility is for settling questions about the demand theory of E. Slutsky (1915). As said, this can fill a volume. There follows an outline of how indirect utility has a part.

Slutsky considered a demand function F with continuous derivatives, and the question of the existence of a utility function ϕ with continuous second derivatives such that, for all p and M, $x = F(p, M)$ is the unique optimal solution to the problem

$$\max \phi(x) : px = M.$$

He introduced coefficients

$$s_{ij} = M\{\partial x_i/\partial p_j + (\partial x_i/\partial M)x_j\}$$

formed from the derivatives of F, elements of the matrix

$$s = M(x_p + x_M x').$$

He showed that the first-order conditions for a maximum,

$$g(x) = \lambda p, \quad px = M,$$

where $x = F(p, M)$ and g is the gradient of ϕ, imply the symmetry of the matrix s. We call this the *Slutsky symmetry condition*. He also showed that the second-order conditions for a maximum imply the condition

$$z \nparallel p \Rightarrow zsz' < 0,$$

where $z \parallel p$ means the vector z is parallel to p, in that $z = tp$ for some scalar t, and $z \nparallel p$ is the denial. This *Slutsky negativity condition* is intermediate between the matrix s being non-positive definite and negative definite, and is different from both. In any case, since $sp' = 0$ is an identity, it is impossible for the Slutsky matrix to be negative definite.

In terms of the normalized demand function $f(u) = F(u, 1)$ Slutsky sought a utility function ϕ such that, for all u, $x = f(u)$ is the unique optimal solution to the problem

$$\max \phi(x) : ux \le 1.$$

With

$$\psi(u) = \max [\phi(x) : ux \le 1]$$

as the indirect utility function associated with ϕ, this requirement on ψ can be stated

$$x = f(u) \Leftrightarrow ux \le 1 \text{ and } \phi(x) = \psi(u).$$

The expression for the *Slutsky matrix* in terms of the normalized demand function $x = f(u)$ ($ux = 1$) allows its factorization into a product

$$s = x_u (1 - u'x'),$$

of the Hessian, or matrix x_u of first derivatives, with the matrix $1 - u'x'$ which, since $ux = 1$, is idempotent and so a projector. This is the projector which resolves any change into an 'income effect' and 'substitution effect'.

The first order maximum conditions used by Slutsky are

$$g(x) = \lambda u, ux = 1,$$

from which $\lambda = g(x)x$, showing that u is determined as a function of x. Thus they imply that the demand function $x = f(u)$ is invertible. This is unsatisfactory, because there is no reason for the question Slutsky considers to be restricted to invertible demand functions. For further discontent, $f(u) = a(ua)^{-1}$ is an example of a demand function derivable from a utility function, that function being

$$\phi(x) = \max [t : at \le x].$$

Despite that, it certainly does not satify the Slutsky negativity condition, since for this demand function *the Slutsky matrix vanishes*.

G. B. Antonelli (1886) and V. Pareto (1894) had dealt with an inverse demand function and with how, with u given as a function of x, from the first-order conditions $g = \lambda u$, the utility ϕ with gradient g could be constructed. V. Volterra (1906), in reviewing Pareto's work, had remarked that the existence of such a function, and so the possibility of the construction, required the *integrability* of the *linear differential form* udx in the sense of the theorem of Frobenius. This required the existence of a function $\lambda(x)$, the *integrating factor*, which made $\lambda u dx$ the total differential $d\phi$ of some function ϕ, the *integral* which should be the required utility function. Frobenius's theorem gave conditions for that in terms of the derivatives of the coefficients u of the differential form. These *classical integrability conditions*, which applied to an inverse demand function, in the earlier form in which they were obtained, are the same as Antonelli's conditions.

An issue with the Slutsky theory is the whereabouts of these integrability conditions, since he works with derivative of the demand function and not of its inverse like the others. To proceed with the demand function the way the inverse function was treated, one would consider the linear differential form $(du)x$ with coefficients $x = f(u)$. Were this integrable, the integral would be a function in the budget space, instead of in the commodity space as formerly. The preoccupation of others with an inverse or an invertible demand function—mostly explicitly, though with Slutsky it was only implicit, as it was also with P. A. Samuelson (1948) and H. S. Houthakker (1950) in their different approach to the same problem—might seem unsuitable. Yet if one deals with a demand function directly, the result is a function in the wrong space. As might be suspected, a clue to resolving this dilemma is in 'The Case of the Vanishing Slutsky Matrix' (Afriat, 1972c), where the demand function involved happens not to have an inverse.

With the derivation of necessary conditions by Lionel W. McKenzie (1957), it comes out in one step that the Slutsky matrix must be symmetric and non-positive definite, because it is identified with the matrix of second derivatives of a cost function. McKenzie does not arrive at the Slutsky negativity condition, for which the matrix being just non-positive definite is not strict enough. That gives better accommodation for the case where the Slutsky matrix vanishes identically, because in this case it is certainly both symmetric and non-positive definite, even though it does not have the Slutsky negativity.

The classical integrability conditions applied to $x = f(u)$ with derivatives $x_{ij} = \partial x_i / \partial u_j$, require that the coefficients

$$x_{ijk} = x_i (x_{jk} - x_{kj}) + x_j (x_{ki} - x_{ik}) + x_k (x_{ij} - x_{ji})$$

all vanish. The identity

$$\Sigma_k x_{ijk} u_k = s_{ij} - s_{ji}$$

(discovered in 1955) shows that the classical conditions imply Slutsky symmetry, and the converse is quite immediate. In that way it appears that *the classical integrability conditions applied to a demand function are equivalent to the symmetry of the Slutsky matrix*.

That leaves an upside-down situation, since we want a utility function in the commodity space and what we have, with the Slutsky symmetry, is the promise of finding a certain function in the budget space. Even that, as proceeding from Frobenius's theorem, is only a limited promise. The theorem does not assure the existence of an integral in more than the local sense, of an integral in some neighbourhoods of any point. It does not tell us the existence of one defined in the entire budget space, which is what is wanted here. There could perhaps be interest in having an integral, if it happened to be the indirect utility for some direct utility, which also happened to meet the requirements for the utility which is sought. But there is no need for an integral to be such a function just on the basis of its existence.

If the differential form $(du)x$ $(x = f(u))$ has an integrating factor μ and integral ψ, we have

$$(du)x\mu = d\psi .$$

Then also $-\psi$ would be an integral, and $-\mu$ the integrating factor. Since $x \geq 0$, one of the pair would be semi-increasing and the other semi-decreasing. We can suppose that ψ is the one which is semi-decreasing. Then a significance found for the Slutsky matrix being non-positive definite is that it is *necessary and sufficient for the integral to be quasi-convex*, that is, for the sets $[u : \psi(u) \leq t]$ all to be convex. As will appear, that is just the condition for the function

$$\phi(x) = \min [\psi(u) : ux \leq 1]$$

derived from ψ to be a direct utility function for which ψ is the indirect utility function, recovered from ϕ by the formula

$$\psi(u) = \max [\phi(x) : ux \leq 1].$$

With ψ quasi-convex, with gradient h, the condition $h = x\mu$ for it to be an integral is also the Lagrange condition which is now *both necessary and sufficient* for u to be an optimal solution to the problem

$$\min \psi(u) : ux \leq 1,$$

that is, for $\phi(x) = \psi(u)$. But this also states that x is an optimal solution to the originally considered problem

$$\max \phi(x) : ux \leq 1.$$

The problem is therefore settled if an integral ψ exists and the Slutsky matrix s is non-positive definite, but we do not yet have an integral. Subject to the symmetry of the Slutsky matrix, Frobenius's theorem provides local integrability. It remains to show that, in the case of a demand function, this implies the required global integrability, or the existence of an integral defined in the entire budget space. Then we have the theorem that, given a demand function $x = F(p, M)$ $(px = M)$ with continuous derivatives, *a necessary and sufficient condition* for the existence of a function ϕ such that, for all p and $M, x = F(p, M)$ if and only if x is an optimal solution for the problem

$$\max \phi(x) : px \leq M$$

is that the Slutsky matrix be symmetric and non-positive definite.

An explanation of the spurious Slutsky negativity condition is that it is implied by the Slutsky matrix being non-positive definite if the demand function is invertible. In requiring the utility function to be differentiable, let alone twice differentiable, Slutsky is requiring the demand function to be that. In 'The Case of the Vanishing Slutsky Matrix' the utility function involved is not differentiable at any point on the ray through the point a, and that ray is the entire range of the associated demand function. The indirect utility function is $\psi(u) = 1/ua$, and this is differentiable everywhere.

A further account of the problem is in *Demand Functions and the Slutsky Matrix* (1980d). This is an outline of features to do with direct and indirect utility and their relationship, elaborated here.

With the approach that has been made to the same problem with reference to a finite collection of demand observations, instead of a demand dunction, differentiability or invertibility is no issue. It does happen that the polyhedral and polytope and so piecewise-linear functions, constructed for purpose of demonstration are in fact differentiable at all interior points of faces, where they are moreover locally linear, and they could be smoothed to be differentiable, to any order.

That construction was made on the side of direct utility, but it could have gone just as well on the side of indirect utility in the budget space. The normalized demands (x_r, u_r) having cross-coefficients D_{rs}, we took any solution $\lambda_r > 0$ and ϕ_r of the inequalities

$$\lambda_r D_{rs} \geq \phi_s - \phi_r,$$

and constructed with it a function ϕ with $\phi(x_r) = \phi_r$. The associated indirect utility function is such that $\psi(u_r) = \phi(x_r)$, and

$$\psi(\varrho^{-1} u_r) - \psi(u_r) \leq \lambda_r(\varrho - 1) \text{ for all } \varrho.$$

We could instead have taken any solution $\mu < 0$ and ψ_r of the system

$$\mu_r D_{rs} \leq \psi_s - \psi_r,$$

for instance $\mu_r = -\lambda_r$ and $\psi_r = -\phi_r$, and proceeded correspondingly, constructing an indirect utility function ψ first, with $\psi(u_r) = \psi_r$, and then the wanted ϕ. That would have served for the required demonstration, though it would have been more roundabout.

5.3   BASIC RELATIONS AND PROPERTIES
This section breaks into more basic parts the structure involved with direct and indirect utility, and with other features of demand analysis.

Relations W and $I \subset W$ between commodity bundles and budget vectors are defined by

$$xWu \equiv ux \leq 1, xIu \equiv ux = 1,$$

by which x is *within* or *on* u. Other relations can be associated with any order R in the commodity space. Let xHu assert that (x, u) is a normal demand compatible with R, so defining a relation $H \subset I$. The relation $T \supset H$, defined by

$$xTu \equiv (\wedge yWu) xRy,$$

asserts that x has the relation R to every bundle y within the budget u; that is, $Wu \subset xR$. Then with $K = T \cap W$, xKu asserts that x is a maximum of R among the bundles within u, so also $K \supset H$. At first we will take R to be an arbitrary binary relation, not necessarily an order.

(i) If R is transitive then $xRy \Rightarrow yT \subset xT$.

Thus,

$$\begin{aligned} xRy &\Rightarrow yRz \Rightarrow xRz && \text{by transitivity of } R \\ &\Rightarrow yR \subset xR \\ &\Rightarrow Wu \subset yR \Rightarrow Wu \subset xR \\ &\Rightarrow y\bar{T}u \Rightarrow x\bar{T}u && \text{by definition of } T \\ &\Rightarrow yT \subset xT \end{aligned}$$

(ii) xT is convex.

Since $X = xR$ is arbitrary, in effect the set

$$[u : Wu \subset X] \subset B$$

is convex for any $X \subset C$. We will show that, for $w \in < u, v >$,

$$Ww \subset Wu \cap Wv,$$

and from this it follows that

$$Wu \subset X \text{ and } Wv \subset X \Rightarrow Ww \subset X,$$

as required. Thus for $w = su + tv$, where $s + t = 1$, $s, t \geq 0$, we have

$$ux > 1 \text{ and } vx > 1 \Rightarrow wx > 1,$$

that is,

$$\bar{W}u \cap \bar{W}v \subset \bar{W}w,$$

and taking complements on both sides gives the required conclusion.

With free disposal, having any $y \geq x$ is at least as good as having x, since the difference $y - x \geq 0$ with x can be disposed of costlessly to leave x. Expressing that, a utility order usually has the *monotonicity* property

$$y \geq x \Rightarrow yRx.$$

A case where xRy and $y > x$ shows that x is a point of *satiation*, since it is as good as another where there is more of everything, so that y is a point of *oversatiation*, since less of everything can be just as good. By R being *insatiable* is meant the impossibility of such a case, that is

$$y > x \Rightarrow x\bar{R}y.$$

Combined with monotonicity, this gives

$$y > x \Rightarrow yPx$$

where P is the strict part of R.

Define $V \subset W$ by

$$xVu \equiv ux < 1,$$

by which the bundle x is said to be *under* the budget u.

(iii)   If R is insatiable, then $T \subset \bar{V}$.

Suppose $x\bar{T}u$ and uVx. Then there exists $y > x$ such that uWy. But then $x\bar{T}u$ implies xRy, which with $y > x$ contradicts the assumption that R is insatiable.

By definition, $H = H' \cap H''$, where

$$xH'u \equiv uy \le 1 \Rightarrow xRy,$$
$$xH''u \equiv yRx \Rightarrow uy \ge 1.$$

In general, H' and H'' are independent, but conditions on R can produce relations between them.

(iv)   If R is insatiable, then $H' \subset H''$.

Supposing $xH'u$ and $uy < 1$; it has to be shown that $y\bar{R}x$. Suppose on the contrary that yRx. From $uy < 1$ we have xRy and also $uz \le 1$ for some $z > y$, and so also xRz, which with yRx and the transitivity of R gives yRz, which with $z > y$ contradicts the insatiability of R. Therefore $y\bar{R}x$. QED

(v)   If R is a complete order and the sets xR are closed then $H'' \subset H'$.

With $xH''u$ and R complete, we have

$$uy < 1 \Rightarrow y\bar{R}x \Rightarrow xRy,$$

so that $Vu \subset xR$. But with xR closed, this implies $Wu \subset xR$. QED

Since H' is the same as the relation now denoted K, $H' \subset H''$ is equivalent to $H = K$, and so, by (iv),

(vi)   If R is an insatiable utility order, then $H = K$.

For another argument, xHu means xKu together with the further requirement

$$yRx \Rightarrow uy \ge 1.$$

But under the hypothesis for R in (iii),

$$xKu \Rightarrow yRx \Rightarrow uy \ge 1,$$

showing that $H \subset K$, and hence $H = K$. To see this, suppose xRy. Then by (i) $xT \subset yT$, and so with xTu, as required by xKu, we have yTu and hence, by (iii), $uy \ge 1$.

While compatibility is defined originally between a demand (x, u) and a utility R, and is asserted by xHu, with R given and reference to it understood, we also say that x is compatible with u. Now we say that a bundle x is *compatible* with a utility R if it is compatible with some budget u; that is, if $xH \ne O$. Similarly a budget u is compatible with R if $Hu \ne 0$.

(vii)   If R is a complete order, and the sets Rx are closed, then

$$u > 0 \Rightarrow Ku \neq O.$$

If $u > 0$, then Wu is compact. Therefore if the sets Rx are closed, then $Ry \cap Wu$ (yWu) is a family of non-empty compact sets. If R is complete, they are nested, so the intersection of a finite collection of them is non-empty. Therefore, being a family of compact sets with the finite intersection property, their intersection is non-empty. Let x be a point of their intersection; that is,

$$x \in \cap [Ry \cap Wu : yWu].$$

Then we have

$$xWu, \quad yWu \Rightarrow xRy,$$

that is, xKu, showing that $Ku \neq O$, as required.

(viii)   If R is an insatiable utility for which the sets xR are closed and concave, then

$$x > 0 \Rightarrow xH \neq O.$$

If $x\overline{R}$ is empty there is nothing more to prove, since then xKu for all $u \in xW$. Therefore suppose $x\overline{R}$ is non-empty. It is convex, since xR is concave, and does not contain x, since R is reflexive. Therefore, by the theorem of the separating hyperplane, there exists $p \neq 0$ such that

$$x\overline{R}y \Rightarrow py \geq px.$$

With R insatiable, we now have

$$y > x \Rightarrow x\overline{R}y \Rightarrow py \geq px.$$

Therefore $p \geq 0$, and hence $px > 0$ if $x > 0$. Now $u = (px)^{-1}p$ is such that $ux = 1$ and $uy < 1 \Rightarrow xRy$, and since xR is closed this implies $uy \leq 1 \Rightarrow xRy$, so we have xKu. But by (vi), with K insatiable this is equivalent to xHu, showing that $xH \neq O$. QED

(ix)   If R is an order such that $xK \neq O$ for all x, then the sets xR are concave.

For any $y \in xR$, since $yK \neq O$ by hypothesis, there exists v such that yKv, that is yTv and yWv. But, by (iii), because R is transitive, xRy and yTv implies xTv; that is, $Wv \subset xR$. Thus for all $y \in xR$ there exists v such that yKv. Any such v is such that $y \in Wv \subset xR$, and this shows that

$$xR = \cup [Wv : xRKv].$$

Therefore xR, being a union of concave sets, is concave. QED

In the next section a relation R in the commodity space is associated with a relation S in the budget space, its adjoint $S = R^*$, and observations to be made now have a bearing there. Such a pair R, S are to express direct and indirect utility. While S then should be derived from R, under suitable conditions R is recoverable from S. Also, given any S with suitable properties, such as are in fact possessed by any relation of the form $S = R^*$, a relation R can be constructed by a similar formula $R = S^*$ which, taken as a direct utility, has S as the associated indirect utility.

First we should note that we already have TW' defined as a relation in the commodity space and $W'T$ as a relation in the budget space. With suitable qualifications, these seem good candidates for R and S. Here the relation T is derived from a given R, and we would need some conditions for the identification $R = TW'$ which would recover R from T.

Since $K = W \cap T$, we have

$$(\vee x) \, xKu \Leftrightarrow (\vee x) \, uW'xTu \Leftrightarrow uW'Tu,$$

so points u, for which $Ku \neq O$, are identified with the reflexive points of $W'T$. Similarly, $xK \neq O$ is equivalent to x being a reflexive point of TW'.

(x) (a) $R \supset TW'$, for any relation R.
    (b) If R is transitive, then

$$yKv \Rightarrow (xRy \Rightarrow xTvW'y).$$

    (c) If R is reflexive, then

$$yKv \Leftarrow (xRy \Rightarrow xTvW'y).$$

Thus, xTu means $Wu \subset xR$, and so

$$xTuW'y \Rightarrow y \in Wu \subset xR \Rightarrow xRy,$$

showing (a). Also, if R is transitive, by (i),

$$xRyKv \Rightarrow xRyTvW'y \Rightarrow xTvW'y,$$

so we have (b). If R is reflexive, so yRy,

$$(xRy \Rightarrow xTvW'y) \Rightarrow yTvW'y \Leftrightarrow yKv,$$

and hence (c).

As a consequence,

(xi) If R is an order, then

$$xK \neq 0 \Leftrightarrow Rx = TW'x.$$

Consequently $R = TW'$ if and only if $xK \neq O$ for all x.

For then $xH \neq O$ if and only if $Rx \subset TW'x$. But in any case, $Rx \supset TW'x$.

5.4   ADJOINT OF A RELATION

Any relation R in the commodity space determines a relation R^* in the budget space, its *adjoint*, given by

$$uR^*v \equiv (\vee xWu) \, (\wedge yWv) \, xRy.$$

If R is a utility order, $S = R^*$ should be the indirect utility order associated with it.

The set Wu is all that can be bought under the budget u, and so the utility of u is at least the utility of any bundle in Wu. It has the same utility as any bundle in Wu, say x, which has highest utility, if there is such a bundle. Then any budget v which allows the purchase of x, and so has at least the utility of x, has at least the utility of u. That shows the sense of the definition of S as representing the indirect utility relation in the budget space corresponding to a given direct utility R.

The x here is a maximum for the order R in the set Wu, that is, it has the relation xKu. In general such x need not exist, but conditions were noted that ensure that one does; that is, that $Ku \neq O$. The limit adjoint dealt with later accommodates the possibility that $Ku = O$.

According to this definition of indirect utility S, it is given by $S = W'T$ where, as in the last section, xTu means that x has the relation R to every bundle within u. We saw that $xK \neq 0$ for all x is just the condition for $R = TW'$, and so to make TW' the direct utility. Now we have $Ku \neq 0$ for all u as the condition for $W'T$ to be effective as the indirect utility.

To identify properties of S either arising from the way in which it is constructed or implied by possible properties for R, it will be taken that R is an arbitrary binary relation, not necessarily an order.

The first note, obvious from the definitions, is that

(i) $uSu \Leftrightarrow Ku \neq 0.$

Thus,

$$uSu \Leftrightarrow (\vee\ x)\ uW'xTu \Leftrightarrow (\vee\ x)\ x(W \cap T)u.$$

The reflexive points of S are just the budgets under which R has a maximum, if it is an order, or in any case contain a point having the relation R to any other.

(ii) If R is transitive, then so is S.

For

$$uSvSw \Leftrightarrow (\vee\ x, y)\ uW'xTvW'yTw.$$

But

$$xTvW'y \Rightarrow xRy, \quad xRyTw \Rightarrow xTw,$$

by definition of T and transitivity of R. Therefore we have

$$uSvSw \Rightarrow (\vee\ x)\ uW'xTw \Rightarrow uSw,$$

so $uSvSw \Rightarrow uSw.$ QED

(iii) If R is complete and transitive, then

$$(uSu \wedge vSv) \Rightarrow (uSv \vee vSu).$$

Thus, *if R is a complete order then its adjoint S produces a complete order of its reflexive points.* By (i) if u, v are reflexive points then xKu, yKv for some x, y. Then xRy or yRx, since R is complete. If xRy, then from yKv we have xTv, by transitivity of R. But from xKu we have $uW'x$ and so now $uW'Tv$; that is, uSv. Similarly, vSu if yRx.

(iv) The free disposal property

$$x \geq y \Rightarrow xRy$$

for R implies that

$$uSu \Rightarrow (u \leq v \Rightarrow uSv).$$

From uSu we have $uW'x\mathit{Tu}$ for some x. Also from $u \leq v$ we have $Wu \supset Wv$. But this with $x\mathit{Tu}$ gives $x\mathit{Tv}$, and so we have $uW'x\mathit{Tv}$, that is uSv. QED

(v) The insatiability property

$$x > y \Rightarrow y\bar{R}x$$

for an order R implies that

$$vSv \Rightarrow (u < v \Rightarrow v\bar{S}u).$$

With vSv we have $vW'z\mathit{Tv}$ for some z. Then from $vW'z$ with $u < v$ we have $uW'x$ for some $x > z$. Suppose if possible that $vW'y$ and yRx for some y. Then zRy follows from $z\mathit{Tv}$ and $vW'y$, and this with yRx and the transitivity of R gives zRx, which is impossible with $x > z$. Hence the supposition is impossible; that is, $vW'y \Rightarrow y\bar{R}x$, and this implies $v\bar{S}u$. QED

(vi) If R is transitive, then $xKu \Rightarrow uS = xT$.

From xKu we have xWu and $x\mathit{Tu}$. Then because

$$uSv \Leftrightarrow (\vee\ y)\ yWu \text{ and } xTv$$

if xTv, by taking $y = x$ we have uSv. Thus $xT \subset uS$. Now suppose uSv, and so yWu and yTv for some y. From yWu with $x\mathit{Tu}$, we have xRy and so, by (i) of the last section, $yT \subset xT$. Therefore from yTv we have xTv. Thus uSv implies xTv showing that $uS \subset xT$, and so now $uS = xT$. QED

(vii) If uSu, then uS is a convex set.

We have this from (vi) because

$$uSu \Rightarrow (\vee\ x)\ xKu$$

and, by (ii) of the last section, the sets xT are convex.

(viii) If R is transitive, then

$$(xKu \wedge yKv) \Rightarrow (uSv \Leftrightarrow xRy).$$

On the left, xWu and $x\mathit{Tu}$ and yWv and yTv. If xRy then, by 5.3(i), $yT \subset xT$, so from yTv we have xTv, and this with xWu give uSv. Conversely, if uSv then, because $uS = xT$ by (vi), we have xTv, and from this with yWv we have xRy.

Just as any relation R in the commodity space has an adjoint R^* in the budget space, where

$$uR^*v \equiv (\vee\ xWu)\ (\wedge\ yWv)\ xRy,$$

so, in a dual fashion, any relation S in the budget space has an adjoint S^* in the commodity space, where

$$xS^*y \equiv (\vee\, yWv)(\wedge\, xWu)\, uSv.$$

Any proposition for the adjoint has its counterpart for the dual adjoint.

For any R in the commodity space, the adjoint of the relation R^* in the budget space is the relation R^{**}, again in the commodity space, where

$$xR^{**}y \Leftrightarrow (\vee\, yWv)\,(\wedge\, xWu)\,(\vee\, x'Wu)\,(\wedge\, y'Wv)\, x'Ry'.$$

(ix) if R is transitive and $xK \neq 0$, then

$$Rx \subset R^{**}x, \quad xR^{**} \subset xR.$$

If R is transitive, then

$$xKu \wedge yRx \Rightarrow xWu \wedge (\wedge\, zWu)\, xRz \wedge yRx$$
$$\Rightarrow xWu \wedge (\wedge\, x'Wu)\, yRx'.$$

Therefore if $xK \neq 0$,

$$yRx \Rightarrow (\vee\, xWu)\,(\wedge\, x'Wu, y' = y)\, y'Rx'$$
$$\Rightarrow (\vee\, xWu)\,(\wedge\, yWv)\,(\vee\, y'Wv)\,(\wedge\, x'Wu)\, y'Rx'$$
$$\Rightarrow yR^{**}x.$$

Thus $Rx \subset R^{**}x$. Now, further,

$$xR^{**}y \Rightarrow (\vee\, yWv)\,(\wedge\, xWu')\,(\vee\, x'Wu')\,(\wedge\, y'Wv)\, y'Rx'$$
$$\Rightarrow (\vee\, yWv)\,(\wedge\, xWu')\,(\vee\, x'Wu')\, x'Ry,$$

since, because yWv, it is possible to set $y' = y$. But if $xK \neq 0$ we have

$$(\vee\, xWu)\,(\wedge\, x'Wu)\, xRx'.$$

Hence, setting $u' = u$,

$$xR^{**}y \Rightarrow (\vee\, x')\, xRx' \wedge x'Ry.$$

But with R transitive this implies xRy. Thus $xR^{**} \subset xR$.

(x) If R is transitive, then

$$(xK \neq 0 \wedge yK \neq 0) \Rightarrow (xRy \Leftrightarrow xR^{**}y).$$

This is a corollary of (iv).

(xi) If R is a utility order such that $xH \neq 0$ for all x, then it is identical with the adjoint of its adjoint, $R = R^{**}$.

5.5 ADJOINT OF A FUNCTION

For any function ϕ in the commodity space the *adjoint function* ϕ^* in the budget space is given by

$$\phi^*(u) = \max\,[\,\phi(x) : ux \leq 1\,],$$

at points where this is defined, such points describing the *adjoint domain* of ϕ, and the domain of ϕ^*. Similarly, the adjoint ψ^* in the commodity space of a function ψ in the budget space is given by

$$\psi^*(x) = \min\ [\psi(u) : ux \le 1].$$

Any function ϕ *represents* the complete order R given by

$$xRy \equiv \phi(x) \ge \phi(y).$$

> THEOREM I If the function ϕ has adjoint ψ, and represents the relation R with adjoint S, then ψ represents S between the points where it is defined, these being the reflexive points of S.

Thus, uSu is equivalent to xKu for some x, and xKu tells us that x is a maximum of ϕ under the constraint $ux \le 1$, the existence of such a maximum being the condition for $\psi(u)$ to be defined. From the definition of ψ and H, for u where ψ is defined,

$$xKu \Leftrightarrow ux \le 1, \quad \phi(x) = \psi(u).$$

Suppose uSu, vSv so that xKu, yKv for some x, y. Then from this, with (viii) of section 5.4,

$$uSu \Leftrightarrow \phi(x) \ge \phi(y) \Leftrightarrow \psi(u) \ge \psi(v).$$

QED

> THEOREM II For any function ϕ and the function ϕ^{**} which is the adjoint of its adjoint,
> $$\phi(x) \ge \phi^{**}(x) \text{ for all } x$$
> and
> $$xK \ne 0 \Leftrightarrow \phi(x) = \phi^{**}(x).$$

From the definition of ϕ^*,

$$ux \le 1 \Rightarrow \phi(x) \le \phi^*(u) \text{ for all } u, x.$$

Therefore from the definition of ϕ^{**} we have the inequality $\phi \ge \phi^{**}$. Also, the equality holds for given x if and only if $\phi(x) = \psi(u)$ and $ux \le 1$ for some u, equivalently $xK \ne 0$.

> THEOREM III For any function ϕ, $\phi^* = \phi^{***}$.

We have $\phi \le \phi^{**}$, by Theorem II, and by similar argument, for any ψ in the budget space, $\psi \ge \psi^{**}$. Applying this to $\psi = \phi^*$, we have $\phi^* \ge \phi^{***}$. But also, directly from $\phi \le \phi^{**}$, it follows that $\phi^* \le \phi^{***}$, so now we have $\phi^* = \phi^{***}$. QED

5.6 LIMIT ADJOINTS

Even if R is a complete order its adjoint S is not generally reflexive, nor is it complete except when restricted to points where it is reflexive. Most of the propositions about the adjoint have a restriction to the reflexive points. But the limit adjoint relation $\dot{S}$, now to be defined as a logical extension of the adjoint, is free from such failures, and has the property that it is reflexive if R is reflexive; and if R is a complete order then $\dot{S}$ is a complete order, which moreover contains S.

This development of the adjoint relation has a counterpart for utility functions. The adjoint $\psi(u)$ of a utility function $\phi(x)$ is not generally defined everywhere. But the limit adjoint function

$$\dot{\psi}(u) = \sup\left[\phi(x) : ux \leq 1\right]$$

agrees with $\psi(u)$ where this is defined, but is itself defined everywhere.

For any relation R, in the commodity space, the *limit adjoint* relation $\dot{S}$ is given by

$$u\dot{S}v \equiv (\wedge\, yWv)\,(\vee\, xWu)\, xRy.$$

While uSv asserts that there exists a bundle of goods x within the budget u which is as good as every y within v, with $u\dot{S}v$ there is the less stringent requirement that, for any given y within v, there exists some x within u which is as good. That holds when R is understood to be a utility order, but in the following no properties are assumed for R which are not stated.

THEOREM I For the adjoint S and limit adjoint $\dot{S}$ of any relation, $S \subset \dot{S}$.

This follows from the tautology (Chapter VI.1)

$$(\vee\, x)\,(\wedge\, y)\,p(x, y) \Rightarrow (\wedge\, y)\,(\vee\, x)\,p(x, y),$$

$p(x, y)$ being any propositional function. But the converse is not valid, so it is not generally the case that $S = \dot{S}$.

THEOREM II If R is transitive then

$$uSu \Rightarrow u\dot{S} \subset uS.$$

With the previous proposition, this shows that the relation produced by $\dot{S}$ between reflexive points of S is indentical with that produced by S, provided R is transitive. Thus,

$$uSu \Rightarrow (\vee\, \bar{x}Wu)\,(\wedge\, yWu)\, \bar{x}Ry.$$

With this $\bar{x}$, by transitivity of R,

$$\begin{aligned}
u\dot{S}v &\Rightarrow (\wedge\, zWv)\,(\vee\, yWu)\, yRz \\
&\Rightarrow (\wedge\, yWv)\, \bar{x}Rz \\
&\Rightarrow (\vee\, xWu)\,(\wedge\, yWv)\, xRy \\
&\Rightarrow uSv.
\end{aligned}$$

THEOREM III If R is complete then $u\bar{S}v \Rightarrow v\dot{S}u$.

Suppose R is complete, that is, $x\bar{R}y \Rightarrow yRx$. Then

$$\begin{aligned}
u\bar{S}v &\Rightarrow (\vee\, yWv)\,(\wedge\, xWu)\, x\bar{R}y \\
&\Rightarrow (\wedge\, xWu)\,(\vee\, yWv)\, x\bar{R}y \\
&\Rightarrow (\wedge\, xWu)\,(\vee\, yWv)\, yRx \\
&\Rightarrow v\dot{S}u.
\end{aligned}$$

THEOREM IV If R is complete, then $\dot{S}$ is complete.

By Theorem III, if R is complete, $\bar{S} \subset S'$. But, by Theorem I, in any case $S' \subset \dot{S}$. Therefore $\bar{S} \subset \dot{S}$. QED

Unless a function $\phi(x)$ has appropriate special properties, the adjoint

$$\phi^*(u) = \max\,[\phi(x) : ux \le 1]$$

need not always be defined everywhere. But the *limit adjoint* function

$$\dot{\phi}(u) = \sup\,[\phi(x) : ux \le 1]$$

is defined everywhere. Also, by definition, it coincides with $\phi^*(u)$ whenever $\phi^*(u)$ exists.

Now we consider a function ϕ with adjoint $\psi = \phi^*$ and limit adjoint which will be denoted $\dot{\psi}$ Also, R is the order represented by ϕ, with adjoint S and limit adjoint $\dot{S}$.

THEOREM V If $xRy \Leftrightarrow \phi(x) \ge \phi(y)$, then

$$u\dot{S}v \Rightarrow \dot{\psi}(u) \ge \dot{\psi}(v),$$
$$(uSu \wedge vSv) \Rightarrow \{\, u\dot{S}v \Leftarrow \psi(u) \ge \psi(v)\,\},$$
$$(u\bar{S}u \wedge vSv) \Rightarrow \{\, u\dot{S}v \Leftarrow \dot{\psi}(u) \ge \dot{\psi}(v)\,\}.$$

With R represented by ϕ,

$$u\dot{S}v \Leftrightarrow (\wedge\, yWv)\,(\vee\, xWu)\phi(x) \ge \phi(y).$$

But, by definition of $\dot{\psi}$,

$$xWu \Rightarrow \phi(x) \le \dot{\psi}(u)$$

and

$$t < \dot{\psi}(u) \Leftrightarrow (\vee\, xWu)t < \phi(x).$$

Hence

$$u\dot{S}v \Rightarrow (\wedge\, yWv)\dot{\psi}(u) \ge \phi(y)$$
$$\Rightarrow \dot{\psi}(u) \ge \dot{\psi}(v).$$

Now, uSu if an only if

$$(\vee\, xWu)\phi(x) = \dot{\psi}(u).$$

Hence, $u\bar{S}u$ if an only if

$$xWu \Rightarrow \phi(x) < \dot{\psi}(u).$$

This proposition shows that $\dot{S}$ coincides with the order represented by $\dot{\psi}$, except that, in the case of a tie in the values of the function, S resolves the tie by giving priority to a point where S is reflexive over one where it is not. Just to this extent, $\dot{S}$ is more highly resolved than the order represented by $\dot{\psi}$.

II.6

Efficiency and Inefficiency

Efficiency is what makes a thing what it is, serving a purpose or realizing a utility; it is a relation between ends and means. Its measure is the extent to which these are matched, so with given ends it would be the choice criterion for the means. It is a pervasive idea, and it would be excessive to regard it as belonging peculiarly to economics.

In a mechanical application of the term, it represents the ratio of useful work performed to the amount of energy expended. This pertains to cases for which the terms are clearly measurable, and proportional. One can take the ratio and state the efficiency achieved; anyone can know exactly what is meant, and possibly can make some use of it. Other applications are not so clear; there are qualities to which numbers cannot be attached, or the objective is nebulous, or there is not the proportionality which permits the useful summary by a single number. Economists and engineers are among those concerned with efficiency, and the term is used frequently by both. From engineeering we have straightforward examples. It is also a main term in economics and does much work in the area; but although it turns up frequently, its meaning can be problematic. The engineering model is also a typical economic model. The comparison is between input and useful output, and an objective is to achieve the greatest possible output from a given input. An engine designer might want to compare the outputs from various designs with the maximum that physical principles allow. A design which realizes the known limit might never be achieved, but better ones are continually produced. Others might be concerned more with the development and production costs and impose a budget constraint. Alternatively, a required performance could be specified, and the objective then would be to minimize the cost of realizing it.

Where engineers test and measure, economists make use of the production function or the utility function. But the grounds for these are less systematic, which can create problems. The production function is understood to specify the maximum possible output obtainable from any given inputs, with a generally available technology. This is not derived by an inspection of technology and calculation, but from data on the activities of firms. As with engines, producers too can be found to be short of efficiency, and so there can be the question of how short. Unlike engines, maximum performance here cannot be calculated from a theoretical model provided by the physical sciences.

The firms themselves make the standard, and provide the data for it. The concern with production functions, and the productivity of firms, creates a peculiar problem that requires its own methodology.

There are similar questions with the utility function. This is a sort of production function, but its magnitude has no meaning; only the order it gives to bundles of goods is significant. The ordinary theory of the consumer is based on utility and unquestioned efficiency. Even when the utility is granted, the perfect efficiency seems an extravagant requirement. The familiar volatilities of real consumers make such intolerance unsuitable.

This chapter deals with some ways in which an allowance can be made for inefficiency in consumers and producers, through an analysis of observations of their activities. The method is related to von Neumann's activity analysis where, from given feasible activities, others are derived on the basis of some model. Here the initial knowledge of feasibilities is a matter of direct observation, with the principle that, if anything has been seen to have been done, then it must have been possible to do it. From observed activities of firms, and the classical model for technology, an activity system can be constructed which gives a limited basis for evaluating the efficiency of activities, in particular the activities of the firms themselves. The construction is the same as von Neumann's, though not necessarily with the additional constant returns to scale assumption in his original formulation. Also, our concern here is with the production function with a single output, though the approach need not be so limited.

Some feasibilities are revealed from observations, and then others are inferred from them on the basis of a model. It is exactly like the revealed preferences of consumer theory, and the parallel goes further. There are revealed infeasibilities also, for the activities which would have given greater profit but were not taken, because they were technologically infeasible, as is supposed or 'revealed'. The absence of contradictions where an activity is revealed simultaneously to be both feasible and infeasible provides a test of the admissibility of the model, just as Houthakker's revealed preference axiom provides a similar test in the case of the consumer.

Models for consumers or producers that accept inefficiency are obtained at first by introduction of a parameter e, between 0 and 1, with the requirement that any activity have an efficiency of at least e. With $e = 1$ there is a return to the usual strict efficiency model. The tests of the data are more relaxed for smaller values of e, and there is an upper limit to the values of e that any given data will accept, which is easily calculated.

In this way there is a determination of upper bounds of efficiencies which should be associated with observed activities, and, quite uninformatively, some will be no better than 1. With a further development, efficiency is taken to have a probability distribution on a certain model, whose parameters, and at the same time all the efficiencies, can be estimated by the principle of maximum likelihood. With this there is the more suitable result that all ativities become represented as inefficient, in some degree. This approach can be compared with a statistical treatment of the speed v in which people run 100 yards. Records are continually broken, so the upper limit v^*, which could give $e = v/v^*$ as the running efficiency of any individual, has not been observed. But an assumption about the distribution of efficiency being on some model carrying parameters enables both v^* and the distribution parameters to be estimated by maximum likelihood, on the basis of a sample of speeds. In the result, v^* would be larger than any observed v. Correspondingly, a production function f is determined, the counterpart of v^*, and any observed production activity (x, y) would be such that $y < f(x)$, and so would be represented as inefficient, $f(x)$ being an estimate of the maximum output attainable with inputs x.

This chapter proceeds along the lines of the finite 'non-parametric' approach to utility construction that has been described, and has application also for production analysis. The construction now makes some sense as an approximation, and in providing a 'frontier' utility function, analogous to the 'frontier production function' familiar in connection with production efficiency measurement.

The approach to inefficiency in consumption and approximate utility (Afriat 1967d, 1972d, 1973e) was influenced by a communication with H. Rubin (1967). On submitting to him the need to accommodate inefficiency, by a relaxation of the inequalities required by perfect efficiency, he proposed the introduction of a single parameter, now identified as a cost efficiency. The similar method (Afriat, 1969f, 1971b) for production analysis, applied to the special case of constant returns, was observed by Charles Geiss (1969) to be equivalent to the method of Farrell (1957) concerning production efficiency measurement. Geiss (1971a, b) recomputed and extended Farrell's results, using the same data. He developed computer programs for carrying out tests of various production models, defined by restrictive properties, and the corresponding efficiency determinations.

This renewed account has reference mainly to Afriat (1967d, 1973e) as concerns consumption, and to Afriat (1971b) for production. Only a part of the material is covered; not included, but for a brief mention, is the maximum likelihood estimation method proposed in Afriat (1971b), based on a probability model for the distribution of efficiency. This was applied by Richmond (1974) with the Cobb-Douglas production function model, and then by others. Most interesting is the development of this method where the function is without parameters and is restricted to having only the classical properties, namely of being non-decreasing and concave.

The approach as concerns consumption has received little attention, but a great deal of attention has been devoted to the production side. Varian (1984) reviews some aspects of the subject and its history, which now has an additional elaboration. Other related items, besides those just mentioned (within the author's awareness), are: Farrell and Fieldhouse (1962), Aigner and Chu

(1968), Hanoch and Rothschild (1972), Charnes, Cooper and Schinner
(1976), Meeusen and van den Broeck (1977), Charnes, Cooper and Rhodes
(1978), Aigner and Schmidt (1980), Charnes, Cooper, Seiford, and Stutz
(1981, 1982). With recent work, the representation provided by this list,
including bibliographies in the articles mentioned, is incomplete.

6.1   CONSUMER INEFFICIENCY

When a utility order R is taken to govern demand, it signifies that demand
must meet efficiency requirements that have reference to R. With a demand
(x, p), px is the money spent, and an efficiency ordinarily required is that
x must have at least the utility of any other bundle y attainable with that expenditure; that is, for all y the condition

$$H' \equiv py \leq px \Rightarrow xRy$$

holds. Another efficiency that can be required is that as much utility as is provided by x should not be attainable with any smaller expenditure, that is, it
should not be possible to find a y such that yRx and $py < px$, or, what is
the same, the condition

$$H'' \equiv yRx \Rightarrow py \geq px$$

is required. In general, these requirements are independent, but relations are
produced between them if R has special properties, as shown in the last chapter.
For instance if R is insatiable, that is, if it is impossible to have xRy while $y < x$,
then $H' \Rightarrow H''$. Also, if R is a complete order and the sets xR are closed, then
$H'' \Rightarrow H'$. Since R has all these properties if it is representable by a continuous
semi-increasing utility function, in that case H' and H'' become equivalent,
and it would seem then that there is no need to deal with more than one of
these conditions. However, even then there is advantage for development in
making both explicit, and dealing with both.

The condition H which is the conjunction of H' and H'', and defines *compatibility* between the demand (x, p) and the utility R, gives the model for
exact efficiency, and now a model is sought where efficiency is achieved only
in some degree. With production, the comparison of observed output with
the maximum possible output with the inputs used, as determined by a production function, provides one type of efficiency measure. It is not one that
is available with utility, which has only an order representation; but the criterion
can have reference instead to cost, and inefficiency can be represented as a
measure of wastage there.

Instead of asking that the utility of x be at least as great as any attainable
with the expenditure px, instead it would have to be as great as any utility
attainable with a fraction epx of the expenditure. In effect, an amount of the
budget not exceeding the remainder $(1 - e)px$ is allowed to be wasted, since
by better programming at least the same utility could have been obtained with
an expenditure not exceeding epx.

With this principle, the utility of x should be at least that attainable with any expenditure not exceeding epx, as stated by the condition

$$H'(e) \equiv py \le epx \Rightarrow xRy,$$

and also it should be impossible to achieve the utility of x with any less expenditure than epx, so for no y should we have $py < epx$ and yRx; or,

$$H''(e) \equiv yRx \Rightarrow py \ge epx.$$

holds. The condition $H(e)$, which is the conjunction of $H'(e)$ and $H''(e)$, for any e between 0 and 1, defines a relation between any demand and utility, of *compatibility at the level of cost efficiency e*.

Evidently for the case $e = 1$ we have $H(1)$ identical with the earlier compatibility condition H. Also, $H(0)$ holds unconditionally; that is, every demand is compatible with every utility at a level of cost efficiency 0. Generally,

$$H(e), \quad e' \le e \Rightarrow H(e'),$$

so any demand and utility which are compatible at a given level of cost efficiency are compatible also at every lower level. Thus, when e decreases from 1 there is increasing tolerance, with complete tolerance when $e = 0$.

In terms of the utility cost function

$$c(p, x) = \inf [py : yRx]$$

derived from the utility order R, a restatement of the condition $H''(e)$ is that

$$c(p, x) \ge epx.$$

When R is restricted to being a complete order for which the sets xR are closed, this implies $H'(e)$, so this condition alone suffices to express the condition $H(e)$. We can define

$$e^* = c(p, x) / px$$

as the cost efficiency of the demand (x, p) as determined by the utility order R. Then $H(e)$ becomes equivalent to the requirement $e^* \ge e$.

In terms of a normalized demand (x, u), for which $ux = 1$, we have

$$uy \le e \Rightarrow xRy, \quad yRx \Rightarrow uy \ge e,$$

as a statement for $H(e)$, and

$$e^* = c(u, x).$$

Since $c(u, x) \le ux$ for all x and u, this always gives $0 \le e^* \le 1$.

6.2 ATTAINABLE EFFICIENCIES

The consistency of a given collection of demand observations (x_t, p_t) requires the existence of a utility order with which they are simultaneously compatible. Now they are *consistent at a level of cost efficiency e* if a utility order exists with which they are simultaneously compatible at that level. Each has a cost efficiency $e_t(R)$ determined in respect to any utility R, and their compatibility at the level e requires $e_t(R) \geq e$ for all t; equivalently $e(R) \geq e$ where

$$e(R) = \min e_t(R).$$

Consistency in the former sense implies the existence of R making $e(R) = 1$. If we introduce

$$e^* = \max_R e(R)$$

as the *critical cost efficiency* for the collection, consistency at the level e implies $e \leq e^*$, and consistency in the original absolute sense implies $e^* = 1$.

The critical cost efficiency coefficient e^* for a collection of demands is therefore an index of their consistency absolutely and at every level of cost efficiency. Even if they are not consistent in the strict sense, they are at some level $e \leq 1$—in fact, any level $e < e^*$. Whether or not they are consistent at the threshhold level e^* is not generally decided, and also not important. In any case, for any $e < e^*$ it is possible to find a utility order R with which they are compatible at the cost-efficiency level e. The question now is how to determine e^*, and then such an R for any $e < e^*$. Though it might not now be obvious, the determinations are quite straightforward and depend on a simple extension of the theory developed for the exact efficiency case.

Enlarging on the result found for strict consistency, it will appear that whenever there exists any utility order compatible with the demands at some cost efficiency level, there also exists one which is represented by a classical utility function, which moreover can be constructed on the same finite polyhedral and polytope models used formerly.

A merit to this present scheme is that, when utility is to be constructed on the basis of demand observations, inconsistency formerly prevented any construction, whereas now some construction can always be made. Before, the fit between the utility and the data was required to be exact, but now it can be approximate, with a discrepancy measured in a way which is economically significant and can be made as small as possible. The result will be an approximate utility function, with discrepancy from fitting all the data exactly stated by $1-e^*$, so when the data are strictly consistent this discrepancy will be zero.

When a best-fitting utility is constructed in this way, every demand (x_t, p_t) of the collection which is the basis for the construction will have an efficiency e_t determined in respect to it. If these are to be regarded as efficiency estimates, they have a poor distribution, since some will have the unlikely value 1. With a prior probability model for the distribution of efficiency, one might proceed differently, by determining distribution parameters, if any, and efficiencies e_t which give maximum likelihoods under the constraint that there exists a utility R which is compatible with (x_t, p_t) at the level e_t, for all t. Should utility be taken on the model of a utility function carrying parameters, these parameters could be estimated at the same time. Though this method has interest, and is applicable also to production, it will not be taken far. The first described approach, which is also a preparation for the second, is more straightforward, and we shall continue with that.

6.3 UTILITY APPROXIMATION

Consider any numbers e_r such that there exists a utility order R which, for all r, is compatible with the demand (x_r, u_r) at the level of cost efficiency e_r. For such numbers,

$$u_r x \leq e_r \Rightarrow x_r R x, \qquad u_r x < 1 \Rightarrow x \bar{R} x_r,$$

in particular,

$$u_r x_s \leq e_r \Rightarrow x_r R x_s, \qquad u_r x_s < 1 \Rightarrow x_s \bar{R} x_r,$$

so with the cross-coefficients $D_{rs} = u_r x_s - 1$ and cost inefficiencies $w_r = 1 - e_r$,

$$D_{rs} + w_r \leq 0 \Rightarrow x_r R x_s, \qquad D_{rs} + w_r < 0 \Rightarrow x_s \bar{R} x_r.$$

The arguments that applied with $w_r = 0$ apply again now, with $D_{rs} + w_r$ in place of D_{rs}. The conclusions are contained in the following theorem. Any numbers e_r are *allowable cost efficiencies* for the given demands if there exists a utility order compatible with them at these levels of cost efficiency. Then the $w_r = 1 - e_r$ are allowable cost inefficiencies. These always exist for any given demands, and complete consistency corresponds to the case where taking all $e_r = 1$, or all $w_r = 0$, is allowable. This theorem gives a characterization of all allowable cost efficiencies. Also, corresponding to any, it gives a construction of examples of utility functions that fit the data as required.

> THEOREM I For any normalized demands (x_r, u_r) $(u_r x_r = 1)$ with cross-coefficients $D_{rs} = u_r x_s - 1$, and any numbers e_r, there exists a utility order which is compatible with (x_r, u_r) at the level of cost efficiency e_r if and only if, with $w_r = 1 - e_r$,
>
> $$D_{rs} + w_r \leq 0, \ldots, D_{tr} + w_t \leq 0 \Rightarrow D_{rs} + w_r = 0, \ldots, D_{tr} + w_t = 0,$$
>
> and, equivalently, there exist numbers λ_r, ϕ_r such that
>
> $$\lambda_r > 0, \quad \lambda_r (D_{rs} + w_r) \geq \phi_s - \phi_r.$$
>
> With any such numbers, the utility functions
>
> $$\phi^o(x) = \min_r \phi_r + \lambda_r (u_r x - e_r)$$
>
> *and*
>
> $$\phi^i(x) = \max \left(\Sigma \phi_r t_r : \Sigma x_r t_r \leq x, \Sigma t_r = 1, t_r \geq 0 \right)$$
>
> fit the data in the way required.

For any allowable e_r there are many such functions, just as there were previously in the case of fully consistent data, with a similar characterization by inner and outer bracket pairs ϕ^i, ϕ^o. The questions now concern the allowable cost efficiencies e_r, and the critical cost efficiency e^*.

If e_r are allowable, then so are any $e'_r \leq e_r$, and so any $e'_r = \min e_s$. The critical cost efficiency for the collection of demands is the upper limit e^* of e such that $e_r = e$ are allowable. Such e are the values that validate the condition $H(e)$ for the existence of a utility compatible with all the demands within the cost efficiency level e. A consequence of Theorem I is that these are also the values e which, with $w = 1 - e$, validate the condition $K(e)$ given by

$$D_{rs} + w \leq 0, \ldots, D_{tr} + w \leq 0 \Rightarrow D_{rs} + w = 0, \ldots, D_{tr} + w = 0.$$

We have to find the upper limit of e, and so the lower limit of w, satisfying this condition. It should be noted that $K = K(1)$, corresponding to $e = 1$ and $w = 0$, is the earlier general consistency test, a counterpart of Houthakker's revealed preference condition.

Let

$$d = \min_{ij \ldots k} \max [D_{ri}, D_{ij}, \ldots, D_{kr}].$$

Then immediately,

$$d > 0 \Rightarrow K, d < 0 \Rightarrow \bar{K},$$

while $d = 0$ leaves K undecided. Moreover,

$$d \leq 0. \Rightarrow .d + w > 0 \Leftrightarrow K(e),$$

where it is understood that $w = 1 - e$. With

$$e^* = \sup [e : K(e)],$$

and $w^* = 1 - e^*$, this shows that

$$d \geq 0 \Rightarrow w^* = 0, \quad d < 0 \Rightarrow w^* = -d,$$

and hence that $w^* = \max [0, -d]$, so proving the following.

THEOREM II   For any given demands with cross coefficients D_{rs}, the upper limit of values of e such that there exists a utility order R compatible with all of them within a level of cost efficiency e is given by $e^* = 1 - w^*$, where

$$w^* = \max [0, -d]$$

and

$$d = \min_{rij \ldots k} \max [D_{ri}, D_{ij}, \ldots, D_{kr}].$$

Given any $e < e^*$, and taking $e_r = e$, utility functions can be constructed as in Theorem I. Whether $K(e)$ holds for $e = e^*$ is not generally decided.

6.4   PRODUCTION EFFICIENCY

If a single activity (x, y) has been observed, where n inputs x have been used to produce a single output y, then it is known that the output y is feasible with the inputs x, by some available means. Without further information it cannot be known whether a greater output would have been possible by any means. Therefore there cannot be any judgement about the efficiency of the activity in producing output from the inputs used. In the concept of a production function f, it determines the maximum output $f(x)$ for any inputs x attainable with the generally available technology. Were it known, it could be used to determine $e = y/f(x)$ as a certain measure of the efficiency of any activity (x, y), where $0 \leq e \leq 1$ since necessarily $y \leq f(x)$. Since other types of efficiency also can be considered, this one is distinguished as *technical efficiency*.

In wanting to make such efficiency measurements, an issue is the availability of the production function. With data of activities (x_r, y_r) $(r = 1, \ldots, m)$ of producers in an industry, econometricians determine a production function f by estimating the parameters in some model. The result is more a statistical predictor of output from given inputs than an assessment of the maximum possible output, and as such is not so suitable for efficiency measurement or comparison. Parametric models of production functions that suit such econometrics are a limited variety, imposing restrictions that reflect no hypothesis about production. But they are all, or mostly, on the classical model, where the function is non-decreasing and concave. Using just that aspect, one can proceed differently, in a way that maintains recognition of the production function as a provider of information about maximum possible output instead of likely output, and so also about efficiency.

The von Neumann approach to representing production possibilities is by means of an activity system generated from a collection of activities on the basis of a model, by taking their closure with respect ot the model. With the observed activities (x_r, y_t) and the classical production model one would take the *classical closure*

$$F = [(x, y) : x \geq \Sigma x_r t_r, \Sigma y_r t_r \geq y, \Sigma t_r = 1, t_r \geq 0].$$

This is an input-output relation where xFy, or $(x, y) \in F$, means that y is producible from x, or (x, y) is a feasible activity. With the production function

$$f(x) = \max [y : xFy]$$

determined from the relation, we have

$$xFy \Leftrightarrow y \leq f(x),$$

so the relation is also represented by this function. It is automatic in the way it is constructed in that it is non-decreasing and concave, and so has the classical properties. Also, $y_r \leq f(x_r)$ for all r, and if f' is any other classical function such that $y_r \leq f'(x_r)$ for all r then $f(x) \leq f'(x)$ for all x.

This function so constructed is therefore the smallest production function on the classical model consistent with the requirement that it provides a bound, if not the maximum, of output attainable with given inputs. With it, therefore, $e_r = y_r / f(x_r)$ is an upper bound for the efficiency of the activity (x_r, y_r). In some cases $e_r = 1$ so there is no 'revealed' inefficiency, but in others possibly $e_r < 1$.

Prior ideas about the distribution of efficiency give some basis for going further with the concept of a production function as telling the maximum of output, more than just a bound, as here. The parallel with the running efficiency of individuals is described in the introduction to this chapter. The beta distribution is a fair model for the distribution of efficiency, consistent with density approaching zero near 0 and 1 with a peak in between, with two parameters related to location of the peak and the concentration around it. Any production function determines efficiencies e_t, and these have a liklihood based on any distribution. Making this likelihood a maximum under the constraint that the function is classical, or on any model, gives a principle for estimating the distribution parameters and the efficiencies, and possibly also function parameters. Without further restriction on its form, the function would not generally be unique, except that always $f(x_r) = y_r e_r$. One such function would be that constructed as before, but now instead from the activities $(x_r, y_r e_r)$. Should the function be taken on some parametric model, the parameters might be uniquely determined at the same time as the distribution parameters and efficiencies, in which case a unique function would be obtained. In any case, the estimates of efficiencies e_t would all be, realistically, strictly less than 1. Whether or not they have fair sense as absolute measures, they might still give a better basis for efficiency comparisons.

In von Neumann's original formulation, the activity system, while based on the classical model, was also conical; that is, it had constant returns to scale. Following that, the activity system generated by the observations (x_r, y_r) would be

$$F = [(x, y) : x \geq \Sigma x_r t_r, \Sigma y_r t_r \geq y, t_r \geq 0]$$
$$= [(x, y) : xy^{-1} \geq \Sigma a_r t_r, \Sigma t_r = 1, t_r \geq 0],$$

where $a_r = x_r y_r^{-1}$ are input bundles for a unit of output. Hence the input possibility set for a unit of output is

$$X = [x : x \geq \Sigma a_r t_r, \Sigma t_r = 1, t_r \geq 0].$$

This set is simply the othoconvex closure of the points a_r, described by points which lie above some point of the convex closure. The efficiency e_r of the activity (x_r, y_r) as provided by this system is determined by $a_r e_r^{-1}$ being the point where the ray to a_r cuts the boundary of this region, which is the unit isoquant for the production function f which represents the input-output relation F. The efficiencies so determined correspond exactly to those obtained by the method of M. J. Farrell (1957). The connection was pointed out by Charles Geiss (1969).

Technical efficiency is a limited view of efficiency, since it takes the inputs x not to be a choice but as given, and the objective is to make the best of them. If the inputs x instead are chosen and have a cost, which becomes the production cost of output, then the unit cost of output could be the efficiency criterion. Then an efficiency is required also in the choice of inputs, since in addition to technical efficiency it should be impossible to obtain the same output with some other inputs which cost less. Such *competitive efficiency* reflects the ability to sell the product at a low price. There is also *profit efficiency*, which compares profit gained with the maximum achievable with the prevailing prices and technology; these two efficiencies coincide in the constant returns case.

Part III

THE COST OF LIVING

III.1

Price and Quantity Levels

The cost of a basket of goods x when the prices are p is the sum $px = \Sigma p_i x_i$, known by every shopper studying an account. There is no general possibility of expressing such a sum simply as a product PX, in effect, as if there were just one good, with quantity X and price P, P depending only on the prices of the goods and X on the quantities bought, say

$$P = e(p), X = f(x).$$

Everyone should agree with that. But the possibility appears to be taken for granted whenever terms like price level or price index are used, as they are constantly in macroeconomic discussions, and every day with regard to the consumer price index (CPI). It can be wondered what sense there should be to the phenomenon.

A price level must have role as a price, so applicable to a quantity, or level, such as the level or standard of living. If P is the price level then PX should be the cost of achieving the quantity level X. But many bundles x, any such that $f(x) \geq X$, achieve the level, and each of these has a cost px. Since any cost can be exceeded freely, cost has unambiguous sense only as minimum cost, and so this cost PX must be the cost of the cheapest bundle that achieves the level;

$$PX = \min \, [px : f(x) \geq X].$$

If this relation holds for all X, so that the expression on the right admits the factorization on the left, then the function f which determines quantity level has the homogeneity or constant returns to scale property

$$f(xt) = f(x)t, \text{ for all } t \geq 0.$$

Then the function e which determines price level is given by

$$e(p) = \min \, [px : f(x) \geq 1] = \min_x px/f(x)$$

Price and quantity levels (P, X) are associated with any demand (p, x), where $P = e(p)$ and $X = f(x)$. Then we have $PX \leq px$, since PX is the minimum cost of attaining the level X of x, while px is simply the cost of x and so at least this minimum; certainly x attains its own level, but there may be cheaper bundles that do also. Consequently the price and quantity function e, f are such that

$$e(p)f(x) \leq px \text{ for all } p, x.$$

Should the demand be cost-efficient, so that achieving the quantity level at a lesser cost is impossible, or no x' exists for which $f(x') \geq f(x)$ while $px' < px$, then, equivalently,

$$f(x') \geq f(x) \Rightarrow px' \geq px \text{ for all } x';$$

then also $PX \geq px$, and so now $PX = px$. Thus an efficient demand (p, x) is distinguished as one that satisfies the condition

$$e(p)f(x) = px.$$

The function f which determines the quantity level, and with it the derived function e which determines price level, puts a constraint on the demand (p, x), if this is to be cost efficient. Since the demand is in principle observable and the function hypothetical, it is suitable to put this relation the other way round and regard the demand as putting a constraint on the function. Then data of many demands will put many simultaneous constraints on the function to be allowed. An issue then is whether such a function exists at all, that is, whether the constraints are consistent. In the case where they are consistent, the functions admitted will be many, or there is an indeterminacy. Such indeterminacy produces an indeterminacy in any price and quantity levels. But the extent of this indeterminacy can be exactly determined.

1.1   PRICE-QUANTITY DUALITY

Let f be conical, having the property

$$f(xt) = f(x)t \ (t \geq 0) \tag{i}$$

by which its graph is a cone. It could be a production function with constant returns to scale, meaning that, if the inputs x are doubled or scaled by any factor t, then so is the output; similarly, it could be a utility function.

For any input x the output is $f(x)$ and so the input for each unit of output, or unit input, is the vector $a(x) = x\{1/f(x)\}$, which by (i) has the property

$$a(xt) = a(x) \ (t \geq 0). \tag{ii}$$

by which it is dependent only on the input proportions, and independent of the scale. If the input prices are p then the cost for each unit of output, or unit cost, is $pa(x) = px/f(x)$. This also depends only on the input proportions, and these can be chosen to make it minimum. The minimum value is a function e of p, the unit cost or price function associated with the production function f, given by

$$e(p) = \min_x px/f(x). \tag{iii-a}$$

From this definition, for all p,

$$e(p) \leq px/f(x) \text{ for all } x$$
$$e(p) = px/f(x) \text{ for some } x$$

or, what is the same,

$$e(p)f(x) \leq px \text{ for all } p, x \qquad \text{(iv)}$$

together with

$$\text{for all } p, e(p)f(x) = px \text{ for some } x. \qquad \text{(v-a)}$$

In addition to (v-a), similar to it but with an exchange of roles between p and x, we have the possible but not generally necessary condition

$$\text{for all } x, e(p)f(x) = px \text{ for some } p \qquad \text{(v-b)}$$

With the relation, K, of conjugacy between p and x, given by

$$pKx \equiv e(p)f(x) = px, \qquad \text{(vi)}$$

(v-a) asserts that $pK \neq 0$ for all p and (v-b) asserts that $Kx \neq 0$ for all x. This relation depends only on proportions, so, for all $s, t > 0, pKx \Rightarrow spKxt$. This is the condition for the input factor proportions specified by x to be cost efficient at the exchange rates specified by the prices p.

Just from the form of its definition (iii-a), regardless of properties of f, the function e is concave conical. Since f is given to be conical, it is concave if and only if it is superadditive: $f(x + y) \geq f(x) + f(y)$. If it is concave then, by the Support theorem, for any x there exists a p for which $f(y) - f(x) \leq p(y - x)$ for all y. Because f is conical, the replacement of y by $y \{ f(x)/f(y)\}$ gives

$$0 \leq py \{ f(x)/f(y) \} - px,$$

showing that

$$px/f(x) \leq py/f(y) \text{ for all } y,$$

showing that (iii-a) holds, for some p, and demonstrating (v-b). Then from (iv) and (v-b) we have, in addition to (iii-a),

$$f(x) = \min_p px/e(p). \qquad \text{(iii-b)}$$

As with e in formula (iii-a), by which e is the conjugate of f, from this formula f must be concave conical. We have seen now that, whatever f, the function e derived from it by (iii-a) is concave conical, and f is recoverable from e by formula (iii-b), or is the conjugate of e, if and only if it is concave conical. Functions related to each other symmetrically in this way, where each is the conjugate of the other, form a dual pair. Examples are given in the next section.

We have seen the following:

THEOREM I (conjugate function duality) For any function f, the function e derived from it by the formula

$$e(p) = \min_x px/f(x)$$

is concave conical, and

$$e(p)f(x) \le px \text{ for all } p, x$$

for all p, $e(p)f(x) = px$ for some x. Also,

$$f(x) \le \min_p px / e(p),$$

and f is recovered from e by the formula

$$f(x) = \min_p px / e(p)$$

if and only if it is concave conical.

If f is differentiable, the gradient of $px / f(x)$ is

$$\nabla \{ px / f(x) \} = \{ 1 / f(x) \} p - \{ px / \{ f(x) \}^2 \} \nabla f(x).$$

If this vanishes, as is required for the relation (vi) to hold, we have

$$\nabla f(x) = \{ f(x) / px \} p$$

and hence, by (vi),

$$\nabla f(x) = \{ 1 / e(p) \} p. \qquad \qquad (\text{vii-a})$$

The relation (vi) is similarly equivalent to

$$\nabla e(p) = x \{ 1 / f(x) \}. \qquad \qquad (\text{vii-b})$$

From (vii-b), the derivatives of e give the inputs for each unit of output when these inputs are chosen in cost efficient proportions. Similarly the derivatives of f give the prices which would make the input proportions cost efficient, the currency unit being the minimum cost of producing a unit at those prices.

THEOREM II (price–quantity duality)   If e, f are any conjugate price and quantity functions, so that

$$e(p)f(x) \ge px \text{ for all } p, x$$

then the condition

$$e(p)f(x) = px$$

for any prices and quantities p, x to be conjugate is equivalent to

$$\nabla e(p) = x \{ 1 / f(x) \}$$

and to

$$\nabla f(x) = \{ 1 / e(p) \} p.$$

1.2   DUAL FUNCTION EXAMPLES

Cobb-Douglas and Cobb-Douglas
A simple illustration of function duality, where functions are related to each other by the formulae 1.1 (iii-a) and 1.1 (iii-b), is provided by the Cobb-Douglas function

$$f(x) = A\Pi_i x_i^{w_i} \qquad \text{(i)}$$

where $w_i > 0$, $\Sigma w_i = 1$. With $X = f(x)$, the derivatives for $x_i > 0$ are given by

$$X_i = Xw_i / x_i \qquad \text{(ii)}$$

Then from 1.1 (vii-a) with $P = e(p)$ we have $X_i = (1/P)p_i$, and 1.1 (v) requires $PX = px$, so that

$$Xw_i / x_i = (1/P)p_i \qquad \text{(iii)}$$

and also

$$p_i x_i = (px)w_i. \qquad \text{(iv)}$$

This last relation shows the constant shares property of the Cobb-Douglas function, the shares being given by the exponents w_i.

Also we have

$$x_i = PXw_i / p_i$$

and so

$$\begin{aligned} X &= A\Pi_i x_i^{w_i} \\ &= A\Pi_i (PXw_i / p_i^{w_i}) \\ &= APX(\Pi_i w_i^{w_i})/(\Pi_i p_i^{w_i}) \end{aligned}$$

giving

$$P = B\Pi_i p_i^{w_i}, \text{ where } AB = \Pi_i w_i^{-w_i}. \qquad \text{(v)}$$

A peculiarity of the Cobb-Douglas, shown here, is that its conjugate is also Cobb-Douglas, and moreover has the same exponents. This symmetry where the functions have the same form is not shared by other examples.

The inequality 1.1 (iv) states that $PX \leq px$ for all p, x. For these functions e, f and with shares denoted $s_i = p_i x_i$, this gives

$$\Pi_i (s_i / w_i)^{w_i} \leq 1$$

for all $s_i \geq 0$, $\Sigma s_i = 1$, or that $\Pi_i s_i^{w_i}$ under these constraints is maximum at $s_i = w_i$.

The assumption that f is concave can be verified as follows. Because f is conical, and differentiable, the condition for it to be concave is that $f(y) \leq \nabla f(x)y$ for all x, y. From (ii), this condition is

$$f(y) \leq \Sigma f(x) w_i y_i / x_i,$$

and so by (i) it is

$$\Pi_i (y_i / x_i)^{w_i} \leq \Sigma w_i (y_i / x_i)$$

which is true by the Theorem of the Mean, which states that an arithmetic mean with any weights is at least the corresponding geometric mean.

Leontief and linear

For another example, the conjugate of a linear function $f(x) = bx$, where $b \in \Omega_n$, is

$$
\begin{aligned}
e(p) &= \min \left[px : bx \geq 1 \right] \\
&= \max \left[t : tb \leq p \right] \text{ by LP duality} \\
&= \max \left[t : t \leq p_i / b_i, \, b_i > 0 \right] \\
&= \min \left[p_i / b_i : b_i > 0 \right],
\end{aligned}
$$

this function having the Leontief form. Alternatively, starting with

$$
e(p) = \max \left[t : tb \leq p \right],
$$

we have

$$
\begin{aligned}
f(x) &= \min \left[px : e(x) \geq 1 \right] \\
&= \min \left[px : p \geq b \right] \\
&= bx.
\end{aligned}
$$

Because of the symmetry between prices and quantities, we could just as well have taken f with the Leontief form, and then the conjugate e would have been linear.

Polyhedral and polytope

A further example, of importance in the next section, is the concave conical polyhedral function

$$
\begin{aligned}
f(x) &= \min b_{(i} x \\
&= \max \left[t : tI \leq bx \right]
\end{aligned}
$$

where $b \in \Omega_n$ has rows $b_{(i}$, and the elements of $I \in \Omega^n$ are all 1. The conjugate is the concave conical polytope function

$$
\begin{aligned}
e(p) &= \min \left[px : bx \geq I \right] \\
&= \max \left[vI : vb \leq p \right] \text{ by LP duality.}
\end{aligned}
$$

Let

$$
f^o(x) = \min \{ px : e(x) \geq 1 \} .
$$

Though we know it, because f is concave conical, it is interesting to verify directly that f is recovered from e by the formula $f = f^o$. As $f \leq f^o$ follows directly from the definition of e from f, it remains to show that $f^o \leq f$. Thus, substituting for e in the formula for f^o,

$$
\begin{aligned}
f^o(x) &= \min \left[px : px' \geq 1, \, bx' \geq I \right] \\
&\leq b_{(i} x \text{ for all } i,
\end{aligned}
$$

because $p = b_{(i}$ is feasible. But this is equivalent to

$$
f^o(x) \leq \min b_{(i} x = f(x).
$$

Again, if f, instead of being polyhedral, had been given the polytope form, its conjugate e would have been polyhedral.

1.3   PRICE AND QUANTITY LEVELS

A pair of function e, f, symmetrically related as shown by 1.1 (iii-a) and 1.1 (iii-b), and so necessarily concave conical and satisfying the functional inequality 1.1 (iv) together with 1.1 (v-a) and 1.1 (v-b), are a *conjugate pair of price and quantity functions*. Such a pair of functions, interpreted in utility terms, serves to give an intelligibility to ideas of 'price level' and 'price index', at the same time showing the inherent restrictions in their use.

Suppose a demand (p_t, x_t) is given as data for each period $t = 1, \ldots, k$, showing the quantities demanded and the prevailing prices. Let (P_t, X_t) be the associated price and quantity levels as determined from any given conjugate functions e, f, so

$$P_t = e(p_t), \quad X_t = f(x_t). \tag{i}$$

For the demands in the various periods all to be represented as cost efficient by the conjugate pair e, f, we require

$$P_t X_t = p_t x_t \text{ for all t.} \tag{ii}$$

By this condition the demands are compatible with e, f; and for present purposes they will be said to be consistent if they are compatible with some such e, f. In any case, (iv) of section 1.1 requires

$$P_s X_t \leq p_s x_t \text{ for all } s, t. \tag{iii}$$

Therefore, assuming (ii), and dividing (iii) by (ii),

$$P_s / P_t \leq p_s x_t / p_t x_t \text{ for all } s, t.$$

With the coefficients

$$a_{ts} = p_s x_t / p_t x_t, \quad b_{ts} = p_t x_s / p_t x_t, \tag{iv}$$

determined from the demand data, the solvability of the inequalities

$$a_{ts} \geq P_s / P_t \text{ for all } s, t \tag{v-a}$$

for the P_t has appeared to be necessary for the consistency of the demands, as mentioned above. It is also sufficient, as will be shown. With (ii), the inequalities (v-a) are equivalent to

$$b_{ts} \geq X_s / X_t, \tag{v-b}$$

and the argument could proceed just as well in terms of these.

Suppose the inequalities (v-a) are solvable, and let P_t be any solution. Then let $b_t = P_t^{-1} p_t$ and

$$f(x) = \min_t b_t x \tag{vi-a}$$
$$e(p) = \min [px : b_t x \geq 1], \tag{vi-b}$$

so these are conjugate functions, of the polyhedral and polytope type dealt with in the last section. Because, by (v-a),

$$b_t x_s = p_t x_s / P_t \geq p_s x_s / P_s = b_s x_s,$$

we have

$$b_s x_s = \min_t b_t x_s .$$

Then, because also

$$b_s x_s = p_s x_s / P_s = X_s ,$$

by (ii), it appears that

$$f(x_s) = X_s .$$

Next we want to show $e(p_s) = P_s$. Thus, because e, f are conjugates,

$$e(p_s)X_s = e(p_s)f(x_s) \le p_s x_s ,$$

so that

$$e(p_s) \le p_s x_s / X_s = P_s .$$

Therefore to prove $e(p_s) = P_s$ it remains to show that $e(p_s) \ge P_s$. We also have

$$b_t x_s / X_s = p_t x_s / P_t X_s \ge 1,$$

by (iii), so that

$$e(p_s) = \min [p_s x : b_t x \ge 1] \le p_s x_s / X_s = P_s ,$$

and now we have the wanted conclusion.

Thus, with any solution P_t of the inequalities (v-a), the existence of which was seen first to be necessary for the consistency of the demands, we have constructed a conjugate pair of function e, f which establishes that consistency. The solvability of these inequalities is therefore both necessary and sufficient for the consistency of the demands. QED

We now have the following:

THEOREM (*constructability*) For any demands

$$(p_t , x_t) \epsilon \Omega_n \times \Omega^n (t = 1, \dots, k)$$

and coefficients

$$a_{rs} = p_s x_r / p_r x_r , \quad b_{rs} = p_r x_s / p_r x_r ,$$

derived from them, let $(P_t , X_t) \epsilon \Omega \times \Omega$ be such that

$$P_t X_t = p_t x_t \text{ for all } t.$$

A necessary and sufficient condition that there exists a conjugate pair of functions e, f such that

$$P_t = e(p_t), \quad X_t = f(x_t)$$

is that

$$a_{rs} \ge P_s / P_r \text{ for all } r, s$$

or, equivalently,

$$b_{rs} \ge X_s / X_r \text{ for all } r, s.$$

Then one pair of such functions is

$$f^*(x) = \min_t p_t x / P_t$$
$$e_*(p) = \min [px : p_t x \geq P_t \text{ for all } t],$$

and another is

$$f_*(x) = \min [px : px_t \geq X_t \text{ for all } t]$$
$$e^*(p) = \min_t px_t / X_t.$$

These functions are such that $e_* \leq e^*$, $f_* \leq f^*$.

1.4 LIMITS OF INDETERMINACY

The given demands (p_t, x_t) with

$$b_{rs} = p_s x_r / p_r x_r, \quad a_{rs} = p_r x_s / p_r x_r,$$

have any (P_t, X_t) as admissible price and quantity levels if

$$P_t X_t = p_t x_t \text{ for all } t, \qquad (\text{i})$$

and

$$b_{rs} \geq P_s / P_r \qquad (\text{ii})$$
$$a_{rs} \geq X_s / X_r. \qquad (\text{iii})$$

Subject to (i), the conditions (ii) and (iii) are equivalent. Therefore with any solution P_t of (ii) the X_t determined from (i) are a solution of (iii), and vice versa.

The demands have any pair of functions (e, f) as admissible price and quantity functions if they are a dual pair of functions such that

$$e(p_t)f(x_t) = p_t x_t \text{ for all } t.$$

A conclusion from the last theorem is that admissible price and quantity levels (P_t, X_t) are identical with levels $P_t = e(p_t)$, $X_t = f(x_t)$ determined from admissible price and quantity functions (e, f). From this, admissible levels exist if and only if admissible functions exist, so the level consistency of the demands can mean either of these conditions.

Given any admissible levels, many admissible level functions exist which have these as their values at the base points p_t, x_t. The different functions can have different values at non-base points, so even when levels at base points are fixed the levels at those points have an indeterminacy, but one already put in limits by the limit functions e^*, e_* and f^*, f_*. But still, the admissible levels themselves, if there are any, are many. Here, therefore, is a further source of indeterminacy in the levels at any points, including the base points. When the indeterminacy at base points is put in limits, the indeterminacy at all other points is also, through the limit functions associated with limit levels. The problem that remains, therefore, concerns the evaluation of level indeterminacy at the base points only. In other words, it concerns the variety of the admissible levels (P_t, X_t) obtained from solutions of the inequalities (ii), or alternatively (iii), since solutions of one or other system are in a correspondence through relation (i).

A particular source of indeterminacy is just scale indeterminacy, which is removed by setting one level to value 1, say $P_1 = 1$. Price indices being ratios of price levels, in effect, then, the levels P_t will become price indices with $t = 1$ as base. The indeterminacy that remains is associated with the ratios $P_{rs} = P_s / P_r$, which can range in a closed interval with upper limit

$$\hat{P}_{rs} = \min [P_s / P_r : b_{ij} \geq P_i / P_j]$$

and lower limit

$$\check{P}_{rs} = 1 / \hat{P}_{sr}.$$

As appears in Chapter V.5, there is also the formula

$$\hat{P}_{rs} = \min_{ij \ldots k} b_{ri} b_{ij} \ldots b_{ks},$$

and the efficient way to calculate the matrix of upper limits is to raise the matrix a to powers in a sense which is a modification of the usual, where addition instead means taking the minimum.

Any level has its full range of indeterminacy only when the other levels are not fixed, since fixing any one level puts a new restriction on all the others. In particular, if one level is given an extreme value, at a limit of the interval to which it is basically restricted, the others will be confined to narrower intervals possibly excluding their basic limits.

Systems of inequalities of the form (i), or (ii), by taking logarithms can be put in the form $a_{rs} \geq x_s - x_r$. Systems of inequalities in this form first arose in the more general form of demand analysis, without the homogeneity restriction suitable to the present topic, treated in Part III. They arose again in the theory of minimum paths in networks, found in Chapter V.5. The mathematics, which contains these different interpretations and applications but is identical in each case, is put best in that usual connection. An expository statement for the present application is in Chapter III.2.

III.2

The True Index

The price index is associated with a narrow concept of the cost of living problem, but it is most familiar and important, for both theory and practice. With
its long history and large literature, and now quite elaborate theory, a sketch
can give the essentials more readily than an extended account. An outline of
the main ideas is described in this chapter. History is touched only where points
are encountered directly, and theorems are brought in discursively and without proof. Other chapters deal with the same matters more fully. The ground
has been trodden so often that what one makes of it might be a personal accident. William Fleetwood, Irving Fisher, and S. S. Byushgens stand out from
the past in this account. Writings of J. R. Hicks, R. G. D. Allen, and Paul
Samuelson form a background, while interest was evoked from J. R. N. Stone,
and from Robin Marris who drew attention to the theorem of Byushgens that
has influenced the other theorems. The 'true index' is an early vague term that
has later acquired the meaning dealt with here.

2.1 THE COST OF LIVING

When prices change, one question concerns how an income should be adjusted
in order to preserve its purchasing power. This has a theoretical interest, and
also a relevance to everyday life, especially when prices are rising. The sense
of the question is not immediate, nor is giving it an answer. The theory of
index numbers offers some intelligibility to the question, and approaches a
solution.

   The data usually allowed for in dealing with this question are demand observations, usually the two for the reference periods themselves, and possibly more.
With several consumption periods, identified as $t = 1, 2, \ldots, T$, let row and
column vectors p_t, x_t give the prices of commodities and the quantities of
them demanded in period t. Then the cost, $C_t = p_t x_t$, of the commodity
bundle x_t at the prices p_t, determines the expenditure on consumption in
period t, which for convenience of statement is equated with income. What
is done in practice draws little from the theory, being governed mostly by social
factors and statistical practicality. The cost of living index in practice is really
somewhat in the nature of a democratic social institution, and should be seen
in that light, in addition to any light coming from the theory. The theory often
associated with the practical index and offered in its support, where it is

identified as a Laspeyres index, has little to do with it; Fleetwood (1707) is much nearer.

One understanding of the cost of living question depends on the supposition that any bundle of goods x has a level of utility, realized through consumption of the goods, representing a standard of living, so that in buying x one is in effect buying a level of utility, or a standard of living. The cost of a standard of living, at any prices for the goods, is the cost of the cheapest bundle of goods that can provide it.

2.2 THE PRICE INDEX

In addition to that understanding, and to some extent independent of it, is the commonly accepted form for giving an answer to the cost of living question, which involves a single number, the price index. The index is associated with any pair of periods, and it specifies a ratio between any incomes that, in those periods and at the prices that prevail, should be accepted as having the same purchasing power. With any periods r and s, a number P_{rs} is associated, with the effect that any incomes E_r and E_s, at the prices p_r and p_s, that should be accepted as having the same purchasing power, must have the relation

$$E_r = P_{rs}E_s.$$

The number P_{rs} is the *price index*, with s as the *base* and r as the *current period*. Generally one would allow a relation which is monotonic increasing, and not necessarily homogeneous linear as here. The price index concept therefore carries with it a special restriction about the relation between equivalent incomes.

With this use of a price index goes the question of how it should be determined. There is then the further question of how any determination, and before that how just the restricted idea of the index itself, fits in with the utility understanding of the purchasing power question it is meant to resolve. In some respects, these questions can be considered both separately and together.

2.3 FORMULAE, AND FISHER'S TESTS

The determination question taken on its own has revolved around a large assortment of formulae coming more from a history of use, than from any theory, or if not actual use then from inclusion among suggestions thrown out by makers of index numbers. Irving Fisher, with his book, *The Making of Index Numbers* (Fisher, 1922), represents the culmination of this phase, which is still not quite dead. In the beginning were the formulae, each with as much right as any other, even though they were subject to favouritism. Fisher classified them and gave Tests to judge their legitimacy, to bring order and discrimination to the prolific host. Though by the standards he laid down they are all illegitimate, he settled on one as his Ideal Index. The reasons he gave for the choice contain a compromise, but a theoretical property discovered for it has interest. That has to do with the utility theory and so belongs to a phase beyond Fisher's usual type of consideration.

A rule about index numbers formulae that has been taken for granted (and must be broken in the generalization for several periods taken simultaneously), is that any one of them should be an algebraical formula in demand data, and that it should depend on demand data only for the two periods to which it refers. The formulae should involve only elementary arithmetic operations — addition, multiplication, and the inverses. Accordingly, P_{rs} should be such a function of the demands (p_r, x_r) and (p_s, x_s) observed for periods r and s. Fisher's Ideal formula is

$$\overline{P}_{rs} = \sqrt{(p_r x_r p_r x_s / p_s x_r p_s x_s)}. \tag{i}$$

It satisfies various of his tests, such as the identity test, $P_{rr} = 1$, and the reversal test,

$$P_{rs} = 1/P_{sr}, \tag{ii}$$

which, by taking $r = s$ implies the former, but not the more stringent chain test

$$P_{rs} P_{st} = P_{rt}, \tag{iii}$$

which implies all the foregoing.

There is a simple sense to these particular tests, which are among a larger collection. If E_r is any income for period r, and E_s is the income with equivalent purchasing power for period s, then we must have

$$E_s = P_{sr} E_r, \tag{a}$$

and E_t is the income equivalent in purchasing power to this for period t, so also

$$E_t = P_{ts} E_s. \tag{b}$$

Then, by transitivity of equivalence, this also has the same purchasing power as E_r in period r, so then also

$$E_t = P_{tr} E_r. \tag{c}$$

Thus, for all E_r, (a) and (b) must imply (c); equivalently, (iii) holds. The underlying thought is that a price index is a ratio of price levels P_r associated with the reference periods. Thus

$$P_{rs} = P_r / P_s, \tag{iv}$$

and from this the conclusion (iii) follows again. Though the term is a part of language, there is still some obscurity about how prices, which are many, should have a single level.

2.4   THE PAASCHE-LASPEYRES INTERVAL

One undoubted way of attaining in period r exactly the standard of living that was enjoyed in period s is to have exactly the same consumption x_s, at the current cost $p_r x_s$. Therefore the income E_r in period r that has the same purchasing power as the income $C_s = p_s x_s$ in period s cannot exceed that cost, because having the income to meet that cost is enough. Accordingly,

$$E_r \leq p_r x_s = (p_r x_s / p_s x_s) C_s.$$

Therefore, if P_{rs} is the price index that in principle gives $E_r = P_{rs} C_s$, we have

$$P_{rs} \leq M_{rs}, \tag{i}$$

where

$$M_{rs} = p_r x_s / p_s x_s \ (\text{Laspeyres}). \tag{ii}$$

In other words, the Laspeyres formula gives an upper bound for the true price index, and this is the classic proposition about price indices. If there is such a thing as a true price index, anything different from it might be a false index or not a price index at all. Even

$$W_{rs} = 1 / M_{sr} = p_r x_r / p_s x_r \ (\text{Paasche}) \tag{iii}$$

is called a price index, and usually there is no claim that either is true. The theory then arrives at proposition that this second formula is a lower bound of the true index; for the true index must obey the reversal law 2.3(ii) and with that, together with (iii) above, the relations

$$W_{rs} \leq P_{rs} \text{ and } P_{rs} \leq M_{rs}$$

become equivalent. Therefore both must be true if one of them is, and therefore both are true since one has been proved. From that argument we have the proposition

$$W_{rs} \leq P_{rs} \leq M_{rs}, \tag{iv}$$

which is central to the theory of index numbers. Also it makes a dilemma, since it is quite possible to find that

$$W_{rs} > M_{rs}, \tag{v}$$

in which case it is impossible to take the Laspeyres and Paasche indices to be upper and lower bounds of anything.

The interval I_{rs} defined by (iv) can be called the Paasche-Laspeyres (P–L) interval, with s as the base and r the current period. The two periods are taken here in detachment from any others, and without any involvement with the demand data associated with others.

There is another way of representing this interval; it is not useful here where the two periods are taken alone, but gains significance when several periods are taken together. It is suitable to use a different notation

$$L_{rs} = p_r x_s / p_s x_s \tag{vi}$$

for what here is the Laspeyres index, because later with many periods this does not have the same significance as now, and ceases to be the counterpart of the Laspeyres index in its role as a limit, even though the L is used out of regard for the present connection. The set C_{rs} of positive solutions of the pair of homogeneous linear inequalities

$$L_{rs}P_s \geq P_r, \; L_{sr}P_r \geq P_s, \qquad \text{(vii)}$$

is a convex cone in the two-dimensional price-level space. Then

$$I_{rs} = [P_r / P_s : (P_r, P_s) \in C_{rs}], \qquad \text{(viii)}$$

this being the set of slopes of the rays in the cone. Alternatively, the P–L interval is the set of values for P_r obtained by cutting the cone by the line $P_s = 1$. Another way of cutting the cone, useful later with many periods when it will be by a hyperplane, is by the line $P_r + P_s = 1$. The section D obtained is in this case a line segment from which the P–L interval I derives again in the same fashion as from the cone C. The counterpart with many periods is a convex polytope lying in the simplex of normalized price-level vectors.

2.5   EXISTENCE TEST

If 2.4 (iv) is true for a true price index, then the existence of a true price index must imply the relation

$$W_{rs} \leq M_{rs} \qquad \text{(i)}$$

between the Paasche and Laspeyres indices, by which the one does not exceed the other. For a restatement,

$$p_r x_r p_s x_s \leq p_r x_s p_s x_r, \qquad \text{(ii)}$$

or, with the notation 2.4(vi),

$$L_{rs} L_{sr} \geq 1, \qquad \text{(iii)}$$

which shows the condition as holding symmetrically between the two periods. Another restatement, which is strange but puts the condition in a form that has a direct generalization to any number of periods, is that the matrix

$$\begin{pmatrix} 1 & L_{rs} \\ L_{sr} & 1 \end{pmatrix} \qquad \text{(iv)}$$

be idempotent in a modified arithmetic where addition means taking the minimum. In other words, now the data must be subject to the test (i) if dealing with a true price index on the basis of the data is to be permitted, at least on a theoretical basis without an allowance for error. Then it can be asked if the test is sufficient for that. In fact, it is necessary and sufficient for the existence of a homogeneous utility that fits the demand data. Moreover, in order for a price index, giving the relation 2.2(i) between equivalent incomes, to be dealt with on the basis of utility, the utility must be homogeneous, with the property where, if one bundle is at least as good as another, then any multiples of them have the same relation. If a true index is to be understood as one determined by any such utility, then there are many such utilities if there are any, and hence many true indices. The true indices describe a closed interval whose end-points can be calculated. They are given by the Paasche and Laspeyres formulae. This is fortunate for the early theory, which gave an answer without having a question, and now we have a question and it gives the answer.

The usually wanted relation between Paasche and Laspeyres is not in itself a theorem, but a test to be applied to the data. For a proper theorem, we have that this test is both necessary and sufficient for the data to admit the existence of a true price index. Any point of the closed interval there is a true price index—*each quite as true as any other*, and that includes the much considered Paasche and Laspeyres end-points as well.

Fisher offered tests for formulae, not tests for the demand data that enter the formulae, that is, tests prior to thinking about a particular formula but rather about the question that any formula is supposed to answer. However, assumptions implicit in the concepts used require the data to be subject to tests if their use is to be admissible. Bringing in such tests makes dilemmas disappear. There is not even any occasion for formula tests, and so no encounter with the simultaneous necessity and impossibility of Fisher's tests when applied to the usual type of formulae, touched on first by A. Wald (1936) and investigated systematically by W. Eichhorn and J. Voeller (1976). When indices are constructed, it should be because the data satisfy the consistency or existence test that permits their construction. Then without question they have the properties they are intended to have, inherited from their construction and the prior condition that permitted it, and so there is no need for a verification afterwards. A question is formulated first and then a formula is found to answer it, instead of the approach *vice versa*. Of course, formula tests can be made into data tests, since the data enter the formula, but even then the distinction just made is still valid. It is incidental that Fisher's tests are tight equations, which moreover cannot generally be satisfied, while the data tests are slack inequalities, a more tolerant allowance, which can be expanded to greater tolerance by admitting consumer inefficiency and error, as in Chapter II.6.

2.6   THEORY AND PRACTICE

Having a homogeneous linear relation between equivalent incomes is the essence of the price index idea, in both theory and practice. That may be too obvious to deserve mention, since it never is mentioned—or a mistake, or a kind of discovery. That it be fitting, as a matter of observation and of definition, is in any case a fundamental thesis in this work.

The simplicity with a price index gives a convenience for common use that compels its adoption. The method by which the index is determined is not constrained by a fixed principle, as might be supposed were it dominated by the theory; it has a freedom associated with the entire circumstances of the matter. The use of a price index at all, and then the value assigned to it, arises out of the social framework. It has the nature of a social and political institution, democratic or otherwise. A dictator could impose the use of a price index, and its value at any time, and the laws for its use; it could make a useful policy instrument in such hands. In a democracy, ideas of equity and impartiality take precedence, as in the election process. The index is based on consumers' own expenditures, giving them a representation—a vote, so to speak. The way those votes are gathered together to arrive at the result need not give universal satisfaction, but it must demonstrate suitable impartiality and other properties, or there might be complaints.

In such respects a comparison can be made with K. J. Arrow's Social Choice and Individual Values theory. That theory, divorced from its unsuitable welfare interpretation, can be regarded as an investigation into an alternative way of conducting a democratic election. First there would be an election to choose an order which the group would give to the candidates, and then the order would choose the candidate, the top one in it being the winner. Each elector would state not just a choice of one candidate but ranked preferences between all candidates. It would be a heavy burden on voters, because no candidate could be simply rejected but preferences would have to be stated between all, including the rejected ones. This is not practical, and even if it were there is no advantage to it over the old-fashioned method. It has nothing to do with welfare, where the advantage should lie, since arbitrary groups, about which we are told nothing further, do not have a welfare criterion. Even with a special group that did in some way have a welfare criterion, this might not be the way to approach it. The unlikelihood of using the procedure has nothing to do with the Impossibility theorem, and that theorem has nothing to do with the self-contradiction of democracy seen by P. A. Samuelson. The theory, though not what it is supposed to be, does not lose interest, however. It draws attention to formal characteristics of the democratic choice process. The CPI as an institution shares some of those.

Understanding the procedure involved in arriving at the CPI can be confused by theory, as it has nothing to do with Paasche, Laspeyres and Fisher. It is closer to Fleetwood who, in a straightforward way without any theory, dealt with a bundle of goods associated with a life-style at no time in particular, and compared its cost in his day to that four centuries earlier. Now the bundle of goods, instead of being for a single individual, is an average for the community. He explained the matter to a student (Fleetwood, 1st edition, 1707) and illustrated that life-style with '4 Hogsheads of Beer, 6 Yards of Cloth, and c'. His remark, 'money is of no other use, than as it is the thing with which we purchase the necessities and conveniences of life . . .', preceded the introduction of utility theory and indicated a need for it. Goods that could be bought are numerous, and bringing in utility reduces their number to one, thereby giving a less ambiguous way of putting his argument. With the CPI, from time to time a bundle of goods is determined and then, as with Fleetwood, its cost is calculated from year to year, so making three dates involved, not the two that occur in theory.

The service the CPI offers is obvious, and so are its flaws. It would be possible to remedy certain defects and improve acceptibility, but at the cost of convenience. The democratic principle is one side of the matter; another is the feelings of those who notice an alteration in the standard of living when prices rise and incomes do not. The utility concept offers a yardstick that should be better than Fleetwood's fixed bundle of goods, which does not recognize the substitution effect in the impact of a price change. Though the utility concept is usually linked to consumer behaviour, this matter is not; it is simply that consumers' feelings, regardless of behaviour, demand a kind of measurement.

2.7 MANY PERIODS

A price index usually is determined for a pair of periods in isolation from others, involving demand data from those periods alone. Price indices so determined for several periods, with such pairwise isolation, are then required, by Fisher's tests, to have a certain consistency together. The tests are an unreasonable imposition considering the isolated determinations, and it is natural that they cannot be satisfied. The problem needs to be reopened from the start by admitting the simultaneous presence of all the data. All we have for two periods is then put in a setting where it is better appreciated. The following is an outline.

The price index concept is an imposition on the broader idea of cost of living. Standard of living has sense with a utility relation R, an order (reflexive and transitive binary relation) in the commodity space, where the statement xRy means a bundle of goods x has at least the standard, or the utility, of y. Provided the sets Rx are closed, the function

$$c(p, x) = \min [py : yRx] \qquad (i)$$

is defined for all $p > O$, and gives the cost at prices p of attaining at least the standard represented by the bundle x. From this definition

$$c(p, x) = py, yRx \text{ for some } y \qquad (ii\text{-}a)$$
$$yRx \Rightarrow c(p, x) \le py \text{ for all } y \qquad (ii\text{-}b)$$

and, because R is reflexive,

$$(iii) \; c(p, x) \le px. \qquad (iii)$$

Another consequence is that $c(p, x)$ is concave conical in p.

A utility R is oversatiated at a point x if

$$y < x, \quad yRx \text{ for some } y,$$

that is, some smaller bundle is at least as good. The contrary is that

$$y < x \Rightarrow \text{not } yRx \text{ for all } y. \qquad (iv)$$

If this holds for all x, R is said to be nonsatiated. Also, R is complete if

$$xRy \text{ or } yRx$$

for all x and y, that is, the relation holds one way or the other between any bundles, equivalently

$$\text{not } xRy \Rightarrow yRx. \qquad (v)$$

The demand (p, x) is represented as cost-efficient by the utility R if

$$c(p,x) = px, \qquad (vi)$$

that is, if the cost of x at the prices p is equal to the minimum cost of attaining at least the standard represented by x. An equivalent statement is that the condition

$$H' \equiv yRx \Rightarrow py \geq px$$

holds; that is, attaining at least the standard requires at least the cost. In the contrapositive form, that is

$$py \leq px \Rightarrow \text{not } yRx. \qquad (\text{vii})$$

This condition can be put alongside the cost effectiveness, or utility maximization, condition:

$$H'' \equiv py \leq px \Rightarrow xRy.$$

The cost efficiency and effectiveness conditions H' and H'' are generally independent, and their combination is

$$H \equiv H' \text{ and } H''.$$

But relations are produced between them under special conditions. They are equivalent if the sets xR are all closed and R is complete and nonsatiated. In that case either condition stands for the combination.

The price index is a concept that in the utility context requires a utility which is homogeneous, or conical; that is,

$$xRy, t > 0 \Rightarrow xtRyt. \qquad (\text{viii})$$

An equivalent condition is that the utility cost function C must admit the factorization

$$c(p,x) = e(p)f(x) \qquad (\text{ix})$$

into product of a function of p alone and a function of x alone. Then from (iii),

$$e(p)f(x) \leq px, \qquad (\text{x})$$

and the condition (vi) for a demand (x, p) to be represented as efficient becomes

$$e(p)f(x) = px. \qquad (\text{xi})$$

Introducing

$$P_r = e(p_r),$$

the costs at any given prices p_r, p_s of attaining a standard of living X are

$$E_r = P_r X, \quad E_s = P_s X.$$

Hence, eliminating X,

$$E_r = P_{rs} E_s$$

where

$$P_{rs} = P_r / P_s.$$

That shows P_{rs} in the role of the price index between situations with the given prices, and indicates how it is determined from any homogeneous utility R in terms of the price function e associated with it.

The cost of living is intelligible in terms of a utility R, and there would be no problem about it if R were given. The cost of living problem arises because usually R is not given. Then the demand data have a bearing on the problem by their being used to provide constraints on any utility R that should be considered, by the requirement that R represent all observed demands as efficient.

The definition of cost of living (i) states it as a minimum cost, so it is inapplicable without that efficiency. In just asking the cost of living question, consumers are making a commitment about how they should be regarded. This use of the data therefore is appropriate; without it, or some more tolerant modification that allows inefficiency and error but still preserves the efficiency framework, all bearings for the question would be lost.

Imposed on this use of the data is the additional requirement, accompanying the insistence on having a price index, that the utility be homogeneous. With the conjugate price and quantity functions e and f that characterize such utility, let us introduce

$$P_t = e(p_t), \quad X_t = f(x_t). \tag{xii}$$

Then the efficiency condition (xi) applied to the observed demands gives

$$P_s X_s = p_s x_s \text{ for all } s \tag{xiii}$$

while (x) gives

$$P_r X_s \le p_r x_s \text{ for all } r, s. \tag{xiv}$$

By division, therefore,

$$L_{rs} \le P_r / P_s \text{ for all } r, s \tag{xv}$$

where

$$L_{rs} = p_r x_s / p_s x_s. \tag{xvi}$$

The existence of numbers P_r that satisfy the inequalities (xv) therefore is necessary for the existence of a homogeneous utility that fits the demand data, and of price indices that are true on the data. The condition is also sufficient. Given any solution P_r, true price indices between all periods are given by

$$P_{rs} = P_r / P_s. \tag{xvii}$$

When these exist let

$$M_{rs} = \min_{ij\ldots k} L_{ri} L_{ij} \ldots L_{ks}. \tag{xviii}$$

The condition for existence is that

$$L_{ri} L_{ij} \ldots L_{kr} \ge 1 \tag{xix}$$

for all $r, i, j, \ldots, k$.

While the L-numbers given by (xvi) might look like Laspeyres price indices, they do not have the same role as limits, except when only two periods are involved. The availability of more data has removed some indeterminacy and narrowed the limits. These numbers can fall ouside limits now effective, and then they are not true indices themselves, unlike the Laspeyres index for two isolated periods. The new limits are obtained by a generalized formula or algorithm involving all the data simultaneously, unlike the Laspeyres and all price index formulae of the type recognized by Fisher. The result is not even conventionally algebraical in the way usually required for a price index.

Powers of a matrix can be redefined as in Section 2.5 for a modified arithmetic where addition means taking the minimum. In raising the L-matrix of order T to successive powers by repeated matrix multiplications in the modified sense, either some power before the Tth will repeat, so making all succeeding powers identical with it, or it will not. That happening is a test for the existence of solutions P_r of the inequalities (xv), equivalent to the condition (xix). Otherwise the series of powers is unending. In the case of termination, the last power obtained determines the matrix M of upper limits. Then the matrix L of lower limits has elements

$$W_{rs} = 1/M_{sr}. \qquad \text{(xx)}$$

The solutions of (xv) are identical with the solutions of either of the derived systems

$$M_{rs} \geq P_r / P_s \text{ for all } r, s \qquad \text{(xxi)}$$

and

$$W_{rs} \leq P_r / P_s \text{ for all } r, s \qquad \text{(xxii)}$$

which exist whenever there are any solutions, which also is just the condition for the existence of these derived systems. With any solution, a price index matrix P is determined from (xvii). The elements of any P-matrix, so obtained, automatically satisfy the Fisher chain test 2.3 (iii). The L-numbers satisfy the multiplicative triangular inequality

$$M_{rs} M_{st} \leq M_{rt} \qquad \text{(xxiii)}$$

and the W-numbers have the similar property with the inequality reversed.

Except in the case of just two periods, the M and W matrices themselves generally are not possible P-matrices. However, their elements do give attainable limits for individual elements of the P-matrices. This comes out of a general extension property of solutions of the system (xxi), or (xxii). Any solution of a subsystem, where the indices range over a subset of periods, can be extended to a solution of the complete system. In particular, starting with a subsystem for two periods r, s the value of P_{rs} can have the full range between W_{rs} and M_{rs}. This is elaborated fully in Chapter V.4.

2.8   PRICE LEVELS

With the relation 2.7(xx), the systems 2.7(xxi) and 2.7(xxii) are equivalent, so we need only think of one of them, and can choose 2.7(xxi). The original system 2.7(xv) is

$$(L) \qquad\qquad L_{rs} P_s \geq P_r \text{ for all } r, s. \qquad\qquad \text{(i)}$$

Then the system 2.7(xxi), obtained by 2.7(xviii), subject to 2.7(xix), is

$$(M) \qquad\qquad M_{rs} P_s \geq P_r \text{ for all } r, s. \qquad\qquad \text{(ii)}$$

This is equivalent to the system (L), the two systems having identical solutions, but the derived coefficients satisfy the multiplicative inequality 2.7(xxi). Any positive solution P_r defines a permissable system of price levels, represented by a point in the price-level space V of dimension equal to the number of periods T. The set C of solutions is a convex polyhedral cone in this space.

When price levels are normalized to have sum 1, they describe a simplex U in the vector space V. This simplex U cuts the cone C in a bounded convex polyhedron, or convex polytope, D. The cone C is recoverable from its section D, being the cone through that section, projecting it from the origin.

Taking price levels to be normalized, and so represented by points in the simplex U, is convenient for computation, and for geometrical representation. We are only concerned with ratios of price levels and these are unaltered by normalization. Every point in the normalized solution set D of the system (M) is a convex combination of a finite set of basic solutions, and so the computational problem requires finding just these. Given any solution P_r we form the matrix of price indices P_{rs} given by 2.7(xvii). Now there will be explorations for a geometrical diagrammatic understanding of the system (M). Dealing with any three periods r, s, t is illustrative of the essential features. Though the associated solution cone C_{rst} is hard to visualize, the normalized solution polytope D_{rst} is much easier and can be represented graphically.

We can refer to any constraint of the system (M) by the two periods involved, so let (M_{rs}) denote the general constraint. There has already been some discussion of the case with two periods, in section 2.4 on the P–L interval. Vectors of price levels for any subset of periods r, s, $\ldots$, understood as representing only the ratios, can be denoted

$$P_{r:s:\ldots} = (P_r : P_s : \ldots). \qquad\qquad \text{(iii)}$$

Because the M-coefficients are given by 2.7(xviii), subject to 2.7(xix), and $L_{rr} = 1$, when these derived coefficients exist we must have

$$(a) M_{rr} \geq 1 \ (b) M_{rs} \leq L_{rs}, \qquad\qquad \text{(iv)}$$

giving also

$$1 \leq M_{rr} \leq L_{rr} = 1 \text{ and consequently } M_{rr} = 1. \qquad\qquad \text{(v)}$$

Also, there is the triangle inequality 2.7(xxiii), and so now

$$M_{rs} M_{sr} \geq M_{rr} \geq 1, \qquad\qquad \text{(vi)}$$

which gives a generalized counterpart of the less strict P–L inequality 2.5(ii). Any period r corresponds to the vertex of the simplex U where $P_r = 1$, and vertices can be labelled by the corresponding periods. Any point on the edge *rs* of the simplex corresponds to a ratio $P_r : P_s$, that is P_{rs} in the notation (ii). Similarly any point in a simplex face *rst* specifies the ratios $P_{r:s:t}$ and so forth for any dimension.

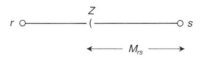

Figure 1

The constraint (M_{rs}) cuts the edge *rs* in a point Z and requires $P_{r:s}$ to lie in the segment Zs, where

$$rZ : Zs = 1 : M_{rs} = P_s : P_r. \qquad (\text{vii})$$

Without ambiguity, we can refer to the segment Zs on the edge *rs* as the segment M_{rs}, as in Figure 1. At the same time, the constraint (M_{rs}) requires $P_{r:s:t}$ to lie in the simplex Zst, and so forth to any dimension.

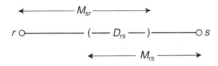

Figure 2

Considering now a pair of constraints (M_{rs}) and (M_{sr}), we have two segments M_{rs} and M_{sr} on the edge *rs*, and (viii) assures that they have a nonempty intersection D_{rs} shown in Figure 2. Because of (iv-b), this lies within the Paasche-Laspeyres interval, and is a generalization of that for when data from other periods are involved. It is generally narrower because any effect of extra data must be to reduce indeterminacy.

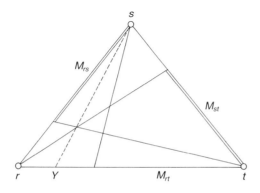

Figure 3

Now consider three constraints associated with the triangle inequality (Figure 3). Two of them produce intervals M_{rs} and M_{st} on rs and st and jointly produce the interval Yt on rt. The triangle inequality requires M_{rt} to be a subinterval of this.

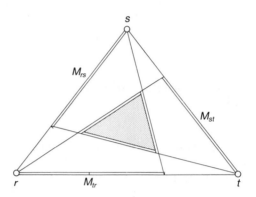

Figure 4

If, instead of M_{rt}, we take M_{tr}, cyclically related to the other two, the resulting joint constraint determines a triangle lying within rst (Figure 4). The other three cyclically related constraints, associated with the opposite cyclical order, determine another triangle, so configured with the first that their intersection is a hexagon, D_{rst} (Figure 5).

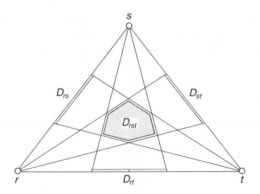

Figure 5

It is seen in this figure that D_{rs} is exactly the projection of D_{rst} from t onto rs. In other words, as $P_{r:s:t}$ *describes* D_{rst}, P_{rs} describes D_{rs}. Or again, for any point in D_{rs} there exists a point in D_{rst} that extends it, in the sense of giving the same ratios concerning r and s. That is the extension property described at the end of section 2.7 (and in Chapter V.4 on minimum paths), and it continues into higher dimensions indefinitely:

> $D_{rs...t}$ is the projection of $D_{rs...tq}$
> from the vertex q of the simplex $rs...tq$
> on to the opposite face $rs...t$. (viii)

That shows how price levels for the periods can be determined sequentially, a further one at a time. Having found any price levels that satisfy the constraints that concern only them, they can be joined by another, so that this is true again. Starting with two periods and continuing in this way, a system of price levels finally will have been found for all the periods. When the data for a price index between two periods involve data also from other periods, and moreover when indices for any subset of periods are to be constructed consistently, these D-polytopes constitute a two-fold generalization of the Paasche-Laspeyres range of indeterminacy of a price index between two periods taken alone.

2.9   FISHER'S FORMULA

This exposition concludes with a mention of the relevance of Fisher's tests to Fisher's index. Let $\bar{P}$ be the matrix of Fisher indices, the elements being determined by the formula 2.3(vi). The question is whether these are true indices. This question can be put in three ways. For the first, one can think of any one element in isolation, and the constraints on utility produced just from the demand data for the two associated periods. The second involves the constraints from all the data, but the indices are still taken in isolation and each is allowed to correspond to a possibly different utility. In the third, the indices must be simultaneously determined from a single utility admitted by all the constraints.

   The first is in the usual framework of just two periods, everything to do with the others being irrelevant. Often the argument is encountered that, with Paasche and Laspeyres as limits (in the sense of bounds) to the true index, Fisher, being their geometric mean, must be a better approximation to it than either. However, they are only bounds, and it is not known whether they are good ones, so the effect of taking the mean is not known. If one were a good approximation and the other not, the result might be not so good. In any case, the true index is not uniquely defined, or defined at all in the context of this argument, and so there are no grounds for speaking of approximations. A simple proposition answering the first question is that, if there exists a true price index at all, then the Fisher index is one. For the existence condition 2.5(i) is that Paasche does not exceed Laspeyres, and then any point in the interval between them, including the end-points, is a true index, each as true as any other. In particular, the geometric mean of the end-points belongs to the interval, and that is the Fisher index.

   For the second question, even if the existence test is fulfilled for any or all the periods, the constraints from the remaining data could narrow the range of true values lying within the Paasche-Laspeyres interval, so as to exclude the Fisher index. That puts the Fisher index, without an auxiliary condition, at a disadvantage in the third question.

S. S. Byushgens (1925) made a new kind of point when he showed that, if a homogeneous quadratic utility could be assumed to prevail, then Fisher's index is exact. The terms of this proposition are significant; in addition to marking the homogeneity inseparable from the price index concept, which is absent in most accounts, it described the sense in which an index could be exact, or true, on the basis of a utility, and showed a link of the theoretical to the more purely statistical approach. The proposition raises the question about whether the quadratic utility hypothesis is admissible on given data. If not, though none the less still true, it becomes vacuous. However, it is admissable if and only if the general price index existence test (2.5(ii), or 2.5(i)) is satisfied. That is the broadest condition for thinking about a price index at all, and just that the Paasche index does not exceed that of Laspeyres.

This theorem, proved in the next chapter, is nice as it stands. But it is not true when there are more than two periods. Something must be added, and the minimum needed is, obvious, namely, the Chain test. My point is that this addition is also enough, as concerns special treatment for Fisher. While with two periods nothing must be added beyond the minimal price index existence test, with more than two we must certainly have the existence test again, though now in the generalized form that has been stated, and obviously also Fisher's chain test, 2.3(ii). In fact, here is all that is needed. The chain test reduces to the reversal test, 2.3(iii), in the case of two periods, and Fisher's index satisfies that test anyway, so we have a generalization of the theorem. This generalization provides a way of answering the third considered question. For a matrix P of true price indices to exist, the existence test on the data is required and then, from the manner of construction that has been described, the chain test is automatically assured. Therefore, if $\overline{P}$ is to be an example of such a P-matrix, the existence test on the demand data is required, and $\overline{P}$ must satisfy the chain test. But, by the generalized theorem, that is enough to assure the existence of a utility for which the matrix P of price indices is identical with $\overline{P}$; in other words, the Fisher indices are true.

III.3

Fisher and Byushgens

If we should ever encounter a case where a theory is named for
the correct man, it will be noted.
George J. Stigler *The Theory of Price* (3rd edition), 1966, p.77

For Irving Fisher, index numbers were formulae of a certain type, and in *The
Making of Index Numbers* (1922) he dealt with the many that had been proposed. Were these answers to a question, their correctness would depend on
the question. But they were answers that had been provided without a definite
question, so making the choice between them was difficult. However, a consistency in understandings about price indices requires a formula to have certain properties, and from these Irving Fisher produced his tests.

Though prices are many, and so there are many levels, the idea of a general
'price level' is often present in arguments, and it appears in models as if it
were a definite number P, when one should like to know how to find the
number. It seems unnecessary to have an absolute price level, and a relative
price level, when one period is taken as base, would serve. The price index,
understood to be a ratio of price levels, should be given by some formula depending on available data. It refers to two periods, distinguished as the *base* and
current periods, say 0 and 1. Whatever the formula, from what it is supposed
to represent and the way it is used, it has the form $P_{10} = P_1 / P_0$, and
therefore, with an exchange of role between base and current periods, it should
be such that $P_{01} = 1 / P_{10}$, which is Fisher's time *reversal test*. It is accepted
that an index formula should involve the demand data (x_0, p_0), (x_1, p_1) for
the two periods to which it has reference, and no more. Many formulae proposed do not satify the reversal test. Also, if one brings in a third period, 2,
there is the *chain test* $P_{10} P_{21} = P_{20}$, and this usually is violated.

The more recent index thinking comes from the utility theory of the consumer,
and it should have a bearing especially on the consumers' price index (CPI).
A main question concerns how much income M_1 is needed at the prices p_1 of
the current period in order to live at the standard attained with some other
income M_0 with the prices p_0 of the base period. A price index P_{01} is
understood to provide the relation $M_1 = P_{10} M_0$ as an answer to this question.
When utility is brought in to give intelligibility, the expenditure $p_0 x_0$ in period
0 has bought the bundle of goods x_0 which provided a standard of living

through its utility; and therefore an income equal to the cost $p_1 x_0$ of that same bundle at the current prices is at least enough to achieve the same standard. Therefore if the answer M_1 provided by the price index is correct for the particular case $M_0 = p_0 x_0$, we must have $p_1 x_0 \leq M_1$, that is $p_1 x_0 \leq P_{10} p_0 x_0$, or, what is the same, P_{10} where

$$\hat{P}_{10} = p_1 x_0 / p_0 x_0.$$

In the same way, $P_{01} \leq \hat{P}_{01}$. But $P_{01} = 1/P_{10}$, and so this is equivalent to $P_{10} \geq \check{P}_{10}$, where $\check{P}_{10} = 1/\hat{P}_{01}$; that is,

$$\check{P}_{10} = p_1 x_1 / p_0 x_1.$$

In a fashion like this, upper and lower bounds have been arrived at for the 'true' index. J. M. Keynes (1930) proceeds similarly, though with some difference (cf. *A Treatise on Money* Vol. I, 'The Method of Limits'). Then there is the familiar argument that, these being 'limits' to the 'true' index, their geometric mean,

$$\overline{P}_{10} = \sqrt{(\hat{P}_{10} \check{P}_{10})},$$

which lies between, must be a better 'approximation' to it than either. For this reason, in addition to his satisfaction of the reversal test, the formula

$$\overline{P}_{10} = \sqrt{(p_1 x_0 p_1 x_1 / p_0 x_0 p_0 x_1)}$$

became Fisher's Ideal Index.

Discussion of the argument so far is contained in the previous chapter, on 'The True Index'. This chapter is concerned with a finding of S. S. Byushgens (1925), 'On a class of hypersurfaces: concerning the 'ideal index' of Irving Fisher'. Robin Marris brought attention to this finding in 1955, and to Irving Fisher's reference to it in *The Making of Index Numbers* (1927 edition, where the author's name appears in the translated form, Buscheguennce). The point made is that Fisher's index is 'exact' if it can be assumed that demand is governed by a homogeneous quadratic utility function. The contents of the paper can be reconstructed from just this remark.

Everything admitted as relating to the theory of the price index up to that point has been described above, where the Laspeyres and Paasche formulae play a part as bounds of the 'true' index; Byushgens's theorem represents a new departure. In a manner of speaking, before, there was an answer without a question, and now there is a definite question for which it comprises the exact answer. Byushgens's theorem raises several questions, touched on in the last chapter; here we deal with one of those. It can be wondered if a utility function required in the hypothesis exists at all. If none does, the theorem remains nice and true, but becomes vacuous.

The homogeneity required in the theorem is essential to dealing with a price index. It represents a restricted understanding of the general cost of living problem, corresponding to the way it is dealt with in practice. To approach the general problem similarly in terms of quadratic utility, one would simply drop the homogeneity. This is done in the next chapter on 'The Four–point Formula'; as complications go, it opens a Pandora's Box.

3.1 BYUSHGENS'S THEOREM

A utility function ϕ which is a homogeneous quadratic has the form

$$\phi(x) = x'hx/2$$

where h, the matrix of second derivatives, or Hessian, is symmetric, $h' = h$. The vector of first derivatives, or gradient, is $g(x) = x'h$. Therefore,

$$\phi(x) = g(x)x/2. \tag{i}$$

Also for any x_0, x_1 we have $x_0' hx_1 = x_1' hx_0$, because h is symmetric, and so

$$g(x_0)x_1 = g(x_1)x_0. \tag{ii}$$

The hypothesis that demand is governed by the utility ϕ requires any observed demand (x, p) to be compatible with it, and so there is the Lagrange condition

$$g(x) = \lambda p.$$

Because of the homogeneity, if ϕ admits any demand (x, p) with $px > 0$ as compatible with it, then it does also every demand (xt, p) for $t \geq 0$, the expansion locus for the prices p being the ray through x. Any point xt on this ray is associated with an income $M = p(xt) = (px)t$, and so $x \{M/(px)\}$ is the point on the ray associated with any given income M, and its utility is

$$\phi(x(M/px)) = \phi(x)\{M/(px)\}^{1/2}.$$

Applied to the demands (x_r, p_r) observed in periods $r = 0, 1$ the condition for incomes M_r at the prices p_r to produce the same utility is that

$$M_1 = P_{10} M_0,$$

where, with $\phi_r = \phi(x_r)$,

$$P_{10} = (p_1 x_1 / p_0 x_0)(\phi_0/\phi_1)^{1/2}$$

appears as the price index, with 0 and 1 as base and current peiods, as determined by the utility ϕ. Therefore in order to learn this price index that is associated with such a ϕ, it is enough just to know the ratio ϕ_1/ϕ_0.

From the Lagrangean conditions $g(x_r) = \lambda_r p_r$ that are required by the hypothesis, by (i) we have $2\phi_r = \lambda_r p_r x_r$, and by (ii), $\lambda_0 p_0 x_1 = \lambda_1 p_1 x_0$, and so

$$\phi_1/\phi_0 = p_0 x_1 p_1 x_1 / p_0 x_0 p_1 x_0.$$

Therefore

$$P_{10} = \sqrt{(p_1 x_0 p_1 x_1 / p_0 x_0 p_0 x_1)},$$

which is Fisher's formula.

The striking thing about this result, apart from the part Fisher's index plays in it, is that we do not need to know anything more about the quadratic utility in order to know the price index, let alone need to construct it. Subject to the hypothesis about the utility, the index is fully determined from the demand data for the two periods. If any utility function required by the hypothesis exists there might be many, even an infinity, of them, and so there would be an indeterminacy in the utility and, it might seem, possibly also in the associated price index. But even then, the price index is fully determinate.

It can still be wondered if any utility function such as is required by the hypothesis exists at all. If none does, the truth of the theorem is unaltered, but it becomes vacuous.

3.2 THE EXISTENCE QUESTION

The gradients of the hypothetical quadratic ϕ at the points x_r are given by $g_r = \lambda_r p_r$ subject to the requirement $g_0 x_1 = g_1 x_0$ which determines the ratio between the Lagrangean multipliers λ_r. The gradients are therefore determined but for an arbitrary multiplier, and the hypothetical quadratic can be taken to be specified to the extent of having these gradients at these points. The question now is whether one exists.

The *Paasche-Laspeyres inequality*, implied by the existence of a price index and so certainly necessary, can be stated

$$p_0 x_0 p_1 x_1 \le p_0 x_1 p_1 x_0.$$

Multiplying this by $\lambda_0 \lambda_1$, it becomes

$$g_0 x_0 g_1 x_1 - g_0 x_1 g_1 x_0 \le 0.$$

The case of equality is excluded for the present and will be dealt with separately later.

Let

$$G = \begin{pmatrix} g_0 \\ g_1 \end{pmatrix}, \ X = (x_0 x_1),$$

so that GX is symmetric, since $g_0 x_1 = g_1 x_0$, with determinant $|GX| \le 0$ by the P–L inequality. Let L be the linear space spanned by the x_r, described by points of the form $x = X\alpha$, which are linear combinations with coefficients given by a vector α. Also let

$$V = [X\alpha : \alpha \ge 0],$$

so this is the convex cone generated by the x_r. The gradient of the quadratic at any point $x = X\alpha$ of L, in particular of V, is $g(x) = \alpha' G$, and the value is

$$\phi(x) = \alpha' GX \alpha / 2.$$

Therefore, provided $|GX| \ne 0$,

$$\phi(x) = \alpha' X' G' (GX)^{-1} GX\alpha / 2 = x' h^* x / 2.$$

where $h^* = G' (GX)^{-1} G$ is symmetric. Thus the function ϕ, already fully defined with restriction to L, has its definition there extended by the homogeneous quadratic ϕ^* with Hessian h^*, so we have $\phi(x) = \phi^*(x)$ for all $x \in L$. Since $X'h^* = G$, the gradient of this quadratic ϕ^* at x_r is g_r, as would be required were it to be the hypothetical quadratic ϕ.

Let $e = X(GX)^{-1}G$. This being such that $e^2 = e$, it is the projector on to its range, parallel to its null space, this being the linear space L spanned by the x_r and the orthogonal complement of the linear space spanned by the g_r. Evidently $h^*e = h^*$, and so by symmetry of h^* also $e'h^* = h^*$, and hence $e'h^*e = h^*$. It follows that, for all x, $\phi^*(x) = \phi^*(ex)$, showing the cylindrical character of ϕ^*, with sections parallel to L. For any x, $ex = X\alpha$ where $\alpha = (GX)^{-1}Gx$, so ex belongs to the linear space L spanned by the x_r, and so the range of ϕ^* is identical with its range when restricted to L.

For any point $x = X\alpha$ of L, $2\phi(x) = \alpha'GX\alpha$. Therefore if $\alpha \geq 0$, so $x \in V$; then $\phi(x) \geq 0$, since $GX \geq 0$. Moreover, because $g_r x_r > 0$, $\phi(x) > 0$ if $x \neq 0$, so ϕ is positive definite on V. However, ϕ takes both positive and negative values, or is indefinite, in L; for the discriminant of the quadratic $\alpha GX\alpha$ is $|GX|$, and for this, being non-negative is equivalent to the P–L inequality. Therefore it vanishes for real α with α_0, $\alpha_1 \neq 0$, determining two values of α_0/α_1, distinct in the case of the strict P–L inequality when this determinant is positive, and coincident when it is zero.

The hypothetical function ϕ has been seen to be positive definite on V, but indefinite on L. Also, it must be quasi-concave at least near the points x_r, and the implications of that must be found. Moreover, there is no possiblity of the function being concave. The condition for a function to be concave is that its Hessian be nonpositive definite. But in the case of a homogeneous quadratic, that property makes the function itself nonpositive definite, which would contradict its being positive definite on V. Also the function, being non-negative definite, is excluded, since this would make it convex. For the hypothetical quadratic to be quasi-concave in a region where it is positive, it must necessarily be an indefinite quadratic, taking both positive and negative values.

Where $\phi(x) \geq 0$, as in some neighbourhood of V, it is possible to introduce $f = \phi^{1/2}$, and this function has the property $f(xt) = f(x)t$, by which it is homogeneous of degree 1, or conical, its graph in that case being a cone. Such a function is quasi-concave if and only if it is concave (Berge, 1963). Therefore, for ϕ to be quasi-concave, we require the Hessian of this function to be non-positive definite.

The gradient of f is $G = (1/2 \, \phi^{3/2})g$, and the Hessian is

$$H = (1/\phi^{-3/2}) (2\phi h - g'g).$$

Therefore, introducing

$$D(x, y) = g(x)xg(y)y - g(x)yg(y)x,$$

because $2\phi(x) = g(x)x$ and $g(y) = y'h$, we have

$$y'H(x)y \leq 0 \Leftrightarrow D(x, y) \leq 0.$$

It is readily seen that, if $D(x, y) \leq 0$ for any x, y, then this holds also when

x, y are replaced by any pair of points in the linear space spanned by them. Also, with

$$|GX| = D(x_0, x_1) < 0,$$

by the strict Paasche-Laspeyres inequality that has been assumed, $D(x, y) < 0$ for all independent $x, y \in L$. Thus, with any points $x = X\alpha, y = X\beta$ in L and $\Gamma = (\alpha, \beta)$, so also $g(x) = \alpha'G, g(y) = \beta'G$, we have

$$D(x, y) = |\Gamma'GX\Gamma| = |GX| \, |\Gamma|^2,$$

so the sign of $D(x, y)$ is invariant and the same as that of

$$|GX| = D(x_0, x_1).$$

It appears from these considerations that, subject to the strict Paasche-Laspeyres inequality, the homogeneous quadratic ϕ^* with Hessian $h^* = G'(GX)^{-1}G$, provided it is taken to represent utility only in some neighbourhood of the convex cone V generated by the points x_r, can serve as the quadratic ϕ in the hypothesis of Byushgen's theorem. To that extent it provides one realization of the hypothesis, and any others must coincide with it in the cone V. It also appears that there is no generally broader way of realizing the hypothesis with a utility represented throughout the commodity space by a homogeneous quadratic. But we have found a qualification for the hypothesis that makes it always realizable subject only to the strict Paasche-Laspeyres inequality.

The P–L inequality is anyway required, this being necessary and sufficient for the homogeneous consistency of the data, or the existence of a compatible homogeneous utility, required anyway for dealing with a price index at all. The exceptional P–L equality case, where the Paasche and Laspeyres indices are equal, still requires consideration. The case is instructive in a broader context apart from this theorem, and is dealt with in the next section.

THEOREM For any pair of demands (x_r, p_r) $(r = 0, 1)$ such that $p_r x_r > 0$, with $\lambda_r > 0$ such that $\lambda_0 p_0 x_1 = \lambda_1 p_1 x_0$ and $g_r = \lambda_r p_r$, and with

$$G = \begin{pmatrix} g_0 \\ g_1 \end{pmatrix}, X = (x_0 \ x_1),$$

the condition $|GX| \le 0$ is equivalent to the Paasche index being at most the Laspeyres index, and is necessary and sufficient for the existence of a compatible homogeneous utility, and for the existence of one moreover representable in a convex neighbourhood of the x_r by a quadratic function. Then, provided $|GX| \ne 0$, and with

$$H = G'(GX)^{-1}G,$$

one such function is the homogeneous quadratic

$$\phi(x) = x'Hx/2$$

with Hessian H, this being positive definite and strictly quasi-convex in the convex conical closure V of the points x_r and having gradient g_r at x_r, and any other such quadratic must coincide with this in V.

3.3 PURCHASING POWER CORRESPONDENCE

On the assumption that preferences determine choices, choices reveal the preferences. That should be so provided the assumption can be maintained and there are no contradictions, from the data or for other reasons, making the assumption untenable. With an absence of contradictions, the source of revelation may be exploited more freely, and when more is assumed about the preferences, the revelations can go still further. We will produce—to go alongside the usual revealed preferences—a *revealed homogeneous preference* principle. (We could just as easily call it a 'revealed separable preferences' or whatever, provided contradictions do not arise.)

Where homogeneity of utility is a part of the assumptions, any observed demand (x, p) reveals that the ray through x is the expansion locus for prices p, so the bundle $x(M / px)$ on this ray is the optimal bundle attainable with income M at those prices. Therefore this bundle has at least the utility of any bundle y attainable with this income, that is, any one such that $py \leq M$. Thus, if R is the hypothetical utility order, with the homogeneity property

$$xRy \Rightarrow xtRyt \ (t \geq 0),$$

we have

$$py \leq M \Rightarrow x(M / px)Ry,$$

for all y and M. Without the homogeneity we would have this just for $M = px$; that is,

$$py \leq px \Rightarrow xRy,$$

as usual, but with the homogeneity we have many more revealed preferences. That is so, provided no contradicitions arise; otherwise, we may have to fall back to the ordinary revealed preferences, or even to having no revealed preferences at all.

Applying revelations from this expanded source to a pair of demands (x_r, p_r) $(r = 0, 1)$, we have

$$x_r (M_r) = x_r (M_r / p_r x_r)$$

as the optimal bundle attainable with any income M_r at the prices p_r, whose utility represents the purchasing power of the income at those prices. Therefore if S is the indirect utility order associated with the hypothetical R, so that

$$M_r^{-1} p_r SM_s^{-1} p_s$$

signifies that the income M_r at the prices p_r has at least the purchasing power of the income M_s at the prices p_s, we have

$$M_r^{-1} p_r SM_s^{-1} p_s \Leftrightarrow x_r (M_r) Rx_s (M_s),$$

and also

$$p_r x_s \, (M_s) \; \leq \; M_r \; \Rightarrow \; x_r \, (M_r) R x_s \, (M_s),$$

where the strict inequality implies the corresponding strict preference. For incomes M_0, M_1 which are to be admitted as equivalent in purchasing power at respective prices, we therefore must have

$$p_r x_s \, (M_s / p_s x_s) \; \geq \; M_r \; (r, \, s \, = \, 0, \, 1 \,);$$

that is,

$$p_1 x_0 / p_0 x_0 \; \geq \; M_1 / M_0 \; \geq \; p_1 x_1 / p_1 x_0 \, .$$

Another way of putting this is that $M_1 \, = \, P_{10} M_0$ where

$$\check{P}_{10} \; \leq \; P_{10} \; \leq \; \hat{P}_{10} \, ,$$

$\check{P}_{10}$ and $\hat{P}_{10}$ being the Paasche and Laspeyres indices. In any case, we have a correspondence between M_0 and M_1 where any value of one corresponds to an interval of values of the other, and *every* value of P_{10} between the Paasche and Laspeyres limits determines a particular one-one subcorrespondence, which can be associated with some homogeneous utility compatible with the given pair of demands, and which so qualifies as a 'true' value. The geometric mean of the limits, which is Fisher's index, is one such value—therefore a true value, but also no truer than any other between these limits. A distinction that Byushgens's theorem gives to this particular value is that it is the one which would be obtained were the associated utility to have a quadratic representation.

The existence of such a utility has been considered, and it was found that, provided the Paasche index is strictly less than that of Laspeyres, a compatible homogeneous utility can be found which has a quadratic representation in a limited sense involving a convex neighbourhood of the points x_r. The threshold case, where the Paasche index equals the Laspeyres, remained to be considered. It will be found that in this case, assuming that the prices p_0 and p_1 are not proportional, any compatible homogeneous utility is essentially not differentiable and so certainly cannot be represented by a quadratic in any neighbourhood of the points x_r.

The P–L equality is necessary and sufficient for the existence of a unique ratio $t_0 / t_1 > 0$ such that, for all t_0, $t_1 > 0$ in that ratio,

$$p_0 x_1 t_1 \; = \; p_0 x_0 t_0, \quad p_1 x_0 t_0 \; = \; p_1 x_0 t_0 \, .$$

Such points $x_0 t_0$ and $x_1 t_1$ are therefore revealed indifferent, so they lie in the same utility surface, and so do all points of the line segment $< x_0 t_0, x_1 t_1 >$ joining them, which therefore lies entirely in that surface. The two hyperplanes

$$p_0 x \; = \; p_0 x_0 t_0, \quad p_1 x \; = \; p_1 x_1 t_1$$

are both supporting hyperplanes to the surface with this segment in common with each other and the surface, and they are distinct hyperplanes, since the prices are not proportional, so denying differentiability of the surface at all points of the segment.

In the further case where the prices are proportional, if p is any price vector proportional to them, px is a homogeneous utility function compatible with the demands, and so the degenerate homogeneous quadratic (px) is compatible also and so realizes the hypothesis in Byushgens's theorem.

3.4 MANY-PERIOD GENERALIZATION

The homogeneous consistency of any demands (x_r, p_r) is defined by the existence of a homogeneous utility which is compatible with all of them. Now we can define *homogeneous quadratic consistency* by the existence of such a utility which, moreover, is representable by a quadratic in a convex neighbourhood of the demand points x_r. We have seen that, for a pair of demands, provided equality between the Paasche and Laspeyres indices is excluded, *homogeneous consistency is equivalent to homogeneous quadratic consistency*. (We can compare this result with the theorem on the equivalence of general and classical consistency, of Chapter II.3.) The neighbourhood qualification in our definition appears suitable because this theorem, which saves Byushgens's theorem from vacuity, would not be true without it.

Byushgens's theorem is as applicable to many periods as to two. But in that more general application, our result as stated, which makes the hypothesis realizable in the case of two periods, is certainly not true. Some further requirement is needed for the realizability, beside the neighbourhood qualification already brought in. It should make a proper restriction with more than two periods, and becomes empty in the special case of two.

One such requirement is obvious, and the question is whether it is all that is needed. It seems fair that Fisher's index should be subjected to Fisher's tests. Usually these tests have been regarded as tests of a formula, which on substitution should produce an identity. Another view is that they provide tests of the data that enter the formula. The reversal test is an identity with Fisher's formula so this is an empty requirement as concerns the data. The more general chain test is not an identity and represents a proper condition on the data when there are more than two periods. With two periods it reduces to the reversal test and so in this case it becomes empty. Here is a case of non-compliance with a Fisher test that is not a disaster but a significant condition on the data.

A. Wald demonstrated a general inconsistency between certain of Fisher's tests, and such inconsistencies have been investigated systematically by W. Eichhorn and J. Voeller (1976). These are bound up with the convention about an index formula that it should involve the demand data for the two reference periods alone. Here we do not follow that convention and such issues cannot arise, since price indices for several periods are determined all together in a way that depends on the data for all the periods simultaneously, and they are automatically all that they should be. That applies also to Fisher's formula when it is exact in the sense of Byushgens's theorem, in providing values associated with a homogeneous utility compatible with the data. In that case the values obtained must satisfy the chain test. The exactness depended on the utility admitting a certain quadratic representation, and the question now is whether the chain test requirement on the Fisher values, in addition to the homogeneous consistency required in the first place, is enough to assure the existence of such a utility. Should that be the case, with the same exclusion of the Paasche-Laspeyres equality, we would have a theorem that reduced in the case of two periods to just what we have already.

Given any numbers P_{rs}, the condition $P_{rs}P_{st} = P_{rt}$, which corresponds to Fisher's chain test for a formula, is necessary and sufficient for them to have the ratio form $P_{rs} = P_r / P_s$, so it can be called the *ratio test*. For, under this condition, we can take $P_r = P_{rt}$ for any fixed t, and then $P_{rs} = P_r / P_s$. Conversely, if the numbers have this form, then obviously the condition must be satisfied.

For the Fisher values

$$P_{rs} = \sqrt{(p_r x_r p_r x_s / p_s x_r p_s x_s)}$$

the ratio test is equivalent to the condition

$$p_r x_s p_s x_t p_t x_r = p_s x_r p_t x_s p_r x_t,$$

which is necessary and sufficient for the existence of numbers $\lambda_r > 0$ with unique ratios such that

$$\lambda_r p_r x_s = \lambda_s p_s x_r,$$

so that with $g_r = \lambda_r p_r$ and

$$G = \begin{pmatrix} g_1 \\ \vdots \\ g_m \end{pmatrix}, \quad X = (x_1 \ldots x_m),$$

the matrix GX is symmetric.

With $L_{rs} = p_r x_s / p_s x_s$, homogeneous consistency requires the existence of a simultaneous solution P_r to the *price-level system* of inequalities $L_{rs} \geq P_r / P_s$. The condition for these inequalities to be solvable is the *cyclical product test*

$$L_{rs} L_{st} \ldots L_{qr} \geq 1$$

for all $r, s, t, \ldots, q$. A necessary condition for this is the *Paasche-Laspeyres test* that $L_{rs} L_{sr} \geq 1$, which is another statement of the Paasche-Laspeyres inequality that the one index does not exceed the other, now holding for all r, s. This condition *by itself is not sufficient for homogeneous consistency*, except for two periods taken alone. However, *its conjunction with the ratio test is sufficient*; for, the ratio test requires the Fisher values to have the form $P_{rs} = P_r / P_s$, and if $L_{rs} L_{sr} \geq 1$ then also $L_{rs} \geq P_{rs}$, showing that the price-level system of inequalities has a solution.

Suppose now that the data accept the ratio test and we have the symmetric positive matrix GX constructed as above, unique but for an arbitrary positive multiplier. A necessary condition for constructing the required quadratic is that $X\alpha = 0 \Rightarrow \alpha'G = 0$ for all α. This is assured, and the further discussion is simplified, if it is taken that GX is a regular matrix. Then we can consider the quadratic with Hessian $H = G'(GX)^{-1}G$; and, subject to the strict Paasche-Laspeyres inequality, $L_{rs}L_{sr} > 1$, an argument along the lines of that used earlier for a pair of demands serves to show that this is a suitable quadratic. The present question paves the way for the question to follow in the next chapter.

III.4

The Four-point Formula

The *expansion locus* associated with any prices is the locus of consumption when income varies while the prices remain fixed. When demand is governed by utility, properties of the utility are reflected in the characteristics of the expansion loci. For instance, if the utility relation $R \subset C \times C$ is homogeneous, or conical, having the property

$$xRy \Rightarrow xtRyt \ (t \geq 0),$$

by which its graph in $C \times C$ is a cone, then also the expansion loci in the commodity space C are cones, possibly just single rays, or lines through the origin. Correspondingly, the relation between incomes that have the same purchasing power at some different prices is homogeneous linear, and so is represented by a line through the origin, now in the *income space*, the space of two dimensions with the incomes as coordinates. We have also called this the *Fleetwood space*, because his method determines points in it, without the compulsion to take ratios of coordinates and otherwise abandon the points, as in effect is done with the CPI. The slope of the line, which in this case completely describes the relation of equivalent incomes, is the *price index* corresponding to the two different price situations. *The idea of a price index for both theory and practice is encompassed in the idea that this relation between equivalent incomes should be homogeneous linear, and so capable of description by a single number—its slope—that number being the price index.* At least, it seems, very suitable to think of it that way. In order for such a relation to be possible when expressed in terms of utility, the utility involved must be homogeneous or conical in the way just stated. Correspondingly, in the commodity space, expansion paths must be rays through the origin. Beyond that, no more can be said of the relation except that it should be monotonic. The price index thus represents a highly restricted idea about purchasing power, or cost of living, with implications about demand behaviour, and about utility when that is brought in.

For a less compromised but still simple approach to the same matter, the relation between equivalent incomes might be taken to be linear, not necessarily homogeneous, and so represented by a line which need not go through the origin. To describe such a relation two numbers are required, the slope and the intercept, instead of just one. Correspondingly, as concerns the expansion that $X\alpha = 0 \Rightarrow \alpha'G = 0$ for all α. This is assured, and the further discussion is simplified, if it is taken that GX is a regular matrix. Then we can consider the quadratic with Hessian $H = G'(GX)^{-1}G$; and, subject to the strict Paasche-Laspeyres inequality, $L_{rs}L_{sr} > 1$, an argument along the lines of that used earlier for a pair of demands serves to show that this is a suitable quadratic. The present question paves the way for the question to follow in the next chapter.

IV.5

General Economic Equilibrium

Schumpeter (1954, p. 500) said 'I do not hold that Bastiat was a bad theorist. I hold that he was no theorist.' That might have been an advantage for Frederic Bastiat (1801–1850), who put the idea of general economic equilibrium very well. He had been about Paris early in the morning, and had seen the milkman doing his rounds, shutters coming down from shops, the baker delivering bread, the inevitable citizen who had just collected a loaf, people were going off to work — it was highly orderly, like clockwork, an exact matching of parts in an elaborate design, an orchestration with a vast number of participants. But where was the designer, or conductor?

Imagination is baffled when it tries to appreciate the vast multiplicity of commodities which must enter tomorrow in order to preserve the inhabitants from falling prey to the convulsions of famine, rebellion and pillage. Yet all sleep, and their slumbers are not disturbed for a single minute by the prospect of such a frightful catastrophe. (Bastiat, 1850)

Bastiat found the ordinary experience remarkable, and raised the question about which the theory of general equilibrium is concerned.

‑'Economy' comes from the Greeks and means management of the household. But households do not manage themselves — there are people in charge, and they do it. Here there seemed to be a large household, highly regulated but with no one in charge, and it was not a unique accident, but happened all the time. Though this matter was so familiar as to be hardly noticed, there was still something needing to be explained. Had Bastiat been with the Incas instead, the question would not have arisen. People *were* in charge there, the Captains of Ten, captains of ten of those, and so forth, collecting and distributing products in a system of warehouses—an elaborate bureaucracy-administered welfare, giving care to the aged, the sick, and those with misfortunes, while any departing from their proper function were skinned alive. Bastiat was not simply concerned with the phenomenon of social order, as such. That really is a commonplace, wherever there are societies, and not just human ones. His concern was with the particular mechanisms imagined to be available, and not to be available, in this case to produce the order.

A system is understood in terms of its parts and their behaviour. An engine is disassembled into parts, which are examined for their individual properties loci in the commodity space C, these would have to be lines, not necessarily through the origin in C. There are two different ways of stating the implications of the linear income relation as concerns utility. First, in terms of the cost function,

$$\varrho(p, x) = \min [py : yRx],$$

this must have the special form

$$\varrho(p, x) = \sigma(p)\phi(x) + \nu(p).$$

For the more restricted homogeneous case, $\nu(p) = 0$, so the cost function admits the factorization

$$\varrho(p, x) = \sigma(p)\phi(x)$$

into a product of a function of prices alone and a function of quantities alone, a *price function* and a *quantity function*. For the homogeneous case the utility surfaces have to be all similar, so just one of them specifies the entire preference relation. In the general linear case, instead two surfaces are required, as elaborated in Chapter III.5.

For just one example of a utility that determines linear expansion loci, we have the general quadratic. For the homogeneous case that plays a part in Byushgens's theorem, these all go through the origin. With a general quadratic these are not necessarily through the origin, but through the centre of the quadratic, if it has one. It will be seen that in dealing with hypothetical quadratic utility on the basis of given demand data, the possible existence of a centre, where the gradient vanishes, is a critical matter, and so is its possible location. Such further complications are avoided in the homogeneous case, where the centre is at the origin, so that we know it exists and also where it is.

On the basis of homogeneous quadratic utility and the usual data provided by a pair of demands for the reference periods, it appears from Byushgens's theorem that price indices are fully determinate, and moreover that they are calculable from the data by Fisher's formula. It is plausible that a similar but less restricted approach to purchasing power could be made on the basis of general quadratics. In dropping the homogeneity of utility, the idea of a price index is abandoned. One would want to construct a general linear relation between equivalent incomes that is consistent with a quadratic that fits given data, and it should be obtained in terms of the data, without having to construct the quadratic. The procedure is suggested by Byushgens's theorem, but carrying it out is not simple and experience of the homogeneous case gives no anticipation of peculiar features encountered. The formulae obtained involve demand data from four periods, instead of the two usual with price index formulae. Why that is so, and why the number is exactly four, will have to be seen. (A remark similar to this did not satify a journal editor, when I submitted a first note on the subject in 1956.) Also, the income purchasing power relation is not fully determinate, and so the formulae have to characterize all the many possibilities. For the special case where the four budgets are parallel in pairs, we do have determinacy, and the formulae become equivalent to Wald's 'New Formula'. The connection was appreciated by H. Houthakker (c. 1960) with the observation that twice two is four. Here, therefore, is a generalization of Wald's formula, which itself is a generalization of Fisher's formula.

A comparison between the homogeneous and non-homogeneous cases, both in general and with quadratics in particular, will serve to indicate what we are about. This involves the finite demand analysis method shown in Part II, which was developed in dealing with this problem though now it is considered on its own. The formula to be obtained has complications, but they have been instructive and have produced that other work as a byproduct.

For any demands (x_r, p_r), with associated expenditures $M_r = p_r x_r$ and budget vectors $u_r = M_r^{-1} p_r$, homogeneous consistency, or the existence of a homogeneous utility compatible with all of them, is equivalent to the existence of numbers P_r such that

$$p_r x_s / p_s x_s \geq P_r / P_s \text{ for all } r, s.$$

As concerns two periods r, s taken alone, these inequalities just require

$$p_r x_s \geq P_r / P_s \geq p_r x_r / p_s x_r;$$

that is, the ratio P_r / P_s must belong to the Paasche-Laspeyres interval

$$I_{rs} = [p_r x_r / p_s x_r, p_r x_s / p_s x_s].$$

When this interval is non-empty, the geometric mean of the end-points, which is the Fisher index, is one of its points, and therefore provides a particular solution. One can always pick this point in dealing with any two periods alone, but not in general for more than two at a time, since a special condition is required, as seen in the last chapter. The condition amounts to an acceptance of Fisher's chain test by Fisher's index. It happens that such a Fisher or *mean solution* can be associated with a quadratic utility, by the theorem in section 3.2. But in any case it is a solution remote from the critical limits. Even when an exact solution is not available for more than two periods, one might want to pick one approximating the model.

A similar way of thinking can apply in the absence of the homogeneity that goes with price indices. It again produces a linkage with quadratics, though in this case they are not homogeneous. The general consistency of the given demands, or the existence of any utility whatsoever that is compatible with all of them, requires the existence of numbers λ_r, ϕ_r which are a solution of the system of homogeneous linear inequalities

$$\lambda_r > 0, \quad \lambda_r D_{rs} \geq \phi_s - \phi_r \quad \text{for all } r, s$$

where the coefficients are given by $D_{rs} = u_r x_s - 1$. For a solution, the numbers are required to be such that the differences $\phi_s - \phi_r$ belong to the intervals

$$(\lambda_r D_{rs}, -\lambda_s D_{sr}).$$

As before, concerning ratios, though now with the arithmetic instead of geometric mean, a particularly well accepted solution might be taken to be one where these differences are not just in these intervals but coincide with their mid-points; that is, where

$$\phi_s - \phi_r = (\lambda_r D_{rs} - \lambda_s D_{sr})/2.$$

Such a *median solution* generally cannot be found for more than four periods, but for fewer than four there are many. For exactly four periods such a solution exists, and also is essentially unique, but for a positive multiplier of the λ_r and a linear transformation of the ϕ_r. As a kind of parallel to Byushgens's theorem, it is found that, if demand is governed by a quadratic utility, then the utilities and marginal utilities determined by it at the demand points x_r correspond to the ϕ_r and λ_r in a median solution, and so as such are essentially unique and can be calculated directly from the data. That is a reason why the formula to be obtained should involve the demand data from four periods, corresponding to the way in which Fisher's formula involves data from two.

The general and homogeneous cases have a correspondence that can be seen with reference to the two systems of inequalities, where the imposition of homogeneity makes a reduction of one to the other. For a utility function ϕ with gradient g, and with

$$\phi_r = \phi(x_r), \quad g_r = g(x_r),$$

we have the Lagrangean conditions $g_r = \lambda_r u_r$, with Lagrange multiplier $\lambda_r = g_r x_r$ since $u_r x_r = 1$. For a linearly homogeneous, or conical, utility we have $g_r x_r = \phi_r$, as Euler's identity, and so $\lambda_r = \phi_r$. Similarly for a homogeneous quadratic, $g_r x_r = 2\phi_r$, and so $\lambda_r = 2\phi_r$. By making these substitutions we obtain corresponding reductions. Thus for the general case we have the system of inequalities

$$\lambda_r(u_r x_s - 1) \geq \phi_s - \phi_r,$$

which with $\lambda_r = \phi_r$ becomes the system

$$u_r x_s \geq \lambda_s/\lambda_r$$

associated with the homogeneous case. Also for the median solution, where

$$\phi_s - \phi_r = \{\lambda_r(u_r x_s - 1) - \lambda_s(u_s x_r - 1)\}/2,$$

with $\lambda_r = 2\phi_r$ we obtain

$$\lambda_r/\lambda_s = u_s x_r/u_r x_s,$$

corresponding to the Fisher or mean solution for the homogeneous case, since now we have the square of a linearly homogeneous function and the index is correspondingly squared.

For the general case, with any *multiplier-level solution* λ_r, ϕ_r we can construct a utility function ϕ, compatible with the given data, with indirect utility function ψ in the budget space B which, from the compatibility, is such that

$\phi(x_r) = \psi(u_r)$. Also $\phi(x_r) = \phi_r$, so the numbers ϕ_r in a solution appear as utility levels. Also, with $g_r = \lambda_r u_r$,

$$\phi(x) - \phi(x_r) \le g_r(x - x_r) \text{ for all } x,$$

so λ_r appears as a Lagrange multiplier making g_r a support gradient of ϕ at the point x_r. Correspondingly, from convex programming theory (with reference to Part V, especially Chapter V.2),

$$\psi(M^{-1}p_r) - \psi(M_r^{-1}p_r) \le (\lambda_r / M_r)(M - M_r),$$

for all incomes M, which in the differentiable case gives

$$\lambda_r / M_r = \partial\psi(M_r^{-1}p_r) / \partial M_r,$$

showing λ_r / M_r as the marginal utility of money in period r. In the homogeneous case we have

$$\psi(M^{-1}p) = M\psi(p),$$

and so

$$\lambda_r = \psi(u_r) = \phi(x_r) = \phi_r.$$

Then the price 'levels' are determined by $P_r = M_r / \lambda_r$, and price indices correspondingly.

The relation between any incomes E_r, E_s that have the same purchasing power at the prices p_r, p_s is determined from the condition

$$\psi(E_r^{-1}p_r) = \psi(E_s^{-1}p_s).$$

Without any qualification about underlying utility, this is simply a monotonic relation. For a homogeneous utility it takes the special homogeneous linear, or 'price index' form $E_r = P_{rs}E_s$ where P_{rs}, the price index, depends on the prices alone. The case we will be concerned with now is where this relation takes the general linear form and, as a case of consistency with that, utility has a quadratic representation, as in Byushgens's theorem, though without the homogeneity.

The result about determinacy of utilities and marginal utilities for a general quadratic utility from demand data for four periods was found in 1955. That in itself represents a generalization of Byushgens's theorem, dealt with in the last chapter. It was a response to the attention that Robin Marris (1955) drew to the theorem, in a consultation about the Paasche-Laspeyres 'spread', and is in my reports or papers (Afriat, 1956a, b, c, 1957b). The determinate values are obtained from what is now called a median solution for multipliers and levels. That terminology was introduced only after the general idea of multiplier-level solutions and their use for constructing utility, with data for any number of periods, was put forward in 1959. The report (Afriat, 1960c) on 'The system of inequalities $a_{rs} > x_s - x_r$' is auxiliary to the mathematics of multiplier-level solutions, including median solutions. This happens also to represent a phase in the theory of minimum paths, now well known. I was then unaware of the connection, as that subject, which comes to the fore with Ford and Fulkerson (1962), had hardly begun. The material is now absorbed into the chapter on minimum paths in Part V, and the aspect to do specifically with median solutions is in this chapter.

The passage from the determinacy theorem to the formula of this chapter was not immediate. On returning to the formula and its theory in order to give this account, though it is dealt with more briefly with secondary aspects put aside, features that were not well developed in the earlier accounts have been elaborated. A stage was represented by three connected reports (Afriat, 1961e), of which one is expository, and was reproduced in the volume in honour of Oskar Morgenstern (Afriat, 1967b), who had sponsored the work. The report on 'Gradient configurations and quadratic functions' (Afriat, 1961c) gives an account of the special questions that arise concerning quadratics, and in this chapter that material has been simplified and condensed. The formula remained as left in 1961, and there has not been a trace of attention to it. This is unlike the background theory of multiplier-level solutions, utility construction and the cost of living problem, which finding the formula provoked and which has had some rediscovery with other writers. Though it was considered eccentric to take time with the 'index number problem' in those days, now of course, with general inflation, it is quite popular, but the subject has an interest of its own.

4.1 MEDIAN MULTIPLIERS AND LEVELS

The characteristic of a quadratic is that its Hessian, or matrix of second derivatives, is constant. Let $\phi(x)$ be a quadratic with gradient $g(x)$ and Hessian h, so h is a constant symmetric matrix, and from Taylor's theorem,

$$\phi(y) - \phi(x) = g(x)(y - x) + (y - x)'h(y - x)/2. \qquad (\text{i})$$

Then

$$g(y) - g(x) = (y - x)'h, \qquad (\text{ii})$$

and so also

$$\phi(y) - \phi(x) = \{g(x) + g(y)\}(y - x)/2. \qquad (\text{iii})$$

From this,

$$g(x)(y - z) + g(y)(z - x) + g(z)(x - y) = 0, \qquad (\text{iv})$$

which can be seen to be equivalent to

$$\{g(x) - g(y)\}(z - w) = \{g(z) - g(w)\}(x - y), \qquad (\text{v})$$

which also follows from (ii) with the symmetry of h. The consequence

$$\{g(x) - g(z)\}(y - z) = \{g(y) - g(z)\}(x - z), \qquad (\text{vi})$$

holding for any fixed z all x, y is sufficient to assure again (v), and (vi), for any vector field $g(x)$. This condition or these equivalents will define the *symmetry* of a vector field. The property is necessary and sufficient for a vector field to be the gradient field of a quadratic.

We will consider vectors g_r associated with given points x_r satisfying conditions corresponding to (iv), (v) and (vi), which in such an application are again equivalent, and the possible quadratics that have these gradients at these points, or admit such a *gradient configuration*.

Should any demands (x_r, p_r) $(r = 0, 1, 2, \ldots)$, with expenditures M_r and budget vectors $u_r = M_r^{-1} p_r$, be compatible with a utility that is represented by a quadratic ϕ in a neighbourhood of the points x_r, we would have $g_r = \lambda_r u_r$ for some Lagrange multipliers $\lambda_r > 0$, where $g_r = g(x_r)$. Therefore, with the utility levels $\phi_r = \phi(x_r)$, we should have

$$\begin{aligned}
\phi_s - \phi_r &= (g_r + g_s)(x_s - x_r)/2 \\
&= \{ \lambda_r u_r (x_s - x_r) - \lambda_s u_s (x_r - x_s) \}/2 \\
&= (\lambda_r D_{rs} - \lambda_s D_{sr})/2,
\end{aligned}$$

where $D_{rs} = u_r x_s - 1$, since $u_r x_r = 1$.

Thus the multipliers and levels λ_r, ϕ_r must satisfy the *median equations*

$$\lambda_r > 0, \quad \phi_s - \phi_r = (\lambda_r D_{rs} - \lambda_s D_{sr})/2,$$

and so be a *median solution*. The *interval inequalities*

$$\lambda_r D_{rs} + \lambda_s D_{sr} \geq 0$$

are then equivalent to

$$\lambda_r D_{rs} \geq \phi_s - \phi_r,$$

and so make a median solution also an ordinary multiplier-level solution for the demands, the existence of which is equivalent to their consistency. Thus *the solvability of the median equations together with the interval inequalities implies the consistency of the demands*.

With any median solution λ_r, ϕ_r and with $g_r = \lambda_r u_r$, we have

$$\phi_s - \phi_r = (g_r + g_s)(x_s - x_r)/2,$$

corresponding to (iii), which has the consequence (v), so we have

$$(g_r - g_0)(x_s - x_0) = (g_s - g_0)(x_r - x_0);$$

that is,

$$g_r(x_s - x_0) - g_s(x_r - x_0) = g_0(x_s - x_r).$$

Equivalently,

$$\lambda_r(D_{rs} - D_{r0}) - \lambda_s(D_{sr} - D_{s0}) = \lambda_0(D_{0s} - D_{0r}).$$

It can be seen now that any four demands $r = 0, 1, 2, 3$ have a median solution which is unique but for an arbitrary positive multiplier, provided that

$$(D_{12} - D_{10})(D_{23} - D_{20})(D_{31} - D_{30}) \neq (D_{21} - D_{20})(D_{32} - D_{30})(D_{13} - D_{10}).$$

For with arbitrary $\lambda_0 > 0$, here are three equations for λ_r $(r = 1, 2, 3)$ which have a unique solution subject to this condition. Then, with the λ_r so obtained and $g_r = \lambda_r u_r$, and with arbitrary ϕ_0, and

$$\phi_r = \phi_0 + (g_0 + g_r)(x_r - x_0) \quad (r = 1, 2, 3),$$

the λ_r, ϕ_r $(r = 0, 1, 2, 3)$ provide a median solution for the four demands. Then the matrices

$$G_0 = [g_r - g_0], \quad X_0 = [x_r - x_0]$$

with $g_r - g_0$ as rows and $x_r - x_0$ as columns, for $r \neq 0$, are such that the 3×3 matrix $G_0 X_0$ which is their product is symmetric.

The intervals inequalities require $\lambda_r > 0$, so that $g_r \geq 0$, and

$$0 \leq g_r(x_s - x_r) + g_s(x_r - x_s)$$
$$= -(g_r - g_s)(x_r - x_s),$$

and so $(g_r - g_s)(x_r - x_s) \leq 0$, in particular $(g_r - g_0)(x_r - x_0) \leq 0$, so making the diagonal elements of $G_0 X_0$ all non-positive. A further case, associated with a concave function, which will be dealt with further, is where $G_0 X_0$ is non-positive definite.

4.2 CENTRE LOCUS

A *centre* of a quadratic is any point c where the gradient vanished; that is, $g(c) = 0$. Then by 4.1(ii), $g(x) = (x - c)'h$ for all x. Then c' is another if and only if $(c - c')h = 0$; that is, $c - c'$ belongs to the null space N of the Hessian h. Thus for a central quadratic the *centre locus* is a linear manifold parallel to N. A *central quadratic* is one for which a centre exists. Any homogeneous quadratic is an example since it has the origin as a centre, and in this case the centre locus is identical with the null space N of the Hessian.

In the case of a *regular quadratic* for which the Hessian is a regular matrix with inverse k we have, again from 4.1(ii),

$$x - kg(x)' = y - kg(y)' \quad \text{for all } x, y$$

so we have a point c such that

$$x - kg(x)' = c \quad \text{for all } x.$$

This point is such that $g(x) = (x - c)'h$ and so $g(c) = 0$; so it is a centre, and moreover a unique centre, since with h regular $c - c' \in N \Rightarrow c = c'$. Thus, any regular quadratic has a unique point as centre. Also, for a central quadratic the centre is unique if and only if the quadratic is regular, that is, has a regular Hessian.

For a quadratic with centre c we now have, corresponding to similar properties in the last section,

$$\phi(x) = \phi(c) + (x - c)'h(x - c) \tag{i}$$

$$g(x) = (x - c)'h \tag{ii}$$

$$\phi(x) = g(x)(x - c)/2 \tag{iii}$$

$$g(x)y - g(y)x = \{ g(x) - g(y) \} c \qquad \text{(iv)}$$

and

$$\{ g(x) - g(z) \} z - g(z)(x - z) = \{ g(x) - g(z) \} c. \qquad \text{(v)}$$

Because h is symmetric, its range R is the orthogonal complement of its null space N. It appears from 4.1(ii) that the *gradient locus* is a linear manifold parallel to R. In the case of a central quadratic this is identical with R, as seen from (ii) here.

There are complications with singular quadratics not present with regular ones. As seen already, while a regular quadratic always has a centre, in fact just one, a singular quadratic might or might not. We call a singular quadratic that does have a centre a *cylindrical quadratic*, with sections parallel to R and generators parallel to N.

Any displacement by a vector in N leaves the gradient unchanged. Resolving the gradient orthogonally into a component in R and a component in N, if there is one, the value is changed in such a displacement only by the component in N. In the case of a cylindrical quadratic, there is no component in N, and so again the value is unchanged. In that case the quadratic has identical values, and gradients, in every linear manifold parallel to R, at points which correspond by displacements parallel to N. Considered as a function in any sectional manifold, parallel to R, and taking any origin and Cartesian coordinates, its values are given by a regular quadratic in the coordinates. Thus a cylindrical quadratic becomes represented by an identical regular quadratic in every sectional manifold.

For a singular quadratic which is not cylindrical, the gradient locus is a linear manifold G which is a parallel displacement of R not identical with R and so not through the origin. If $\bar{g}$ is the foot of the perpendicular from the origin on to G, so necessarily $\bar{g}$ belongs to N; for any g in G, we have that $g - \bar{g}$ is both in R and perpendicular to $\bar{g}$, and G is described by all points of the form $\bar{g} + r$ where $r \in R$. The locus of points $\bar{x}$ where $g(\bar{x}) = \bar{g}$ is a linear manifold N which is a parallel displacement of N, the *parabolic axis* of the quadratic, cutting every sectional manifold in a unique point where the gradient is $\bar{g}$.

Consider again vectors g_r associated with points x_r. If any quadratic with centre c has these gradients at these points, then, by (iv),

$$g_r x_s - g_s x_r = (g_r - g_s)c.$$

These are the *centre equations* for the gradient configuration (g_r, x_r), and the *centre manifold* is the linear manifold of points c which are solutions. If any solution exists, then necessarily

$$g_r x_s - g_s x_r + g_s x_t - g_t x_s + g_t x_r - g_r x_t = 0,$$

corresponding to 4.1(iv); and, equivalently, corresponding to 4.1(vi), the matrix $G_0 X_0$ introduced at the end of section 4.1 is symmetric, this being the general gradient symmetry condition, equivalent to

$$G_0 x_r - (g_r X_0)' = G_0 x_0 - (g_0 X_0)'.$$

For an equivalent statement of the centre equations, subject to this symmetry, we have

$$G_0 x_0 - (g_0 X_0)' = G_0 c.$$

The centre equations have a solution $c = 0$ if and only if $g_r x_s = g_s x_r$, which is the homogeneous gradient symmetry condition; equivalently, $G_0 x_0 = (g_0 X_0)'$.

For any quadratic that admits the gradient configuration H with elements (x_r, g_r) its gradient at any point $x_\alpha = x_0 + X_0 \alpha$ on the linear manifold through the x_r, or *base manifold*, must be given by the point $g_\alpha = g_0 + \alpha' G_0$ on the linear manifold through the g_r, or *gradient manifold* of the configuration. But the gradient at any point is unique, and so, for consistency with admission of H by some quadratic, we must have

$$x_\alpha = x_\beta \quad \Rightarrow \quad g_\alpha = g_\beta$$

for all vectors α, β and, equivalently,

$$X_0 \alpha = 0 \quad \Rightarrow \quad \alpha' G_0 = 0$$

for all vectors α.

Should we have $g_\alpha = 0$ for some α, every quadratic that admits H has $c = x_\alpha$ as a centre, and so is a central quadratic.

In any case, subject to the symmetry of $G_0 X_0$, at any point x_α which is a solution of the centre equations, and so in the intersection of the centre and base manifolds, the gradient g_α is such that $g_\alpha X_0 = 0$, and so if not null is perpendicular to the base manifold. For such a solution requires $-(g_0 X_0)' = G_0 X_0 \alpha$, which, with the symmetry of $G_0 X_0$, is equivalent to $g_\alpha X_0 = 0$.

For a *regular gradient configuration* H, $G_0 X_0$ is a regular symmetric matrix. In this case there is a unique point $\bar{c} = x_\alpha$ where the centre manifold cuts the base manifold. As just seen, the gradient $\bar{g} = g_\alpha$ at this point, if not null, is perpendicular to the base manifold. Thus, with the regularity, for a solution x_α to the centre equations, we must have

$$\alpha = -(G_0 X_0)^{-1} X_0' g_0';$$

and therefore

$$\bar{c} = x_0 - X_0 (G_0 X_0)^{-1} X_0' g_0'$$

and

$$\bar{g} = g_0 - g_0 X_0 (G_0 X_0)^{-1} G_0 = g_0 (1 - e),$$

where

$$e = X_0 (G_0 X_0)^{-1} G_0$$

is idempotent, and therefore the projector on to its range parallel to its null space, these being the range of G_0 and the null space of X_0. Then $1 - e$ is the complementary projector, on to the null space, or the orthogonal complement of the range, of X_0, parallel to the range of G_0, and we have $\bar{g}$ as the image of g_0 by this.

For any quadratic that admits the gradient configuration H and has a point c as its centre, at any point x_α of the base manifold, where the gradient is g_α, the value must, by (iii), be given by

$$\phi_\alpha = C + g_\alpha(x_\alpha - c)/2,$$

where $C = \phi(c)$ is the value at the centre.

4.3   LINEAR PURCHASING POWER

Consider a regular quadratic ϕ. It must have a unique centre c and so have the form

$$\phi(x) = C + (x - c)'h(x - c)/2,$$

where h is the Hessian, symmetric and regular, and $C = \phi(c)$. The gradient is $g(x) = (x - c)'h$.

For the compatibility of a normalized demand (x, u), for which $ux = 1$, with a utility represented near x by ϕ it is necessary that $g(x) = \lambda u$ for some $\lambda > 0$; that is,

$$(x - c)'h = \lambda u,$$

and so if k is the inverse of h, also symmetric, we have

$$x - c = ku'\lambda.$$

From $ux = 1$, therefore,

$$1 - uc = uku'\lambda,$$

and so

$$x - c = ku'(1 - uc)/uku'.$$

Hence with $u = M^{-1}p$ we have

$$x - c = kp'(M - pc)/pkp',$$

which shows that the locus of demand x as income M varies while prices p remain fixed is a line through c, with direction kp'. Thus the expansion loci determined by a regular quadratic utility are all lines going through its centre.

The utility attained by an income M when the prices are p is

$$C + (M - pc)^2/2pkp',$$

that is, $\psi(M^{-1}p)$, where

$$\psi(u) = C + (1 - uc)^2/2uku'$$

is the indirect utility function obtained from ϕ.

If it is given that the quadratic is compatible with some four demands $(x_r, p_r)(r = 0, 1, 2, 3)$, with expenditures $M_r = p_r x_r$ and budget vectors $u_r = M_r^{-1}p_r$, then, as shown in section 4.1 and subject to the stated regularity, the Lagrange multipliers λ_r corresponding to the normalized demands (x_r, u_r) are fully determined, but for an arbitrary multiplier of no importance, and then so are the ϕ_r, but for an additive constant which is fixed by assigning ϕ_0 arbitrarily.

The quadratic then admits the gradient configuration (x_r, g_r) where $g_r = \lambda_r u_r$, and so its centre c must satisfy the centre equations

$$g_r x_s - g_s x_r = (g_r - g_s)c.$$

The compatibility of the quadratic with the given demands has further implications about the location of the centre, and so also about its value C at the centre consistent with the value given arbitrarily to ϕ_0. Here two cases become distinguished, as will be dealt with further. Also we have

$$1 - u_r c = u_r k u_r' \lambda_r.$$

Any incomes E_r, E_s that have the same purchasing power at the prices p_r, p_s as decided by the utility ϕ must be such that

$$\psi(E_r^{-1} p_r) = \psi(E_s^{-1} p_s);$$

equivalently,

$$(E_r - p_r c)^2 / p_r k p_r' = (E_s - p_s c)^2 / p_s k p_s'.$$

Now since

$$u_r = M_r^{-1} p_r, \quad g_r = \lambda_r u_r, \quad u_r k u_r' = (1 - u_r c)/\lambda_r,$$

this is equivalent to

$$(\lambda_r E_r / M_r - g_r c)^2 / g_r (x_r - c) = (\lambda_s E_s / M_s - g_s c)^2 / g_s (x_s - c).$$

But with $C = \phi(c)$ and $\phi_r = \phi(x_r)$,

$$\phi_r - C = g_r(x_r - c), \quad \lambda_r = g_r x_r,$$

and so with $\Delta_r = E_r / M_r - 1$ this is equivalent to

$$\{\lambda_r \Delta_r + 2(\phi_r - C)\}^2 / (\phi_r - C) = \{\lambda_s \Delta_s + 2(\phi_s - C)\}^2 / (\phi_s - C).$$

These relations holding for all r and s imply one or other of two possible cases:

(1) $C > \phi_r$ for all r (elliptical case),
(2) $C < \phi_r$ for all r (hyperbolic case).

The reason these are distinguished as elliptical and hyperbolic is given more fully in the next section. In case (1) take

(1') $\theta_r = -(C - \phi_r)^{1/2},$

and in case (2) take

(2') $\theta_r = (\phi_r - C)^{1/2}.$

The reason for this procedure will be seen below. In either case the purchasing power relation comes into the form

$$(\lambda_r \Delta_r / \theta_r - \lambda_s \Delta_s / \theta_s) / 2 = \theta_r - \theta_s.$$

For any value of the undetermined parameter C that provides one or other of the two cases, here is a proper increasing linear relation between Δ_r and Δ_s and so between equivalent incomes E_r and E_s at prices p_r and p_s, for all $r, s = 0, 1, 2, 4$. For any permitted value of C they are a consistent system of relations for all four periods, so that determining E_s from any E_r and then E_t from E_s gives the same result as determining E_t directly from E_r.

Let Δ_{rs} be the value of Δ_r obtained by taking $E_s = M_s$; that is, $\Delta_s = 0$, so

$$\lambda_r \Delta_{rs} / 2 = \theta_r{}^2 - \theta_r \theta_s.$$

Then we have

$$(\lambda_r \Delta_{rs} - \lambda_s \Delta_{sr}) / 2 = \phi_s - \phi_r,$$

in the elliptical case, which should be compared with the median equations

$$(\lambda_r D_{rs} - \lambda_s D_{sr}) / 2 = \phi_s - \phi_r,$$

used initially to determine the λ_r and ϕ_r from the D_{rs}. Were the Δ_{rs} now given instead of the D_{rs}, the same λ_r and ϕ_r could be recovered from them in the same way. We also have

$$(\lambda_r D_{rs} + \lambda_s D_{sr}) / 2 = \theta_s^2 + \theta_r^2 - 2\theta_r \theta_s,$$
$$= (\theta_r - \theta_s)^2,$$

and so, corresponding to the interval inequalities, also

$$\lambda_r D_{rs} + \lambda_s D_{sr} \geq 0,$$

and consequently now, going further still with the parallel between the original D_{rs} and the determined Δ_{rs},

$$\lambda_r \Delta_{rs} \geq \phi_s - \phi_r,$$

which are the multiplier-level inequalities with the Δ_{rs} in place of the D_{rs}. The interval inequalities are required in the hyperbolic case also, as will be found in section 4.5.

4.4   CRITICAL LOCATIONS

For a regular quadratic utility ϕ representing utility in some convex neighbourhood of the points x_r, the expansion loci are all lines concurrent in the quadratic's unique centre c. Gradients are positive, and in describing these lines in the direction of increasing income, and so of increasing utility, they all point either towards the centre or away from it. With C as the value at the centre, in the one case $\phi_r < C$ for all r and in the other $\phi_r > C$ for all r. These cases have already been designated as elliptical and hyperbolic.

The first-order Lagrangean conditions required by compatibility of the hypothetical utility with the given demands have been the basis for developments so far. But the second-order conditions have implications also, from requiring the quadratic to be quasi-concave near the points x_r. In the first case $(x - c)'h(x - c)$ is negative and quasi-concave in a neighbourhood, and this can be so if and only if h is non-positive definite, which with h regular is equivalent to its being negative definite. In the other case this function is positive and quasi-concave in a neighbourhood. By the same argument used in Chapter III.3 for the homogeneous case, but with the quadratic centre taken as origin, the condition for this is that

$$g(x)(x - c)g(y)(y - c) \le g(x)(y - c)g(y)(x - c)$$

for all x, y in the neighbourhood, and necessarily in this case h is an indefinite matrix, with a quadratic form taking both positive and negative values.

In the first case the utility surfaces are ellipsoids and in this they are hyperboloids, so here is the sense of the terminology for distinguishing the cases. In the homogeneous case dealt with earlier in connection with Fisher's index, and Byushgens's theorem about it, the elliptical case cannot arise and so only the hyperbolic case had to be dealt with, but now both must be investigated.

With the median equations for determining the multipliers and levels associated with quadratics, after the λ_r have been determined, the ϕ_r become fully determined after one of them has been assigned a value arbitrarily. Then the centre equations limit the possible locations of the hypothetical quadratic to a linear manifold. These further second-order considerations now put a further restriction on the possible locations of the centre, with the effect of putting a condition on the possible value C of the quadratic at its centre c consistent with its having the values ϕ_r at the points x_r. The implications are different in the two distinguished cases, which will be dealt with separately.

The parabolic case is where the centre is at infinity and so the expansion lines, having this as a common point, are parallel. This is a common limiting form for both the elliptical and hyperbolic cases, but with no need for a complete coincidence in the limit since the limiting expansion directions could be different in either case. In the one case where C has the ϕ_r as lower bounds it is approached when $C \to \infty$, and in the other case, where the ϕ_r are upper bounds, when $C \to -\infty$.

The purchasing power relation obtained in the last section contains C as an undetermined parameter, and becomes fully determined when C is assigned a value consistent with one case or the other. The object now is to find the legitimate values of C in the two distinguished cases. In the elliptical case we will find a lower limit $\bar{C}$ for C, greater than the lower bounds ϕ_r that it has already, and all $C > \bar{C}$ are admitted, so it is possible to make C arbitrarily large. We will evaluate the purchasing power relation in the limit as $C \to \infty$, and find a certain monotonicity characteristic for the approach. The hyperbolic case will have a similar treatment.

The following is involved in the evaluation of limits:

LEMMA For any numbers a, b and all $C > a, b$, the function

$$F(C) = C - \{(C - a)(C - b)\}^{1/2}$$

has derivative $F'(C) < 0$ and so is monotonic decreasing if $a \neq b$, and in any case

$$F(C) \to (a + b)/2 \, (C \to \infty).$$

The derivative is

$$F'(C) = 1 - \{(C - a)(C - b)\}^{-1/2} \{(C - a) + (C - b)\}/2$$
$$= [\{C - a)(C - b)\}^{1/2} - (1/2)\{(C - a) + (C - b)\}]/\{(C - a)(C - b)\}.$$

The numerator is the defect of the arithmetic mean of two positive numbers from their geometric mean. But this is always nonpositive, and is zero if and only if the two numbers are equal, by the Theorem of the Mean.

The last part follows from the expression

$$F(C) = (a + b - ab/C)/(1 + \{(1 - a/C)(1 - b/C)\}^{1/2}.$$

COROLLARY If $C < a, b$ and
$$F(C) = -C - \{(a - C)(a - C)\}^{1/2}$$
then
$$F(C) > 0 \text{ if } a \neq b,$$
and in any case
$$F(C) \to -(a + b)/2 (C \to -\infty).$$

4.5 ELLIPTICAL CASE

Any quadratic ϕ that admits the *gradient configuration* with elements (x_r, g_r), so that $g(x_r) = g_r$, must have gradient g_α at a point x_α of the base manifold, where

$$x_\alpha = x_0 + X_0\alpha, \quad g_\alpha = g_0 + \alpha'G_0,$$

and the matrices X_0 and G_0, with columns $x_r - x_0$ and rows $g_r - g_0$ $(r \neq 0)$, are such that their product $G_0 X_0$ is symmetric.

If ϕ has centre c, this must lie on the centre manifold of the gradient configuration and so be such that

$$G_0 x_0 - (g_0 X_0)' = G_0 c.$$

With the values ϕ_r determined from the median solution, with ϕ_0 assigned arbitrarily, we have a *function skeleton* with elements (x_r, g_r, ϕ_r). For any quadratic ϕ which admits this skeleton, so that $g(x_r) = g_r$ and $\phi(x_r) = \phi_r$, if $C = \phi(c)$ is the value at its centre c, the value ϕ_α at any point x_α of the base manifold is given by

$$\begin{aligned}
2(\phi_\alpha - C) &= g_\alpha(x_\alpha - c) \\
&= (g_0 + \alpha'G_0)(x_0 + X_0\alpha - c) \\
&= g_0(x_0 - c) + \alpha'(G_0 x_0 - G_0 c)' + g_0 X_0\alpha + \alpha'G_0 X_0\alpha \\
&= 2(\phi_0 - C) + 2g_0 X_0\alpha + \alpha'G_0 X_0\alpha.
\end{aligned}$$

Therefore

$$\phi_\alpha = \phi_0 + g_0 X_0\alpha + \alpha'G_0 X_0\alpha/2.$$

Provided $G_0 X_0$ is regular, and with

$$H_0 = G_0'(G_0 X_0)^{-1} G_0,$$

one particular quadratic that extends the function so determined on the base manifold to the entire commodity space is

$$\phi(x) = \phi_0 + g_0(x - x_0) + (x - x_0)' H_0(x - x_0)/2.$$

It has gradient $g(x) = g_0 + (x - x_0)' H_0$ with the value $g(\bar{c}) = \bar{g}$.

By taking any point c of the centre manifold which is not in the base manifold, and any value C, and adjoining the element $(c, 0, C)$ to the function skeleton and repeating this construction, we have another extension which has the point c as centre, and where the function value is C.

The case where a central quadratic ϕ admitted by the skeleton is concave, and so a maximum at its centre, requires $\phi_\alpha < C$ for all α, and so the matrix

$$H = \begin{pmatrix} 2(\phi_0 - C) & g_0 X_0 \\ (g_0 X_0)' & G_0 X_0 \end{pmatrix}$$

must be negative definite. For this, a necessary and sufficient condition is that $G_0 X_0$ be negative definite, and so regular, and

$$|H| / |G_0 X_0| < 0.$$

But

$$|H| = |G_0 X_0| \{ 2(\phi_0 - C) - g_0 X_0(G_0 X_0)^{-1} X_0' g_0' \}.$$

Therefore this condition is that $G_0 X_0$ be negative definite and $C > \bar{C}$ where

$$\bar{C} = \phi_0 + g_0 X_0(G_0 X_0)^{-1} X_0' g_0' / 2.$$

But with

$$\bar{c} = x_0 - X_0(G_0 X_0)^{-1} X_0' g_0'$$

we have

$$\bar{C} = \phi_0 - g_0(x_0 - \bar{c})/2$$
$$= C + g_0(x_0 - c)/2 - g_0(x_0 - \bar{c})/2$$
$$= C + g_0(\bar{c} - c)/2,$$

so that

$$\bar{C} - C = g_0(\bar{c} - c)/2.$$

Thus $C > \bar{C}$ is equivalent to $g_0 c > g_0 \bar{c}$.

Since $\bar{c}$ in any case lies on the centre manifold and c is required to also it follows that $G_0(c - \bar{c}) = 0$. Therefore with

$$\bar{g} = g_0 \{ 1 - X_0(G_0 X_0)^{-1} G_0 \},$$

we have $(\bar{g} - g_0)(c - \bar{c}) = 0$, and so the condition is also equivalent to $\bar{g} c > \bar{g} \bar{c}$.

Given that $G_0 X_0$ is negative definite, so is its inverse, and so from the formula for $\bar{C}$ it appears that $\bar{C} > \phi_0$. Since the original order of the given demands is arbitrary, ϕ_0 could just as well be ϕ_r; from this also, $\overline{C} > \phi_r$ for all r. Thus $\overline{C}$ is an improvement on the ϕ_r as lower bounds of C admissible in the elliptical case, and it is moreover the best lower bound or lower limit.

4.6   HYPERBOLIC CASE

Now we will deal similarly with the hyperbolic case. For a function ϕ to be concave at a point x, the gradient $g(x)$ must be a support gradient there; that is,

$$\phi(y) - \phi(x) \leq g(x)(y - x) \quad \text{for all } y.$$

This implies it is also a quasi-support there; that is,

$$g(x)y \leq g(x)x \Rightarrow \phi(y) \leq \phi(x) \quad \text{for all } y,$$

and this is the condition for ϕ to be quasi-concave at x. If ϕ is a homogeneous quadratic, so that $\phi(x) = g(x)x/2$, this condition in a region where the function is positive is equivalent to

$$g(x)xg(y)y \leq g(x)yg(y)x$$

for all x and y in the region. If ϕ is a quadratic with centre c, so that $\phi(x) = g(x)(x - c)$, the corresponding condition is that

$$g(x)(x - c)g(y)(y - c) \leq g(x)(y - c)g(y)(x - c).$$

For a compatible quadratic in the hyperbolic case, this condition is required for all points in the convex closure of the demand points x_r, in particular for these points themselves; that is,

$$g(x_r)(x_r - c)g(x_s)(x_s - c) \leq g(x_r)(x_s - c)g(x_s)(x_r - c).$$

This last condition is necessary but not sufficient. On the basis of it we can seek conditions on C for the hyperbolic case, but possibly not all those that are required.

We have $g_r(x_s - c) = g_s(x_r - c)$ and also

$$\begin{aligned}
g_r(x_s - c) &= g_r(x_s - x_r) + g_r(x_r - c) \\
&= \lambda_r u_r(x_s - x_r) + 2(\phi_r - C) \\
&= \lambda_r D_{rs} + 2(\phi_r - C),
\end{aligned}$$

and so the condition is equivalent to

$$\{\lambda_r D_{rs} + 2(\phi_r - C)\}^2 \geq 4(\phi_r - C)(\phi_s - C).$$

From the median equations,

$$\lambda_r D_{rs} + \phi_r - \phi_s = (\lambda_r D_{rs} + \lambda_s D_{sr})/2 = \lambda_s D_{sr} + \phi_r - \phi_s;$$

and with this, and

$$I_{rs} = (\lambda_r D_{rs} + \lambda_s D_{sr})/2,$$

so that $I_{rs} = I_{sr}$, and the interval inequalities are stated $I_{rs} \geq 0$, the condition becomes

$$(C - \phi_r)I_{rs} \leq (I_{rs} + \phi_s - \phi_r)/4.$$

If $I_{rs} = 0$ for all r, s, the conditions are satisfied for all C. If $I_{rs} < 0$ for any r, s, the condition implies $C > \phi_r$, contradicting $C < \phi_r$ required for the hyperbolic case. Otherwise the conditions add nothing to the requirement $C < \phi_r$ that we have already.

In this last case, multiplier-level inequalities

$$\lambda_r D_{rs} \geq \phi_s - \phi_r$$

hold, since the median equations make them equivalent to the interval inequalities

$$\lambda_r D_{rs} + \lambda_s D_{sr} \geq 0;$$

that is, $I_{rs} \geq 0$. This case requires these to hold for all r, s and to hold strictly for some r, s.

It has appeared that for admission of a compatible quadratic in any case, elliptical or hyperbolic, it is necesssary that the median multipliers be determined all positive and that the interval inequalities be satisfied, and so consequently the multiplier-level inequalities also.

Given this, for the elliptical case to be admitted it is necessary and sufficient that the matrix $G_0 X_0$ be non-positive definite. Then, for C to be the value at the centre of some compatible regular quadratic that admits the skeleton (x_r, g_r, ϕ_r), it is necessary and sufficient that $C > \bar{C}$.

The values of C so admitted for the elliptical case give determinations of the purchasing power relation, which carries C as a parameter. We will be able to find the limiting position of this linear relation as $C \to \infty$.

With all this, the analysis of the elliptical case is exhausted in a satisfactory way. The hyperbolic case has not yet been so yielding, and must be taken further.

The compatibility of a quadratic with centre c in the hyperbolic case requires the existence of a solution $t_r > 0$ of the inequalities

$$u_r(x_s - c)/u_r(x_r - c) \geq t_r/t_s \ (r, s = 0, 1, 2, 3).$$

With $g_r = \lambda_r u_r$, and also $g_r(x_s - c) = g_s(x_r - c)$ since c must be on the centre manifold, these are equivalent to

$$g_s(x_r - c)t_s \geq g_r(x_r - c)t_r,$$

and, since $g_s(x_r - x_s) = \lambda_s D_{sr}$, also to

$$\{\lambda_s D_{sr} + g_s(x_s - c)\} t_s \geq g_r(x_r - c)t_r,$$

and, since $g_r(x_r - c) = 2(\phi_r - C)$, also to

$$\{\lambda_s D_{sr} + 2(\phi_s - C)\} t_s \geq 2(\phi_r - C)t_r.$$

But for a median solution,

$$\lambda_s D_{sr} + 2\phi_s = \lambda_{rs} D_{rs} + 2\phi_r.$$

Here this is equivalent to

$$\lambda_r D_{rs}/2(\phi_r - C) + 1 \geq t_r/t_s.$$

With

$$K_{rs} = \lambda_r D_{rs} / 2 (\phi_r - C) + 1,$$

since $D_{rr} = 0$, necessary and sufficient conditions for the solvability of these inequalities are that

$$H_{ri} H_{ij} H_{jk} H_{kr} \geq 1 \, (r, i, j, k = 0, 1, 2, 3).$$

What these mean for C seems not immediately obvious. However, collecting terms on the left, and clearing denominators, the coefficient of C^4 is zero, and that of C^3 is a negative multiple of

$$\lambda_r D_{ri} + \ldots + \lambda_k D_{kr}.$$

But this is positive as a consequence of the median equations together with the strict interval inequalities. It follows that there exists some C^* such that these conditions are satisfied for all $C < C^*$.

4.7 PARABOLIC LIMITS

For determining the income E_r in period r that has the same purchasing power as any income E_s in period s, the purchasing power relation found in section 4.3 gives

$$\lambda_r \Delta_r = \lambda_s \Delta_s \theta_r / \theta_s + 2 (\theta_r^2 - \theta_r \theta_s),$$

where $\Delta_r = E_r / M_r - 1$. There is one such relation for every admissible value of C

A proviso for any admissibility at all is that the median multipliers λ_r, say when λ_0 is arbitrarily assigned the positive value 1, all be determined positive and satify the interval inequalities $\lambda_r D_{rs} + \lambda_s D_{sr} > 0$. The matrix $G_0 X_0$ constructed from the median multipliers, necessarily symmetric, then has negative diagonal elements. This so far is the test for *quadratic consistency* of the given four demands, or for the existence of a compatible utility representable near the demand points x_r by a quadratic.

With that granted, two cases are distinguished. One, the elliptical case, requires an additional test for admissibility, which is that the matrix $G_0 X_0$ be negative definite. That being granted, the critical central value C is necessarily such that $\overline{C} > \phi_r$ for all r. Then any value $C > \overline{C}$ is admissible and determines $\theta_r = - (C - \phi_r)^{1/2}$ and therefore the associated purchasing power relation.

The remaining hyperbolic case requires no additional test. There is some $C^* \leq \min \phi_r$ such that any $C < C^*$ is admissible, and in this case we take $\underline{\theta}_r = (\phi_r - C)^{1/2}$. Though we do not have an explicit formula for C^* as for $\overline{C}$, we know it exists and how to calculate it.

Thus, subject to quadratic consistency, we have the hyperbolic range $[-\infty, C^*]$ for C and, subject to $G_0 X_0$ being negative definite, also the elliptical range $[\overline{C}, \infty]$. Corresponding to any C so admitted, we have a consistent relation connecting equivalent incomes E_r in the four periods.

The limiting parabolic case is where the centre is at infinity, making the expansion lines all parallel, since they pass through the centre. We can evaluate the limiting purchasing power relations for both elliptical and parabolic cases as limits when $C \rightarrow +/-\infty$.

The factor θ_r / θ_s approaches the limit 1 monotonically as $C \rightarrow +/-\infty$. For the term $\theta_r^2 - \theta_r \theta_s$ we have limits $+/- (\phi_s - \phi_r) / 2$ approached monotonically from above as $C \rightarrow +/-\infty$. In each case $+$ is for the elliptical case and $-$ for the hyperbolic. Thus we have the limiting relations

$$\lambda_r \Delta_r +/- \phi_r = \lambda_s \Delta_s +/- \phi_s.$$

With $c(p, x)$ as the utility cost function for any compatible utility, while $M_{rs} = p_r x_s$ is simply the cost of the bundle x_s of period s at the prices of period r, $E_{rs} = c(p_r, x_s)$ is the cost at those prices of the utility of x_s, or the cost at the prices of period r of living at the standard of period s. Compatibility of the utility with the demand (x_r, p_r) requires the coincidence $M_{rr} = E_{rr}$. While the coefficient $D_{rs} = M_{rs} / M_{rr} - 1$ compares bundle costs, $\Delta_{rs} = E_{rs} / E_{rr} - 1$ compares utility costs. Since $M_r = M_{rr} = E_{rr}$, these numbers are $D_{rs} = M_{rs} / M_r - 1$ and $\Delta_{rs} = E_{rs} / M_r - 1$, and because $C(p, x) \le px$ for all p and x we have $\Delta_{rs} \le D_{rs}$.

The income M_s spent at the prices p_s in period s purchased the cost of living represented by the bundle x_s, and so the income E_{rs} at the prices p_r should have the same purchasing power as the income M_s at the prices p_s. To determine E_{rs} with respect to compatible quadratic utilities we take $E_s = M_s$, that is $\Delta_s = 0$, in the purchasing power relation obtained and so determine the corresponding Δ_r, that is

$$\Delta_{rs} = 2(\theta_r^2 - \theta_r \theta_s) / \lambda_r,$$

and then take $E_{rs} = M_r(1 + \Delta_{rs})$.

There is one such value of Δ_{rs} for every permissible value of C, and for all $\Delta_{rs} \le D_{rs}$. For the elliptical case there is the value $\overline{\Delta}_{rs}$ corresponding to the critical value $\overline{C}$ of C. As C increase from $\overline{C}$ to ∞, Δ_{rs} decreases monotonically and approaches the limit $(\phi_s - \phi_r) / \lambda_r$. For the hyperbolic case where C decreases from its critical value C^* to $-\infty$, Δ_{rs} decreases from the corresponding value Δ^*_{rs} to the limit $-(\phi_s - \phi_r) / \lambda_r$.

4.8   DEMONSTRATION: FISHER'S DATA

```
1 DATA The Four-point Formula
2 '
9 '
10 GOSUB 1000:GOSUB 100:END
11 '
79 '____ rotate
80 SWAP I,J:SWAP J,K:RETURN
89 '____ count
90 Z=1+(Z MOD 3):RETURN
91 '
99 '_____ cycle coefficients
```

```
100 FOR I=1 TO 3:FOR J=1 TO 3:A(I,J)=D(I,J)-D(I,0)
110 NEXT J,I:I=1:J=2:K=3:U=1:V=1
120 FOR R=1 TO 3:B(I)=D(0,K)-D(0,J):U=U*A(J,K):V=V*A(K,J)
130 GOSUB 80:NEXT:W=UV
199 '___ multipliers
200 PRINT#1,CR$,"Multipliers";CR$:M(0)=1:PRINT#1,1,:FOR R=1 TO 3
210 M=B(I)*A(J,I)*A(K,I)+B(J)*A(K,J)*A(J,I)+B(K)*A(J,K)*A(K,I)
220 M=M/W:M(I)=M:PRINT#1,M,:GOSUB 80:NEXT:PRINT#1,
299 '___ levels
300 PRINT#1,CR$,"Levels";CR$:L(0)=0:PRINT#1,0,:FOR I=1 TO 3
310 L(I)=(M(0)*D(0,I)-M(I)*D(I,0))/2:PRINT#1,L(I),:NEXT
399 '___ gradients
400 FOR I=0 TO 3:FOR K=1 TO N:P(I,K)=M(I)*P(I,K):NEXT K,I
499 '___ relative
500 FOR I=1 TO 3:FOR K=1 TO N
510 X(I,K)=X(I,K)X(0,K):P(I,K)=P(I,K)-P(0,K):NEXT K,I
599 '___ critical matrix
600 PRINT#1,CR$;CR$,"Critical matrix";CR$:FOR I=1 TO 3:FOR J=1
TO 3
610 A=0:FOR K=1 TO N:A=A+X(I,K)*P(J,K):NEXT:A(I,J)=A
620 PRINT#1,A,:NEXT:PRINT#1,:NEXT
649 '___ determinant
650 I=1:J=2:K=3:E=1:D=0
660 FOR R=1 TO 3:D=D+E*A(1,I)*A(2,J)*A(3,K):GOSUB 80:NEXT
670 IF E=1 THEN E=1:I=2:J=1:GOTO 660
680 PRINT#1,CR$,"Determinant",D;CR$
699 '___ inverse
700 FOR I=1 TO 3:FOR U=1 TO 3
710 Z=I:GOSUB 90:J=Z:GOSUB 90:K=Z
720 Z=U:GOSUB 90:V=Z:GOSUB 90:W=Z
730 D(U,I)=(A(J,V)*A(K,W)-A(J,W)*A(K,V))/D:NEXT U,I
749 '___ critical value
750 FOR I=1 TO 3:B=0:FOR K=1 TO N
760 B=B+X(I,K)*P(0,K):NEXT:B(I)=B:NEXT
770 M=0:FOR I=1 TO 3:FOR J=1 TO 3
780 M=M+B(I)*D(I,J)*B(J):NEXT J,I:M=-M/2
790 PRINT#1,,"Critical value";M;CR$;CR$
798 '
799 '_____ utility-cost limits
800 PRINT#1,"Relative cross-costs: utility";CR$
809 '___ lower
810 PRINT#1,"Lower limits";CR$:FOR I=0 TO 3:FOR J=0 TO 3
820 A(I,J)=1+(L(J)-L(I))/M(I):PRINT#1,A(I,J),:NEXT:PRINT#1,:NEXT
849 '___ upper
850 PRINT#1,CR$"Upper limits";CR$:FOR I=0 TO 3
860 L(I)=SQR(2*(ML(I))):M(I)=-L(I)/M(I):NEXT
870 FOR I=0 TO 3:FOR J=0 TO 3:D(I,J)=1+M(I)*(L(J)-L(I))
880 PRINT#1,D(I,J),:NEXT:PRINT#1,:NEXT:PRINT#1,CR$:RETURN
998 '
999 '_____ initialize - read data
1000 DEFINT I,J,K,N:READ A$,B$,C$,N
1010 LF$=CHR$(10):FF$=CHR$(12):CR$=CHR$(13):ESC$=CHR$(27)
1020 DIM P(3,N),X(3,N),E(3,3),D(3,3),A(3,3),B(3),L(3),M(3)
1099 '
1100 PRINT FF$,A$;CR$:INPUT"screen, printer or disk (s/p/d)";O$
1110 IF O$="p" THEN O$="LPT1:" ELSE IF O$="d" THEN O$="A:FPF"
ELSE O$="SCRN:"
1120 CLS:OPEN O$ FOR OUTPUT AS #1
```

```
1199 '
1200 PRINT#1,A$;CR$;CR$;B$;CR$;C$;CR$
1210 PRINT#1,,"Periods";CR$:FOR I=0 TO 3:READ X$
1220 PRINT#1,I;" ";X$,:NEXT:PRINT#1,CR$
1299 '
1300 PRINT#1,"Price and Quantity Data - four
periods,";N;"commodities";CR$
1310 FOR I=0 TO 3:PRINT#1,,"Period";I;CR$
1320 FOR J=1 TO N:READ P(I,J):PRINT#1,P(I,J),:NEXT:PRINT#1,
1330 FOR J=1 TO N:READ X(I,J):PRINT#1,X(I,J),:NEXT:PRINT#1,
1340 PRINT#1,:NEXT:PRINT#1,
1399 '
1400 PRINT#1,,"Cross-costs: goods";CR$
1410 FOR I=0 TO 3:FOR J=0 TO 3:E=0:FOR K=1 TO N
1420 E=E+P(I,K)*X(J,K):NEXT:E(I,J)=E:PRINT#1,E,:NEXT:PRINT#1,:N-
EXT
1499 '
1500 PRINT#1,CR$,"Relative cross-costs: goods";CR$
1510 FOR I=0 TO 3:FOR J=0 TO 3:X=E(I,J)/E(I,I)
1520 D(I,J)=X1:PRINT#1,X,:NEXT:PRINT#1,:NEXT
1599 '
1600 FOR I=0 TO 3:FOR K=1 TO N:P(I,K)=P(I,K)/E(I,I):NEXT
K,I:RETURN
4998 '
4999 '_____ the data
5000 DATA Four kinds of fuel - 1913 & 1916-18
5010 DATA Irving Fisher - The Making of Index Numbers
5020 '
5030 DATA    4       :' N= number of commodities
5040 DATA    1913, 1916, 1917, 1918        :' 4 periods  0, 1, 2, 3
5090 '
5100 DATA       5.0636, 1.27,    3.03,    .1233    :' P0
5105 DATA       6.9,    477,     46.3,    10400    :' X0
5109 '
5110 DATA       5.2906, 2.07,    4.78,    .1217    :' P1
5115 DATA       6.75,   502,     54.5,    12640    :' X1
5119 '
5120 DATA       5.6218, 3.58,    10.66,   .1242    :' P2
5125 DATA       7.83,   552,     56.7,    14880    :' X2
5129 '
5130 DATA       6.5098, 2.4,     7,       .1695    :' P3
5135 DATA       7.69,   583,     55,      15680    :' X3
```

```
The Four-point Formula

Four kinds of fuel - 1913 & 1916-18
Irving Fisher - The Making of Index Numbers

              Periods

0 - 1913        1 - 1916        2 - 1917        3 - 1918

Price and Quantity Data - four periods, 4 commodities

              Period 0

5.0636          1.27            3.03            .1233
6.9             477             46.3            10400
```

Period 1

5.2906	2.07	4.78	.1217
6.75	502	54.5	12640

Period 2

5.6218	3.58	10.66	.1242
7.83	552	56.7	14880

Period 3

6.5098	2.4	7	.1695
7.69	583	55	15680

Cross-costs: goods

2063.338	2395.366	2747.193	2879.343
2510.889	2873.65	3265.987	3418.651
3531.689	3985.965	4472.697	4664.128
3276.618	3772.721	4294.832	4492.021

Relative cross-costs: goods

1	1.160918	1.331431	1.395478
.8737632	1	1.13653	1.189655
.7896106	.8911773	1	1.0428
.7294307	.8398718	.9561024	1

Multipliers

1	.149656	1.295474	1.164477

Levels

0	.1530234	.3019927	.3552749

Critical matrix

$-1.578923E-02$	$-2.934116E-02$	$-3.231207E-02$
$-2.934071E-02$	$-5.887733E-02$	$-6.747752E-02$
$-3.231173E-02$	$-6.747791E-02$	$-8.040662E-02$

Determinant $-1.093649E\ 07$

Critical value .9776764

Relative cross-costs: utility

Lower limits

1	1.153024	1.301993	1.355275
.8668962	1	1.129577	1.175924
.7668864	.8850079	1	1.04113
.694906	.8263155	.9542437	1

Upper limits

1	1.159531	1.329807	1.395215
.8725571	1	1.136026	1.188278
.7883566	.8907308	1	1.041974
.729205	.8385131	.9551831	1

III.5

Wald's 'New Formula'

A. Wald (1939) escaped from the then current insistence that the cost of living should be settled by a price index. When a utility function is given, it is possible to determine the relation between incomes that have the same purchasing power at different prices. Generally this could be any monotonic relation. Use of a price index requires it always to be a homogeneous linear relation, a line through the origin, for which the price index gives the slope.

With this price index assumption it is implicit that expansion paths are lines through the origin of the commodity space. Therefore when demands (x_r, p_r) $(r = 0, 1)$ to be associated with the utility are given as data, it is given that the ray L_r through x_r is the expansion path for the prices p_r. In effect we have expansion data (L_r, p_r) $(r = 0, 1)$ where L_r is the expansion path for the prices p_r given as a line through the origin. Wald instead took the given expansion paths L_r to be general lines in the commodity space. With that assumption, the price index expression of purchasing power is abandoned. Now the relation between incomes that have the same purchasing power must be a general linear relation, with an intercept as well as a slope, so two numbers are required to define it instead of just one. Wald observed that quadratic utility functions have linear expansion loci. He then showed that, with demand data in the form of a pair of linear expansions (L_r, p_r) $(r = 0, 1)$ and the hypothesis that these belong to some quadratic utility, the relation between incomes M_r that have the same purchasing power at the prices p_r, as decided by such a utility, is a fully determinate linear relation. His 'New Formula' is the procedure for arriving at that relation from the given data. He noted that, when the lines L_r happen both to go through the origin, this becomes a homogeneous linear relation, whose slope is given by Fisher's price index formula.

It is evident that Wald's theorem with its formula has a close relation to the theorem of S. S. Byushgens (1925) about Fisher's formula and homogeneous quadratic utility, which is the subject of Chapter III.3. It is possible to obtain Byushgens's theorem as a corollary of Wald's theorem, as Wald's note about the Fisher index, and the quadratic utility connection, immediately suggests. But also, it is possible to arrive at Wald's theorem as a corollary of Byushgens's theorem, and in doing that to produce an equivalent of Wald's formula which is very much simpler than the original, and also makes the connection with Fisher's formula completely transparent. For a proper generalization of these theorems and formulae, we have the Four-point Formula and its theory of the last chapter. The focus for Wald's formula is not generality, but the special form of its data.

A certain number D will be determined from the expansion data, the *discriminant*. Its sign and whether or not it is non-zero are central to issues about Wald's formula which will be dealt with. Certain points c_r are determined on the lines L_r, which are unique if the discriminant is non-zero. These are the *critical points* on the expansion lines, which are fundamental to our entire discussion. They give the formula a framework in which much more can be brought out about it.

We will be able to put Wald's formula in a new *marginal price index* framework, where price indices have non-homogeneous counterparts. Replacing commodity bundles in the formulae by *marginal bundles*, we have such counterparts for the Laspeyes, Paasche and Fisher indices. The 'Fisher marginal price index' so obtained is *identical* to that obtained from Wald's formula. Also, the Laspeyres and Paasche counterparts have a role as marginal price index limits, corresponding exactly to the role of the original formulae in the context of price indices. In the case where quantities and marginal quantities have the same ratios — which is the homogeneous case with the data, when the expansion lines are rays through the origin—the marginal price indices become simply price indices, given again by the usual formulae.

This marginal price index concept, beside being illuminating about the nature of price indices, also has a statistical workability. That is shown to some extent in *The Price Index* (Afriat, 1977b). There I used the usual expenditure data to calculate both average and marginal price indices, the average index coinciding, in principle, with the ordinary CPI. When the data confirm the homogeneous case, these would be identical. Otherwise, their comparison shows the departure from homogeneity, reflecting a possible *bias* inherent in the use of the average index.

5.1 LINEAR EXPANSIONS

The demand data are now given in the form of a pair of *linear expansions* (L_r, p_r) $(r = 0, 1)$, L_r being a line in the commodity space which is the locus of consumption when the prices are p_r, different points of the line corresponding to different levels of income.

If a_r and b_r are any two points determining the line L_r, then, since different points correspond to different incomes, necessarily $p_r a_r \neq p_r b_r$, and we can suppose $p_r a_r < p_r b_r$. Then $d_r = b_r - a_r$ is a displacement on the line specifying its direction, such that $p_r d_r > 0$. The line is now described by points $x_r = a_r + d_r t_r$, t_r being a parameter. The income associated with the point x_r is $M_r = p_r x_r$.

Because $p_r d_r \neq 0$, there is one point of the line, the *income origin*, for which the associated income is zero. Since a_r is an arbitrary point of the line, it can for simplicity be taken to be this point, so we have $p_r a_r = 0$.

The displacement d_r describes the *marginal consumption pattern* when the prices are p_r, or the incremental proportions in which demand is affected by a increment of income. With linear expansion this is fixed for all increments, at all levels of income. The increment of demand for any unit increment of income, when the prices are p_r, is $e_r = d_r(p_r d_r)^{-1}$. This is the *unit incremental bundle* for the prices p_r. It has the same direction, or pattern, as d_r and is moreover such that $p_r e_r = 1$. Every additional unit of income goes towards buying one of these bundles (I discuss the sense of this assumption in Chapter II.1. 2).

Any point of the line is now given by $x_r = a_r + e_r M_r$, where

$$p_r x_r = p_r a_r + p_r e_r M_r = 0 + 1 M_r = M_r,$$

since also $p_r a_r = 0$, so the parameter M_r of any point of L_r is identical with the income associated with it.

Wald offered the suggestion that the expansion loci associated with a quadratic utility are lines. Then, with demand data given in the form of a pair of linear expansion (L_r, p_r) ($r = 0, 1$), he supposed these to be associated with some quadratic utility. He then showed that the relation between incomes M_0, M_1 that have the same purchasing power at the prices p_0, p_1 on the basis of such utility is determinate, by obtaining a formula for it in terms of the given data.

This result is straightforward as it stands but, without knowing that the hypothesis is realizable, it is also possibly vacuous. Whether the expansion lines are admitted in their entirety as providing demand data, or only some parts of them, will be found to be critical for the more basic consistency question of whether there is *any* utility that is compatible with the data. Even when that is settled, in whatever fashion that provides the consistency needed in order to proceed at all, there is the further question about the existence of some such compatible utility that is moreover representable by a quadratic.

Characteristics of the expansion loci of quadratics are glossed over in the offer that they are lines. Generally any one is a part—if not a whole then half—of a linear manifold, then, moreover, truncated in the commodity space. The dimension is 1 in the case of a regular quadratic, for which the Hessian is regular, and otherwise is greater by the nullity of the Hessian. Therefore, if the expansion loci of the quadratic are to be contained in the lines L_r and not in manifolds of higher dimension containing these, the quadratic must be regular. But a regular quadratic has a unique point, its centre, where the gradient vanishes, and all its expansion lines must go through this. In that case the lines L_r must intersect, in a point c which is the centre of the regular quadratic to which they belong. If they do not intersect they cannot contain complete expansion loci of any quadratic utility. To save the theorem from vacuity the lines, if they are to represent expansion loci of some compatible quadratic, need to be cut and then enlarged. Should the loci that result lie outside the commodity space, the vacuity is then inescapable.

5.2 REVEALED PURCHASING POWER

The linear expansion (L_r, p_r) consists in the collection of demands (x_r, p_r) where $x_r \in L_r$. For any M_r there is just one for which $p_r x_r = M_r$, given by $x_r = a_r + e_r M_r$. Any restriction to a part of L_r is expressed by a restriction of M_r to some range.

Consistency of all the demands provided by the pair of linear expansions might be denied, so there might not exist any utility compatible with all of them. But consistency might be obtained when the ranges of the incomes M_r are suitably restricted. Now we can consider demands (x_r, p_r) with incomes M_r and relations between them that must be produced by any utility R that is compatible with them, or possibly with some range including them.

The purchasing power of the income M_r at the prices p_r is the utility of the bundle x_r that it buys at the prices. Then purchasing power relations between incomes on the basis of any compatible utility are concluded from any 'revealed preference' relation between the bundles they buy. Thus, from $p_r x_s \leq p_r x_r$ we have $x_r R x_s$, or the 'revealed preference' of x_r to x_s, and so M_r has at least the purchasing power of M_s at the respective prices. And from $p_r x_s < p_r x_r$ it is concluded that the purchasing power of M_r is strictly greater.

Since $p_r x_r = M_r$ and $x_r = a_r + e_r M_r$ where $p_r a_r = 0$ and $p_r e_r = 1$, the relation $_s\leq_r$ of *revealed relative purchasing power* at the prices of periods r and s, defined by

$$M_s \, _s\leq_r M_r \equiv p_r a_s + p_r e_s M_s \leq M_r,$$

reveals that income M_r at prices p_r has at least the purchasing power of M_s at prices p_s, and $_s<_r$ defined by

$$M_s \, _s<_r M_r \equiv p_r a_s + p_r e_s M_s < M_r$$

reveals that it is greater. For consistency, it is required that

$$M_r \, _r<_s M_s \Rightarrow \sim M_s \, _s\leq_r M_r,$$

this condition corresponding to Samuelson's revealed preference axiom.

We can also define the relation $_r=_s$ of *revealed purchasing power equivalence* by

$$M_r \, _r=_s M_s \equiv M_r \, _r\leq_s M_s \text{ and } M_s \, _s\leq_r M_r.$$

This signifies necessary equivalence with respect to every compatible utility. The relation $_r\sim_s$, defined by

$$M_r \, _r\sim_s M_s \equiv \sim M_r \, _r<_s M_s \text{ and } \sim M_s \, _s<_r M_r,$$

denies revealed inequivalence and so leaves open the possibility of equivalence with respect to some compatible utility. This relation establishes a many-many correspondence between points of L_r and L_s through the correspondence of their associated incomes. In general, a point of L_r corresponds to a segment of points of L_s, if it corresponds to any. Though now we have only a pair of linear expansions as data, and $r, s = 0$ or 1 only, the present concepts have

scope when there is any number, also without the restriction that they be linear.
    The requirement for revealed preference consistency is that inequalities

$$p_0 a_1 + p_0 e_1 M_1 \leq M_0, \quad p_1 a_0 + p_1 e_0 M_0 \leq M_1$$

imply the equalities. Should this be denied for any M_0 and M_1 then corresponding points on L_0 and L_1 cannot be simultaneously admitted as part of the data.
    For possibly equivalent incomes M_0 and M_1, we have

$$p_0 a_1 + p_0 e_1 M_1 \geq M_0, \quad p_1 a_0 + p_1 e_0 M_0 \geq M_1.$$

These inequalities produce a correspondence between M_0 and M_1 in which any value of one in general corresponds to an interval of values of the other, and, by assocition with points of L_0 and L_1, any point of one corresponds to a segment of the other.

5.3   THE CRITICAL POINTS

Now we consider the possibility of finding a pair of points c_0, c_1 on L_0, L_1 which are revealed indifferent, without bearing the restriction that these belong to the commodity space. We require

$$p_0 c_1 = p_0 c_0, \quad p_1 c_0 = p_1 c_1.$$

But, with $C_0 = p_0 c_0$ and $C_1 = p_1 c_1$, these equations are

$$p_0 a_1 + p_0 e_1 C_1 = C_0, \quad p_1 a_0 + p_1 e_0 C_0 = C_1,$$

which can be stated

$$\begin{pmatrix} 1 & -p_0 e_1 \\ -p_1 e_0 & 1 \end{pmatrix} \begin{pmatrix} C_0 \\ C_1 \end{pmatrix} = \begin{pmatrix} p_0 a_1 \\ p_1 a_0 \end{pmatrix}.$$

Hence, introducing

$$D = \begin{vmatrix} 1 & -p_0 e_{-1} \\ -p_1 e_0 & 1 \end{vmatrix} = 1 - p_0 e_1 p_1 e_0$$

as the *discriminant* for the given data, the condition $D \neq 0$ is necessary and sufficient for the existence and uniqueness of a solution C_0, C_1 to the equations. This condition defines the *regular case*, and the unique points c_0, c_1 so determined under it are the *critical points* on the expansion lines L_0, L_1. The *singular case* where $D = 0$ will be considered later.
    Subtracting the equations for the critical points from the inequalities determining incomes M_0, M_1 that are possibly equivalent in purchasing power, we obtain

$$p_0 e_1 (M_1 - C_1) \geq M_0 - C_0, \quad p_1 e_0 (M_0 - C_0) \geq M_1 - C_1.$$

Any compatible utility would determine a relation of purchasing power equivalence between M_0 and M_1 which gives a positive association between them, and which is a sub-relation of this. Consistency, which provides a compatible utility, therefore requires

$$p_0 e_1 > 0, \quad p_1 e_0 > 0.$$

With this given, the relation implies one or other of the two possibilities

$$M_0 \le C_0 \text{ and } M_1 \le C_1 \tag{i}$$
$$M_0 \ge C_0 \text{ and } M_1 \ge C_1. \tag{ii}$$

Another way of stating the relation between M_0 and M_1 so obtained is that

$$M_1 - C_1 = P_{10}(M_0 - C_0)$$

where in the first case

$$1/p_0 e_1 \ge P_{10} \ge p_1 e_0,$$

and in the second case

$$1/p_0 e_1 \le P_{10} \le p_1 e_0.$$

The existence of any M_0, M_1 different from C_0, C_1 having the relation obtaining in the first case therefore implies $1/p_0 e_1 > p_1 e_0$, that is, $D < 0$. Similarly $D > 0$ if they have the relation obtaining in the second case. It follows that only one of the two possible cases can occur, depending on the sign of the discriminant, the first or the second according to whether $D < 0$ or $D > 0$, respectively.

We distinguish *elliptical, parabolic* and *hyperbolic* cases by the possibilities $D < 0$, $D = 0$ and $D > 0$. Thus the regular case $D \ne 0$ just excludes the parabolic case, which will be dealt with later. The critical points, which exist and are unique in the regular case, cut the expansion lines each into two rays, going forwards to higher incomes and backwards to lower. It has appeared that points on the two lines which are possibly indifferent for some compatible utility always belong to the backward rays in the elliptical case and to forward rays in the hyperbolic case. It can also be seen that points on the opposite rays in either case are involved in revealed preference inconsistencies. Their exclusion is therefore required if the demand data are to be consistent.

On this basis, therefore, it is fitting to truncate the given expansion lines at their critical points, leaving the forward or backward rays according to the case. This process can be called *critical reduction* of the data. The demand data that so result, which consist of a pair of rays with vertices at the critical points, are always consistent, and to every point on one ray there corresponds a non-empty closed interval of points on the other which could be indifferent to it for some compatible utility.

Of course, critical reduction might eliminate all parts of the given expansion lines that lie in the commodity space, so that in effect there are no data left. That can happen only in the elliptical case, and then just when a critical point falls outside the commodity space.

For any quadratic ϕ with gradient g, it should be noted that if $g(x) = \lambda p$, $g(y) = \mu p$ then for any point $z = x\varrho + y\sigma$ where $\varrho + y\sigma = 1$, this being any point on the line L joining x and y, we have

$$g(z) = \varrho g(x) + \sigma g(y) = \nu p,$$

where $\nu = \varrho \lambda + \sigma \mu$. This is either always zero or is zero for just one point z of L, and it is constant if $\lambda = \mu$.

THEOREM For a pair of linear expansions (L_r, p_r) with unique critical points $c_r \epsilon L_r$ $(r = 0, 1)$, if ϕ is a quadratic with gradient g such that $g(x_r) = \lambda_r p_r$ for some λ_r at two distinct points $x_r \epsilon L_r$ $(r = 0, 1)$ then

$$\phi(c_0) = \phi(c_1), \quad g(x_0) = g(c_1) = 0.$$

From the hypothesis, $g(c_r) = \mu_r p_r$ for some μ_r, and so

$$\phi(c_0) - \phi(c_1) = \{\mu_0 p_0 + \mu_1 p_1\}(c_0 - c_1)/2 = 0,$$

because the c_r are critical points, such that $p_r c_s = p_r c_r$. Then further, for any $x_r \epsilon L_r$, $g(x_r) = \lambda_r p_r$ for some λ_r. Therefore

$$\phi(x_0) - \phi(c_0) = (\lambda_0 p_0 + \mu_0 p_0)(x_0 - c_0),$$
$$\phi(x_0) - \phi(c_1) = (\lambda_0 p_0 + \mu_1 p_1)(x_0 - c_1),$$

and with $d_0 = x_0 - c_0$ these now give $\mu_0 p_0 d_0 = \mu_1 p_1 d_0$, and hence $\mu_0 = \mu_1 p_1 e_0$. By the same argument $\mu_1 = \mu_0 p_0 e_1$. But $D \neq 0$ since the critical points are unique, and so it follows that $\mu_0 = \mu_1 = 0$, and hence $g(c_0) = g(c_1) = 0$.

This theorem shows the significance of the critical points as concerns compatible quadratics. If ϕ is compatible with some demand (x_r, p_r) where $x_r \epsilon L_r$ then $g(x_r) = \lambda_r p_r$ for some $\lambda_r > 0$, and so c_r is the unique point on L_r where $g(c_r) = 0$. Note that, with x_r on one side of the critical point, $\lambda_r < 0$ for any $x_r \epsilon L_r$ on the other side and so ϕ cannot be compatible also with the demand (x_r, p_r). This gives a reflection on the process of critical reduction of the data by which one half of the expansion lines are rejected from it, to leave a pair of rays R_0, R_1 with vertices at the critical points.

The *critical transversal* T of the expansion lines joins their critical points. It is described by points $c = c_0 \alpha_0 + c_1 \alpha_1$ where $\alpha_0 + \alpha_1 = 1$. From $p_r c_s = p_r c_r$, it follows that $p_r c = p_r c_r$ for all $c \epsilon T$. Also

$$g(c) = \alpha_0 g(c_0) + \alpha_1 g(c_1) = 0,$$

and

$$\phi(c) - \phi(c_0) = \{g(c) + g(c_0)\}(c - c_0)/2 = 0.$$

Thus, ϕ is constant and its gradient vanishes everywhere on T.

5.4 MARGINAL PRICE INDICES, AND LIMITS

Because the given data consist of linear expansions, there is no need to consider only compatible utilities for which the expansion loci are all linear. But it is natural to do so, and since quadratics have linear expansion loci these can be included as possible examples.

For utility functions that do have linear expansion loci, the purchasing power relation takes the linear form

$$M_1 - C_1 = P_{10}(M_0 - C_0),$$

for some constants C_0, C_1 and P_{10}, these being independent of the incomes, and depends only on the prices p_0, p_1. We call P_{10} the *marginal price index* determined by such a utility. With that known, the relation between M_0 and M_1 becomes fixed when the intercept $C_1 - P_{10} C_0$ is also known. We have seen that, with critical reduction of the data, replacing the lines L_0, L_1 by rays R_0, R_1 with vertices at the critical points, the resulting data are consistent, and then we can take $C_0 = p_0 c_0$, $C_1 = p_1 c_1$ with P_{10} indeterminate between certain upper and lower limits $\hat{P}_{10}$ and $\check{P}_{10}$. In the hyperbolic case, the relation has validity only for $M_0 > C_0$, and the formulae for these limits are

$$\hat{P}_{10} = p_1 e_0 = p_1 d_0 / p_0 d_0, \quad \check{P}_{10} = 1/p_0 e_1 = p_1 d_1 / p_0 d_1 ;$$

in the elliptical case, the formulae are exchanged, and $M_0 < C_0$ for validity. In either case,

$$\overline{P}_{10} = \sqrt{(\hat{P}_{10} \check{P}_{10})}$$

is a particular value for P_{10} which lies between the limits appropriate to the case. One could single out many such particular values between the limits, in fact any point between them. We will see that each corresponds to some compatible utility which has linear expansion loci. P_{10}, without other merit, just happens to be the marginal price index that would be obtained from any compatible quadratic utility, should one exist. Therefore simply by picking it we have Wald's 'New Formula', which was derived on the basis of a hypothetical quadratic utility, but is now in a revealing disguise, with new qualifications about validity, depending on the sign of the discriminant, the reduction of the data necessary to make it consistent, and the restriction on income range.

The formulae for the marginal price index limits are impressively like the Paasche and Laspeyres formulae of price index theory, and their role as limits is similar also. Out of respect for that connection though the source is alien it seems suitable to call them the *Laspeyres and Paasche marginal price index formulae*. The connection that is immediately evident in this way should be taken further. Then the geometric mean of the limits not only looks like Fisher's formula but also has an association with quadratic utility, connecting it with the relation obtained by Wald. That is quite like Byushgens's theorem about Fisher's formula and its association with homogeneous quadratic utility. In fact, the difference can be represented as corresponding simply to a change of origin for commodity bundles, from the origin in the commodity space to one of the critical points or, just as well when the expansion lines do not intersect so that these are distinct, to any point on the critical transversal T which joins them. We can see that, because we know that the gradient of any compatible quadratic must vanish at any point c of T, so that the quadratic has c as a centre, and is equivalent to—or translatable into—a homogeneous quadratic with c as origin.

A displacement on L_r is given by $d_r = x_r - c_r$, for any $x_r \epsilon L_r$. Then, for any $c \epsilon T$,

$$C_r = p_r c_r = p_r c$$

and

$$p_r(x_s - c_s) = p_r(x_s - c),$$

and so

$$p_r e_s = p_r(x_s - c)/p_r(x_r - c).$$

Then the 'Fisher' (or Wald) marginal price index counterpart is

$$\bar{P}_{10} = \sqrt{\{p_1(x_0 - c)p_1(x_1 - c)/p_0(x_0 - c)p_0(x_1 - c)\}},$$

and the relation based on this, which by implication from the quadratic associaton must coincide with Wald's 'New Formula', is

$$M_1 - p_1 c = \bar{P}_{10}(M_0 - p_0 c).$$

If the lines L_r intersect in the origin, then we have $c = 0$, and if they do not interesect but the critical transversal T passes through the origin, then we can take $c = 0$. Then the marginal price index counterpart of Fisher's index simply becomes Fisher's price index, and the equivalent income relation becomes the homogeneous relation

$$M_1 = \bar{P}_{10} M_0.$$

At the same time, the quadratic whose gradient vanishes at c must, now with $c = 0$, be a homogeneous quadratic, but for an additive constant, so we have Byushgens's theorem. The argument can be reversed, by taking a point $c \in T$ as origin so that Byushgens' theorem can be applied, and then we arrive at Wald's formula directly in the above form. Doing that depends on the critical point concept and the results associated with it, and so there is no suggestion here that Wald's formula was anything but 'New'.

A characteristic of the homogeneous case is that the elliptical case amounts to inconsistency. Critical reduction of the data leaves a pair of rays pointing from the origin outside the commodity space. Truncation of the expansion lines in the commodity space after critical reduction therefore leaves no data at all. So a consistency with homogeneity requires the hyperbolic case. The familiar roles of the Laspeyes and Paasche formulae as upper and lower limits which belong to this case are exchanged in the elliptical case. For a perspective with the Four-point Formula of the last chapter, there the centre of the quadratic has an indeterminacy, with a consequent indeterminacy in the purchasing power relation; whereas here, with a pair of expansion lines, the centre is determinate by identification with a critical point.

Part IV
LOGIC OF PRICE

IV.1

Opportunity Models

A model for an economic situation should show the courses of action possible in it. The interest might be in the choice of the action to be taken, and the criteria that are effective. But choice presupposes opportunity, and there is always a model for that, even when it might be in part understood without explanation. The market itself is an important factor in choice, and is usually present where economics is concerned. The idea of such a market, where goods are available in any desired quantities at some given prices, constitutes a model which might be taken for granted. As with models, it might represent an oversimplification. Another major sector of opportunity is based on production technology. Here, usual means of expression has been the production function. At first that was simply

$$Y = F(K, L)$$

where the factors distinguished were capital and labour, and then more generally

$$y = f(x_1, \ldots, x_n).$$

In having possession of $x_1, \ldots, x_n$, there is the opportunity to have y instead, provided by the technology represented by the function f. Joining it with the market opportunity sector, manufacturers exploit such an opportunity for a profit.

The things which can be done, and between which a choice has to be made, are *activities*. Von Neumann (1945; first published in 1938) introduced the concept of an activity vector, whose elements showed what was gained and lost in its performance, and of an *activity system*. His linear activity system provided an approach to production which, in contrast to the production function, made the representation of joint production completely natural. It is a finite construction with scope because of approximation properties, and it brings production into the linear programming framework. With production functions used for econometrics, a difficulty arises from the poverty of parametrically defined functions to serve as models. With the von Neumann production model that issue is avoided. It is avoided also with the polyhedral and polytope utility functions used here for demand analysis, which are counterparts of his production model.

T. C. Koopmans (1951b) gave the linear activity system a different development which has its own interests and which will be considered also, especially for the axiomatic basis that can be given to it.

1.1   THE PRODUCTION FUNCTION

A production function is usually taken to be a non-decreasing function, which serves to represent that an increase of inputs does not result in less output. This can also be understood to show *free disposal* on the input side, in that the input increase can always be eliminated without impairing output from the remainder. On the ouput side, free disposal would mean that with any possible output any lesser output is also possible, since any part of the output can be abandoned costlessly. With this, the production function simply tells us the maximum possible output from the inputs, so it should be understood to determine the relation $y \leq f(x)$ between input x and output y by which one is feasible with the other. Perfect efficiency of operations with the technology represented by f would require $y = f(x)$. To express diminishing marginal returns, a production function f is required to be a concave function. That property requires the points (x, y) where $y \leq f(x)$ to describe a convex set. A *classical production function* has these monotonicity and convexity properties, expressing both free disposal and diminishing returns.

A consequence of the classical properties is that any point x^* for which $f(x) \leq f(x^*)$ for some $x > x^*$ must be such that $f(x) \leq f(x^*)$ for all x. In this case, $y^* = f(x^*)$ is an absolute ceiling for output, which cannot be exceeded with any inputs. The existence of a ceiling is denied when f is *semi-increasing*, i.e.

$$x < x' \Rightarrow f(x) < f(x'),$$

where $x < x'$ means $x_i < x_i'$ for all i. This condition is stronger than the requirement

$$x \leq x' \Rightarrow f(x) \leq f(x')$$

for f to be *non-decreasing*, where $x \leq x'$ means $x_i \leq x_i'$ for all i. Also, it is not as restrictive as when f is taken to be an *increasing* function, that is, when

$$x \lneq x' \Rightarrow f(x) < f(x')$$

which is commonly assumed for production and utility functions, where $x \lneq x'$ means $x \leq x'$ and $x \neq x'$. An unsuitability of this last assumption is found in the real possibility that an increase of some input might not contribute at all to output without an increase in some other input on which its usefulness depends.

A defect of the production function is that it represents only *separate production*, where one good alone is the output from the process. Production is typically *joint production*, where there are many simultaneous outputs, and with any given inputs there are many output possibilities. From the nature of the process, in producing some things the production of some other things might be inevitable. These are *by-products* where they have some value, otherwise *wasteproducts*, like the smoke that goes up the chimney.

1.2   GENERAL INPUT-OUTPUT

A step towards representing joint production takes the form of a *transformation locus*, possibly represented as a locus $t(x_1, \ldots, x_n) = 0$, where the x's now can be positive or negative depending whether a good is an output or an input. By solving this for one variable in terms of the others, we have some sort of production function, although with an ambiguity about which goods are inputs and which outputs. But at least, now several goods might be produced rather than just one. Another understanding of the transformation locus is that $t(x) \leq 0$ describes all bundles of goods x attainable by the available means, in other words a *production possibility set*. In the difference between any two production possibilities, some goods are gained but some others are lost, these reflecting outputs and inputs. Though the transformation locus does service for some theoretical purposes, it is not so suitable for a closer description of production operations.

Usually a producer's facilites are dedicated to producing outputs of certain goods and using others as inputs. Another, rather more modern, type of expression gives a restriction $g(-x, y) \leq 0$ on input and output vectors $x \geq 0, y \geq 0$ where the function g is non-decreasing. In any case, there is an input-output relation R, and here, because of the monotonicity of g, it has the property

$$x' \geq xRy \geq y' \Rightarrow x'Ry',$$

expressing free disposal on the sides of input and output. On the input side this means that, if y is producible from x then it is also producible from any $x' \geq x$, and, to bring in the output side, so is any $y' \leq y$. Here it is explicit which goods are used up in the process and which ones are produced, even though some of these might be the same. But, for a possible standard form which is always available, all goods could still be represented on both the input and output sides, with only some of them being effective on each side in any particular case.

With any input-output relation R we now have $xR = [y : xRy]$ as the output possibility set for any input vector x, and $Ry = [x : xRy]$ as the input possibility set for any output vector y, while xRy states that y is producible from x, or that the input-output (x, y) is feasible. This is a proper generalization of the production function, which now corresponds to the case where the output vector y has just one element. As with a production function, requiring R to be convex expresses diminishing marginal returns and, what amounts to the same, increasing marginal costs. A *classical input-output relation* is one with this property together with the free-disposal monotonicity.

1.3   VON NEUMANN'S ACTIVITY SYSTEM

Von Neumann (1945) brought forward this production relation concept together with the finite algebraical way of constructing such relations. That was in connection with his economic model, but the formulation itself is a distinct influence beyond that particular application. Leontief's model is an obvious example, involving a simplification. The finitistic approach dealt with here in demand analysis can be related to it, since the utility functions that enter have the same polyhedral or polytope construction. Von Neumann gave a finitely constructive method which brings production analysis very readily into the linear programming framework. At the same time, the scope of the constructions is not so very limited, since they can approximate the entire class of production relations with the classical properties.

In one formulation, an activity vector is simply a vector $z = (z_1, \ldots, z_n)$ whose element z_i is the amount of good i gained in performing it, or $-z_i$ is the amount lost, so that good i is an output if $z_i > 0$ and an input if $z_i < 0$. The goods which disappear have been transformed into those that appear in their place, and what we have is a *transformation activity*. With another formulation, the activity is described by an input vector $a = (a_1, \ldots, a_n)$ and an output vector $b = (b_1, \ldots, b_n)$, both non-negative. In this case we have an *input-output activity*. This is the original formulation of von Neumann, while the other has been pursued by Koopmans. When it is understood that only a certain subset of some p of the n possible goods serve as inputs, and similarly some q are outputs, the input and output vectors a and b can be truncated correspondingly to these dimensions. Then for the case $p = 1$, what we have can also be represented by a production function.

In the idea of an activity system, which gives a use to this activity concept, from any activities that are given to be possible, further possible activities can be derived, or generated. This simple idea has a fair scope, since much that is ordinarily understood in the way of models for production and market operations can be approached by means of it.

An activity system can be defined as the collection A of all activities that can be derived from some given set G, the *base set*. This set could be finite, so the system generated from it has a finite description even though the collection A of all activities in it is not finite. The principle of generation corresponds simply to some basic assumption about the set A. For instance if, to express constant returns to scale, A is taken to be a cone, so that

$$a \, \epsilon \, A, \quad t \geq 0 \Rightarrow at \, \epsilon \, A,$$

then from any $a \, \epsilon \, G$ one would generate $at \, \epsilon \, A$ for all $t \geq 0$. With the basic assumption that A is convex, G would generate its convex closure; or, if free disposal is a further assumption, then G would generate its orthoconvex closure. Any mixture of assumption about A produces a principle of generating A from some base set G, possibly finite even though A is not. Bearing on this is the way (in Chapter II.4 on 'Separable Utility') utility functions have been constructed from available data on the basis of separability assumptions. Associated with the convexity which is a general expression of diminishing returns is the fact that, even though some A may not be generated completely accurately from any finite set, it can be approximated, and also can be put within the bounds of a smaller polytope set and a larger polyhedral set, both of which are finitely generated and whose difference can be made small. The bracket functions which have a part in the finite demand analysis shown in earlier chapters are an illustration. In the case of production, where, unlike with utility, quantities of goods are directly observable, the matter becomes simpler still, as was found in the efficiency measurement considerations of Chapter II.6. There is the additional point, which was developed already in the demand context and which applies more generally, that diminishing returns may be not a law of nature but rather a law for efficient economic operations, and so the assumption, even when it is without other validity, should be consistent with observable behaviour.

The von Neumann formulation of an activity as described by an input and an output vector, forming a pair (x, y), makes it suitable to represent the activity set as a binary relation R between inputs and outputs, so that $(x, y) \in R$ is stated xRy. With the Koopmans formulation a different adoption is suitable. With the view that any economic activity should be described as a transformation of goods, an economic position, or state, should correspond to an endowment of goods. Joined with that are the transformation possibilities, which can bring about their replacement by other goods and so give access to another state. That would make seeking a favourable position what economics is about, and, according to how one defines a state, it is bound to be true. There should be a relation T, the *transformation possibility relation*, where xTy means that goods x, identifying one position, are transformable into goods y, making another. With Koopmans's activity formulation,

$$V = [y - x : xTy]$$

would be the activity set, and with the linear activity system model he adopts, this set is a finitely generated convex cone. He excludes getting something for nothing—the 'impossibility of the Land of Cochaigne'—which means that no element of it is semi-positive. While the elements of V are the source of feasible activities, to perform any activity a while having goods $x \geq 0$ it is necessary that $x + a \geq 0$; that is, for the performance of any activity to be feasible, the inputs required must not exceed availability. Therefore, with the activity cone V given, the transformation possibility relation T would be determined by the formula

$$xTy \equiv x, y \geq 0, \quad y - x \in V.$$

This is a very different model from that considered by von Neumann. Any relation T so defined from a convex cone would be reflexive and transitive and so an order, whereas von Neumann's input-output relation R, even if suitable growth possibilities could make it reflexive, would not be transitive and anyway has no such general properties. We will consider a set of properties of any relation T so determined from a Koopmans activity cone, and their plausible sense or interpretation, and find that they are completely characteristic of such relations, and independent, so providing an axiomatic basis for the model.

With the Koopmans model, market activities can be incorporated along with production activities. Buying and selling activities would be represented separately, with possibly different prices. Reversible activities are identified by their belonging to the vertex manifold of the cone, as would be buying and selling without a price difference, and free disposal activities are any belonging to the non-positive orthant. Though market operations are usually separated from production, the connection can be recognized just as well, since for an individual agent the effect is the same. In either case, some goods are given up and others take their place. It is necessary to go from individual to global accounts to recognize the difference: that the goods sold have not completely disappeared but are now in the possession of someone else, and still that is not necessarily of any concern to the seller. The consumables at home are outputs from the factors delivered in going to work, regardless of any technology involved. Whatever its internal structure, with markets and whatever, the entire economy is represented in theory as an elaborate transformer serving the production of utility.

A distinctive limitation of the transformation possibility relation based on the Koopmans activity system, associated with its transitivity, is that time essentially has no part in it. If xTy were to mean that y is producible from x in a single production period, then from xTy and yTz we might conclude that z is producible from x—first make y from x and then make z from y. However, while we might be assured that achievement is possible in *two* production periods, there is no assurance of the possiblity in one, and so xTz cannot be concluded. From that consideration, T, being transitive, cannot have reference to what is possible within a particular period.

1.4 AXIOMATICS OF KOOPMANS'S SYSTEM

Various properties for a transformation possibility relation T are considered now, each having a sense intelligible on its own which can be judged for plausibility as an assumption. It will be found that the collection of these properties is necessary and sufficient for the representation of T by a Koopmans activity system V, where

$$xTy \Leftrightarrow x, y \geq 0, \quad y - x \in V.$$

The state of an economic agent is described by possessions or capacities of various kinds. These might not all be of the material kind but they can still be pictured as a heap of goods $x \geq 0$, transformable subject to the relation T which tells the accessibility of one state from another:

P1 process: $xTyTx \Rightarrow xTz$.

P2 separation: $xTy, \quad z \geq 0 \Rightarrow (x + z)T(y + z)$.

P3 scale: $xTy, \quad t \geq 0 \Rightarrow (xt)T(yt)$.

P4 disposal: xTo.

P5 economy: $o\bar{T}x \Rightarrow x = 0$.

P6 continuity: T is closed.

The names for these axioms are connected with some sense of validity with explanation as follows.

P1 process: $xTyTx \Rightarrow xTz$
If y is producible from x and z from y, a possible process for producing z from x consists in first producing y from x and then z from y; and so z is producible from x, though there cannot be any account of time needed, if any.

P2 separation: $xTy, \quad z \geq 0 \Rightarrow (x + z)T(y + z)$
Imagine a heap of goods; separate it into two parts, modify one part and put the two heaps together again. The axiom asserts that the possible modifications of the one part are the same as when it is alone without any possible external interference from the presence of the other part; the other part does not get in the way, which seems a fair assumption in some circumstance but not all.

A consequence with P1 is the additivity

$$xTy, \quad zTw \Rightarrow (x+z)T(y + w).$$

P3 scale: $xTy, \quad t \geq 0 \Rightarrow (xt)T(yt)$
Feasibility is independent of the scale of operations; equivalently, T is a cone, and with the additivity which is a consequence of P1 and P2 it is a convex cone.

P4 disposal: $x\bar{T}o$
It is possible to dispose of everything. A consequence with P2 is free disposal,

$$x \geq y \Rightarrow xTy,$$

in particular reflexivity $x\bar{T}x$, which with the transitivity P1 makes T an order relation.

P5 economy : $o\bar{T}x \Rightarrow x = 0$
Nothing is producible from nothing. The denial of this, together with P3, would make some good available in unlimited quantities at no cost. It would not be an economic good, and such goods can always be dropped from accounts without upsetting anything, so validating the axiom. A consequence with P2 is that

$$x \lesssim y \Rightarrow x\bar{\bar{T}}y,$$

so it is impossible to gain a good without sacrificing another—corresponding to Koopmans's 'impossibility of the Land of Cockaigne' (an imaginary land of luxury and idleness described in a French satire of the 1300s, according to *The World Book Dictionary*).

P6 continuity: T is closed

The practical significance is that accounts have limited precision, so that $x_r \to x$ means there exists some m such that $x_r = x$ for all $r > m$.

With the consequence of P1, P2 and P3 that T is a convex cone, this makes T a closed convex cone.

A consequence of P2 and P3 is that

$$x' \geq x, \quad t \geq 0, \quad (y' - x') = (y - x)t . \Rightarrow . xTy \Rightarrow x'Ty'.$$

But since $x' > 0$ implies that, for all x, $x's > x$ for some $s > 0$, from this we have

$$x, x' > 0, \quad [y' - x' > = [y - x > . \Rightarrow . xTy \Leftrightarrow x'Ty',$$

where

$$[x > = [xt : t \geq 0]$$

denotes the ray through any vector x. Therefore, for any x, let

$$V_x = [(y - x)t : xTy, t \geq 0].$$

Then we have

$$x, x' > 0 \Rightarrow V_x = V_{x'},$$

in other words, the cone generated by all possible displacements $y - x$ from a point x subject to xTy is the same for all $x > 0$. Let this cone be V, so that

$$x > 0 \Rightarrow V_x = V.$$

We now have

$$x > 0 \Rightarrow (xTy \Leftrightarrow y - x \in V, \quad y \geq 0).$$

With P6, that T is closed; it follows that V is closed and also that

$$xTy \Leftrightarrow y - x \in V, \quad x, y \geq 0.$$

But now with P1, asserting that T is transitive, it follows that

$$a, b \in V \Rightarrow a + b \in V.$$

Since V is constructed as a cone, this shows that it is a convex cone.

The argument so far contributes to the following.

THEOREM For a binary relation T in the commodity space to be such that it is closed and

$$xTx, xTyTz \Rightarrow xTz,$$
$$xTy, \quad z \geq 0 \Rightarrow (x + z)T(y + z),$$

and

$$xTy, \quad t \geq 0 \Rightarrow (xt)T(yt),$$

it is necessary and sufficient that there exists a closed convex cone V such that

$$xTy \Leftrightarrow x, y \geq 0, \quad y - x \in V.$$

We have shown the necessity, and the converse is obvious.

With Koopmans's system we have a closed convex cone V as the activity set, which in fact is finitely generated, but that is not essential to present considerations. To express that it contains disposal activities for all goods, we have the condition

$$-C \subset V, \tag{i}$$

where C is the commodity space, or the non-negative orthant of the activity space, and so $-C$ is the non-positive orthant. Were there disposal activities for only some goods, then C would be replaced by a corresponding face. Similary, for the 'impossibility of the Land of Cockaigne' there is the condition

$$V \cap C = O, \tag{ii}$$

O here being the null cone consisting of the origin alone. But now, given a transformation possibility relation T represented as in the theorem by a closed convex cone V, the disposal axiom P4 for T is equivalent to the condition (i) on V, and the economy axiom P5 is equivalent to (ii). Thus, if we add P4 and P5 to the requirement for T in the theorem, the corresponding requirement for V is simply that it be a Koopmans activity cone. Thus we have P1–P6 as a complete characterization of relations T so represented by such a type of cone V. A consequence of (ii) is that V is a proper cone, whose dual cone U is non-null, and a consequence of (i) is that $U \subset C$. Thus, an equivalent representation of T is by means of a proper non-negative closed convex cone U such that

$$xTy \,. \Leftrightarrow .\, x, y \geq 0, \quad u \in U \Rightarrow ux \geq uy.$$

IV.2

Leontief's Input-Output

Economic actions can be regarded as transformations of some kind; goods are turned into other goods, or a cost into a return. A change from one economic position to another takes place; there is an input-output operation where some x is the input or cost, and some y the output or return. A common general idea is present, and 'transformation' is a suitable term for it, and so is input-output. Output without input is outside economics—rather for the magician. Any ordinary producer of an output is also the consumer of an input, as is understood in the references made in economics to production, and similarly to consumption. The terms are used to distinguish the types of agents involved, and not to say that they are doing anything completely different.

Input-output is a general idea, and at the same time the term has a unique association with the special input-output method of Leontief. The method is offered as a means for grasping structure — as in 'The Structure of the American Economy'. The simplest sense of structure is provided by the blueprint, a means for reproducing the object in all its characteristics, simulating it or knowing it completely. That cannot apply here. In another sense, one can regard structure as a line that has been drawn somewhere in the area described, and then it is important to know where it is drawn, and why just there. This question is not frequently asked about the Leontief system, possibly because without doing research one can know the answer. But the question is still of interest, especially since the method is so well established. Peter F. Drucker (1981), in his essay 'Toward the next economics', in the volume on *The Crisis in Economic Theory* edited by Daniel Bell and Irving Kristol, no place for tolerance, describes it as 'one of the most advanced tools of modern economics'.

Understanding the basis for such acceptance cannot be simple. The exact quantitative sense in which the model might be understood is of course questionable, since it is outstanding that the method can always be applied regardless of such sense. This is a weakness—and a certain strength. But to take the calculation aspect going beyond the *Tableau Economique* of Quesnay (1758) as absurd would put aside the wisdom with which it might be applied, and those ritual needs whose representation in economics is both familiar and inevitable. When planning decisions must be made in the face of outstanding ignorance of system characteristics, the input-output method might offer a kind of rescue. The theory of the method shows a logic that is nice and remarkable. That the method has peculiar strengths is well appreciated, but where they all lie is less readily stated. To throw an inkpot at the wall and call the result the structure of anything would not be impressive, and this method has impressed many.

The source for the theory in the last section of this chapter is David Gale (1960b), *The Theory of Linear Economic Models*. This gathers the main theory of the Leontief matrix in a way that is close to economics and free of unwanted elaborations. I taught, or, more definitely, learnt, from that book for a number of years and my debts are not all as easily pointed out as here.

2.1 QUESNEY'S 'TABLEAU ECONOMIQUE'

The economy is divided into n sectors, 1, . . ., n. The division could have a purely accounting basis, possibly from some importance for national administration that requires data in that form to be available, and have no other significance. It could also be a division based on technology, as it must be if the Leontief model is going to have a validity. But the input-output method can always be applied without any regard for the basis of the division. There is a strength in the method here, and also good reason for pausing before using it.

Each sector i has an output X_i which is to be accounted. Amounts X_{ij} of this go to all sectors j in the economy, to serve as input for their outputs. The aggregate of these represents intermediate demand, used up in the production process. The remainder Y_i, which represents net output for the economy, goes to the remaining final demand sector. As accounting identities, we have

$$X_i = \Sigma_j X_{ij} + Y_i \quad \text{for all } i,$$

all entries being non-negative, and in money terms. In the manner of Quesnay with his *Tableau Economique*, this accounting data can be set out in a table (see Table 1).

Table 1

Supply	Intermediate demand sector inputs			Final demand
	1 ...	j ...	n	
1 X_1	X_{11} ...	X_{1j} ...	X_{1n}	Y_1
⋮ ⋮		⋮ ⋮ ⋮		⋮
i X_i	X_{i1} ...	X_{ij} ...	X_{in}	Y_i
⋮ ⋮		⋮ ⋮ ⋮		⋮
n X_n	X_{n1} ...	X_{nj} ...	X_{nn}	Y_n
Sector outputs	X_1 ...	X_j ...	X_n	

2.2 THE LEONTIEF MATRIX

A step taken by Leontief with this accounting scheme was to represent the output x of any sector as a function of the inputs x_i obtained from all the sectors, the function depending on the sector. Moreover, the function was taken to have the special form

$$x = \min\ [\,x_i\,/\,a_i : a_i > 0\,],$$

the parameter vector $a \geq 0$ depending on the sector.

With such a production function, for any output x to be feasible with inputs x_i it is required that

$$x \leq x_i\,/\,a_i \quad \text{for all } i,$$

and so the minimum inputs for any output x are

$$x_i = a_i x.$$

The assumption of efficiency in the use of inputs requires these to be the observed inputs found with any observed output. Then, with any observation of inputs x_i and an output $x > 0$, the coefficients are immediately determined by

$$a_i = x_i\,/\,x.$$

This principle can be applied to every sector in the economy, using the data on inputs and outputs provided by the accounting table. Thus, for sector j the coefficients determined are

$$a_{ij} = X_{ij}\,/\,X_j\,.$$

Accompanying this determination is the assumption that, for any other possible ouput x_j in sector j, the inputs must be $a_{ij}x_j$.

From the accounting identity in section 2.1 and the definition of the coefficients, we have

$$X_i = \Sigma_j a_{ij} X_j + Y_i\,,$$

or, in matrix form,

$$X = aX + Y,$$

giving

$$Y = (1 - a)X. \qquad\qquad (\text{i})$$

This is an identity, true just from the definition of its terms and representing no special assumption. But when, in considering any other possible output x, the relation

$$y = (1 - a)x \qquad\qquad (\text{ii})$$

is entertained for determining the net output y, the assumptions made have their effect.

The Leontief input-output method is embodied in the step from the identity (i) to the general relation (ii). When (ii) is accepted, a vista opens for choice and planning.

2.3 PRODUCTION PLANNING

The activity in the separate sectors is specified by the gross output vector x and the model requires $x \geq 0$. A part ax of the output x is used up as necessary input in the activity that produces it, to leave a net output $y = x - ax$. In the closed Leontief economy dealt with here, the outputs x are the source of the inputs ax needed to produce them, so we must also have $x \geq ax$. Thus, for any x to represent a feasible activity of the economy, it is required that

$$x \geq ax, \, x \geq 0.$$

The economy is described by the Leontief matrix $a \geq 0$, but for an arbitrary matrix $a \geq 0$ no such feasible x generally need exist; the economy described by it could be incapable of any activity, and so not be viable. However, the matrix a is constructed from a transaction table associated no doubt with an actually existing and, so one must assume, viable economy. Then, from the way it is constructed, we already have $X \geq aX$ for the particular vector X in the data table, from the identity (i), because we have $Y \geq 0$ for the final demand vector.

A matrix $a \geq 0$ for which such feasible x exist can be distinguished from an arbitrary matrix $a \geq 0$ as being a proper, or viable, Leontief matrix, and it has been seen that the Leontief construction of the matrix from a transaction table with all entries non-negative always produces one.

With a positive final demand Y in the transaction table, more than just viability is assured. The production process has demonstrated that it can not only not use up all that it produces in producing what it produces (unlike Sraffa's subsistence economy), but it can leave a positive net output of all goods that have a part in the process. All goods are producible in that they have a positive output with some feasible activity; or the economy is productive, satisfying the condition

$$x > ax \quad \text{for some } x \geq 0.$$

Any feasible activity x results in a non-negative final output y determined from the relation (ii); and

$$[y : y = (1 - a)x, \, x \geq 0, \, y \geq 0]$$

is the set of feasible final outputs for the economy. A planner could be concerned about whether this set contains some particular final output y which is desirable, and to know an activity x that will produce it. About such questions the Leontief system has remarkable properties, which will be developed in the following sections. It is immediate that in a productive economy some $y > 0$ are feasible, but it is not so immediate that any given $y \geq 0$ is feasible, and that the activity which produces it is unique.

A good r is producible if $y_r > 0$, and all goods are if $y > 0$, for some feasible final output y. A good s depends on a good r if $a_{rs} > 0$, that is, if good r is needed as an input for its production. A property of the Leontief system is that no producible good depends on a non-producible one. Therefore there is a sub-economy, and a submatrix, that involves only the producible goods, in other words a productive subeconomy. That makes it suitable, when considering viable economies, to consider especially those which are productive.

2.4 LEONTIEF AND ZENO

At the start, the tortoise is at a point 100 yards ahead of Achilles, who runs ten times as fast. Achilles runs to the point, but when he gets there the tortoise is at another point, leaving him short by 10 yards. When Achilles gets to that further point the tortoise has moved again, and is at a point 1 yard ahead . . . and so forth, indefinitely. As Zeno offered, Achilles never catches up with the tortoise, but we think he does, and this conflict makes Zeno's Paradox.

A translation will be made into Leontief input-output terms. First, it will be done with one good so as to follow Zeno exactly, and the generalization for many goods then follows.

For an output of 10 bushels of corn 1 bushel is required as input, no doubt eaten by the harvesters. A Farmer wants 100 bushels and when it is harvested he finds only 90, so he harvests another 10, and finds 9, and so forth. Zeno would say he never gets the 100. However, we know the Farmer should have gone out to produce exactly

$$x = (1 - 0.1)^{-1} 100 = 100/0.9 = 111.11. . .$$

from the start. Then he would finish up with

$$y = 0.9 \times 111.11 . . . = 99.999 . . . \text{ bushels.}$$

That does seem a bit short. But if he had planned for any more he would have had an unwanted surplus. Perhaps the Farmer was right after all. The paradox. . .

A Planner wants the economy to meet a demand y. He orders the sectors to produce an output $x = y$, but the result is $x - ax$, since ax of the output got used up as input to produce it. Therefore he orders a further ay, making $x = y + ay$, and finds instead

$$x - ax = y + ay - ay - a^2 y$$
$$= y - a^2 y,$$

so now the shortage is $a^2 y$. He increases the order again, now by this amount, making

$$x = y + ay + a^2 y$$

and still he is short, since ax gets used up, leaving

$$x - ax = y - a^3 y,$$

and so forth. Continuing in this way m times, the output ordered from the sectors will be

$$x = y + ay + . . . + a^{m-1}y$$

and the result will be $x - ax = y - a^m y$, making a shortage of $a^m y$.

It is quite possible that the situation will be getting worse and worse with every renewed effort to achieve the production goal. The Planner must give up, perhaps wishing he had never started. However, providence (in the form of the Perron-Frobenius theorem on the dominant root of a non-negative matrix joined with Oldenburger's theorem on the convergence of matrix powers) intervenes.

The condition for the economy to be productive, which is that $x > ax$ for some $x \geq 0$, is exactly the condition on a matrix $a \geq 0$ which assures that $a^m \to 0$ ($m \to \infty$). Then at some point the Planner will find the shortage $a^m y$ negligible and be satisfied with what he has got. Like the Farmer he has followed a commonsense and efficient procedure:

$$0 \text{ let } x = 0$$
$$1 \text{ if } x = y + ax \text{ then end}$$
$$2 \text{ let } x = y + ax, \text{ goto } 1$$

Had the Planner been mathematically informed, he might have done something tedious and costly, like inverting a matrix. For if that condition holds, then $1 - a$ is a regular matrix, and, moreover, the inverse is given by

$$(1 - a)^{-1} = 1 + a + a^2 + \ldots,$$

showing that it is a non-negative matrix. In that case,

$$x = (1 - a)^{-1} y$$

is non-negative for every non-negative y, and is the unique x for which $y = (1 - a)x$, for any given y.

In the next section we arrive at the same conclusions without a dependence on excessive outside theorems.

2.5 PRODUCTIVE SYSTEMS

THEOREM For any non-negative matrix a,
$ax < x$ for some $x \geq 0$
if and only if
$(1 - a)^{-1}$ exists and is non-negative.

This is the main theorem of the Leontief input-output method. With the input – output matrix a of the Leontief model, ax is the input needed for any output $x \geq 0$, so $y = (1 - a)x$ is the net output. Of interest is the solubility of this relation for $x \geq 0$, for any given $y \geq 0$. We can call this condition the Leontief regularity of the system, or of the matrix a which describes it.

A good r is producible if

$$x \geq ax, \ x_s > a_s x \text{ for some } x \geq 0.$$

The economy is productive if all goods are producible, either separately or, what by addition is equivalent, simultaneously together, that is, if $x > ax$ for some $x \geq 0$. The economy is semi-productive if some goods are producible, or if $x \gtrsim ax$ for some $x \geq 0$.

Good r is dependent on good s, for its production, if $a_{rs} > 0$ and otherwise is independent. In a semi-productive system, the producible goods are all independent of the non-producible ones. For suppose s is producible, so we have the above condition, but r is not, so also $x_r = a_r x$. Replacing x_s by $x_s - \epsilon$, for sufficiently small ϵ the same conditions hold except that, if $a_{rs} > 0$, we have $x_r > a_r x$, that is, good r appears as producible, contrary to hypothesis, so necessarily $a_{rs} = 0$. It follows that with a semi-productive system, by ignoring non-producible goods, there is a reduction to a productive subsystem, where all goods are producible. An irreducible system is one where there is no proper subset of goods which are dependent on each other and on no others. We know that such a system is productive if and only if it is semi-productive, so the distinction between these conditions disappears.

Now it will be seen that a productive system, where $x > ax$ for some $x \geq 0$, has the property $y \geq ay \Rightarrow y \geq 0$, for all y. Thus suppose

$$x > ax, \; x \geq 0 \qquad\qquad\text{(i)}$$
$$y \geq ay. \qquad\qquad\text{(ii)}$$

Then we want to deduce $y \geq 0$. If on the contrary $y_i < 0$ for some i then

$$-\theta = \min y_i / x_i = y_r / x_r < 0,$$

for some r, where $\theta > 0$. Then $z = y + x\theta$ is such that $y \geq 0$ but $x_r = 0$. Then also

$$z = y + x\theta > ay + ax\theta = az \geq 0,$$

so $z > 0$ and there is a contradiction. Hence $y \geq 0$. QED. We have proved:

LEMMA If a is productive then, for all x,

$$x > ax \Rightarrow x \geq 0.$$

Now, moreover,

COROLLARY (I) If a is productive, then $1 - a$ is regular.

For if $(1 - a)x = 0$ for any x, then by the lemma we have both $x \geq 0$ and $-x \geq 0$, and so $x = 0$.

COROLLARY (II) If a is productive then for all $y \geq 0$, there exists a unique $x \geq 0$ for which

$$(1 - a)x = y.$$

Because $1 - a$ is regular, by corollary (i), for all y there exists x for which $(1 - a)x = y$. Then $x \geq 0$ if $y \geq 0$, by the lemma.

From corollaries (i) and (ii), the theorem follows.

2.6 COMPUTER DEMONSTRATION

```
1 DATA          Leontief's Input-Output
2 '
3 '            Hyperion & IBMPC : BASICA
9 '
10 GOSUB 1000:GOSUB 100:END
11 '
90 K$="":WHILE K$="":K$=INKEY$:WEND
95 IF K$=ESC$ THEN END ELSE RETURN
98 '
99 '_____ main
100 FOR I=1 TO N:T=Y(I):FOR J=1 TO N
110 T=T+A(I,J)*X(J):NEXT:PRINT#1,TAB(H*I)T;
120 IF X(I)<>T THEN T(I)=T:F=1
130 NEXT:PRINT#1,:IF F=0 THEN PRINT#1,EF$:RETURN ELSE F=0
140 FOR I=1 TO N:X(I)=T(I):NEXT:IF LEN(INKEY$) THEN GOSUB 90
150 GOTO 100
159 '
999 '_____ init
1000 DEFINT F,I,J,N:READ A$,N:H=12
1010 EF$=CHR$(3):LF$=CHR$(10):FF$=CHR$(12)
1020 CR$=CHR$(13)
1030 CLS:PRINT,A$;CR$
1099 '
1100 INPUT"screen, printer or disk (s/p/d)";O$
1110 IF O$="p" THEN O$="LPT1:" ELSE IF O$="d" THEN O$="IOF"
ELSE O$="SCRN:"
1120 CLS:OPEN O$ FOR OUTPUT AS #1
1199 '
1200 PRINT#1,,A$;CR$:DIM A(N,N),X(N),Y(N)
1210 PRINT#1,"IO coefficients";CR$
1299 '
1300 FOR I=1 TO N:FOR J=1 TO N:READ A(I,J)
1310 PRINT#1,TAB(H*J)A(I,J);:NEXT:PRINT#1,:NEXT
1330 PRINT#1,CR$;"Net output";CR$
1399 '
1400 FOR J=1 TO N:READ Y(J)
1410 PRINT#1,TAB(H*J)Y(J);:NEXT
1430 PRINT#1,CR$;CR$;"Gross output";CR$
1900 RETURN
1998 '
1999 '_____ data
2000 DATA 3:' =N
2009 '_____ data A
2010 DATA       .3,       .2,       .1
2020 DATA       .2,       .1,       .3
2030 DATA       .2,       .4,       .1
2899 '_____ data Y
2900 DATA       1,        2,        3
```

```
            Leontief's Input-Output

IO coefficients

            .3          .2          .1
            .2          .1          .3
            .2          .4          .1
```

Net output

| 1 | 2 | 3 |

Gross output

1	2	3
1	2	3
2	3.3	4.3
2.69	4.02	5.15
3.126	4.485	5.661
3.4009	4.772	5.9853
3.5732	4.95297	6.18751
3.681305	5.06619	6.31458
3.749087	5.137254	6.394195
3.791597	5.181802	6.444139
3.818253	5.209741	6.475454
3.83497	5.227261	6.495093
3.845452	5.238248	6.507408
3.852026	5.245138	6.51513
3.856148	5.249459	6.519974
3.858734	5.252168	6.523011
3.860355	5.253867	6.524915
3.861371	5.254933	6.526109
3.862009	5.255601	6.526859
3.862409	5.256019	6.527328
3.86266	5.256282	6.527622
3.862816	5.256447	6.527807
3.862915	5.25655	6.527923
3.862977	5.256615	6.527996
3.863016	5.256656	6.528041
3.86304	5.256681	6.528069
3.863055	5.256697	6.528087
3.863065	5.256707	6.528099
3.863071	5.256714	6.528106
3.863075	5.256717	6.52811
3.863077	5.25672	6.528113
3.863078	5.256722	6.528115
3.86308	5.256723	6.528116
3.86308	5.256723	6.528117
3.863081	5.256724	6.528117
3.863081	5.256724	6.528117

IV.3

The Market

The market is central to economic experience, so far as we are concerned. Because of that, it is hard to think of a social order without it. Often there is some attempt to do so at the beginning of textbooks, where Robinson Crusoe appears, but it fades quickly. One hears that the Incas had no market, and accepts it as just another remarkable thing about them, like their having never invented the wheel.

The market is just the term for where there are buyers and sellers and goods bearing a price. The surface is simple, but much economic thought is concerned with what might be imagined underneath. A function of the market, and the cause for it, is the enlargement of choice; it is a classic part of economic choice (another being production). The transactions of economics occur in ordinary history, so the statistics of prices and quantities of goods transacted are only a fragment of any story. But the market is a distinct general phenomenon, present in all kinds of circumstances. To understand it as such, and as being unconditioned by very special circumstances, it should in some way be cut off for a separate consideration. Though one is then in an imaginary world, demonstrating the market phenomenon in such a well-defined, abstract world may go some way towards providing an explanation. The market is a completely commonplace phenomenon. For it to occur, it is outstanding that no planning committee, or other agency, is required to take part. Markets just happen, and they seem to grow in almost any soil. The conditions entertained therefore should be simple and flexible. For a theory, some such conditions have to be explored.

The possibility of a market cannot be isolated from the process of original realization. An existing possible arrangement is tantalizing in the absence of a way of getting to it from some, perhaps any, position. The *tâtonnement*, or tentative groping process of Walras, or something like it, is therefore an essential part of the matter. The pure existence possibility has to be joined with some operational finding process. That requires a kind of roughness, overriding disturbances, so as to embody the stability of the self-regulated market system, without which it could not in practice exist.

The considerations are necessarily abstract, intended only to reflect something of the form of common experience. A simplest representation therefore could be quite adequate. Here we introduce the idea of a linear market, and all wanted features have an expression by it. Generality still has some value, especially if it is costless, and when linear market functions are replaced by more general continuous ones the main results are reproduced. Then, instead of finite algebra from theory of distribution matrices, known in connection with the Markov processes, we use the KKM lemma shown in Chapter VI.3, in much the way that H. W. Kuhn uses it to prove the Brouwer Fixed-point theorem. This is not microeconomic theory that offers a picture of the system built from ultimate parts, but something more primitive.

3.1   THE LOGIC OF PRICE

That a good has a price P is demonstrated when a transaction takes place in which it has that price. There is no real alternative sense in which a good can have a price. It means nothing that cabbages are $1 per pound if no one, or rather no two, are buying and selling at that price. Goods left on the shelf with a price tag on them do not have a price until they are sold. Those tags are at most just factors in the *tâtonnement*. There are countless other goods on the shelf, some of them not yet invented.

In the transaction there is a buyer and a seller, and, even though two are present, what is bought and what is sold are the same thing. There seems no escape from that. In other words, supply S equals demand D: $S = D$. This is not an equation with content. It just connects two names that have been given to the same thing. But why give the same object two different names? It would be logical to give it one, say the transaction quantity Q.

We have a transaction price P and quantity Q for a good. Both are observable, and they are observed together. But economists give Q two different names, S and D, and then talk about S and D separately as if they were distinct entities, which could, moreover, exist apart. There is a puzzle here, or some confusion—possibly on the part of the writer.

It could be wondered (from limitless curiosity) why any price should be just P and not higher or lower. Since the market is central to economics, it is in some way understandable that there should be an attempt to give an explanation of price, even a complete one. But what kind of explanation can there be? To explain a change in a price is a more modest endeavour than explaining a price. The same is true with regard to the neck of the giraffe. The elongation is well understood in terms of evolutionary mechanisms (despite some debate about that); but no biologist attempts a complete explanation of the giraffe. Economists, of the fundamentalist kind, have greater courage. They offer an explanation of price, of all prices; or, rather, a form for an explanation has been proposed (perhaps more than one). But carrying out a realization of the form is a further matter, having much less attention. One may ask what content there could be just in the proposal about form, and whether there is anything in it that can be known to be true or false, or neither.

A main doctrine about a price in settled times was that it should be settled. A price was part of the order of things like fowls of the air and beasts of the field; there was such a thing as a proper chicken and it had a proper price. The price could be known and counted on; it could enter into plans for a dinner or the allocation of a budget. This is a rational position, and practical, but it is not one that can always be enjoyed, because unsettled times produce changes also in prices. The interest then is still practical: not why prices should all be absolutely what they are, but how they might change. This is as with the giraffe. There can still be the question of why there should be any offer to explain all prices, and even whether there really is an explanation.

3.2 SUPPLY AND DEMAND

Teach a parrott to say Supply and Demand and there you have an economist.
Stephen Leacock, *Literary Lapses*

Whether or not this statement deserves approval, it suggests a pleonasm, since we decided that supply and demand are the same thing. They are not equal, but are indistinguishable. That is a matter of inescapable logic, since what means buying something to a buyer means selling something to a seller, and these two things happen to be identical. All the same, though the two things are one, it is outstanding that the same cannot be said of the buyer and the seller. These are two separate individuals. In fact, since the transaction is voluntary on both sides, it seems something of a coincidence that they got together; for theory there is not just the chance but the matter to be explained.

This apparent chance has an extension to the aggregate, where it looks as if an unlikely coincidence must occur in order to have a price at all, because those willing to buy must be exactly matched by those willing to sell. It seems implausible that everyday economic life, where the price phenomenon is a commonplace, should be based on such a precarious balance. Theory should deal with the possibility of the fine arrangement; and, since feasibility is of incomplete interest without an idea of how it is realized, it should also deal with the process for arriving at it. Now, however, the concern is with elements rather than aggregates.

The encounter between buyer and seller might in reality have some significant effect on each. If this is of a special and individual kind it must be ignored, and for purposes of theory we should deal with simple automata. A simplicity in the encounter is assured if the only recognizable interface between buyer and seller is the price. For a start, it is supposed that the buyer and the seller in their separateness each have a definite potentiality for their part in the transaction which takes place, already existing and then realized from the encounter. A shape for such assumptions is provided by the following:

(i) Anyone willing to buy a unit of a good at some price P would be willing to buy it also at any lower price.

(ii) Anyone willing to sell a unit at price P would also be willing to sell it at any higher price.

These are norms, consistent with price being an incentive to sell and a disincentive to buy, and not absolute laws. We know from Veblen about ostentatious expenditure, and ostentatious charity could be a fair addition to that. The situation is not different from Newton's when he made uniform motion a norm. Non-uniform motion causes attention to forces, if any can be found, and here ostentation is to Veblen what gravitation was to Newton. These assumptions express a free disposal: the buyer who pays less is free to dispose of the difference leaving a situation which is the same and therefore as acceptible as when P has been paid, and similarly on the side of a seller.

If P_b is the upper limit to prices at which the buyer would be willing to buy a unit and P_s as the lower limit at which the seller would sell then simultaneous willingness both sides requires $P_s < P < P_b$, and hence $P_s < P_b$. Characteristics of buyer and seller are represented by Figure 1.

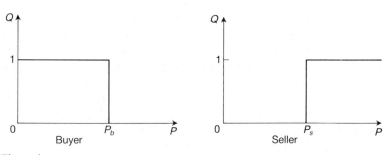

Figure 1

Superimposed, the regions under the graphs have to intersect for simultaneous consent to a transaction quantity at some price, which then can be anywhere between P_b and P_s. Otherwise at least one refuses and there is no transaction (see Figure 2).

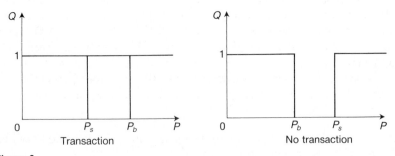

Figure 2

When successive further units are brought in we get declining and rising step functions, and if the units are small and numerous these become general monotonic curves, the supply and demand curves for buyer and seller. There is better sense to going further with this by bringing in notions about a market and these individuals being in one.

3.3 PRICE FORMATION

> So put forward . . . not just text and bare authorities, because our discourse
> must relate to the sensible world and not to one on paper.
>
> **Galileo,** translated by **Stillman Drake**

It was taught that the Heavens were created fixed for all time. Galileo looked at the sky more closely than others because he had a telescope, and he found a difference. He reported what he saw instead of what he read, saying that Aristotle would have done the same—though that did not save him from trouble. Economists might seem to be vulnerable in many ways to his objection, but they have escapes. Important data of their sensible world concern form, not hard to get but evident from ordinary experience; no measurements are needed to know it, or read it. Also, things on paper are a part of economics because they affect behaviour and events; they are a real part of the real world. There is a voluminous recording and manipulation of economic data, but nothing of what in the main passes for economic theory really depends on it. It has no relation to Galileo's measurements. In part of its nature it is near to ritual, in some form indispensible to social decision-making as from time immemorial. The empiricism of natural scientists is different from 'empirical work' in economics.

These possible views are entertained in connection with price theory based on supply and demand, in order to evaluate rather than object to it. The theory relies on ideas, of the kind in the last section that have obvious reference to experience, and we know what they mean. But there is a transition at some point, and there can be questions about the result. For instance, if the final theory were true there would be no way of knowing it, and so there can be a question about the sense of offering it as true, or even as possibly true. As for its being false, in our particular economies we know that it is, at least to an extent, because for instance prices are subject to various regulations. Also, time is a complication that makes the theory even difficult to interpret. None the less, and perhaps properly, the theory of prices and their equilibrium (in an unknown and unknowable framework) is given an important place in economic theory. Whether or not there should be a complaint exactly here, there can be one of another order about the 'welfare' appendages to this theory.

The matters in the last section have a local and individual reference, but dealing with an economy signifies a global framework of information and competition. Stephen Leacock brings that out in 'Boarding House Geometry', another of his *Literary Lapses*. He sets out the argument in the manner of

Euclid, with a few Postulates, and then Propositions. The former go something like this:

POSTULATES:

A landlady is an oblong angular figure which is equal to anything.
Boarding house sheets produced however far each way will not meet.
A pie is produced any number of times . . .

and so forth. Then comes the first Proposition, and its proof:

PROPOSITION: All boarding house rents are equal.

The proof is by the method of *reductio ad absurdum*, by which a hypothesis is impossible if it has impossible consequences:

PROOF: Suppose, if possible, that the rents are not equal. Then one is greater than the other. Then the other is less than it might have been, which is absurd etc. QED

The absurdity is from the landlady's side, and it could have gone just as well from the the tenant's side—i.e. the other is greater than it might have been, . . . Leacock takes for granted the assumptions about buyers and sellers of the last section. While there are transactions in a good at price P, no seller will sell at a lower price and no buyer will buy at a higher one. Since joint consent is needed, there will be no transactions at a price above or below P, and the good has a single price, P. There is a global equalization, a global information situation having been presupposed.

Should buyers willing to buy at the price be exausted before sellers willing to sell, then if further transactions take place they will be at a price that brings in more buyers and thereby a lower price, though not one so low as to cut out all sellers. Those sellers who are within their threshold and prepared to sell at a lower price will take part, and those who were at or beyond it will not. In going to a lower price demand rises and supply falls; similarly with the reverse situation, in which further transactions would take place, if at all, at a higher price. At any point the price is what it is because all who would be buyers at that price find sellers and all sellers, buyers. There might be none of either. But it makes no sense to say that cabbages are £1 per kilo if there is a would-be buyer at the price who cannot find a seller, or a seller who cannot find a buyer. The price being P depends on the balance $S = D$. If both sides of this equation are zero, as when buyers and sellers are far apart and there are none for a range of prices, it would not be precarious; otherwise it is, and there are movements. This is a dynamic picture giving some sense to movements. It does not depend on a knowledge of the total numbers that would buy or sell at whatever price; whatever these might be, should it make sense even to refer to them, they can be recognized to be continually changing. At any moment one can in principle know the prevailing price P and the transaction quantity Q which is simultaneously both supply and demand; and that is all.

The theory of price as determined by the equality of supply and demand postulates that supply and demand are functions $S = S(P)$, $D = D(P)$ of the possible price P, and the prevailing price P is determined by the condition $S(P) = D(P)$. If this theory is offered as having an empirical basis, there is a problem about knowledge of these functions, since only one point is observable on each, the point (P, Q). If the price P ever changes, it must be because the functions have changed and so are no longer observable; instead, a new single point can be observed on the new 'functions'. If the functions do not change they cannot be observed, and if they do change they cannot be observed either.

3.4 MARKET FUNCTIONS

The market in which goods have a price at which they are bought and sold is a commonplace phenomenon. With it there can be the idea, even if not the exact experience, of a settled market where, day after day, the prices and transaction quantities are the same. If we can think of a market as we do because of experience, we can also think of a settled market; it is a logical possiblity arising from the terms of description of markets, and it makes an ideal reference.

With a settled market, the possibility can be entertained of its being made up of settled individuals with fixed supply and demand functions. That is an imaginable possibility, in fact, one that is already imagined in price theory. A market of some sort is known to be a real possibility in some real circumstances. Now it can be asked if a market is a logical possibility in some ideal logically possible circumstances with fair provisors that do not ask anything positively contradicted from experience. This is an important first question for a theoretical understanding of the market system. A negative answer would be a great surprise and would make the market phenomenon thoroughly mysterious. Markets are found everywhere, in principle self-created and self-governed without any centralized intervention; and one would have to wonder what it is in the real world and not in the imagined world that makes them possible. With a positive answer there is, in addition to peace of mind, a central finding about the nature of markets, showing the known real possibility matched by an intrinsic theoretical possibility.

To develop the question, consider functions which give the vector S of differences between aggregate supply and aggregate demand for all goods as determined by the vector p of all the prices. These are *market functions*, given in the form of excess supply functions, so $D(p) = -S(p)$ would be excess demand functions.

In principle, the economy is composed of individuals each with such a function $s(p)$, and the market function S is a sum of all the individual functions s. At any prices, each individual buys some goods and sells others, paying for purchases with receipts from sales, so that demands match supplies in exchange value and there is the individual *budget constraint* $ps(p) = 0$. Then, for their sum, $pS(p) = 0$, which is called *Walras's Law*.

The prices $p > 0$ are significant only as determining exchange rates between goods from their ratios. Since the functions s depend only on the ratios, we have $s(tp) = s(p)$ for all $t > 0$. Summing, the function $S(p)$ is defined for all $p > 0$ and such that $S(tp) = S(p)$ for all $t > 0$.

The market functions $S(p)$ are now defined for all $p > 0$ and are such that

$$pS(p) = 0, \ S(tp) = S(p)(t > 0).$$

The market feasibility question, or the existence of some feasible prices, is now the question of whether or not there exists some prices $p > 0$ for which aggregate supply equals aggregate demand for every good, or the excess supplies are simultaneously all zero, that is

$$S(p) = 0.$$

It is not enough to know that such prices should exist; a further issue is how they would be found. After all, no one is doing the computing but the economy itself. The law of supply and demand, that the price of a good falls if it is in excess supply and rises if it is in excess demand, is an available principle which, put in a suitable form, should amount to a computational algorithm.

3.5   INTERCEPT AND SLOPE

The market functions $S_i(p)$ in the form described are too general for economic sense, and for the wanted existence. First, *continuity* will be assumed. The economy is taken to be finite, with a *finite supply capacity* in any good j. Consequently $S_j(p)$ should have a finite upper limit, or be bounded above. There is no need to think that $S_j(p)$ should be bounded below. On the contrary, when the price p_j is small demand can be unbounded above, and since supply is bounded above the difference S_j would approach $-\infty$. A moderate form for this possible assumption is that $S_j < 0$ if p_j is small, which will be called the *intercept condition*.

Because $S(tp) = S(p)$, the values of $S(p)$ at all points $p > 0$ are the same as the value at the corresponding point in the interior of the normalized price simplex

$$\Delta = [p : p \geq 0, pI = 1].$$

Values of excess supplies of goods determined by their own prices are given by

$$e_j(p) = p_j S_j(p).$$

These market *value functions* are such that $e_j(tp) = te_j(p)$ and, from Walras's law, $\Sigma e_j = 0$. Since $e_j \leq S_j$ if $p_j \leq 1$, we have that they are bounded above in Δ. From Walras's law, $e_j = -\Sigma_{i \neq j} e_i$, and so *from their being bounded above it follows that they are also bounded below*, even though the S_j need not be.

The excess supply value functions e_j, being continuous and bounded in the interior of the simplex Δ, have unique continuous extensions which include the boundary, and the functions can now be taken to have that extension. Then a restatement of the intercept condition is that $e_j < 0$ if $p_j = 0$. With this and Walras's law, for $p \in \Delta$,

$$p_j = 1 \Leftrightarrow p_i = 0 \, (i \neq j)$$
$$\Rightarrow e_i < 0 \, (i \neq j)$$
$$\Rightarrow e_j = -\Sigma_{i \neq j} \, e_i > 0.$$

so *the intercept condition, implies that also $e_j > 0$ if $p_j = 1$.*

With the intercept condition, it therefore follows immediately from continuity that, for all $p_i \, (i \neq j)$, there exists some $p_j > 0$ for which $e_j(p) = 0$. For, since e_j takes positive and negative values as p_j varies, *it must be zero for some p_j*, by Bolzano's theorem. The issue then is whether a $p > 0$ moreover exists for which $e_j(p) = 0$ for all j simultaneously. That this existence can be affirmed will be shown later using the KKM lemma proved in Chapter VI.3. Here therefore are quite loose economically motivated conditions under which feasible prices must exist for the economy.

Further conditions considered now, consistent with (in fact, implying) the foregoing, are therefore not essential for the existence of prices, but they serve an easy consideration of the process for arriving at them. For the special case of a linear market, dealt with in the next section, they are already implied by the foregoing. More than requiring e_j to be positive when p_j is large and negative when p_j is small, the variation of e_j is required to be monotonic in a suitable sense. Prices are significant only to the extent of their ratios, and varying one price affects its ratios with all others. An increase in one price amounts to a lowering of all other prices relative to it. Instead of asking first that e_j be increasing in p_j it can be required to be decreasing in all $p_i \, (i \neq j)$. From Walras's law it then follows that e_j is increasing in p_j. When price normalization is maintained, prices cannot be given independent variations, and the *slope condition* so formulated applies to prices free of the normalization restriction.

3.6 LINEAR MARKETS

A special market model is the *linear market* model, in which the excess supply value functions $e_j = p_j S_j$ are the elements of the vector e given in the linear form $e = pa$, where a is a constant matrix. Then Walras's law, that $eI = 0$ for all p, requires $aI = 0$. Then the price existence question is whether $p > 0$ exists for which $pa = 0$. For, with $p_j > 0$, $e_j = 0$ is equivalent to $S_j = 0$. We will consider the question in this section, and also the next, where it will be approached by a method that shows at the same time how such prices can be arrived at following the law of supply and demand, like the *tâtonnement* of Walras.

With this model,

$$S_j = a_{jj} + \Sigma_{i \neq j} p_i a_{ij} / p_j,$$

so a_{jj} is the supply capacity limit for good j in the economy, approached asymptotically as $p_j \to \infty$. This means the same when prices are restricted to be normalized and $p_j \to 1$, ratios of other prices being fixed while normalization is preserved. The *finite supply capacity* assumption is therefore *an automatic part of this model*. The intercept condition requires $e_j < 0$ if $p_j = 0$, that is,

$$\Sigma_{i \neq j} p_i a_{ij} < 0 \quad \text{for all} \quad p_i \, (i \neq j),$$

so it is equivalent to

$$a_{ij} < 0 \, (i \neq j).$$

But the slope condition is equivalent to this also. Thus, for the linear market model, *the slope and intercept conditions are equivalent*. With Walras's law, they both imply

$$a_{jj} > 0 \text{ for all } j,$$

that is, a *positive supply capacity limit* for every good.

The units for goods are at present arbitrary. When $u_j > 0$ present units of good j are made the new unit, the price p_j becomes $p_j u_j$, and the excess supply quantity S_j becomes S_j / u_j, so the excess supply value $e_j = p_j S_j$ is *unaltered*. With the new units, the elements a_{ij} of the matrix a are replaced by a_{ij} / u_i; in particular, a_{jj} is replaced by a_{jj} / u_j. Since $a_{jj} > 0$, we can take $u_j = a_{jj}$ and so choose new units to make $a_{jj} = 1$. It can be understood now that the system has been normalized by this choice of units to make $a_{jj} = 1$ for all j. That is, for any good, *the supply capacity limit has been made the unit of amount*.

For any $p_i \, (i \neq j)$, the excess supply curve for good j is a rectangular hyperbola with the lines $p_j = 0$ and $S_j = 1$ as asymptotes (see Figure 3). The curve cuts the line $S_j = 0$ where

$$p_j = -\Sigma_{i \neq j} p_i a_{ij} = p_j - \Sigma_i p_i a_{ij} = \Sigma_i p_i b_{ij},$$

the coefficients b_{ij} being given by

$$b_{ij} = -a_{ij} > 0 \, (i \neq j), \, b_{jj} = 1 - a_{jj} = 1 - 1 = 0,$$

so that $b = 1 - a \geq 0$.

The condition for $S_j = 0$ for all j is therefore $p = pb$. Since Walras's law requires $aI = 0$, we have $bI = I$. Thus b, being such that $b \geq 0$ and $bI = I$, is a square row distribution matrix, or a transition matrix as in a Markov process. Because $b_{ij} > 0 \, (j \, i)$, it is irreducible, and so, by the equilibrium theorem for Markov processes shown in chapter V.5, *there exists a unique normalized price vector p for which $p = pb$, and moreover this is positive*. That is, there exist prices p_j, with ratios uniquely determined and all positive, for which $e_j = p_j S_j = 0$ for all j. Since $p_j > 0$, this is equivalent to $S_j = 0$ for all j, as required.

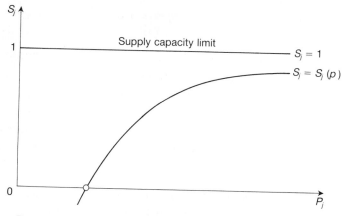

Excess supply curve for good *j* prices of other goods being fixed

Figure 3

3.7 'TÂTONNEMENT'

From the theory of distribution matrices, with *b* irreducible, we not only have the existence of a unique and positive normalized price vector p^* for which $p^* = p^*b$; we also know that it can be found, starting with any initial *p*, by repeatedly replacing *p* by *pb*. That is,

$$pb^t \rightarrow p^* \ (t \rightarrow \infty),$$

whatever the initial *p*. An explanation of this process, where *p* is adjusted each time to *pb*, is that, given any prices *p* for all the goods, *the price of each good is altered to exactly the price that would clear its market were all the other prices to remain unaltered*. The other prices do not remain the same, but all are readjusted by the same principle simultaneously, and so none come out quite as intended. But, with the indefinite repetition of the process, there is a convergence to the right prices which clear all markets simultaneously. This might be a fair model for the process of arriving at p^*, were there some agency in the economy for its realization; in any case, a knowledge of the matrix *b* would be essential. We have no idea of such an agency, with that kind of knowledge, and this is not the sort of thing to be entertained for the automatic self-regulation of the market.

Excess supply or demand is known not by a fixed identifiable individual or agency, but in a scattered decentralized way, as soon as a buyer of a good cannot find a seller or a seller a buyer at the price of the last transaction. That price then is no longer the price. The possible price rises or falls, in the minds and readiness of unfulfilled buyers or sellers (in the one case or the other), until a transaction takes place, when it becomes the actual price; and so forth. A consistency with this picture is required; it is not exactly the *tâtonnement* of Walras, but is more or less the same—and there is no need for the usual auctioneer.

The adjustment model to be considered is stated by

$$p_j{}^* = p_j - v_j e_j,$$

where the $v_j > 0$ are reaction coefficients, or *adjustment velocities*. For a restatement, $r^* = rc$, where $r_j = p_j / v_j$ and

$$c_{ij} = - v_i a_{ij} \geq 0 \ (i \neq j), \ c_{jj} = 1 - v_j a_{jj} = 1 - v_j.$$

Thus $cI = I$, since $aI = 0$. Also, $c \geq 0$ provided $v_j \leq 1$ for all j. In that case c is a distribution matrix, and so as before, starting with any p, and corresponding r, indefinite repetition of the adjustment produces a convergence, with limit r^* for which $r^* = r^*c$, that is $p^{**} = p^*$, equivalently $e(p^*) = 0$, or equivalently $S(p^*) = 0$.

The velocities must be positive, to produce an alteration in the prices. Also, they cannot be so large as to make any price become negative. At any rate, over-reaction can be expected not to lead to an eventual settled state, but to produce endless turmoil in the prices; to produce not a final order, but a perpetual chaos. With our particular normalization, involving a choice of units, the requirement for an orderly convergence takes the form $0 < v_i \leq 1$. This is an entirely satisfactory result, as it stands. We could also allow the v_i to vary freely in time, provided the upper and lower limits as time $\rightarrow \infty$ be positive and less than 1. But then we need a theorem about the convergence of infinite products of distribution matrices, instead of the familiar theorem about the convergence of powers.

3.8 CONTINUOUS MARKETS

Consider continuous excess supply value functions $e_i = p_i S_i$ defined on the normalized prices simplex Δ such that

$$\Sigma e_i = 0, \quad p_i = 0 \Rightarrow e_i < 0,$$

that is, satisfying Walras's law and the interscept condition. We will show that $S_i = 0$ for all i, for some $p > 0$.

Let $C_i = [p : e_i \geq 0]$, so these are closed sets since the functions e_i are continuous, and for any subset V of the goods, or of vertices of the simplex, let $C_V = \cup_{i \, \epsilon \, V} C_i$. The face of the simplex on the vertices V is

$$\Delta_V = [p : i \, \epsilon \, \overline{V} \Rightarrow p_i = 0].$$

It will be shown that $\Delta_V \subset C_V$ for all V and hence, by the KKM lemma of Chapter VI.3, $\cap C_i \neq O$. But any $p \, \epsilon \cap C_i$ is by definition such that $e_i(p) \geq 0$ for all i. Since $e_i = 0$, this is equivalent to $e_i = 0$ for all i. By the intercept condition this implies $p_i > 0$ and so is equivalent to $S_i(p) = 0$ for all i, as required.

Thus, for any $p \, \epsilon \, \Delta$,

$$p \, \epsilon \, \Delta_V \Leftrightarrow i \, \epsilon \, \overline{V} \Rightarrow p_i = 0 \qquad \text{\textit{definition of left}}$$
$$\Rightarrow i \, \epsilon \, \overline{V} \Rightarrow e_i \leq 0 \qquad \text{\textit{intercept condition}}$$
$$\Rightarrow \Sigma_{i \, \epsilon \, \overline{V}} e_i \leq 0 \qquad \text{\textit{inequality sum}}$$

$\leftrightarrow \Sigma_{i \epsilon V} e_i \geq 0$ *Walras's law*
$\Rightarrow e_i \geq 0$ for some $i \epsilon V$ *inequality sum*
$\leftrightarrow p \epsilon C_i$ for some $i \epsilon V$ *definition of C_i*
$\leftrightarrow p \epsilon C_V$ *definition of C_V*

and so we have $\Delta_V \subset C_V$. QED

3.9   UNIQUENESS AND STABILITY

Suppose market functions e_i are continuously differentiable and such that

$$e_{ij} = \partial e_i / \partial p_j < 0 \ (j \neq i).$$

This *slope condition*, though different, is similar to the familiar gross substitutes condition on excess demand.

Now from Walras's law $\Sigma_i e_i = 0$, we have $\Sigma_i e_{ij} = 0$, and so also $e_{ii} > 0$. Because the e_i are homogeneous of degree 1 they satisfy Euler's identity

$$\Sigma_j e_{ij} p_j = e_i,$$

with the consequence that $e_i < 0$ if $p_i = 0$. Thus, *the slope condition implies the intercept condition* and so, by the theorem of the last section, we have the existence of $p^* > 0$ for which $e_i(p^*) = 0$ for all i. We will be able to deduce also the uniqueness of such p^* from the following stability considerations.

Consider the differential price adjustment system

$$\dot{p}_i = - v_i e_i(p),$$

where the *reaction coefficients*, or velocities, are any constants $v_i > 0$. Since replacing p_i by p_i / v_i corresponds to a change of the arbitrary physical units, we can suppose the change already made, so in effect the coefficients v_i become all equal to 1 and the system becomes simply

$$\dot{p} = - e(p).$$

Given any initial $p(0)$ in the interior of Δ, this has a unique solution $p(t)(t \geq 0)$, and the intercept condition assures us that this remains in the interior of Δ. We want to show that

$$p(t) \rightarrow p^* \ (t \rightarrow \infty).$$

In other words, p^* is a globally stable equilibrium, in the differential adjustment process, and hence also the unique equilibrium.

For a small time interval τ the adjustment process is approximated by the finite difference system

$$p' - p = - \tau e(p),$$

where p becomes p' after time τ. Thus we have $p' = f(p)$ where

$$f(p) = p - \tau e(p),$$

so $e(p^*) = 0$ is equivalent to $f(p^*) = p^*$.

For the derivatives of f_i we have

$$f_{ii} = 1 - \tau e_{ii}, f_{ij} = -\tau e_{ij} > 0 (j \neq i),$$

and

$$\Sigma_i f_{ij} = 1 - \tau_i e_{ij} = 1.$$

Thus the derivative matrix g of f is a positive row distribution matrix provided

$$\tau < 1/e_{ii}.$$

From continuity of the derivatives and compactness of Δ, τ can be made small enough to make this so for all p. Then with g positive and continuous, and Δ compact, the elements of g have a lower bound $\mu > 0$.

Now consider the r-fold iterated image

$$f^{(r)}(p) = f(f(\ldots f(p)\ldots)));$$

that is,

$$f^{(0)}(p) = p, \quad f^{(r)}(p) = f(f^{(r-1)}(p)) \quad (r = 1, 2, \ldots).$$

The derivative matrix, by the chain rule, is

$$g^{(r)} = g^1 \ldots g^r,$$

where g^s is g evaluated at $f^{(s-1)}(p)$. Then, by section V.5.4, for all $p, q \in \Delta$,

$$|(q - p)g^{(r)}| < |q - p|(1 - \mu)^r.$$

We should conclude from this that, for any $\epsilon > 0$, there exists s such that, for all $p, q \in \Delta$,

$$|f^{(r)}(q) - f^{(r)}(p)| < \epsilon$$

for all $r > s$, and hence that $f^{(r)}(p)(r \to \infty)$ converges to a constant function, with the single value p^* since in any case this must be one of its values. In other words, p^* is a stable equilibrium in the finite adjustment system $p' = f(p)$.

The differential system and the finite difference systems have the same equilibria. The finite difference systems are stable and approximate the differential system for small τ. It follows that the differential system is also stable.

IV.4

Sraffa's Prices

In Chapter I of Piero Sraffa's *Production of Commodities by Means of Commodities: Prelude to a Critique of Economic Theory* (1960), entitled 'Production for Subsistence', the same production is repeated every period and everything produced is used up in producing what is produced. (The elusive steady state sought by ecologists must be like this.) The complete intelligibility is undone when prices are introduced; it is not said what purpose they serve, as if one should know. These are not prices in the ordinary sense of when a market transaction takes place.

Being clear about some matters can spoil them for higher thought—Sraffa's book certainly has not done that. It is a canonical text serving a revival of interest in the *theory of value,* whatever that is—it seems to be an inheritance from earlier thought, and a later concentration of Ricardo, whose significance is quite uncertain. Prices are not regarded as having anything to do with market transactions, competition and the equilibrium of supply and demand. They are required to express the principle that the value of anything is justly measured by the value that has gone into its making, so that there is the *value equation,* i.e. value of input equals value of output. A rate of surplus is introduced later, and then the value of output is a multiple of the value of input. It is a uniform rate across sectors, suggesting a background of competition rather alien to this thought. The kind of principle intended—whether it has anything to do with real prices or is a moral formula for proper prices, or anything else— is an issue. For Sraffa in the application to his particular model it happens to be a precise formula determining unique prices. He barely escapes imposing too many conditions on them and certainly cannot require more. In the background, and giving motive to the enquiry, is the labour theory of value, a doctrine of sorts more than a theory, and that goes further. It asserts that the value of anything is ultimately equal to the labour that has gone into making it; so it implies the same principle expressed by the value equation, but if it tells us anything a further condition has been added about the nature of the unit. Since the value equation alone makes prices fully determined, there is no room for further conditions, and with production models different from Sraffa's there are too many already. There is an obstacle to the application of the theory, since the arithmetic of it is impossible.

It is an accident of his special Chapter I model that the simultaneous constraints on prices imposed by Sraffa are not inconsistent. He counts independent equations and variables and finds the numbers equal, concluding that prices with the wanted consistency property do exist. Walras did the same for prices which should clear all markets simultaneously, and Abraham Wald a hundred years later pointed out that the counting argument is ineffective, so initiating the modern theory, which goes further with the mathematics though not much further with the economics. Sraffa has linear equations for which the counting is useful. But prices which must satisfy them should also be non-negative, even positive. That might be supposed, though without knowing the significance of the prices it is impossible to know this with certainty. If this is an exercise in labour value arithmetic, the fruit is to find that the arithmetic is impossible. Sraffa's model, like Leontief's, has separate production of all goods, and if it is modified to allow joint production then the value equation alone produces an inconsistency, without any requirement about the unit. The same is true when a rate of surplus is allowed.

It might be a pity to encounter difficulties only when coming to Sraffa's arithmetic, and not before. It may fairly be asked what importance should be given to sense and logic. Here is another formula or slogan, like the 'greatest happiness for the greatest number', or the optimality of competitive equilibrium, which might lack sense but not influence. The words can be used, joined with equations where those are appreciated, and still they have effect of a stirring symbol, or a flag. Robinson and Eatwell (1973, p. 3), dealing with 'Metaphysics and science', call the greatest good formula 'metaphysics', but it is not that, and the same can be said of Sraffa's prices. But while those other formulae are insubstantial and give slight opportunity for an investigation, Sraffa's prices produce questions, beside whatever else, about the mathematics of his arguments. The affinity with von Neumann's economic model is well recognized, and the trinity of Marx, von Neumann and Sraffa have been canonized. On such lines, in the association with von Neumann, Sraffa's thought leads to an expression of the Maximum Doctrine of Perfect Competition much better than is found in textbooks where the Walrasian system is given that duty. The maximality is now in the physical terms wanted by the physiocrats, and behaviour concerns competition and profit. That Sraffa's ideas should find a coherence in that particular context, revealing them in a way as crypto-capitalist, is surprising.

First we consider the existence question in his Chapter I. A theorem from the theory of Markov processes—applied to distributions not now of probability but of goods to sectors—shows the general existence of non-negative prices satisfying the required conditions, imposed by the value equation. The further condition for these to be unique and positive is that the economy be irreducible, or that no independent sub-economy should exist. Joined with this condition is an elaboration quite like the *tâtonnement* of Walras for arriving at the prices, though it has nothing to do with the relation of supply and demand, which now are fixed. If in any period the prices are not exactly right, the shortages and surpluses of value for sectors which occur are compensated by price adjustments for the next period. Each price is adjusted for the right amount, as concerns income from output and regardless of the other prices being adjusted at the same time. Therefore it turns out not to be quite the right amount, and the process must be repeated endlessly, but there is a convergence. For a parallel with the Walrasian equilibrium and stability, Sraffa's prices are represented in a framework where they appear as equilibrium prices — with a global stability, moreover. After dealing with the case concerning a surplus, and joint production, the relation with Leontief and von Neumann is considered.

4.1 PRODUCTION FOR SUBSISTENCE

The economy produces some n goods, in the same quantities in any period. The production quantity of each can be made the unit, so the amount of any good produced in a period always equals 1. There are n sectors in the economy, each producing just one of the goods. Any good produced can be an input for the production of any other, and the total amount of a good that is used up in the production of all goods exactly equals the total amount produced. The chosen units makes this 1 in each case.

Let a_{ij} be the amount of good i used up in the production of good j. Since the total amount used up exactly equals the amount produced, we have

$$a_{ij} \geq 0, \ \Sigma_j a_{ij} = 1 \quad \text{for all } i.$$

The matrix a with these elements is a distribution matrix, each of its rows being a distribution vector since the elements of it are non-negative and sum to 1. The distribution in any one row shows how the good produced by one sector is distributed to all sectors. For the matrix a we now have

$$a \geq 0, \ aI = I \tag{i}$$

where I is the column vector with n elements all 1.

If the goods have prices p_i, the value of the amount a_{ij} of good i used as an input in the production of good j is $p_i a_{ij}$, and so the total value of inputs is $\Sigma_i a_{ij}$. The output is one unit of good j, with value $p_j 1 = p_j$. Therefore on Sraffa's principle, that *the value of output equals the value of input*, it is required that

$$\Sigma_i p_i a_{ij} = p_j \quad \text{for all } j;$$

that is,

$$pa = p \tag{ii}$$

where p is the vector of the prices. Only the ratios of the prices are important for this condition. If they should be non-negative and not all zero, so that their sum is positive, then by dividing them by their sum their ratios are unaltered but their sum is made equal to one. Then p is such that

$$p \geq 0, \ pI = I \tag{iii}$$

and so is a distribution vector. Since prices are values of the outputs, this vector represents a distribution of value over the sectors, or an income distribution.

Sraffa suggests that, because of (i), any $n - 1$ of the n equations stated by (ii) imply the remaining one, so that there are $n - 1$ independent equations to determine $n - 1$ unique ratios of the prices. A valid conclusion from the condition $aI = I$ in (ii) is that the equations (ii) are satisfied by some $p \neq 0$. The uniqueness depends on the rank of $a - 1$. A proper question is about the existence, and the uniqueness, of a solution of (ii) subject to (iii) or, possibly more suitably, to

$$p > 0, pI = I. \qquad\qquad (\text{iii}')$$

That there generally exists a solution subject to (iii) is known immediately from the theory of Markov processes, by Theorem I of section V.5.1. Any prices which are such a solution are called *Sraffa's prices* (a phrase, invented by this writer, whose echo might be heard — with a different commentary — at symposia in Naples). The further issue about solutions subject to (iii'), that is, about the existence of positive Sraffa's prices, involves the irreducibility condition, put in economic terms in the introduction here, and discussed in chapter V.5 on 'Distribution Matrices'. It is settled, again, by a theorem from the theory of Markov processes, Theorem II of section V.5.1. From it, we have that the irreducibility is necessary and sufficient for both existence and uniqueness.

The Sraffa matrix a is a Quesnay *tableau économique*, and because of the choice of units making outputs all 1 it is also a Leontief input-output matrix. The special feature of the Sraffa subsistence economy is that the outputs equal the inputs so that net outputs are all zero. In terms of the input-output theory of section IV.2.6, this may not be a productive economy, or even a semi-productive one, since no goods are produced finally. In any case, we cannot freely think that Sraffa's economy is a Leontief economy, where there is a choice of activity on the linear model, even though, for that matter, Leontief did take such a liberty with similar data.

A subgroup E of sectors, with complement D, is an *independent sub-economy* if

$$a_{ij} = 0 \text{ for } i \in D, j \in E.$$

That is, sectors which are in E use no inputs produced by sectors which are not. Such a sub-economy would, out of self-interest, were such a thing understandable here, break away from the others and possibly become a better-than-subsistence economy on its own. Irreducibility means the non-existence of such a sub-economy. It guarantees the existence of positive Sraffa's prices, and is implied by their existence. It is also equivalent to Sraffa's prices being unique.

4.2 INTERDEPENDENCE AND STABILITY

With the Sraffa distribution matrix a, and any prices p,

$$v = pa - p$$

is the vector of value losses to sectors, and $-v$ the gains, or profits. The algebraical sum of the losses, or the gains, is zero. For with $aI = I$ we have

$$vI = paI - pI = pI - pI = 0.$$

There is a loss to sector i if $v_i > 0$ and a gain or profit if $v_i < 0$, and the total of losses equals the total of gains, as in a zero-sum game, so the winners take away from the losers. With Sraffa's prices we have $v = 0$, and so no such imbalance, but equilibrium. Whenever $v \neq 0$ there is inequity, exploitation; forces are present—if not for revolution, then for a change of prices. The price p_i which determines the value of the product of sector i can be adjusted to compensate the current loss v_i by making it $p_i^+ = p_i + v_i$ in the next period. The prices therefore become

$$p^+ = p + v = p + (pa - p) = pa.$$

The new losses and gains generally will not be zero and the process must be repeated, indefinitely, producing a series of prices pa^t ($t = 0, 1, 2, \ldots$). Sraffa's prices p^* always exist. But under a certain condition, which also assures they are unique and positive, we have

$$pa^t \to p^* \; (t \to \infty),$$

so the series is always convergent, to a limit which is independent of the initial prices p and equal to the Sraffa price vector p^*, so we have $v \to 0$. The required condition is more than the irreducibility of the Sraffa distribution matrix a, only to exclude the periodic case dealt with in the last section of chapter V.5. In that special case there can be chains of dependence which close into cycles involving a subgroup of sectors, leaving others outside the circle. It is reflected by some power of the the matrix a being reducible, even if a is not. If there is such a power at all it will occur before the nth. In that case the prices would tend to run through a cycle of values, and so to oscillate indefinitely instead of converging, even though the various values on the cycle converge. Contrivance is needed to produce such a case, and if it is excluded then irreducibility is the required convergence condition. One way of excluding it is to require all powers up to the nth to be irreducible. The condition has a direct economic sense which extends to other models, beside Sraffa's and Leontief's. The concern of it is interdependence between sectors, so it is relational rather than quantitative, and it is also readable directly from Quesnay's *tableau économique*.

4.3 PRODUCTION WITH A SURPLUS

A Quesnay table has the form $T \, Y \, X$ where T is the transaction table, X the gross product vector and Y the net product, or surplus after the factors of production have been replaced. All entries are taken to be non-negative and there is the accounting identity

$$TI + Y = X.$$

We have chosen the units to make $X = I$. Then the Leontief coefficients are

$$a_{ij} = T_{ij} / X_j = T_{ij},$$

so $a = T$ and the transaction matrix T already is the Leontief matrix. Thus we have

$$aI + Y = I,$$

the matrix a being ambiguously the Sraffa, Leontief and Quesnay matrices simultaneously. In the subsistence case there is no surplus so that $Y = 0$ and hence $aI = I$. In any case, $aI \leq I$, since it is understood that $Y \geq 0$. The surplus or net product is

$$Y = I - aI = (1 - a)I,$$

and some goods are produced with a surplus if $aI \leq I$, and all are if $aI < I$.

For the case of production with a surplus, Sraffa introduces a rate of profit r simultaneously with prices p by means of the condition

$$(1 + r)pa = p$$

which makes the value of output in any sector the profit factor $e = 1 + r$ times the value of the inputs.

Sraffa argues that here are n independent equations to uniquely determine n unknowns, the profit factor e and $n - 1$ independent ratios of the prices p. These are not linear equations in all the variables, so the existence question is not so straightforward, and is even less so if prices are taken to be semi-positive, as expressed by

$$p \geq 0, \quad pI = 1.$$

The Perron-Frobenius theorem on non-negative matrices shows that his conclusion is correct as concerns existence provided a is irreducible. Also, under this condition, if r is given the smallest possible value for any solution, then the corresponding p is unique and positive.

For another view, consider an interest factor i across a production period when the prices are $p \geq 0$. The costs of the inputs are given by ipa and the returns on outputs by p, and so the profits by $p - ipa$. Then

$$e = \inf [i : ipa \geq p, p \geq 0, pI = 1]$$

is the lower limit of interest factors consistent with nonpositive profits. Since p is restricted to a compact set it is attained for some p, and so is a minimum. With any prices p, the minimum interest factor is

$$e(p) = \min [i : ipa \geq p],$$

and then

$$e = \min [e(p) : p \gtrless 0].$$

Then we have

$$epa \gtrless p, \quad p \ge 0, pI = 1$$

for some p, and for all p', and e',

$$e'p'a \gtrless p', \quad p' \gtrless 0 \Rightarrow e' \ge e.$$

Sraffa's problem now has a resolution for the case where a is irreducible; for then, moreover

$$epa = p, \quad p \gtrless 0,$$

and such p with the normalization $pI = 1$ is unique. With this background we see Sraffa's profit rate rather as the minimum interest rate at which a positive profit is impossible at any prices.

Sraffa's profit rate is introduced in value terms without reference to a growth rate in the real terms of production. It lacks sense without such an anchor because, for all we know or have been told, there is nothing one can do with value except buy goods. In any case, we should see if Sraffa's value profit rate has, accidentally, any definite relation to the real growth rate. The growth factor is the largest multiple of inputs which can be replaced by outputs, or does not exceed them, so in Sraffa's economy it is

$$g = \max [t : aIt \le I].$$

We have $g \ge 1$ since $aI \le I$; also $g > 1$ only if $aI \le I$, and otherwise $g = 1$. In any case $aIg \le I$, and so

$$paig \le pI = 1.$$

Also, from $epa \ge p$ it follows that

$$epaI \ge pI = 1,$$

and hence

$$(paI)g \le (paI)e.$$

With $aI \gtrless 0$ and $p \gtrless 0$ we have $paI \gtrless 0$, and it follows that $e \ge g$. The case $e \gtrless g$ is likely in Sraffa's economy, where there is no choice of activity. Here, therefore, there might be a proof that Sraffa's economy is inflationary, were it possible to give inflation a meaning in this model.

4.4 JOINT PRODUCTION

Instead of having n goods each produced separately by n sectors, suppose there are n sectors each of which jointly produces many goods from a possible m. Let $a_{ij} \ge 0$, $b_{ij} \ge 0$ be the input and output of good i by sector j. In a subsistence economy the total input and output of any good i are equal, so with this common total taken as the unit of amount for each good we have

$$\sum_j a_{ij} = 1, \quad \sum_j b_{ij} = 1 \quad \text{for all } i;$$

that is,

$$aI = I, \quad bI = I.$$

Also $a \geq 0, b \geq 0$ so a, b are a pair of rectangular row-distribution matrices, of order $m \times n$. The original model of Sraffa corresponds to the case where $m = n$ and b is the unit matrix.

Any prices p are required to be non-negative and with sum 1,

$$p \geq 0, \quad pI = 1,$$

and the value equation between input and output in every sector requires

$$pa = pb.$$

In the case of Sraffa's subsistence economy such prices would be ordinary Sraffa prices, and their existence is assured. But in the more general case with joint production there is no such assurance. With

$$\Pi = [p : p \geq 0, pI = 1]$$

as the price simplex, consider the polytopes

$$A = [pa : p \in \Pi], \quad B = [pb : p \in \Pi]$$

which are the convex closures of the rows of a, b lying in the distribution simplex

$$\Delta = [d : d \geq 0, Jd = 1]$$

where J is the row vector with n elements all equal to 1. The existence of consistent prices immediately implies that A and B intersect, and there is no general reason why they should. One could divide the simplex Δ into two parts linearly, so that both parts are convex, and take the rows of a in one part and of b in the other. Their convex closures would then be disjoint. In the special case of Sraffa we have $\Delta = B$ so that $A \subset B$, and so of course this cannot be done. Sraffa's economy has generalizations in which consistent prices still must exist. One is where $m > n$ and some n of the goods are produced entirely by some n different sectors; in other words, each sector has a monopoly in the production of at least one good.

4.5   VARIABLE ACTIVITY

A principle about value is invalidated as a general principle if it requires very special circumstances for its applicability, and we saw that Sraffa's cannot generally be applied to a subsistence economy with joint production. Also, a rate of profit for production with a surplus is introduced purely in value or money terms, without any explicit relation to the real terms of production. In his model the profit rate can exceed the physical growth rate. From experience, this might signify an inflationary situation, but here it cannot, since there is no sure way to interpret inflation in this model, where prices have significance only through their ratios. We are not told what happens to the profit and surplus, and without other guidance they seem useless. Sraffa in his preface emphasizes that the production plan is fixed, in order to guard against any presumption that he is dependent on constant returns. Then the surplus cannot be used to expand production, and we do not know what happens to it. Sraffa might be forced to allow variable activity to give a destination to the surplus and profit, and we are also. Another observation is that his positive profit rate has an alternative meaning: it is also the minimum interest rate which makes positive profit impossible at any prices. Zero profit is associated in theory with perfect competition—an uncongenial model in this setting—but if one adopts the latter meaning a way is open for resolving these difficulties.

As usual, irreducibility, the non-existence of an independent sub-economy, will play a part, and this is suitable if an economy is a proper unit arising from an interdependence between the parts. Sraffa distinguishes *basic goods* essential to the production of all others and *luxury goods*, which are not essential to any. In an irreducible economy all goods are basic if not from direct dependence of other goods on them then indirectly from chains of dependence. He remarks that there are no luxury goods in a subsistence economy because every output immediately becomes an input, although they can arise when there is a surplus. There cannot be any luxury goods if the economy is irreducible. But this would imply that the smoke issuing from factory chimnies is a luxury! There can be some grievance about the smoke, but not that sort.

The obvious way of introducing variable activity is to turn the Sraffa economy into a Leontief economy. This is especially easy, since the Sraffa matrix is already, with the quantity units that have been adopted, also a Leontief matrix.

4.6 SRAFFA AND LEONTIEF

Since the output quantities have been made the units, the vector I with all elements 1 is the output vector, and aI is the input vector. The subsistence case is where $aI = I$. When a is regarded as a Leontief matrix the output can be any $x \geq 0$, and ax is the input required for it. The Sraffa model then corresponds to the case where only $x = I$ is allowed.

In reality, production takes time, and inputs come before outputs. If the outputs supply inputs it must be for the next round of production. The output x_t in period t is the resource for the input ax_{t+1} in the next period, and cannot be exceeded by it. The output in one period puts a condition on the possible output in the next, and for a series of outputs to be feasible it is required that

$$x_t \geq ax_{t+1}, \qquad t = 0, 1, 2, \ldots$$

The condition for successive outputs x, y to be feasible is that $x \geq ay$, and for growth by a factor θ it is required that $y \geq x\theta$, so we have

$$x \geq ay \geq ax\theta .$$

Thus $x \geq ax\theta$ is a necessary condition for growth θ of an output x. Also it is sufficient since, given this condition, we can take $y = x\theta$, and then $x \geq ay$, $y \geq x\theta$ as required.

Any output $x \geq 0$ is associated with a growth factor

$$g(x) = \max [\theta : x \geq ax\theta] = \min [x_i / a_{(i}x : a_{(i}x \geq 0],$$

so

$$x \geq ax\theta \Leftrightarrow \theta \leq g(x).$$

The function $g(x)$ depends only on the ratios of the elements of x. Also, $x \geq 0$ is equivalent to $x \geq 0$ and $Jx \geq 0$, J being a row vector with elements all 1. The range of $g(x)$ therefore is unaltered by restriction to the set

$$X = [x : x \geq 0, Jx = 1].$$

The set X is compact and $g(x)$ is continuous in it, and so attains a maximum. The system therefore has a maximum growth factor, for all possible outputs $x \geq 0$, given by

$$\begin{aligned} g &= \max [g(x) : x \geq 0] \\ &= \max [\theta : x \geq ax\theta, x \geq 0, Jx = 1]. \end{aligned}$$

With a Leontief matrix a, in Chapter IV.2, we considered conditions $ax \leq x$ for some $x \geq 0$, $ax \geq x$ for some $x \geq 0$, and $ax < x$ for some $x \geq 0$. These are required for the economy to be capable of, respectively, at least subsistence, to be semi-productive, maintaining levels of all goods with a surplus of some, and to be productive, with a surplus of all, respectively. If the economy is irreducible, the last two conditions are equivalent. A main input-output theorem is that the last condition is necessary and sufficient for the inverse of $1 - a$ to exist and be non-negative. Now that growth has been brought in, the conditions are just telling us about g, the first that $g \geq 1$ and the last that $g \geq 1$. Also, the way the theorem is formulated is artificial. It makes sense when production has no reference to time; if it does, then outputs are required to supply the inputs that produced them as if they were available for that purpose in advance of their own production. Another form for the theorem is that

$$|1 - ga| = 0,$$

and a necessary and sufficient condition for the inverse of $1 - \theta a$ to exist and be non-negative is that $\theta < g$.

Outputs replace inputs, and for the fixed production economy the replacement is stated to be physical; then the prices which are introduced have no function. An alternative view is that the cost $pa_{j)}x_j$ of input of any industry j is borrowed at the beginning of the production period, and paid back with interest from the return $p_j x_j$ on output x_j at the end. If the interest factor is θ the profit is $(p_j - \theta pa_{j)})x_j$. Perfect competition denies positive profit in equilibrium, so θ is an admissible interest factor if

$$\theta pa_{j)} \geq p_j \quad \text{for all } j,$$

that is, if $\theta pa \geq p$. Solvency of industry j requires a non-negative profit, and so if the rate of profit on output is negative it will not produce; that is,

$$\theta pa_{j)} > p_j \Rightarrow x_j = 0.$$

With $\theta pa \ge p$ this condition is equivalent to $\theta pax = px$.

The considerations given to the maximum growth factor apply similarly to the minimum interest factor for the system, given by

$$h = \min [\theta : \theta pa \ge p, p \ge 0, pI = 1].$$

We now have a maximum growth factor g and a minimum interest factor h and some quantities x and prices p with which they are achieved. For these we have

$$axg \le x, \quad hpa \ge p.$$

Industry solvency requires, moreover, that $hpax = px$.

Having introduced prices and hypothetical criteria for an equilibrium such as nonpositive profit and solvency, we can proceed similarly with the growth factor. Equilibrium is not significant in the absence of a mechanism with forces that produce and maintain it, and ideas associated with perfect competition are relevant here. Such a picture would amount to a computational algorithm for the equilibrium, in the way that the Walrasian *tâtonnement* is an algorithm for prices that clear markets, though here we deal with a different model.

Output goods in one period are demanded only as inputs in the next, and if the growth of any good exceeds the maximum overall rate there would be an unusable surplus of it. Excess supply in equilibrium makes a free good, so we have

$$a_{(i}xg \le x_i \Rightarrow p_i = 0 \quad \text{for all } i.$$

With $axg \le x$, this condition is equivalent to $paxg = px$.

We now have

$$axg \le x, \quad paxg = px,$$
$$hpa \ge p, \quad hpax = px,$$

and consequently also

$$paxg = px = hpax.$$

If $pax = 0$, it follows that also $px = 0$. But with a irreducible, this combination is impossible. Therefore $pax \gtrless 0$, and it follows that $g = h$. With θ as the common value of g and h, our conditions imply

(M)	$ax\theta \le x, \quad x \gtrless 0,$
(W)	$\theta pa \ge p, \quad p \gtrless 0,$

and these imply $px \ge pax\theta \ge px$, so all the conditions follow from these.

The issue now is whether all the conditions entertained can be satisfied simultaneously, or, what now is the same, whether there exist p, x and θ which satisfy M and W.

It is noted that M and W are the Kuhn-Tucker conditions for the function

$$r(p, x) = px / pax \qquad (p \ge 0, x \ge 0)$$

to have a saddle point, with saddle value θ. This function is well defined provided

$$pax = 0, \; px = 0 \qquad (p \geq 0, x \geq 0)$$

is impossible, as it is since a is irreducible. With the function well defined, the question is whether it has a saddle point.

The conditions make sense even when a is a rectangular matrix, and in fact the existence question is unaffected. It is a special case of the similar question for the von Neumann model dealt with in the next section. That model incorporates joint production, and the numbers of goods and of industries, or activities, that produce them are not restricted to equality. But now we have an irreducible square matrix, and an appeal can be made to the Perron-Frobenius theorem. The conclusion is that the conditions can be satisfied, moreover, with the equalities

$$ax\theta = x, \quad \theta pa = p,$$

and θ is identified not only with the maximum growth factor and the minimum interest factor, but also with Sraffa's profit factor. Also, p provides Sraffa's prices. The profit rate is at least the rate of surplus, and, with the restriction to the single activity $x = I$ of the fixed production economy, it cannot be granted that it is not greater.

4.7   SRAFFA AND VON NEUMANN

With the input and output matrices a and b of section 4.4, suppose now they are rectangular of order $m \times n$, so m goods are produced by n sectors without the restriction $m = n$. The Sraffa economy with separate production is now the case where $m = n$ and $b = 1$. The subsistence case is where $aI = bI$ and there is a surplus of output over input if $aI \leq bI$. With variable activity these conditions become less important, and only signify the existence of some quantities with a growth factor of at least 1.

Sraffa's prices p and profit π are subject to conditions $\pi pa = pb$, but these are not generally consistent, and no such prices and profit need exist. An alternative is to think in terms of an interest factor as in the last section. With zero profit, the criterion for solvency, as the maximum profit there are conditions $\pi pa \geq pb$ instead. These are easier to solve, and even too easy. For any prices there exists an interest factor which makes them satisfied. There is no prospect of using these conditions to determine prices, since any prices will do. A limitation on the interest rate is needed. One that is suitable—perhaps even for a capitalist economy—is that it should not exceed the real rate of growth. Without an objective for growth, there is an ambiguity about the rate of growth, by any measure, and the proportional sense used here has a limited significance. But at least, if positive quantities of all goods are growing at a positive rate, then every quantity for every good will be exceeded eventually—or the opposite if the rate is negative, so that there is contraction instead of expansion.

Now we shall describe the linear activity model with joint production due to von Neumann, which extends the Sraffa and Leontief models. Growth is defined with it as reference. The growth factor, and quantity side of the model, fit symmetrically, as a dual, to the interest factor and price side, which have already been touched. A central point is the feasibility of making an interest factor, with some prices, not exceed a growth factor with some quantities, and the uniqueness which results. The theorem of von Neumann offers this with some provisors. At first, with activities fixed, each sector j has an input vector $a_{j)}$ and output vector $b_{j)}$. One way to make this variable is by introducing an activity parameter t_j, making an input $a_{j)}\, t_j$ and output $b_{j)}\, t_j$. The parameter, or activity intensity, is not now restricted to the value 1 but can take any value $t_j \geq 0$. With t as the activity vector, the total input x and output y of the economy are given by $x = at,\; bt = y$. The system so described is called a linear activity system, and is an innovation of von Neumann. By taking b with a single row we have many inputs and one output, and so a production function for one good. But the system gives service especially as a model for joint production. The output goods need not be the same as the input goods, though here the m goods listed can include all goods.

Another way to read this system is that at is the vector of minimum inputs required to perform the activity t, and bt the vector of maximum outputs from the activity. Then, with x as the vector of quantities available to serve as inputs, they must be at least enough to support the activity t, so that we have the constraint $x \geq at$. Another understanding of this constraint is that it expresses free disposal on the input side, or that the excess of availability over requirement can be eliminated without constraint or cost. One could have this and keep the formulation with equations instead of inequalities by introducing disposal activities with input and no output, but this way is more suitable. Similarly, we have the constraint $bt \geq y$ on the output side, showing that outputs can be bt or anything less, and so incorporating free disposal on that side. Thus, in order that any input and ouput x and y with an activity t to be feasible, it is required that

$$x \geq at, \quad bt \geq y.$$

Therefore, for any given x, y, the output y with input x is feasible provided there exists an activity t which satisfies these simultaneous constraints. Thus the input-output relation R for the economy across a single production period is defined by

$$xRy \equiv x \geq at,\, bt \geq y \quad \text{for some } t.$$

In particular, $a_{j)}\, R b_{j)}$, this corresponding to the case where only sector j is active; and $(at)R(bt)$ is a further case. Free disposal on both sides is expressed by

$$x' \geq xRy \geq y' \;\Rightarrow\; x'Ry'$$

or, using the relation product, by $\geq R \geq \;\subset R$.

Growth can be formulated as for input or for output, or for activity. It makes no difference to growth factors, and activity suits best. Activities t admit a growth factor θ if $at\theta \leq bt$. We already have that prices p admit an interest factor π if $\pi pa \geq pb$. With the constraint $\pi \leq \theta$ making the interest rate at most the growth rate, a question of consistency arises, whether such p, t, π and θ exist.

The conditions

$$\pi pa \geq pb, \quad p \geq 0,$$
$$at\theta \leq bt, \quad t \geq 0,$$

imply

$$\pi pat \geq pbt \geq at\theta.$$

Therefore if it can be granted that $pat > 0$, it would follow that $\pi \geq \theta$ and hence $\pi = \theta$, and hence also

$$\pi pat = pbt = pat\theta.$$

It would be enough to know that

$$pat = 0, \quad pbt = 0 \qquad (p \geq 0, t \geq 0)$$

is impossible; for from the last relation $pbt = 0$ if $pat = 0$, and so $pat = 0$ would be denied. This wanted impossibility amounts to a generalization applicable to a rectangular matrix pair a, b of the condition for a single square matrix a to be irreducible. It reduces to that condition when these are square matrices and $b = 1$. It is a generalization arrived at by pursuing the economic sense of irreducibility, the non-existence of an independent sub-economy, with this more general model. For his existence theorem von Neumann required the stronger condition $a + b > 0$, which amounts to saying that every good is either an input or an output in every activity, but this condition can replace it. Conditions that are not mentioned, but are also needed, are

$$p > 0 \Rightarrow pa \geq 0, \quad t > 0 \Rightarrow bt > 0.$$

For another view, the conditions being considered are equivalent to

(W) $\qquad\qquad \pi pa \geq pb, \quad \pi pat = pbt,$
(M) $\qquad\qquad at\theta \leq bt, \quad pat\theta = pbt,$

together with $\pi \leq \theta$, which with irreducibility implies that $\pi = \theta$. Part of (W) is the condition

$$\pi pa_{j)} \geq pb_{j)} \quad \text{for all } j,$$

for π to be a permissible interest factor with the prices p, making zero profit the maximum attainable by any sector j. With that, the second part is equivalent to

$$\pi pa_{j)} > pb_{j)} \Rightarrow t_j = 0,$$

that is, sectors which do not achieve solvency cease activity. Here are equilibrium conditions of perfect competition. The total profit in all sectors of the economy when the activities are t is $(pb - \pi pa)t = 0$, so if not all profits are zero then some will be positive and some negative. With free movement of resources from the insolvent sectors to profitable ones the economy will come to rest only when these conditions are satisfied. The survivors will all be solvent, each with zero profit since the total is zero.

Another competitive mechanism is on the side of the goods. They are supplied by output and demanded by input, which are related by the growth factor θ. The total value for all goods of the difference between supply and demand at the prices p is $p(bt - at\theta) = 0$. Total excess supply value being zero, if it is not zero for all then for some it will be positive and others negative. If the prices are free to rise and fall according to the law of supply and demand, when the economy is at rest any good i still in excess supply must be a free good; that is, $p_i = 0$, so there is the condition

$$b_{(i}t > a_{(i}\theta \Rightarrow p_i = 0.$$

With the condition

$$b_{(i}t \geq a_{(i}\theta \quad \text{for all } i$$

for θ to be a possible growth factor, with the activity t, this is equivalent to $pbt = pat\,\theta$. The considered conditions are interpreted in this way as equilibrium conditions for perfect competition. When the growth rate determined by the conditions is identified with the maximum rate, some sort of realization for the offerings of the Maximum Doctrine of Perfect Competition is obtained.

IV.5

General Economic Equilibrium

Schumpeter (1954, p. 500) said 'I do not hold that Bastiat was a bad theorist. I hold that he was no theorist.' That might have been an advantage for Frederic Bastiat (1801–1850), who put the idea of general economic equilibrium very well. He had been about Paris early in the morning, and had seen the milkman doing his rounds, shutters coming down from shops, the baker delivering bread, the inevitable citizen who had just collected a loaf, people were going off to work — it was highly orderly, like clockwork, an exact matching of parts in an elaborate design, an orchestration with a vast number of participants. But where was the designer, or conductor?

Imagination is baffled when it tries to appreciate the vast multiplicity of commodities which must enter tomorrow in order to preserve the inhabitants from falling prey to the convulsions of famine, rebellion and pillage. Yet all sleep, and their slumbers are not disturbed for a single minute by the prospect of such a frightful catastrophe. (Bastiat, 1850)

Bastiat found the ordinary experience remarkable, and raised the question about which the theory of general equilibrium is concerned.

'Economy' comes from the Greeks and means management of the household. But households do not manage themselves — there are people in charge, and they do it. Here there seemed to be a large household, highly regulated but with no one in charge, and it was not a unique accident, but happened all the time. Though this matter was so familiar as to be hardly noticed, there was still something needing to be explained. Had Bastiat been with the Incas instead, the question would not have arisen. People *were* in charge there, the Captains of Ten, captains of ten of those, and so forth, collecting and distributing products in a system of warehouses — an elaborate bureaucracy-administered welfare, giving care to the aged, the sick, and those with misfortunes, while any departing from their proper function were skinned alive. Bastiat was not simply concerned with the phenomenon of social order, as such. That really is a commonplace, wherever there are societies, and not just human ones. His concern was with the particular mechanisms imagined to be available, and not to be available, in this case to produce the order.

A system is understood in terms of its parts and their behaviour. An engine is disassembled into parts, which are examined for their individual properties conditions of perfect competition. The total profit in all sectors of the economy when the activities are t is $(pb - \pi pa)t = 0$, so if not all profits are zero then some will be positive and some negative. With free movement of resources from the insolvent sectors to profitable ones the economy will come to rest only when these conditions are satisfied. The survivors will all be solvent, each with zero profit since the total is zero.

Another competitive mechanism is on the side of the goods. They are supplied by output and demanded by input, which are related by the growth factor θ. The total value for all goods of the difference between supply and demand at the prices p is $p(bt - at\theta) = 0$. Total excess supply value being zero, if it is not zero for all then for some it will be positive and others negative. If the prices are free to rise and fall according to the law of supply and demand, when the economy is at rest any good i still in excess supply must be a free good; that is, $p_i = 0$, so there is the condition

$$b_{(i}t > a_{(i}\theta \Rightarrow p_i = 0.$$

With the condition

$$b_{(i}t \geq a_{(i}\theta \quad \text{for all } i$$

for θ to be a possible growth factor, with the activity t, this is equivalent to $pbt = pat\theta$. The considered conditions are interpreted in this way as equilibrium conditions for perfect competition. When the growth rate determined by the conditions is identified with the maximum rate, some sort of realization for the offerings of the Maximum Doctrine of Perfect Competition is obtained.

III.4

The Four-point Formula

The *expansion locus* associated with any prices is the locus of consumption when income varies while the prices remain fixed. When demand is governed by utility, properties of the utility are reflected in the characteristics of the expansion loci. For instance, if the utility relation $R \subset C \times C$ is homogeneous, or conical, having the property

$$xRy \Rightarrow xtRyt \ (t \geq 0),$$

by which its graph in $C \times C$ is a cone, then also the expansion loci in the commodity space C are cones, possibly just single rays, or lines through the origin. Correspondingly, the relation between incomes that have the same purchasing power at some different prices is homogeneous linear, and so is represented by a line through the origin, now in the *income space*, the space of two dimensions with the incomes as coordinates. We have also called this the *Fleetwood space*, because his method determines points in it, without the compulsion to take ratios of coordinates and otherwise abandon the points, as in effect is done with the CPI. The slope of the line, which in this case completely describes the relation of equivalent incomes, is the *price index* corresponding to the two different price situations. *The idea of a price index for both theory and practice is encompassed in the idea that this relation between equivalent incomes should be homogeneous linear, and so capable of description by a single number—its slope—that number being the price index.* At least, it seems, very suitable to think of it that way. In order for such a relation to be possible when expressed in terms of utility, the utility involved must be homogeneous or conical in the way just stated. Correspondingly, in the commodity space, expansion paths must be rays through the origin. Beyond that, no more can be said of the relation except that it should be monotonic. The price index thus represents a highly restricted idea about purchasing power, or cost of living, with implications about demand behaviour, and about utility when that is brought in.

For a less compromised but still simple approach to the same matter, the relation between equivalent incomes might be taken to be linear, not necessarily homogeneous, and so represented by a line which need not go through the origin. To describe such a relation two numbers are required, the slope and the intercept, instead of just one. Correspondingly, as concerns the expansion and the way in which they fit together. From that, everything about the engine is known. Engineers have always been trained to think like that; it is successful in the physical sciences, and extends to the economics which grew after Newton. An engine is not disassembled into ultimate parts to the full extent conceivable, but into significant units as far as the engine is concerned—the components from which the system is built. They might still be complex in themselves, but what happens internally is unimportant. The outward performance is what concerns the system, the outside input-output behaviour. The same is done with the economy, though what we have in this case is not as clear as with a mechanical engine which someone has designed and made, and so is knowable perfectly well in principle and almost as well in practice. But, considering the reasonable objectives, this does not matter. There is a general phenomenon to be explained, and the explanation can be offered only by demonstrating it in some fashion with an imaginary model, an economy-like engine that is invented.

Two kinds of components are distinguished, *producers* and *consumers*. In fact, both of these components both produce and consume, simultaneously, so this terminology does not reveal the distinction intended. Products are distinguished as *intermediate*, which become inputs for some further production, and *final*, which do not. The 'consumers' are distinguished as being producers of final products, each producing one, the utility which, being the motive, acts to make a maximum. The entire flow of production goes towards the production of these utilities of consumers, and is consumed in their production. The producer-consumer terminology serves well, even though the producers are as much consumers as are the consumers, and logically it might fit even better the other way round. Producers are subordinates of the consumers, being owned by them. What they do is governed by their utility to their owners, and from here the profit motive of producers derives without additional assumption.

These consumers are free agents; anything they do is voluntary and they act for their own interests, their utilities, serving no one but themselves. They do not even know the states and interests of other agents so as to have any regard for them. Yet they are bound together through their own separate interests, and settle down in an orderly fashion in a general and stable equilibrium—that is what has to be demonstrated to satisfy Bastiat. Adam Smith's well known remark tells us the same thing: 'We owe our bread not to the benevolence of the baker but to his self-interest.' Then there is the doctrine of the Invisible Hand: with all these selfish people gathered together, chaos might have been the expected result, but instead there is order, as if the economy were governed by an Invisible Hand. The expression is not to suggest an outside intervention, defeating the idea of a self-regulated system, but the opposite. More has been seen in the Invisible Hand than was intended by Adam Smith. It has been taken to be like a production manager who directs the economy to produce its maximum possible output. But the economy has many outputs—all the separate utilities of those self-interested consumers who are without a notion of collective welfare or output—so it is impossible to know what this could mean. There seems to be an unfortunate association with the Maximum Doctrine of Perfect Competition, which had much currency then as now. The only competition in Walrasian equilibrium models is that which produced Stephen Leacock's 'All boarding-house rents are equal' proposition (section IV.3.3). The *General Competitive Analysis* of K. J. Arrow and F. Hahn (1972) is not so general; the term 'competitive', frequently used in general equilibrium theory does very little work there—unless it is exhausted from honouring the memory of the dead Maximum Doctrine.

The theory of the market of Chapter IV.3 is more basic than microeconomic theory such as this, and is independent of it. The existence of individual traders is recognized there, but little is assumed about them and they are quite featureless. They need not even be the completely self-interested consumers of classical doctrine. Here they are definitely in the picture, and make the main point of it. Bastiat actually saw them going about their activities and wondered how they came to be so organized. The assumptions made about them are consistent with the market model of Chapter IV.3, and are illustrative of it without being required by it. There can be a concurrence with the view of Schumpeter (1954, p. 134):

... utilitarian hypotheses are unnecessary but harmless. For instance we can state and discuss properties of economic equilibrium without introducing them. But if we do introduce them the results are not materially affected, hence not impaired.

After customary attention to Robinson Crusoe, we go to Edgeworth's Box and its generalizations, such as are associated with MacKenzie, and with Arrow and Debreu. In the Cobb-Douglas world the theory becomes elementary, and consistent with the linear market model developed in Chapter IV.3. Main points are still represented, but now they are dealt with more simply by finite algebra, and everything can be calculated.

5.1   CRUSOE'S DEVELOPMENT

Robinson Crusoe by himself makes a model for the opposite of a market economy. He should be no different from the typical individual, except for his unusual situation. We will use him for describing the economic individual, even though at first he is taken away from the market where the individuals later appear. We start with the isolation usually associated with him and consider effects as the situation develops.

Crusoe escapes from the shipwreck with a bundle of goods b and a customary way of life from before the event, represented by another bundle of goods a (see Figure 1). The shock of the gap between anything less than b which was available, and everything greater than a which would satisfy custom, sent him into adaptive explorations. In the reduced condition of his arrival, feasibility lay in an intolerantly small region, and the survival contour C bounding it was encountered at every turn. He was at first continually close to that contour,

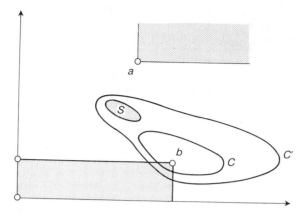

Figure 1   Crusoe's development

in states of exhaustion or starvation, or both. But he did not quite cross over, and eventually become more settled and organized, so the contour *C* receded to *C'*, diminishing the hazards and the pressure of his proximity to it. In the secure interior of a widened feasibility he became knowledgeable and discriminating about locations. Fair proportions between his needs and the activities required to supply them were discovered, and the adaptive search mechanisms required to steer away from the survival contour in the days when that was everywhere near fell into atrophy. He had found a settled way of life, *S*.

That story might look somewhat different from the ordinary textbook story of the economic individual, and perhaps it is; and it should be seen where any difference lies. If Crusoe works too much, he perishes from exhaustion, and if not enough, then from starvation, and if he acts in the wrong way, then from both. There is a survival-feasibility region in his activity space, small when he first arrived but luckily not empty, despite his wretched condition. The diagram shows the corresponding region in the activity space. The bundle *b* of his earlier custom is far out of reach. He would soon die of exhaustion if driven by old habit to work for anything like it. He would not get anywhere near it, and should he have it by chance it would not be best for the new situation, as he would find. After he adjusts to his new situation, his activity space is enlarged, and his vulnerability to hardships is diminished, and so a larger range of activities become feasible. He has more choice and develops preferences beyond just survival. Eventually, as a fruit of a lot of accidents, he settles down in a small region or point *S*, his general equilibrium and new habit, the sort of thing that biologists call a 'niche'.

This is a ragged story, and what else should one do about Crusoe? To suppose he has comprehensive preferences between things unknown to him would be irrational. The effort to find out about all those things in order to make useless judgements about them would soon exhaust and derange him — like any ordinary creature in equilibrium, he accepts, or prefers, the nature or niche that he has. The shipwreck, of course, disturbed Crusoe's equilibrium, but now he is in equilibrium again.

There is already a model for Crusoe, and it can be developed, without making it any more precise, by imposing features which are mathematically specific. That has already been done, for instance, in the use of a diagram (Figure 1). One could pretend that one knew all those curves, and one could also give him preferences between everything in the world. We could thus turn him into a respectable economic individual — even rational, as some say.

In the common way to put it, activity is what Crusoe chooses, on the basis of a valuation of effects. These might be separated into costs and benefits, input and output, x and y, constrained by feasibility and giving a value $U(x, y)$. We can always redefine U to have value $-\infty$ in the case of infeasibility, so feasibility can be understood to be incorporated in the constraint $U > -\infty$; and survival is a necessary condition for feasibility, so no more need be said about that either. Crusoe maximizes U and we suppose some value $U > -\infty$ is attainable. In fact, Crusoe is devoted to hunting as much as to its material results and does not count the cost. The unalterable separation of variables into goods and bads, benefits and costs, though often useful, can also be awkward. In Crusoe's case, hunting is a good when taken in a fair measure and proportion with other things and a bad otherwise. Most creatures exist not altogether for input-output but according to their nature, or niche, like 'the lillies of the field, which toil not nor do they reap'. Even a profit-making firm can be viewed in that way.

The first theoretical individual is simply a consumer, dealing only in benefits, or input x, and a utility $U(x)$, which is an output of service to no one else and has no market. When the individual is put to work later there must be some other output, y. But to be more flexible, instead of distinguishing input and output, x and y both non-negative, one can deal with an activity vector z with elements positive or negative, and a utility $U(z)$.

5.2 EDGEWORTH'S BOX

Edgeworth's box diagram is a way of representing all possible distributions of two goods to two individuals (see Figure 2). A pair of diagonally opposite corners of a unit square are associated with the individuals 1, 2 and the directions of the sides are associated with the goods 1, 2.

Lines through any point X of the square parallel to the sides cut the sides in points dividing them in proportion to the division of the goods between the individuals. The points of the square, or box, therefore correspond to distributions of the goods to the individuals. If the total quantities of the goods being allocated are made the units of quantity, the distributions also specify actual amounts of goods allocated to the individuals. If x_{ij} is the amount of good i allocated to individual j corresponding to a point X in the box, then we have

$$x_{11} + x_{12} = 1, \quad x_{21} + x_{22} = 1,$$

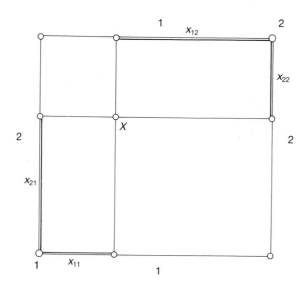

Figure 2   Edgeworth's Box

making the matrix x with these elements a 2×2 distribution matrix. Its ith row is a distribution specifying how good i is distributed to individuals. The vector x_j with elements x_{ij}, from column j of the matrix is the bundle of goods held by individual j. These bundles are such that $x_1 + x_2 = I$, where I is the vector with elements all 1.

In this way we think of a point X of the box as a distribution matrix x. Put this way, we have an immediate generalization for any numbers m of goods and n of individuals, the 'hyperbox' dealt with in the next section. The advantage of the original box is its diagram, which provides a means for illustrating all general features.

In moving from one point x in the box to another y, one individual receives more of some good and the other less, and the gain of one equals the loss of the other. There is a transfer of goods between the individuals, the total quantities held by them remaining unchanged. This reveals a useful characteristic of the diagram.

These individuals and goods can be taken to make up an economy whose state is specified by an allocation, represented by a point x in the box. A measure of welfare in the economy—were there such a thing—therefore would be a function $U(x) = U(x_1, x_2)$ of the state. With the distribution constraint $x_1 + x_2 = I$ this could be represented as a function of x_1, or of x_2. Were this function to govern, an optimal point for the economy would be one where this function is a maximum. But, as there are two independent individuals, so there are two views about welfare and its measure, stated by two utility functions $U_1(x) = U_1(x_1)$, $U_2(x) = U_2(x_2)$.

The sense of these functions is that any action taken by the individuals can only be so as to increase their own utility functions. An assumption about the functions, beside continuity, is that they are semi-increasing; that is, they increase when all their arguments are increased. Therefore neither individual would simply dispose of goods by giving them to the other, because this would represent a loss. One individual would possibly consent to giving a good to the other on condition of a return in another good; there would have to be an exchange. Moreover, an exchange contract requires joint consent from both sides, and this would be forthcoming only if it is of benefit to both sides.

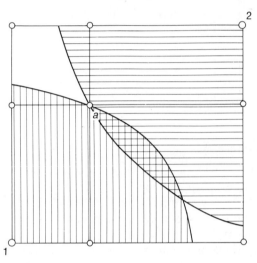

Figure 3   Exchange set

Starting from a given initial position represented by a point a in the box, we can now consider all possible exchanges that could take place. The set of points in the box attainable by them is the *exchange set* (Figure 3)

$$E(a) = [x : U_1(x) > U_1(a), U_2(x) > U_2(a)],$$

which is associated with the initial point a. If this set is empty, so that no voluntary exchanges can take place and there can be no movement from the point a, then a is a point of *exchange equilibrium* (Figure 4). The set C of exchange equilibria defines the *contract locus*. For any $a \in C$, we have

$$U_1(x) \geq U_1(a) \Rightarrow U_2(x) \leq U_2(a);$$

that is,

$$\max \{ U_2(x) : U_1(x) \geq U_1(a) \} = U_2(a)$$

and also

$$U_1(x) > U_1(a) \Rightarrow U_2(x) < U_2(a)$$

and, equivalently, the same with 1, 2 interchanged.

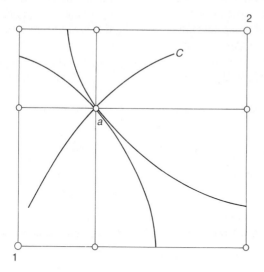

Figure 4   Exchange equilibrium

Introducing preference relations

$$xP_j y \equiv U_j(x) < U_j(y) \qquad (j = 1, 2)$$

for the individuals and their intersection

$$P = P_1 \cap P_2,$$

we have $E(a) = aP$, that is, the exchange set $E(a)$ is simply the set $aP = [x : aPx]$ of points x in the box to which the initial point a has the relation P. The joint preference or *Pareto relation* P is irreflexive and transitive and so is a strict order. A point has this relation to another point if both individuals agree that the other is superior or is an acceptable successor to the first.

Any points $x, y, \ldots$ form an *exchange series* if each has the next as an acceptible successor, if it *has* a successor; that is, $xPyP\ldots$. Because of transitivity, every term is a successor of all earlier ones. Any term which is an exchange equilibrium cannot have a successor and so must terminate the series. An infinite exchange series therefore cannot contain any term which is an equilibrium. However, for any point of the box, *either it is an exchange equilibrium or it has a successor which is*. Thus, if a is not, so that aP is not empty and aPb for some b, let c be a solution to the problem

$$\max U_1(x) : U_2(x) \geq U_2(b),$$

which exists since functions are continuous and regions compact. Then $aPbPc$ so that aPc, but cP is empty.

We can think of the Edgeworth box economy, with two individuals traders and two goods, just as well as an economy where two goods — the utilities — are produced separately but sharing the same two inputs—the goods whose fixed amounts make the box. A unit of each of the inputs is available and is to be shared between the producers. Edgeworth's rigid box does not permit free disposal of the inputs, but it is natural to consider it. The input resource space is then not just the bundle I with a unit of each good, but also includes anything less. An input allocation x is feasible if the total inputs xI do not exceed availability; that is, $xI \leq I$, so

$$A = [x : x \geq 0, xI \leq I]$$

is the set of feasible *allocations*, while

$$D = [x : x \geq 0, xI = I]$$

is the subset of complete allocations, or *distributions*, corresponding to points of the box. With any input allocation x to the producers the output is the vector

$$U(x) = U_1(x_1), U_2(x_2)$$

in the output or utility space (see Figures 5 and 6). Then, with A as the input possibility set, the output possibility set is the image

$$U(A) = [U(x) : x \epsilon A],$$

in the output space. With restriction to the box D of distributions, the image would be the subset $U(D) \subset U(A)$. Though it is not so natural to consider this, the box diagram makes reference to D easy.

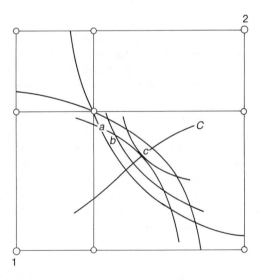

Figure 5   Input possibilities

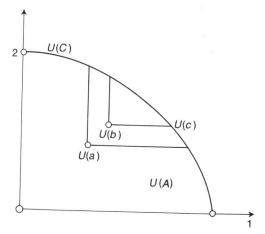

Figure 6   Output possibilities

Were the box contracted by replacing the bundle I of units by a smaller bundle, $U(A)$ and $U(D)$ would contract also. While $U(A)$ already includes all points associated with such contractions, $U(D)$ does not. A property of $U(A)$ not necessarily shared by $U(D)$ is that

$$z \in U(A), z' \leq x \Rightarrow z' \in U(A),$$

by which it is an *orthogenous* set. However, $U(A)$ is derivable as the *orthogenous closure* of its subset $U(D)$,

$$U(A) = [z' : z' \leq z, z \in U(D)].$$

In fact, the image $U(C)$ of the contract locus C serves just as well as a subset of $U(A)$ from which $U(A)$ can be drived as its orthogenous closure. This follows from the proposition stated earlier, that every point in the box which is not an exchange equilibrium has a successor which is. Moreover, the contract locus image is the *smallest* such subset.

5.3   THREE SENSES OF EQUILIBRIUM

The utility curves have been drawn convex for the sake of simplicity and also because the property has some importance now, but it had no importance up to this point. An assumption about utility functions that has been used is that they are semi-increasing. This condition is intermediate between their being increasing and non-decreasing and it makes the utility possibility set orthogenous. Now we assume utility functions to be concave. A consequence is that the utility possibility set is convex. Since it is already orthogenous, that makes it *orthoconvex* and so a typical production possibility set.

Were there a social welfare function for the economy, it would govern choice, and so take the place of the individual utilities in any decision. The individuals would have no choices to make, but could only produce utility as directed using the inputs given to them in the optimal plan; they would be enslaved to the central objective. There would be no semblance of individual liberty, and it is very odd that welfare functions are usually brought in to demonstrate the merits of the free economy beyond the freedom—in fact, cancelling it. An apparent welfare type of function in the following should not be taken as such, or as serving that idea at all—more the contrary—and with it we have the sense of the usual textbook optimality conditions.

We already have one kind of equilibrium in which the individuals, finding no exchange contract that benefits both, are unwilling to exchange. They remain at rest in the current position, which is one of *exchange equilibrium*, such points describing the contract locus. Now such points will be seen to be equilibria in two further senses. One is that some (social welfare!) function defined in the utility space is at a maximum; the other is that there exist prices which leave the two traders independently in equilibrium where they are, each unwilling to trade at those prices. We can call one *centralized equilibrium* and the other *decentralized equilibrium*. Separate from this, we later shall have an equilibrium concept applied to prices, having reference to any point in the box and not just the contract locus. That is yet another situation in which the possible movement applies to the prices. It is not to be confused with what we have already, even though there is a relationship. We can call the prices that produce the decentralized equilibrium *equilibrating prices*, distinguishing them from the equilibrium prices of this other sense. It is true that equilibrium prices for any point of the box are associated with a point of the box which is on the contract locus, and they are equilibrating prices for that point; but that is another concept and the distinction in view holds none the less.

With Edgeworth's box there is no production and only a transfer of goods, whose total quantities remain unchanged. Though much is illustrated with it, not everything is. When production is brought in, a further global 'optimality' appears. This is that the total output of the economy in equilibrium is at the maximum possible when it is valued at the equilibrium prices themselves. This might be construed as a fulfilment of some significant optimality doctrine, and it should not be. The equilibrium prices were not known in advance of the equilibrium, as a welfare criterion should be—in any case, something will be at a maximum anywhere one cares to choose. Consider the following:

PROPOSITION: x is optimal.

Proof Let $f(x) = 1$, $f(y) = 0$ ($y \neq x$). Now f is maximum at x. Therefore, x is optimal. QED

Some optimalities that are offered are no more impressive than this, as can be obscured by greater sophistication in the choice of f, and the complex conditions for it to be maximum.

Consider any point c which is on the contract locus, that is, a point of exchange equilibrium. It corresponds to a point $U(c)$ which is on the boundary of the utility possibility set $U(A)$, which is convex. Therefore, by the theorem of the supporting hyperplane, there exists a nonconstant linear function $W(U)$ in the utility space whose maximum in the set $U(A)$ is at the point $U(c)$. We now have $U = U(c)$ as a solution to the problem

$$\max W(U) : U \epsilon U(A),$$

that is, $x = c$ is a solution to

$$\max W(U(x)) : x \epsilon A,$$

which is the problem

$$\max W(U(x)) : xI \leq I, x \geq 0.$$

Now because W is linear and the utility functions are concave, and the constraints are linear, this is a convex programming problem. Because $xI < I$ for some $x \geq 0$, Slater's condition is satisfied. Hence, for some p, we have the programming optimality conditions, of Chapter V.2:

$$cI \leq I, p \geq 0, pcI = pI,$$

together with

$$c \geq 0, W(U(x)) - pxI \leq W(U(c)) - pcI \text{ for all } x \geq 0.$$

The existence of a p so that these conditions are satisfied is necessary and sufficient for c to be an optimal solution.

Now,

$$x = (x_1, x_2), xI = x_1 + x_2, U(x) = (U_1(x_1), U_2(x_2)),$$

and W has the form

$$W(U(x)) = w_1 U_1(x_1) + w_2 U_2(x_2), \quad (w_1, w_2) \neq 0.$$

Because $U(A)$ is orthogenous and so attains it maxumum under $U \leq U(c)$ at $U = U(c)$, we conclude that $(w_1, w_2) \geq 0$. Also, if $U(c)$ is not on the boundary of the utility space we must have $(w_1, w_2) > 0$. The optimality conditions imply that

$$c_i \geq 0, \quad w_i U_i(x_i) - px_i \leq w_i U_i(c_i) - pc_i \quad \text{for all } x_i \geq 0,$$

for $i = 1, 2$. But with $p \geq 0$, $w_i > 0$, here we have optimality conditions for the two separate problems

$$\max U_i(x_i) : px_i \leq pc_i, x_i \geq 0 \quad (i = 1, 2),$$

making $x_i = c_i$ their solutions.

Conversely from here, with $p \geq 0$ and $c_1 + c_2 = I$, we infer the existence of $w_i > 0$ to satisfy the original conditions. In this way we have seen *the equivalence of centralized equilibrium*, involving some overall value function W, *and decentralized equilibrium*, involving some prices p and bearing on the individuals separately, and we have noted that *both are implied by exchange equilibrium*. With the observation that they imply exchange equilibrium we have that *all three conditions are equivalent*. We observe that, because the prices *p* provide a line in Edgeworth's box separating the preferred regions of the individuals, and since these regions are separate, there is no mutually acceptable exchange contract; in other words, they are at a point of exchange equilibrium. The decentralized equilibrium conditions show that at the prices *p* neither individual wants to buy or sell anything, so these are equilibrating prices for a decentralized equilibrium.

The prices *p* first appeared as Lagrange multipliers associated with the constraints $xI \leq I$ in the centralized problem. They are also marginal values of the goods in the economy, value being determined by the maximum value of *W*. If the function

$$F(z) = \max \left[W(U(x)) : xI \leq z, x \geq 0 \right]$$

is differentiable at $z = I$ then these prices provide its derivatives, and in any case

$$F(z) - F(I) \leq p(z - I) \quad \text{for all } z,$$

which implies the former when *F* is differentiable. This is in harmony with the doctrine about wages, or factor prices, reflecting marginal social product; but *W* is meaningless as a criterion of social value.

5.4   FEASIBLE PRICES

With the equilibrating prices associated with any contract point, neither individual wants to buy or sell anything. The supply and the demand for any good at those prices are zero and so certainly they are equal. At points of the box not on the contract locus there are no such prices, making supplies and demands all zero; then there can be a question about the existence of prices just making them equal.

With any point *a* of the box and any prices *p*, the budget lines of the traders are represented simultaneously by a line in the box through *a*. Prices being non-negative, this line lies in two quadrants of the box, upper left *A* and lower right *B*. Trader *i* would trade to replace the initial bundle a_i by a bundle x_i which has the same value at the prices but makes utility U_i a maximum, that is, which solves the programming problem

$$\max U_i(x_i) : px_i = pa_i, x_i \geq 0.$$

Assuming the utility curves to be strictly convex, x_i is determined as a continuous single-valued function $x_i(p)$ of *p*. The net supply of goods from trader *i* is $s_i = a_i - x_i$, also a continuous function of *p*; or $d_i = -s_i$ is the net demand. From the budget constraint, $ps_i = 0$. The excess supply in the economy, or the aggregate of net supplies, is given by

$$S = s_1 + s_2 = (a_1 + a_2) - (x_1 + x_2) = aI - xI.$$

From the budget constraints it follows that $pS = 0$, this being Walras's law. The issue is whether there exist prices *p* which make $S = 0$. Because $aI = I$, this requires $xI = I$.

The discussion of Chapter IV.3 could be made to apply now, but that is hardly suitable. Our problem is simple because there are only two goods, and so from Walras's law if one market is cleared then so is the other automatically. We therefore have to find prices which make supply equal to demand for just one of the goods. When we can find two price positions making excess demand for one good in one position positive and in the other position negative, then because of continuity we can know that there is some position in between where the excess is zero.

Because of the convexity of the utility curves, any trader has equilibrating prices at any point of the box, by the support theorem. But, except at a point on the contract locus, the equilibrating prices of the traders at the same point are different. Let p_1, p_2 be equilibrating prices for traders 1, 2 at a point a. We can assume that these are normalized so that $p_i I = 1$ ($i = 1, 2$). At prices p_1 the supplies and demands of trader 1 for all goods are all zero. Then trader 2 will demand one good and supply the other in some positive quantities, say will demand good 2 and supply good 1 as in Figure 7, where the demand point of trader 2 falls in the lower right quadrant B which contains the intersection of the preferred regions of the traders, as it must from convexity and support considerations. Thus, good 2 is in excess demand and good 1 is in excess supply at the prices p_1. Similarly, at the prices p_2, and it has to be argued that in this case there is the opposite situation, with good 1 in excess demand and good 1 in excess supply. We only have to see that the demand point of trader 1 falls in the same quadrant B, and it must since this contains the jointly preferred region, from the same considerations that applied before. Our conclusion is that there exist some normalized prices p on the segment joining p_1, p_2 where neither good is in excess supply or demand.

We could argue more cumbersomely by considering limiting situations as the price line varies continuously between horizontal and vertical positions. This has a correspondence with the argument in Chapter IV.3. Another alternative is as follows. With smooth and strictly convex utility curves, the contract locus is a curve with a unique price line associated with each of its points, which varies continuously as the curve is described. It cuts the boundary of the jointly preferred region in two points where the associated price lines fall on opposite sides of the original point a. Therefore by continuity there exists a point c on the contract curve in between these where the associate price line goes through a.

When the traders trade at the equilibrium prices p they are left at a point c on the contract locus. At that point the Edgeworth box economy is in equilibrium in the three senses of the last section, and moreover the equilibrium prices p now act as equilibrating prices for the decentralized equilibrium holding there.

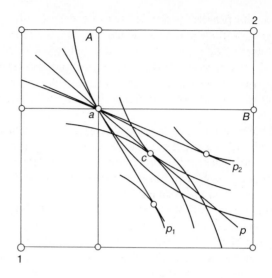

Figure 7

5.5   A COBB-DOUGLAS WORLD

The Edgeworth box discussion can be elaborated in a simple way algebraically
by taking the individual utility functions to have the Cobb-Douglas form

$$U_j(x_j) = A_j \Pi_i x_{ij}{}^{w_{ij}},$$

where

$$A_j > 0, \quad w_{ij} \geq 0, \quad \Sigma_i w_{ij} = 1.$$

Then explicit formulae can be found for its various terms.

The notation used is suited for the hyperbox generalization dealt with in
the next section where i, j have ranges 1 to m, 1 to n. For the present we still
have $m = 2$, $n = 2$ and assume $w_{ij} > 0$.

With $U_j > 0$ we must have $x_{ij} > 0$, and then

$$\partial U_j / \partial x_{ij} = U_j w_{ij} / x_{ij}.$$

Then the demand problem

$$\max U_j(x_j) : px_j = M_j$$

for individual j with income $M_j > 0$ and prices $p > 0$ produces positive
utility and so has the solution

$$x_{ij} = w_{ij} M_j / p_i.$$

At a point a of the box, with prices p, the income of individual j is
$M_j = pa_j$. With this value the demanded x_j is determined as a function of
p. The individual supplies a_j and demands x_j. Therefore for aggregate supply
to equal aggregate demand it is required that $aI = xI$. But $aI = I$ for a point

of the box, so this requires $xI = I$. Then from the demand functions, by summing over j,

$$p_i = \Sigma_j w_{ij} M_j;$$

that is, $p' = wM$, p being a row vector and M a column vector. We already have $M' = pa$, and so $p = paw'$ is the condition for equilibrium prices. This condition will be elaborated in the next section where the numbers of goods and traders are arbitrary.

The condition for a to be a point of the contract locus is that $x = a$ for the equilibrium prices p associated with a. Thus for trader 1 the quantities must satisfy

$$a_{11} = w_{11} M_1 / (w_{11} M_1 + w_{12} M_2),$$

$$a_{21} = w_{21} M_1 / (w_{21} M_1 + w_{22} M_2).$$

We can eliminate M_1 / M_2 between these relations and so obtain a relation between a_{11} and a_{21} describing the contract curve. Taking the lower and left edges of the box as x and y axes, so that $x = a_{11}$, $y = a_{21}$, we find

$$y = mx / \{ 1 + (m - 1) x \}$$

where

$$m = w_{11} w_{22} / w_{12} w_{21} .$$

If the want-coefficients (w_{11} , w_{12}), (w_{21} , w_{22}) of the two individuals are the same, we have $m = 1$, and then $y = x$ describes the contract curve; it is simply the diagonal of the box joining the two opposite origins. If the wants of the individuals are very different, then m is close to either 0 or ∞, and the curve still joins the origins but is distant from the diagonal on one side or the other.

Applying as much to the hyperbox of the next section as now, the formula

$$c_{ij} = w_{ij} M_j / \Sigma_j w_{ik} M_k$$

gives a parametric representation of points c on the contract locus in terms of the distribution of income M_j to the traders. Calculation of the utilities $U_j (c)$ with these values for c provides a parametric representation of the boundary of the utility possibility set, or of the utility transformation curve, or surface. The (social welfare!) function

$$W = A \Pi_j U_j M_j ,$$

a Bergson-Samuelson type of welfare function, and a Cobb-Douglas function of the utilities, whose exponents are given by the income distribution associated with a point c on the contract locus, attains a maximum in the box, or hyperbox, at the point $x = c$. It has derivatives

$$\partial W / \partial x_{ij} = (WM_j / U_j)(U_j w_{ij} / x_{ij}) = W (M_j w_{ij} / x_{ij}) = W p_j ,$$

so optimality conditions for the problem

$$\max W (x) : xI \leq I, x \geq 0$$

are satisfied with Wp as the vector of Lagrange multipliers associated with the constraints.

5.6 THE HYPERBOX

We now consider an economy with any m goods $i = 1, \ldots, m$ and n traders $j = 1, \ldots, n$. When there are just two of each, the Edgeworth diagram can be referred to. But everything considered for the special case has a counterpart for the general case, without any loss of simplicity; the diagram is lost but all the ideas are maintained, and significant features emerge that are not well represented in the special case. The issue of reducibility, of some subgroup of traders being independent of the others by having all possessions between them that are related to their own wants, is poorly represented when there are just two traders and two goods. As before, the individual utility functions have the Cobb-Douglas form. This assumption exactly produces the linear market model investigated in Chapter IV.3, and so everything there applies also here. A further illustrative feature is provided by the matrix w formed by the exponents in the functions. Since the exponents for any one trader which form a column of this matrix are non-negative and sum to 1, each column is a distribution vector, so making this an $m \times n$ rectangular distribution matrix. It is the *want matrix*, its elements expressing the relative weight or intensity with which any trader wants any good. It is such that $w \geq 0$, $Jw = J$ where J is a row vector of any order whose elements are all 1. Another similar rectangular distribution matrix that is involved is the *endowment matrix a*. This is a point in the *hyperbox* which is the generalized counterpart of Edgeworth's box whose rows tell how the goods in the economy are distributed to the traders. This is such that $a \geq 0$, $aI = I$, where I is like the vector J but a column vector instead. The two rectangular distribution matrices a and w, one with distributions by rows and the other columns, give all the parameters for the generalized Edgeworth box economy being considered. The product aw' of the one distribution matrix with the transpose of the other is a square distribution matrix, like the transition probability matrix of a Markov process. These distribution matrices have nothing to do with probability, but theorems available from probability theory can be applied to obtain required results. Reducibility of aw' in the sense applied to a stochastic matrix is equivalent to a similar reducibility which applies to a and w simultaneously and has an economic sense. The irreducibility of aw' or of the pair a, w in the equivalent sense is necessary and sufficient for positive equilibrium prices to exist, and for these to be unique. The three senses of equilibrium of section 5.3, generalized and subject to irreducibility, are again equivalent. Irreducibility is also the condition for the global convergence of the *tâtonnement* process for finding them, dealt with in Chapter IV.3.

Prices are given by a row vector p, and $pI = 1$ tells that they are normalized prices with sum 1. With the allocation a trader j has a bundle of goods a_j from column j, with a value $M_j = pa_j$ which is the income for determining the trader's budget constraint. The column vector M with these elements has transpose $M' = pa$. Because, with normalized prices, $M'I = paI = pI = 1$, the elements sum to 1 so this is a distribution vector, telling us the *income distribution* of traders which is associated with the distribution of goods a and prices p. The demand for goods i by trader j is

$$x_{ij} = w_{ij} M_j / p_i$$

and the supply is a_{ij}. The aggregate excess supply for good i is therefore

$$S_i = \Sigma_j (a_{ij} - w_{ij} M_j / p_i)$$

and so, since $\Sigma_j a_{ij} = 1$, the excess supply value $e_i = p_i S_i$ is given by

$$e_i = p_i - \Sigma_j w_{ij} \Sigma_k p_k a_{kj},$$

that is, $e = pb$ where $b = 1 - aw'$. Because $aw'I = aI = I$, Walras's law, stated by the identity $e(p)I = 0$ for all p, is verified. Also if $p_i = 1$, so that $p_j = 0$ ($j \neq i$) because of price normalization, then $S_i = 1$, so the supply capacity limit of every good is 1. Thus we have the normalized linear market functions of Chapter IV.3 with coefficients $b = 1 - aw'$. Everything said there can apply now, including about the existence and uniqueness of equilibrium prices p making $S(p) = 0$, about the *tâtonnement* process and its reaction coefficients v, and about the role of irreducibility in all that. Equilibrium prices p are such that $p = paw'$, and are associated with an income distribution M by the relations $M' = pa, p' = wM$ which also give $M = a'wM$. After solving for p, M is determined. Alternatively, one could solve for M in this last relation and then determine p.

Now it will be seen what the irreducibility condition of Chapter IV.3 signifies in terms of the allocation and want matrices a and w, which describe the economy. A subgroup T of traders constitutes an *independent sub-economy* if the traders between them own all the goods they want. For a statement of that,

$$(j \in T, \quad w_{ij} > 0) \Rightarrow (a_{ik} > 0 \Rightarrow k \in T);$$

in other words, if trader j is in the group and wants good i, then any trader k who has some of good i must be in the group. The traders in the group will have no dealings with those outside it since they want nothing the outsiders have. However, those in the group might have things the others want. The economy is *reducible* if such an independent sub-economy exists, and otherwise is *irreducible*. We have to connect this economic sense of reducibility, which applies to a pair of rectangular distribution matrices, with the reducibility condition that familiarly applies to a single square distribution matrix.

With S as the complement of T, the considered condition is equivalent to

$$(j \in T, \quad k \in S) \Rightarrow (w_{ij} > 0 \Rightarrow a_{ik} = 0).$$

Because the terms are non-negative, the right side here is equivalent to $w_{ij} a_{ik} = 0$ for all i, and because a sum of non-negative terms is zero if and only if each term is zero this is equivalent to

$$(w'a)_{jk} = \Sigma_i \, w_{ij} \, a_{ik} = 0.$$

The condition therefore is

$$(j \in T, \quad k \in S) \Rightarrow (a'w)_{kj} = 0,$$

showing a reduction of the square matrix $w'a$ in the usual sense.

The reduction condition has been stated with reference to a group of traders, but it can also be expressed in terms of a group of goods. Consider a group G of goods owned entirely by traders who want no others, that is

$$(i \in G, \quad a_{ij} > 0) \Rightarrow (w_{kj} > 0 \Rightarrow k \in G),$$

and, equivalently, with H the complement of G,

$$(i \in G, \quad k \in H) \Rightarrow (aw')_{ik} = 0,$$

showing a reduction of aw'. Given the first condition on a group T of traders one can form the group

$$G = [i : w_{ij} > 0, j \in T]$$

of all goods that are wanted by any of them. Also, given the second condition in terms of a group G of goods,

$$T = [j : a_{ij} > 0, i \in G]$$

is the set of all traders who own any of them. Then the one condition in terms of one group is equivalent to the other condition in terms of the other, and to the condition stated for the matrix $w'a$ and to that for the matrix aw'. In other words a and w having the form

$$a = G\begin{array}{|cc} \hline T & \\ \hline . & 0 \\ . & . \end{array} \qquad w = G\begin{array}{|cc} \hline T & \\ \hline . & . \\ 0 & . \end{array}$$

is equivalent to $a'w$ having the form

$$a'w = T\begin{array}{|cc} \hline T & \\ \hline . & . \\ 0 & . \end{array}$$

and to aw' having the form

$$aw' = G\begin{array}{|cc} \hline G & \\ \hline . & 0 \\ . & . \end{array}$$

Because a and w are distribution matrices, a by rows and w by columns, so are aw' and $a'w$, by rows and columns respectively, and these moreover are square. Theorems from the theory of Markov processes can therefore apply to $a'w$ and aw', and the irreducibility condition of that theory, applying usually to the matrix of transition probabilities, is now translated into the economic irreducibility condition stated directly in terms of the allocation and want-matrices a and w.

5.7 PRODUCTION AND PROFIT

A limitation of Edgeworth's box and the hyperbox generalization is that, except for utility, the goods, which are factors in the production of utility, are represented as having been already produced, and there is no account of their production. Exchange of goods between traders makes no alteration of the total quantities in the economy as a whole, but it does alter the quantities held by any individual trader involved. From the local point of view of the trader who is without interest in that global fact, the effect is the same as with production where some goods are gained and others lost.

Without production, Crusoe has just the bundle of goods b rescued from the shipwreck, and from free disposal also anything less, $y \leq b$, so this is his production possibility set. The goods being useful, the only efficient output is the original bundle b, so at this point he has no production decision to make. If he had access to a market, he might be able to trade bundle b for a better bundle c, as illustrated in Figure 8.

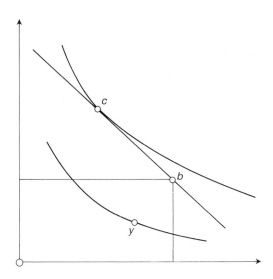

Figure 8

Again in isolation, with some means of production he need not settle for point b but can choose a point y from a larger set B, and would solve the problem

$$\max U(x) : x = y, y \in B,$$

obtaining a solution z, as in Figure 9.

If now he has access to a market where the prices are p, he could trade any produced bundle y for a bundle x with better utility, and solve the problem

$$\max U(x) : px = py, y \in B,$$

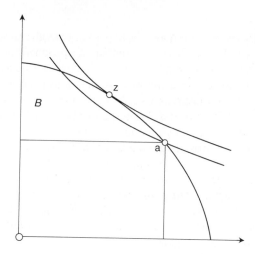

Figure 8

obtaining a solution y, as in Figure 10. It could be offered, equivalently, that
he first solve the maximum profit problem

$$\max py : y \epsilon B$$

in managing his means of production, the 'capitalist' type (where these have
nothing directly to do with his personal utility), and then the utility problem

$$\max U(x) : px = py.$$

The utility maximization requires the maximum possible profit from the capitalist production, so this is not an independent assumption. In solving this
problem for any prices p, x and y are determined as continuous functions $x(p)$
and $y(p)$ of p, the suitable convexity assumptions about A and U being provided. These demand and supply functions satisfy the budget constraint
$px(p) = py(p)$, showing that things demanded are paid for by things supplied; or, with $s(p) = y(p) - x(p)$ as net supply, we have the budget constraint $ps(p) = 0$.

   This model for the individual generalizes that used in the Edgeworth box,
or pure exchange economy. There is a return to that model when the production possibility set B shrinks to the original $[y : y \leq b]$. In this case the production function $y(p)$ becomes a constant $y(p) = b$.

   The *profit function* for the production possibility set B is

$$b(p) = \max[py : y B].$$

characterized by being closed, concave and conical; so with this differentiable,
with gradient $b'(p)$, there is the Euler identity

$$pb'(p) = b(p).$$

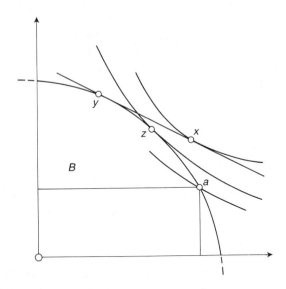

Figure 10

Also, the gradient coincides with the production function, $y(p) = b'(p)$, and so $b(p) = py(p)$.

Taken immediately, the new model still provides a defective representation of the consumer-individual who produces as well as consumes, and of the producer-plant that consumes as well as produces. That would be so only from habits deriving from confinement to Edgeworth's box, and from the commodity space of consumer theory where it is forgotten that the consumer should also be a producer—that is, of other goods beside personal utility. Also, the rigid input-output situation, in which it is already settled which goods are inputs and which other ones are outputs, is unsuitable. Instead, it ought to be allowed that in some price situations a consumer would employ a gardener, and in others would take a job as a gardener.

The cure is simple and consists in permitting negative values to coordinates of the vectors x and y. These then are not non-negative input and output vectors, but *activity vectors* with elements not so restricted. Should we wish always to represent supply as positive, x would be replaced by $-x$, giving $s = x + y$ as the individual's total supply, or $-s$ as demand. Just as the slave plant has an activity set B, the personal plant that produces utility beside other things has an activity set A, suitably stated just as concerns the other things, since with any $x \in A$ we are given $U(x)$ as the maximum feasible utility output.

It might appear that this separation of productive plant in command of the individual into two parts, associated with A and B, is spurious, a meaningless complication; B should just as well be incorporated and buried in the representation as a part of A. Were the individual without transferable 'capitalist' property, there is a good point here, except that, were the individual a slave, incorporating A into B and forgetting about the utility would be more suitable. The separation therefore is significant or not depending on accidents of the economic order. As concerns mathematics it is not; whatever we do, we have a framework in which the arguments of Chapter IV.3 on 'The Market' can be brought to bear.

A further elaboration of the capitalist order is found in the Arrow-Debreu model, but it reduces mathematically to what we already have. There are several firms in the economy, with activity sets B_i and associated profit functions $b_i(p)$, and our individual has a share σ_i ($0 \le \sigma_i \le 1$) in the ith, providing an 'unearned' — not directly involved in utility production — income $b(p) = \Sigma\sigma_i b_i(p)$. But this function $b(p)$ is again closed, concave and conical, like the others, and so qualifies as a profit function, associated with some production possibility set, say B, easily identified; so we return again to the form with which we started.

With the resolution $x = x^+ - x^-$ of the activity vector $x \in A$ into input and output parts $x^+, x^- \ge 0$ (before we replaced x by $-x$ to make a point), x^+ is the true consumption of the consumer individual, and x^- together with $U(x)$ represents production. In x^- we have 'labour' and other products apart from utility. An observation conveniently made here is about the 'disutility of labour' which is a most common assumption in economics, concordant with Quesnay's 'labour-pain', which ignores a part of experience. From ideas that are freely accepted about production, it is unnecessary. Production is generally joint production, many goods being produced together. It is possible for one good to be a by-product of another, more of one being accompanied by more of the other—for instance the smoke that goes up the factory chimney, though it could be more useful. An opposite possibility is where, with given inputs, a gain in one output involves a sacrifice in another. Recognizing that utility and labour are joint outputs in the model, both possibilities can be allowed, and both are familiar from experience, as everyone knows.

5.8   LESSONS IN EDGEWORTH'S BOX

Edgeworth introduced the box diagram, familiar to every economics student, to illustrate the gains from trade, and the general equilibrium of a market economy.

To represent trade, at least two traders, and two goods are needed. His diagram deals with the simplest possible model of a trading economy. The numbers of traders and of goods are at a minimum; two in each case. Also, no production takes place, in which quantities of some goods are lost as inputs and gained as outputs, to alter the totals that exist in the system.

For each good, therefore, the fixed total quantity of it can be made the arbitrary unit of amount. The amounts that the traders have of either of the goods is then given by two fractions whose sum is 1. If one trader A has amounts x, y, of the two goods, X and Y, then the other, B, has $1 - x$, $1 - y$.

Taking a unit square, and associating opposite corners, say SW and NE, with the traders A and B, any point in the box has coordinates with either corner as origin and sides of the square as axes. If the coordinates with origin A are x, y, then the coordinates with origin B are $1 - x$, $1 - y$. The ways the goods can be divided between the traders are therefore described by points of the box in a one-one correspondence. This is the basic principle of the box diagram. It gives the means for a graphical representation of all features in the theory of the Edgeworth economy, illustrative of the same features for more elaborate models. Here the model is realized in a computer program, which has the appropriate graphic output with any system parameters.

The system is described by the initial possessions of the traders, and their wants, the satisfaction of which is the motive for any trade. If quantities x_I, y_I represent the initial possessions of trader A, then $1 - x_I$, $1 - y_I$ represent those of trader B; we have an initial point in the box, designated (x_I, y_I).

As for the wants, these are expressed by the governing of a trader by a utility function, to the effect that any voluntary action would be to increase it. The arguments of the function are quantities of goods possessed, so any trade in these must be to make the value greater.

For the purpose of illustration, we consider traders with utility functions having the form $z = x^w y^{1-w}$ (see the definition in line 11 of the program), with one parameter w, where $0 \leq w \leq 1$. The want of any trader for the goods X, Y is expressed by the distribution of weight w, $1 - w$ on them. For the two different traders A, B the want parameter w is given two values a, b. The difference, or spread, between the traders, as concerns their wants, is indicated by the coefficient

$$m = (1/b - 1)/(1/a - 1)$$

(def in line 14), which is the parameter for different contract curves that could arise, were the traders' wants to vary (constructed at 200 using the def in 13), as shown in Lesson 2. In the case $m = 1$, which applies when $a = b$, the contract curve coincides with the box diagonal. Towards its extremes, 0 and ∞ , for instance when one trader is only interested in one good, and the other trader only in the other, the contract curve departs increasingly steeply, one way or the other, away from the diagonal.

The contract curve for the traders is determined only by the parameter m. Thus, with coordinates taken with respect to the origin for trader A, it is given by

$$y = 1/[1 + m(1/x - 1)].$$

With the functions thus associated with the traders, at any point x, y in the box they have utilities

$$A = x^a y^{1-a}, B = (1-x)^b (1-y)^{1-b}.$$

These are coordinates of a point in a further space, the *utility space*, which is the space of final outputs of the system, namely the traders utilities. As the box is described, this point, taken with the points below it, attainable by free disposal, describes a set in the utility space, the utility-possibility set, or *utility set* for the system. Initially, with $x = x_I$, $y = y_I$, we have the initial utilities $A = A_I$, $B = B_I$, from which any trade should produce a gain. For the figure in Lesson 4, instead of utility z, which is concave, and conical (linearly homogeneous), and so not strictly concave, we take the square root $\sqrt{z}$, which is a strictly concave function. This makes the utility set look better, with its boundary strictly convex, instead of flat. That alters nothing as far as concerns the rest of the program, where for simplicity we deal with the conical utility, and it illustrates a theorem on the shape of the utility set.

With every utility image, we draw horizontal and vertical lines bounding the points below it, as evident in the figure produced for Lesson 4. It is because free disposal of goods, and so of utility, would admit also those points as utility-possibilities. The theorem on the convex shape of the utility set, which depends on the traders' utility functions being concave, requires this; otherwise the utility set could have holes in it.

By plotting the contours of constant utility in the box for one trader, and then the other, we have the *indifference curves* produced for Lesson 1. The locus of tangency of the curves is the *contract curve*, one of the variety of possible curves illustrated in Lesson 2. The contract curve, in the box, or *commodity space*, has an image in the *utility space* identical with the forward boundary of the utility set. Any point not on the curve, such as the chosen initial point in the box, has an image lying under the boundary, as shown in Lesson 4. The forward horizontal and vertical lines through the image bound the part of the utility set which is the image of the contract region in the box, shown in Lesson 3. Any trade should produce a move into this part of the utility set, away from the original utility, which is marked. In particular there is the point, also marked in the figure, reached when the economy, having true prices, goes to a position of general equilibrium. A remark concerning popular comment about this point: even though both traders are better off there than they were before, there is nothing further about this point to single it out, for instance as 'optimal' in some way, except that it is just an accident of the system, in which they have each participated, separately and voluntarily for their own gain. There is no other social value in this model.

At any point in the box, each trader gives the goods an exchange rate based on utility. It is the rate at which the goods may be substituted, one for the other, while maintaining the same level of utility, or their *substitution rate*. These rates may differ between the traders, at any point, and points on the contract curves are distinguished *by* their coincidence. In the general equilibrium of the economy, they also coincide with the market exchange rates, and, were there any producers, with the technical exchanges rates for every one. Thus, in general equilibrium, the many exchange rates that may be distinguished all coincide.

If the goods have prices, these are important only through their ratio, which provides a market exchange rate between the goods. They can be normalized with sum 1, and so be given by p, $1 - p$, where $0 \leq p \leq 1$.

With such prices, at a point (x, y) in the box, the exchange values available to the traders, for the goods that the have, are

$$M = px + (1 - p)y, \quad N = p(1 - x) + (1 - p)(1 - y),$$

for which $M + N = 1$. From the partition of goods, we have this partition of 'income'. The traders would each demand goods of highest use value attainable with these exchange values. Thus trader A would demand quantities

$$x_A = Ma/p, \quad y_A = M(1 - a)/(1 - p),$$

in exchange for the quantities x, y, since these maximise A's utility under the exchange budget constraint. Similarly, B would demand

$$x_B = Nb/p, \quad y_B = N(1 - b)/(1 - p),$$

in exchange for $1 - x$, $1 - y$.

The idea of market prices is that they are an offer to any trader to buy or sell freely at the exchange rates they specify. But the traders can only buy or sell by trade with each other. The offer cannot be upheld if a buyer cannot find a seller, or a seller a buyer, and for *true prices* this cannot happen. In this abstract economy, we know exactly what any trader would want to buy or sell, when faced with any prices, so we can test if any proposed prices are true or not, and possibly find some that are. These are also called *equilibrium prices*, because they are associated with a balance of supply and demand, but they may be called true for a radical emphasis; that actual market prices have to be true, or the offer is not an offer, which is a contradiction in terms.

For good X, the net market supply, or supply reduced by demand, is

$$
\begin{aligned}
X &= [x - x_A] + [(1 - x) - x_B] \\
&= 1 - x_A - x_B \\
&= L_X + L_Y - L_Y/p
\end{aligned}
$$

where

$$L_X = 1 - xa - (1 - x)b, \quad L_Y = ya + (1 - y)b.$$

When $p \to 0$, we have $X \to -\infty$; supply falls and demand rises, eventually overtaking supply and tending to ∞. When $p \to 1$, X increases and $\to L_X$; L_X is the *supply capacity limit* of good X, approached asymptotically as its exchange rate with the other good approaches ∞.

Similarly for good Y, the net supply is

$$
\begin{aligned}
Y &= [y - y_A] + [(1 - y) - y_B] \\
&= 1 - y_A - y_B \\
&= L_X + L_Y - L_X/(1 - p),
\end{aligned}
$$

and we have L_Y as the supply capacity limit. There is the identity

$$pX + (1 - p)Y = 0,$$

as required by Walras's law. The figure for Lesson 6 shows the two supply curves plotted, with $Q = X$ for one, and $Q = Y$ for the other. They cross the $Q = 0$

axis simultaneously at $P = P_e$. The X-curve goes to $-\infty$ at $P = 0$, and the Y-curve at $1 - p = 0$, and they reach their maxima, L_X and L_Y, at the other extremes.

From the formulae for the supply capacity limits, $1 - L_X$ and L_Y are averages of a, b with weights x, $1 - x$ and y, $1 - y$. Hence they are bounded between the min and max of a, b. Since these are bounded between 0 and 1, it follows that L_X and L_Y are also.

For true prices, it is required that $X = 0$, $Y = 0$ simultaneously. This is the case just for $p = p_e$, where

$$p_e = L_Y / (L_X + L_Y).$$

If any considered prices are not true, they may be subjected to an adjustment process $p^* = f(p)$, where old prices p are replaced by new prices p^*. Taking new prices then as the old, this replacement may be repeated indefinitely. According to the Law of Supply and Demand, for the adjustment of prices, a price should rise when there is excess demand for the good, and fall when there is excess supply. In consistency with this, we can take

$$p^* = p - spX,$$

where pX is net market supply of good X valued at its own price, and s a reaction parameter, the *tâtonnement speed*. As applied to the other good, this is equivalent to the identical process, where

$$1 - p^* = 1 - p - s(1 - p)Y,$$

as seen from Walras's law, the speed parameter being the same. If we abandon price normalization, we could proceed just as well with a different adjustment speed for the other good, but for simplicity we will keep it the same.

We now have

$$p^* = p - s[p(L_X + L_Y) - L_Y],$$

that is,

$$p^* = pR + sL_Y,$$

where

$$R = 1 - s(L_X + L_Y).$$

For all $s > 0$, $p^* = p$ if and only if $p = p_e$; in other words, p_e is the unique equilibrium in this dynamic adjustment process. Now we consider the stability; that is, starting with any p, we consider whether or not $p \to p_e$.

By subtracting the relation

$$p_e = p_e R + sL_Y,$$

we get

$$p^* - p_e = (p - p_e)R.$$

Hence, starting with any $p = p_0$, *after t* iterations we have

$$p^* - p_e = (p_0 - p_e)R^t,$$

so that

$$p^* \to p_e \ (t \to \infty) \text{ if and only if } |R| < 1.$$

But $|R| < 1$ is equivalent to

$$0 < s < S, \text{ where } S = 2/(L_X + L_Y),$$

and so we have this condition on the speed parameter s, with a *speed limit* S, under which there is a stability of the adjustment process. Obviously we need $s > 0$, or there is no adjustment; also, adjustment cannot be too violent, with an over-reaction to excess supply or demand, or, besides prices being forced to become negative, any deviation from equilibrium would only become amplified. But here, concerning stability, there is a generous allowance, with a speed limit S which is at least 1, since L_X and L_Y are at most 1. Also, for prices to remain non-negative under adjustment, it is required that $1 - sX \geq 0$. Hence, since $X \leq L_X$, it is enough to have $s \leq 1/L_X$, and hence enough to have $s \leq 1$. Therefore, though it could be pushed further in most cases, a speed limit set to 1 assures, in any case, both the continued non-negativity of prices, and stability. The highest speed limit that gives this safety, in the case of the current economy, is determined as the minimum of $1/L_X$ and $2/(L_X + L_Y)$. This is the speed limit advertised, among the statistics in Lesson 9.

There is one particular speed, $s = 1/(L_X + L_Y)$, with which, whatever the initial prices, the first iteration will always produce a jump straight to the equilibrium. This is exactly half the stability speed limit S. We can distinguish speeds as high or low according to whether they are above or below this critical speed. Low speeds produce a steady adjustment towards equilibrium, in contrast with high speeds which produce an oscillation around it. The figures for Lesson 7 show examples of both.

Lessons in
Edgeworth's Box

1. Indifference Curves and the Contract Curve
2. Contract curves for various traders
3. The Contract Set
4. The Utility Set
5. The Offer Curves
6. Supply and Demand
7. Tatonnement
8. General Equilibrium
9. Statistics

choose 1–9

Edgeworth's Box

```
                                      Traders
                              possessions      wants

                              A      B         A      B
              Goods    X     .25    .75       .75    .7
                       Y     .8     .2        .25    .3
```

```
              utilities    .334370 .5044892
              starting prices    .45     .55
              tatonnement speed 1.9    speed limit 1.946472
              supply capacity limits  X  .2875   Y  .74

          Do you want to change anything (y or n)?
          1. The initial allocation of goods to traders
          2. The traders' wants
          3. The starting prices
          4. The tatonnement speed
```

Edgeworth's Box

```
                                      Traders
                              possessions      wants

                              A      B         A      B
              Goods    X     .25    .75       .75    .7
                       Y     .8     .2        .25    .3
```

```
              utilities    .334370 .5044892
              starting prices    .45     .55
              tatonnement speed 1.9    speed limit 1.946472
              supply capacity limits  X  .2875   Y  .74

          In equilibrium:
              prices          .720194 .2798054
              possessions
                          Traders    A       B
                      Goods    X    .420608 .579392
                               Y    .360869 .6391305
              utilities    .404804 .5967021
```

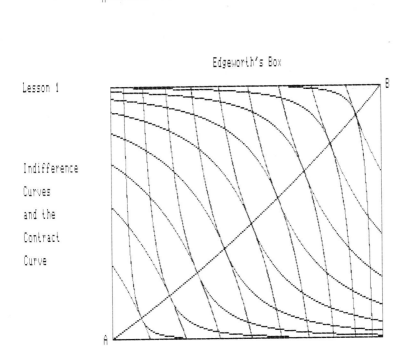

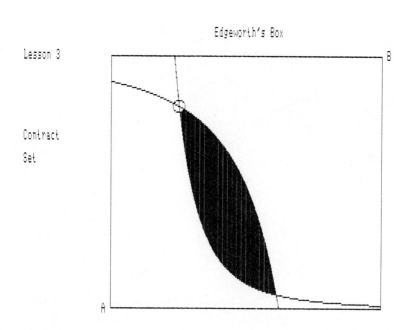

Edgeworth's Box

Lesson 4

Utility
Set

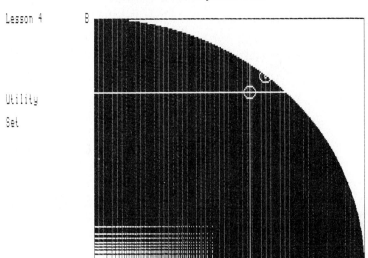

Edgeworth's Box

Lesson 5

Offer
Curves

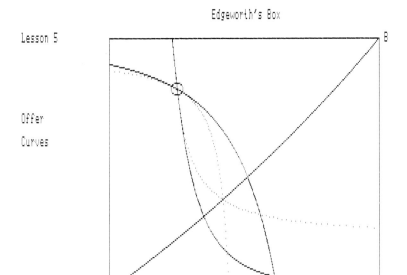

Logic of Price

Edgeworth's Box

Lesson 6

Supply
&
Demand

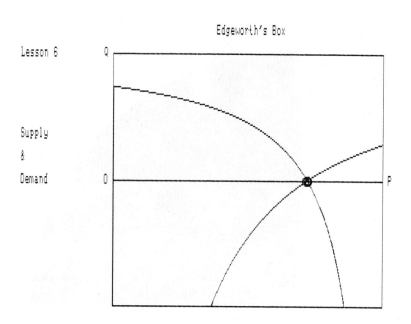

Edgeworth's Box

Lesson 7

Tatonnement

speed = 1.8

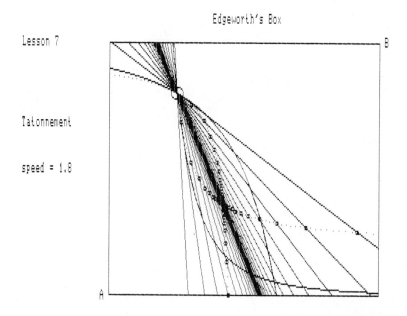

Edgeworth's Box

Lesson 7

Tatonnement

speed = .2

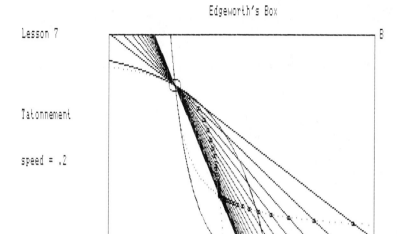

Edgeworth's Box

Lesson 8

General
Equilibrium

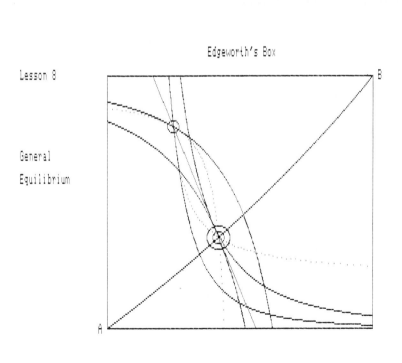

```
1 DATA 5,20
2 DATA"          EBOX.BAS               ",,,
3 DATA"                                 "
4 DATA"          Lessons in            ",
5 DATA"        __ Edgeworth's Box __    ",,,,,,,
6 DATA"                                 "
7 DATA"<Space> to pause                 "
8 DATA"<Space> to continue, <CR> to rerun, <Esc> to exit",*
9 '
10 DEFINT F-H,J,K,N,U,V:DIM Q(1)
11 DEF FNZ=X^W*Y^(1-W)
12 DEF FNI=(Z/X^W)^(1/(1-W))
13 DEF FNC=1/(1+M*(1/X-1))
14 DEF FNM=(1/WB-1)/(1/WA-1)
15 DEF FNX=LX+LY-LY/P
16 DEF FNY=LX+LYLX/(1-P)
17 DEF FNE=P*FNX
18 DEF FNT=P-S*FNE
50 GOTO 1000
59 '
60 LOCATE,C:PRINT Z;:C=C+8:RETURN
69 '--- plot line
70 TX0=-X/DX:TX1=(1-X)/DX:TY0=-Y/DY:TY1=(1-Y)/DY
71 IF TX0>0 THEN SWAP TX0,TX1
72 IF TY0>0 THEN SWAP TY0,TY1
73 IF TX0>TY0 THEN T0=TX0 ELSE T0=TY0
74 IF TX1>TY1 THEN T1=TX1 ELSE T1=TY1
75 X0=X+DX*T0:Y0=Y+DY*T0:X1=X+DX*T1:Y1=Y+DY*T1
76 LINE(A+U*X0,B+VV*Y0)-(A+U*X1,B+V-V*Y1)
77 RETURN
79 '--- plot curve
80 D=(Y-Y0)*V:Y0=Y:PSET(A+X*U,B+V-Y*V)
81 IF ABS(D)>1 THEN LINE-STEP(0,D)
82 IF LEN(INKEY$) THEN GOSUB 90
83 RETURN
89 '--- pause, input
90 LOCATE,,0:K$=INPUT$(1)
91 IF K$=ESC$ THEN 9999 ELSE IF K$=CR$ THEN RETURN 9998 ELSE RETURN
98 '
99 '--- 1: indifference curve
100 Y0=1-F:FOR T=1/U TO 1 STEP 1/U:X=T:Y=FNI
110 IF Y>1 THEN 140 ELSE IF Y<1/V THEN RETURN
120 IF F THEN X=1-X:Y=1-Y
130 GOSUB 80
140 NEXT:RETURN
159 '
199 '--- 2: contract curve
200 Y0=0:FOR X=1/U TO 1 STEP 1/U
210 Y=FNC:GOSUB 80:NEXT:RETURN
219 '
299 '--- 3: contract set
300 X=XI:Y=YI:XS=A+X*U:YS=B+V-Y*V
310 IF F THEN W=WB:X=1-X:Y=1-Y ELSE W=WA:CIRCLE(XS,YS),10
320    Z=FNZ:GOSUB   100:F=1-F:IF   F   THEN   300   ELSE
PAINT(XS+16,YS+16),H:RETURN
398 '
399 '--- 4: utility set
400 M=FNM:FOR T=1/U TO 1 STEP 1/U:X=T:Y=FNC
```

```
410 W=WA:ZA=SQR(FNZ):W=WB:X=1-X:Y=1-Y:ZB=SQR(FNZ)
420 LINE(A,B+V)-(A+U*ZA,B+V-V*ZB),,B
430 IF LEN(INKEY$) THEN GOSUB 90
440 NEXT:RETURN
498 '
499 '--- 5: offer curves
500 FOR T=.5 TO 89.5 STEP .5:P=COS(T*RAD):P=P*P
510 X=XI:Y=YI:W=WA:IF F THEN X=1-X:Y=1-Y:W=WB
520 M=P*X+(1-P)*Y:XO=M*W/P:YO=M*(1W)/(1-P)
530 IF FZ AND F=0 THEN DX=XOX:DY=YO-Y:GOSUB 70
540 X=XO:Y=YO:IF X<0 OR X>1 OR Y<0 OR Y>1 THEN 570
550 IF F THEN X=1-X:Y=1-Y
560 IF FZ THEN CIRCLE(A+U*X,B+V-V*Y),3 ELSE PSET(A+U*X,B+V-V*Y)
570 F=1-F:IF F THEN 510 ELSE IF FZ THEN RETURN
580 NEXT:RETURN
598 '
599 '--- 6: supply & demand
600 Q(F)=-1:FOR P=1/U TO 1 STEP 1/U
610 IF F THEN Q=FNY ELSE Q=FNX
620 IF Q<1 THEN 650
630 D=(QQ(F))*V/2:Q(F)=Q:X=A+U*P:Y=B+V/2V*Q/2
640 PSET(X,Y):IF ABS(D)>1 THEN LINE-STEP(0,D)
650 F=1-F:IF F THEN 610
655 IF LEN(INKEY$) THEN GOSUB 90
660 NEXT:CIRCLE(A+U*PE,B+V/2),10:RETURN
698 '
699 '--- 7: tatonnement
700 GOSUB 510:P1=FNT:IF LEN(INKEY$) THEN GOSUB 90
710 IF ABS(P-P1)<0 THEN RETURN ELSE P=P1:GOTO 700
798 '
799 '--- 8: general equilibrium
800 X=XI:Y=YI:DX=XEX:DY=YE-Y:GOSUB 70
810 Z=AE:F=0:GOSUB 100:Z=BE:F=1:GOSUB 100:F=0:RETURN
898 '
899 '--- 9: statistics
909 ' initial possessions, wants &c
910 LOCATE 9:C=42
911 Z=XI:GOSUB 60:Z=1-XI:GOSUB 60:Z=WA:GOSUB 60:Z=WB:GOSUB 60
912 LOCATE 10:C=42
913 Z=YI:GOSUB 60:Z=1-YI:GOSUB 60:Z=1-WA:GOSUB 60:Z=1-WB:GOSUB 60
920 LOCATE 12:C=40:Z=SQR(AI):GOSUB 60:Z=SQR(BI):GOSUB 60
921 LOCATE 13:C=46:Z=PS:GOSUB 60:Z=1-PS:GOSUB 60
922 LOCATE 14:C=45:Z=S:GOSUB 60:C=C+11:Z=SL:GOSUB 60
923 LOCATE 15:C=54:Z=LX:GOSUB 60:C=C+4:Z=LY:GOSUB 60
924 LOCATE 17:RETURN
929 ' in equilibrium
930 LOCATE 18:C=42:Z=PE:GOSUB 60:Z=1-PE:GOSUB 60
940 LOCATE 21:C=50:Z=XE:GOSUB 60:Z=1-XE:GOSUB 60
941 LOCATE 22:C=50:Z=YE:GOSUB 60:Z=1-YE:GOSUB 60
950 LOCATE 23:C=40:Z=SQR(AE):GOSUB 60:Z=SQR(BE):GOSUB 60
990 RETURN
998 '
999 '===== init
1000 EB$="Edgeworth's Box":RESTORE 1010
1010 READ A, B, U, V, WA, WB, XI, YI, E, N, PS, S
1020 DATA 152,20, 464,175, .75, .7, .25, .8, 1.5, 12, .45, 1.35
1030 READ    PI,        O,      XX
1040 DATA 3.1415926, .000001, 1
```

```
1099 '
1100 ESC$=CHR$(27):CR$=CHR$(13):CRR$=CR$+CR$:RAD=PI/180
1199 '
1200 X=XI:Y=YI:LX=1-X*WA-(1-X)*WB:LY=Y*WA+(1-Y)*WB
1210 W=WA:AI=FNZ:X=1-X:Y=1-Y:W=WB:BI=FNZ
1220 PE=LY/(LX+LY):SS=2/(LX+LY):SP=1/LX
1230 IF SS<SP THEN SL=SS ELSE SL=SP
1240 P=PE:X=XI:Y=YI
1250 M=P*X+(1-P)*Y:XE=M*WA/P:YE=M*(1-WA)/(1-P)
1260 X=XE:Y=YE:W=WA:AE=FNZ
1270 X=1-XE:Y=1-YE:W=WB:BE=FNZ:IF FR THEN FR=0:RETURN
1399 '
1400 KEY OFF:SCREEN 0
1405 IF XX THEN XX=0:RESTORE:GOSUB 7000
1410 RESTORE 7100:GOSUB 7000:K=ASC(K$)
1420 IF K<49 OR K>57 THEN 1210 ELSE K=K-48
1499 '
1500 SCREEN 2:LINE(A,B)-STEP(U,V),,B
1510 RESTORE 9100:GOSUB 9000
1520 LOCATE 1,42:PRINT EB$;:LOCATE 3,1
1530 PRINT"Lesson";K;:LOCATE 10,1
1899 '
1900 ON K GOSUB 2100,2200,2300,2400,2500,2600,2700,2800,2900
1910 GOSUB 90:GOTO 1200
1919 '
1999 '--- 1
2100 PRINT"Indifference";CRR$;"Curves";CR$:W=WA
2110 FOR Z=.1 TO 1 STEP .1:GOSUB 100
2120 NEXT:F=1-F:IF F THEN GOSUB 80:W=WB:GOTO 2110
2130 GOSUB 90:PRINT"and the";CRR$;"Contract";CRR$;"Curve"
2140 M=FNM:GOSUB 200:RETURN
2199 '--- 2
2200 PRINT"Contract";CRR$;"Curves";
2210 M=1/E^N:FOR T=-N TO N:GOSUB 200
2220 M=M*E:NEXT:RETURN
2299 '--- 3
2300 PRINT"Contract";CRR$;"Set";:H=1
2310 GOSUB 300:H=0:RETURN
2399 '--- 4
2400 PRINT"Utility";CRR$;"Set";
2410 RESTORE 9110:GOSUB 9000
2420 GOSUB 400:X=SQR(AI):Y=SQR(BI)
2430 CIRCLE(A+U*X,B+V-V*Y),10,0
2440 LINE(A+U*X,B+V)-(A+U*X,B+V-V*Y),0,B
2445 LINE(A,B+V-V*Y)-(A+U*X,B+V-V*Y),0,B
2450 LINE-STEP(80,-40),0,B
2460 ZA=SQR(AE):ZB=SQR(BE)
2470 CIRCLE(A+U*ZA,B+V-V*ZB),10,0
2480 CIRCLE(A+U*ZA,B+V-V*ZB),2,0:RETURN
2499 '--- 5
2500 PRINT"Offer";CRR$;"Curves"
2510 GOSUB 2310:GOSUB 500:GOSUB 2140:RETURN
2599 '--- 6
2600 PRINT"Supply";CRR$;"&";CRR$;"Demand"
2610 RESTORE 9120:GOSUB 9000
2620 LINE(A,B+V/2)-STEP(U,0)
2630 GOSUB 600:RETURN
2699 '--- 7
```

```
2700 PRINT"Tatonnement";CRR$;CRR$;"speed =";S
2710 GOSUB 2310:GOSUB 500:FZ=1:P=PS
2720 GOSUB 700:FZ=0:GOSUB 90:M=FNM:GOSUB 200:RETURN
2799 '--- 8
2800 PRINT"General";CRR$;"Equilibrium"
2810 GOSUB 2510:P=PE:GOSUB 800
2820 CIRCLE(A+U*XE,B+V-V*YE),10
2830 CIRCLE(A+U*XE,B+V-V*YE),20:RETURN
2899 '--- 9
2900 PRINT"Statistics":RESTORE 9130:GOSUB 9000
2905 LINE(A-3,B-2)-STEP(U+6,V+4),,B
2910 RESTORE 7200:FR=1:GOSUB 7005
2920 GOSUB 910:GOSUB 90:IF K$="y" OR K$="Y" THEN 4000
2930 FR=1:GOSUB 7010:GOSUB 930:RETURN
3999 ' changes
4000 RESTORE 7400:GOSUB 7005
4005 K=ASC(K$):IF K<48 OR K>52 THEN 4010 ELSE K=K-48
4010 LOCATE 23,23:ON K GOSUB 4110,4120,4130,4140
4090 LOCATE 23,23:PRINT SPACE$(40);:FR=1:GOSUB 1200:GOTO 2910
4099 '
4110 INPUT"allocation of good X to trader A";Z:IF Z THEN XI=Z
4111 LOCATE 23,23:INPUT"allocation of good Y to trader A";Z:IF
     Z THEN YI=Z
4113 RETURN
4120 INPUT"weight of good X for trader A";Z:IF Z THEN WA=Z
4121 LOCATE 23,23:INPUT"weight of good X for trader B";Z:IF Z
     THEN WB=Z
4123 RETURN
4130 INPUT"starting price";Z:IF Z THEN PS=Z:RETURN ELSE RETURN
4140 INPUT"tatonnement speed";Z:IF Z THEN S=Z:RETURN ELSE
     RETURN
6998 '
6999 '--- text
7000 CLS
7005 READ R,T:LOCATE R
7010 READ L$:IF L$<>"*" THEN LOCATE,T:PRINT L$:GOTO 7010
7020 IF FR THEN FR=0:RETURN ELSE GOSUB 90:RETURN
7099 '
7100 DATA 4,20, Lessons in, Edgeworth's Box,,
7110 DATA 1. Indifference Curves and the Contract Curve
7120 DATA 2. Contract curves for various traders
7130 DATA 3. The Contract Set
7140 DATA 4. The Utility Set
7150 DATA 5. The Offer Curves
7160 DATA 6. Supply and Demand
7170 DATA 7. Tatonnement
7180 DATA 8. General Equilibrium
7190 DATA 9. Statistics,,,,
7195 DATA choose 1-9,*
7199 '
7200 DATA 5,22
7210 DATA"                              Traders              "
7220 DATA"                      possessions      wants       ",
7230 DATA"                       A      B      A      B      "
7240 DATA"       Goods   X                                   "
7250 DATA"               Y                                   ",
7260 DATA"       utilities                                   "
7270 DATA"       starting prices                             "
```

```
7275 DATA"       tatonnement speed          speed limit          "
7280 DATA"       supply capacity limits  X               Y       ",
7285 DATA" Do you want to change anything (y or n)?               ",*
7290 DATA" In equilibrium:                                        "
7300 DATA"      prices                                            "
7310 DATA"      possessions                                       "
7320 DATA"                       Traders    A        B            "
7330 DATA"              Goods    X                                "
7340 DATA"                       Y                                "
7350 DATA"       utilities                                        ",*
7399 '
7400 DATA 17,22
7410 DATA" Change what?                                           "
7420 DATA" 1. The initial allocation of goods to traders         "
7430 DATA" 2. The traders' wants                                  "
7440 DATA" 3. The starting prices"
7450 DATA" 4. The tatonnement speed                              ",*
7460 DATA"
7499 '
8999 '--- markers
9000 READ II:FOR I=1 TO II:READ R,C,L$
9010 LOCATE R,C:PRINT L$;:NEXT:RETURN
9100 DATA 2,  25,18,A,   3,79,B
9110 DATA 4,  25,18,O,   3,79," ",  3,18,B,  25,79,A
9120 DATA 5,  25,18," ", 3,79," ",  3,18,Q,  14,18,O, 14,79,P
9130 DATA 2,  25,18," ", 3,79," "
9939 '
9998 RETURN 1200
9999 CLS:SCREEN 0:KEY ON:END
```

HBOX.BAS

_____The Hyperbox_____
m goods and n traders

further lessons from
Edgeworth's Box

<Space> to pause
<Space> to continue, <CR> to rerun, <Esc>
to exit

output to screen, printer or disk (s, p, or d)?

Hyperbox Economy

Totals of goods, and distribution to traders

7	.1428572	.2857143	.5714286
13	.6153846	.3076923	7.692308E−02
7	.5714286	.1428572	.2857143

Weights of traders' wants for goods

.1111111	.3333334	.5
.6666667	.1666667	.3333334
.2222222	.5	.1666667

Initial Utilities

.5146629	.2045413	.2609087

Supply capacities of the economy

.6031746	.5128205	.7539683

Tatonnement speed limits

1.657895	1.95	1.326316

Current speeds

1	1	1

Starting prices

1	2	3

Tatonnement: excess supplies, new prices

Supplies	−.5775337	−.4038463	.4617419
Prices	1.577534	2.807693	1.614774
Supplies	−2.948192E−02	3.797091E−02	−3.721997E−02
Prices	1.624042	2.701082	1.674876
Supplies	−7.016704E−03	2.363704E−03	2.991676E−03
Prices	1.635438	2.694697	1.669865

| Supplies | −1.169369E−03 | 6.743744E−04 | 5.695224E−05 |
| Prices | 1.63735 | 2.69288 | 1.66977 |

| Supplies | −2.163202E−04 | 1.0968E−04 | 3.509224E−05 |
| Prices | 1.637705 | 2.692585 | 1.669712 |

| Supplies | −3.893674E−05 | 2.052635E−05 | 5.096197E−06 |
| Prices | 1.637768 | 2.692529 | 1.669703 |

| Supplies | −7.078052E−06 | 3.673136E−06 | 9.834766E−07 |
| Prices | 1.63778 | 2.692519 | 1.669701 |

| Supplies | −1.2815E−06 | 6.034971E−07 | 1.639128E−07 |
| Prices | 1.637782 | 2.692518 | 1.669701 |

| Supplies | −2.235174E−07 | 1.117587E−07 | −2.980232E−08 |
| Prices | 1.637782 | 2.692517 | 1.669701 |

Equilibrium Prices

| 1.637782 | 2.692518 | 1.669701 |

Final allocation of goods to traders

| .1930129 | .3124009 | .4945865 |
| .7044257 | 9.501229E−02 | .200562 |

Final utilities

| .5314368 | .51075 | .3038508 |

```
1 DATA 5,16
2 DATA"                    HBOX.BAS        ",
3 DATA"               __The Hyperbox__
4 DATA"          m goods & n traders     ",
5 DATA"          further lessons from
6 DATA"             Edgeworth's Box       ",,,
7 DATA"
8 DATA"<Space> to pause
9 DATA"<Space> to continue, <CR> to rerun, <Esc> to exit",,*
10 DATA"output to screen, printer or disk (s, p, or d)? ",*
14 '
15 DEFINT I-K
16 DIM W(9,9),X(9,9),XO(9,9),XE(9,9),P(9),PO(9),PI(9),PE(9)
17 DIM UO(9),UE(9),M(9),S(9,9),SL(9),E(9),V(9),VL(9),H$(11)
50 GOTO 1000
59 '
79 '- text
```

```
80 READ R,C:CLS:LOCATE R
81 READ L$:IF L$<>"*" THEN PRINT#1,TAB(C);L$:GOTO 81
82 GOSUB 90:RETURN
89 '- pause, input
90 K$=INPUT$(1):IF FE THEN PRINT#1,K$;CR$
91 IF K$=ESC$ THEN 9999 ELSE IF K$=CR$ THEN RUN ELSE RETURN
98 '
99 '--- exchange values
100 FOR J=1 TO N:T=0:FOR I=1 TO M
110 T=T+P(I)*XO(I,J):NEXT:M(J)=T:NEXT:RETURN
199 '--- initial utilities uo
200 PRINT#1,H$(3):FOR J=1 TO N:T=1:FOR I=1 TO M
210 T=T*XO(I,J)^W(I,J):NEXT:UO(J)=T
220 PRINT#1,TAB(16*J);T;:NEXT:RETURN
299 '--- final utilities ue
300 PRINT#1,H$(11):FOR J=1 TO N:T=1:FOR I=1 TO M
310 T=T*XE(I,J)^W(I,J):NEXT:UE(J)=T
320 PRINT#1,TAB(16*J);T;:NEXT:RETURN
399 '--- traders' offers
400 GOSUB 100:FOR I=1 TO M:FOR J=1 TO N
410 X(I,J)=M(J)*W(I,J)/P(I):S(I,J)=XO(I,J)-X(I,J)
420 NEXT J,I:RETURN
499 '--- market supply
500 GOSUB 400:PRINT#1,S$;:FOR I=1 TO M:T=0:FOR J=1 TO N
510 T=T+S(I,J):NEXT:E(I)=P(I)*T
520 PRINT#1,TAB(16*I);T;:NEXT:PRINT#1,:RETURN
599 '--- tatonnement
600 FOR I=1 TO M:P(I)=PI(I):NEXT:GOSUB 500:F=0
610 PRINT#1,P$;:FOR I=1 TO N:PI(I)=P(I)-V(I)*E(I)
615 PRINT#1,TAB(16*I);PI(I);
620 IF ABS(P(I)-PI(I))>0 THEN F=1
630 NEXT:IF LEN(INKEY$) THEN GOSUB 90
640 PRINT#1, CR$:IF F THEN 600 ELSE PRINT#1,H$(9)
650 FOR I=1 TO
M:PE(I)=P(I):PRINT#1,TAB(16*I);PE(I);:NEXT:PRINT#1,CR$
660 PRINT#1,H$(10):FOR I=1 TO M:FOR J=1 TO N
670 XE(I,J)=X(I,J):PRINT#1,TAB(16*J);XE(I,J);:NEXT
J,I:PRINT#1,CR$
680 GOSUB 300:GOSUB 90:RETURN
998 '
999 '======== init
1000 ESC$=CHR$(27):CR$=CHR$(13):CRR$=CR$+CR$
1010 O=.000001:FE=1
1015 OPEN "SCRN:" FOR OUTPUT AS #1
1019 '
1030 RESTORE 1050:READ H:FOR I=0 TO H:READ H$
1035 H$(I)=H$+CR$:NEXT:READ S$,P$
1039 '
1050 DATA 11,Hyperbox Economy
1051 DATA"Totals of goods, and distribution to traders
1052 DATA Weights of traders' wants for goods
1053 DATA Initial Utilities
1054 DATA Supply capacities of the economy
1055 DATA Tatonnement speed limits
1056 DATA Current speeds
1057 DATA Starting prices
1058 DATA"Tatonnement: excess supplies, new prices
1059 DATA Equilibrium Prices
```

```
1060 DATA Final allocation of goods to traders
1061 DATA Final Utilities
1069 DATA Supplies, Prices
1099 '
1100 CLS:KEY OFF:RESTORE:GOSUB 80:GOSUB 81:O$=K$
1110 IF O$="s" OR O$="S" THEN O$="SCRN:"
1120 IF O$="p" OR O$="P" THEN O$="LPT1:"
1130 IF O$="d" OR O$="D" THEN O$="B:HBOX.OUT"
1140 IF LEN(O$)=1 THEN O$="SCRN:"
1190 CLOSE1:OPEN O$ FOR OUTPUT AS #1
1199 '--- read m goods, n traders
1200 RESTORE 5000:READ M,N:CLS:PRINT#1,,SPC(8);H$(0)
1209 '--- xo initial possessions, and totals
1210 PRINT#1,H$(1):RESTORE 5110
1220 FOR I=1 TO M:T=0:FOR J=1 TO N:READ XO(I,J)
1230 T=T+XO(I,J):NEXT:XO(I,0)=T:NEXT
1239 '--- normalize xoI=I
1240 FOR I=1 TO M:FOR J=1 TO N
1250 XO(I,J)=XO(I,J)/XO(I,0):NEXT
1260 FOR J=0 TO N:PRINT#1,TAB(16*J);XO(I,J);:NEXT J,I:GOSUB 90
1299 '--- w wants
1300 PRINT#1,H$(2):RESTORE 5210
1310 FOR I=1 TO M:FOR J=1 TO N
1320 READ W(I,J):NEXT J,I
1329 '--- normalize Jw=J
1330 FOR J=1 TO N:T=0:FOR I=1 TO M
1340 T=T+W(I,J):NEXT:FOR I=1 TO M
1350 W(I,J)=W(I,J)/T:NEXT I,J
1360 FOR I=1 TO M:FOR J=1 TO N
1370 PRINT#1,TAB(16*J);W(I,J);:NEXT J,I:GOSUB 90
1379 '--- initial utilities
1380 GOSUB 200:GOSUB 90
1399 '--- a market clearing matrix
1400 FOR I=1 TO M:FOR K=1 TO M:T=0
1410 FOR J=1 TO N:T=T+XO(I,J)*W(K,J)
1420 NEXT:A(I,K)=T:NEXT K,I
1499 '--- supply capacities
1500 PRINT#1,H$(4):FOR I=1 TO N:SC(I)=1A(I,I)
1510 PRINT#1,TAB(16*I);SC(I);:NEXT:GOSUB 90
1599 '--- speed limits
1600 PRINT#1,H$(5):FOR I=1 TO N:VL(I)=1/SC(I)
1610 PRINT#1,TAB(16*I);VL(I);:NEXT:GOSUB 90
1699 '--- v tatonnement speeds
1700 PRINT#1,H$(6):RESTORE 5300
1710 FOR I=1 TO N:READ V(I)
1720 PRINT#1,TAB(16*I);V(I);:NEXT:GOSUB 90
1799 '--- po initial prices
1800 PRINT#1,H$(7):RESTORE 5400
1810 FOR I=1 TO N:READ PO(I):PI(I)=PO(I)
1820 PRINT#1,TAB(16*I);PO(I);:NEXT:GOSUB 90
1899 '
2000 PRINT#1,H$(8):FE=0:GOSUB 600
4899 '
4999 ' goods, traders
5000 DATA 3, 3
5099 ' possessions
5110 DATA 1, 2, 4
5120 DATA 8, 4, 1
```

```
5130 DATA 4, 1, 2
5199 ' wants
5210 DATA 1, 2, 3
5220 DATA 6, 1, 2
5230 DATA 2, 3, 1
5299 ' current speeds
5300 DATA 1, 1, 1
5399 ' initial prices
5400 DATA 1, 2, 3
9998 '
9999 CLOSE#1:CLS:KEY ON:END
```

Von Neumann's Economic Model

Among the several interesting features of the von Neumann model, the most important may simply be its method of formulation. This represents the start of the 'activity analysis' approach which, joined with linear programming, makes a framework for stating and analysing a wide range of problems. Unlike the old production function for a single output, this method deals naturally with joint production. For some the model, or models of its type with whatever elaborations or simplifications, gives a scheme for modelling economies, and planning, as with the Leontief input-output method. Then there is the model itself, as a model of theoretical economics, and an auxiliary of doctrines. It has become a classic, alongside the equilibrium model of Walras, and its descendents like the McKenzie and Arrow-Debreu models, and other, different models that descend from the so-called Maximum Doctrine of Perfect Competition of Quesnay and the physiocrats, found in some fashion in the usual textbooks. Affinity with the last seems closest, though at the same time we find the association of von Neumann with Sraffa and Marx.

Aside from such matters, the model can also be looked at simply as a theory about a pair of rectangular non-negative matrices. As such, it is remarkable enough. It is a related system in the theory of systems of linear inequalities, showing striking similarity and contrast with the linear programming system, and some connection with matrix games and the Minimax theorem. As developed by G. L. Thompson and R. L. Weyl, it shares a perspective with the Perron–Frobenius theorem about the dominant root of a non-negative matrix, and generalized eigenvalue problems. Though von Neumann's original proof for the model is now replaced by finite algebraical methods, the topological existence theorem he proposed for it was a new type, generalizing the Brouwer fixed point theorem, that now has other uses. S. Kakutani straightforwardly proved a special case, still a generalization of Brouwer's theorem, from which von Neumann's Intersection theorem immediately follows.

This account includes a computational algorithm, named the Stretch algorithm, that had at first seemed quite different from others. However, with identification of the stretch parameter with the game value on which a method of G. L. Thompson is based, the two methods become associated.

The monograph by O. Morgenstern and G. L. Thompson (1976), besides giving an ample report of what we have about the model, contains notes on history, and an extensive bibliography. Reference is made also to D. Gale (1960), for his treatment, and to Afriat (1974) for certain features of this account. Test examples for the algorithm have been taken from the first two works. I am indebted to Gerald Thompson for his communications, and Juliet Howland for guidance in less familiar reaches of the subject.

6.1 ACTIVITY SYSTEM

Von Neumann dealt with *activities*, that have inputs and outputs, and with a *linear activity system* in which activities are generated by combination of basic activities, with various intensities. Thus, basic activity j has input and output vectors $a_{j)}$, $b_{j)}$ given by the jth columns of non-negative matrices a, b. These may be combined with intensities t_j, forming the activity vector $t \geq 0$ and its elements. The resulting activity requires inputs $\Sigma a_{j)} t_j = at$ for its performance, and then has output $\Sigma b_{j)} t_j = bt$. Allowing free disposal on the sides of both input and output, if x is the vector of goods available to supply inputs, then $x \geq at$ is the condition for feasibility of activity t, and the output is any $y \leq bt$. Therefore the condition for y to be producible from x is that there exists some activity t such that $x \geq at$, $bt \geq y$. Hence inputs and outputs have the *input-output relation R* defined by

$$xRy \equiv (\vee\ t) \, x \geq at, \ bt \geq y.$$

In von Neumann's economic model, such a relation determines the input-output possibilities in any production period. The outputs of one period supply the inputs for the next. Hence $x_1 \, Rx_2 \, R \ldots$ is the condition for $x_1, x_2, \ldots$ to be a possible path of the economy, described in terms of goods. Then the input-output relation across N production periods is the relation holding between endpoints of paths of that length. This is the power relation R^N, where

$$R^1 = R, \ R^N = RR^{N-1},$$

the product of two relations being such that $x(AB)y$ means $xAzBy$ for some z.

The system admits a *growth factor r*, for some vector of goods x, if $xRxr$ for some $x \geq 0$. In that case $xRxrRxr^2 R \ldots Rxr^N$, which implies $xR^N xr^N$. Thus the growth factors for R^N include, and may exhaust, all the values r^N, where r is a growth factor of R.

For an activity t_1 in one period to generate an activity t_2 in the next, the available output bt_1 from the one must suffice to provide the needed input at_2 for the next. Such activites therefore have the relation G defined by

$$t_1 Gt_2 \equiv bt_1 \geq at_2.$$

Then $t_1 Gt_2 G \ldots$ is the condition for $t_1, t_2, \ldots$ to be a possible activity path; and $t_1 G^N t_2$ asserts that an activity t_1 can generate an activity t_2 N periods later.

Any activity $t \geq 0$ can grow by a factor r if $tGtr$, that is, $bt \geq atr$. But then, taking $x = at$, we have $x \geq at$, $bt \geq xr$, that is, $xRxr$. Given that $at \geq 0$ if

$t \geq 0$, which is condition (a) dealt with in section 3, we also have $x \geq 0$. Conversely, $xRxr$ is equivalent to $x \geq at$, $bt \geq xr$ for some t, and so implies $bt \geq atr$, that is, $tGtr$. Also, $t \geq 0$ if $x \geq 0$ and $r > 0$. Thus we see that, subject to (a), the growth factors for the system are the same whether they be defined with reference to goods or to activities.

6.2 DUAL SYSTEM

In a period when there is an input x when the prices are p, and an output y when the prices are q, the profit, or return from output reduced by cost of input, is $qy - px$. The principle of equilibrium when profits fall to zero leads to the consideration of prices p, q which provide non-positive profit. Such prices have the relation R^* given by

$$pR^* q \equiv xRy \Rightarrow px \geq qy.$$

This defines the *dual system* R^* determined from the system R.

Since

$$x \geq at, bt \geq y \Rightarrow px \geq qy, \text{ for all } x, y \text{ and } t,$$

non-negativity of all elements being understood, is equivalent to $pa \geq qb$, we have $R^* = S$, where S is the relation defined by

$$pSq \equiv pa \geq qb.$$

The relation between R and its dual $S = R^*$ is symmetrical, in that R is recovered as the dual $R = S^*$ of S by the same principle that S derives from R; in other words, $R^{**} = R$. Thus,

$$pa \geq qb \Rightarrow px \geq qy, \text{ for all } p,$$

is equivalent to

$$x \geq at, bt \geq y, \text{ for some } t,$$

that is, to xRy. Hence, with S^* defined by

$$xS^* y \equiv pSq \Rightarrow px \geq qy,$$

we have $R = S^*$.

In the same way that G, as a relation between successive activities, is associated with R, where sGt means $bs \geq at$, so a relation H is associated with S, where

$$uHv \equiv (\lor p) u \geq pb, pa \geq v.$$

Just as R, S are related as dual systems, so are G, H. Thus, $H = G^*$, and $G = H^*$, where

$$uG^* v \equiv sGt \Rightarrow us \geq vt, \quad sH^* t \equiv uHv \Rightarrow us \geq vt.$$

For the sense of the relation H, we should consider prices p prevailing between consecutive production periods, at the end of one and the beginning of the other. With these prices, $u \geq pb$ and $v \leq pa$ are vectors of at least the returns and at most the costs associated with basic activities. We require that the return from output of activity s in one period should finance the cost of input required by activity t in the next, such that sGt, so $us \geq vt$ is required.

Regarding these four relations, dual in pairs, we also find that when the system (a, b) is exchanged with its reciprocal (b', a'), there is an exchange between R and H, and between S and G.

6.3 IRREDUCIBILITY

For any *von Neumann pair* (a, b), of non-negative rectangular matrices, of the same order, we consider various conditions. The first two are stated in three equivalent ways.

(a) $a_{j)}$ is semipositive,
        at is semipositive if t is semipositive,
        pa is positive if p is positive,

that is,

every activity has some good as an input.

(b) $b_{(i}$ is semipositive,
        pb is semipositive if p is semipositive,
        bt is positive if t is positive,

that is,

every good is an output of some activity.

For a *regular* von Neumann pair, these two conditions hold. Transposing and exchanging a and b, we have another regular pair, the *reciprocal* of the first.

A subset $R \subset [1, \ldots, m]$ of the goods is *independent* if, for some subset $C \subset [1, \ldots, n]$ of activities,

for all $i \in R'$, $a_{ij} = 0$ for all $j \in C$.
for all $i \in R$, $b_{ij} > 0$ for some $j \in C$,

In other words, there are some activities that require no other goods as inputs that also have all the goods as outputs. With a suitable ordering of goods and activities, the input and output matrices have the form

$$a = \begin{pmatrix} a_{00} & a_{01} \\ O & a_{11} \end{pmatrix}, \qquad b = \begin{pmatrix} b_{00} & b_{01} \\ b_{10} & b_{11} \end{pmatrix},$$

where O is null, and the rows of b_{00} are semipositive. In that case, given that (a, b) is a regular system, so also is the system (a_{00}, b_{00}). We say (a, b) is *irreducible* if no proper independent subset of goods exists (Gale 1960, p. 314). This is a third considered property:

(c) (a, b) is irreducible.

In other words,

there exists no proper independent subset of goods, which are all that are required as inputs by some activities, which also have them all as outputs.

When a is square, and $b = 1$, the identity matrix, this condition becomes the same as the irreducibility found in the Perron–Frobenius (1932) theorem on the dominant root of a non-negative matrix. Instead of this more economically significant condition introduced by Gale (1960), von Neumann dealt with the condition $a + b > 0$, which makes the funtion *pbt/pat* well defined for all semipositive t and p, and states that, in every activity, every good is either an input or an output. The 'absence of gap cycles' condition of Afriat (1974) is a weakening of it, sufficient to assure that $(R^N)^* = (R^*)^N$. The conditions (a) and (b), missing in the argument of von Neumann (1937), though necessary for it as discussed by Afriat (1974)), were brought forward by Kemeny, Morgenstern and Thompson (1956).

We can assume that goods by themselves are without volition whereas activities, or possibly groups of them, interpreted as individual firms, might be allowed to have it. We may take independent activities to produce all the goods they require as inputs, while these are not produced by any other activities. Then irreducibility can be defined by the non-existence of a proper independent subset of activities. Instead, $b_{01} = O$, while (a_{00}, b_{00}) is again a regular subsystem. This is the same as the original reducibility applied to the reciprocal system (b', a').

6.4   ADMISSIBLE FACTORS

Subject to condition (a), any semipositive activity t is associated with a unique growth factor

$$r(t) = \max\ [r : bt \geq atr],$$

the maximum factor with which it can be made to grow. This is such that, for all r and semipositive t,

$$bt \geq atr \Leftrightarrow r \leq r(t).$$

We have

$$r(t) = \max\ [r : b_{(i}t \geq a_{(i}tr]$$
$$= \max\ [r : b_{(i}t/a_{(i}t \geq r, a_{(i}t > 0]$$
$$= \min\ [b_{(i}t/a_{(i}t : a_{(i}t > 0].$$

With condition (a), making also at semipositive, this is well-defined, and finite. Thus

$$\text{(a) implies } r(t) < \infty \text{ for all semipositive } t.$$

Also, (b) makes bt positive if t is positive, and so we have

$$\text{(b) implies } r(t) > 0 \text{ for all positive } t.$$

Another characterization of $r = r(t)$ is that $bt \geq atr$ while not $bt > atr$.
    Now we can define

$$\bar{r} = \sup\ r(t), \quad \dot{r} = \sup_{t > 0} r\ (t),$$

so in any case $\dot{r} \leq \bar{r}$. Given (b), so that $bt > 0$ for $t > 0$, we have $\dot{r} > 0$.

Similarly, subject to (b), any semipositive price vector p is associated with an interest factor

$$s(p) = \min \; [s : pb \le spa].$$

This is the minimum interest factor which, with the prices, makes a positive profit impossible. With condition (b), by which pb is semipositive for semipositive p, this is well defined, positive, and such that

$$pb \le spa \Leftrightarrow s \ge s(p).$$

Now we have

$$s(p) = \max \; [pb_{j)} /pa_{j)} : pa_{j)} > 0],$$

and we can introduce

$$\bar{s} = \inf s(p), \; \dot{s} = \inf_{p \,>\, 0} s(p),$$

so in any case $\dot{s} \ge \bar{s}$. Given (à), so that $pa > 0$ for $p > 0$, we also have $\dot{s} < \infty$.

The following gather the main remarks made above.

THEOREM   (a) $\Rightarrow r(t) < \infty$ for all $t \ge 0$,
         (b) $\Rightarrow r(t) > 0$ for all t > 0,
         $\dot{r} \le \bar{r}$, (b) $\Rightarrow \dot{r} > 0$,

THEOREM   (b) $\Rightarrow s(p) > 0$ for all $p \ge 0$,
         (a) $\Rightarrow s(p) < \infty$ for all $p > 0$,
         $\dot{s} \ge \bar{s}$, (a) $\Rightarrow \dot{s} < \infty$.

6.5.   FACTOR BOUNDS

THEOREM   If (a, b) is regular and irreducible then any growth and interest factors r and s are such that $r \le s$.

If $r = 0$, there is nothing more to prove. Hence let $r > 0$. Suppose, as required for r and s, that

$$bt \ge atr, \; pb \le spa,$$

for some semipositive t, p. Then, with regular (a, b), at is semipositive, and so also bt, since $r > 0$. Also

$$rpat \le pbt \le spat.$$

Hence, for the required conclusion, it is sufficient to show that $pat > 0$.

From condition (a) required for regularity, we have $at \ge 0$. Hence, with $r > 0$, we have $bt \ge atr \ge 0$, and so $bt \ge 0$.

Now let

$$R = [i : b_{(i}t > 0], \; C = [j : t_j > 0].$$

Because bt is now semipositive, R is non-empty. For $i \, \epsilon \, R'$, we have $b_{(i}t = 0$ and, since

$$b_{(i} \geq a_{(i}tr \geq 0, r > 0,$$

also $a_{(i}t = 0$. Thus

$$0 = a_{(i}t \geq a_{ij}t_j \geq 0,$$

so that $a_{ij} = 0$ for $j \, \epsilon \, C$. It follows that R is an independent subset of goods. Hence, by the irreducibility, it cannot be a proper subset. Therefore, since it is non-empty, its complement is empty, showing that $bt > 0$. Hence $pbt > 0$, from which it follows that $pat > 0$, QED.

Only the (a)-part of (a, b) being regular enters in this result. With the similar, dual definition of irreducibility, which has reference to an independent subgroup of activities, in which there is an exchange of roles between rows and columns, and between a and b, the (b)-part bears similarly, and there is the same conclusion.

This theorem is a minor elaboration on the argument of Gale (1960, p. 135). More explicitly, the following was shown.

> THEOREM   For an irreducible von Neumann pair (a, b), the conditions $bt \geq atr$, $t \geq 0$, together with $r > 0$ and $at \geq 0$, imply $bt > 0$.

6.6   LIMIT RECIPROCITY

> THEOREM   For all v, either
>
> (i) $bt \geq atv$ for some $t \geq 0$,
>
> or
>
> (ii) $pb < vpa$ for some $p \geq 0$,
>
> and not both.

This follows from the theorem that, for any matrix c, either $ct \geq 0$ or $pc < 0$ have semipositive solutions, and not both. An account of the theorem is in A. W. Tucker (1956), Ky Fan (1956), and D. Gale (1960).

> COROLLARY   (i) $\bar{r} \geq \dot{s}$.

If $v > \bar{r}$ then, by definition of $\bar{r}$, (i) does not have a solution. Therefore, by the theorem, (ii) does. But evidently then $pb \leq vpa$ does also for some $p > 0$, so that $v \geq \dot{s}$. Thus we have

$$v > \bar{r} \Rightarrow v \geq \dot{s},$$

and this gives the wanted conclusion.

> COROLLARY   (ii)   (a) $\Rightarrow \bar{r} = \dot{s}$.

If $v > \dot{s}$ then, for $v > v' > \dot{s}$,

$$pb \leq v'pa \text{ for some } p > 0,$$

by definition of $\dot{s}$. But then, from (a), we have $pa > 0$, and hence also $pb < vpa$, so (ii) has a solution. Hence, by the theorem, (i) does not, showing that $v \geq \bar{r}$. Thus we have

$$v > \dot{s} \Rightarrow v \geq \bar{r},$$

from which it follows that $\dot{s} \geq \bar{r}$, which, with Corollary (i), gives the required conclusion.

COROLLARY (iii) $bt \geq at\bar{r}$ for some $t \geq 0$.

For any s, if (ii) has a solution with $v = s$, then it does also for all v in some open neighbourgood of s. Hence the set of such s is open, and its complement is closed. But, by the theorem, the complement is the set of v for which (i) has a solution. This is an interval with limits 0 and $\bar{r}$. It follows that $\bar{r}$ belongs to this set, QED. Gale (1960, p. 312, n.) instead proposes a compactness argument.

In the same way, or as reciprocals of the foregoing, these being the same propositions as applied to the reciprocal system (b', a'), we have

$$\bar{s} \leq \dot{r}, (b) \Rightarrow \bar{s} = \dot{r},$$

and also

$$pb \leq \bar{s}pa \text{ for some } p \geq 0.$$

COROLLARY (iv)   If the system is regular then

$$0 < \dot{r} = \bar{s} \leq \dot{s} = \bar{r} < \infty ,$$

and if also it is irreducible then moreover

$$\dot{r} = \bar{s} = \dot{s} = \bar{r}.$$

From Corollary (ii), together with remarks made in section 5, we have the first part. Then from Corollary (iii) with the theorem of section 5, $\bar{r} \leq \bar{s}$, and so we have the second part.

6.7   VON NEUMANN FACTOR

A *von Neumann factor* is any number which is simultaneously a growth and interest factor, that is, any v such that the conditions

$$(\text{VN}) \ bt \geq atv, t \geq 0, pb \leq vpa, p \geq 0,$$

have solutions.

Since, by Corollary (iii) of the last section, the first has a solution with $v = \bar{r}$, and similarly the second has a solution with $v = \bar{s}$, it appears that these conditions have a simutaneous solution if and only if $\bar{s} \leq v \leq \bar{r}$. Now by Corollary (iv) of the last section, we have the following.

THEOREM   If the system is regular then the set of von Neumann factors is the non-empty bounded closed interval with $\bar{s}$ and $\bar{r}$ as its upper and lower limits.

From this, again with Corollary (iv):

THEOREM   If the system is regular and irreducible, then a von Neumann factor exists, is unique, and coincides simultaneously with the maximum growth factor $\bar{r}$ and the minimum interest factor $\bar{s}$.

The von Neumann conditions (VN) can be stated in an equivalent form, for the irreducible case, in which they have sense as economic equilibrium conditions:

$$p_i \geq 0, \; b_{(i}t \geq a_{(i}tr, \; b_{(i}t > a_{(i}tr \Rightarrow p_i = 0,$$

$$t_j \geq 0, \; pb_{j)} \geq spa_{j)}, \; pb_{j)} > spa_{j)} \Rightarrow t_j = 0,$$

together with

$$p_i > 0 \text{ for some } i, \; t_j > 0 \text{ for some } j.$$

In the irreducible case, they determine r and s uniquely, with $r = s$. Here we see that any unprofitable activities are inactive, and any overproduced goods are free. These conditions may be compared with the similar optimality condition for a dual pair of LP problems

$$(M) \; \max px: ax \leq q, \; (W) \; \min uq: ua \geq p.$$

Thus, the conditions

$$u_i \geq 0, \; a_{(i}x \leq q_i, \; a_{(i}x < q_i \Rightarrow u_i = 0,$$

$$x_j \geq 0, \; ua_{j)} \geq p_j, \; ua_{j)} > p_j \Rightarrow x_j = 0,$$

are necessary and sufficient for x and u to be optimal solutions of the problems (M) and (W), in which case $px = uq$.

Only the ratios of elements being significant, nothing is altered if we understand the vectors $t \geq 0$, $p \geq 0$ to be normalized so that the sum of their elements is 1, making them distribution vectors. With I as a column vector with elements all 1, and J such a row vector, we can require

$$pI = 1, \; p \geq 0, \; Jt = 1, \; t \geq 0,$$

putting no constraint on the ratios of elements and implying the vectors are semipositive. Such t and p describe spaces Δ and ∇, which are simplices of dimension $n - 1$ and $m - 1$.

The (VN) conditions imply $patv \leq pbt \leq vpat$, and hence $pbt = vpat$. We may now consider conditions, stated

$$pMt \equiv bt \geq atr, \; pbt = patr, \; p \in \nabla,$$

$$tWp \equiv pb \leq spa, \; pbt = spat, \; t \in \Delta.$$

It is implicit in them that $r = r(t)$ and $s = s(p)$, so they define relations M, N between t, p. The (VN) conditions are equivalent to these relations holding simultaneously for some t, p with the further requirement that $r = s$, that is, $r(t) = s(p)$. However, if $pbt > 0$, this equality is not an additional imposition on the conditions, but is implied. The original existence and uniqueness argument of von Neumann (1937) dealt in this way with these relations, by a topological method, with the assumption that $a + b > 0$ which assured that $pbt > 0$ and hence $r = s$ in any solution. His argument depended on the sets $Mt \subset \nabla$ and $Wp \subset \Delta$ being non-empty for all $t \epsilon \Delta$ and $p \epsilon \nabla$. For this to be so, the regularity conditions (a) and (b), of Kemeny, Morgenstern and Thompson (1956), are required. Less is required now for the existence question, while condition (c) for irreducibility replaces von Neumann's condition to provide uniqueness.

Von Neumann based his argument on the theorem, which he formulated, whether or not his proof is accepted, that if A, B are simplices and R, $S \subset A \times B$ are closed and such that the sets xR, Sy are non-empty convex for all $x \epsilon A$, $y \epsilon B$, then xRy, xSy for some x, y. Kakutani (1941) straightforwardly proved the special case where $B = A$, and $S = D$, the diagonal $D \subset A \times A$ for which xDy means $x = y$. This assures the existence of x such that xRx. He deduced von Neumann's theorem from this case by applying it to the relation

$$(x, y)T(x', y') \Leftrightarrow xRy', x'Sy.$$

6.8   STRETCH ALGORITHM

With any $t > 0$, we may take $r = r(t)$, so that $r \leq \bar{r}$. Then, characterizing such r, we have $bt \geq atr$, but not $bt > atr$. Were it the case that $r < \dot{r}$, we would then be able to find t' such that $bt' > at'r$, so giving all the inequalities a positive slack. In particular, a t' could be found to *stretch* the inequalities by making the minimum slack a maximum. Then with $r' = r(t')$ we have $r < r' \leq \bar{r}$, and r' can replace r for a repetition, provided also $r' < \dot{r}$.

In general we have $\dot{r} \leq \bar{r}$. But in the regular irreducible case, to be considered first, we have $0 < \dot{r} = \bar{r} < \infty$. In this case there is a unique von Neumann factor v, coinciding with $\bar{r}$ and $\dot{r}$, and also with $\bar{s}$ and $\dot{s}$. With the above process, at any stage we have a t providing an $r \leq v$. It would be apparent when $r = v$, because there would be a termination. Otherwise, $r < v$. In that case, we can find a t' such that $bt' > at'r$, so that, with $r' = r(t')$, we have $r < r' \leq v$. Replacing r by r' and repeating the process, the bounded monotonic increasing sequence thus obtained, $r, r', \ldots$ is convergent with v. One could proceed just as well on the dual side, dealing with interest factors, to obtain a monotonic decreasing sequence $s, s', \ldots$ convergent with v.

This method for the irreducible case, and the one of Gerald L. Thompson (1974), described also in Morgenstern and Thompson (1976), and below, seem to have roughly the same efficiency, as we both agree. Despite some differences, the two methods are closely connected, as will become apparent. The question is whether there is any important difference. Whether or not, this method still may have interest. Even a brief consideration of it discloses the largely neglected distinction of the four numbers $\dot{r}, \bar{s}, \bar{r}, \dot{s}$ and their relationships, dealt with here, and also in Afriat (1971).

For the reducible case, when the regularity conditions (a) and (b) are met but condition (c) is not met, and we may have $\bar{s} = \dot{r} < \bar{r} = \dot{s}$, the object is to determine the limits $\bar{r}, \bar{s}$ of the no longer unique von Neumann factor.

Without prior inspection of the model, the present method can detect a failure of any of the conditions (a), (b) and (c). Though not to be approached here, a development of it, as also of Thompson's method, may serve for analysing decomposition structure, finding the irreducible subsystems and the associated von Neumann factors.

Consider any v, either a growth factor, when $v = r(t)$, or an interest factor, when $v = s(p)$, and a von Neumann factor when both apply. Let $c = b - va$. With v as a growth factor, the stretch operation consists of maximizing e, subject to $Ie \leq ct, t \in \Delta$. When v is an interest factor, it consists of minimizing e, where $eJ \geq pc, p \in \nabla$. In each case we have an LP problem. But the two problems thus obtained are dual LP problems, which would be simultaneously solved if either were solved, given the same value for e, by the LP Duality theorem. This renders immaterial the ambiguity concerning the nature of v.

The LP problems are

(M) max $e : Ie - ct \leq 0, Jt = 1, t \geq 0,$
(W) min $e : eJ - pc \geq 0, pI = 1, p \geq 0.$

These are dual problems, and both are feasible. Therefore both have optimal solutions, with the same optimal values. Since the values have already been equated together in these statements, being represented by the same variable e, the required solutions are characterized by simultaneous solutions (t, p) of the constraints, and provide the well defined unique *stretch parameter* $e = pct$, associated with v. We distinguish three cases; $e > 0, e = 0, e < 0$.

If $e = 0$, it determines that v is a von Neumann (VN) factor, equivalently, $\bar{s} \leq v \leq \bar{r}$, in which case there may be a termination, especially in a known case of irreducibility, when necessarily $\bar{s} = \bar{r}$. Otherwise, if $e > 0$, then v is a growth factor, and not an interest factor, and *vice versa* if $e < 0$. Thus, $e > 0$ is equivalent to

$$bt > atv, t \geq 0, \qquad\qquad (i)$$

having a solution, which implies $v < \dot{r}$, and to

$$pb \leq vpa, p \geq 0, \qquad\qquad (ii)$$

not having a solution, which is equivalent to $v < \bar{s}$. Here again we come to the conclusion that $\bar{s} \leq \dot{r}$. Moreover, in the irreducible case, $\bar{s} = \dot{r}$, by Theorem 6, Corollary (iv), so in this case we also have the converse, and (i) having a solution becomes equivalent to $v < \dot{r}$. With this in view, the description for this case, at the start of this section, becomes fully explicit. We will consider how to proceed without irreducibility as a prior assumption, after describing Thompson's approach.

Thompson formulated the problem of finding the von Neumann factor as finding a value for v such that $c = b - va$ is the payoff matrix of a fair game: one for which the game value is zero. Any first impression of novelty given by the present method is diminished, though not altogether to zero, by the discovery that the stretch parameter is equivalent to the game value of Thompson's approach. The next two sections deal with the relevant game theory, and with it, the LP method. The formulae for finding the max-min and min-max values M and W and the strategies, in section 10, are identical with the stretch parameter formulae (M) and (W) above.

Thompson's method is now easily described. In view of the equivalence of our stretch parameter and his game value, it amounts, in present terms, to the following: Starting with some v_0, v_1 having stretch parameters $e_0 < 0$, $e_1 > 0$, so that the von Neumann factor lies between them, we take $v = (v_0 + v_1)/2$, and determine its value e. If, within the limit of attainable precision, $e = 0$, then v is the von Neumann factor, and so the process terminates. Otherwise, if $e < 0$ we take $v_0 = v$ and if $e > 0$ then $v_1 = v$, so producing closer limits for the von Neumann factor. This process is repeated with the new limits v_0, v_1 and so forth, to termination, which may also be when $v_0 = v_1$, within the limits of attainable precision, as must eventually happen, in fewer than an easily evaluable finite number of iterations, since the interval with v_0, v_1 as limits is halved at each step.

In Part I of the following, we have $e \geq 0$ always, and a monotonic increasing series of values v converging to $\dot{r} = \bar{s}$. In Part II we have $e \leq 0$, and a monotonic decreasing series of v converging to $\dot{s} = \bar{r}$. Reducibility is discovered if it is found that $\bar{s} < \bar{r}$. In any case, the von Neumann factors describe the interval with limits $\bar{s}$, $\bar{r}$. In the irreducible case these limits coincide, and the two parts give the same result.

(I):

    0   $t = I$
    1   $v = r(t)$, $c = b - va$
    2   solve (M) to determine t, e
    3   if $e = 0$ then end; $\bar{s}$ found
    4   goto 1

(II):

    0   $p = J$
    1   $v = s(p)$, $c = b - va$
    2   solve (W) to determine p, e
    3   if $e = 0$ then end; $\bar{r}$ found
    4   goto 1

Because of their duality, and simultaneous solution, there is no practical distinction between the problems (M) and (W). An alternative termination, for either part, is at the step where no change is found in v.

Following Thompson's approach, having determined v_+, v_0, v_- with $e >$, $=$, < 0, one could proceed as follows:

(I):

    1 $v = (v_+ + v_0)/2$, solve for e
    2 if $e > 0$ then $v_+ = v$ else $v_0 = v$
    3 if $v_+ = v_0$ then end; $\bar{s}$ found
    4 goto 1

(II):

    1 $v = (v_- + v_0)/2$, solve for e
    2 if $e < 0$ then $v_- = v$ else $v_0 = v$
    3 if $v_- = v_0$ then end; $\bar{r}$ found
    4 goto 1

With either approach, the terminating LP problems provide von Neumann activity and price vectors t and p, corresponding to the von Neumann factor that has been found.

6.9 MATRIX GAMES

For a zero-sum two person matrix game, the payoff function has the form *uax*, where a is an m x n-matrix, and probability vectors u and x describe the strategies of the two players.

Let I be the column m-vector with elements all 1, and J the similar row n-vector, so that, for row and column probability vectors u and x, there are the constraints

$$uI = 1, u \geq 0; Jx = 1, x \geq 0.$$

We can suppose the payoff results in gain to the u-player, who has m pure strategies, associated with the rows of the matrix a, and loss to the x-player, with n pure strategies associated with the columns. An *equilibrium solution* is then a pair u, x such that

$$vax \leq uax \leq uay$$

for all v, y. In other words, it is a max–min saddle point (u, x) of the function. Then the saddle value $t = uax$ is the *value* of the game, which is a *fair game* if $t = 0$.

While in general, for any function of x and u, we just have

$$\max_u \min_x \leq \min_x \max_u,$$

for the existence of a saddle-point it is required that

$$\max_u \min_x = \min_x \max_u.$$

Von Neumann's *Minimax theorem* asserts the existence of a saddle point, or an equilibrium, for any zero-sum two person matrix game.

In the case of the finite game obtained by restriction to pure strategies, this would not be true. Thus consider:

$$
\begin{array}{ccc}
 & 1: & 2: \\
\end{array}
$$

$$
\begin{array}{cccc}
1: & 2 & 4 & \geq 2 \\
2: & 3 & 1 & \geq 1 \\
 & \leq 3 & \leq 4 &
\end{array}
$$

The max-min strategy, of the maximizing x-player, is $i = 1$, with value 2, and the min–max strategy for the minimizing x-player is $j = 1$, with value 2, so in this case we have

$$
\max_i \min_j a_{ij} = 2 < 3 = \min_j \max_i a_{ij},
$$

and there is no saddle point. However, there is a saddle point when mixed strategies, which are distributions over pure strategies, are allowed. In certain cases, there may be a solution in pure strategies. Thus consider:

$$
\begin{array}{ccc}
 & 1: & 2: \\
\end{array}
$$

$$
\begin{array}{cccc}
1: & 3 & 4 & \geq 3 \\
2: & 2 & 1 & \geq 1 \\
 & \leq 3 & \leq 4 &
\end{array}
$$

In this case,

$$
\max_i \min_j a_{ij} = 3 = \min_j \max_i a_{ij},
$$

so 3 is the saddle value, for the saddle point $(1, 1)$.

6.10 LP SOLUTION

With any strategy u for the max-player, the worst possible outcome is where uax is minimum. The max–min strategy u makes this minimum a maximum, M, so making the worst that can happen as favourable as possible. Similarly the min-player has a min–max strategy x, providing a value W. From the general relation between a min–max and max–min, $M \leq W$. In the present case, by the Minimax theorem, the values obtained are equal, $M = W$, so these defensive strategies provide a saddle-point of the payoff function, or a Nash solution of the game. The saddle-value S, given by both M and W, defines the value of the game. This is zero in the case of a fair game.

The problem of finding the solution strategies u, x is represented by a pair of LP problems. Then, since they are dual problems, the Minimax theorem follows from the LP Duality theorem.

For all u,

$$
\min \left[uax : Jx = 1, x \geq 0 \right] = \max \left[t : tJ \leq ua \right],
$$

as follows from LP duality. More directly,

$$
uax = \Sigma ua_{j)} x_j
$$

is an average of numbers $ua_{j)}$ with weights x_j. This attains a minimum when all weight is concentrated on the smallest number. Hence the value is

$$\min ua_{j)} = \max \ [t : t \leq ua_{j)} \ ],$$

whence the stated formula.

Now for

$$M = \max_u \min_x uax \ (uI = 1, u \geq 0, Jx = 1, x \geq 0)$$

we obtain

$$M = \max \ [t : tJ \leq ua, uI = 1, u \geq 0].$$

Similarly,

$$W = \min \ [t : It \geq ax, Jx = 1, x \geq 0].$$

These are dual LP formulae and so, by the LP Duality theorem, $M = W$.

A simplification of these formulae is applicable when $a > 0$. In any case, replacing a by $a + tIJ > 0$ for large values of t replaces uax by

$$u(a + tIJ)x = uax + tuIJx = uax + t,$$

and therefore S by $S + t$, leaving the solution strategies unchanged. The qualification $a > 0$ therefore involves no essential limitation. With it, we have

$$M = \max \ [t : tJ \leq ua, uI = 1, u \geq 0, t \geq 0].$$

Hence, with the substitution $v = t^{-1}u$,

$$M = \max \ [t : J \leq va, vI = t^{-1}, v \geq 0],$$
$$= 1/\min \ [vI : va \geq J, v \geq 0].$$

Therefore, by solving the LP problem

$$(M) \ \min vI : va \geq J, v \geq 0,$$

we determine the value $S = (vI)^{-1} > 0$ and strategy $u = v(vI)^{-1}$. Similarly we have the problem

$$(W) \ \max Jy : ay \leq I, y \geq 0,$$

to determine $x = (Jy)^{-1}y$.

In any case, problem (W) is feasible, and, if $a > 0$, then so is (M). Hence they have solutions, obtainable simultaneously by Dantzig's Simplex algorithm.

6.11 PERRON–FROBENIUS AND VON NEUMANN

The von Neumann theory, for a pair of rectangular non-negative matrices (a, b), as with the economic model, or a single rectangular matrix, in the Minimax theorem of game theory, shares a perspective with the Perron–Frobenius theorem about a single square non-negative matrix a, concerning the dominant root. To begin with, we have the following, for a square non-negative matrix a.

THEOREM If $\bar{r} = \max \ [r : x \geq axr, x \gtrless 0]$, then

$$x \geq ax\bar{r}, x \gtrless 0 \Rightarrow x = ax\bar{r}.$$

$$(\text{Gale 1960, p. 317}).$$

Suppose, on the contrary, that $S = [i : x_i > a_{(i}x\bar{r}]$ is non-empty. In any case S' must be non-empty, since otherwise $\bar{r}$ could be increased, and so would not be maximum. We can suppose x chosen to make S as large as possible.

Then $a_{kj}x_j = 0$ for all $k \in S'$, $j \in S$. For suppose $a_{kj}x_j > 0$ for some $k \in S'$, $j \in S$. Then a small decrease in x_j would preserve the elements of S while adjoining the further element k, so increasing the size of S, which is impossible.

Now let the x_k for $k \in S'$ all be replaced by 0. For $i \in S$, we still have $x_i > a_{(i}x\bar{r}$, while for $k \in S'$ we simply have $0 \equiv 0$. But this again means that $\bar{r}$ could be increased, which is impossible. Consequently, S must be empty, QED.

The *multiplicity* of a characteristic value is its multiplicity as a root of the characteristic polynomial. The *rank* is the dimension of the corresponding space of characteristic vectors. For any matrix, this is at most the multiplicity. A *simple* characteristic value has multiplicity 1; hence its rank also is 1. A *dominant root* is one whose modulus is a maximum. According to the Perron–Frobenius theorem, any irreducible square non-negative matrix a has a dominant root $\bar{r}$ which is real and simple, and a corresponding characteristic vector $\bar{x}$ which is positive; moreover, if

$$r(x) = \min [a_{(i}x/x_i : x_i > 0],$$

then

$$\bar{r} = \max [r(x): x \geq 0],$$

this value being attained at $x = \bar{x}$. For an equivalent formula,

$$r(x) = \max [r: ax \geq xr], \bar{r} = \max [r(x): x \geq 0],$$

and so

$$\bar{r} = \max [r : xr - ax \leq 0, Jx \leq 1, x \geq 0].$$

Here we see the reciprocal of the dominant root as the von Neumann factor for the system $(a, 1)$. The existence and uniqueness of the von Neumann factor for this special system, subject to irreducibility, therefore follow from the Perron–Frobenius theorem. Equally, the dominant root can now be determined by the LP methods that have been described for the von Neumann factor, which are simpler than having to solve a polynomial. However, the usual, still simpler, method of finding $\bar{r}$ and $\bar{x}$ is to start with any $x \geq 0$, such as $x = I$, and repeatedly replace x by $ax(Jax)^{-1}$. Then $x \to \bar{x}$, and $a\bar{x} = \bar{x}\bar{r}$ determines $\bar{r}$.

The conditions (section 7) for a von Neumann solution (t, p, v), with a system (a, b), are equivalent to

$$p_i \geq 0, b_{(i}t \geq a_{(i}tv, p_i > 0 \Rightarrow b_{(i}t = a_{(i}tv = 0,$$

$$t_j \geq 0, pb_{j)} \leq vpa_{j)}, t_j > 0 \Rightarrow pb_{j)} = vpa_{j)} = 0,$$

together with

$$p_i > 0 \text{ for some } i, t_j > 0 \text{ for some } j.$$

Subject to irreducibility, these determine a unique v. Let

$$R = [i: p_i > 0], C = [j: t_j > 0],$$

so these sets are non-empty. Then, with a, b replaced by the submatrices in these rows and columns, and p, t truncated similarly, we have

$$bt = atv, t > 0, pb = vpa, p > 0.$$

Given the subsytem (a, b), also irreducible, by that assumption for the original, these equations have a positive solution for a unique positive v. Granting that the matrices are square, as the case must be with suitable qualifications, we have the shape of a generalization of the Perron–Frobenius theory, concerning a matrix pencil $a - \lambda b$, such as has been investigated by Gantmacher (1959), instead of $a - \lambda 1$, and of which the von Neumann theory is already a generalization. Thompson (1975a, b), Weyl (1964, 1968, 1970), Thompson and Weyl (1969, 1970, 1971, 1972), and Dell, Weyl and Thompson (1971), pursue such a generalization, which is made a basis for computation of von Neumann solutions by Weyl. Morgenstern and Thompson (1976, p. 56) give an outline of the history of proofs and computations.

6.12   BASIC PROGRAM

This program is for the algorithm

```
0   r = 0
1   c = b - ar
2   solve min Jx: cx ≥ I, max uI: uc ≤ J
3   r′ = r, r = r(x)
4   if r ≠ r′ then 1
5   end
```

On termination, the von Neumann factor, and the activities and prices, are determined from

$$Jx = v^{-1} = uI, t = x(Jx)^{-1}, p = (uI)^{-1}u.$$

The program runs as intended in tests with irreducible examples, but should be replaced by another that includes the dual side, for reducible cases.

```
1 DATA 2,15
2 DATA"              VNM.BAS                  ",
3 DATA"              Von Neumann's
4 DATA"              Economic Model           ",*
5 '
6 '                  sna nov 85
9 '
10 '
15 DATA "<Space> to continue, <CR> to rerun, <Esc> to exit ",,*
16 DATA "output to screen, printer or disk (s, p, or d)? ",,*
17 DATA "data in memory",,"do you want a directory (y or
n)?",,*
18 DATA "Which model? ",,*
```

```
19 DATA "termination-r active (y or n)?",,*
20 DATA "termination-r resolution (1E-N, N=0-9, <Space> for
default 6)?",,*
21 DATA,"continue (y or n)? ",,*
22 DATA "alternative calculation of activities & prices (y or
n)",*
29 '
49 '
50 DEFINT GK,M,N
51 DIM
A(20,20),B(20,20),C(20,20),D(20,20),G(20),H(20),X(20),U(20)
52 GOTO 1000
59 '
90 IF FI THEN FI=0:INPUT K$ ELSE K$=INPUT$(1)
91 IF K$=ESC$ THEN 9999 ELSE IF K$=CR$ THEN RUN
92 FX=K$="x" OR K$="X":YES=K$="y" OR K$="Y" :NO=NOT YES:RETURN
93 RETURN
98 '
99 '--- find pivot column S, or optimum
100 L=00:FOR J=1 TO N:C=C(0,J)
110 IF C<0 AND L>C THEN L=C:S=J
120 NEXT:IF L=00 THEN PRINT#1,"result ",:GOSUB 330:FF=1:RETURN
129 '--- find pivot row R, or problem unbounded
130 L=00:FOR I=1 TO M
140 IF C(I,S)>0 THEN Q=C(I,0)>/C(I,S)>:IF L>Q THEN L=Q:R=I
150 NEXT:IF L=00 THEN PRINT#1,"termination-a":FF=0:RETURN
155 P=C(R,S)>:PRINT#1,"pivot element";P;"in
row";R;"column";S;CR$
159 '--- pivot on C produces new tableau D
160 FOR I=0 TO M:FOR J=0 TO N
170 D(I,J)=C(I,J)C(I,S)*C(R,J)/P
180 IF I=R THEN D(I,J)=C(I,J)/P
190 IF J=S THEN D(I,J)=C(I,J)/P
200 IF I=R AND J=S THEN C(I,J)=1/P
210 NEXT J,I:SWAP H(S),G(R):' register the exchange
219 '--- D becomes C for another loop
220 GOSUB 300:FOR I=0 TO M:GOSUB 320:FOR J=0 TO N:C(I,J)=D(I,J)
230 PRINT#1,TAB(4+J*TT)C(I,J);:NEXT:PRINT#1,:NEXT:PRINT#1,
240 IF LEN(INKEY$) THEN GOSUB 90
250 GOTO 100
251 '
259 '--- identify variables, basic or non-basic
260 IF FB THEN V=H(J) ELSE V=G(I)
270 IF V>N THEN V$="U":V=VN ELSE V$="X"
280 V$=V$+MID$(STR$(V),2):RETURN
299 '--- basic labels
300 FB=1:FOR J=1 TO N:GOSUB 260
310 PRINT#1,TAB(6+J*TT)V$;:NEXT:PRINT#1,:RETURN
319 '--- non-basic labels
320 IF I THEN GOSUB 260:PRINT#1,V$; ELSE FB=0
325 RETURN
329 '----- results
330 PRINT#1,"Value:";:Z=-C(>0,0)>
335 IF FE THEN PRINT#1,Z:Z=1 ELSE Z=1/Z:PRINT#1,Z
340 PRINT#1,CR$,"Solution:"
350 FB=0:FOR I=1 TO M:GOSUB 260:PRINT#1,,,V$;" =";
360 IF LEFT$(V$,1)="X" THEN X(V)=-C(I,0)*Z:PRINT#1,X(V)
365 IF LEFT$(V$,1)="U" THEN U(V)=0:PRINT#1,U(V)
```

```
370 NEXT:FB=1:FOR J=1 TO N:GOSUB 260:PRINT#1,,,V$;" =";
380 IF LEFT$(V$,1)="U" THEN U(V)=C(O,J)*Z:PRINT#1,U(V)
385 IF LEFT$(V$,1)="X" THEN X(V)=0:PRINT#1,X(V)
390 NEXT:RETURN
391 '
399 '--- ax, bx
400 FOR I=1 TO M:AX=0:BX=0:FOR J=1 TO N
410 AX=AX+A(I,J)*X(J):BX=BX+B(I,J)*X(J)
420 NEXT:AX(I)=AX:BX(I)=BX:NEXT
439 '--- new t
440 T=00:FOR I=1 TO M
445 IF AX(I)>0 AND BX(I)/AX(I)<T THEN T=BX(I)/AX(I)
450 NEXT:NT=NT+1:PRINT#1,CR$;"Round";NT;": T =";T;" DT
=";T-TO;CR$
455 IF FO THEN PRINT CR$;"Round";NT;": T =";T;" DT =";TTO;CR$
456 IF LEN(INKEY$) THEN GOSUB 90
460 IF FX OR (FR AND T/TO-1<O) THEN GOSUB 700
465 TO=T
469 '--- c = b - at
470 FOR I=1 TO M:D(I,0)=-1+FE:FOR J=1 TO N:D(O,J)=-1+FE
475 D(I,J)=(1-2*FE)*(B(I,J)-T*A(I,J)):NEXT J,I:IF FE THEN
RETURN
480 FOR J=1 TO N:H(J)=J:NEXT:' basic are 1 to N
485 FOR I=1 TO M:G(I)=N+I:NEXT:' non-basic are N+1 to N+M
490 IF FE THEN RETURN ELSE GOSUB 220:IF FF THEN 400 ELSE TV=T
499 '--- alternative calculation of x & u
500 GOSUB 800
510 RESTORE 22:GOSUB 991:IF NO THEN 640
520 FE=1:GOSUB 470:M=M+1:N=N+1
530 D(O,N)=-1:FOR I=1 TO M:D(I,N)=1:NEXT
540 D(M,0)=-1:FOR J=1 TO N:D(M,J)=1:NEXT
550 D(0,0)=0:D(M,N)=0:PRINT#1,
599 '--- transpose
600 IF M>N THEN L=M ELSE L=N
610 FOR I=1 TO L:FOR J=0 TO I-1
620 SWAP D(I,J),D(J,I):NEXT J,I
625 SWAP M,N:GOSUB 480
629 '
630 GOSUB 220:GOSUB 800
639 '
640 RESTORE 21:GOSUB 991
650 IF NO THEN RETURN
660 RESTORE 20:GOSUB 995
670 IF FE THEN FE=0:SWAP M,N:M=M1:N=N-1
675 GOSUB 470:RETURN
689 '
699 '--- termination-r or x
700 TV=T:GOSUB 800:IF FX THEN PRINT#1,"Termination-x"
705 IF FX=0 THEN PRINT#1,CR$;"Termination-r, resolution";O
710 RESTORE 21:GOSUB 991
720 IF NO THEN FX=0:RETURN 510
730 IF FX THEN FX=0 ELSE FR=0
740 RETURN
799 '--- results
800 PRINT#1,CR$,"Von Neumann factor =";TV
810 IF FE THEN PRINT#1,CR$;"activities"; ELSE PRINT#1,CR$;"
prices =";
815 X=0:FOR J=1 TO N-FE:X=X+X(J):NEXT
```

```
820 FOR J=1 TO N-FE:PRINT#1,TAB(J*TT);X(J)/X;:NEXT
825 IF FE THEN PRINT#1,CR$;"    prices"; ELSE
PRINT#1,CR$;"activities =";
830 U=0:FOR I=1 TO M-FE:U=U+U(I):NEXT
835 FOR I=1 TO M-FE:PRINT#1,TAB(I*TT);U(I)/U;:NEXT
840 PRINT CR$:RETURN
849 '--- data?
850 RESTORE 2000:READ VN$:RESTORE 17
851 IF VN$="*" THEN VN$="No " ELSE VN$=VN$+".VNP "
852 PRINT#1,,VN$;:GOSUB 991:RETURN
979 '
980 PRINT#1,TAB(CC);L$:IF FO THEN PRINT TAB(CC);L$
985 RETURN
989 '--- text
990 READ RR,CC:CLS:LOCATE RR
991 READ L$:IF L$<>"*" THEN GOSUB 980:GOTO 991
992 IF FP THEN GOSUB 90 ELSE FP=1
993 RETURN
994 '--- resolution
995 GOSUB 991:IF K$=" " THEN RETURN ELSE K=ASC(K$)-48
996 IF K<0 OR K>9 THEN RESTORE 20:GOTO 995 ELSE O=1/10^K:RETURN
998 '
999 '============ init
1000 ESC$=CHR$(27):CR$=CHR$(13):CRR$=CR$+CR$
1005 O$="SCRN:":TT=14:O=.00001:OO=1E+32:' =Inf
1006 IF O$<>"SCRN:" THEN FO=1
1010 OPEN O$ FOR OUTPUT AS 1:KEY OFF:GOSUB 990:GOSUB 991:O$=K$
1020 IF O$="p" OR O$="P" THEN O$="PRN:"
1021 IF O$="S" OR O$="s" THEN O$="SCRN:"
1022 GOSUB 850:IF NO THEN 1060
1029 '
1030 CLS:PRINT#1,CRR$,"Von Neumann model directory";CRR$
1035 FILES"B:*.VNP":PRINT#1,,:FI=1:CC=14:GOSUB 991:IF K$="" THEN
1060
1040 PRB$="B:"+K$+".VNP"
1045 PRINT#1,CR$;"loading ";PRB$;" ... RUN again, then <CR> at
this point"
1050 CLOSE#1:MERGE PRB$
1059 '
1060 RESTORE 19:GOSUB 991:IF YES THEN FR=1:GOSUB 995
1099 '
1100 CC=0:RESTORE 2000:READ
VN$:PRB$=VN$+".VNP":SLN$="B:"+VN$+".VNS"
1101 IF O$="D" OR O$="d" THEN O$=SLN$ ELSE IF O$=" " THEN
O$="SCRN:"
1102 IF O$="SCRN:" THEN FO=0 ELSE FO=1
1103 IF O$=SLN$ THEN PRINT#1,"Output written to disk file ";O$
1110 CLOSE#1:OPEN O$ FOR OUTPUT AS #1
1120 RESTORE 2000:CC=0:PRINT:FP=0:GOSUB 991:READ M,N
1130 PRINT#1,CR$,"rows for activities, columns for goods"
1199 '
1200 RESTORE 2110:PRINT#1,CR$;"Input Matrix a:";CR$
1210 FOR I=1 TO M:FOR J=1 TO N:READ A(I,J)
1220 PRINT#1,TAB(TT*J);A(I,J);:NEXT J,I:PRINT#1,
1230 RESTORE 2210:PRINT#1,CR$;"Output Matrix b:";CR$
1240 FOR I=1 TO M:FOR J=1 TO N:READ B(I,J)
1250 PRINT#1,TAB(TT*J);B(I,J);:NEXT J,I:PRINT#1,:GOSUB 90
1299 '
```

```
1300 NT=1:T=0:PRINT#1,CR$;"Round 1 :   T = 0";CR$:T0=0
1310 IF LEN(INKEY$) THEN GOSUB 90
1320 GOSUB 470:GOSUB 90
1399 '
1999 '---------- input and output matrices
2000 DATA MT165,,"Morgenstern & Thompson p. 165",
2009 '
2010 DATA" Activities:   Laying            Hatching          Labour"
2015 DATA"      Goods:   Laying            Hatching
     Labour",*
2099 '
2100 DATA 3, 3 :' M, N
2110 DATA        1,       0,       1
2120 DATA        1,       4,       1
2130 DATA        4,       8,       0
2199 '
2210 DATA        1,      12,       0
2220 DATA        5,       0,       0
2230 DATA        0,       0,       4
2999 '
9999 CLOSE#1:CLS:KEY ON:END
```

6.13 PROBLEMS

(1)
```
1999 '--------- input and output matrices
2000 DATA GALE,,"Gale, Theory of Linear Economic Models, p.
315",
2009 '
2010 DATA" testing    t = 2^1/3 = 1.259921"
2020 DATA"  x = (2^-1/3, 2^-2/3, 1), u = (1, 2^-1/3, 2^-2/3,
0)"
2030 DATA"    = (   1/t,  1/t^2, 1)    = (1,     1/t,  1/t^2,
0)",*
2099 '
2100 DATA 3, 4 :' M, N
2110 DATA        0,       1,       0,       0
2120 DATA        1,       0,       0,       1
2130 DATA        0,       0,       1,       0
2199 '
2210 DATA        1,       0,       0,       0
2220 DATA        0,       0,       2,       0
2230 DATA        0,       1,       0,       1
```

(2)
```
2000 DATA MT24,,"Morgenstern & Thompson p. 24",
2009 '
2010 DATA" Activities:  Laying Eggs, Hatching Chickens"
2015 DATA" Goods:          Chickens,              Eggs",*
2099 '
2100 DATA 2, 2 :' M, N
2110 DATA        1,       0
2120 DATA        1,       4
2199 '
2210 DATA        1,      12
2220 DATA        5,       0
```

```
(3)
2000 DATA MT27,,"Morgenstern & Thompson p. 27",
2009 '
2010 DATA" Activities:  Laying          Hatching          Labour"
2015 DATA"     Goods:   Laying          Hatching          Labour"
2099 '
2100 DATA 3, 3 :' M, N
2110 DATA      1,       0,       1
2120 DATA      1,       4,       1
2130 DATA      4,       8,       0
2199 '
2210 DATA      1,      12,       0
2220 DATA      5,       0,       0
2230 DATA      0,       0,       2

(4)
2000 DATA MT26,,"Morgenstern & Thompson p. 26",
2009 '
2010 DATA" Activities:  Wheat   Laying  Hatching"
2015 DATA"     Goods:   Wheat   Laying  Hatching",*
2099 '
2100 DATA 3, 3 :' M, N
2110 DATA      1,       0,       0
2120 DATA      1,       1,       0
2130 DATA      1,       1,       4
2199 '
2210 DATA      9,       0,       0
2220 DATA      0,       1,      12
2230 DATA      0,       5,       0

(5)
2000 DATA MT54,,"Morgenstern & Thompson p. 54",
2009 '
2010 DATA" Factors  1, 2, 3 and 4"
2015 DATA" x = (.25, .25, .25, .25),   u = (0, 0, 0, 1)",*
2099 '
2100 DATA 4, 4 :' M, N
2110 DATA      1,       0,       0,       0
2120 DATA      6,       1,       0,       0
2130 DATA      0,       1,       1,       0
2140 DATA      0,       1,       1,       1
2199 '
2210 DATA      4,       0,       0,       0
2220 DATA      2,       3,       0,       0
2230 DATA      0,       2,       2,       0
2240 DATA      2,       0,       6,       1
```

6.14 DEMONSTRATIONS

VNM.BAS

Von Neumann's
Economic Model

<Space> to continue, <CR> to rerun, <Esc> to exit

output to screen, printer or disk (s, p or d)?

Von Neumann model directory

Which model?
Output written to disk file B:GALE.VNS
GALE

Gale, Theory of Linear Economic Models, p. 315

    testing   t = 2^1/3 = 1.259921
    x = (2^-1/3, 2^-2/3, 1), u = (1, 2^-1/3, 2^-2/3, 0)
      = (1/t,   1/t^2, 1)   = (1,   1/t, 1/t^2, 0)

            rows for activities, columns for goods

Input Matrix   a:

0	1	0	0
1	0	0	1
0	0	1	0

Output Matrix   b:

1	0	0	0
0	0	2	0
0	1	0	1

Round 1 : T = 0

	X1	X2	X3	X4
0	-1	1	1	1
U1 -1	1	0	0	0
U2 -1	0	0	2	0
U3 -1	0	1	0	1

pivot element 1 in row 1 column 1

	U1	X2	X3	X4
-1	1	-1	-1	-1
X1 -1	1	0	0	0
U2 -1	0	0	2	0
U3 -1	0	1	0	1

pivot element 1 in row 3 column 2

	U1	U3	X3	X4
-2	1	1	1	0
X1 -1	1	0	0	0
U2 -1	0	0	2	0
X2 -1	0	1	0	1

pivot element 2 in row 2 column 3

	U1	U3	U2	X4
-2.5	1	1	.5	0
X1 -1	1	0	0	0

```
X3 -.5            0              0              1              0
X2 -1             0              1              0              1
```

result -

                    Value: .4

                    Solution:
                              X1 = .4
                              X3 = .2
                              X2 = .4
                              U1 = .4
                              U3 = .4
                              U2 = .2
                              X4 = 0

Round 2 : T = 1

and so forth, nine rounds .....

```
                    U1             U3             U2             X4
    -569775.3   145221.7       182967.9       115262.4       37746.16
X1 -182967.9    59916.63       75492.31       47556.92       15574.69
X3 -115262.4    37746.16       47556.92       -1             9810.757
X2 -145221.7    47556.92       59916.63       37746.16       12361.71
```

result -

                    Value: 1.755078E-06

                    Solution:
                              X1 = .3211228
                              X3 = .2022945
                              X2 = .2548754
                              U1 = .2548754
                              U3 = .3211228
                              U2 = .2022945
                              X4 = 0

Round 10 : T = 1.25992

termination-r, resolution .00001

                    Von Neumann factor = 1.25992

      prices = .4125991   .3274801   .2599208   0
  activities = .3274801   .2599208   .4125991

MT24

Morgenstern & Thompson p. 24

  Activities: Laying Eggs, Hatching Chickens
       Goods: Chickens,   Eggs

                    rows for activities, columns for goods

```
Input Matrix   a:

                      1                0
                      1                4

Output Matrix   b:

                      1               12
                      5                0

Round 1 :   T = 0

                          X1              X2
        0              1                1
U1 -1              1               12
U2 -1              5                0

pivot element 5 in row 2 column 1

                          U2              X2
      .2               .2              -1
U1 -.8             -.2              12
X1 -.2             -1                0

pivot element 12 in row 1 column 2

                          U2              U1
    -.2666667         .1833333       8.333334E-02
X2 -6.666667E-02 -1.666667E-02 -1
X1 -.2             -1                0

result -

                Value: 3.75

                Solution:
                                X2 = .25
X1 = .75
U2 = .6875
U1 = .3125

Round 2 :   T = 2.142857   DT = 2.142857

   and so forth for 9 rounds .....

result -
                Value: 1.114273E05

                Solution:
                                X2 = .1145484
                                X1 = .6872886
                                U2 = .4009189
                                U1 = .4009182

Round 10 :   T = 2.999998   DT = 9.775162E06

termination-r, resolution .00001
```

```
Continue to termination-x (y or n)?

            Von Neumann factor = 2.999998

    prices =  .8571426       .1428574
activities =  .4999996       .5000004


MT165

Morgenstern & Thompson p. 165

 Activities: Laying          Hatching        Labour
     Goods:  Laying          Hatching        Labour

            rows for activities, columns for goods

Input Matrix  a:

            1               0               1
            1               4               1
            4               8               0

Output Matrix  b:

            1               12              0
            5               0               0
            0               0               4

Round 1 :  T = 0

...

Round 13 :  T = 1.302773    DT = 4.887581E-06


            Von Neumann factor = 1.302773

    prices =  .318397        7.399818E-02   .6076048
activities =  .3771603       .377161        .2456788

Termination-r, resolution .00001

continue (y or n)?
```

Part V

OPTIMAL PROGRAMMING

V.1

Optimal Programming

from the Concise Oxford Dictionary of Current English

'Choice' and 'optimum' are terms that give little trouble in everyday use, and everyone seems to understand them. But encounter further discussion about them, and the need arises to consult a dictionary. Voltaire made fun of Leibniz with Dr Pangloss, but the Optimism has become solemn doctrine in economics. The more mathematical works do not resolve the matter, as might be hoped, but help to petrify it further. Today, Leibniz's doctrine is applied not to the entire universe, which might be going too far for local importance, but to the economy, and perhaps to election results. This approach has created a fertile field for the collaboration of economist and philosophers. Whatever the problems that should concern us, a cheap solution resides in the dictionary, and in the saving unambiguity of the subject known as 'optimal programming'.

When there is a criterion for deciding the better and the worse among possibilities, a search can be made for the best, or optimum. This is a commonplace pursuit taking many forms. The special form of optimal programming dealt with in this chapter is typical of economics.

For a simpler type of example, suppose there is a heap of stones and one is to be chosen from it to serve as an anchor. For that to be feasible, a stone must have such a shape that a rope can be attached to it. With a stone x taken in hand and inspected for feasibility, $Q(x)$ can denote affirmation. Feasibility granted, the criterion for a good anchor is weight. When two stones x, y are held one in each hand, a judgement can be made about which is the heavier. Let xWy signify that x is found to be at least as heavy as y. Should a weighing scale be available, it would also be possible to determine the weight $w(x)$ of any stone x. Then the weight relation W would be represented by the weight function w, in that

$$xWy \Leftrightarrow w(x) \geq w(y).$$

But even with w available, only the relation W so represented by it and expressing preferences for stones in their use as anchors is relevant to the choice to be made. This illustrates the point that, though a numerical objective function might be dealt with, only the order represented by it is essential. Similarly, in demand theory, the indifference map (which actually is a preference map) suffices to describe choice behaviour. Appreciating that is, in some accounts, a notable achievement of Pareto, and a page of calculus can be given to it.

A possibility x is optimal if it is feasible and at least as good as any other that is feasible:

$$Q(x), \quad Q(y) \Rightarrow xWy.$$

That is, x is a maximum of the order W in the feasible set Q. In terms of the function w,

$$Q(x), \quad w(x) = \max [w(y) : Q(y)],$$

or x is a maximum of the function w under the feasibility constraint Q. The problem of finding such x can be denoted

$$\max w(x) : Q(x).$$

Preferences govern selection and rejection, and infeasibility simply means sure rejection, so it also can be made a part of the preference criterion. Any stones for which use as an anchor is not feasible can instead be admitted among the feasible ones but given bottom priority, all equally. The special consideration of feasibility is in that way put aside, any feasible stone in former terms now being preferred to any infeasible one. The relation R defined by

$$xRy \equiv xWy \text{ or } \sim Q(y),$$

is an order relation, and optimality of x is just that xRy for all y, that is, x is a maximum of R. Or, with the function u given by

$$u(x) = w(x) \text{ if } Q(x), \quad u(x) = 0 \text{ if } \sim Q(x),$$

optimality of x just means that it is a maximum of u. Such elimination of the feasibility criterion by incorporating it into the preference criterion is like a procedure in optimal programming, which can be more elaborate. In that procedure, without altering the optimal solution, constraints are dropped but a cost of resources based on their shadow prices is introduced into the objective function. The Optimal Programming theorem of this chapter is concerned with just this. An aspect of the theorem is its generality, since it requires no restrictive assumptions whatsoever on the activity set A or the output and input functions f and g defined on it. When convexity, differentiability, or linearity assumptions are introduced in succeeding chapters, dealing with convex programming, the Kuhn-Tucker theory, and linear programming, the roles of these extra assumptions become clear.

As a shadow price, the Lagrange multiplier has a further economic meaning, in the way it enters into the new context, for instance in Kuhn-Tucker conditions. It is also a marginal value or derivative, where we have differentiability, but it is not dependent on differentiability, and has additional features. It gives a basis for the ideas about decentralized planning, realizing a plan by selling the centrally managed resources freely, instead of allocating them in a fixed way to be used according to the plan. Practical or not, the scheme has doctrinal value in mixed economies, reconciling the planning principle with the prevalence of markets.

Our top-down approach goes from the general and elementary in this chapter towards the more special and elaborate that comes later. The economic language assists thinking, and is where the interest lies, but imposes no limitation.

The example with the stones and their weights, though without other features, illustrates main ideas about optimization. The form of problem to be considered has scope for a type of problem that occurs widely in economics. Statements about it are in economic terms for the sake of exposition and preparation for applications — as said, that does not impose a restriction. Arguments will have reference to a productive firm choosing its activity. For typical economics applications the activity set A is in a Euclidean space, and frequently the variables have a non-negativity restriction. At first no restrictions at all will be put on A or on the input and output functions, g and f. Then, with the assumptions for convex and linear programming, it is possible to isolate the roles of these assumptions in later results. That applies especially to Slater's condition in convex programming, and to the Kuhn-Tucker conditions for the differentiable case that, subject to the constraint qualification, characterize all optimal solutions. Then it applies to linear programming, peculiarities of which make it outstanding both mathematically and for the many applications.

The optimal programming problem, now understood, represents the classic situation where there is no ambiguity at all about the better or worse among possibilities, and so none also about the best, or optimum. The theory of the consumer maximizing utility under a budget constraint would fit, but for the want of information about the utility being maximized, which requires it to be dealt with hypothetically. Doctrines about optimization of an economy under perfect competition or other conditions fit less well because of the absence of a global output criterion that would give them sense. Putting that issue aside as the 'aggregation problem' alters nothing, since we do not know what the problem is, and approaching it in terms of a welfare function or voting procedure does not help either. If in some way a global economic objective could be agreed upon, it would be assumed that one would know what it is in advance, and then one would be less likely to think that achieving it could be automatic.

In the experience of choice, for an individual or alternatively in a social and political context, many objectives can have a bearing simultaneously. These need not be aggregated, so as to turn the many conflicting objectives into a single one which can be made a basis for choice; rather, there is some decision about how much satisfaction each objective requires, which could be a matter of habit and expectation, or political agreement. Following an arrival at such agreement, the issue would be the simultaneous feasibility of the multiple requirements, not any global optimality. Adam Smith argued about the co-ordinating and organizing effectiveness of market forces and not the efficiency entertained in welfare economics that must depend on a criterion in the output space, which we do not have. The latter argument has gained favour among market polemicists — if they are defenders of liberty, then new recruits are needed.

The theorem of this chapter and the exposition of optimal programming related to it has an advantage for the economic context. This has been put by A. C. Williams (1974), reviewing an account (Afriat, 1969b) based on class notes at Purdue University, 1967–8:

This paper amounts to a complete reformulation of mathematical programming theory. The emphasis is on economic motivation and the language that of production theory. For example, one begins by defining, for a given maximization problem, a support solution which is defined as a set of prices that allow the constraints to be included in the objective function. The support solution is, of course, the set of Lagrangian multipliers. Rather than establish the existence and interpret the results, as is customary, the author defines what the economic context would demand, and then derives the conditions of their existence. One benefit to be obtained from this approach is that the role of convexity in mathematical programming is more clearly identified. The overall benefit is that of formulating programming theory completely in an economic context. (Williams, 1974)

There is a connection, as concerns our theorem, with work of F. J. Gould (1967), on 'Extensions of Lagrange multipliers in nonlinear programming'. We gathered that from a discussion of the subject in Chapel Hill, North Carolina, in 1969.

1.1 BOUNDS, LIMITS AND MAXIMA

Terms required in optimal programming, and the theorem of this chapter, are reviewed here. This section also serves to illustrate usages with binary relations, which fit this and similar topics.

Bounds

For numbers x, y such that $x \leq y$, y is an upper bound of x, and x is a lower bound of y. A set S has x as an upper bound if x is an upper bound of all its elements, as stated by

$$S \leq x \equiv y \in S \Rightarrow y \leq x,$$

and similarly by $x \geq S$. Then

$$S \leq \ = \ [x : S \leq x]$$

is the set of upper bounds of S, and so is $\geq S$. The upper bounds of any set $S \subset \mathbf{R}$ form a set $S \leq \ \subset \mathbf{R}$, $\mathbf{R}$ being the real numbers. Similarly, any S has a set of lower bounds $S \geq$, and so $S \leq \ \geq$, or $\leq \geq S$, or $\leq (S \leq)$, is the set of lower bounds of the set of upper bounds of S. From the definitions, all the elements of a set are lower bounds of all its upper bounds, so

$$S \subset S \leq \ \geq \ .$$

It follows that

$$S \neq O \Rightarrow S \leq \ \geq \ \neq O.$$

If a set is empty it has every number for an upper bound, and conversely, so

$$S = O \Leftrightarrow S \leq \ = \mathbf{R}.$$

Hence, because $\mathbf{R} \geq \ = O$, that is, $\mathbf{R}$ has no lower bounds, we have

$$S = O \Rightarrow S \leq \ = \mathbf{R} \Rightarrow S \leq \ \geq \ = O$$

and so now

$$S = O \Leftrightarrow S \leq \ \geq \ = O.$$

Consequently, if S is non-empty, and bounded above, then $S \leq$ is bounded below, and non-empty, and conversely.

Maxima

An upper bound of a set which is also an element of it defines a maximum, or greatest element. Thus, for x to be a maximum of S, we have

$$x \in S, \quad y \in S \Rightarrow y \leq x.$$

The maxima of S therefore form the set

$$\max S = S \cap S \leq.$$

There cannot be more than one maximum, and so we need not distinguish between max S and the single element in it, if there is one. But there need not be one. Thus the function max S is single valued when it is defined, but it is not always defined. Similar remarks apply to the minimum.

If a set has a maximum then it is both non-empty and bounded, but the converse is not true, for example $[x : x < 0]$. However, for a set that has the special form $S \leq$ the converse does apply, as the following asserts:

THEOREM OF THE LEAST UPPER BOUND If a non-empty set has an upper bound then it has a least upper bound.

In other words, if $\geq S$ is non-empty and bounded (or the same for S, since this has been noted equivalent, with boundedness from above in one case and below in the other), then it has a minimum.

Limits

The function max S is not defined for every set, nor even for sets which are non-empty and bounded. But the Theorem of the Least Upper Bound assures that min $\geq S$ is defined for all non-empty and bounded S. Whenever max S is defined so is min $\geq S$, and then moreover they are equal,

$$\text{max } S = \text{min } \geq S.$$

For the left, being an upper bound, cannot be less than the right, since this is the least. Also, the left, being an element of the set, cannot exceed the right, since this is a bound. Hence the two sides are equal.

The least upper bound is also called the upper limit, or *supremum*, and denoted

$$\text{sup } S = \text{min } \geq S = {\geq}S \cap {\leq}{\geq}S.$$

It is characterized by the property that no element of S exceeds it, but some element exceeds anything less; that is, $x = \text{sup } S$ is equivalent to

$$y \leq x \text{ for all } y \in S,$$

together with

$$t < x \Rightarrow y > t \text{ for some } y \in S.$$

A further element ∞ is introduced as a symbolic upper bound of all real numbers, so

$$x \in \mathbf{R} \Rightarrow x < \infty ,$$

and similarly with $-\infty$ as a lower bound. With $\mathbb{R}$ denoting $\mathbf{R}$ with these two further elements adjoined to it, every $S \subset \mathbf{R}$ is now bounded in the sense of having a bound in the new set $\mathbb{R}$, and so determines a non-empty $\geq S \subset \mathbf{R}$. The function sup S, first defined only for non-empty bounded sets $S \subset \mathbf{R}$, and with values in $\mathbb{R}$, is now defined for all $S \subset \mathbf{R}$, with values in $\mathbb{R}$. For the cases where formerly sup S was not defined, where S is empty or unbounded, sup S is now defined with values ∞ or $-\infty$. We have

$$\text{sup } S = -\infty \text{ for } S \text{ empty}$$
$$\text{sup } S = \infty \text{ for } S \text{ unbounded},$$

and otherwise the value is in $\mathbf{R}$,

$$-\infty < \text{sup } S < \infty \text{ for } S \text{ non-empty and bounded}.$$

In that way, sup S is defined for all $S \subset \mathbf{R}$, with values in $\mathbb{R}$.

Function bounds

Bounds, and so limits and maxima, are defined with reference to an order. For the real numbers, in the absence of other indication, relative magnitude is the order that is understood. But one can as well consider an arbitrary set D and any order R in it. With xRy meaning priority of x over y, as with $x \geq y$, any $x \in D$ is a bound of a subset $S \subset D$, in the order R, according to the condition

$$xRS \equiv y \in S \Rightarrow xRy.$$

Then $RS = [x : xRS]$ is the set of upper bounds of S, and $(RS)R$ is the set of lower bounds of the upper bounds. As before, $S \subset (RS)R$, because the elements of S are all lower bounds of its upper bounds. We have max $S = S \cap RS$, and formerly we would have

$$\sup S = \min RS = RS \cap (RS)R.$$

But for an arbitrary order R we do not have the benefit of the Theorem of the Least Upper Bound, which is a property of the real numbers with their natural order, and we do not have sup S defined whenever S and RS are nonempty, as formerly. But we do if the order is represented by a real-valued function f, where

$$xRy \Leftrightarrow f(x) \geq f(y).$$

Thus, with $f: D \rightarrow \mathbf{R}$ and any $S \subset D$,

$$f(S) = [t: t = f(x), x \in S]$$
$$= [f(x) : x \in S]$$

is the set of values attained by f in S. It is nonempty if S is nonempty, and is bounded if f is bounded in S. Then sup $f(S)$ is always defined, with values in $\mathbf{R}$:

$$\sup f(S) = \infty \text{ means } f \text{ is unbounded in } S,$$

that is, if for all $t \in \mathbf{R}$, $f(x) > t$ for some $x \in S$,

$$\sup f(S) = -\infty \text{ means } S \text{ is empty,}$$

and otherwise

$$-\infty < \sup f(S) < \infty ,$$

that is, sup $f(S) \in \mathbf{R}$. The statement $s = \sup f(S)$ means

$$x \in S \Rightarrow f(x) \leq s$$

together with

$$t < s \Rightarrow f(x) > t \text{ for some } x \in S,$$

that is, s is a bound of f in S and any smaller number is not. Whether $s \in f(S)$, that is, whether $s = f(x)$ for some $x \in S$, is not generally decided; should it be the case, then we have $s = \max f(S)$.

1.2   PROGRAMMING PROBLEM OF A FIRM

An individual agent, possibly a productive firm, is capable of a variety of activities, describing a space A. Any activity uses up resources which must be available if it is going to be performed, and also has a value or output, which is the gain from performing it. The firm has certain resources available and its objective is to obtain the greatest possible value from their use, by suitable choice of an activity. An optimal activity is one that achieves the maximum value attainable with the available resources, and finding that is the optimal programming problem.

Whatever the resource availability, any activity is efficient for output—in the sense of cost effectiveness—if no greater output value is attainable with the resources it uses. An optimal activity therefore must be efficient for output, and moreover must meet a resource availability restriction. An efficiency can also apply on the side of available resources—in the sense of cost efficiency—when the resources are completely used up by the activity which produces maximum output from them.

The performance of any activity x in the activity space A requires a certain minimum of resources, given by a vector function $g(x)$. The m elements $g_i(x)$ are the costs in terms of the m factors needed for its performance. The availability of resources to meet these costs puts a constraint on activities which are feasible, so these m functions have a role as *constraint functions*.

The value or output of the activity is a function $f(x)$, this being the *objective function* for the problem. The available resouces are given by a vector q, and so if the minimum resources z needed for the performance of an activity are not to exceed availability, we must have $z \leq q$. Hence for the feasibility of any activity x it must satisfy the vector constraint $g(x) \leq q$, or, in terms of elements, it must satisfy the simultaneous constraints

$$g_i(x) \leq q_i, \qquad i = 1, \ldots, m.$$

The *feasible activities* with resources q therefore form the subset

$$A(q) = [x : g(x) \leq q]$$

of A, which is the intersection of the subsets

$$A_i(q) = [x : g_i(x) \leq q_i].$$

An output t is feasible with resources q if it is the output of a feasible activity, or anything less. Thus, the set of *feasible values* is

$$V(q) = [t : t \leq f(x), x \in A(q)]$$
$$= [t : t \leq f(x), g(x) \leq q].$$

The programming problem of the firm, denoted (M), is stated as

$$(M) \qquad \max f(x) : g(x) \leq q.$$

The activity space A being the domain of definition of the functions, there is no need to remark here, and elsewhere, that x belongs to this space. Thus the problem (M) is to find an maximum x of the objective function $f(x)$ subject to the resource constraints, or in the set $A(q)$ of feasible activities. Any such x, should one exist, is an *optimal solution* to the problem, and $t = f(x)$ is the *optimal value*. If feasible solutions exist, that is, should $A(q)$ be nonempty, we have a *feasible problem*; and otherwise an *infeasible* problem.

An optimal solution is a feasible solution that gives at least as high a value as any other. Let $M(x)$ stand for the assertion that x is an optimal solution to the problem (M), so

$$M(x) \equiv g(x) \leq q, \quad g(y) \leq q \Rightarrow f(y) \leq f(x).$$

Then $t = f(x)$, the output value of the optimal activity, which is the optimal value for the problem, is the maximum element in the set $V(q)$ of feasible values, or the maximum feasible value; it both belongs to the set and is an upper bound of it;

$$t \epsilon V(q), \quad s \epsilon V(q) \Rightarrow s \leq t.$$

Evidently, while optimal solutions might be many, the optimal value is unique.

An activity x is efficient for output if it is impossible to achieve greater value with any other activity that requires no more resources than it does; that is,

$$g(y) \leq g(x) \Rightarrow f(y) \leq f(x).$$

Any activity which is optimal must be efficient for output, but we do not have the converse.

Resources q are efficient for input if it is impossible to do as well with less. Introducing the upper limit

$$v(z) = \sup V(z) = \sup [f(x) : g(x) \leq z]$$

of the set of feasible values, the condition is

$$z \leq q \Rightarrow v(z) < v(q).$$

Any resources exactly used up by an efficient activity must be efficient for input. But there could be an optimal activity associated even with inefficient resources, if that activity does not necessarily use them all up; for in that case one could do just as well with less.

1.3 OPTIMAL PROGRAMMING THEOREM

The theorem to be dealt with, which has its background in the foregoing, will now be stated. Then there is a discussion of its various terms, preliminary to the proof.

THEOREM For an arbitrary set A and functions

$$f: A \rightarrow \mathbf{R}, \; g: A \rightarrow \mathbf{R}^m$$

and vector $q \epsilon \mathbf{R}^m$, and the function

$$w: \mathbf{R}^m \rightarrow \mathbb{R}$$

given by

$$w(z) = \sup[f(x) : g(x) \leq z],$$

let conditions on any $x \epsilon A$ and $u \epsilon \mathbf{R}_m$ be defined by

$$C(x, u) \equiv g(x) \leq q, u \geq 0, ug(x) = uq$$
$$L(x, u) \equiv f(y) - ug(y) \leq f(x) - ug(x)$$
$$D(u) \equiv w(z) - uz \leq w(q) - uq$$
$$M(x) \equiv g(x) \leq q, g(y) \leq q \Rightarrow f(y) \leq f(x).$$

Then

$$C(x, u) \& L(x, u) \Leftrightarrow D(u) \& M(x).$$

The activity set A, the output and input functions f and g defined in it and the vector q make the basis for the programming problem:

(M) $\max f(x) : g(x) \leq q.$

The statement $M(x)$ in the theorem is just that x is an optimal solution of the problem. The statement $D(u)$ involves the function w which is associated with the problem, and is about a vector u. Any u for which it is true will be called a *support solution* for the problem.

An interesting consequence of the theorem is that

$$D(u) . \Rightarrow . M(x) \Leftrightarrow C(x, u) \& L(x, u).$$

Given any support solution u, necessary and sufficient conditions for x to be an optimal solution are stated on the right. This shows a similarity with the usual Lagrange method for determining a maximum of a function subject to constraints, by means of conditions involving x together with further variables, the 'Lagrange multipliers'. The parallel with the Lagrangean method goes far, even to the extent of the identification of Lagrangian multipliers with derivatives of the maximum function. But this theorem has other features, to be noted further, especially in the last section.

1.4   INPUT–OUTPUT

A possible view of the optimal programming problem is that a two-stage production process is being optimized. In the first stage an activity x is produced from the initial resource input q. In the second stage the activity becomes an input from which a final output value t is obtained. The problem is to obtain a maximum final output from the the given initial input, by choosing the intermediate activity suitably. When the initial input q and possible final ouput t obtainable from it are connected by a production function v, in the relation $t \leq v(q)$, the optimization problem shows an internal mechanism on which the production function v, giving the maximum possible output, is based.

The activity output and input functions $f: A \rightarrow \mathbf{R}$, $g: A \rightarrow \mathbf{R}^m$ determine relations $F \subset \mathbf{R} \times A$, $G \subset A \times \mathbf{R}^m$ where

$$tFx \equiv t \leq f(x), \quad xGz \equiv g(x) \leq z.$$

These are input-output relations, for which xGz means that activity x is producible from the input z and tFx means that output value t is producible from the activity x. Then tFx and xGz together, stated $tFxGz$, means that t is producible from z in a two stage production process, activity x being the intermediate output. The relations F and G determine a product relation $FG \subset \mathbf{R} \times \mathbf{R}^m$, where

$$t(FG)z \equiv tFxGz \text{ for some } x.$$

Then $V = FG$, which gives the relation between initial input and final output, expresses the two-stage process as a single step. With $tF = [x : tFx]$, and similarly with Gz, we have $tF \cap Gz$ as the set of possible activities intermediate between the input z and the output t, and

$$tVz \Leftrightarrow tF \cap Gz \neq O,$$

so the input-output (z, t) is feasible provided this set of possible intermediates in nonempty.

From the way F is defined, it has the property

$$t' \leq tFx \Rightarrow t'Fx,$$

which, using the relation product notation, can also be stated $\leq F \subset F$; that is, given any output that is feasible with given x, any smaller output is also feasible. Put another way, the difference with the smaller output can always be disposed of; this expresses free disposal on the output side. Similarly, G has the property

$$xGz \leq z' \Rightarrow xGz',$$

by which if an input z suffices to produce an activity x then so does any larger input. This expresses free disposal on the input side. As a consequence for the product relation $V = FG$,

$$t' \leq tVz \leq z' \Rightarrow t'Vz',$$

which can also be stated $\leq V \leq \; \subset V$, and expresses free disposal on both sides. Another statement of free disposal on the input side for V is that

$$z \leq z' . \Rightarrow . xVz \Rightarrow xVz',$$

that is

$$z \leq z' \Rightarrow Vz \subset Vz',$$

where $Vz = [t : tVz]$ is the set of output possibilies with the input z; having more inputs does not eliminate any output possibilities.

From the definitions of F, G from f, g, they are such that

$$f(x)Fx, \quad xGg(x) \text{ for all } x,$$

from which it follows that

$$f(x)Vg(x) \text{ for all } x.$$

It also follows that Fx is always nonempty, since it contains $f(x)$, and hence that Vz is nonempty if and only if Gz is nonempty. For the programming problem (M), Gq is the set of feasible solutions, and so feasibility of the problem is equivalent to Vq being nonempty.

1.5 OUTPUT LIMIT FUNCTION

Because of free disposal of output, the output possibility set Vz, being such that

$$t \epsilon Vz \; \& \; t' \leq t \Rightarrow t' \epsilon Vz,$$

has the form of an interval in $\mathbf{R}$, with lower limit $-\infty$, and upper limit

$$v(z) \;=\; \text{sup } Vz.$$

The interval is completely described by $v(z)$ when it is known whether or not $v(z) \; \epsilon \; Vz$. In this case the limit is attained and so a maximum, so $v(z) = \text{max } Vz$, and we have

$$Vz \;=\; [\, t : t \le v(z)\,],$$

and, in the contrary case

$$Vz \;=\; [\, t : t < v(z)\,].$$

The function $v: \mathbf{R}^m \rightarrow \mathbf{R}$ so defined is the output *limit function*, or simply the value function, associated with the programming problem (M). If the problem has an optimal solution x then $f(x) = v(q)$. If the problem is infeasible, in which case Vq is empty, then $v(q) = -\infty$; and $v(q) = \infty$ means it is unbounded; that is, the objective function can be made arbitrarily large without violating the constraints.

In the last section it was noted that

$$z \le z' \;\Rightarrow\; Vz \subset Vz',$$

and from this it follows that

$$z \le z' \;\Rightarrow\; v(z) \le v(z'),$$

so *the limit function is always non-decreasing*. Also, because $f(x)\, Vg(x)$ for all x, it satisfies the functional inequality

$$f(x) \;\le\; v(g(x)) \text{ for all } x.$$

1.6   SUPPORT GRADIENTS AND MARGINAL VALUES

A function $v: \mathbf{R}^m \rightarrow \mathbf{R}$ has $l \; \epsilon \; \mathbf{R}$ as a bound in a subset $S \subset \mathbf{R}^m$ if $v(z) \le l$ for all $z \; \epsilon \; S$, and l is, moreover, a limit if also no smaller number is a bound. This most usual definition, in which a bound of a function is just a number, can be extended to permit a bound to be another function, in particular a linear function. Thus a *linear bound* of v in S is any linear function $l: \mathbf{R}^m \rightarrow \mathbf{R}$ such that

$$z \, \epsilon \, S \;\Rightarrow\; v(z) \le l(z);$$

that is, the linear function l lies above the function v at every point of S. If also it equals f at some point $q \; \epsilon \; S$, so that $v(q) = l(q)$, it is called a *linear support* of f in the set S, *at the point q* (see Figure 1).

A linear function has the form $l(x) = ux + c$ where $u \; \epsilon \; \mathbf{R}_m$ is its gradient and $c \; \epsilon \; \mathbf{R}$ is a constant. The gradient of a linear support defines a *support gradient*, of the function *at the point*. Thus, if u is a support gradient of v at a point q, we have that $l(x) = ux + c$, for some c, is a support of v at q; that is,

$$v(z) \le uz + c \text{ for all } z$$
$$v(q) = uq + c.$$

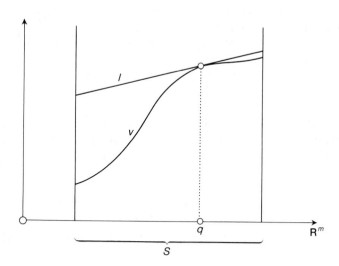

Figure 1   Support at q

Subtracting the equation from the inequality gives

$$v(z) - v(q) \le u(z - q) \text{ for all } z.$$

This condition, which is just the condition $D(u)$ in the theorem which defines a support solution to the problem (M), therefore is necessary. It is also sufficient. For if it holds, let $l(x) = v(q) + u(z - q)$; then we have $l(q) = v(q)$ immediately, and $v(z) \le l(z)$ for all z by hypothesis. Thus, the considered condition $D(u)$ *is necessary and sufficient for u to be a support gradient of the function v at the point q.*

Because the limit function v is non-decreasing, *any support gradient* of it at any point, in particular the point q, *must be non-negative,* so we have

$$D(u) \Rightarrow u \ge o.$$

For, with v non-decreasing,

$$z \ge q \Rightarrow 0 \le v(z) - v(q) \le u(z - q),$$

and hence

$$z \ge q \Rightarrow uz \ge uq,$$

or, equivalently, taking $a = z - q$,

$$a \ge o \Rightarrow ua \ge 0.$$

But this implies $u \ge 0$; for taking $a_i = 1$ and $a_j = 0 \, (j \ne i)$, so that $a \ge o$ and $ua = u_i$, it follows that $u_i \ge 0$, for each i.

Without further assumptions there is no general reason for v to have a support gradient at q. However, as dealt with in the next chapter, if f is concave and the elements of g are all convex, then v must be concave. Then, by the support theorem for concave functions, if v is finite in the neighbourhood of q, it must have a support and hence a support gradient there. Then, further, v is differentiable at q if and only if the support gradient is unique, and then the differential gradient is identical with that unique support gradient. In that case we have identification of the elements of the support gradient with marginal values of the inputs, that is, with partial derivatives of v at q. However, unlike marginal values, the support gradient concept is not dependent on differentiability. Moreover, while differentiability means the existence of a local linear approximation, without regard for the sign of the error, with a linear support the function is always overestimated, so the error is always one sided, not just locally but also globally.

A remarkable features of linear programming is the identification of support solutions with dual optimal solutions; to differentiate the maximum function of one problem you solve the dual. The classic paper of A. C. William (1962) on 'Marginal values in linear programming' takes this further.

1.7 COMPLEMENTARITY

Given $u \; \epsilon \; \mathbf{R}_m$ and $z \; \epsilon \; \mathbf{R}^m$ for which

$$u \geq 0, \; z \geq 0, \qquad\qquad (\text{i})$$
$$uz = 0, \qquad\qquad (\text{ii})$$

from (i) it follows that

$$u_i z_i \geq 0 \qquad\qquad (\text{i}')$$

and (ii) is equivalent to

$$\Sigma u_i z_i = 0. \qquad\qquad (\text{ii}')$$

But a sum of non-negative terms is zero if and only if each term is zero. Hence (i′) implies the equivalent of (ii′) to

$$u_i z_i = 0 \text{ for all } i. \qquad\qquad (\text{ii}'')$$

Now with (i), (ii″) is equivalent to

$$u_i \geq 0 \; \Rightarrow \; z_i = 0,$$

and to

$$z_i \geq 0 \; \Rightarrow \; u_i = 0.$$

These last conditions, which are equivalent to each other under (i), express *complementary slackness*, by which two associated variables cannot both be positive, or slack, simultaneously.

Applying this to the condition

$$C(x, u) \equiv u \geq o, \; g(x) \leq q, \; ug(x) = uq,$$

which appears in the Theorem, by putting $z = q - g(x)$, we find that it is equivalent to

$$(a) \, u_i \geq 0, \, g_i(x) \leq q_i \, (b) \, g_i(x) < q_i \Rightarrow u_i = 0.$$

In other words, with (i) stated by (a), (ii) is equivalent to the complementary slackness condition (b). In the context of optimality, if a constraint is slack, or the resource not fully used up by the optimal activity, then the associated support variable, the shadow price or marginal value, must be zero.

1.8   SHADOW PRICE DECENTRALIZATION

When the support solution condition $D(u)$ in the Theorem, which requires u to be a support gradient of v at q, is put in the form

$$v(z) - uz \leq v(q) - uq \text{ for all } z,$$

it has another sense. It is as if the firm does not have resources q imposed on it for the performance of its activities, but can buy them freely at prices u. This is not a real market, but a shadow or imaginary one, and the prices are *shadow prices*. The return on any resources z, when they are used optimally, is $v(z)$ and uz is the cost of buying them, so $v(z) - uz$ is the profit from operations with inputs z. The condition $D(u)$ tells us that the factor prices u are such that maximum profit attainable with them is attained at the point $z = q$. It is as if the planning authority wanted to give the firm q to carry out the plan implemented on the basis of the problem (M). Now with the new arrangement, the firm chooses $z = q$ anyway, but with apparent freedom governed only by profit, and the result is just the same. This seems to offer a method for implementing a plan not by dictatorship, but by creating an incentive situation such that, even with free agents freely pursuing their own profit, the planned result will still be the outcome. Put one way, the condition $D(u)$ leads to pure mathematical thoughts, while put this other way it takes a political tone. But being governed by a totally determining objective is not freedom; if not slavery, it is dedication. The firm pictured here is at any rate a dedicated automaton, with fixed objectives, whether they be centralized or not, and without any freedom of choice at all.

The condition $L(x, u)$ in the Theorem,

$$f(y) - ug(y) \leq f(x) - ug(x) \text{ for all } y,$$

has a similarity with $D(u)$. But while with condition D the internal activity x of the firm is not on the surface, and is only implicit in the function v and must be optimized to determine any value of v, it is the explicit concern in condition L. Any activity y has a return $f(y)$ and a cost $ug(y)$ from buying the resources $g(y)$ needed to perform it at the shadow prices u. Hence the profit on activity y is $f(y) - ug(y)$, and this is to be made a maximum without any constraints. The condition L tells us that this unconstrained maximum is attained at $y = x$. The constraints $g(y) \leq q$ in the problem (M) have been dropped, but the objective function has been modified by introduction of a cost. The Theorem shows that, with a suitable choice of the shadow prices u, the new unconstrained problem will have the same optimal solution as the original problem (M) with constraints.

The Slater constraint qualification, together with the convexity conditions on the functions f and g, accounted in the next chapter, serve to guarantee the existence of the suitable u. With the activity set A described by the non-negative vectors in $\mathbf{R}^n$, or as the space Ω^n, Ω being the non-negative numbers, and with the functions f and g given as differentiable, when the constrained problem is transformed into one without constraints, the optimality conditions can be stated in terms of derivatives. In that way, the Kuhn-Tucker optimality conditions are produced.

1.9 PROOF OF THE THEOREM

The Theorem discussed at some length is elementary, as seems assured by the absence of special assumptions, and the proof is fairly immediate.

To prove

$$D(u) \,\&\, M(x) \Rightarrow C(x, u) \,\&\, L(x, u),$$

assume the left-hand side. A restatement of $M(x)$ is that

$$g(x) \le q, \tag{i}$$
$$f(x) = v(q), \tag{ii}$$

since this states that x satisfies the constraints and is where f attains its upper limit under them. From $D(u)$, immediately,

$$u \ge 0, \tag{iii}$$

as was seen in section 1.5. Because v is non-decreasing, as found in section 1.5, and $D(u)$ holds, a consequence of (i) and (iii) is that

$$0 \le v(g(x)) - v(q) \le u \{ g(x) - q \} \le 0,$$

showing that

$$v(g(x)) = v(q), \tag{iv}$$
$$ug(x) = uq. \tag{v}$$

With (i), (iii) and (v), we have $C(x, u)$, so it remains to show $L(x, u)$.

From section 1.5, $f(y) \le v(g(y))$ for any y, and so, using this with (iv), $D(u)$ and then (v),

$$f(y) - f(x) \le v(g(y)) - v(q) \le u \{ g(y) - q \} = u \{ g(y) - g(x) \},$$

so we have

$$f(y) - f(x) \le u \{ g(y) - g(x) \} \tag{vi},$$

which is $L(x, u)$. QED

For the converse, suppose the right-hand side, so now we have (i), (iii), and (v) together with (vi), and want to deduce the condition on the left. From

(vi), (v), and (iii) it follows that

$$g(y) \le q \Rightarrow f(y) \le f(x),$$

and this with (i) gives $M(x)$. It remains to deduce $D(u)$.

From $M(x)$ we have $f(x) = v(q)$. Hence from (vi) with (v),

$$f(y) - v(q) \le u(g(y) - q).$$

From this, with (iii),

$$g(y) \le z \Rightarrow f(y) - v(q) \le u(z - q),$$

and hence

$$\sup [f(y) : g(y) \le z] - v(q) \le u(z - q),$$

which is $D(u)$. QED

1.10 LAGRANGE MULTIPLIERS

Lagrange's 'method of undetermined multipliers' applies to a function f of several variables x subject to contraints, for which a maximum is required. The constraints can be stated $g(x) = q$ where the vector q is constant. Ordinarily one might distinguish independent and dependent variables under the constraints, and then, by substitution for the dependent variables in f, one has a function of independent variables whose derivatives must vanish. Instead, Lagrange offered an elegant procedure without the arbitrary distinction between variables. The method involves the introduction of further variables u, the 'undetermined multipliers' associated with the constraints. With n function variables and m constraints we then have $m + n$ variables (x, u). Lagrange's method depends on $m + n$ relations to determine these, and so on the n function variables x which are among them and should give the required maximum. The remaining m variables u, the 'undetermined multipliers', may be determined just as well. But originally they were just part of this device for determining a maximum and their values had no interest even if they could be determined. The multipliers in fact have a further significance, as derivatives that tell us how the maximum value varies as the constraints deviate owing to a variation of q. They therefore have an importance in economic problems. For, in addition to the value obtainable from given resources, one might also wish to know the 'marginal value' of any resource, the extra value obtainable when a unit of it is added. The Lagrangean method is therefore quite natural for the 'Marginalist Revolution', and the 'multiplier' has become a part of economic language; it is also the concept that underlies 'shadow price', 'implicit value' and similar expressions.

The most typical economic maximum problem is formulated differently from that dealt with by Lagrange. Rather, the constraints take the form of inequalities, expressing the condition that some resource availability must not be exceeded; also, functions involved have convexity properties required by diminishing marginal returns. The theory of such problems is different and does not depend on what we have for Lagrange's classical problem. Despite the difference, there is impressive similarity, from the role of 'multipliers', so one can think that here is Lagrange's method again. But about these new multipliers, new things can be said. In either case, classical or new, the required maximum is associated with multipliers enabling certain conditions to be satisfied. There is this similarity, but the premises and conclusions related to such conditions are different. The two lines come together, but it is a mistake to see coincidence, and it is proper to make the treatments entirely separate instead of trying to deduce one from the other. The difference is appreciated in the difference between the proofs of main points, in which one case is dealt with straightforwardly by differential calculus and the other, convex programming, requires instead the Theorem of the Separating Hyperplane. Again, one is entirely concerned with differentiable functions while the other in its main part is not, though the differentiable case treated by H. W. Kuhn and A. W. Tucker is most familiar. Reassuring for the connection, there are special problems where both lines are applicable, and then the multipliers involved are identical. But even then more can be said about the multipliers than would come simply from the classical case. Our review of the classical and new multiplier theories will make clear the cleavages and connections; we will also see the peculiar, remarkable features of the matter in the context of linear programming.

Following the ordinary method of distinguishing independent variables and eliminating dependent variables, we can, without further thought, arrive at Lagrange's method from a consideration of the derivatives which the multipliers happen to represent. In that way, apart from other possible merit, the multipliers become at the same time identified with those derivatives. Though this is not a usual procedure, it is a counterpart for classical multipliers of an argument that is essential for the new multipliers of optimal programming theory.

It is convenient now to denote the n function variables by z, reserving x for independent variables among these. Lagrange's problem is to determine a maximum of $f(z)$ subject to m constraints, stated

$$g(z) = q. \tag{i}$$

Variables are column vectors, and all functions are understood to be differentiable, so, for instance, g has an $m \times n$ derivative matrix denoted g_z with elements $g_{ij} = \partial g_i / \partial z_j$. As necessary for z to be a maximum (or minimum, in any case a stationary point), Lagrange concluded that

$$f_z = u g_z \text{ for some } u; \tag{ii}$$

in other words, the n conditions

$$f_j = \Sigma_i u_i g_{ij} \qquad (j = 1, \ldots, n).$$

Together with the m conditions

$$g_i = q_i \qquad (i = 1, \ldots, m)$$

provided by the constraints (i), we have $m + n$ *Lagrange conditions* on the $m + n$ variables

$$u_i \; (i = 1, \ldots, m), \qquad z_j \; (j = 1, \ldots, n).$$

Lagrange's method depends on the idea that these $m+n$ conditions can be solved to determine the $m+n$ variables, and therefore the n variables z_j which are among these. Put another way, the multipliers u_i can be eliminated (and so left 'undetermined') and the conditions obtained then solved for the z_j.

With independent and dependent variables x and y under the constraints, the variables have a partition $z = (x, y)$, and we have a function $f(x, y)$ under constraints $g(x, y) = q$ that determine y as a function $y = Y(x, q)$. Then $g(x, Y(x, q)) = q$ is an identity and so, by differentiation with respect to x,

$$g_x + g_y Y_x = 0, \qquad (\text{iii})$$

and with respect to q, $g_y Y_q = 1$; and since from here g_y and Y_q are inverse matrices we also have

$$Y_q g_y = 1. \qquad (\text{iv})$$

For any q the constrained values of f are described by $f(x, Y(x, q))$ as x varies without restriction. The x–derivatives must vanish for a stationary point; that is,

$$f_x + f_y Y_x = 0. \qquad (\text{v})$$

Assuming that this condition determines a unique point x for any q, the stationary points for various q are described by a function $x = X(q)$. Then the corresponding stationary values of f are given by the function

$$F(q) = f(X(q), Y(X(q), q)),$$

with derivatives

$$\begin{aligned} F_q &= f_x X_q + f_y (Y_x X_q + Y_q) \\ &= (f_x + f_y Y_x) X_q + f_y Y_q = f_y Y_q \end{aligned} \qquad \text{by (v)}.$$

Hence

$$\begin{aligned} F_q g_x &= (f_y Y_q) g_x \\ &= (f_y Y_q)(-g_y Y_x) & \text{by (iii)} \\ &= -f_y (Y_q g_y) Y_x = -f_y Y_x & \text{by (iv)} \\ &= f_x & \text{by (v)} \end{aligned}$$

and also

$$F_q g_y = (f_y Y_q) g_y = f_y (Y_q g_y) = f_y \qquad \text{by (iv)}.$$

It has now been seen that

$$F_q g_x = f_x, \quad F_q g_y = f_y,$$

that is, $f_z = F_q g_z$, which is (i) with $u = F_q$. Thus we have Lagrange's conditions, together with the identification $u = F_q$ for the multipliers.

For any x, the existence of u so that (x, u) satisfy Lagrange's conditions

(i) and (ii) is the condition for x to be a stationary point. It is therefore necessary for x to be a maximum, or a minimum, and on its own is not sufficient for x to be either. Solutions of Lagrange's conditions, if any, provide the stationary points, possibly many, without information that any should be a maximum.

An important case is where the Lagrangean conditions have a unique solution (x, u) and where also, on some grounds, a maximum is known to exist. It can be concluded that x is the unique maximum.

Given any stationary point x, such as could be found from a solution of Lagrange's conditions, and so obtained by a condition on first derivatives at x, one can possibly find out if it is a local maximum, or a maximum in some neighbourhood of x under the constraints, by an examination of further conditions bringing in higher derivatives at x. However, no conditions on derivatives simply *at* the point x will tell us anything about x except in the local sense. There is no way of knowing whether x is a global maximum simply from a satisfaction of some condition on derivatives at x, of any order. Of course in economics a maximum is significant only in the global sense. Fortunately, typical functions of economics have convexity properties that enable one to go further on the basis of local conditions. Connected with this, any stationary point of a convex, or concave, function is necessarily a global minimum, or maximum, so in such cases first-order conditions are enough. This matter plays a part in the further theory of Lagrange multipliers in the more typically economic context of convex programming.

The Lagrangean method is made intelligible geometrically in the following way, first where there is one constraint. Consider a point x on the constraint surface C, this being a particular level surface of the function g. Consider the level surface L of the function f through x. If these surfaces crossed over at x, there would be points of C lying on either side of L, where f is greater and less than it is at x, so x would be neither a maximum nor minimum of f on C. Hence, if x is such a maximum these surfaces cannot so cross over. Then it is necessary that the tangent hyperplanes to these surfaces at x do not cross over at x. Then these must coincide, in which case the normals, specified by the directions of the gradients of the functions, must coincide; that is, $f_x = ug_x$ for some multiplier u. A similar argument applies where there are many constraints: the tangent manifold of C at x must not cross over the tangent hyperplane of L and so must be contained in it.

A most usual way of arriving at Lagrange's method is by the Leibnizian type of argument with 'differentials'. This can be taken further to show second-order sufficient conditions for a local maximum. With some x that satisfies the constraints, for a differential dx to satisfy the constraints it is required that $g_x\,dx = 0$. For a maximum of f at x under the constraints, we require $df = f_x\,dx \leq 0$ for all such differentials dx; that is,

$$g_x\,dx = 0 \Rightarrow f_x\,dx \leq 0 \qquad \text{for all } dx,$$

which is immediately equivalent to

$$g_x \, dx = 0 \Rightarrow f_x \, dx = 0 \qquad \text{for all } dx,$$

which, by a theorem of linear algebra, is equivalent to

$$f_x = u g_x \qquad \text{for some } u,$$

which is Lagrange's condition. With this satisfied,

$$df = u g_x \, dx + dx' f_{xx'} \, dx \, / \, 2,$$

to second order. Therefore in order to have

$$g_x \, dx = 0 \Rightarrow df \le 0,$$

as is required for x to be a maximum locally, the condition

$$g_x \, dx = 0 \Rightarrow dx' f_{xx'} \, dx \le 0$$

is necessary, and

$$g_x \, dx = 0, \ dx \ne 0 \Rightarrow dx' f_{xx'} \, dx < 0$$

is sufficient for x to be a locally unique maximum. Both these last conditions can be expressed in terms of principal determinants of the matrix

$$\begin{pmatrix} 0 & g_{x'} \\ g_x & f_{xx'} \end{pmatrix}.$$

We also have, subject to Lagrange's conditions holding while there is a variation of q, that $df = u \, dq$, which shows again the sense of the multipliers as derivatives.

Lagrange's method can be described, with reference to the 'Lagrangean function'

$$L(x, u) = f(x) - u\{ g(x) - q \},$$

as requiring the x and u derivatives to be set to 0. This way of putting it is without significance except as a cookbook statement. One first learns about setting derivatives to zero when there are no constraints, and now, even though there are constraints, one can with confident familiarity do it again, even with the impression that the Lagrangean function should be at a maximum as if the recipe had that sense. There is better occasion for something like this in convex programming, where u is fixed so as to make x a maximum of the Lagrangean.

A problem with inequality constraints is stated as

$$(M) \qquad \qquad \max f(x) : g(x) \le q,$$

the functions being defined in a set A. It can be imagined that A is an *activity* set, and the performance of any $x \in A$ gives a return $f(x)$ and has a cost in terms of various resources given by the vector $g(x)$, so for *feasibility* this must not exceed the available stock q, so that $g(x) \le q$ is required. The problem is to find an *optimal solution*, an activity x that gives the greatest return attainable with the available resources, as asserted by the condition

$$M(x) \equiv g(x) \leq q,\, g(y) \leq q \Rightarrow f(y) \leq f(x).$$

The *limit function* associated with the problem is

$$F(z) = \sup\,[f(x) : g(x) \leq z],$$

and a *support solution* u is defined by the condition

$$D(u) \equiv F(z) - F(q) \leq u(z - q) \text{ for all } z,$$

equivalent to u being a support gradient of F at the point $z = q$.

Support solutions correspond to Lagrange multipliers in that they are variables associated with the constraints that give a means for characterizing optimal solutions. Thus, for a pair (x, u), *complementary slackness* is defined by

$$C(x, u) \equiv g(x) \leq q,\, u \geq 0,\, ug(x) = uq,$$

and a *shadow solution* by

$$S(x, u) \equiv f(x) - ug(x) \geq f(y) - ug(y) \qquad \text{for all } y.$$

For the latter, equivalently, u is fixed to make x a maximum of the Lagrangean function associated with the problem. An important proposition, not requiring any assumptions whatsoever about the set A or the functions f and g defined in it, is that any given pair (x, u) is a shadow solution with complementary slackness if and only if x is an optimal solution and u a support solution, that is,

$$M(x)\ \&\ D(u) \Leftrightarrow C(x, u)\ \&\ S(x, u),$$

as restates the Theorem of this chapter, proved in the last section. For characterizing optimal solutions by means of the condition on the right-hand side, the outstanding issue therefore is the existence of a support solution. We will find this guaranteed under conditions natural for economics at least.

A *convex problem* is one where f is a concave function and the elements of g are convex. The only importance is to make the limit function F concave. Then it has a linear support, and so a support gradient providing a support solution, at any interior point of the region where it is finite. Now with $F(q)$ finite, Slater's condition which requires $g(x) < q$ for some x assures that q is exactly such a point. Thus for a convex problem with Slater's condition, and with $F(q)$ finite, as it must be if an optimal solution exists, we do have the existence of a support solution, and therefore a characterization of all optimal solutions by means of shadow solutions with complementary slackness.

It is a short step from here to the characterization by means of Kuhn-Tucker conditions. These apply to a problem where the activity set A is a space of non-negative vectors, and the functions are differentiable. All that has to be known further is that for a differentiable concave function $\phi(x)$ subject to $x \geq 0$ to be a maximum it is necessary and sufficient that

$$\phi_x \leq 0, \quad x \geq 0, \quad \phi_x x = 0.$$

Applied to the Lagrangean $f(x) - u\{g(x) - q\}$, with u fixed and non-negative and x restricted non-negative, the conditions $S(x, u)$ for a shadow solution become

$$f_x - ug_x \leq 0, \quad x \geq 0, \quad (f_x - ug_x)x = 0,$$

and so now, with complementary slackness $C(x, u)$, we have the Kuhn-Tucker conditions. In case $x > 0$, the conditions just obtained reduce to $f_x = ug_x$, in other words, ordinary Lagrange conditions, with the support solution u providing the multipliers.

With F concave, it is *differentiable at a point q if and only if it has a unique support gradient u there*, and then the support gradient coincides with the differential gradient, $u = F_q$. Thus uniqueness of support solutions is associated with differentiability of the limit function F at the point q. The identification $u = F_q$ that can be made in this case is comparable with the identity of classical Lagrange multipliers with derivatives of the stationary value function. But this new multiplier theory, even for the Kuhn-Tucker case, in no way depends on the differentiability of the limit function. Also, for the linear approximation near q that is available in the differentiable case, we know more about it in that the error is always positive, or that it overestimates the limit function, not just locally but everywhere. Thus, $D(u)$ asserts that $F(z) - uz$ is maximum at $z = q$, so with F differentiable we have $F'(q) - u = 0$. The linear function approximating F at q therefore is $l(z) = F(q) + u(z - q)$ with error $l(z) - F(z)$ which, according to $D(u)$, is positive at every point, unless zero.

Consider now a standard linear programming (LP) problem

$$(M) \qquad\qquad \max px : ax \leq q, x \geq 0.$$

Another characterization for support solutions of LP problems can be noted, coming from the homogeneity. Thus, with F as the limit function of (M), the condition for u to be a support solution becomes

$$F(q) = uq, \quad F(z) \leq uz \text{ for all } z.$$

Since (M) is a convex problem, the foregoing will apply to it. Also it has the required form for application of the Kuhn-Tucker conditions, which, following the way we expressed them before with some rearrangement in the second line, become

$$ax \leq q, \quad u \geq 0, \quad uax = uq,$$
$$ua \geq p, \quad x \geq 0, \quad uax = px.$$

We know from the foregoing that (x, u) is a solution of these conditions if and only if x is an optimal solution and u a support solution of the problem (M).

There is a symmetry in the situation that enables these conditions to be read differently. With an exchange of role between x and u they become Kuhn-Tucker conditions for the problem

(W) min $uq : ua \geq p, u \geq 0,$

and so they hold if and only if u is an optimal solution and x a support solution of (W). It follows that *the support solutions of either problem are identical with the optimal solutions of the other*.

Of course, (M) and (W) are a standard dual pair of LP problems, and so, by the LP Duality Theorem, one has an optimal solution if and only if the other does. Hence *any LP problem has a support solution if and only if it has an optimal solution*. Most remarkable is the method for finding support solutions for an LP problem—as it were, differentiating the limit function, or finding the 'Lagrange multipliers'—by finding optimal solutions for another LP problem; and we know how to do that.

V.2

Convex Programming

If x is a solution of the classical Lagrange problem

$$\max f(x) : g(x) = q,$$

then there exists a vector u, of Lagrange multipliers associated with the constraints, for which x and u satisfy the conditions

$$f'(x) = ug'(x), \quad g(x) = q.$$

But for any x, u that satisfy these conditions it is not generally necessary for x to be a solution of the problem. A case without this defect occurs where the problem is known on some grounds to have a solution, and also the solution of the conditions is found to be unique. Then the problem solution must be unique and given by the solution of the conditions. Rather the opposite situation is found with the economic type problem

$$\max f(x) : g(x) \leq q,$$

and the conditions

$$u \geq 0, g(x) \leq q, ug(x) = uq,$$
$$f(y) - ug(y) \leq f(x) - ug(x) \text{ for all } y.$$

If any x, u satisfy these conditions then x is necessarily an optimal solution of the problem, as is known from the theorem of the last chapter, which also tells us about the u involved. However, given any optimal solution x, generally it is not assured that there exists a u such that x, u together satisfy the conditions. The disadvantage here is opposite to that found before with the classical Lagrangean method. Were this assurance granted, the solutions to the conditions would describe all optimal solutions of the problem.

The assumptions of convex programming give the wanted assurance, so that under them optimal solutions are completely characterized by these stated conditions. They require first the activity set A to be in $\mathbf{R}^n$, and the functions f and g, which are defined in A to have certain convexity properties. The properties happen to fit the economic interpretation that has been given f and g. Like a typical output or production function, f is required to be concave. An ordinary cost function being convex, this is the property required of the functions which are elements of g. As will be proved, a consequence of these assumptions so far is to make the limit function v concave; also, that is their only importance. No monotonicity properties are required of f and g, but v is in any case a non-decreasing function just from the way it is defined. With v non-decreasing and concave, it has all the properties of a classical production function.

If the problem has an optimal solution it must be feasible, so the constraints $g(x) \leq q$ have a solution, any optimal solution being one. A further assumption for convex programming is that, more than just being feasible, the problem must be amply feasible, in that there even exist some x for which $g(x) < q$; it should have feasability even with quantities of all inputs to spare. Then q could be reduced to some $q' < q$ and still the problem would be feasible with the new constraints $g(x) \leq q'$. That is *Slater's condition*.

With

$$Q = [\, z : g(x) \leq z, x \in A \,] = [\, z : v(z) > - \infty \,]$$

as the set of points z where the constraints $g(x) \leq z$ have a solution, making $v(z)$ finite, the role of Slater's condition is to assure that the problem is not at the threshold of infeasibility, that q is not on the boundary of Q, beyond which feasibility ceases and v takes the value $-\infty$. By the Support Theorem for a concave function, concerning the existence of supports at interior points of the domain where it is defined and finite, v must have a support at q and hence a support gradient u. As seen (section V.1.6), support gradients of v at q are identical with the u that make the condition $D(u)$ true. By the theorem in section V.1.3 these then are the vectors u which, together with any optimal solution x of the problem, satisfy the considered conditions. So it appears that under these conditions the optimal solutions of the problem are identified with the x that appear in solutions of the conditions, and moreover the u which appear with them are identified with support gradients for the limit function v at q. With differentiable functions f and g and the activity vector x restricted non-negative, those conditions can be expressed in terms of derivatives; in that way the Kuhn-Tucker conditions are derived.

Another characterization of the x, u that satisfy the conditions is that they make a max-min saddle point of the Lagrangean function

$$L(x, u) = f(x) - u\{g(x) - q\},$$

subject to $x \in A$, $u \geq 0$. That is not of general interest for convex programming; but it takes a peculiar form in linear programming, where, because of a symmetry between dual problems, the same function is ambiguously the Lagrangean function of one problem and, with an exchange of the roles of variables and multipliers, also of the other. A conclusion is that *optimal solutions of either problem are identical to the support solutions of the other*.

A set is convex if it contains the linear segment joining any pair of its points. A hyperplane is the locus where a linear function take a constant value. Associated with it, having the hyperplane as its face, is the linear *half-space*, where the function does not exceed the value. For any set, a *bounding half-space* is one that contains it, and if also the face touches the set at any point it is a *supporting half-space*, at that point. A characteristic property of a closed convex set, important for convex programming, is that every point on the boundary is a maximum of some linear function; what is the same, there is a supporting half-space there. It follows that a closed convex set is identical with the intersection of its supporting half-spaces.

A convex polyhedron is the intersection of a finite collection of half-spaces. Convex sets can be approximated by convex polyhedra, by taking a finite dense enough set of points on the boundary and the intersection of the supports at them. From this, showing the proximity of the two topics, convex programming problems can be approximated by linear programming problems, and also they are just linear problems where the number of constraints is not finitely restricted. The involvement of linear and convex programming with economic problems is connected with the half-space feature, because half-spaces in economics commonly express a scarcity.

2.1 CONVEXITY

Given any two points $x, y \in \mathbf{R}^n$, as t describes the interval $<0, 1>$, $z = x + (y - x)t$ describes the line segment $<x, y>$ having end-points x, y. With $s = 1 - t$, the points of the segment are given by $z = xs + yt$ where $s, t \geq 0$, $s + t = 1$. A linear combination where the coefficients are nonnegative and sum to one being called a *convex combination*, the points of the interval are the convex combinations of its end-points.

A set $S \subset \mathbf{R}^n$ is convex if

$$x, y \in S \Rightarrow <x, y> \subset S;$$

that is, if any points belong to S, then so does the entire segment joining them. Another statement is that

$$x, y \in S, \quad s, t \geq 0, \quad s + t = 1 \Rightarrow xs + yt \in S.$$

The characteristic property of a closed convex set S is that *every point b on the boundary of S is a maximum in S of some non-constant linear function*; for some $u \in \mathbf{R}_n$, $u \neq 0$,

$$x \in S \Rightarrow ux \leq ub.$$

This restates the Theorem of the Supporting Hyperplane. The hyperplane has equation $ux = ub$, it has a common point b with S, and contains S entirely on one side of it. This theorem, especially as applied to functions, is the main theorem needed for convex programming.

The convexity property originally defined for sets is made to apply to a function through the convexity of some associated set. The graph of a function $f: A \to \mathbf{R}$ is the set

$$[(t, x) : t = f(x)] \subset \mathbf{R} \times A.$$

The function f is regarded as a binary relation and therefore as a set, given by the graph, by using the statement tfx for $t = f(x)$. The set $\mathbf{R} \times A$ is a prism, or cylinder, with sections given by A. The function graph, now also denoted f as well as the function, determines two parts of the prism lying above and below it and having it as their common boundary. These are just the product relations $\geq f$ and $\leq f$. For $t \geq fx$ means $t \geq sfx$ for some s, which means $t \geq s = f(x)$, that is $t \geq f(x)$. Thus $\geq f$ is the region above the graph, and similarly $\leq f$ is the region below. Either of these two regions is sometimes called the *epigraph* of the function. To distinguish them, $\geq f$ lying above the graph f could well be called the *catagraph* and $\leq f$, lying below, the *anagraph*; also, one could do without such terms and call them simply the above-graph and below-graph regions.

The function f is a *convex function* if the region $\geq f$ above the graph is convex, and a *concave function* if the region $\leq f$ below is convex. In an earlier terminology it would be convex downwards in the one case and upwards in the other. Evidently f is concave if $-f$ is convex.

The condition for any $S \subset \mathbf{R} \times A$ to be convex is that

$$(s, x), (s', x') \in S, t, t' \geq 0, t + t' = 1$$
$$\Rightarrow (st + s't', xt + x't') \in S.$$

If also, for all $x \in A$, there exists $s \in \mathbf{R}$ such that $(s, x) \in S$, a consequence is the convexity of A. The condition for $(s, x) \in \leq f$ is that $s \leq f(x)$ and $x \in A$. Hence for $\leq f$ to be convex, or for the function f to be concave, the domain A must be convex and

$$s \leq f(x), s' \leq f(x'), t, t' \geq 0, t + t' = 1$$
$$\Rightarrow st + s't' \leq f(xt + x't').$$

This last condition, whose sense requires the function domain A to be convex, is equivalent to

$$f(x)t + f(x')t' \leq f(xt + x't')$$

for all $t, t' \geq 0, t + t' = 1$, the convexity of the domain now being implied, since arguments of the function must be understood to lie in it. Thus concave functions are characterized by their satisfying this functional inequality, and convex functions are similarly, with the inequality reversed.

The Support Theorem for a concave function is that it has a linear support at every interior point of its domain. Thus, with f concave and a an interior point of its domain A, there exists a linear function $l: \mathbf{R}^n \to \mathbf{R}$ such that

$$f(x) \leq l(x) \text{ for all } x \in A, \quad f(a) = l(a).$$

This is proved by the Theorem of the Supporting Hyperplane in the form stated earlier. Since $\leq f$ is convex and $(f(a), a)$ is a boundary point, also of the closure of $\leq f$ if this set is not closed, there exists $(s, u) \neq 0$ such that

$$sf(a) + ua \geq st + ux \text{ for all } t \leq f(x).$$

This immediately implies $s \geq 0$. Also, $s = 0$ is impossible, since were it not then, necessarily, $u \neq 0$ and we would have

$$ua \geq ux \text{ for all } x \in A,$$

implying that a is on the boundary of A, contrary to our hypothesis. Therefore $s > 0$, and taking $v = s^{-1}u$, it follows that

$$f(a) + va \geq f(x) + vx,$$

and hence that $l(x) = f(a) + v(x - a)$ is a linear support to f at a, showing the required existence. QED. Section V.1.6 amplifies about a vector v being a support gradient of a function f at a point a.

An addition to this background in convexity is useful for convex programming. A concave function can have many support gradients at a point; they form a convex set, which at an interior point of the domain must also be closed and bounded. The Differentiability Theorem for concave functions is that any concave function is differentiable at exactly those points where it has a unique support, and then the differential gradient is identical with the support gradient. Also, if the function is differentiable in an open set it must be continuously differentiable there.

Differentiability at a point is a local condition, about the function being locally linear or having a linear approximation near the point—it looks flat nearby, like the earth. But having a support is a global condition. From the Differentiability Theorem we have that, if $f: A \to \mathbf{R}$, where $A \subset \mathbf{R}^n$, is concave and differentiable, with gradient $g: A \to \mathbf{R}_n$, then

$$l(x) = f(x') + g(x')(x - x')$$

is not just a locally approximating linear function at any x', as required by the differentiability, but also is a support there, globally. So we have $f(x) \leq l(x)$; that is,

$$f(x) \leq f(x') + g(x')(x - x') \text{ for all } x, x'.$$

This condition on a function and its derivatives is therefore necessary for it to be concave. It is also sufficient. For with it the function admits the expression

$$f(x) = \min_{x'} f(x') + g(x')(x - x')$$

where it is the minimum of a collection of linear functions in x, and any function having such a form is necessarily concave.

The strata of a function f are the sets

$$S_t = [x : f(x) \geq t],$$

in this case upper strata, though lower strata are defined similarly. Evidently

$$t' \geq t \Rightarrow S_{t'} \subset S_t.$$

Also, as readily seen, the strata of a concave function are all convex sets.

2.2 PROGRAMMING CONVEXITY THEOREM

THEOREM   For any set $A \subset \mathbf{R}_n$ and functions

$$f: A \to \mathbf{R}, g: A \to \mathbf{R}^m,$$

and the function $v\colon \mathbf{R}^m \to \mathbf{R}$ where

$$v(z) = \sup \, [f(x) : g(x) \le z],$$

if f is concave and the elements of g are convex, then v is concave.

For any $z, z' \in A$, and

$$t, t' \ge 0, \, t + t' = 1, \tag{1}$$

it has to be shown that $v(z)t + v(z')t' \le v(zt + z't')$. For this, by assuming

$$s < v(z)t + v(z')t', \tag{a}$$

for any s, it is enough then to show the consequence

$$s < v(zt + z't'). \tag{b}$$

We have by the hypothsis about f and g that, for any x, x',

$$f(x)t + f(x')t' \le f(xt + x't'), \tag{2}$$
$$g(x)t + g(x')t' \ge g(xt + x't'), \tag{3}$$

and, by definition of v, for any z,

$$g(x) \le z \Rightarrow f(x) \le v(z) \text{ for all } x, \tag{4}$$

and also, for any r

$$r < v(z) \Rightarrow g(x) \le z, f(x) > r \text{ for some } x. \tag{5}$$

With $(1)-(5)$, and assuming (a), we want now to deduce (b).

From (1) it follows that $t > 0$ or $t' > 0$, so that from (a) there exist r, r' for which

$$s = rt + r't', \tag{i}$$
$$r < v(z), r' < v(z'). \tag{ii}$$

By (5) applied to (ii), for some x, x'

$$g(x) \le z, f(x) > r; g(x') \le z', f(x') > r'. \tag{iii}$$

Because $t, t' \ge 0$, from (1), it follows from (iii) that

$$f(x)t + f(x')t' > rt + r't',$$

and so, by (4) with (i),

$$f(xy + x't') > s. \tag{iv}$$

Again from (iii), by (1),

$$g(x)t + g(x')t' \le zt + z't',$$

so that, by (5),

$$g(xt + x't') \le zt + z't',$$

and hence by (4)

$$f(xt + x't') \le v(zt + z't'). \tag{v}$$

Now from (iv) and (v), (b) follows. QED

2.3   SLATER'S CONDITION

The optimal programming problem is feasible if the constraints have some solution, that is if $g(x) \leq q$ for some x, in which case $v(q) > -\infty$. Slater's condition requires moreover that $g(x) < q$ for some x.

An immediate equivalent of Slater's condition is that, for some $q' < q$, $g(x) \leq q'$ for some x, that is $v(q') > -\infty$.

THEOREM   For a bounded convex problem Slater's condition implies that the limit function v is bounded $< \infty$ everywhere and has a support at q.

For a bounded problem, $v(q) < \infty$, and Slater's condition requires

$$-\infty < v(q') \text{ for some } q' < q.$$

Then v is finite in the open set

$$Q = [z : q' < z < q].$$

For in any case v is non-decreasing (section V.1.6), so that

$$z \in Q \Rightarrow -\infty < v(q') \leq v(z) \leq v(q) < \infty.$$

Because the problem is convex, the limit function v is concave, by the Convex Programming Theorem (section V.1.2). Since now v is finite and concave in the open set Q, by the Support Theorem (section V.2.1) it has a support at every point. A support being a linear upper bound, the existence of one anywhere makes v bounded $< \infty$ everywhere. It follows now that

$$Q' = [z : q' < z]$$

is an open neighbourhood of q where v is finite. Hence, again by the Support Theorem, it has a support there. QED

As remarked (section V.1.6), the gradient of any support, or any support gradient, of the limit function v at q is simply any u for which the condition $D(u)$ holds, or which is a support solution of the problem. Slater's condition thus assures the existence of a support solution for any bounded convex problem.

This Theorem can apply to the support characterization of optimal solutions of convex problems, since any problem with an optimal solution must be bounded.

2.4   OPTIMALITY THEOREM

THEOREM   For a convex problem that satisfies Slater's condition any optimal solution x is characterized by the existence of a u with which it satisfies the conditions

$$u \geq 0,\ g(x) \leq q,\ ug(x) = uq,$$
$$f(y) - ug(y) \text{ is maximum at } y = x.$$

This is the main theorem on convex programming. Little is needed now for its proof. The Optimal Programming Theorem (section V.1.3) shows that, for any problem whatsoever, the stated conditions are equivalent to x being an optimal solution and u being a support solution. The conditions holding with any u therefore are sufficient for x to be an optimal solution; and then moreover the u must be a support solution. All that is required now for the conditions to be also necessary is the existence of a support solution. But by the theorem of the last section, the convexity assumptions together with Slater's condition assure that.

2.5   NON-NEGATIVE MAXIMA

THEOREM   For a concave function f which is differentiable with gradient g, a necessary and sufficient condition for x to be a maximum of f subject to the non-negativity constraint is that

$$x \geq 0, \quad g(x) \leq 0, \quad g(x)x = 0.$$

This condition has to be shown equivalent to

$$x \geq 0, \quad x' \geq 0 \Rightarrow f(x') \leq f(x). \tag{i}$$

First, it will be shown to imply (i).

Because f is concave,

$$f(x') \leq f(x) + g(x)(x' - x) \text{ for all } x'. \tag{ii}$$

The condition in the theorem requires $g(x)x = 0$, and with this (ii) reduces to

$$f(x') \leq f(x) + g(x)x'. \tag{iii}$$

Also, $g(x) \leq 0$ is required, and it follows that

$$x' \geq 0 \Rightarrow g(x)x' \leq 0 \Rightarrow f(x) + g(x)x' \leq f(x),$$

which with (iii) gives

$$x' \geq 0 \Rightarrow f(x') \leq f(x),$$

so (i) follows. QED

To prove the converse, now suppose (i). The function f is understood to be defined for $x > 0$, and so Slater's condition is automatic for the convex problem

$$\max f(x) : -x \leq 0.$$

Therefore, by the theorem of the last section, there exists a vector u such that

$$u \geq 0, \quad -x \leq 0, \quad ux = 0,$$
$$x \geq 0, \quad x' \geq 0 \Rightarrow f(x') + ux' \leq f(x) + ux.$$

But a consequence of

$$f(x') - f(x) \leq -u(x' - x) \text{ for all } x' > 0,$$

with the differentiability of f at x, is that $u = -g(x)$, and with this we now have the conditions in the theorem.

The conditions reflect the complementary slackness dealt with earlier (section V.1.7), equivalent to

$$x_j \geq 0, \quad g_j(x) \leq 0, \quad x_j > 0 \Rightarrow g_j(x) = 0.$$

Therefore, should it happen that $x > 0$, or the maximum is at an interior point of the region where the variables are non-negative, so that the constraints are slack at that point and it will make no difference if they are dropped, we would have $g(x) = 0$; that is, the gradient vanishes. The vanishing of the gradient of a differentiable function without constraints is generally a necessary but not sufficient condition for a maximum. But here, with a concave function, it is also sufficient. Moreover, generally with any function the derivatives can express only a local condition, but here we have a global condition. That reflects the important property of a concave function by which any local maximum is necessarily also a global maximum. And the examination of second derivatives to discriminate between a maximum or a minimum at a point where the first derivatives vanish, which generally has application, is immaterial in the case of a concave function.

2.6 THE KUHN-TUCKER CONDITIONS

THEOREM For a differentiable convex problem with the constraint qualification and the variables restricted non-negative, a necessary and sufficient condition for any x to be optimal is that, together with some u, it satisfies the conditions

$$u \geq 0, \quad g(x) \leq q, \quad ug(x) = uq,$$
$$x \geq 0, f'(x) \leq ug'(x), \quad f'(x)x = ug'(x)x.$$

These are the *Kuhn-Tucker (KT) conditions*. This theorem follows from the theorems of sections 2.4 and 2.5. With f concave and the elements of g convex, and with $u \geq 0$, $h(x) = f(x) - ug(x)$ is concave as a function of x. Since the functions f and g are differentiable, so is this, and the gradient is $h'(x) = f'(x) - ug'(x)$. With the variables restricted non-negative, the activity set A is $[x : x \geq 0]$. The conditon in section 2.4 that $f(x) - ug(x)$ be at a maximum in the activity set, when put in the form given in section 2.5, becomes

$$x \geq 0, \quad h'(x) \leq 0, \quad h'(x)x = 0;$$

that is,

$$x \geq 0, f'(x) - ug(x) \leq 0, \quad \{f'(x) - ug'(x)\}x = 0,$$

and so the theorem is proved.

The two lines of the KT conditions are different, but they have a similarity in that both of them require a complementarity slackness, in the form that has been discussed already (section V.1.7). In terms of elements,

$$u_j \geq 0, \quad g_j(x) \leq q_j, \quad g_j(x) < q_j \Rightarrow u_j = 0,$$
$$x_i \geq 0, \quad f_i(x) \leq ug_i(x), \quad f_i(x) < ug_i(x) \Rightarrow x_i = 0.$$

The relation between the two lines gains remarkable similarity, and symmetry, when they are applied to a linear programming problem. The LP problem is obtained from the KT problem

$$\max f(x) : g(x) \le q, x \ge 0$$

by giving the objective and constraint functions the linear forms $f(x) = px$, $g(x) = ax$ where $p \in \mathbf{R}_n$ and $a \in \mathbf{R}_n^m$, so the problem becomes the standard-max LP problem

$$\max px : ax \le q, x \ge 0.$$

Then for the derivatives we have $f'(x) = p$, $g'(x) = a$, so the KT conditions are

$$u \ge 0, ax \le q, uax = uq,$$
$$x \ge 0, p \le ua, up = uax.$$

The two lines in the KT conditions are distinguishable, with distinct roles and without any symmetry between them in the general case. But there is a symmetry in this linear case, which is brought out better when with minor rearrangement the conditions are restated as

(m) $u \ge 0, ax \le q, uax = uq,$
(w) $x \ge 0, ua \ge p, uax = px.$

Considering the pair of problems

(M) $\max px : ax \le q, x \ge 0,$
(W) $\min uq : ua \ge p, u \ge 0,$

each one has the combination of (m) and (w) as its KT conditions. With problem (M) they would come in the order (m), (w) as already seen, and with (W) they would come in the order (w), (m), so the two parts of the conditions exchange their roles, without altering their conjunction.

Together, (M) and (W) form a standard dual pair of LP problems. Problem (M) is put in the form of a standard max-problem, and (W) in that of a standard min-problem. It can be recognized that the distinction between the max- and min-problems is just a way of expressing them and nothing more; either problem can be put either way. Thus

$$\min x'(-p') : x'(-a') \le -q', x' \ge 0,$$

a prime signifying transposition, is (M) stated as a standard min-problem; it is the same problem (M) written in the same form as (W); the only reason it is not written that way is that it is not so neat. This consideration also shows that the relation between the problems is symmetrical; each has the same relation to the other, or in going from one to the other one could just as well go from the other to the one: if (M) is the primal and (W) the dual, by the same principle (W) could be the primal and (M) the dual. Either of the problems with its dual forms the same symmetrical pair. When one is distinguished as the primal it can only be a matter of interpretation, possibly in relation to some application. Both problems (M) and (W) derive from the data scheme formed by the $(m + 1) \times (n + 1)$ matrix

$$A = \begin{pmatrix} 0 & -p \\ -q & a \end{pmatrix}.$$

If A is replaced by $-A'$ we have the same pair of problems but they exchange places, (M) then being stated as the min-problem and (W) as the max.

The condition $L(x, u)$, of section V.1.3, applied to the linear problem (M), is that

$$x \geq 0, \quad x' \geq 0 \Rightarrow px' - uax' \leq px - uax.$$

By the non-negative maximum theorem of section 2.5, this condition is equivalent to the second part (w) of the KT conditions. But this can also be seen simply and directly. For a restatement of the considered condition is that

$$x \geq 0, \quad x' \geq 0 \Rightarrow (p - ua)(x' - x) \leq 0,$$

and by taking $x' = 2x$ and $(1/2)x$, we find that $(p - ua)x = 0$; with this the condition reduces to $x' \geq 0 \Rightarrow (p - ua)x' \leq 0$, which implies $p - ua \leq 0$.

Any x, u satisfy (m), (w) if and only if x is an optimal solution and u a support solution for problem (M). We know this from the general Optimal Programming Theorem (section 1.3), together with the argument just given, as well as from the KT theorem. But now, from the symmetry, x is just as well a support solution for problem (W), and u an optimal solution. The solvability of the KT conditions bears equally and simultaneously on both the problems. The contribution of convex programming (CP) theory to LP is just that the constraint qualification for a problem assures the existence of a support solution. It tells us nothing about the existence of an optimal solution, which with the existence of a support solution would be equivalent to the solvability of the KT conditions.

The Lagrangean functions associated with the problems (M) and (W) are

$$px - u(ax - q), \quad uq - (ua - p)x,$$

where the Lagrange multipliers are given by u for the first and x for the second. But these happen to be the same function,

$$L(x, u) = px + uq - uax.$$

This function therefore can be understood ambiguously to be the Lagrangean function of either problem — or of both simultaneously. Another way of characterizing any solution x, u of the KT conditions is that it is a non-negative max-min saddle point of this function, that is

$$x \geq 0, \quad u \geq 0;$$
$$x' \geq 0, u' \geq 0 \Rightarrow L(x', u) \leq L(x, u) \leq L(x, u').$$

A peculiarity of LP theory is that the constraint qualification has no part in it; the existence of an optimal solution is equivalent to the existence of a support solution, and to the solvability of the KT conditions, which is equivalent to the same for the dual. Also, the finiteness of the limit value $v(q)$ is equivalent to the existence of an optimal solution. These and other propositions peculiar to LP, without a counterpart for general convex programming, are dealt with in the next chapter.

Linear Programming

The applications of linear programming in economics, games, operations research (OR), and engineering are well known, so its usefulness does not need to be stressed; also, it has an importance for theory. The range of its uses needs some explanation, since LP might appear quite limited by linearity and compromised for applications. The convex problem is nothing other than the linear problem where the number of constraints is not finitely restricted, as was remarked in the last chapter and will be elaborated further. Convex problems can be approximated by linear problems, and solved by LP methods. These circumstances show a further range for LP that might not at first be apparent. Though convexities pervade economics, the point of the matter might be not here, but more primitive than that. It could be, as is the case for every counting device, that material heaps are additive:

quantity (heap 1 + heap 2) = quantity (heap 1) + quantity (heap 2),

such as applies to the abacus, to the bill at a supermarket or in a factory where available men and machines are assigned to tasks. In the allocation of scarce resources there is a confinement to a linear halfspace. The wide applicability of linear and convex programming might come from that.

A linear halfspace in $\mathbf{R}^n$ is a locus where some non-constant linear function does not exceed a certain value; for some $u \in \mathbf{R}_n$, $u \neq 0$, and $t \in \mathbf{R}$, it is the locus of x where $ux \leq t$. The boundary of the halfspace, its face, is the hyperplane with equation $ux = t$. In economics non-negativities frequently apply, such as to market prices p or physical quantities x, so instead of being in spaces $\mathbf{R}^n$ and $\mathbf{R}_n$ these points are in the non-negative orthants, or quadrants in the case of two dimensions, Ω^n and Ω_n, Ω being the non-negative numbers. The value of any bundle of goods $x \in \Omega^n$ at prices $p \in \Omega_n$ is the product $px \in \Omega$. With such non-negativity constraints, halfspaces and hyperplanes are restricted to their parts where they intersect the non-negative orthant. The standard LP constraint restricts to a halfspace. The non-negativity restriction on a coordinate is such a case, the restriction being to a coordinate halfspace, whose face is a coordinate hyperplane.

Halfspaces being convex and any intersection of convex sets being convex, any intersection of halfspaces is convex. The intersection of any finite collection of halfspaces is a *convex polyhedron*, and the region defined by the simultaneous constraints in an LP problem is an example.

A standard max-problem has the form

(M)   max $px : ax \leq q, x \geq 0$,

where $p \in \mathbf{R}_n$, $q \in \mathbf{R}^m$ and $a \in \mathbf{R}_n^m$, n being the number of program variables and m the number of constraints. With the ith row, jth column and i, jth element of a denoted

$$a_{(i} \in \mathbf{R}_n, \quad a_{j)} \in \mathbf{R}^m \quad \text{and} \quad a'_{ij} \in \mathbf{R},$$

for $i = 1, \ldots, m$ and $j = 1, \ldots, n$ the constraints which are stated together by $ax \leq q$, and by

$$a_{1)} x_1 + \ldots + a_{n)} x_n \leq q,$$

are stated separately as

$$a_{(i}x \leq q_i, \quad i = 1, \ldots, m.$$

The problem (M) is associated with the LP tableau

$$A = \begin{pmatrix} 0 & -p \\ -q & a \end{pmatrix}$$

with $m + 1$ rows and $n + 1$ columns, numbered $0, 1, \ldots, m$ and $0, 1, \ldots, n$. The Simplex Algorithm for solving LP problems, originated by George Dantzig, has a basic step, the pivot operation. This acts on any tableau to produce a series which terminates in one that shows a solution, if there is one, and otherwise shows that there is no solution.

Given any linear functions l_r, the function

$$f(x) = \min_r l_r(x) = \max [t : t \leq l_r(x)]$$

is concave. For the regions below the graphs we have

$$\leq f = \cap_r \leq l_r,$$

and since the $\leq l_r$ are halfspaces, $\leq f$ is a convex polyhedron and f is a *polyhedral concave function*. A polyhedral convex function is obtained by exchanging max and min. Thus, with linear functions l_{is}, the functions

$$g_i(x) = \max_s l_{is}(x)$$

are all polyhedral convex functions, forming a vector g. Then the problem

(MC)   max $f(x) : g(x) \leq q$

has the form of a *polyhedral convex programming problem*. None the less, *it can be restated as the LP problem*

(ML)   max $t : t \leq l_r(x), l_{is}(x) \leq q_i$.

3.1   LINEAR INEQUALITIES

The algebra of linear inequalities will be initiated without an immediate concern with linear programming. Instead, the interest is in two theorems about Completion and Consistency for systems of linear inequalities. These are not proved directly but are consequences of a theorem which will be proved in the next section. The main LP theorems are encountered, including the LP Duality Theorem, which then appears equivalent to each of them. First we consider basic operations with inequalities.

The non-negative numbers are closed under addition and multiplication: if s and t are non-negative then so are $s + t$ and st. For any numbers a and b, the relation $a \leq b$ signifies that $b - a \geq 0$. Consequently we have three *basic rules* for deriving inequalities from inequalities. The first rule is inference by transitivity:

$$a \leq b, \ b \leq c \Rightarrow a \leq c. \tag{i}$$

For if $b - a, c - b \geq 0$ then so is the sum $c - a \geq 0$. For the other two rules, inequalities can be multiplied by non-negative numbers, or added together:

$$a \leq b, \ t \geq 0 \Rightarrow at \leq bt, \tag{ii}$$
$$a \leq b, \ c \leq d \Rightarrow a + c \leq b + d. \tag{iii}$$

Thus (ii) is by closure of the non-negative numbers under multiplication. For (iii), from the left-hand side we have $a + c \leq b + c, \ b + c \leq b + d$ by closure under addition, and hence the right-hand side by (i). For an equivalent, extended, form of rules (ii) and (iii), following from them and including them as cases, we have

$$(+) \qquad\qquad a_i \leq b_i, \ t_i \geq 0 \Rightarrow \Sigma a_i t_i \leq \Sigma b_i t_i.$$

In this form they can be applied directly to the system of simultaneous linear inequalities

$$a_{(i}x \leq q_i, \ i = 1, \dots, m,$$

that is, the system

$$(A) \qquad\qquad\qquad ax \leq q.$$

Given any simultaneous solution x of A and any $u_i \geq 0$, it is concluded from $(+)$ that x is also a solution of

$$\Sigma u_i a_{(i}x \leq \Sigma u_i q_i.$$

For a matrix statement,

$$ax \leq q, \ u \geq 0 \Rightarrow uax \leq uq.$$

Now using also transitivity (i), if x satisfies the system of inequalities A then also it must satisfy every inequality of the form $px \leq t$ where $p = ua, t \geq uq$ for some $u \geq 0$. The new collection (B) of inequalities of this form, all of which are implied by the finite collection (A) by the three basic rules, and which inludes (A) as a subset, can be called the *basic completion* of (A):

$$(B) \qquad\qquad p = ua, \ t \geq uq, \ u \geq 0 \Rightarrow px \leq t$$

Evidently, repeatedly taking the basic completion produces no larger collection. However, one could define a *completion* (C) of (A) in another way which does not involve reference to the basic rules. An inequality $px \leq t$

belongs to the collection (C) if every x which is a simultaneous solution of the inequalities in (A), or (B) since we know this amounts to the same, is also a solution of it. Thus (C) contains (B), and for all we know at this point it might be larger. The proposed Completion Theorem for systems of linear inequalities is that it is not larger: *the basic completion is complete.* Another way of putting it is that all linear inequalities that are implied by (A) can be derived from (A) by the three basic rules.

All theorems which follow concern a matrix $a \in \mathbf{R}_n^m$, vectors $q \in \mathbf{R}^m$, $b \in \mathbf{R}_n$ and a number $t \in \mathbf{R}$.

THEOREM I (*completion*)   If $ax \leq q$ for some x, then

$$ax \leq q \Rightarrow px \leq t \text{ for all } x \tag{I-a}$$

if and only if

$$p = ua, \ t \geq uq \text{ for some } u \geq 0 \tag{I-b}$$

K. Fan (1956, *p.* 109) refers to this as a well-known theorem of J. Farkas (1902). In the terms we are using now, the theorem tells us that there is no distinction between the completion and the basic completion of finite system of linear inequalities, or that (C) = (B). The part (B) $\subset$ (C), or that (I-b) $\Rightarrow$ (I-a), has been seen already, and the other part is more substantial. This theorem will not be proved directly or immediately, but will be eventually by proving equivalence with some other theorem which will be proved. Now we consider another possible theorem.

An issue with any system of simultaneous inequalities is its consistency, or the existence of a solution. One way that a system can be insoluble is by containing an inequality that on its own is insoluble, such as $0x \leq t$ where $t < 0$, since any solution to this would give the impossible conclusion $0 < 0$. Because the solutions of (A) and (B) are identical, one way of showing that (A) is insoluble might be to show that (B) is insoluble just because it includes an impossible inequality like this. It can be asked whether this way is always available when (A) is insoluble. The proposed Consistency Theorem asserts that it is.

The condition for system (B) to include such an impossible inequality is that

$$ua = 0, \ uq < 0 \text{ for some } u \geq 0,$$

and the contrary is

$$ua = 0 \Rightarrow uq \geq 0 \text{ for all } u \geq 0,$$

so the following is a statement of the theorem that is in view.

THEOREM II (*consistency*)

$$ax \leq q \text{ for some } x \tag{II-a}$$

if and only if

$$ua = 0 \Rightarrow uq \geq 0 \text{ for all } u \geq 0. \tag{II-b}$$

K. Fan (1956, p. 100) gives this theorem. Without now proving it, and regardless of its happening to be true, Theorem I on Completion will be deduced from this Consistency Theorem, and LP theorems will be encountered at the same time. First we prove:

COROLLARY If $ax \leq q$ for some x, then

$$ax \leq q \Rightarrow px < t \text{ for all } x \qquad (i)$$

if and only if

$$ua = p, uq < t \text{ for some } u \geq 0. \qquad (ii)$$

The condition (i) means the system

$$ax \leq q, \ -px \leq -t$$

is inconsistent. By Theorem II an equivalent condition is that the system

$$va - sp = 0, \ vq - st < 0, \ v \geq 0, \ s \geq 0$$

is consistent. With any solution we must have $s > 0$; for $s = 0$ would give

$$va = 0, \ vq < 0, \ v \geq 0$$

and this, by Theorem II, implies that the system $ax \leq q$ is inconsistent, contrary to hypothesis. With $s > 0$ we have $u = s^{-1} v$ as a demonstration of (ii). Thus under the stated hypothesis Theorem II implies the equivalence of (i) and (ii). QED

The continuation now involves the pair of LP problems

$$(M) \qquad\qquad \max px : ax \leq q$$

and

$$(W) \qquad\qquad \min uq : ua = p, u \geq 0.$$

These are dual LP problems as commonly understood, though that means nothing until a value for regarding them as such comes out of theorems that follow. Also, the principle by which any LP problem can be associated with a dual problem has a symmetry, making any problem the dual of its dual, which is not immediately apparent with the incomplete symmetry between the forms of (M) and (W). However, the distinction of form between (M) and (W) is inessential, since either problem can be restated in the form of the other. For instance, (W) can be restated as the problem

$$\max -uq : ua \leq p, \ -ua \leq -p, \ -u \leq 0.$$

which has the form of (M). Then, governed by our example of the dual of a problem of the form (M), the dual would be

$$\min py - pz - 0t : ay - az - Jt = -q, y, z, t \geq 0,$$

which is the same as the problem

$$\max p(z - y) : a(z - y) + Jt = q, y, z, t \geq 0,$$

which, with $x = z - y$, is equivalent to our original problem (M). The same principle which makes (W) the dual of (M) now makes (M) the dual of (W). That shows the underlying symmetry in the duality association, which is not at first apparent from the way (M) and (W) have been stated. Though the rule for deriving the dual of a problem has reference to its form, really the distinction of form is inessential and later the rule will be developed in a way which encompasses the present one and applies to a problem in any form.

The set of feasible values of problem (M) is

$$V = [px : ax \leq q],$$

and by the hypothesis in Theorem I this is nonempty. The set of bounds for problem (M), or upper bounds of this set, is

$$T = [t : ax \leq q \Rightarrow px \leq t].$$

Boundedness of problem (M) means that this set is nonempty. Suppose the problem is both feasible and bounded, that is, that both V and T are nonempty. Then by the Theorem of the Least Upper Bound, T contains a least element m. Morever,

$$T = [t : m \leq t]$$

so it is a closed set. The set of strict upper bounds is

$$S = [t : ax \leq q \Rightarrow px < t].$$

These being upper bounds, we have $S \subset T$; also, if T is nonempty then so is S. By the corollary,

$$S = [t : ua = p, uq < t, u \geq 0].$$

From this,

$$t \,\epsilon\, S \Rightarrow t' \,\epsilon\, S \text{ for all } t' > t \text{ and for some } t' < t,$$

showing that S is an open set.

Now we consider whether m, the least upper bound or upper limit of the set V, is an element of V and so the greatest element, or maximum, in V. If not, then every upper bound of V is also a strict upper bound, so $S = T$. But S has been shown to be open while T is closed, so this is impossible. Hence m belongs to V, so it is a feasible value for the problem M, and being the greatest it is the optimal value.

The following has been proved.

> THEOREM III (*LP solubility*)   If a linear programming problem is both feasible and bounded, then it has an optimal solution.

Immediately from the definitions involved, the converse is true for any optimal programming problem. However, this theorem is a special feature of LP, which is not available even for convex problems. Though neglected in many LP accounts, it is found in Dantzig (1963).

It is elementary that, if one problem of a dual pair is feasible, then the other is bounded; for, if x, u are feasible solutions of (M), (W), then we have

$$uax = px, \ uax \leq uq$$

and so

$$px \leq uq,$$

showing that *feasible values of one problem are bounds for feasible values of the other*. Thus, (M) *is bounded if* (W) *is feasible*. Also it appears from the corollary that if (M) is feasible and bounded then (W) is feasible; for, (i), for some t, is required for (M) to be bounded. But by the corollary, with (M) feasible, this is equivalent to (ii) which implies that $ua = p$ for some $u \geq 0$; that is, (W) is feasible. Hence we have:

THEOREM IV   Any linear programming problem is bounded if and only if the dual is feasible.

We now have that, if one problem has an optimal solution, so it is feasible and bounded, then by Theorem IV the other is bounded and feasible and hence by Theorem III has an optimal solution. Thus, *one problem has an optimal solution if and only if the other does*. Then, moreover, *the optimal values are equal*. For let m, w be the optimal values of problems (M), (W). Feasible values of one problem are bounds for the other, as remarked. Therefore, because these are feasible values, we have $m \leq w$. Because they are optimal, (i) is equivalent to $t > m$ and (ii) implies $t > w$. Since, by the corollary, (i) and (ii) are equivalent, it follows that

$$t > m \Rightarrow t > w \text{ for all } t$$

and hence that $m \geq w$, showing that $m = w$. We have proved:

THEOREM V (*LP duality*)   For any dual pair of linear programming problems, one has an optimal solution if and only if the other does, and then the optimal values are equal.

It can be seen now that Theorem I is deducible from consequences that have been found from Theorem II, and so is a consequence of Theorem II. The case in Theorem I where (M) is unbounded is, by Theorem III, identical with the case where (W) is infeasible. In this case both (i) and (ii) in Theorem I are denied and there is nothing more to prove. For the contrary case let v be the common optimal value for (M) and (W) provided by Theorem IV, so $w = v = m$. Then, by Theorem IV, both (i) and (ii) are equivalent to $t \geq v$, and hence are equivalent. QED

An additional remark for the case where an LP problem is unbounded, concerning the determination of directions in which it is unbounded, is made in section 3.4. It can be noted here that if problem (M) is infeasible then, by Theorem II,

$$va = 0, \ vq < 0 \text{ for some } v \geq 0.$$

Hence if (W) is feasible and w is any feasible solution, so that $wa = p$, $w \geq 0$, then, with $u = w + tv$ for all $t \geq 0$, we have

$$ua = (w + tv)a = wa + tva = p, \; u \geq 0,$$

so also u is a feasible solution; and, moreover,

$$uq = (w + tv)q = wq + tvq \to -\infty \; (t \to \infty),$$

so the problem (W) is unbounded. The solutions v therefore give directions in which the problem would be unbounded, were it feasible.

Finally, we see that Theorem V, the LP Duality Theorem which was deduced from Theorem II, implies Theorem II on solubility of systems of linear inequalities, so these two theorems are deducible from each other. Consider the dual pair of problems

(M)   max $0x : ax \leq q$,

(W)   min $uq : ua = 0, \; u \geq 0$.

Problem (M) has an optimal solution if and only if it is feasible, any feasible solution then being optimal, with value 0. By the LP Duality Theorem, (M) having an optimal solution is equivalent to the same for (W), with the same optimal value, 0; that is,

$$\min \, [uq : ua = 0, \, u \geq 0]$$

exists and has value 0; in other words

$$ua = 0 \Rightarrow uq \geq 0 \text{ for all } u \geq 0.$$

Thus the solubility of $ax \leq q$ is equivalent to this condition, which is just what Theorem II asserts. Thus Theorem II follows from Theorem IV. QED

In the next section we prove a theorem from which Theorem II, and so also all its consequences found in this section, can be deduced. An alternative approach to proof is by means of the Simplex Algorithm, of George B. Dantzig, which is not only a means for solving LP problems but also a basis for proof of all the LP theorems, including the LP Duality Theorem which was already seen to be equivalent to Theorem II.

That both problems in a dual pair can be infeasible is shown by the following example:

(M)   max $x_1 + x_2 + 0 + 0 : (u_1) \; 2x_1 - x_2 + 0 + 0 \leq 0$
$(u_2) - x_1 + x_2 + 0 + 0 \leq 0$
$(u_3) \, 0 + 0 + 2x_3 - x_4 \leq 0$
$(u_4) \, 0 + 0 - x_3 + x_4 \leq 0$
$x_1, x_2, x_3, x_4 \geq 0$

and

(W)   min $0 + 0 + 0 + 0 : (x_1) \, 2u_1 - u_2 + 0 + 0 \geq 1$
$(x_2) - u_1 + u_2 + 0 + 0 \geq 1$
$(x_3) \, 0 + 0 + 2u_3 - u_4 \geq 0$
$(x_4) \, 0 + 0 - u_3 + u_4 \geq 0$
$u_1, u_2, u_3, u_4 \geq 0$

3.2 SEPARATION THEOREMS

THEOREM I (*linear separation*) Any point either belongs to the convex closure of a given finite set of points or is linearly separated from them, and not both.

With $A = \langle a_1 \dots a_n \rangle$, it has to be shown that either $q \in A$ or, for some $u, uq > ua_i$ for all i, and not both. Clearly not both. For if $q \in A$, that is if

$$q = \Sigma a_i t_i \text{ where } t_i \geq 0,\ \Sigma t_i = 1,$$

then $uq = \Sigma(ua_i)t_i$, so uq is an average of the ua_i , and we have

$$\min ua_i \leq uq \leq \max ua_i .$$

Since not both, it remains to show that the denial of the first case implies the second. The proof will be by induction on the number n of points, and is illustrated in Figure 1. The theorem is obviously true for $n = 1$. Assume now that it is true for n. It will be deduced for $n + 1$, and then the theorem will be proved.

Let b be the $(n + 1)$th point, and let $B = \langle a_1 \dots a_n b \rangle$. Suppose q is not in B, so that $q \neq b$ and also q cannot be in A. Then by hypothesis there exists a hyperplane Π separating q from A. If this also separates q from b and

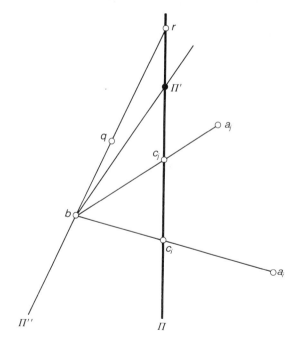

Figure 1

therefore from B, there is nothing more to prove. Therefore suppose the contrary. In that case Π must separate b from A, so the segments $<ba_i>$ all cut Π, say in points c_i. Since $q \neq b$ three cases can be distinguished: (i) the ray from b through q cuts Π, (ii) the reverse ray does, or (iii) the line bq is parallel to Π. These possibilities are exclusive and exhaustive and can be taken in turn.

The first case is simple, for in this case the hyperplane through b parallel to Π separates q from B. To consider the next case, let $C = <c_1 \ldots c_n>$, and let r be the point where the ray from b to q cuts Π. Then r cannot be in C, since in this case q would be in B contrary to our initial assumption. Since r is not in C, by the inductive hypothesis there exists a hyperplane Π' in Π which separates r from C. Then the hyperplane Π'' joining Π' to b separates q from b.

For the remaining case, the hyperplane through b parallel to Π only has to be rotated a small amount at b to produce a hyperplane that separates q from B. Since Π separates b from A, let u be the gradient of Π, so $ub > ua_i$ for all i and, since bq is parallel to Π, also $uq = ub$. Because $(b-q)'(b-q) > 0$, with $v = (q-b)'$ we have that $vq > vb$ and hence, with $w = u + tv$ and $t > 0$, that

$$wq = uq + tvq > ub + tvb = wb.$$

Provided t is small, we still have $wb > wa_i$ for all i. Thus w provides the required linear separator, the hyperplane through b with this gradient separating q from B. The theorem is now proved.

A restatement of Theorem I is that

either
(I-a) $ax = q, \ Jx = 1$ for some $x \geq 0$
or
(I-b) $ua < uqJ$ for some u
and not both.

The proof, like the theorem, is easily stated and understood in geometrical terms. It could be restated algebraically, but then it is cumbersome, and also, an interest of it is in the geometrical understanding it contributes to the proof of the next theorem. That theorem is dealt with algebraically, but for want of a diagram it is not so readily understood geometrically, except that the same idea is followed.

Theorem I is a finite algebraic version of the Theorem of the Separating Hyperplane for convex sets, provable by methods of finite algebra. The next theorem is a homogeneous, or conical, counterpart, more directly usable than the first in many applications, especially in linear programming. Also, Theorem I can be deduced from it.

THEOREM II (*conical separation*)   For any $a \in \mathbf{R}_n^m$ and $q \in \mathbf{R}^m$,
either
(II-a) $ax = q$ for some $x \geq 0$

or

(II-b) $ua \leq 0, \ uq > 0$ for some u

and not both.

It is obvious geometrically, and fairly immediate algebraically, that Theorem I follows from Theorem II (we will show the reverse later). Geometrically, we take a new origin at a point outside the space V in which the figure involved in Theorem I lies, apply Theorem II to the new figure, and then take the intersection in V of the hyperplane through the new origin that is so obtained. The algebraical argument follows this idea. A restatement of (I-a) is that

$$\begin{pmatrix} J \\ a \end{pmatrix} x = \begin{pmatrix} 1 \\ q \end{pmatrix}, \quad x \geq 0,$$

where J is a row of 1's. Every vector has been given a new coordinate, with value 1, so extending the original space and representing it as the section of the new space where this coordinate is 1. Now by Theorem II either such x exists or there exist s, u such that

$$(s \ u) \begin{pmatrix} J \\ a \end{pmatrix} \leq 0, \quad (s \ u) \begin{pmatrix} 1 \\ q \end{pmatrix} > 0;$$

that is,

$$sJ + ua \leq 0, \ s + uq > 0,$$

which implies $uq > ua_i$ for all i, as required for (I-b).

We can also proceed another way. A restatement of (I-a) is that

$$(a - qJ)x = 0 \quad \text{for some } x \geq 0,$$

By Theorem II, the denial of this is equivalent to

$$u(a - qJ) < 0 \quad \text{for some } u,$$

and hence to (I-b).

By writing (II-a) in the form

$$ax \leq q, \ -ax \leq -q, \ -x \leq 0,$$

and applying Theorem 3.1.II, it is immediate that Theorem II follows from Theorem 3.1.II. Also, Theorem II follows from Theorem 3.1.I simply as a case of it where $q = 0$, $t = 0$. These theorems, together with the LP Duality Theorem, are deducible from each other. But the one that has the best direct proof is the present Theorem II. A way of understanding its method is more or less represented by the geometrical argument given here for Theorem I.

There is a clear geometrical picture of the theorem, even if not so for the proof. Since $ax = \Sigma a_i x_i$, the set $A = [ax : x \geq 0]$ is the set of non-negative combinations of the columns of the matrix a, and is the convex cone generated by the columns, with vertex the origin, or projecting them from the origin. The theorem is that either the vector q belongs to this cone, or it is separated from the cone by a hyperplane through its vertex, the origin. The following excellent proof derives from an account provided by D. Gale (1960b), who tells me it was suggested from writings of H. Weyl.

The two possibilities in the theorem are exclusive, since a consequence of both is that $uax = uq$ and $uax \geq 0 > uq$. This is impossible, so it remains to show that the denial of the first implies the second. The proof is by induction on n. The theorem is obviously true for $n = 1$. Assume it now for n. Introducing a further vector b, a denial of the first possibility in the theorem for the case $n + 1$ is that

$$\Sigma a_i x_i + by \neq q \quad \text{for all } x_i, y \geq 0.$$

A consequence is that

$$\Sigma a_i x_i \neq q \quad \text{for all } x_i \geq 0.$$

From this, by the inductive hypothesis, there exists u for which

$$ua_i \leq 0 \quad \text{for all} i, uq > 0.$$

If also $ub \leq 0$, there is nothing more to prove. Therefore suppose $ub > 0$, and consider

$$c_i = b(ua_i) - a_i(ub),$$
$$r = b(uq) - q(ub).$$

We have

$$\Sigma c_i x_i \neq r \quad \text{for all } x_i \geq 0;$$

for otherwise we would have

$$\Sigma \{ b(ua_i) - a_i(ub) \} x_i = b(uq) - q(ub)$$

and so, since $ub \neq 0$,

$$\Sigma a_i x_i + b\{ uq - \Sigma(ua_i)x_i \} / ub = q.$$

But with

$$ua_i \leq 0, x_i \geq 0, uq > 0, ub > 0,$$

here we would have a contradiction of our initial assumption. Therefore, by the inductive hypothesis again, for some v,

$$vc_i \leq 0 \quad \text{for all } i, vr > 0.$$

Let

$$w = (vb)u - (ub)v.$$

Then

$$\begin{aligned} wa_i &= (vb)(ua_i) - (ub)(va_i) \\ &= v\{ b(ua_i) - a_i(ub) \} \\ &= vc_i \\ &\leq 0 \end{aligned}$$

and

$$wb = 0,$$

and

$$wq = vr \geq 0.$$

Thus we have, for some w,

$$wa_i \leq 0, \ wb \leq 0, \ wq > 0.$$

QED

The correspondence with terms in the argument for Theorem I is evident. But with this theorem there are simplifications, since the distinction between cases needed for Theorem I is immaterial and the algebraical statements, were they produced for Theorem I, are simpler here.

The idea of the proof is as follows (see Figure 1). If the convex cone generated by the a_i and b excludes q then so does the convex cone generated by the a_i. Then by the inductive hypothesis there exists a half-space U which includes the a_i but excludes b and q. Then the rays joining b to the a_i and q intersect the hyperplane face of U in points c_i and r. Then the cone generated by the c_i excludes r. Hence, again by the inductive hypothesis, there exists a halfspace V which separates r from the c_i. Then the halfspace W whose face is the hyperplane which joins b to the intersection of the faces of U and V includes the a_i and b but excludes q.

This theorem, now proved, can be a basis for the proof of all theorems about systems of simultaneous linear inequalities, including all LP theorems and theorems about convex polytopes and polyhedra. It is deducible from the LP Duality Theorem, so when that theorem is proved by means of the Simplex Algorithm it will have another proof.

3.3 THEOREMS OF ALTERNATIVES

This chapter provides theorems about systems of linear inequalities needed in connections other than linear programming. Some such theorems will now be derived from those already proved.

Alternative possibilities are labelled by variables associated with their constraints which enter the constraints of their opposites. The association has a duality pattern in which $\leq$ constraints are associated with variables ≥ 0, $=$ constraints with unrestricted variables, and $\geq$ constraints with variables > 0.

THEOREM I (*proper cone*) Either

(u)   for all q, $ax = q$ for some $x \geq 0$

or

(x) $ua \leq 0$ for some $u \neq 0$

and not both.

A *proper cone* is a cone which is different from the entire space. The first possibility (u) is that the convex cone A generated by the columns of a is the entire space, in which case it is not a proper cone, and the alternative is that the cone lies in a closed halfspace U cut by a hyperplane through the origin.

The alternative of (u), by Theorem 3.2.II, is that

for some q, $ua \leq 0$, $uq > 0$ for some u.

Immediately, this is equivalent to the second case (x).

THEOREM II (*pointed cone*)   Either

(u) $ax = 0$ for some $x \geq 0$

or

(x) $ua < 0$ for some u

and not both.

The set $V = [q : q \in A, -q \in A]$ is a linear manifold, the *vertex manifold* of the cone A, and its dimension is the *vertex dimension* of A. The cone is *pointed* if its vertex dimension is 0. Assuming that no column of a is null, the first possibility (u) is that the cone is not pointed. The second case (x) is that the columns of a all lie in an open halfspace cut by a hyperplane through the origin; according to the theorem, this is a necessary and sufficient condition for the cone to be pointed.

The case (u) in the theorem is equivalent to

$$ax = 0, \ Jx = 1 \text{ for some } x \geq 0.$$

By Theorem 3.2.II, the alternative is that

$$ua + sJ \leq 0, \ u0 + s1 > 0 \quad \text{for some } u, s$$

and this is equivalent to the second case (x) in the theorem.

THEOREM III   Either

(u) $ax \leq 0$ for some $x \geq 0$

or

(x) $ua > 0$ for some $u \geq 0$

and not both.

Either a semi-positive combination of the points is in the non-negative orthant, or they are separated from the non-negative orthant by a hyperplane.

Case (x) is equivalent to the solvability of

$$ax \leq 0, \ -Jx \leq -1.$$

By Theorem 3.1.II the opposite is the solvability of

$$ua - sJ = 0, \ u0 + s(-1) < 0, \ u \geq 0, \ s \geq 0,$$

which is equivalent to (u).

THEOREM IV   Either

(u) $ax \geq 0$ for some x

or

(x) $ua = 0$ for some $u > 0$

and not both.

Either the linear space spanned by the columns of a cuts the non-negative orthant in some point other than the origin, or there is a closed halfspace which excludes the non-negative orthant except the origin, and includes the columns of a with at least some points in its interior.

Let b be a matrix whose rows are a spanning set of solutions of $ua = 0$, so that

$$ua = 0 \Leftrightarrow u = vb \text{ for some } v.$$

Then the colums of a are the same for the solutions of $by = 0$; that is,

$$by = 0 \Leftrightarrow y = ax \text{ for some } x.$$

Hence $ax \geq 0$ for some x means that $by = 0$ for some $y \geq 0$, and $ua = 0$ for some $u > 0$ means that $vb > 0$ for some v. But by Theorem II these conditions are alternatives.

THEOREM V The set of q for which the system $ax \leq q$ is consistent is closed.

The inconsistency of $ax \leq q$, by Theorem 3.1.II, is equivalent to the consistency of

$$ua = q, uq < 0, u \geq 0.$$

For any u the set of q for which $uq < 0$ is open. Therefore, a union of open sets being open, the union of these sets for all u for which $ua = 0$, $u \geq 0$ is open, so the complement is closed. QED

An independent proof is as follows. The set V of (x, y) such that $ax \leq y$ is a closed convex polyhedral cone. It is the projection from the origin of its intersection U on the unit sphere, which is compact, so U is compact. Hence its y–projection U_y is closed. Therefore the cone projecting U_y is closed. But this is the y-projection V_y of V, so V_y is closed. QED

We can use this theorem to deduce Theorem 3.2.II from Theorem 3.1.I, the more immediate opposite having been done already. The inconsistency of the system $ax = q$, $x \geq 0$ is equivalent to that of

$$(\theta a)x + 0t = q, Jx + 1t = 1, t \geq 0, x \geq 0,$$

for all $\theta \geq 0$. By Theorem 3.2.I, this is equivalent to the consistency of

$$sJ + \theta ua \leq 0, s1 + u0 \leq 0, s + uq > 0;$$

that is,

$$\theta ua \leq -sJ, s \leq 0, uq > -s.$$

If $s = 0$ we have the required conclusion immediately. Otherwise the solubility of this system is equivalent to that of

$$ua \leq rJ, uq = 1$$

for all $r > 0$. For $r \geq 0$ let

$$U_r = [u : uq = 1, ua \leq rJ]$$

so that $U_r \neq 0$ for $r > 0$. But $[r : U_r \neq 0]$ is closed, by Theorem V. It follows that $U_0 \neq 0$. QED

THEOREM VI (*LP feasibility*)   Either

(u) $ax \leq q$ for some $x \geq 0$

or

(x) $ua \geq 0,\ uq < 0$ for some $u \geq 0$

and not both.

We are able to conclude from this theorem that, if an LP problem is infeasible and the dual problem is feasible, then the dual is unbounded. Hence, a feasible LP problem is bounded if, and only if, the dual also is feasible.

The system (u) can be restated

$$ax + y = q,\ x \geq 0,\ y \geq 0.$$

Then by Theorem 3.2.II its opposite is

$$ua \geq 0,\ u \geq 0,\ uq < 0.$$

THEOREM VII (*LP Slater qualification*)   Either

(u) $ax < q$ for some $x \geq 0$

or

(x) $ua \geq 0,\ uq \leq 0$ for some $u \geq 0$

and not both.

We have the Slater constraint qualification, which is important for convex programming, now as it would apply to an LP problem, and conditions equivalent to its denial.

Case (x) can be restated

$$ua \geq 0,\ -uq \geq 0,\ u \geq 0.$$

Then by Theorem III the opposite is that

$$ax - qt < 0,\ x \geq 0,\ t \geq 0.$$

has a solution. If $t = 0$ then we have $ax < 0$, and then $ax < qt'$ for small t', so there also exists a solution with $t > 0$. If $t > 0$ then $ax' < q$ with $x' = x(1/t)$. Thus in any case $ax < q$ for some $x \geq 0$. QED

Theorem 3.2.II has been used as a basis for all other theorems proved about systems of linear inequalities. A proposition will be added now which amounts to a restatement, or an interpretation. It provides a symmetrical expression of the duality principle for convex sets, though in this case it is with a finite algebraical limitation.

For any set $A \subset \mathbf{R}^n$, the set

$$A^* = [\,u : x \in A \Rightarrow ux \leq 0\,] \subset \mathbf{R}_n$$

is a convex cone. Similarly, any $B \subset \mathbf{R}_n$ determines a convex cone $B^* \subset \mathbf{R}^n$. Evidently $C \subset C^{**}$ for any set C in either space, and also $C \subset D \Rightarrow D^* \subset C^*$. Therefore $(C^{**})^* \subset C^*$. But also, $C^* \subset (C^*)^{**}$. It follows that $C^{***} = C^*$ for any set C.

Calling C^* the *dual* of C, it appears that any set of the form $D = C^*$ for some C, or any set which is the dual of some set, is necessarily a convex cone. Moreover, it is the dual of its dual, so with its dual forms a dual pair of convex cones, or a pair where each is the dual of the other. Any convex cone which, being the dual of its dual, belongs to a dual pair can be called *regular*. We have just seen that any set of the form $D = C^*$ is a regular convex cone. There is also the general theorem, not now to be considered, that *a convex cone is regular if and only if it is closed*. The remark to be made now about Theorem 3.2.II is that it asserts any convex polytope cone, or one of the form $A = [ax : x \geq 0]$, to be regular. The dual obviously is $B = [u : ua \leq 0]$, and the dual of this is $C = [y : ua \leq 0 \Rightarrow uy \leq 0]$. Theorem 3.2.II tells that $C = A$.

3.4 POLYHEDRA AND POLYTOPES

The asymptotic cone

A convex polyhedron has the form $P = [x : ax \leq q]$. For any point x and vector y specifying a direction,

$$[x, y> = [x + yt : t \geq 0]$$

is the ray, or halfline, with vertex at x and going in the direction of y. If $[x, y> \subset P$ we have that x is a point of P and so also is every point reached from x by movement in the direction of y, making the polyhedron unbounded in that direction from x. For any x let

$$V(x) = [y : [x, y> \subset P],$$

so that this is the set of directions of rays with vertex x that lie entirely in P. This set is a convex cone, defining the asymptotic cone of P at x.

For $[x, y> \subset P$, we have

$$a(x + yt) \leq q \quad \text{for all } t \geq 0,$$

and a necessary and sufficient for this is that

$$ax \leq q, ay \leq 0.$$

Introducing

$$V = [y : ay \leq 0],$$

which is a convex cone, we have

$$x \in P, y \in V$$

as a statement of this condition, so we have

$$V(x) = V \text{ for all } x \in P.$$

The asymptotic cone $V(x)$ therefore is a constant V at all points $x \in P$. The constant V defines the *asymptotic cone* of the convex polyhedron P.

It should be remarked, even though it is not of immediate concern, that this definition and constancy property of the asymptotic cone applies not only to a convex polyhedron but equally well to any closed convex set.

We have found the following:

THEOREM I   The asymptotic cone of the convex polyhedron
$$P = [x : ax \le q]$$
is the polyhedral convex cone
$$V = [y : ay \le 0],$$
with the property that the ray $[x, y >$ with vertex at x and in the direction of y lies entirely in P if and only if $x \in P$ and $y \in V$.

For a bounded polyhedron P, V is the null cone containing the single element 0. If P has a nonempty complement then so does V. If P is itself a cone with vertex v, or with v as any point of its vertex manifold if this is not a pointed cone, then V is simply the translation $V = P - v$ of P which brings v to the origin.

The normal cone

The support function of P is
$$s(p) = \sup [px : x \in P] = \sup [px : ax \le q].$$

The condition that $s(p) > -\infty$ for some P is equivalent to the same for all p, and to $P \ne O$, and to the consistency of the system $ax \le q$. We will assume that P is proper, that is, that neither it nor its complement is nonempty. In that case we have $s(p) > -\infty$ for all p. Also $s(p) < \infty$ for some p; that is,
$$N = [p : s(p) < \infty]$$
is nonempty. For instance, one could take $p = a_{(i}$ and then $s(p) = q_i$. Also, it is assumed that P is of full dimension n, or solid, this just requiring that $ax < q$ for some x.

It was proved in section 3.1 that a feasible LP problem is bounded if and only if the dual is feasible, so now we have
$$s(p) < \infty \leftrightarrow ua = p \text{ for some } u \ge 0,$$
and hence
$$N = [ua : u \ge 0].$$

This is a convex polytope cone, the *normal cone* of P. It is the dual of the convex polyhedral cone $V = [y : ay \le 0]$ which is the asymptotic cone of P.

Polyhedral faces

The polyhedron P is described by points x where $ax \le q$; that is,
$$a_{(i} \le q_i \text{ for all } i.$$

A *face* of it is a locus where, for some k, moreover
$$a_{(k} = q_k.$$

The faces therefore are convex polyhedra lying on the boundary of P, of lower dimension.

Any face P' of P has an asymptotic cone V', and since $P' \subset P$ we have $V' \subset V$.

Now we can see that

$$P = <\cup P'> + V;$$

that is:

THEOREM II Any convex polyhedron is the sum of the convex closure of its faces and its asymptotic cone.

If P is not proper and solid there is nothing to prove, so we suppose the contrary. Because the $P' \subset P$ and P is convex, we have $\cup P' \subset P$ and then $<\cup P'> \subset P$; in other words, P contains the convex closure of the union of all its faces P'. Also $x + V \subset P$ for any $x \in P$, and hence

$$<\cup P'> + V \subset P.$$

It remains now to show that

$$P \subset \; <\cup P'> + V,$$

or that any $x \in P$ has the form $x = y + z$ where $y \in <\cup P'>$, $x \in V$.

If x is on the boundary and so in some face P', we already have that. Therefore, P being solid, consider x in the interior of P, so that $ax < q$. With P proper, so is V. Hence let z' be any point in the complement of V. Then $x' = x + z't$ is on the boundary of P for some $t > 0$, and so is in some face P'. Now consider $z'' = -z'$. If also this belongs to V then take $y = x', z = -z't$ and then we have $x = y + z$ where $y \in P$, $z \in V$ as required. Otherwise $x'' = x + z''t \in P''$ where P'' is another face. Now we have $x \in <x', x''>$, so $x \in <P' \cup P''>$ and hence $x \in <\cup P'>$, as required.

Basis theorem

The general solution of a system of equations $ax = q$ can be put in the finite form

$$x = y + \Sigma z_j t_j$$

where y is a particular solution and the z_j are a basic set of solutions of the reduced system $az = 0$, finite in number. The next theorem is a step towards a counterpart of this for a system of linear inequalities, the general solution of $ax \le q$ having the finite form

$$x = \Sigma y_i s_i + \Sigma z_j t_j \text{ where } \Sigma s_i = 1, s_i, t_j \ge 0,$$

so $x = y + z$ where y describes a convex polytope and z a convex polytope cone.

THEOREM III Any convex polyhedron P is the sum $P = Q + V$ of a convex polytope Q and a convex polyhedral cone V.

Evidently V must be the asymptotic cone.

The proof is by induction on the dimension n of the polyhedron. The theorem is obviously true for dimension 1. Suppose it true for dimensions $< n$ and let P be of dimension n.

Any face P' of P is of dimension $< n$ and so, by the inductive hypothesis, $P' = Q' + V'$ where Q' is a polytope and V' the asymptotic cone, for which $V' \subset V$ since $P' \subset P$. Now by Theorem II,

$$P = <\cup P'> + V = <\cup(Q'+V')> + V = <\cup Q'> + \Sigma V' + V.$$

But $\Sigma V' + V = V$ since all $V' \subset V$. Also the number of faces is finite, so $Q = <\cup Q'>$ is a polytope. Hence $P = Q + V$ where Q is a polytope and V a polyhedral cone. QED

COROLLARY The convex polytopes and the bounded convex polyhedra are identical.

For if a convex polyhedron is bounded then its asymptotic cone must be the null cone.

To arrive at the above-mentioned finite statement of the general solution of a system of linear inequalities, it remains to show the identity between the convex polyhedral cones and the convex polytope cones, or cones of the form $V = [x : ax \leq 0]$ and $V = [bt : t \geq 0]$. Here is an outline for a proof based on the foregoing.

If the cone is a linear manifold then the wanted result is a conclusion from elementary linear algebra. Therefore since any cone is the sum of its vertex manifold and a pointed cone, it suffices to consider a pointed cone. Any pointed polyhedral cone is the projection of a bounded polyhedron, which by the foregoing theorem is also a polytope generated by its vertices, which also generate the cone, so making it a polytope cone. QED

3.5 LP DUALITY
LP problems (M) and (W) have been linked together, and one value in doing that comes from the LP Duality Theorem, Theorem 3.4.IV, which involves them together. A defect lies in the lack of symmetry from their different forms. But this was relieved by observing that (W) can be restated in the form (M), in which form it is associated with a problem in the form (W), and this happens to be a restatement of problem (M). The unsymmetrical distinction of form is inessential to the association, which really is symmetrical, and the rule of association can be redeveloped to make this explicit.

It can be seen that the same principle associates together the problems

(M)   max $px : ax \leq q, x \geq 0,$
(W)   min $uq : ua \geq p, u \geq 0.$

The problem (M) here is already in the form of the first considered (M) when one puts the constraints as $ax \leq q$, $-1x \leq 0$. Then by the first principle it is associated with the problem

$$\text{min } uq + v0 : ua - v1 = p, u, v \geq 0.$$

But $ua - v = p, v \geq 0$ is equivalent to $ua \geq p$ so this is the present problem (M).

We call the present (M) a standard max problem and (W) a standard min. The max problem can be rewritten in the form of the min problem and vice versa, so again this is a distinction not between problems but just between how they are written. The two problems are associated with the LP tableau

$$T = \begin{pmatrix} 0 & -p \\ -q & a \end{pmatrix}.$$

When T is replaced by $T^* = -T'$ we obtain the same pair of problems except that they change places, the max problem appearing in the form of a min problem and vice versa. The relation by which any problem form has a dual, of which it is moreover the dual, is perfectly symmetrical, corresponding to the property $T^{**} = - (-T')' = T$.

There is more importance attaching to this formulation than to symmetry, together with a preservation of the LP Duality Theorem. The identification of 'support' or 'Lagrangean multiplier' solutions of one problem, dealt with in Chapters V.1 and V.2, with optimal solutions of the other problem, depends on it. Also, an implementation of the Simplex Algorithm consists of 'pivot' operations with the tableau T.

We now know how to form the dual of an LP problem by putting it in any one of four possible forms, instead of one or two as at first. One would be enough, since any problem can be put in any of the forms. But the rule can be put so as to apply instead directly to any LP problem, including the mixed form where the constraints include equations and inequalities and where some variables are restricted non-negative and others not. Consider a problem

$$(M) \quad \max p_0 x_0 + p_1 x_1 : (u_0) \ a_{00} x_0 + a_{01} x_1 \leq q_0$$
$$(u_1) \ a_{10} x_0 + a_{11} x_1 = q_1$$
$$x_0 \geq 0.$$

The n program variables x are partitioned into n_0 variables x_0 which are restricted non-negative and n_1 other variables x_1. The m constraints are associated with m variables u which serve as their labels and will be program variables for the dual problem. They are partitioned into m_0 inequalities labelled by dual variables u_0 which will be restricted non-negative in the dual problem, and m_1 equations labelled by u_1. The dual problem is

$$(W) \quad \min u_0 q_0 + u_1 q_1 : (x_0) \ u_0 a_{00} + u_1 a_{10} \geq p_0$$
$$(x_1) \ u_0 a_{01} + u_1 a_{11} \geq p_1$$
$$u_0 \geq 0.$$

This is established by putting (M) in standard form. To do that, any equation $L = R$ is replaced by two inequalities $L \leq R$, $-L \leq -R$, and an unrestricted variable X is replaced by the difference $X' - X''$ of two restricted variables $X', X'' \geq 0$. Then the dual can be formed by the rule for standard problems and it reduces to this. As with constraints in (M) and variables in

Optimal Programming

(W), the constraints in (W) are labelled by the program variables for (M), these being restricted non-negative for inequalities and not restricted for equations.

This rule for mixed problems, as concerns form, is more general than the other cases from which is was derived, since it encompasses them, but as concerns problems themselves it has no greater generality but is identical.

3.6 THE PIVOT OPERATION

Any matrix a can be taken to provide a relation $y = ax$, variables x being independent and y dependent. If $a_{rs} \neq 0$ there can be an exchange making y_s become one of the independent variables and x_s one of the dependent. If x' denotes the vector x with x_s replaced by y_r and similarly y' is y with x_s in place of y_r, we obtain a relation $y' = a'x'$, a' being the new matrix of coefficients.

The operation on the matrix a for deriving the matrix a', with a given r and s, is called the *pivot operation*, with r as the *pivot row*, s the *pivot column*, and a_{rs} the *pivot element*. As will be established, it can always be done provided that $a_{rs} \neq 0$, and the rule for carrying it out is shown by the scheme

$$\begin{pmatrix} e & f \\ g & h \end{pmatrix} \rightarrow \begin{pmatrix} e^{-1} & -e^{-1}f \\ ge^{-1} & h - ge^{-1}f \end{pmatrix}.$$

On the left-hand side we have typical elements of the original matrix a, e being the pivot element, f another element in the pivot row, g another in the pivot column and h an element not in either. On the right-hand side are corresponding elements of the new matrix a' obtained by the pivot operation.

This scheme can also be read in an extended fashion as describing a *block-pivot* operation, where the pivot e is any regular square submatrix of a instead of a single element. With the pivot block in leading position, on the left the matrix a is partitioned and on the right the resulting matrix partitioned similarly. Any combination of elementary pivot operations can be expressed as a single block-pivot operation. Conversely, any block-pivot operation can be broken down into a combination of elementary ones. Because in the result we have expressions like e^{-1} and $e^{-1}f$, this scheme is also suitable for basic computations of linear algebra, inverting a matrix, or solving linear equations, in addition to evaluating a determinant as a product of pivot elements.

The elementary relations in $y = ax$ can be stated as

$$y_r = a_{rs}x_s + \Sigma_{j \neq s} a_{rj}x_j, \tag{i}$$

$$y_i = a_{is}x_s + \Sigma_{j \neq s} a_{ij}x_j \quad (i \neq s). \tag{ii}$$

Provided $a_{rs} \neq 0$, (i) can be solved for x_s and the expression substituted in (ii). Thus, from (i),

$$\begin{aligned} x_s &= a_{rs}^{-1} y_r + \Sigma_{j \neq s} (- a_{rs}^{-1} a_{rj})x_j \\ &= a'_s y_r + \Sigma_{j \neq s} a'_{rj}x_j, \end{aligned}$$

where

$$a'_{rs} = a_{rs}^{-1}, \ a'_{rj} = -a_{rs}^{-1}a_{rj} \qquad (j \neq s).$$ (i′)

Then, substituting in (ii),

$$\begin{aligned}
y_i &= a_{is}\{a_{rs}^{-1}y_r + \Sigma_{j \neq s}(-a_{rs}^{-1}a_{rj})x_j\} + \Sigma_{j \neq s}a_{ij}x_j \\
&= a_{is}a_{rs}^{-1}y_r + \Sigma_{j \neq s}(a_{ij} - a_{is}a_{rs}^{-1}a_{rj})x_j \\
&= a'_{rs}y + \Sigma_{j \neq s}a_{i'j}x_j \qquad\qquad (i \neq r)
\end{aligned}$$

where

$$a'_{is} = a_{is}a_{rs}^{-1}, \ a_{ij} = a_{ij} - a_{is}a_{rs}^{-1}a_{rj} \ (i \neq r, j \neq s)$$ (ii′)

From (i′) and (ii′) we have the scheme stated earlier, with

$$e = a_{rs}, f = a_{rj}, g = a_{is}, h = a_{ij}.$$

Similarly, a relation $v = ua$ can be subjected to an exchange between independent and dependent variables u_r and v_s. Again, this is possible provided $a_{rs} \neq 0$. It is found that the coefficient matrix a' in the new relation $v' = u'a'$ obtained by this exchange is identical with the matrix a' found previously for the exchange between y_r and x_s. Therefore, *the pivot operation can be regarded as simultaneously producing an exchange between variables y_r and x_s in one relation and between v_s and u_r in the other*. In the context of the Simplex Algorithm, where pivot operations apply to a tableau associated with a dual pair of LP problems, the pivot operation can be looked at from the sides of both problems simultaneously. With soluble problems, when the algorithm terminates a solution of both problems is read from the final tableau.

The pivot rule can be derived more briefly in the following way, which serves at once for both the elementary and the block operation. Suppose we have relations

$$\begin{aligned}
y_0 &= a_{00}x_0 + a_{01}x_1, \\
y_1 &= a_{10}x_0 + a_{11}x_1,
\end{aligned}$$

where a_{00} is a regular square matrix, the *pivot block*, or the pivot element in the elementary case. The pivot operation will exchange the roles of the x_0 and y_0 variables as dependent and independent. From the pivot-row relations,

$$x_0 = a_{00}^{-1}y_0 - a_{00}^{-1}a_{01}x_1,$$

and by substitution of this in the other,

$$y_1 = a_{10}a_{00}^{-1}y_0 + (a_{11} - a_{10}a_{00}^{-1}a_{01})x_1.$$

Thus

$$\begin{aligned}
x_0 &= b_{00}y_0 + b_{01}x_1, \\
y_1 &= b_{10}y_0 + b_{11}x_1,
\end{aligned}$$

where

$$\begin{aligned}
b_{00} &= a_{00}^{-1}, & b_{01} &= -a_{00}^{-1}a_{01}, \\
b_{10} &= aa_{00}^{-1}, & b_1 &= a_{11} - a_{10}a_{00}^{-1}a_{01}.
\end{aligned}$$

3.7   THE SIMPLEX ALGORITHM

A standard LP problem

$$(M) \qquad\qquad \max px : ax \le q, x \ge 0$$

can be restated

$$\max px + 0y : ax + y = q, x \ge 0, y \ge 0.$$

The n original variables x are joined by the m 'slack' variables associated with the constraints, so now there are $m+n$ variables. By the constraints they are all restricted to be non-negative. Relations between them are stated by

$$-r = 0 - px\,(= \min) \qquad\qquad\qquad (\mathrm{i})$$
$$-y = -q + ax\,(\le 0).$$

The objective function r is included in the place it has in the scheme though discussion does not concern it now, and unlike others subsequently it remains dependent or 'nonbasic'. Here the relations are shown solved for the y variables in terms of the x; they are in a form where the y variables are determined by the x variables, or the x variables are *basic* and they are *nonbasic*. But by pivot operations the relations become solved differently. They are put in a form where some other n variables from the $m + n$ are the basic variables, and the remaining m variables, whose values are uniquely determined by their values, are the nonbasic variables.

Any values for the variables which satisfy these relations constitute a solution. A *feasible solution* is one where the values are moreover all non-negative. A *basic solution* is one where the values for a set of n basic variables are zero. The values of the remaining m nonbasic variables are then uniquely determined, and if these are non-negative we have a *basic feasible solution*.

The relations as given initially by (1) provide the initial basic solution $x = 0$, $y = q$. Should it happen that $q \ge 0$, as is often the case with problems originating from economics, then this initial basic solution is also a feasible solution, and so a basic feasible solution. The objective function is already expressed in terms of the initial basic variables x, and its value is 0.

Pivot operations can make some other n variables basic, and express both the other nonbasic variables and the objective function in terms of them. When those basic variables are set to zero we immediately have the values of both the nonbasic variables and the objective function. The objective function, or variable r, is included as a nonbasic variable, and it remains nonbasic because pivot elements are never in the first row of the tableau. Also they are never taken in the first column.

The Simplex Algorithm starts with the relations betweeen the variables as initially given, and with the initial basic solution so provided. Pivot operations, exchanging nonbasic variables, then give movements from one base to a neighbouring one in succession, guided by a criterion.

If the initial basic solution is not feasible, an initial part of the algorithm concerns going from it to a basic feasible solution, if there is one, or finding that the problem is infeasible, in which case the algorithm terminates. At any point where the algorithm already has a basic feasible solution, one possiblity is to find that the problem is unbounded, in which case the algorithm terminates. Otherwise the criterion requires movement to another basic feasible solution where the objective function does not decrease. If that is not possible, the current basic solution is also the unique optimal solution, as will be seen, and the algorithm terminates.

An issue with the Simplex Algorithm is the possiblity of cycling, or going indefinitely through a cycle of solutions where the objective function remains constant. For simplicity we put this aside by a *regularity assumption* which requires that no more than n variables can be made zero simultaneously. Since the n basic variables are zero in a basic solution this means the nonbasic variables are all nonzero. As a result, movement from one basic solution to another either increases or decreases the objective function. Then the criterion requires movements that increase the objective function, and if none is possible the optimum has been found and the algorithm terminates.

If the initial basic solution is not a feasible one, because it makes some nonbasic variables negative, the Simplex Algorithm as already stated can be applied to finding a basic feasible solution from which it can proceed further, or to finding that the problem is infeasible. Pivot operations can be chosen so as to maintain non-negativities already achieved but increase some remaining negative nonbasic variable, just as the objective function is increased at the later stage. Should a negative nonbasic variable reach its maximum and still be negative, the problem is infeasible. Otherwise, at some point a basic feasible solution will be found, and the algorithm can enter the next stage.

Though there are others, this describes one implementation of the Simplex Algorithm method. Here the primary reference is to one problem in a dual pair, which in that sense is distinguished as the primal problem, and the other as the dual. The reference could have been the other way round, and in any case when the algorithm terminates the results will be the same and the distinction spurious. Here on the dual side we have the problem

$$(W) \qquad \min uq : ua \geq p, u \geq 0,$$

which can be restated

$$\min uq + v0 : ua - v = p, u \geq 0, v \geq 0,$$

and provides the scheme

$$s = 0 - uq \ (= \max) \qquad (2)$$
$$v = -p + ua \, (\geq 0)$$

which, having the same tableau, is acted on simultaneously with the other one.

The algorithm is not only a computational device; all the theorems of linear programming are implicit in it, from considerations about the ways in which it terminates. The objective functions for primal and dual are equal at every stage, since both are given by the corner element in the tableau. Any pivot operation has an interpretation for one problem and the other simultaneously, as remarked in the last section, and the terminating optimality conditions are the same. Whenever an optimal solution is found for one problem, an optimal solution is also found for the other, and the objective functions are equal — so we have the LP Duality Theorem. The condition for termination in the infeasibility of one problem is the same as for unboundedness of the other, so, for another theorem, one problem is feasible if and only if the other is bounded. For a further instance, any problem is always found to be either infeasible or unbounded or to have an optimal solution. The case of a problem which is feasible and bounded and does not have an optimal solution therefore cannot arise, which is another LP theorem. These arguments, and also the conclusions, are associated with George B. Dantzig.

At any stage with the Simplex Algorithm there is a current LP tableau A. Either it is final by one of the criteria for termination, or a new tableau B is produced from it by a pivot operation that exchanges a basic and a nonbasic variable, so the pivot element is not in the first row or the first column. Initially $A = T$, so the routine goes

    0 let $A = T$
    1 if A is final then end
    2 pivot $A \rightarrow B$, let $A = B$
    3 goto 1

Any tableau A obtained in the process represents a basic solution. We have 0 for all the basic variables, and the negatives of the nonbasic variables are given by the first column $A_{0)}$, with elements A_{io}, so this is a basic feasible solution if $A_{io} \leq 0$ for all $i \neq 0$. The regularity assumption which excludes nonbasic zeros then makes $A_{io} < 0$ for all $i \neq 0$. The objective function enters like one of the nonbasic variables, even though it does not have exchanges with basic variables, so the negative of the objective function is the corner element A_{00}.

Suppose the basic solution provided by A is feasible. The question now is whether a pivot element can be found which produces a new tableau B with a basic solution which is both feasible and makes the objective function greater.

If A_{rs} is to be the pivot element, r and s being the pivot row and column, first we must have $A_{rs} \neq 0$. Then, as shown in section 3.6, for the coefficients in the new tableau B we have

$$B_{ro} = -A_{rs}^{-1} A_{ro} \qquad \qquad (\text{i})$$
$$B_{io} = A_{io} - A_{is} A_{rs}^{-1} A_{ro} \qquad \qquad (\text{ii})$$
$$= A_{io} + A_{is} B_{ro} \qquad (i \neq r).$$

and, in particular,

$$B_{oo} = A_{oo} - A_{os} A_{rs}^{-1} A_{ro}. \qquad \qquad (\text{iii})$$

Given that

$$A_{io} < 0 \text{ for all } i,$$

we want, if possible,

$$B_{io} < 0 \text{ for all } i, B_{oo} < A_{oo}.$$

Therefore from (i) we require $A_{rs} < 0$, and then from (iii), having this with $A_{ro} < 0$, we require $A_{os} < 0$.

Should it happen that $A_{oj} \geq 0$ for all $j \neq 0$, so that this last is impossible, the optimality conditions are satisfied and the algorithm terminates. Otherwise it is possible to choose a pivot column s for which $A_{os} < 0$. Now we consider our choice of the pivot row s with $A_{rs} < 0$ which moreover makes $B_{io} < 0$ for all $i \neq 0$.

By (ii), we require

$$A_{io} \leq A_{is} A_{rs}^{-1} A_{ro} \text{ for all } i \neq 0.$$

Should it be the case that $A_{is} \geq 0$ for all $i \neq 0$, no negative pivot in this column can be chosen, let alone satisfy this requirement. But it does not matter, since we have conditions showing that the problem is unbounded, and therefore the algorithm terminates. Otherwise s can be chosen making

$$A_{rs}^{-1} A_{ro} = \min \ [A_{is}^{\ -1} A_{io} : A_{is} < 0].$$

Then all the requirements are met for the next pivot operation.

3.8 BASIC PROGRAM

```
1 DATA Linear Programming
2 DATA The SIMPLEX ALGORITHM
3 '
10 ' BASICA : Hyperion & IBM-PC
11 '
19 '_____
20 CLS:KEY OFF:GOSUB 1000:KEY ON:END
21 '
99 '_____ find pivot column S, if optimum then end
100 L=OO:FOR J=1 TO N:A=A(O,J)
110 IF A<O AND L>A THEN L=A:S=J
120 NEXT:IF L=OO THEN PRINT#1,"Optimum found -":GOSUB 900:RETURN
198 '
199 '_____ find pivot row R, if unbounded then end
200 L=OO:FOR I=1 TO M
210 IF A(I,S)>O THEN Q=-A(I,O)/A(I,S):IF L>Q THEN L=Q:R=I
220 NEXT:IF L=OO THEN PRINT#1,"Problem unbounded":RETURN
230 P=A(R,S):PRINT#1,"pivot element";P;"in row";R;"column";S;CR$
298 '
299 '_____ pivot on A produces new tableau B
300 FOR I=0 TO M:FOR J=0 TO N
310 B(I,J)=A(I,J)-A(I,S)*A(R,J)/P
320 IF I=R THEN B(I,J)=A(I,J)/P
330 IF J=S THEN B(I,J)=-A(I,J)/P
340 IF I=R AND J=S THEN B(I,J)=1/P
350 NEXT J,I:SWAP D(S),C(R):' register exchange
```

```
398 '
399 '_____ B becomes A for another loop
400 GOSUB 600:FOR I=0 TO M:GOSUB 700:FOR J=0 TO N:A(I,J)=B(I,J)
410 PRINT#1,TAB(4+J*T)A(I,J);:NEXT:PRINT#1,:NEXT:PRINT#1,:GOTO
100
496 '
497 '_____ sbrs
499 '_____ identify variables, basic or nonbasic
500 IF FB THEN V=D(J) ELSE V=C(I)
510 IF V>N THEN V$="U":V=V-N ELSE V$="X"
520 V$=V$+MID$(STR$(V),2):RETURN
599 '_____ basic labels
600 FB=1:FOR J=1 TO N:GOSUB 500
610 PRINT#1,TAB(6+J*T)V$;:NEXT:PRINT#1,:RETURN
699 '_____ non-basic labels
700 IF I THEN GOSUB 500:PRINT#1,V$; ELSE FB=0
710 RETURN
898 '
899 '_____ print the result
900 PRINT#1,CR$,"Optimal value:";-A(0,0)
910 PRINT#1,CR$,"Optimal solution:";CR$
920 FB=0:FOR I=1 TO M:GOSUB 500:PRINT#1,,,V$;" =";
930 IF LEFT$(V$,1)="X" THEN PRINT#1,-A(I,0) ELSE PRINT#1,0
940 NEXT
950 FB=1:FOR J=1 TO N:GOSUB 500:PRINT#1,,,V$;" =";
960 IF LEFT$(V$,1)="U" THEN PRINT#1,A(0,J) ELSE PRINT#1,0
970 NEXT :RETURN
998 '
999 '_____ init
1000 DEFINT C,D,I,J,K,M,N,R,S,T
1010 READ A$,B$,T,OO,C$,M,N:DATA 14, 1E32 :' OO=INF
1020 LF$=CHR$(10):FF$=CHR$(12):CR$=CHR$(13)
1090 PRINT FF$,A$;" : ";B$;CR$
1099 '
1100 INPUT"screen, printer or disk (s/p/d)";O$
1110 IF O$="p" THEN O$="LPT1:" ELSE IF O$="d" THEN O$="LPF" ELSE
O$="SCRN:"
1120 CLS:OPEN O$ FOR OUTPUT AS #1
1199 '
1200 PRINT#1,,A$;" : ";B$;CR$;CR$;C$;CR$
1210 DIM A(M,N),B(M,N),C(M),D(N)
1220 FOR I=0 TO M:FOR J=0 TO N:READ B(I,J):NEXT J,I
1230 FOR J=1 TO N:D(J)=J:NEXT:' basic are 1 to n
1240 FOR I=1 TO M:C(I)=N+I:NEXT:GOTO 400:' nonbasic are N+1 to
N+M
1998 '
1999 '_____ LP Problem
2000 DATA "Dorfman, Samuelson & Solow    p. 86 ",   3,  4:' = M, N
2100 DATA     0,        -60,      -60,     -90,     -90
2110 DATA     -1500,    100,      100,     100,     100
2120 DATA     -100,     7,        5,       3,       2
2130 DATA     -100,     3,        5,       10,      15
```

Linear Programming : The SIMPLEX ALGORITHM

Dorfman, Samuelson & Solow   p. 86

	X1	X2	X3	X4
0	-60	-60	-90	-90
U1 -1500	100	100	100	100
U2 -100	7	5	3	2
U3 -100	3	5	10	15

pivot element 10 in row 3 column 3

	X1	X2	U3	X4
-900	-33	-15	9	45
U1 -500	70	50	-10	-50
U2 -70	6.1	3.5	-.3	-2.5
X3 -10	.3	.5	.1	1.5

pivot element 70 in row 1 column 1

	U1	X2	U3	X4
-1135.7				
14	.4714286	8.571428	4.285714	21.42857
X1 -7.142857	1.428571E-02	.7142858	-.1428572	-.7142858
U2 -26.42857	-8.714286E02	-.8571429	.5714286	1.857143
X3 -7.857143	-4.285715E03	.2857143	.1428572	1.714286

Optimum found -

  Optimal value: 1135.714

  Optimal solution:

                          X1 = 7.142857
                          U2 = 0
                          X3 = 7.857143
                          U1 = .4714286
                          X2 = 0
                          U3 = 4.285714
                          X4 = 0

V.4

Minimum Paths

Getting from one point to another at a minimum of some cost, possibly just distance, or time, is a problem that arises in many contexts. It could be a traveller on a journey, or a switching system making a connection, or flows in a network, or still other situations less obvious. The minimum path problem is of interest both in itself and as a type of optimization question that has many applications. But that alone is not the reason for its inclusion here. The need comes instead from its connections with problems in economics that appear to have nothing at all to do with minimum paths—with demand analysis and the theory of price indices. Though these subjects have to do with optimal choice, their connection with the minimum path problem resides in the algebra that arises when matters pertaining to them are taken to have reference to a finite scheme of demand data as dealt with in Parts II and III. There had been no notice of that connection originally (c. 1960); and only later, in communications with Jack Edmunds (1973) at the University of Waterloo, did it appear that accidentally something had been done about minimum paths. Features in the now familiar minimum path theory had been present already in that other context, wherein they bore a different interpretation and had some further relevant elaboration. In the demand and index number applications there is no explicit dealing with minimum paths, and it occurs only from the accident of an identity between the mathematics involved on both sides. In this chapter the minimum path problem is dealt with directly, and the subject is pursued for its own interest as well as for the applications found other chapters.

The problem is illustrated, and fully described, by an electric car travelling in a mountainous area which discharges batteries going uphill and charges them going down. (The example of a diesel engine and a flywheel for recapturing energy when breaking would serve also—as with buses in Sweden.) From any point to another attainable from it on some path there is a cost, positive or negative and depending on the path. The problem is to find the path on which the cost, in one case electricity, is a minimum; rather, it is to find all minimum paths, between all points, and the costs associated with them. Obviously, if the cost going round any cycle is negative, by describing the cycle repeatedly, we have an infinite supply of free energy, and a *perpetuum mobile*. In that case the cost of going anywhere can be made an indefinitely large profit, and there is no such thing as a minimum path. For minimum paths to exist, a non-negative cost on any cycle is necessary, and also sufficient.

For the given data in the problem there is a matrix a where the element a_{rs} is a cost associated with any known path from r to s. It would be enough to enter data just for the basic paths which are the immediate or direct connections, and to put ∞ elsewhere. In computations ∞ is just any suitably large number exceeding any path cost that will arise. In the end, when minimum path costs have all been found, any remaining ∞ will signify a point is unattainable from another at any cost.

A main question concerns the efficient means for determining the *minimum cost matrix b* from the original data matrix a, and in addition for being able to construct the series of nodes that makes the minimum path from any point to any other. As a method for the latter, following an idea of T. C. Hu (1969)—which exploits an essential element of the original Ford and Fulkerson (1982) method—in the course of computations we construct the connection matrix c which determines $k = c_{ij}$ as the first node encountered in going from i on the minimum path that leads to j. Starting in the same way with k one can determine the next node $l = c_{kj}$ from there and so forth, so forming the complete series leading to j.

The element b_{rs} of the derived matrix b is the minimum cost for going from r to s, and with this we wish also to determine the path, for which the costs associated with its direct segments add up to the minimum total cost. The computation of the *derived matrix b*, and at the same time the *connection matrix c*, is accomplished by means of the Power Algorithm, by which the original matrix a is raised to successive powers in a sense belonging to a modified arithmetic where *multiplication means addition and addition means taking the minimum*. This terminates as soon as a power is repeated by its successor, and the last power obtained is then b. With n nodes, or locations, so that the matrix is $n \times n$, the *termination must happen before the nth power* if at all; otherwise the series of powers is unending and the elements tend to $-\infty$. A record kept in the course of the algorithm about where to go next from any point in going towards another, provides the connection matrix c for the problem which allows construction of the series of nodes that make up any minimum path.

A program in BASIC for the Power Algorithm is given at the end of the chapter. This also computes the series of nodes in any wanted minimum path. It is illustrated by the problem of getting around in Berkeley in minimum time, taken from Bellman, Cooke and Lockett (1970, p. 86). Before that, we have a program for the original algorithm of Ford and Fulkerson (1962) for finding all minimum paths leading to a single node (and more efficient for just that purpose), stated in a way that leads directly to all features of the later algorithm.

The starting point for the demand and index number applications is with the system of inequalities

(a) $$a_{rs} \geq x_s - x_s$$

which have an association with the minimum path problem, in this case arrived at afterwards, although for those concerned primarily with minimum paths it went more the other way round. These inequalities have an importance for demand analysis which is shown in Part II, and in the multiplicative form $a_{rs} \geq x_s / x_r$ also for price indices, as appears in Part III. The condition for the existence of solutions of the system (a) is simply the cyclical non-negativity that occurs in the minimum path problem and gives the existence of the derived, or 'minimum cost', coefficients b_{rs}. Then with these we have the derived system

(b) $$b_{rs} \geq x_s - x_s,$$

which has exactly the same solutions as (a) but the coefficients of which satisfy the triangle inequality

$$b_{rs} + b_{st} \geq b_{rt}.$$

The equality holds just when s lies on a minimum path from r to t.

Because of the triangle inequality, when the derived system (b) exists and has been constructed, special solutions for system (b), and so identically for the original system (a), are immediately available and, for any k, are given by

$$x_i = b_{ki}, \text{ or } x_i = -b_{ik}.$$

Fiedler and Ptak (1967) call any solution of the inequalities (a) a *subpotential*, and we also call it a *scale* for the system. With 'potential' levels determined from any solution, the cost of going directly from r to s is at least the gain in potential. We can say that a subpotential is *exact*, or critical, in going from r to s if the equality holds. A minimum path is characterized by the existence of a subpotential which is exact along it. Related to that, and obtained with an immediate proof, we have the linear programming formula

$$b_{ij} = \min [\, x_j - x_i : a_{rs} \geq x_s - x_s \text{ all } r, s \,],$$

which expresses a minimum cost as a minimum subpotential difference, for all subpotentials of the system. Jack Edmunds (1973) brought this formula to attention and proved it by flow argument, using a flow-decomposition theorem. Together with my own, which is completely different, this proof is included here, with related theory about flows and transportation networks.

Systems which have the triangle inequality are characterized by the *extension property* of solutions, by which any solution for a subset of nodes can be extended to a solution for the complete set. Hence solutions can be found step by step, starting from two and bringing in a further node each time. Another such characterization is by the idempotence of the coefficient matrix with the modified arithmetic used in the Power Algorithm.

4.1 CONNECTION COSTS

Consider a network with n nodes, indexed by the numbers 1 to n, and values $a_{rs} > -\infty$ associated with the directed edges (r, s), forming a matrix a. These values are interpreted as costs in going from one node r to another s, and it is taken that $a_{rr} = 0$. A value $a_{rs} = \infty$ signifies that there is no direct connection, or at least no as-yet-noted connection, from r to s. However, any chain of connections (r, i), (i, j), $\ldots$, (k, s) makes a path $r, i, j, \ldots, k$, s that establishes a connection from r to s, and the associated cost is

$$a_{rij\ldots ks} = a_{ri} + a_{ij} + \ldots + a_{ks}.$$

There are many paths, and one which has minimum cost can be chosen, should there be one. If there are no paths with a finite cost, as would be shown by this minimum being infinite, then s is inaccessible from r. With a connected network every node is accessible from any other, on some path with a finite cost. A special case is where $a_{rs} < \infty$ for all r, s. This case alone is important for applications in other chapters, though we do not require it in this one.

A minimum path is one which, among all paths with the same end-points, has minimum cost. Evidently, all segments of a minimum path must themselves be minimum paths. The existence of minimum paths will be considered now.

If one path ends where another begins, the two join together to make another path, from where the one begins to where the other ends and going through the point where they join, with a cost which is the sum of their costs,

$$a_{r\ldots s} + a_{s\ldots t} = a_{r\ldots s\ldots t}.$$

A cycle, or loop, is a path that ends where it begins. It can be described equally well starting at any point of it and ending again at that point, the cost being the same in each case. Thus $r, i, j, \ldots, k, r$ is a cycle and the cost of describing it once is

$$a_{rij\ldots kr} = a_{ij\ldots kri} = \ldots = a_{krij\ldots k}.$$

Given any cycle, and its cost, a new cycle is produced when it is described repeatedly m times, starting from any one of its points and ending at the same point, this cycle having m times the cost of the original. Therefore if any cycle has a negative cost and is described m times, as $m \to \infty$ we have a series of cycles where the cost $\to -\infty$.

A cycle on any node in a path can be added to the path, to give a new path with the same extremities. If the path cost is finite and the cycle cost is negative then the new path will have a lower cost. Therefore, given any path with a finite cost, if there is a negative cycle on any of its nodes it cannot be a minimum path, and by repeating the cycle the cost approaches $-\infty$, so no minimum path exists which has the same extremities. Consequently

> THEOREM There can be no minimum path from a point to another which is accessible from it through some point on which there is a negative cycle.

Any points that lie together on some negative cycle are such a case. In the case of a connected network, where every point is accessible from any other, at a finite cost, we have that the absence of negative cycles is necessary for any minimum paths to exist at all. Should the existence of any negative cycle be established, it would be possible to go from any point to any other with an arbitrarily large profit, by going *via* a point of the cycle and winding round the cycle enough times before going on to the destination.

COROLLARY No minimum paths exist in a connected network that has a negative cycle.

4.2 PERPETUUM MOBILE IMPOSSIBLE

A simple path is one that contains no repeated elements. The segment of a path between two occurrences of the same elements represents a loop in the path, so freedom from loops is the same condition. Cancelling a loop in a path leaves a path with the same extremities but the cost has been reduced by the cost of the loop, or of the cycle of elements it describes. Thus,

$$a_{ri\ldots tu\ldots tj\ldots s} = a_{ri\ldots tj\ldots s} + a_{tu\ldots t}.$$

Therefore if the cost on the cycle is non-negative, the cost of the path is not increased by the cancellation. Consequently, if the path were a minimum path it would remain one. By repeated cancellation of loops, a path with the same extremities as the original will finally be obtained which is free of loops, or simple. It follows that minimum paths, if they exist, can be found among just the simple paths, provided the costs on cycles are non-negative. But the number of simple paths is finite, so minimum simple paths always exist, from any point to any other. With cyclical non-negativity the costs of these are lower bounds for the costs of all paths with the same extremities; in other words, they are minimum paths. Thus we have:

THEOREM I Cyclical non-negativity implies the existence of a minimum path from any point to any other, and that it can be chosen simple.

Evidently, if the costs of cycles of more than one element are all positive, a minimum path not only can be but must be simple. For in this case the cancellation of a loop in a path would reduce the cost, so the presence of a loop in a minimum path is impossible.

In addition to the condition

(*Cyclical non-negativity*)
$$a_{ri} + a_{ij} + \ldots + a_{kr} \geq 0, \qquad \text{for all } r, i, j, \ldots, k$$

we can also consider

(*Simple cyclical non-negativity*)
$$a_{ri} + a_{ij} + \ldots + a_{kr} \geq 0 \qquad \text{for all distinct } r, i, j, \ldots, k.$$

From immediate form, the first is not a finite condition, and it implies the second. The second is finite, since the number of series of distinct elements taken from 1 to n is

$$\Sigma_1^n n(n-1)\ldots(n-k+1),$$

which is finite. Rather, the condition applies to cyclic series of distinct elements and the number of these is less, and is given by

$$\Sigma_1^n \binom{n}{1}(k-1)! = \Sigma_1^n (n-k+1)\ldots n/k.$$

Fortunately, the second condition, which is finitely testable, also implies the first, so the two conditions are equivalent and the first has a finite test after all; for any cycle is resolvable into a combination of simple cycles. Therefore the cost on any cycle is a sum of costs on simple cycles, so if these are non-negative then so is their sum. We now have:

THEOREM II Cyclical non-negativity is equivalent to simple cyclical non-negativity and is necessary and sufficient for the existence of a minimum path from any point to any other.

As understood, a minimum path can still have an infinite cost attached to it, signifying that the end is inaccessible from the beginning by any path.

4.3   THE TRIANGLE INEQUALITY
The cyclical non-negativity condition is stated by

$$a_{ri\ldots r} \geq 0 \text{ for all } r, i, \ldots$$

and since $a_{rr} = 0$ it is equivalent to

$$\min_{i\ldots} a_{ri\ldots r} = 0 \text{ for all } r.$$

Provided this condition holds, the minimum paths all exist, and from the matrix a of direct path costs it is possible to derive the matrix b of minimum costs:

$$b_{rs} = \min_{i\ldots} a_{ri\ldots s},$$

where $-\infty < b_{rs} \leq \infty$ and, from the remark just made,

$$b_{rr} = 0 \text{ for all } r.$$

As seen in the last section, whenever they exist, minimum paths can always be found among the simple paths, and so the minimization here can be over $i, \ldots$ distinct from each other and from r, s and so made finite. Because the direct path, with cost a_{rs}, is one possible path from r to s, we have

$$b_{rs} \leq a_{rs} \text{ for all } r, s.$$

Since

$$a_{ri\ldots tj\ldots s} = a_{ri\ldots t} + a_{tj\ldots s},$$

we have

$$
\begin{aligned}
b_{rs} &= \min_t \min_{i \ldots j \ldots}\; a_{ri \ldots tj \ldots s} \\
&\le \min_{i \ldots j \ldots}\; (a_{ri \ldots t} + a_{tj \ldots s}) \\
&= b_{rt} + b_{ts}
\end{aligned}
$$

and hence:

($The\ triangle\ inequality$)

$$
b_{rt} + b_{ts} \ge b_{rs} \text{ for all } r,\, s,\, t.
$$

An equivalent statement is that

$$
b_{ri \ldots s} \ge b_{rs},
$$

from which it follows that

$$
\min{}_{i \ldots}\; b_{ri \ldots s} = b_{rs}.
$$

Thus, when the process by which b is derived from a is applied to b, the result is again b. This reproduction is a test of the triangle inequality, and had the inequality been a property of a we would have had $b = a$. The triangle inequality on any matrix assures the cyclical non-negativity required for the existence of the derived matrix, and makes it the same as the original.

> THEOREM I Cyclical non-negativity is necessary and sufficient for the existence of the derived matrix of minimum path costs, and when this exists it always satisfies the triangle inequality. If the original matrix satisfies the triangle inequality then the derived matrix exists and is identical with it.

The triangle equality

$$
b_{rt} + b_{ts} = b_{rt}
$$

is the condition for t to be on some minimum path going from r to s. Similarly,

$$
b_{ri \ldots s} = b_{rs}
$$

is the condition for $i, \ldots$ to be a series of nodes lying on some minimum path from r to s, or to be a route connecting r to s.

4.4   ROUTES
A condition U on any series of nodes is defined by

$$
U(r, i, \ldots, s) \equiv a_{ri \ldots s} = b_{rs}.
$$

This is just the condition for the series to be a minimum path. Successors in a minimum path have the relation V given by

$$
rVs \equiv a_{rs} = b_{rs},
$$

so we have

$$
rVs \Leftrightarrow U(r,s).
$$

Also,

$$U(r, i, \ldots, s) \Rightarrow rViV \ldots Vs,$$

that is, any U-series is a V-chain, but not conversely. We can define a condition W by

$$W(r, i, \ldots, s) \equiv b_{ri \ldots s} = b_{rs}.$$

It means that the series is a subseries of some U-series, so the elements lie in order on some minimum path, such a series being called a *route*. Any U-series is a W-series and any subseries of a W-series is a W-series. Not every V-chain is a U-series, but we have the following

THEOREM I A V-chain is a U-series if and only if it is a W-series.

While a route, or W-series, shows only some nodes encountered in some minimum path, or U-series, with costs in traversing from one to the other given by the derived matrix b, a minimum path, or U-series, shows all nodes, with costs given by the original matrix a. For a route to be a minimum path, it is required that successive nodes be a direct connection, with costs given by the original matrix a, beside being efficient so that the costs are also given by b; in other words, successive nodes have the relation V.

Also, we have:

THEOREM II If every subseries of three terms of a series is a W-series, then so is the series.

The proof is by induction on the number m of terms. The case $m = 3$ is verified. Suppose the theorem to be true for m terms and let $r, \ldots, s, t$ be a series of $m + 1$ terms that satisfies the hypothesis in the theorem. Then $r, \ldots, s$ is a series of m terms that does so also, and hence, by the inductive hypothesis, we have

$$b_{r \ldots s} = b_{rs}. \tag{i}$$

By assumption concerning any subseries of three terms,

$$b_{rst} = b_{rt}, \tag{ii}$$

so now we have

$$
\begin{aligned}
b_{r \ldots st} &= b_{r \ldots s} + b_{st} && \text{by def.} \\
&= b_{rs} + b_{st} && \text{by (i)} \\
&= b_{rst} && \text{by def.} \\
&= b_{rt} && \text{by (ii).}
\end{aligned}
$$

and hence $b_{r \ldots st} = b_{rt}$. QED

Any series of nodes being a totally ordered subset $J \subset I$ of the set I of all nodes, it is described by a binary relation $T \subset J \times J$ which is a total order, transitive, simple, and complete. That is,

$$iTjTk \Rightarrow iTk, \quad iTj \wedge jTi \Rightarrow i = j$$

and

$$i, j \in J \Rightarrow iTj \lor jTi.$$

Therefore (J, T) can specify a series of nodes, where it is understood that $J \subset I$ and $T \subset J \times J$, and that T is such a relation.

THEOREM III For any series of nodes (J, T), a necessary and sufficient condition for it to be a route is that there exist numbers x_i ($i \in J$) such that

$$iTj \Rightarrow b_{ij} = x_j - x_i.$$

Then for any such numbers,

$$i, j \in J \Rightarrow b_{ij} \geq x_j - x_i.$$

The condition is sufficient. For if it holds then

$$iTjTk \Rightarrow b_{ij} = x_j - x_i, \ b_{jk} = x_k - x_j.$$

Also, since T is transitive,

$$iTjTk \Rightarrow iTk \Rightarrow b_{ik} = x_k - x_i.$$

Hence we have

$$iTjTk \Rightarrow b_{ij} + b_{jk} = b_{ik},$$

and from this, by Theorem I, the required conclusion follows.

The condition is also necessary. Let o be the first element in the series, so that

$$o \in J, i \in J \Rightarrow oTi.$$

Let $x_i = b_{oi}$ ($i \in J$), so that $x_o = 0$. Then, on the assumption that the series is a route, so that any subseries is also, we have

$$
\begin{aligned}
iTj &\Rightarrow oTiTj \\
&\Rightarrow b_{oi} + b_{ij} = b_{oj} \\
&\Rightarrow b_{ij} = x_j - x_i,
\end{aligned}
$$

showing the sufficiency.

Regarding the last remark, given such numbers, since T is complete for any i, j we have iTj, in which case $b_{ij} = x_j - x_i$, or jTi, in which case $b_{ji} = x_i - x_j$. But we have $b_{ij} + b_{ji} \geq 0$ for all i, j, so in either case we have $b_{ij} \geq x_j - x_i$. QED

Associated with any finite order T is the successor relation S, its intransitive base, or the intransitive subrelation of which it is the transitive closure.

THEOREM IV For any series of nodes formed by a set J with successor relation S, a necessary and sufficient condition that it be a minimum path is that, for some numbers x_i ($i \in J$),

$$i, j \in J \Rightarrow b_{ij} \geq x_j - x_i, \tag{i}$$
$$iSj \Rightarrow a_{ij} = x_j - x_i. \tag{ii}$$

If we have a minimum path, then $iSj \Rightarrow a_{ij} = b_{ij}$, so the necessity follows from Theorem III. To consider the sufficiency, suppose such numbers exist. Because $a_{ij} \geq b_{ij}$, from (i) for any $r, i, j, \ldots, k, s \in J$, we have

$$a_{ri} \geq x_i - x_r, \ a_{ij} \geq x_j - x_i, \ \ldots, \ a_{ks} \geq x_s - x_k,$$

so by addition

$$a_{r \ldots s} \geq x_s - x_r,$$

from which it follows that

$$a_{r \ldots s} \geq b_{rs} \geq x_s - x_r. \tag{iii}$$

Let T be the transitive closure of S, so rTs means that, for some $i, j, \ldots, k \in J$, $rSiSjS \ldots kSs$ and so, by (ii),

$$a_{ri} = x_i - x_r, \ a_{ij} = x_j - x_i, \ \ldots, \ a_{ks} = x_s - x_k,$$

so by addition

$$a_{r \ldots s} = x_s - x_r.$$

Hence, with (iii), we have

$$rTs \Rightarrow a_{r \ldots s} = b_{rs} = x_s - x_r,$$

with the consequences

$$rSs \Rightarrow a_{rs} = b_{rs},$$
$$rTs \Rightarrow b_{rs} = x_s - x_r.$$

The required conclusion now follows from Theorems I and III.

4.5 SCALES

Numbers x_i ($i \in I$) attached to the nodes such that

$$\text{(a)} \qquad a_{ij} \geq x_j - x_i \ (i, j \in I)$$

define a *scale x* for the system with cost matrix a. It represents the cost of going from one node to the other as being at least the scale difference. Fiedler and Ptak (1967) use the term *subpotential* instead of scale. In mechanics, potential difference determines the work done in movement from one point to the other, and the sense here is that the cost should be at least the potential difference, or work required.

THEOREM I If x is a scale, then, for any path
$$a_{rij \ldots ks} \geq x_s - x_r.$$

That is, the cost on any path is at least the scale difference of the end points. For we have

$$a_{ri} \geq x_i - x_r, \ a_{ij} \geq x_j - x_i, \ \ldots, \ a_{ks} \geq x_s - x_k,$$

so by addition we have the result.

COROLLARY The existence of a scale implies cyclical non-negativity.

For if $r = s$ then $a_{ri \ldots r} \geq x_r - x_r = 0$, so the cost on any cycle is non-negative.

THEOREM II If a scale exists, then the derived system exists.

For by Theorem 4.2.II, or Theorem 4.3.I, cyclical non-negativity implies the existence of the derived system, and from this together with Theorem I's Corollary, the theorem follows.

THEOREM III If the derived system exists, then the scales for the two systems are identical.

By Theorem I, if x is any scale for the original system, that is, any solution of the system of inequalities (a), then we have

$$\min\,_{ij\ldots k}\,a_{rij\ldots ks} \geq x_s - x_r\,,$$

and since

$$b_{rs} = \min_{ij\ldots k} a_{rij\ldots ks}\,,$$

we have that x is a solution of the system

(b) $\qquad\qquad\qquad b_{ij} \geq x_j - x_i\ (i, j \in I),$

so x is also a scale for the derived system. But $a_{ij} \geq b_{ij}$ for all i, j, so any solution of (b) is also a solution of (a). Thus the solutions of the two systems (a) and (b) are identical. QED

THEOREM IV The derived system, when it exists, always has a scale.

For, by Theorem 4.3.I, the derived system, when it exists, always satisfies the triangle inequality

$$b_{rs} + b_{st} \geq b_{rt}\,.$$

Therefore, for any k, taking

$$x_i = b_{ki}\ \text{for all}\ i,$$

or, alternatively,

$$x_i = -b_{ik}\ \text{for all}\ i,$$

we have a solution x of (b). We can call these special scales the *basic scales*, there being two associated with each node, and can distinguish the first as the forward basic scale, associated with node k, and the second as the backward basic scale. We have $x_k = 0$ in each case.

THEOREM V Cyclical non-negativity implies the existence of a scale.

For it implies the existence of the derived system, by Theorem 4.3.I. The derived system, when it exists, always has a scale, by Theorem IV. Morover, any scale of the derived system must be a scale also for the original, by Theorem 4.3.I. Therefore cyclical non-negativity implies the existence of a scale for the original. QED

From the foregoing we have the following:

THEOREM VI For any system, cyclical non-negativity is necessary and sufficient for the existence of a scale, and for the existence of the derived system, and then the scales for the two systems are identical.

Associated with any system (a), having n nodes, is the set $P(a) \subset \mathbf{R}^n$ of its scales, or subpotentials, which is the convex polyhedron given by

$$P(a) = [x : a_{ij} \geq x_j - x_i].$$

By Theorem VI, cyclical non-negativity is necessary and sufficient for this to be nonempty; then the derived system (b) exists, and $P(a) = P(b)$. In that case, without ambiguity, P can denote both $P(a)$ and $P(b)$.

With $I \in \mathbf{R}^n$ as the vector with all elements 1, E the line through this described by points It ($t \in \mathbf{R}$), and

$$x + E = [x + y : y \in E]$$

the parallel translation of this line through any point x, we have

$$x \in P \Rightarrow x + E \subset P.$$

In other words, if any point x belongs to P, then so does the entire line through x parallel to E. This shows that *the set P is a prism, whose generators are lines parallel to E*.

A right-section of the prism P is its section by any hyperplane perpendicular to its generators, such a hyperplane being any locus on which $x_i = $ constant. The prism is recoverable from any right-section by taking the union of all lines through its points parallel to E. In this way the prism is completely described by any right-section, in particular by the one given by

$$Q = [x : x \in P, \ \Sigma x_i = 0].$$

Because P is a convex polyhedron, so is the section Q. The right sections, since they are translations of each other, are either all bounded or all unbounded. Now it will be seen that Q is bounded, and hence, by Theorem 3.4.III, Corollary, it must be a convex polytope. Thus, from

$$a_{ij} \geq x_j - x_i, \ \Sigma x_i = 0,$$

it follows that

$$\Sigma_i a_{ij} \geq nx_j, \ \Sigma_j a_{ij} \geq -nx_i,$$

and hence that, for all j,

$$(\Sigma_i a_{ij}) / n \geq x_j \geq - (\Sigma_i a_{ji}) / n,$$

which gives the required conclusion.

Any convex polytope is expressible as the set of convex combinations, or the convex closure, of a unique and finite set of points, these being its extreme points, or vertices. Thus, when we have identified the scales for the system (a) which are the vertices of Q, we will have a finite description of all the scales. Any vertex of Q is a point of intersection of some $n - 1$ faces. Any face lies in a supporting hyperplane of P from among the hyperplanes

$a_{ij} = x_j - x_i$ which are also among the hyperplanes $b_{ij} = x_j - x_i$, and so for which $a_{ij} = b_{ij}$; that is, iVj, the relation V having been introduced in the last section. By Theorem 4.5.III, for any W-series of n nodes $r, i, j, \ldots, k, s$, the associated hyperplanes

$$b_{ri} = x_i - x_r, \; b_{ij} = x_j - x_i, \; \ldots, \; b_{ks} = x_s - x_k,$$

these all being supporting hyperplanes of P, intersect in a point x on the boundary of Q, possibly a vertex. Such a kind of idea may give some approach to dealing with vertices, but we have been unable to take it further. It seems natural to consider the basic scales, defined above in this section, as having some possible role in the question.

4.6 EXTENSION THEOREM

A system $(a : I)$, given by a set of nodes I and a matrix a, has $(A : J)$ as a subsystem if $J \subset I$ and

$$A_{ij} = a_{ij} \; (i, j \; \epsilon \; J).$$

If the given system is cyclically non-negative, then so are all its subsystems, and so all have derived systems. But the derived system $(B : J)$ of a subsystem $(A : J)$ is not generally the corresponding subsystem of the derived system; that is, we do not generally have

$$B_{ij} = b_{ij} \; (i, j \; \epsilon \; J),$$

but only

$$B_{ij} \geq b_{ij} \; (i, j \; \epsilon \; J).$$

However, if the original system satisfies the triangle inequality, then so do all the subsystems, and so they are all identical with their derived systems. In that case we do have the considered correspondence—and, according to the next theorem, in only that case:

> THEOREM I For any given system, a necessary and sufficient condition that the derived system of any subsystem be the corresponding subsystem of the derived system is that the given system satisfy the triangle inequality.

The sufficiency has been remarked, and the necessity comes from a consideration of subsystems on two and three nodes. If the triangle inequality is not satisfied, then

$$a_{rs} + a_{st} < a_{rt}$$

for some r, s, t. Then the subsystem A on r, t has $B_{rt} = a_{rt}$, but the subsystem A on r, s, t has $B_{rt} < a_{rt}$, so not both can be equal to b_{rt}, thereby showing the necessity.

Now we consider another completely characteristic, though not quite so immediate, property of systems with the triangle inequality. That is the *scale extension property*, by which every scale for a subsystem can be extended to a scale for the complete system. In other words, for any subset $J \subset I$, with complement K, and any x_i ($i \in J$) such that

$$a_{ij} \geq x_j - x_i \ (i, j \in J),$$

it is always possible to find x_i ($i \in K$) so that

$$a_{ij} \geq x_j - x_i \ (i, j \in I).$$

THEOREM II If a system satisfies the triangle inequality, then it has the scale extension property.

When it is shown that a scale for a subsystem on $m - 1$ nodes can be extended to a scale for a larger system which includes one more node, the more general extension possibility will follow by induction. It is enough to consider a system on nodes $1, \ldots, n$ and subsystems on nodes $1, \ldots, m$ for $m \leq n$. Let x_i ($i < m$) be such that

$$a_{ij} \geq x_j - x_i \ (i, j < m). \tag{i}$$

Then it is required to show the existence of an x_m so that

$$a_{ij} \geq x_j - x_i \ (i, j \leq m), \tag{ii}$$

given the triangle inequality

$$a_{ij} + a_{jk} \geq a_{ik} \text{ for all } i, j, k.$$

The triangle inequality implies that $a_{ii} \geq 0$ for all i. This together with (i) being given, (ii) is equivalent to

$$a_{im} \geq x_m - x_i \ (i < m),$$
$$a_{mj} \geq x_j - x_m \ (j < m),$$

and hence to

$$x_j - a_{mj} \leq x_m \leq x_i + a_{im} \ (i, j < m).$$

Therefore for such x_m to exist, it is necessary and sufficient that

$$x_j - a_{mj} \leq x_i + a_{im} \ (i, j < m);$$

that is, that

$$a_{im} + a_{mj} \geq x_j - x_i \ (i, j < m).$$

But from (i), together with the triangle inequality,

$$a_{im} + a_{mj} \geq a_{ij} \geq x_j - x_i \ (i, j < m),$$

so this condition is satisfied, showing the existence of the required x_m. QED

THEOREM III Any system that has a scale and also the scale extension property must satisfy the triangle inequality.

If the hypothesis applies to the system, then it must also apply to every subsystem, in particular any subsystem on three nodes, say r, s, t, and its subsystems on two nodes. Because a scale exists for the complete system, we have

$$a_{rs} + a_{sr} \geq 0.$$

So choosing any x_r, x_s for which

$$a_{rs} = x_s - x_r,$$

we then have also

$$a_{sr} \geq x_r - x_s,$$

and so a scale for the subsystem on the nodes r, s. By the extension property this can be extended to a scale for the system on r, s, t. That is, there exists t for which

$$a_{rt} \geq x_t - x_r, \ a_{ts} \geq x_s - x_t;$$

equivalently,

$$x_s - a_{ts} \leq x_t \leq x_r + a_{rt}.$$

Such x_t exists only if

$$x_s - a_{ts} \leq x_r + a_{rt},$$

that is, if

$$a_{rt} + a_{ts} \geq x_s - x_r.$$

But $a_{rs} = x_s - x_r$, so this implies that $a_{rt} + a_{ts} \geq a_{rs}$. QED

The combination of Theorems II and III gives

> THEOREM IV For any system with a scale, the scale extension property is equivalent to the triangle inequality.

It only has to be added that any system with the triangle inequality has a scale, as is shown in the argument for Theorem 4.5.IV, using Theorem 4.3.I.

4.7 THE LP FORMULA

A scale x, for a system with matrix a, is *critical* on an edge (r, s) if $a_{rs} = x_s - x_r$.

> THEOREM I Any system with the triangle inequality has a scale that is critical on any given edge.

As in the argument for Theorem 4.6.III, there exists a scale for the subsystem on the two nodes of the edge which is critical on the edge. The system has the scale extension property, by Theorem 4.6.IV, so it has a scale which is an extension of this one for the subsystem, and so is critical on the edge.

A restatement of this theorem is that if b satisfies the triangle inequality then

$$b_{rs} = \max \ [x_s - x_r : b_{ij} \geq x_j - x_i, \ i, j \in I].$$

From this we obtain:

> THEOREM II For any system with matrix a the minimum path costs, when these exist, are given by
> $$b_{rs} = \max \ [x_s - x_r : a_{ij} \geq x_j - x_i, \ i, j \in I].$$

For when the b_{rs} exist, in which case, by Theorem 4.3.I they must satisfy the triangle inequality, so that the foregoing applies, the constraints in this formula and the one before have identical solutions, by Theorem 4.5.VI; so from the first we have the second. QED

It can be noted that the LP problem on the right-hand side is in any case bounded, a_{rs} being a bound. By a theorem of Dantzig, any LP problem has an optimal solution if and only if it is both feasible and bounded. Therefore the max here exists if and only if the constraints have a solution, that is, if the system has a scale, which by Theorem 4.5.VI is just the condition for the b_{rs} all to exist. Thus the left and right-hand sides exist always together, and here, moreover, we have the equality.

This theorem has three other proofs which are of interest for their methods and interpretations. One follows in the next section and the others later. Now we make another use of the scale extension theorem, combining it instead with Theorem 4.4.IV to give another characterization of minimum paths:

THEOREM III A necessary and sufficient condition for any series of nodes to be a minimum path is that there exists a scale which is critical on all its edges.

If J is the set of nodes in the series and S the successor relation, the condition stated in the theorem is that there exists a scale x such that

$$iSj \implies a_{ij} = x_j - x_i .$$

But Theorem 4.4.IV asserts exactly that, except that the scale is for a subsystem, on the nodes J, and not of the system but the derived system b. By Theorem 4.3.I the derived system satisfies the triangle inequality and so, by Theorem 4.6.II, it has the scale extension property. Therefore this scale has an extension to the complete system b. But by Theorem 4.5.VI the two systems have the same scale, so this is also a scale for a, with the considered properties. That proves the necessity. If a has such a scale then, so does b and so does the subsystem of b on the nodes J, so providing the condition required by Theorem 4.4.IV and proving the sufficiency.

4.8   FLOW ARGUMENT

In Theorem 4.7.II the problem of determining the minimum path costs is formulated as the LP problem

$$(M) \qquad \max x_s - x_r : (u_{ij})\ x_j - x_i \le a_{ij} \text{ all } i, j.$$

It is immaterial whether or not the x_i are restricted non-negative, since they enter the constraints only through their differences; and if x_i is a solution, then so is $x_i + c$, and c can be made large enough for this to be non-negative. The dual (W) of this problem, by the rule where constraints in (M) are associated with dual variables u_{ij}, and the constraints in the dual (W) are associated with the variables x_j in (M), is given by

(W)   min $\Sigma_{ij} u_{ij} a_{ij}$: (x_k) $\Sigma_i u_{ik} - \Sigma_j u_{kj} = p_k$ for all k,

where

$$p_r = -1, \ p_s = 1, \ p_k = 0 \ (k \neq r, k \neq s).$$

Had the x_i been restricted non-negative, the constraints here would have been $\geq p_k$. But since $\Sigma_k p_k = 0$, the equalities would then be implied.

The dual variables u_{ij} can be interpreted as flows in the directed edges (i, j) of the network. Then

$$s_k = \Sigma_j u_{kj}$$

is the total flow out of node k, and

$$d_k = \Sigma_i u_{ik}$$

the flow in; so

$$D_k = d_k - s_k$$

is the net flow in, or $S_k = -D_k$ is the net flow out. The constraints state that

$$D_r = -1, \ D_s = 1, \ D_k = 0 \ (k \neq r, k \neq s).$$

In other words, node r is a source for a unit flow, s a sink for the same amount, and at all other nodes flow in equals flow out, so they are neither sources nor sinks.

With a_{ij} as the rate of cost for flows in the edge (i, j) for any i, j,

$$C = \Sigma_{ij} u_{ij} a_{ij}$$

is the total cost for the flow system represented by the u_{ij}. Then the dual problem (W) seeks the flow with minimum cost which has r as the only source and s as the only sink, and flow value unity.

We will consider feasible solutions x and u to primal and dual, and find that the corresponding feasible values are equal, and equal to b_{rs}, so they are optimal solutions, and b_{rs} is the optimal value, as is to be proved.

Let J be the set of nodes on a minimum path from r to s, and S the successor relation, so that

$$b_{rs} = \Sigma_{iSj} a_{ij}.$$

By Theorem 4.7.III, there exists a solution x to the constraints for (M) such that

$$iSj \Rightarrow a_{ij} = x_j - x_i.$$

Then

$$\Sigma_{iSj} a_{ij} = x_s - x_r,$$

and so $b_{rs} = x_s - x_r$. Thus b_{rs} is a feasible value for problem (M). When we show that this is also an feasible value for (W) it will be seen to be the optimal value for both problems.

Thus, take $u_{ij} = 1$ if iSj and $u_{ij} = 0$ otherwise. In other words, consider a unit flow along the edges of the given path and no flow elsewhere in the network. This flow system is a feasible solution for problem (W), and the corresponding feasible value is

$$C = \Sigma_{ij} u_{ij} a_{ij} = \Sigma_{iSj} a_{ij} = b_{rs},$$

so that b_{rs} is a feasible value for both problems. QED

This proof does not use the LP Duality Theorem, and its basis is instead Theorem 4.7.III. Another proof, which is to follow, uses the LP Duality Theorem together with a theorem on the decomposition of flows. Its method is to solve (W) and find the b_{rs} that is the optimal value, which then, by the Duality Theorem, must also be the optimal value for problem (M).

4.9 ELEMENTARY DECOMPOSITION

Any non-negative matrix u represents a flow system where the flow in any directed edge (i, j) of the network is given by the element u_{ij}. The net flow out of node k is

$$v_k = \Sigma_j u_{kj} - \Sigma_i u_{ik},$$

and the net flow into k is $-v_k$. The flow is from a *source* if $v_k > 0$ and to a *sink* if $v_k < 0$. If $v_k = 0$, so that the flow into k exactly equals the flow out, then node k is neither a source nor a sink, but a junction with flow value

$$w_k = \Sigma_j u_{kj} = \Sigma_i u_{ik},$$

provided this is not zero. Otherwise k has no part in the flow system u. If there are no sources or sinks then u is a *closed flow*, where every node involved is a only a junction. Because

$$\Sigma_k v_k = \Sigma_k \Sigma_j u_{kj} - \Sigma_k \Sigma_i u_{ik} = 0,$$

we have that

$$w = \Sigma_{v_k > 0} v_k = \Sigma_{-v_k > 0} -v_k$$

is both the total flow from sources and the total flow to sinks, and defines the *flow value* $w \geq 0$ of the system u. In the case of a closed flow, we have $w = 0$; equivalently, $v_k = 0$ for all k, and, again equivalently,

$$\Sigma_j u_{kj} = \Sigma_i u_{ik} \text{ for all } k.$$

A matrix is *sum-symmetric* by this last condition. Doubly stochastic matrices comprise the special case where these sums are all 1. Thus, closed flows are distinguished by the flow matrix u being sum-symmetric.

A flow where there is a unit flow on the directed edges of a simple cycle and zero flow elsewhere will be called an *elementary closed flow*. Let C denote the successor relation on a simple cycle. The characteristic matrix of this relation is also the matrix for the flow round the cycle, and is sum-symmetric. It also can be denoted C, so the elements are

$$C_{ij} = 1 \text{ if } iCj, \; C_{ij} = 0 \text{ otherwise.}$$

Such a matrix which describes a unit flow in a simple cycle can be called an *elementary cyclic matrix*. Any permutation being a product of disjoint cyclic permutations, any permuation matrix is a sum of such matrices associated with disjoint cycles. The theorem of G. D. Birkhoff on doubly stochastic matrices is that they describe the convex polytope which is the convex closure of the permutation matrices. An analogous though more elementary theorem is that *sum-symmetric matrices describe the convex polytope cone generated by non-negative combinations of the elementary cyclic matrices.*

In terms of flows, any closed flow is an non-negative combination of elementary closed flows. Thus, any closed flow u has the form

$$u = \Sigma_C \theta_C C$$

where θ is a non-negative function defined on the simple cycles C. This is the *elementary decomposition theorem for closed flows.*

The cost associated with the flow in any cycle C is

$$\Sigma_{ij} C_{ij} a_{ij} = \Sigma_{iCj} a_{ij},$$

and the cyclical non-negativity condition would make this non-negative. Therefore the cost

$$\Sigma_{ij} u_{ij} a_{ij} = \Sigma_C \theta_C \Sigma_{iCj} a_{ij},$$

associated with the closed flow u also would be non-negative. Thus, on the basis of the decomposition theorem, we have:

THEOREM I Cyclical non-negativity implies non-negativity of the cost of any closed flow.

A flow where there is a unit flow in the edges of a simple path and zero flow elsewhere will be called an elementary open flow. Such a flow has a single source and single sink, the first and last elements in the path, and flow value unity.

Let S be the successor relation on a simple path. Then the cost associated with the path, or the flow in it, is

$$\Sigma_{ij} S_{ij} a_{ij} = \Sigma_{iSj} a_{ij} \geq b_{rs},$$

where b_{rs}, assuming this exists, is the minimum path cost from the source r to the sink s. The equality is attained for some simple open flow with r, s as source and sink.

An extension of the decomposition theorem for closed flows is that *any flow with flow value unity is a sum of a convex combination of elementary open flows from sources to sinks and a closed flow.* Applying this to any flow u with a single source and sink r, s and flow value unity, since the cost associated with the closed flow is non-negative, as already remarked, the cost of u is at least b_{rs}, being at least an average of the costs on all simple paths from r to s, all of which are at least this value. But this value has been seen to be attainable, so it is the minimum cost for all flows, as stated. In other words, this is the optimal value for the LP problem (W) in section 4.8. Therefore, by the LP

Duality Theorem, it is also the optimal value for the problem (M), of which it is the dual. That proves again the formula in Theorem 4.7.II.

Consider a problem where demands d_k, or supplies $-d_k$, at the nodes k are given and it is required to find a flow u of minimum cost which is consistent with these requirements. The constraints are

$$\Sigma_i u_{ik} - \Sigma_j u_{kj} \geq d_k,$$

and for these to be feasible it is necessary that

$$\Sigma_k d_k \leq 0,$$

that is,

$$\Sigma_{d_k > 0} d_k \leq \Sigma_{-d_k > 0} -d_k,$$

so total demand must not exceed total suuply. The condition is also sufficient. If w is the flow value for any feasible flow, we must have

$$\Sigma_{d_k > 0} d_k \leq w \leq \Sigma_{-d_k > 0} -d_k.$$

Also, given any such w, the flow u with

$$u_{ij} = -d_i d_j / w \text{ if } d_i < 0 \text{ and } d_j > 0, \ u_{ij} = 0 \text{ otherwise}$$

satisfies the constraints and has flow value w.

The problem considered is stated

(W) $\qquad \min \Sigma_{ij} u_{ij} a_{ij} : \Sigma_i u_{ik} - \Sigma_j u_{kj} \geq d_k, \ u_{ij} \geq 0,$

and the dual is

(M) $\qquad \max \Sigma_k d_k x_k : x_j - x_i \leq a_{ij}.$

Subject to cyclical non-negativity, problem (M) is feasible, and then it is equivalent to the problem

(M') $\qquad \max \Sigma_k d_k x_k : x_j - x_i \leq b_{ij},$

with dual

(W') $\qquad \min \Sigma_{ij} u_{ij} b_{ij} : \Sigma_i u_{ik} - \Sigma_j u_{kj} \geq d_k, \ u_{ij} \geq 0.$

With both problems feasible, both have optimal solutions. Since (M) is equivalent to (M'), (W) is also equivalent to (W') where a has been replaced by the derived matrix b.

The scale values x_k can be regarded as prices at the nodes subject to the competitive requirement that the price difference between one node and another does not exceed the transport cost rate. The profit from return on demand reduced by cost of supply, at local prices, is $\Sigma_k d_k x_k$, and problem (M) is to determine prices that make this maximum. The dual problem (W) solves the transport problem involved in realizing this objective.

An appeal to the flow decomposition theorem shows that a problem of the form (W'') where b satisfies the triangle inequality is equivalent to the reduced problem (W'') of the same form obtained when all nodes which are not sources

or sinks are eliminated. Then the same must be true for the dual problem (M'),
which is then equivalent to a similarly reduced problem (M''). When there
is only one source r and one sink s and a unit flow, so that we have $d_r = 1$,
$d_s = 1$ and all other $d_k = 0$, the reduced problems are simply

$$(\mathrm{M}'') \qquad \max x_s - x_r : x_s - x_r \leq b_{rs},$$
$$(\mathrm{W}'') \qquad \min b_{rs} u_{rs} : u_{sr} \geq 1, \ -u_{rs} \geq -1, \ u_{ij} \geq 0,$$

with optimal value b_{rs}. This being also the optimal value for problem (M)
with the special d_k, we have Theorem 4.7.II again. But generally the problem (W'') has the form of the Hitchcock problem, or the standard transport
problem.

4.10   FORD AND FULKERSON

The 'shortest chain algorithm' of Ford and Fulkerson (1962, p. 30) determines all minimum paths leading to a given node s. It will be restated in a
way leading readily to an algorithm for determining all minimum paths, from
any node to any other.

At any stage, any node i has a label in the form (c_i, x_i). Initially all the
$c_i = 0$, and all $x_i = \infty$ except that $x_s = 0$. If at any stage of the algorithm
it is found that

$$x_i > a_{ij} + x_j$$

for some i, j, then x_i is replaced by a_{ij} and c_i by j. There is a halt when there
is nothing more to do. The x_i so produced give the minimum path distance
from any node i to the given destination node s. Also, $c(i) = c_i$ is the first
node encountered in the minimum path going from i to s, and so $c(c(i))$
is the next, and so forth. In that way the entire series of nodes leading to node
s is determined.

This algorithm has many models for its implementation, depending on how
one scans for the next step needing to be carried out, if there is one. If, for
any i, the basic step is carried out for all j, we are in effect performing the
operation

$$y_i = \min_j a_{ij} + x_j, \ x_i = y_i.$$

With this, a j will be found for which

$$y_i = a_{ij} + x_j,$$

and then, when the operation is completed, $c_i = j$.

In the notation where addition means taking the minimum and multiplication means addition—that is, where new sum means usual min and new product means usual sum — we have

$$y_i = \Sigma_j a_{ij} x_j, \ x_i = y_i$$

as a restatement of the operation. By saving the new value of the x_i as the
values of the y_i, and doing this for all i, and *then* replacing all the old values

of the x_i by the new ones given by the y_i, we have the operation

$$y = ax, \; x = y.$$

In effect, x is replaced by ax. This simplicity of statement provides the value of the modification of arithmetic — which otherwise might seem bizarre.

With the initial x chosed, as already stated, for the given node s, the first value of y is $a_{s)}$, the sth column of the matrix a. The algorithm now has the form

$$
\begin{array}{ll}
0 & y = a_{s)} \\
1 & x = y, \; y = ax \\
2 & \text{if } x = y \text{ then end else } 1
\end{array}
$$

With the new arithmetic, we still have associativity of addition and multiplication and the distributivity of multiplication over addition, valid as for the old, which enables matrix powers to be defined. Then when, for any s, the algorithm terminates, we have a vector $x = a^m a_{s)}$ with the property $ax = x$, for some m, and consequently also for all larger m. Therefore, for any large enough m,

$$a(a^m a_{s)}) = a^m a_{s)} \text{ for all } s.$$

But anyway, for any m and s,

$$a^m a_{s)} = (a^{m+1})_{s)}$$

and so we have

$$a(a^{m+1})_{s)} = (a^{m+1})_{s)} \, .$$

But

$$a(a^{m+1})_{s)} = (a^{m+2})_{s)} \, .$$

So this gives

$$(a^{m+2})_{s)} = (a^{m+1})_{s)} \text{ for all } s,$$

for all large enough m, which is equivalent to

$$a^{m+2} = a^{m+1} \, .$$

From these considerations, one way of applying the algorithm for all s, and so to determine all minimim paths, is stated by the routine

$$
\begin{array}{ll}
0 & c = a \\
1 & b = c, \; c = ab \\
2 & \text{if } b = c \text{ then end else } 1
\end{array}
$$

This is not as efficient as dealing with each node separately, since termination for some s is settled earlier than for others and this is disregarded. For just the matter of determining minimum path values, this routine can be improved, but not if it is required to know also the actual series of nodes that make up any minimum path.

4.11 SHORTEST PATH ALGORITHM IN BASIC

```
1 DATA    Shortest Path Algorithm (Ford and Fulkerson, p.130)
2 '
3 '                       main step restated as
4 '             Y=AX where PROD means SUM and SUM means MIN
5 '
6 '                  Hyperion & IBM-PC : BASICA
9 '
10 GOTO 1000
11 '
80 K$="":WHILE K$="":K$=INKEY$:WEND:RETURN
89 '
90 V$="":GOSUB 80
91 WHILE K$<>CR$:V$=V$+K$:PRINT#1,K$;:GOSUB 80:WEND
92 V=VAL(V$):RETURN
98 '
99 '_____ x=y, y=ax, if x<>y then repeat else end
100 GOSUB 200:FOR I=1 TO N:Y=X(I):FOR J=1 TO N
110 T=A(I,J)+X(J):IF Y>T THEN Y=T:C(I)=J
120 NEXT:IF X(I)<>Y THEN Y(I)=Y:F=1
130 NEXT:IF F=0 THEN RETURN ELSE F=0
140 IF LEN(INKEY$) THEN GOSUB 90
150 GOTO 100
169 '
199 '___ distance & connection to base, x=y
200 FOR I=1 TO N:X(I)=Y(I)
210 IF X(I)=INF THEN X$="." ELSE X$=STR$(X(I))
220 PRINT#1,TAB(H*I)X$;C(I);:NEXT:PRINT#1,:RETURN
798 '
799 '_____ to where?
800 PRINT#1,CR$;"shortest distances and connections to ";
810 GOSUB 90:S=V:FOR I=1 TO N:Y(I)=INF:C(I)=0:NEXT:Y(S)=0
820 PRINT#1,CR$;CR$;"algorithm steps";CR$:RETURN
899 '_____ from where?
900 PRINT#1,CR$;"to";S;"from ";:GOSUB 90:IF V=0 THEN END
910 R=V:X=X(R):C=C(R):IF X=INF THEN PRINT#1,"no path":GOTO 900
920 IF C=0 THEN PRINT#1,,"no distance":GOTO 900
930 PRINT#1,,"total distance";X
940 IF C=S THEN PRINT#1,,"direct path":GOTO 900
950 PRINT#1,,,"from";R;"to";C;"distance";X(R)-X(C)
960 R=C:C=C(R):IF C THEN 950 ELSE 900
998 '
999 '_____ init
1000 DEFINT A-Z:READ A$,B$,N:H=10:INF=9999
1010 LF$=CHR$(10):CR$=CHR$(13)
1020 CLS:PRINT,A$;CR$
1099 '
1100 PRINT"screen or disk (s/d)?.";:GOSUB 80
1110 IF K$="d" OR K$="D" THEN O$="SPF" ELSE O$="SCRN:"
1120 CLS:OPEN O$ FOR OUTPUT AS #1
1199 '
1200 PRINT#1,A$;CR$;CR$;B$;CR$:DIM A(N,N),X(N),C(N)
1210 PRINT#1,"original distances";CR$
1299 '
1300 FOR I=1 TO N:FOR J=1 TO N:READ V$
```

```
1310 IF V$="." THEN A(I,J)=INF ELSE A(I,J)=VAL(V$)
1320 PRINT#1,TAB(H*J)V$;:NEXT:PRINT#1,:NEXT
1899 '
1900 GOSUB 800:GOSUB 100:PRINT#1,CR$;"shortest distances -":GOTO
900
1998 '
1999 '_____ data
2000 DATA "Bellman, Cooke and Lockett (1970), p. 86", 6 :' =N
2001 ' getting around Berkeley in minimum time
2009 '___ data A
2010 DATA       0,       28,       50,       .,       .,       .
2020 DATA       .,        0,        .,       46,       .,       .
2030 DATA       .,        .,        0,       27,       52,       .
2040 DATA       .,       46,       27,        0,       .,       .
2050 DATA       .,        .,       37,        .,        0,       16
2060 DATA       .,        .,        .,       17,       26,        0
```

Shortest Path Algorithm (Ford and Fulkerson, p. 130)

Bellman, Cooke and Lockett (1970, p. 86)

original distances

```
    0         28        50         .         .         .
    .          0         .        46         .         .
    .          .         0        27        52         .
    .         46        27         0         .         .
    .          .        37         .         0        16
    .          .         .        17        26         0
```

shortest distances and connections to 3

algorithm steps

```
  . 0       . 0       0 0       . 0       . 0       . 0
  50 3      . 0       0 0       27 3      37 3      . 0
  50 3      73 4      0 0       27 3      37 3      44 4
```

shortest distances -

```
to 3 from 2    total distance 73
                              from 2 to 4 distance 46
                              from 4 to 3 distance 27

to 3 from 4    total distance 27

               direct path

to 3 from 6    total distance 44
                              from 6 to 4 distance 17
                              from 4 to 3 distance 27
```

```
1 DATA         "Minimum paths:- the Power Algorithm"
2 '
3 '       MATRIX POWERS where PROD means SUM and SUM means MIN
4 '
5 '                   Hyperion & IBM-PC : BASICA
```

```
9  '
10 GOTO 1000
11 '
80 K$="":WHILE K$="":K$=INKEY$:WEND:RETURN
89 '
90 V$="":GOSUB 80
91 WHILE K$<>CR$:V$=V$+K$:PRINT#1,K$;:GOSUB 80:WEND
92 V=VAL(V$):RETURN
98 '
99 '_____ if b<>ab then b=ab and repeat else end
100 FOR J=1 TO N:FOR I=1 TO N:X=B(I,J):FOR K=1 TO N
110 T=A(I,K)+B(K,J):IF X>T THEN X=T:C(I,J)=K
120 NEXT:X(I)=X:NEXT
130 IF X(J)<0 THEN PRINT"Divergent - negative cycle on";J:END
140 FOR I=1 TO N:IF B(I,J)<>X(I) THEN B(I,J)=X(I):F=1
150 NEXT I,J:P=P+1:PRINT#1,P;:IF F THEN F=0:GOTO 100
160 PRINT#1,CR$;CR$;"minimum costs";CR$:E=2:GOSUB 300
170 PRINT#1,CR$;"connections";CR$:E=3:GOSUB 300:RETURN
298 '
299 '_____ pr A, B or C
300 FOR I=0 TO N:IF I THEN PRINT#1,I;
310 FOR J=1 TO N
320 IF I THEN V=-(E=1)*A(I,J)-(E=2)*B(I,J)-(E=3)*C(I,J) ELSE V=J
330 IF V=INF THEN V$="." ELSE V$=STR$(V)
340 PRINT#1,TAB(H*J)V$;:NEXT:PRINT#1,:IF I=0 THEN PRINT#1,
350 NEXT:PRINT#1,:RETURN
798 '
899 '_____ from where to where?
900 PRINT#1,CR$;"path from ";:GOSUB 90:IF V=0 THEN END ELSE R=V
910 PRINT#1," to ";:GOSUB 90:IF V=0 THEN END ELSE S=V
920 B=B(R,S):IF B=INF THEN PRINT#1,,"no path":GOTO 900
930 PRINT#1,,"total cost";B
940 C=C(R,S):IF C=S THEN PRINT#1,,,"direct path":GOTO 900
950 PRINT#1,,,"from";R;"to";C;"cost";B(R,C)
960 R=C:C=C(R,S):IF C THEN 950 ELSE 900
998 '
999 '_____ init
1000 CLS:DEFINT A-Z:READ A$,B$,N:H=10:INF=9999
1010 LF$=CHR$(10):CR$=CHR$(13)
1099 '
1100 PRINT,A$;CR$;CR$;"screen or disk (s/d)? ";:GOSUB 80
1110 IF K$="d" OR K$="D" THEN O$="PAF" ELSE O$="SCRN:"
1120 CLS:OPEN O$ FOR OUTPUT AS 1
1199 '
1200 PRINT#1,A$;CR$;CR$;B$;CR$:DIM A(N,N),B(N,N),C(N,N),X(N)
1210 PRINT#1,"original costs";CR$
1220 FOR I=1 TO N:FOR J=1 TO N:READ V$
1230 IF V$="." THEN A(I,J)=INF ELSE A(I,J)=VAL(V$)
1240 B(I,J)=INF:IF I=J THEN B(I,J)=0
1250 NEXT J,I:E=1:GOSUB 300
1299 '
1300 PRINT#1,"powers ... ";:GOSUB 100:GOTO 900
1998 '
1999 '_____ data
2000 DATA "Bellman, Cooke and Lockett (1970), p. 86", 6 :' =N
2001 ' getting around Berkeley in minimum time
2009 '___ data A
```

```
2010 DATA      0,      28,     50,     .,      .,      .
2020 DATA      .,      0,      .,      46,     .,      .
2030 DATA      .,      .,      0,      27,     52,     .
2040 DATA      .,      46,     27,     0,      .,      .
2050 DATA      .,      .,      37,     .,      0,      16
2060 DATA      .,      .,      .,      17,     26,     0
```

Minimum paths:- the Power Algorithm

Bellman, Cooke and Lockett (1970, p. 86)

original costs

	1	2	3	4	5	6
1	0	28	50	.	.	.
2	.	0	.	46	.	.
3	.	.	0	27	52	.
4	.	46	27	0	.	.
5	.	.	37	.	0	16
6	.	.	.	17	26	0

powers ... 1 2 3 4 5

minimum costs

	1	2	3	4	5	6
1	0	28	50	74	102	118
2	.	0	73	46	125	141
3	.	73	0	27	52	68
4	.	46	27	0	79	95
5	.	79	37	33	0	16
6	.	63	44	17	26	0

connections

	1	2	3	4	5	6
1	0	2	3	2	3	3
2	0	0	4	4	4	4
3	0	4	0	4	5	5
4	0	2	3	0	3	3
5	0	6	3	6	0	6
6	0	4	4	4	5	0

path from 6 to 1   no path

path from 2 to 6   total cost 141
                          from 2 to 4 cost 46
                          from 4 to 3 cost 27
                          from 3 to 5 cost 52
                          from 5 to 6 cost 16

path from 1 to 2   total cost 28
                          direct path

V.5

Distribution Matrices

Non-negative numbers that sum to 1 describe a distribution of some kind. It could be a distribution of probability, or of goods in an economy, as here. A *distribution vector* being one whose elements describe a distribution, a row vector p is a distribution if $p \geq 0$ and $pI = I$, where I is a column vector with elements all 1. A *distribution matrix* is one whose rows, or alternatively columns, are all distribution vectors. Often we have a rectangular distribution matrix since the number of goods is not necessarily the number of sectors in which they are distributed. In this chapter we deal with a square row-distribution matrix. With a Markov process the distribution matrix involved is formed by the transition probabilities, and is square. The original interest of distribution matrices derives from this context, and so does the theory. In such a probability context they are called stochastic matrices. By a *transition matrix* here we will mean a square distribution matrix, free of the probabilistic connection.

For a typical Markov process, individuals in a population have n possible states, and from one period to the next an individual in state i will make a transition to state j with probability a_{ij}, so that

$$a_{ij} > 0, \ \Sigma a_{ij} = 1 \text{ for all } i.$$

Of p_i individuals in state i in one period, $p_i a_{ij}$ will be in state j in the next, so $\Sigma p_i a_{ij}$ will be the total going into state j. Thus, if p is the distribution of individuals over states in one period, then in the next it will be pa. An *equilibrium distribution* is one that is preserved period after period. Thus, for p^* to be an equilibrium, it should be a distribution vector such that $p^* a = p^*$. Main theorems about transition matrices concern the existence and stability of an equilibrium. This is just like in the theory of general economic equilibrium. In fact, such theorems have an application there, as was shown in Chapters IV.3 and IV.5. In dealing with Sraffa's prices in chapter IV.4, in addition to the existence question that arises, the stability of an adjustment process is settled by the same means. Shortage or surpluses of value going to sectors in one period, because the prices are not correct, are compensated by price adjustments in the next. Each price is adjusted regardless of the adjustments of the others, as if they were to remain the same. But the others also are adjusted, so each must be readjusted endlessly, but there is a convergence. This is quite like the Walrasian *tâtonnement*; in a special case, each price is adjusted so as to clear its own market were the other prices to remain fixed, but they also are adjusted, and so forth. But still, Sraffa's prices have nothing to do with the equilibrium of supply and demand, since in this model these are fixed and unalterable. Both orders now have an equitable share in equilibrium and stability.

In studies about general equilibrium in a Cobb-Douglas world, found in Chapter IV.4, again we have distribution matrices, though in this case they are not square but rectangular. Many goods are distributed to many individuals, and weights associated with the wants of the individuals are distributed over the goods. Though the two distribution matrices so obtained are rectangular, they multiply together to give a square one to which available theorems apply, with implications for the existence and stability of positive equilibrium prices. Arguments applied to distribution matrices also have useful applications in the Leontief input-output model, and more generally in the von Neumann model. Irreducibility conditions familiar from the theory of Markov processes translate into the (welcome or not) one-interdependent-world situation envisaged in economics, with consequences for prices instead of probabilities.

For a greatly simplified and satisfactory theory of markets, we have our linear model, which still gives a full representation of the main questions; and, instead of apparatus from topology and differential equations, there is a dependence on nothing more elaborate than the finite algebra of distribution matrices. Even when we drop the linearity, distribution matrices show up again, in dealing with global stability of a flexible type of adjustment process that obeys the Law of Supply and Demand.

5.1 EQUILIBRIUM

The distributions on n objects describe the $(n-1)$ simplex

$$S = [p : pI = 1, p \geq 0].$$

The indices $1, \ldots, n$ are labels for its vertices, and subsets of vertices specify the faces. For another description, the simplex is the locus of centroids when a unit mass is distributed to its vertices. Each vertex becomes the centroid or centre of gravity when the entire mass is concentrated on it, and a face is described when the mass is concentrated on a subset of vertices. When negative weights are permitted, we have the barycentric coordinates familiar in analytic geometry, which sum to 1, with a triangle and more generally a simplex of reference. The effect of the non-negativity restriction is to confine points to the region given by the simplex itself, instead of having them range in the carrier space of the simplex.

A distribution matrix a can be regarded as a mapping $a: S \rightarrow S$ of the simplex into itself, any point $p \in S$ having an image $pa \in S$. For, given that $a \geq 0$, $aI = I$, if $p \geq 0$, $pI = 1$, so that $p \in S$, and $q = pa$, then $q \geq 0$ and also

$$qI = (pa)I = p(aI) = pI = 1,$$

so that also $q \epsilon S$. An equilibrium is a fixed point in the mapping, one which coincides with its image, or such that pa = p. The following theorem shows the existence of an equilibrium.

> THEOREM I (*existence*) If $a \geq 0$ and $aI = I$, then $pa = p$ for some p such that $p \geq 0$ and $pI = 1$.

By Theorem 3.1.III, with $a - 1$ transposed in place of a, either we have this required conclusion or, alternatively,

$$ax < x \text{ for some } x. \tag{i}$$

Therefore it is enough to show that the hypothesis in the theorem excludes this alternative.

Should there be such x as in (i), let $x_r = \min x_i$, so that

$$x_i - x_r \geq 0 \text{ for all } i.$$

Then, because $a \geq 0$, we have

$$\Sigma a_{ri}(x_i - x_r) \geq 0 \tag{ii}.$$

Also, $aIx_r = Ix_r$ and so, subtracting this from (i),

$$a(x - Ix_r) < x - Ix_r,$$

which gives, in particular,

$$\Sigma a_{ri}(x_i - x_r) < x_r - x_r = 0,$$

contradicting (ii) and so denying (i). QED

5.2 IRREDUCIBILITY

A subset G of the indices $1, \ldots, n$ specifies a face S' of the distribution simplex S, so if H is the complementary subset, then

$$p \epsilon S' \Leftrightarrow p_j = 0 \text{ for all } j \epsilon H.$$

The transition matrix a is *reducible* on S' if $S'a \subset S'$, that is if $p \epsilon S' \Rightarrow pa \epsilon S'$, or the image of every point in S' is also in S'. In this case we have

$$\Sigma_{i \epsilon G} p_i a_{ij} = 0 \text{ for } j \epsilon H.$$

Since a sum of non-negative terms is zero if and only if each term is zero, this is equivalent to

$$p_i a_{ij} = 0 \text{ for } i \epsilon G, j \epsilon H,$$

and this, being true for all $p \epsilon S'$, is equivalent to

$$a_{ij} = 0 \text{ for } i \epsilon G, j \epsilon H.$$

Reducibility of a therefore means the existence of a subset G of vertices, with complement H, for which this is true.

The term applies similarly to a Leontief input-output matrix where there is an independent subgroup of sectors, whose required inputs are supplied entirely by their own outputs. Some arguments about a transition matrix apply just as well to a Leontief matrix.

THEOREM I (*uniqueness*) For any transition matrix a with an equilibrium p, to have $p > 0$ it is necessary and sufficient that a be irreducible, and then and only then is the equilibrium p unique.

Let $G = [j : p_j > 0]$, so that G is nonempty, since $p \geq 0$ and $pI = 1$, and the complement H being nonempty denies $p > 0$. Then, since $p = pa$, we have

$$\Sigma_{i \epsilon G} p_i a_{ij} = 0 \ (j \epsilon H).$$

Since $p_i a_{ij} \geq 0$, this is equivalent to

$$p_i a_{ij} = 0 \ (i \epsilon G, j \epsilon H),$$

which, since $p_i > 0 \ (i \epsilon G)$, is equivalent to

$$a_{ij} = 0 \ (i \epsilon G, j \epsilon H).$$

Here we have that a is reducible if H is nonempty. Therefore if a is irreducible H must be empty; that is, $p > 0$. Also if a is reducible, say again on the set G, and p an equilibrium, with

$$w = \Sigma_{j \epsilon G} p_j, \ q_j = (1/w)p_j \ (j \epsilon G), \ q_j = 0 \ (j \epsilon H),$$

q would be a new equilibrium where $q > 0$ is denied. Therefore irreducibility is also necessary in order always to have $p > 0$ for an equilibrium.

With irreducibility, the equilibrium p must be unique. For were q another, let

$$t = \min p_i / q_i, \ r = p - tq$$

so that $r \geq 0$ while $r_i = 0$ for some i, and also $ra = r$, which, unless $r = 0$, implies reducibility. Hence $r = 0$, that is $p = tq$, which with $pI = 1$, $qI = 1$ implies $t = 1$ and $p = q$. QED

A positive element $a_{ij} > 0$ expresses a connection from i to j. With an input-output matrix it decides dependence in production of one good i on another j. In a Markov process it signifies accessibility of one state from another. These relations, which have this first direct significance, also usually have an equally important extended significance in which, as is clearly suitable for accessibility and dependence, they are required to be transitive. Then any chain of direct dependence or connection produces a correspondingly significant relation between the end-points of the chain. The extended relation, the transitive closure of the direct relation, can be put in terms of powers of the matrix.

For a preliminary, consider non-negative matrices a, b with product $c = ab$, and relations A, B and C defined by

$$iAj \equiv a_{ij} > 0, \ iBj \equiv b_{ij} > 0, \ iCj \equiv c_{ij} > 0.$$

The product AB of relations A, B is defined by

$$i(AB)j \equiv (\lor k) \ iAkBj.$$

Note the relation $C = AB$, which is an obvious consequence of the matrices being non-negative. From this we have that, if a is a transition matrix and A the relation associated with it in this way, then the relation so associated with its power a^m is simply the power A^m of the relation. Therefore, the transitive closure of a relation being the union of its powers, for the transitive closure T of the relation A, we also have

$$iTj \Leftrightarrow (\vee\, m)b = a^m\, ,\; b_{ij} > 0.$$

That is, the relation is equivalent to some power having the i, jth element positive. By a non-negative matrix which is *transitively positive* we can mean one for which this relation holds for all i, j.

If a non-negative matrix is reducible, then all its powers are similarly reducible, so i, j exist for which $a_{ij}^m = 0$ for all m, and it cannot be transitively positive. Irreducibility is therefore an obvious necessary condition for a non-negative matrix to be transitively positive, and according to the next theorem it is also sufficient.

THEOREM II (*irreducibility*) A non-negative matrix is transitively positive if and only if it is irreducible.

It will be shown that, if the matrix is not transitively positive, then it is reducible. Thus, suppose $a_{ij}^m = 0$ for all m, for some i, j. Let

$$H = [\, k : a_{ik}^m = 0 \text{ for all } m\,],$$

so we have $j \,\epsilon\, H$, and let K be the complement of H. Then K is non-empty since $a_{ik} > 0$ for some k. Take $k \,\epsilon\, K$, so we have $a_{ik}^m > 0$ for some m. Then with this we have that

$$a_{kj} > 0 \;\Rightarrow\; a_{ij}^{m+1}\, ,$$

and the conclusion would contradict that $j \,\epsilon\, H$. It follows that

$$k \,\epsilon\, K,\, j \,\epsilon\, H \;\Rightarrow\; a_{kj} = 0,$$

showing that a is reducible. QED

In section 5.5 it will appear that, except in the periodic case dealt with there, irreducibility implies that some power of the matrix has a positive column. The effect of that conclusion for the convergence of powers is found in section 5.4. In the next section we shall deal with the simpler case in which the convergence is assured by the matrix or some power of it being positive.

5.3 POWERS AND LIMITS

A linear combination of vectors where the coefficients are non-negative with sum 1, and so describe a distribution, is variously called an average, a convex combination, or a *mixture* of the vectors. The last term is suitable here. If p is a distribution vector, then the row vector pa, which is the linear combination of the rows of the matrix a with coefficients given by p, is a mixture of these rows. A mixture of distributions is itself a distribution, and so if, moreover, *a* is a distribution matrix, having rows which are distributions, then *pa* is a distribution. Thus, if $a \geq 0 \, aI = I$, so *a* is a distribution matrix, and if $p \geq 0$, $pI = 1$, so *p* is a distribution vector, and $q = pa$ so *q* is a mixture of the rows of *a*; then we have $q \geq 0$ and

$$qI = (pa)I = p(aI) = pI = I,$$

showing that *q* is also a distribution.

The base distributions where one coordinate is 1 and all others are 0 are the vertices of the distribution simplex *S*. Any distribution *p* is a point in *S* and is a mixture of these, *p* itself giving the coefficients. These are also the barycentric coordinates of the point with *S* as simplex of reference, often used in analytic geometry. For any point of the space the coodinates sum to 1, and points that are in the reference simplex itself are where they are all non-negative.

Now we consider a transition matrix *a*, this being any square distribution matrix. Such a matrix has powers, and evidently these are all transition matrices. Since a transition matrix *a* has rows which are distributions, so that they are points of *S*, *pa* is the same mixture of these points as *p* itself is of the vertices of *S*, the coefficients in both case being given by *p*. These points given by the rows of *a* determine another simplex *A* lying in *S*. This is the image $A = Sa$ of *S* in the mapping $a: S \rightarrow S$ where any $p \in S$ has an image *pa*.

This image of *S* could be of lower dimension so not all these points would be vertices, but for an illustration altering nothing essential we can suppose not. This is a regularity assumption, making the inverse of the mapping single valued. The condition is that, for all *v*,

$$vI = 0 \Rightarrow va = 0,$$

or the rows of *a* be simplicially independent, none of them being a mixture of, or in the convex closure of, the others. Then *Sa* could serve as simplex of reference for its image $(Sa)a = Sa$. The coordinates of the vertices of *Sa* with *Sa* as simplex of reference would be the same as the coordinates of the vertices of *Sa* with *S* as simplex of reference, these being given in each case by the rows of *a*. With that sense the situation of Sa^2 in *Sa* is similar to the situation of *Sa* in *S*. Then also Sa^2 can be the simplex of reference for describing S^3 and so forth, with the same remarks at each stage. Just as $Sa \subset S$, so also $Sa^2 \subset Sa$, and similarly further, with a repeated contraction from one image to its successor. Since the volume of each simplex relative to that of the simplex of reference depends only on the coordinates, which here are the same in each case, the ratio *R* of the volume of each simplex Sa^m to that of its predecessor is fixed, and also $R \leq 1$ because we have a contraction.

We now have a series of images A_m for which

$$A_0 = S, \; A_m = A_{m-1} a \; (m = 1, 2, \ldots),$$

and so

$$A_m = Sa^m \; (m = 0, 1, 2, \ldots).$$

Because $a^m = aa^{m-1}$, the rows of a^m are mixtures of the rows of a^{m-1}, with coefficients given by the rows of a. It follows that

$$A_m \subset A_{m-1}(m = 1, 2, \ldots),$$

so each image is a contraction of its predecessor. Also since the mixture-coefficients, or barycentric coordinates, are always given by the rows of a and so are independent of m, the situation of A_m in A_{m-1} is similar to that of A_{m-1} in A_{m-2}, and ... and finally to that of $A = Sa$ in S. These progressive contractions together with the repeated similarity, give a geometrical picture of what happens when a transition matrix is raised to powers, making easily plausible the results that follow.

If $a > 0$, the contractions of each simplex are to its interior and it is plausible that A_m should contract to a point as $m \to \infty$. From our regularity assumption, made for the sake of illustration, though otherwise one could take relative volumes, the simplex volumes are all positive. But the ratio of successive volumes is a constant $R \leq 1$, so the volume of A_m is proportional to R^m. Unless one simplex lies exactly over the other, because there is just a permutation of the vertices, in which case they all do, we have $R < 1$, and we would have that if $a > 0$. In that case volumes $\to 0$ as $m \to \infty$, as is at least consistent with A_m contracting to a point. Of course, it is not volume but linear dimensions that must diminish to zero, and that will be shown.

The significance of $A_m = Sa^m$ contracting to a point, say p^*, is that the rows of a^m all converge to p^*, so a^m converges to a matrix where the rows are all identical with each other. Also, starting with any p ϵ S whatever and forming the sequence

$$p_0 = p, p_m = p_{m-1} a \ (m = 1, 2, \ldots),$$

we always have

$$p_m \to p^* \ (m \to \infty).$$

The sequence always converges, and the limit is independent of the starting point. Here is a close analogy to the *tâtonnement* of Walras and the global stability of general equilibrium prices. In fact, we have an application there, in which the required irreducibility condition is interpreted as denying the existence of any completely self-contained sub-economy. There is a similar development in the consideration of Sraffa's prices, and a similarity again in connection with the von Neumann and Leontief models, where irreducibility becomes an expression of the hanging-together or interdependence of all parts of the economy.

It is known that the rows of a matrix are all closely equal when the elements in any column are. The closeness of the elements in a column is decided by the closeness of the maximum and minimum elements, and deducing that is served by the following theorem:

THEOREM I Let a be a distribution matrix and let $y = ax$. If the smallest element of a is a_w and the largest and smallest elements of x and y are x_m, x_w and y_m, y_w, then

$$x_w + a_w(x_m - x_w) \le y_w \le y_m \le x_m - a_w(x_m - x_w).$$

Because the rows of a are distributions, each element

$$y_i = \Sigma a_{ij} x_j$$

is an average of the elements of x, the weights being given by row i of a. With $a_{ij} \ge a_w$ the minimum weight in row i is at least a_w and therefore also the maximum weight is at most $1 - a_w$. Therefore a lower bound of y_i is obtained by assigning weight $1 - a_w$ to x_w and weight a_w to x_m, and an upper bound is obtained by exchanging these weights, so we have

$$(1 - a_w)x_w + a_w x_m \le y_i \le (1 - a_w)x_m + a_w x_w,$$

from which the required conclusion.

COROLLARY (I) $\quad x_w \le y_w \le y_m \le x_m$
and
$$y_m - y_w \le (1 - 2a_w)(x_m - x_w).$$

This is an immediate consequence of the theorem. Here a is a general row-distribution matrix, not necessarily square. Now consider a sequence of such matrices a, b, ... with minimum elements a_w, b_w, ...

COROLLARY (II) If $y = \ldots bax$ (r factors), then y_m and y_w are non-increasing and non-decreasing with r, and

$$y_m - y_w \le (1 - 2a_w)(1 - 2b_w) \ldots (x_m - x_w).$$

The special case in which the factors are all the same, and so their products are powers of some matrix, necessarily square, making it a transition matrix, is the usual one in the theory of Markov processes. But in general equilibrium stability theory there is a use for results concerning infinite products of transition matrices.

COROLLARY (III) If a is a transition matrix and $y = a^r x$ then y_m, y_w are non-increasing and non-decreasing with m and

$$y_m - y_w \le (1 - 2a_w)^r(x_m - x_w).$$

This is the classical result, and we have seen that a more general result is obtainable just as well when the matrix power is replaced by any product of distribution matrices, and there is no need for these to be square.

COROLLARY (IV) The series y_m, y_w ($r = 1, 2, \ldots$) are convergent, and if $a > 0$, then their limits are equal, and positive.

The series being monotonic by Corollary (ii), the convergence follows from the theorem on the convergence of monotonic series. If $a > 0$, so that $0 < a_w < 1$, then $1 - 2a_w < 1$. Hence by Corollary (ii) the difference of y_m, y_w converges to 0, and so the limits must be equal. Moreover, because y_w is positive and non-decreasing, the limits must be positive.

It is now easy to draw wanted conclusions from the theorem and its corollaries. A rule of matrix algebra is that $(ab)_{j)} = ab_{j)}$, or the jth column in a matrix product ab is the product of a with the jth column of b. Therefore

$$a^r a_{j)} = (a^{r+1})_{j)},$$

so with $x = a_{j)}$ and $y = a^r x$ we have $y = (a^{r+1})_{j)}$. Then, from the theorem and corollaries, if $a > 0$ then, for all j, $y_i \to p_j^* (m \to \infty)$ for all i; that is, $(a^r)_{(i} \to p^* (r \to \infty)$ for all i, or the rows of a^r are all convergent and have the same limit p^*.

THEOREM II   If a is a positive transition matrix, then a^r ($r \to \infty$) is convergent and the limit matrix is positive and has all its rows equal.

The limit matrix has the form $a^* = Ip^*$, where p^* is a distribution vector since it is a limit of distribution vectors.

COROLLARY (I)   If a is a positive transition matrix, then for any distribution vector p the series pa^r ($r \to \infty$) is convergent, and the limit is positive and independent of p.

For, with $pI = 1$, the series is convergent with limit

$$pa^* = p(Ip^*) = (pI)p^* = p^*,$$

which is independent of p.

COROLLARY (II)   Any positive transition matrix has a unique equilibrium, which moreover is positive.

The last corollary shows the existence of a positive equilibrium p^*, so it remains to show uniqueness. If p is any equilibrium we have $pa^r = p$, and so in the limit as $r \to \infty$, we have $pIp^* = p$, giving $p^* = p$.

COROLLARY (III)   There are the same conclusions for a transition matrix for which some power is positive.

If $a^s > 0$ let θ be the smallest element, and let $y = a^r x$. Then for $r = ks$ we have

$$y_m - y_w \le (1 - 2\theta)^k (x_m - x_w).$$

In any case y_m and y_w are non-increasing and non-decreasing, and this shows that their difference converges to zero.

Similar arguments give the following:

THEOREM III   If a, b, ... is any sequence of transition matrices for which the minimum elements have a positive lower limit, then the infinite product . . . *ba* is convergent, to a transition matrix which is positive and has all its rows equal.

The next section concerns a matrix which, instead of being positive, just has a positive column. The effect of that condition is to exclude a face of the reference simplex S from its image in the mapping $a: S \rightarrow S$. There is a contraction again with volume ratio $R < 1$, and again plausibility that the iterated image should contract to a point. The case of a positive matrix is the further case in which every column is positive, so that every face is excluded and the image of the base simplex must lie in its interior. Similar considerations apply just as well to infinite products instead of powers.

5.4 CONVERGENCE

Now there will be an improvement on the convergence criterion found in the last section. Instead of the transition matrix or some power of it being positive, it is just required that the matrix, or some power of it, have a positive column.

For any vector v for which $vI = \Sigma v_i = 0$, let

$$|v| = \Sigma |v_j| .$$

So $v = 0$ if $|v| = 0$. If a is a distribution matrix then $aI = I$, so if v is such a vector then $vaI = vI = 0$, so va is also such a vector, and we can consider $|va|$.

THEOREM I If a is a distribution matrix and a_k is the smallest element in column k, and if v is any vector for which $vI = 0$, then

$$|va| \leq |v| (1 - a_k).$$

It can be taken that

$$\Sigma_i v_i a_{ik} \geq 0, \qquad (i)$$

since otherwise v can be replaced by $- v$. Then, first by (i) and then by

$$a_{ij} \geq 0, \qquad (ii)$$

$$\Sigma_j a_{ij} = 1, \qquad (iii)$$

and, by definitions of $|v|$ and a_k,

$$\Sigma v_i = 0, \qquad (iv)$$

we have

$$
\begin{aligned}
|a| &= \Sigma_{j \neq k} |\Sigma_i v_i a_{ij}| + \Sigma_i v_i a_{ik} & \text{by (i)} \\
&\leq \Sigma_{j \neq k} \Sigma_i |v_i| a_{ij} + \Sigma_i v_i a_{ik} & \text{by (ii)} \\
&= \Sigma_j \Sigma_i |v_i| a_{ij} - \Sigma_i (|v_i| - v_i) a_{ik} & \\
&\leq |v| - \Sigma_i (|v_i| - v_i) a_k & \text{by (iii)} \\
&= |v| (1 - a_k) & \text{by (iv)}
\end{aligned}
$$

COROLLARY (I) If $e = \max_k \min_i a_{ik}$, then

$$|va^m| \leq |v|(1-e)^m.$$

COROLLARY (II) If a or some power of it has a positive column, then

$$va^m \to 0 \ (m \to \infty).$$

In any case, $|va| \leq |v|$, so $|va^m|$ is non-increasing with m and so, by the theorem on monotonic series, this series is convergent. It remains to see that under the stated conditions the limit is 0, so va^m is convergent with limit 0. If a has a positive column, then $e > 0$, and since also $e \leq 1$ we have $(1-e)^m \to 0$, showing by Corollary (i) that the limit is zero. The remaining part of the argument is similar to one found at the end of the last section, depending on monotonicity and with the foregoing applied instead to the power.

THEOREM II (*convergence*) If a is a transition matrix having an equilibrium p^*, and if it or some power of it has a positive column, then the equilibrium is unique, and for all p such that $pI = 1$ the series pa^m ($m \to \infty$) is convergent, and the limit is independent of p and given by p^*.

Let $v = p - p^*$, so that $vI = 0$ and $va^m = pa^m - p^*$. Then $va^m \to 0$, so that $pa^m \to p^*$. If p were another equilibrium, we would have $p = pa^m$, so that $p = p^*$.

Let a_r ($r = 1, 2, \ldots$) be a series of row-distribution matrices, and let e_r be associated with a_r the way e has been associated with a. Thus e_r is the maximum of the minimum elements of the columns of a_r, so that $0 \leq e_r \leq 1$, and $e_r > 0$ signifies that a_r has a positive column. Now for any vector v such that $vI = 0$, by Theorem I we have

$$|a_1 \ldots a_m| \leq |v|(1-e_1) \ldots (1-e_m).$$

Introducing

$$\bar{e} = \overline{\lim}\ e_r\ (r \to \infty),$$

it follows that $\bar{e} > 0$ is sufficient to assure that

$$va_1 \ldots a_m \to 0\ (m \to \infty),$$

and so, given that it exists, the limit of $pa_1 \ldots a_m$ is independent of p; an equivalent conclusion is that

$$a_1 \ldots a_m \to a^*$$

where a^* is a matrix whose rows are all equal, and so has the form $a^* = Ip^*$.

5.5   PERIODIC CASE

A matrix a is periodic, with period h, if there exists a partition S_r ($r = 1, \ldots, h$) of $1, \ldots, n$ such that $a_{ij} = 0$ unless $i \in S_r, j \in S_{r+1}$ for some r or $i \in S_h$, $j \in S_1$. Such a matrix has the form

$$a = \begin{pmatrix} 0 & a_1 & 0 & \cdots & 0 \\ 0 & 0 & a_2 & \cdots & 0 \\ \cdots & \cdots & \cdots & \cdots & \cdots \\ 0 & 0 & 0 & \cdots & a_{h-1} \\ a_h & 0 & 0 & \cdots & 0 \end{pmatrix}$$

and then

$$a^h = \begin{pmatrix} a_1 a_2 \ldots a_h & 0 & \cdots & 0 \\ 0 & a_2 a_3 \ldots a_1 & \cdots & 0 \\ \cdots & \cdots & \cdots & \cdots \\ 0 & 0 & \cdots & a_h a_1 \ldots a_{h-1} \end{pmatrix}$$

which is reducible. Therefore if all powers up to order n are irreducible the matrix cannot be periodic.

THEOREM I If a transition matrix is irreducible then either it is periodic or some power has a positive column.

Let a be an irreducible transition matrix. Then by Theorem 5.2.II it is transitively positive so that, for any j, we have $a_{jj}^m > 0$ for some m, making the set

$$E = [m : a_{jj}^m > 0]$$

nonempty. Let h be the highest common factor of the elements of E.

If $a_{ij}^m > 0$ for $m = r, s$, then h divides $r - s$; for, since a is transitively positive, we also have $a_{ji}^t > 0$ for some t and it follows that $a_{jj}^{r+t}, a_{jj}^{s+t} > 0$. Then h divides $r + t$ and $s + t$ and so it divides $r - s$; that is,

$$r - s \equiv 0 \ (\mathrm{mod}\ h).$$

It follows that the h sets

$$S_r = [i : a_{ij}^t > 0, t \equiv r\,(\mathrm{mod}\ h)]\ (r = 1, \ldots, h)$$

are disjoint. Also, because a is irreducible and so transitively positive, every element belongs to one of them. Hence they form a partition.

First consider the case $h > 1$ where the elements of E are not relatively prime. If $a_{ik} > 0$, and $i \in S_r$, so that

$$a_{kj}^t > 0 \text{ for some } t \equiv r\,(\mathrm{mod}\ h),$$

then we have $a_{ij}^{t+1} > 0$, and hence $j \in S_{r+1}$ if $r < h$ and $j \in S_1$ if $r = h$. It appears thus that a is periodic, with period h.

Now suppose $h = 1$ so that the elements of E are relatively prime integers, and consequently any sufficiently large positive integer s has an expression in the form

$$s = \Sigma_{r \in S}\, rm_r$$

where the m_r are positive integers; so we have that, for some s,

$$a_{jj}^m > 0 \text{ for all } m \geq s.$$

But for all i there exists a t_i for which $a_{ij}^{t_i} i > 0$. Let $t = \max t_i$. Then for any i we have $a_{ij}^{s+t} > 0$. For let $u = t - t_i$, so that $u \geq 0$. Then we have $a_{jj}^{s+u} > 0$ and $a_{ij}^{t_i} i > 0$ and hence $a_{ij}^{s+u+t_i} i > 0$. But $s + t = s + t_i + u$, whence the conclusion. Thus, column j of a^{s+t} is positive, and the theorem is proved.

COROLLARY If all powers up to the nth are irreducible then some power has a positive column.

For, as remarked, in this case the matrix cannot be periodic.

We can now put together the consequences of irreducibility and of a power having a positive column. Any transition matrix has an equilibrium p^*, by the theorem of section 5.1. Irreducibility, by Theorem 5.2.I, implies that it is unique and positive. If a power has a positive column then, by Theorem 5.3.II, $pa^m \rightarrow p^*$ ($m \rightarrow \infty$) for any initial distribution p. This implies that $a^m \rightarrow Ip^*$ ($m \rightarrow \infty$), and with $p^* > 0$ it follows that $a^m > 0$ for all large m. The last condition implies that a^m is irreducible for all m, from which, by the last theorem, we have again the conditions with which we started, so proving equivalence with them.

THEOREM II For any transition matrix the following conditions are equivalent,
(i) all powers up to the nth are irreducible,
(ii) all large powers are positive,
(iii) the matrix is irreducible and some power has a positive column.

5.6 COMPUTER GRAPHICS

```
1 DATA Distribution Matrix - POWERS
2 '
3 ' Hyperion & IBM-PC : BASICA
9 '
10 GOTO 1000
11 '
90 K$="":WHILE K$="":K$=INKEY$:WEND
95 IF K$=ESC$ THEN SCREEN 0:KEY ON:END ELSE RETURN
98 '
99 '_____ B=BA, draw B, repeat
100 FOR I=1 TO 3:FOR J=1 TO 3:T=0:FOR K=1 TO 3
110 T=T+B(I,K)*A(K,J):NEXT:T(J)=T:NEXT
120 FOR J=1 TO 3:B(I,J)=T(J):NEXT J,I
130 GOSUB 200:P=P+1:LOCATE 3,1
140 PRINT"power";P;:IF LEN(INKEY$) THEN GOSUB 90
150 GOTO 100
199 '_____ calculate the vertices
200 FOR I=1 TO 3:FOR K=0 TO 1:X=0
210 FOR J=1 TO 3:X=X+B(I,J)*U(J,K)
220 NEXT:X(I,K)=X:NEXT K,I
230 FOR K=0 TO 1:X(0,K)=X(3,K):NEXT
299 '_____ draw the simplex
300 FOR I=1 TO 3:LINE(X(I-1,0),X(I-1,1))-(X(I,0),X(I,1)),1
310 NEXT:RETURN
```

```
998 '
999 '_____ initialize
1000 CLS:KEY OFF:SCREEN 2:ESC$=CHR$(27)
1010 READ H$:LOCATE 1,28:PRINT H$;
1020 DEFINT I,J,K,P,U,X
1100 DIM A(3,3),B(3,3),U(3,1),X(3,1),T(3)
1199 '___ base simplex
1200 FOR I=1 TO 3:FOR K=0 TO 1:READ U(I,K):NEXT K,I
1210 DATA 320,16,80,200,560,200
1299 '___ which?
1300 LOCATE 3,72:INPUT"example ",E
1310 IF E THEN FOR I=1 TO 9*E:READ R:NEXT
1999 '___ read it
2000 FOR I=1 TO 3:B(I,I)=1:FOR J=1 TO 3
2010 READ A(I,J):NEXT J,I
2099 '___ draw the base
2100 GOSUB 200:GOTO 100
4999 '
5000 '_____ examples
5005 'symmetric
5010 DATA   .1,   .1,   .8,   .1,   .8,   .1,   .8,   .1,   .1
5015 'eccentric
5020 DATA   .1,   .2,   .7,   .2,   .7,   .1,   .7,   .1,   .2
5025 'rotate
5030 DATA   .9,.075,.025,.025,   .9,.075,.075,.025,   .9
5035 'oscillate
5040 DATA   .1,   .1,   .8,   .2,   .7,   .1,   .7,   .1,   .2
5045 'spiral
5050 DATA   .1,   .1,   .8,   .6,   .3,   .1,  .05,  .85,   .1
5055 '?
5060 DATA    0,   .9,   .1,   .1,    0,   .9,   .9,   .1,    0
5065 '?
5070 DATA    0,  .95,  .05,  .05,    0,  .95,  .95,  .05,    0

1 DATA       Markov Process - EQUILIBRIUM
2 '
3 '           Hyperion & IBM-PC : BASICA
9 '
10 GOSUB 1000:GOSUB 100:END
11 '
90 K$="":WHILE K$="":K$=INKEY$:WEND
95 IF K$=ESC$ THEN END ELSE RETURN
98 '
99 '_____ main
100 FOR J=1 TO N:P(J)=Q(J):NEXT
110 FOR J=1 TO N:Q=0:FOR I=1 TO N
120 Q=Q+P(I)*A(I,J):NEXT:PRINT#1,TAB(H*J)Q;
130 IF Q(J)<>Q THEN Q(J)=Q:F=1
140 NEXT:PRINT#1,:IF F=0 THEN RETURN ELSE F=0
150 IF LEN(INKEY$) THEN GOSUB 90
160 GOTO 100
169 '
999 '_____ init
1000 DEFINT F,I,J,N:READ A$,N:H=12
1010 ESC$=CHR$(27):LF$=CHR$(10):FF$=CHR$(12):CR$=CHR$(13)
1020 CLS:PRINT,A$;CR$
1099 '
1100 PRINT"screen, printer or disk (s/p/d)? ";:GOSUB 90
```

```
1110 IF K$="p" THEN O$="LPT1:" ELSE IF K$="d" THEN O$="MPF" ELSE
O$="SCRN:"
1120 CLS:OPEN O$ FOR OUTPUT AS #1
1199 '
1200 PRINT#1,,A$;CR$:DIM A(N,N),P(N),Q(N)
1210 PRINT#1,"Transition probabilities"
1299 '
1300 FOR I=1 TO N:FOR J=1 TO N:READ A(I,J)
1310 PRINT#1,TAB(H*J)A(I,J);:NEXT:PRINT#1,:NEXT
1330 PRINT#1,CR$;"Initial distribution"
1399 '
1400 FOR J=1 TO N:READ Q(J)
1410 PRINT#1,TAB(H*J)Q(J);:NEXT
1430 PRINT#1,CR$;CR$;"Subsequent distributions"
1900 RETURN
1998 '
1999 '_____ data
2000 DATA 3:' =N
2009 '___ data A
2010 DATA       .3,      .3,      .4
2020 DATA       .2,      .2,      .6
2030 DATA       .1,      .7,      .2
2899 '___ data Q
2900 DATA       .2,      .3,      .5
```

Markov Process - EQUILIBRIUM

Transition probabilities

.3	.3	.4
2	.2	.6
.1	.7	.2

Initial distribution

.2	.3	.5

Subsequent distributions

.17	.47	.36
.181	.397	.422
.1759	.4291	.395
.17809	.41509	.40682
.177127	.421219	.401654
.1775473	.4185397	.403913
.1773634	.4197113	.4029254
.1774438	.419199	.4033572
.1774087	.419423	.4031684
.177424	.4193251	.4032509
.1774173	.4193679	.4032149
.1774202	.4193491	.4032306
.177419	.4193573	.4032237
.1774195	.4193538	.4032267
.1774193	.4193553	.4032254
.1774194	.4193546	.403226
.1774194	.419355	.4032258
.1774194	.4193548	.4032259
.1774194	.4193549	.4032258
.1774194	.4193549	.4032259
.1774194	.4193549	.4032259
.1774194	.4193549	.4032259

power 49   example 6

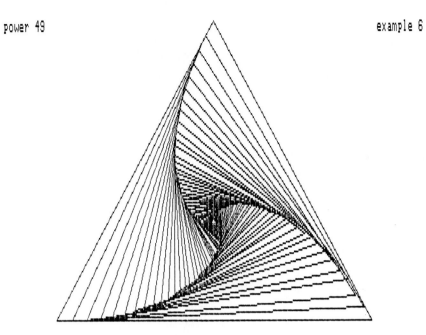

Figure 1 Distribution Matrix-Powers

Part VI

GENERAL MATHEMATICS

VI.1

Calculus of Propositions

---

0 (Nothing)
1 make two copies
2 attach a Yin to one and a Yang to the other
3 join them
4 goto 1

Shao Yung's Program

The use of logical notation in this book is informal, for the sake of simplicity, and not in order to follow rules that do not serve that end. Many sources offer a background to the calculus of propositions and, what amounts to a restatement of the same matter, to elementary set theory. Less available are accounts of the algebra of relations that suits our material; that subject arises out of elementary set theory when the sets have the form of subsets of a Cartesian product. The account given in the next chapter is needed for present purposes, and an outline of Boolean logic is included now for the sake of completeness. It is more straightforward, and there is some de-mystification, when propositional calculus is put not in terms of propositions and their truth and falsehood, but as arithmetic with 0 and 1. That is the way we will do it. Put another way, the basic form that the subject takes is a *dichotomy*, wherever there is a distinction of two possibilities—what they might be called besides 0 and 1 hardly matters. This is simple, even as simple as possible, and yet, what can be made out of it is not very limited. This hardly needs comment, and in any case there is the program at the beginning of this chapter, a source of digital thought in ancient China, not to mention the digital computer, as may be gathered from *The Ring of Linked Rings* (Afriat, 1982a), and A. K. Dewdney (1984).

A *Boolean variable* is one that takes the values 0 or 1 and a *Boolean function* is a function $e = f(e_1, \ldots, e_n)$ whose arguments e_i and value e are all Boolean variables. Everything in the subject amounts to a discussion of Boolean functions. By *substitution* of one function in another is meant making the value of the one function one of the arguments of the other. The resulting function is a *compound* of the two functions. Repeated substitutions with various functions produce a compound of the functions involved. Thus, further compounds are produced by taking compounds of compounds. Three particular Boolean functions are given by

$$\sim a = 1 - a, \ a \wedge b = ab, \ a \vee b = a + b - ab,$$

and are called *negation, conjunction* and *disjunction*. We also denote $\sim a$ by $\bar{a}$. These are the elementary Boolean functions, or *Boolean operations*, and a *Boolean compound* is any compound of these. Because any Boolean function can be expressed as a Boolean compound—in many ways, moreover—these three functions or operations have a special importance. By taking compounds of just these three, all possible Boolean functions are produced.

A Boolean variable e can be associated with any matter requiring a Yes $= 1$ or No $= 0$; issuing the Yes or No can be described as making up one's mind about the matter. An importance for Boolean functions comes from ways this may be done, where the final e depends on several independent $e_1, \ldots, e_n$. The matter can be termed a *proposition*, to be decided True or False. Its being one or the other might depend on the outcomes for several other propositions, or matters. Instead of $c = a \wedge b$ where a, b and c are Boolean variables, one might put $r \Leftrightarrow p \wedge q$ where p, q and r are the propositions with which these are associated. The only difference is one of terminology; the meaning is the same.

A Boolean function can be defined either as a compound of others that have been defined, or by a *truth table*. This is a table that tells its value for all possibilities of the arguments. With n arguments there are 2^n possibilities, corresponding to the n-bit binary numbers, and they can be listed by counting in binary from $0 \ldots 0 = 0$ to $1 \ldots 1 = 2^n - 1$. Though we defined $a \wedge b$ simply as the product ab it can also be defined without reference to arithmetic from the truth table

a	b	$a \wedge b$
0	0	0
0	1	0
1	0	0
1	1	1

When we have a set of objects U and a function P defined on them whose value $P(x)$ for any object $x \in U$ is a Boolean variable, we have a *propositional function*. Other terms are used for the same idea. With a *predicate* P the statement $P(x)$ tells us something about x which can be true or false. Given any particular $a \in U$, $p = P(a)$ is a *proposition*, to be decided true or false. With a *subset* $A \subset U$, any $x \in U$ either is or is not an element of A, so $x \in A$ is just another way of stating a propositional function. We could say that $A = [x : P(x) = 1]$ is the *truth set* of the propositional function P, or that P is the *characteristic function* of the set A, so that $x \in A$ means the same as $P(x) = 1$. There is a change of notation and terminology for the same matter.

We can just as well have a propositional function $P(x, y)$ of two arguments $x \in U, y \in V$ and correspondingly a subset $R \subset U \times V$, of the Cartesian product $U \times V$ of the two sets U, V. Here R is the truth set of P, and P the characteristic function of R, so $P(x, y) = 1$ means the same as $(x, y) \in R$. But now we call R a *binary relation* and use the notation xRy for $(x, y) \in R$, with the statement that x has the relation R to y. Similarly, one can have a propositional function of some n arguments, or an n-ary relation. In this way the theory of relations comes directly out of propositional or set theory, with additional features included only because subsets of a Cartesian product are dealt with.

1.1 THE BOOLEAN LAWS

A part of the logical reasoning that is done in the head could be described as mental Boolean arithmetic—perhaps with tables learnt by heart, or by an appeal to laws, or rules, such as have long had attention, especially from George Boole (1815 – 1864) in *The Laws of Thought*.

We have $\bar{0} = 1$, $\bar{1} = 0$, and $\bar{\bar{a}} = a$, this being the *law of double negation*. Also,

$$a \wedge \bar{a} = 0, \qquad a \vee \bar{a} = 1,$$

these being the *laws of complementarity*. The *laws of identity* are

$$a \wedge 0 = 0, \qquad a \vee 0 = a$$

and

$$a \wedge 1 = a, \qquad a \vee 1 = 1.$$

All these come immediately from the formulae defining the operations. Because $a^2 = a$ for any Boolean variable a we have the *laws of idempotence* for conjunction and disjunction:

$$a \wedge a = a, \qquad a \vee a = a.$$

Then there are the *commutativity laws*:

$$a \wedge b = b \wedge a, \qquad a \vee b = b \vee a,$$

and *associativity laws*:

$$a \wedge (b \wedge c) = (a \wedge b) \wedge c,$$
$$a \vee (b \vee c) = (a \vee b) \vee c.$$

The last can be seen from symmetry of the expression

$$a \vee (b \vee c) = a + b + c - bc - ca - ab + abc.$$

Now

$$\overline{a \vee b} = 1 - a \vee b = (1 - a)(1 - b) = \bar{a} \wedge \bar{b}$$

so that

$$\overline{a \vee b} = \bar{a} \wedge \bar{b};$$

and replacing a, b by $\bar{a}$, $\bar{b}$ and using the law of double negation from this, we have also

$$\overline{a \wedge b} = \bar{a} \vee \bar{b}$$

These are De Morgan's laws, or the *laws of duality* between conjunction and disjunction. From this,

$$a \wedge (a \vee b) = (a \vee a) \wedge (a \vee b)$$
$$= a \vee (a \wedge b),$$

and, because $a^2 = a$, also

$$a \wedge (a \vee b) = a(a + b - ab) = a,$$

and so we have the *laws of absorption*:

$$a \wedge (a \vee b) = a, \qquad a \vee (a \wedge b) = a.$$

1.2 NORMAL FORMS

For Boolean variables a, b let a^b mean a if $b = 1$ and $\bar{a}$ if $b = 0$. Then a^a is always 1, since $a = 1$ if $a = 1$ and $\bar{a} = 1$ if $a = 0$. Also $a^b = 0$ if $b \neq a$. For in this case if $b = 1$ then $a = 0$ and $a^b = a = 0$, and if $b = 0$ then $a = 1$ and $a^b = \bar{a} = 0$.

Now for Boolean vectors

$$a = (a_1, \ldots, a_n), \qquad b = (b_1, \ldots, b_n)$$

let

$$\wedge a^b = \wedge_i a_i^{b_i},$$

so by definition of $\wedge$ also

$$\wedge a^b = \Pi_i a_i^{b_i}.$$

Then from the foregoing,

$$\wedge a^a = 1, \qquad \wedge a^b = 0 \text{ if } a \neq b,$$

and hence if $b \neq c$ then

$$(\wedge a^b) \wedge (\wedge a^c) = \wedge_i (a_i^{b_i} \wedge a_i^{c_i}) = 0,$$

from which it follows that always

$$(\wedge a^b) \vee (\wedge a^c) = (\wedge a^b) + (\wedge a^c).$$

Hence, for any Boolean function f,

$$\vee_{f(u) = 1} (\wedge e^u) = \Sigma_{f(u) = 1} (\wedge e^u)$$

and this is $\wedge e^e = 1$ if $f(e) = 1$ and 0 if $f(e) = 0$; in other words

$$f(e) = \vee_{f(u) = 1} (\wedge e^u).$$

This is the *disjunctive normal form* of f. It really amounts to a truth table listing all the cases where f is 'true' or equal to 1; we have it immediately, simply from that consideration.

Applying this to $\bar{f}$,

$$\bar{f}(e) = \vee_{f(u) = 0} (\wedge e^u),$$

from which, by taking negations on both sides,

$$f(e) = \wedge_{f(u) = 0}(\overline{ve^u}),$$

where $\overline{ve^u} = v_i \overline{e_i^{u_i}}$. This is the *conjunctive normal form* for f.

Either of these normal forms shows that every Boolean function is expressible as a compound of the three basic Boolean functions, or operations: negation, conjunction, and disjunction. In other words, the Boolean functions obtained by taking compounds of these three exhaust all possible Boolean functions.

1.3 THE CONDITIONAL

The *conditional* is the Boolean compound $\rightarrow$, given by

$$a \rightarrow b = \overline{a} \vee b.$$

Therefore also

$$a \rightarrow b = (1 - a) + b - (1 - a)b = 1 - a + ab,$$

and the table for its values, the 'truth table', is

a	b	$a \rightarrow b$
0	0	1
0	1	0
1	0	1
1	1	1

For another description, $a \rightarrow b = 1$ just when $a \le b$. This shows that $a \rightarrow b$ is the characteristic function of the Boolean relation $a \le b$, which is equivalent to $a = ab$. From this, and amounting to the same thing, $b = 1$ if $a = 1$. Thus $a \rightarrow b$ being true signifies that b is true if a is true.

As remarked before, it is more customary to have propositions in place of the Boolean variables used here. But then, all that is said concerns the truth values of the propositions represented by Boolean variables, and what is said is just the same. It is more straightforward when Boolean functions are understood simply arithmetically. Their use as concerns propositions is then an application, and with that use there are conventions. The assertion of a Boolean variable a means that it has the value $a = 1$, and to deny this is to give it the value $a = 0$. Thus, an assertion of $a \rightarrow b$ means that b is asserted *conditionally* on the assertion of a.

The formula $(\overline{a} \vee b)$ for the conditional is already in conjunctive normal form. The disjunctive normal form, which can be read directly from the truth table from the cases for which it is true, is

$$(a \wedge b) \vee (\overline{a} \wedge b) \vee (\overline{a} \wedge \overline{b}),$$

and similarly, the disjunctive normal form for the negation is $(a \wedge \overline{b})$.

From the conditional is derived the *biconditional* $\leftrightarrow$, which is the symmetric Boolean function given by

$$a \leftrightarrow b = (a \to b) \wedge (b \to a).$$

Therefore, from the definition of $\to$, it is given as a Boolean compound by

$$a \leftrightarrow b = (\bar{a} \vee b) \wedge (a \vee \bar{b}),$$

where it is already in conjunctive normal form. The truth table is

a	b	$a \leftrightarrow b$
0	0	1
0	1	0
1	0	0
1	1	1

Evidently $a \leftrightarrow b$ is the characteristic function of the Boolean relation $a = b$. From this table the disjunctive normal form is $(\bar{a} \wedge \bar{b}) \vee (a \wedge b)$.

1.4 TAUTOLOGIES

A *tautology* is a universally asserted Boolean formula, in other words one for which the value is identically 1. For instance, $a \vee \bar{a}$ is a tautology, because $a \vee \bar{a} = 1$ for all a. Thus, because $a^2 = a$ for a Boolean variable,

$$a \vee a = a + (1 - a) - a(1 - a) = 1 - a + a^2 = 1.$$

If T is a tautology, then so also is $1 \to T$, because to assert this is to assert that T is a tautology, and if it is then so is $1 \to T$, and so for that matter is

$$1 \to [\, 1 \to \{ \, \ldots \, (1 \to T) \, \ldots \, \} \,],$$

although this is no great addition to the stock of tautologies. A most simple, and useless, tautology is $0 \to a$.

The Boolean laws of section 1.1 were stated as arithmetic identities, but they all provide tautologies. For instance De Morgan's duality law

$$\overline{a \wedge b} = \bar{a} \vee \bar{b}$$

gives the tautology

$$\overline{a \wedge b} \leftrightarrow (\bar{a} \vee \bar{b}),$$

and this, being a tautology, means that

$$\{ \overline{a \wedge b} \leftrightarrow (\bar{a} \vee \bar{b}) \} = 1 \text{ for all } a, b.$$

From given tautologies further ones can be deduced. For instance, if p and $p \to q$ are tautologies then so is q. Here the 'reasoning' itself depends on a tautology, called *modus ponens*,

$$\{ p \wedge (p \to q) \} \to q,$$

which, because propositions really enter only through their truth values, we would rather put as

$$\{ a \wedge (a \to b) \} \to b,$$

this expression being identically 1.

We have a system of formulae, some of which are tautologies. New ones can be discovered from others that are known. They are the 'theorems' of the system, but unlike theorems of general mathematics there is never any mystery about how they can be proved or disproved. As proper Boolean formulae in the first place, their values can be computed for all the 2^n possibilities with their n arguments, and we have a tautology when every value is a 1. Tautologies need not receive such treatment. That is like Cartesian geometry when ingenuity is defeated, and one sure way of proving a Euclidean theorem is to take coordinates and do it algebraically.

The Boolean laws provide important tautologies, and now others will be considered:

(i) $\qquad\qquad b \to (a \vee b), \qquad (a \wedge b) \to a.$

(ii) $\qquad\qquad \{(a \vee b) \to b\} \leftrightarrow \{(a \vee b) \leftrightarrow b\},$
$\qquad\qquad \{a \to (a \wedge b)\} \leftrightarrow \{a \leftrightarrow (a \wedge b)\}.$

(iii) $\qquad\qquad \{(a \vee b) \to b\} \leftrightarrow (a \to b),$
$\qquad\qquad \{a \to (a \wedge b)\} \leftrightarrow (a \to b).$

(iv) $\qquad\qquad \{(a \vee b) \leftrightarrow b\} \leftrightarrow (a \to b),$
$\qquad\qquad \{a \leftrightarrow (a \wedge b)\} \leftrightarrow (a \to b).$

Order properties of the conditional:

$\qquad\qquad a \to a \qquad\qquad\qquad\qquad\qquad\qquad$ *reflexivity*
$\qquad\qquad (a \to b) \vee (a \to b) \qquad\qquad\qquad$ *completeness*
$\qquad\qquad \{(a \to b) \wedge (b \to a)\} \to (a \leftrightarrow b) \qquad$ *asymmetry*

(v) $\qquad\qquad \{(a \to b) \wedge (b \to c)\} \to (a \to c) \qquad$ *transitivity*

Equivalence properties of the biconditional:

(vi) $\qquad\qquad a \leftrightarrow a \qquad\qquad\qquad\qquad\qquad\qquad$ *reflexivity*
$\qquad\qquad (a \leftrightarrow b) \to (a \leftrightarrow b) \qquad\qquad\qquad$ *symmetry*
$\qquad\qquad \{(a \leftrightarrow b) \wedge (b \leftrightarrow a)\} \to (a \leftrightarrow b) \qquad$ *transitivity*

Law of bounds:

$\qquad\qquad 0 \to a, \qquad a \to 1,$
$\qquad\qquad (a \to b) \vee \{(a \wedge c) \to (b \wedge c)\},$

(vii) $\qquad\qquad (a \to b) \vee \{(a \vee c) \to (b \vee c)\}.$

Law of the least upper bound:

$\qquad\qquad a \to (a \vee b), \qquad b \to (a \vee b),$

(viii) $\qquad\qquad \{(a \to c) \wedge (b \to c)\} \to \{(a \vee b) \to c\}.$

Law of the greatest lower bound:
$$(a \wedge b) \to a, \qquad (a \wedge b) \to b,$$

(ix) $\qquad \{ (c \to a) \wedge (c \to b) \} \to \{ (c \to (a \wedge b)) \}.$

Law of the contrapositive:

(x) $\qquad (a \to b) \to (\bar{b} \to \bar{a}).$

Modus ponens:

(xi) $\qquad \{ a \wedge (a \to b) \} \to b.$

(formulated by Crisippus, c. 230 BC)

(xii) $\qquad \{ (a \vee b) \to c \} \leftrightarrow \{ (a \to c) \wedge (b \to c) \},$
$\qquad \{ (a \wedge b) \to c \} \leftrightarrow \{ (a \to c) \vee (b \to c) \}.$

1.5 EXISTENTIAL AND UNIVERSAL QUANTIFIERS

A Boolean formula $f(x)$ where x is the vector of its n arguments is itself an example of a propositional function. One way of asserting it to be a tautology, that is, of asserting $f(x)$ *for all* x, is to take the conjunction $\wedge_x f(x)$ of all its 2^n values, for $x = 0\ldots0$ to $1\ldots1$, and assert that this true or has the value 1. Similarly, asserting the disjunction $\vee_x f(x)$ means asserting $f(x)$ *for some* x, or that there exists an x for which $f(x)$ is true, or 1.

In the same way with any propositional function $p(x)$ $(x \in U)$, the conjunctions and disjunctions $\wedge_x p(x)$ and $\vee_x p(x)$ mean '$p(x)$ *for all* x' and '$p(x)$ *for some* x'. A sometimes more convenient notation for the conjunction is $(\wedge x)p(x)$, or, when a set $Q \subset U$ to which x is restricted is to be made explicit, $(\wedge x \in Q)p(x)$, and also $\wedge \{ p(x) : x \in Q \}$, and what we have then is the same as $\wedge_x \{ (x \in Q) \to p(x) \}$. In terms of the propositional function $q(x)$ which is the characteristic function of Q, or has Q as its truth set, $\wedge_{q(x)} p(x)$, $\wedge [p(x): q(x)]$, and $\wedge_x \{ q(x) \to p(x) \}$ mean again the same, or with P as the truth set of $p(x)$ we have simply $Q \subset P$. Which notation and terminology is used on an occasion is a matter of custom and convenience. Often, $q(x) \to p(x)$ without other comment will mean $\wedge_x \{ q(x) \to p(x) \}$.

With $\vee_x p(x)$ there are similar alternatives. Thus, $\vee_{x \in Q} p(x)$, or $\vee [p(x) : x \in Q]$, means '$p(x)$ *for some* x in Q', and, what is the same, $\vee_x \{ p(x) \wedge q(x) \}$, or $P \cap Q \neq O$.

Properties of these *existential* and *universal quantification* operators will now be considered. From tautology (i) of the last section,

$$\{ \wedge_x p(x) \} \to p(y), \qquad p(y) \to \{ \vee_x p(x) \},$$

are tautologies meaning that

$$\wedge_y [\{ \wedge_x p(x) \} \to p(y)], \qquad \wedge_y [p(y) \to \{ \vee_x p(x) \}] \qquad \text{(i)},$$

are true.

By de Morgan,

$$\sim \{ \wedge_x p(x) \} \leftrightarrow \vee_x \sim p(x), \tag{ii}$$

and, dually,

$$\sim \{ \vee_x p(x) \} \leftrightarrow \wedge_x \sim p(x),$$

or, contrapositively,

$$\vee_x p(x) \leftrightarrow \sim \{ \wedge_x \sim p(x) \} . \tag{ii$'$}$$

Consider now a propositional function $p(x, y)$ of two variables $x \in U, y \in V$. This would be the characteristic function of a binary relation between U, V. From the associativity and commutativity laws for $\wedge$ and $\vee$,

$$\wedge_x \{ \wedge_y p(x, y) \} \leftrightarrow \wedge_{x,y} p(x, y) \tag{iii}$$
$$\vee_x \{ \vee_y p(x, y) \} \leftrightarrow \vee_{x,y} p(x, y).$$

From the tautology $p(x, y) \rightarrow \vee_y p(x, y)$ follows

$$\wedge_x p(x, y) \rightarrow \wedge_x \vee_y p(x, y),$$

and so

$$\vee_y \wedge_x p(x, y) \rightarrow \wedge_x \vee_y p(x, y). \tag{iii$'$}$$

However, the converse is not true. For instance, let $p(x, y)$ mean $y = x^+$ where $x \in [0, 1, 2]$ and $0+ = 1, 1+ = 2, 2+ = 0$, so x^+ is the successor of x when 0, 1, 2 are taken in a cyclical order. Every point has a successor but there is no point which is a sucessor to all, so $\wedge_x \vee_y p(x, y)$ is asserted while $\vee_y \wedge_x p(x, y)$ is denied.

Similarly, we have

$$\wedge_x \{ p(x) \wedge q(x) \} \leftrightarrow \{ \wedge_x p(x) \wedge \wedge_x q(x) \} , \tag{iv}$$

$$\vee_x \{ p(x) \vee q(x) \} \leftrightarrow \{ \vee_x p(x) \vee \vee_x q(x) \} ,$$

and also

$$\vee_x \{ p(x) \wedge q(x) \} \rightarrow \{ \vee_x p(x) \} \wedge \{ \vee_x q(x) \} \tag{iv$'$}$$

but not the converse; and

$$[\{ \vee_x p(x) \} \rightarrow q] \leftrightarrow [\wedge_x \{ p(x) \rightarrow q \}], \tag{v}$$
$$[\{ \wedge_x p(x) \} \rightarrow q] \leftrightarrow [\vee_x \{ p(x) \rightarrow q \}].$$

1.6 PREDICATES AND SETS

Propositional functions and sets have different notations; there is no other difference between them, except perhaps a way of thinking in which sets are visualized, as with the Venn diagrams. When statements $x \in A$ and $p(x) = 1$ mean the same, we say that p is the *characteristic function* of A, and A the *truth set* of p, and any statements about one can be translated for the other. Making $x \in p$ mean $p(x) = 1$, thereby using p also to denote the truth set of the propositional function, might be logical, but it could be confusing and is not customary.

'Predicate' is a word which signifies yet another manner of expression for the same thing, like 'propositional function' and 'set'. A predicate P applies to some object x, so $P(x)$ is a statement that tells us something about x. The statement is an affirmation, corresponding to $p(x) = 1$ with a propositional function or $x \in A$ with a set, and the denial would be stated $\sim P(x)$, or $\bar{P}$.

We have a set when we can tell that we have an elements of it. Set algebra can start with a set U, the *universe of discourse*, without comment on how we get it. Sets are a fact of experience, and in the end there has to be a reliance on that without being formal about it. There is no need, and there might not be any sense, to refer to the complement of U. Now we deal with subsets of U and correspondingly with propositional functions defined on U.

Predicate, propositional function, and set are the same first idea, which concerns objects—which are recognized and given names for reference—in whatever there is to tell about them. Since an object involves the idea already from the general recognition it has from its many appearances, it has no priority, or even difference. There is no more about this first idea except the Boolean form with two values—affirm or deny, or whatever.

With regard to a binary relation $R \subset U \times V$, this is defined as a subset of a Cartesian product, but the statement xRy is used to affirm that objects x, y have such a relationship, meaning that $(x, y) \in R$. This expression corresponds to using R as a predicate. It suits binary relations generally and fits customary usages like $x \leq y$, instead of $\leq (x, y)$. With a ternary relation $R \subset U \times V \times W$, one would quite likely use $R(x, y, z)$ to assert that objects x, y, z are so related. Here we recognize a set $R \subset U$ as a unary relation, and as a predicate, and $R(x)$ would mean the same as $x \in R$.

We have treated Boolean operations simply as arithmetic operations with Boolean variables, and should note usages with them where propositions are concerned. It is straightforward that, when propositional functions are substituted for the arguments in a Boolean operation, and generally any Boolean formula, a propositional function is obtained, for instance, $r(x) = p(x) \wedge q(x)$.

With another use, propositions take the place of the arguments in a Boolean formula. The result then is a proposition, something to be affirmed or denied, and just the statement of it signifies affirmation. It is called a *compound proposition* with the others as its *constituents*. Whether a proposition is affirmed or denied can be represented by a Boolean variable, and the sense of this proposition is that its affirmation or denial is related to those for its constituents as the value of the Boolean formula is related to its arguments. Therefore when the affirmation or denial of each of its constituents is settled, so also is its own; and, according to whether it is affirmed or denied, certain combinations of that for the constituents are admitted.

Given a Boolean function $e = f(a, b, \dots)$ and any subsets $A, B, \dots \subset U$, we now have a sense for $E = f(A, B, \dots)$ as another subset. When a set is said to be given, we take it that we know, formally or informally, when we have an element of it. We define a set formally by laying out a rule by which anyone can know when they have an element of it. Thus,

$$x \in E \equiv f(x \in A, y \in B, \ldots)$$

is a formal definition of the set E; for instance,

$$x \in A \wedge B \equiv (x \in A) \wedge (x \in B),$$

the $\equiv$ signifying that the already intelligible logical expression on the right-hand side tells us the sense of the expression with something new in it on the left-hand side. It just happens that from custom we write $A \wedge B$ differently, as $A \cap B$. This helps to remind us that A and B are sets, and similarly with other Boolean operations as applied to sets. Alternatively, in terms of the characteristic functions of the sets, we have

$$e(x) = f(a(x), b(x), \ldots).$$

We can define an algebra of propositional functions by

$$(a \wedge b)(x) = a(x) \wedge b(x),$$

and so forth. Then $A \cap B$ is the truth set of $a \wedge b$.

With this scheme, all the laws of Boolean algebra that have been stated for the arithmetic operations have counterparts where they are stated for sets.

1.7   SHAO YUNG'S PROGRAM

```
1 DATA The SEQUENCE of SHAO YUNG
2 '
10 GOSUB 1000:GOTO 500
99 '~~~~~~~~
100 LINE(X-3,Y)-(X-2,Y),1
110 LINE(X-1,Y)-(X+1,Y),B(I)
120 LINE(X+2,Y)-(X+3,Y),1
150 I=I+1:RETURN
199 '~~~~
200 FOR I=0 TO N:B(I)=1-B(I)
210 IF B(I) THEN I=0:RETURN ELSE NEXT
299 '~~~~
300 FOR I=0 TO N:B(I)=0:NEXT:I=0:RETURN
498 '
499 '~~~~~~~~
500 FOR N=0 TO 5:K=2^(N+1)-1
510     FOR X=M-5*K TO M+5*K STEP 10
520             FOR Y=L TO L+N:GOSUB 100
600             NEXT Y:GOSUB 200
610     NEXT X:L=L+16:GOSUB 300
620 NEXT N
629 '~~~~~~~~
900 K$="":WHILE K$="":K$=INKEY$:WEND
910 SCREEN 0:KEY ON:END
998 '
999 '~~~~~~~~~~~~~~~~~~·~
```

```
1000 DEFINT A-Z:L=20:M=320:DEFSNG P:PI=3.14159
1010 DIM B(5):KEY OFF:SCREEN 2
1100 CIRCLE(M,L),24,,,,2/5:CIRCLE(M,L),3
1110 CIRCLE(M+12,L),10,,0,PI,0,2/5
1120 CIRCLE(M-12,L),10,,PI,0,0,2/5
1200 READ S$:LOCATE 7,29:PRINT S$:L=88:RETURN
```

Algebra of Relations

Relations are defined as subsets of a Cartesian product, or as predicates involving several objects, and so everything in the Boolean theory of the last chapter should apply to them, any further elaborations coming just from there being more than one variable. Binary relations in particular, which hold for a pair of objects x and y, have the convenient notation xRy, by which it is said that x has the relation R to y. These play a part in many areas in economics, especially demand and production, and choice theory, and they form the subject matter of the present chapter. Just as simple sets with the operations and notations that go with them provide a language for dealing with sets, so it is with relations, although the latter appear to be less familiar in economics. A free use of the notation is found in K. J. Arrow's *Social Choice and Individual Values* (1951), and it was uncommon then. Understanding relations as sets and treating them as such was unusual, and so was operating with them in ways peculiarly associated with binary relations. In addition to a limited use of the notation, order and equivalence relations comprised the range of the matter in evidence in economic writing. A need for additional facilities came from the 'revealed preference' method of P. A. Samuelson (1948), with the development given to it by H. S. Houthakker (1950). When I read the paper (my first moment in economics), circulating as a reprint in 1953 at the Department of Applied Economics, Cambridge, irreflexivity of a transitive closure definitely seemed the proper way to express Houthakker's 'semi-transitivity' condition. The transitive closure is indispensable to that subject, and it has flourished there since; Hirofumi Uzawa's independent use must have originated at about the same time. In a chance discussion of this matter in 1954, C. Davis, my class contemporary who worked in logic, mentioned the order refinement theorem of Szpilrajn (1930). The finite version of this plays an essential part in the finite demand and index theory dealt with in Parts II and III, and it has also done service in many hands (unaware, apparently, of how it came to this subject). Demand and choice theory stimulated an attention to binary relations, which affects elementary matters, as the following illustrates.

We call any relation R an *order* if it is reflexive and transitive; xRx and $xRyRz \Rightarrow xRz$. It has a *converse*, R', a *complement*, R, and a *converse complement*, R'. It also has *symmetric* and *antisymmetric* parts, $E = R \cap R'$ and $P = R \cap R'$, which partition it, since $E \cap P = O$ and $E \cup P = R$. For example, the relation $\leq$ between numbers has $=$ and $<$ as its symmetric and antisymmetric parts. This relation has additional properties which, stated as for R, are that it is *complete*, and *simple*; that is,

$$x R y \vee y R x, \text{ and } x R y \wedge y R x \Rightarrow x = y.$$

These additional properties would make R a *total order*, like $\leq$. As with $<$, P is irreflexive and transitive, so making it a *strict order*. The fact that P has these properties for any order R, without R having to be complete, is taken for granted by some, like M. Drazin and E. M. L. Beale (1956), but for a long time it was widely absent from the literature on demand and choice theory. It is needed for an untroublesome economical way of organizing ideas, without which useless questions arise. When indifference is dealt with as an absence of preference, whether or not it is transitive becomes as issue. Here, E is the indifference relation for the preference relation R, so it is automatically transitive and there is no issue about that. The non-comparison relation is $\bar{R} \cap \bar{R}'$, and this need not be transitive if R is not complete. One can often find indifference and preference dealt with axiomatically as if they were separate matters, and then there can be a long list of axioms. Here, in one stroke, all is covered in the statement that R is an order, reflexive and transitive. That automatically makes E an equivalence and P a strict order; we also have the *absorption* properties, $RE \subset R$, $PE \subset P$, $RP \subset P$ and so forth.

Apparatus of binary relations is natural also for production, especially joint production. An input-output relation, extending the idea of a production function, is a binary relation R between inputs and outputs, where $x R y$ means that y is producible from x, xR is the *output-possiblity set* for an input x, and Ry the *input-possibility set* for an output y, which in the case of a production function, is the region above the y-isoquant. For multistage production, if A and B are input-output relations where the output of A is an intermediate output that provides the input for B, then the *product relation AB*, where $x(AB)z$ means that $(\vee y)xAyBz$, is the input-output relation between initial inputs and final outputs. If these relations are of the von Neumann type, then the dual relations between input and output prices that make positive profits impossible are such that the dual of a product is the product of the duals, $(AB)^* = A^* B^*$. For the von Neumann economic model, the input-output relation across m production periods is the *mth* power R^m of the relation R across one period, and its dual $(R^m)^*$ is the corresponding power $(R^*)^m$ of the dual R^*. Binary relations here are not only convenient as language and notation, but natural to sense and content. They provide an advantageous way of putting many things, and even the only way for some; like elementary sets, they provide a useful vocabulary for some parts of economics.

2.1   OPERATIONS WITH RELATIONS

With a pair of sets A, B one can form the *Cartesian product*

$$A \times B = [(x, y) : x \in A, y \in B],$$

which is the set with elements (x, y) where the first term x is in A and the second in B. This is as with Descartes, who, by taking coordinates x, y in the plane, identified geometric points with points (x, y) of the set $\mathbf{R} \times \mathbf{R}$, where in this case A and B are both the set $\mathbf{R}$ of the real numbers. Also, any n sets A_i $(i = 1, \ldots, n)$ have an n-fold Cartesian product $\times_i A_i$ with elements $(x_1, \ldots, x_n)$ where $x_i \epsilon A_i$; for instance, with $A_i = \mathbf{R}$ we have the n-dimensional Cartesian space $\mathbf{R}^n$.

A *binary relation* between sets A and B, or with these as its first and second *domains*, is any subset $R \subset A \times B$. The statement xRy, or that x *has the relation R to y*, simply means $(x, y) \epsilon R$, and in that case necessarily $x \epsilon A$ and $y \epsilon B$. Similarly, $R \subset \times_i A_i$ defines an *n*-ary relation, and $R(x_1, \ldots, x_n)$ is the statement that $x_1, \ldots, x_n$ are so related, meaning that $(x_1, \ldots, x_n) \epsilon R$. But we will be concerned mostly with binary relations.

With a binary relation $R \subset U \times V$, the statement $x, y, \ldots Rz$ can mean $xRz, yRz, \ldots$ and similarly $xRy, z, \ldots$ means $xRy, xRz, \ldots$. Also, $xRyRz \ldots$ means $xRy, yRz, \ldots$.

The set of elements *to which x is related* in R is denoted $xR = [y : xRy]$, and the set *which is related to x* is $Rx = [y : yRx]$. Necessarily, $Rx \subset U$, $xR \subset V$; also, if $xR \neq 0$, then $x \epsilon U$, and if $Rx \neq 0$ then $x \epsilon V$. If $A = [x : xR \neq 0]$, $B = [x : Rx \neq 0]$, then we have $A \subset U$, $B \subset V$ so that $A \times B \subset U \times V$, and now also $R \subset A \times B$.

Since binary relations with the same domains U, V are all subsets of the set $U \times V$, as such all the operations and then also all the laws of set algebra can apply to them. Thus, any relation $R \subset U \times V$ has a *complement R*, as a subset of $U \times V$, for which, with any $x \epsilon U$ and $y \epsilon V$,

$$x\overline{R}y \Leftrightarrow \sim xRy.$$

Also, any two relations R, S have an *intersection* and *union*, which are the relations $R \cap S$ and $R \cup S$ for which

$$x(R \cap S)y \Leftrightarrow xRy \wedge xSy, \quad x(R \cup S)y \Leftrightarrow xRy \vee xSy.$$

But there are other operations that apply peculiarly to binary relations as such, which will now be considered.

First, any $R \subset U \times V$ determines a *converse* relation $R' \subset V \times U$, defined by

$$xR'y \equiv yRx.$$

The complement of the converse is identical with the converse of the complement; that is, $(\sim R)' = \sim (R')$. For

$$x(\sim R)'y \Leftrightarrow y(\sim R)x \Leftrightarrow \sim yRx \Leftrightarrow \sim xR'y \Leftrightarrow x\{\sim(R')\}y.$$

Hence there is no ambiguity in the expression $\overline{R}'$, for the *converse complement* of R. Evidently the operation of taking the converse is distributive over intersection and union;

$$(R \cap S)' = R' \cap S', \quad (R \cup S)' = R' \cup S'.$$

Now, further, any $R \subset U \times V$ and $S \subset V \times W$ determine a *product relation* $RS \subset U \times W$, defined by

$$x(RS)y \equiv (\vee z)xRySz.$$

From this definition,

$$x(RS)z \Leftrightarrow xR \cap Sz \neq 0.$$

The product operation is associative, $R(ST) = (RS)T$. Also there are the distribution laws

$$R(S \cap T) \subset RS \cap RT, \quad R(S \cup T) = RS \cup RT.$$

Also, $(RS)' = S'R'$, and

$$R \subset S \Rightarrow RT \subset ST.$$

These are easily proved; for instance,

$$
\begin{aligned}
xR(S \cap T)z \quad &\Leftrightarrow \quad (\vee y)xRy(S \cap T)z \\
&\Leftrightarrow \quad (\vee y)xRy \wedge ySz \wedge yTz \\
&\Rightarrow \quad xRSz \wedge xRTz \\
&\Leftrightarrow \quad x(RS \cap RT)z,
\end{aligned}
$$

and so $R(S \cap T) \subset RS \cap RT$.

The product operation being associative, there is no ambiguity in the expression $R_1 \ldots R_n$ for an n-fold product when this makes sense, which is when the second domain of any one factor is the same as the first of the next.

A relation $R \subset U \times U$, where the two domains are the same set U, we call a relation in or between the elements of U. Any relations in same set all have products, which are again relations in that set so we can form extended products, in particular powers R^m ($m = 1, 2, \ldots$), where

$$R^1 = R, \quad R^{m+1} = RR^m.$$

The product operation with relations is not generally commutative. However, products of powers of the same relation are commutative,

$$R^m R^n = R^{m+n} = R^{n+m} = R^n R^m.$$

An R-*chain* is a series $x, y, \ldots, z$ in which each element has the relation R to its successor; that is, $xRy \ldots Rz$. It has *length* m if there are $m + 1$ elements. This chain has *extremities* x and z, and connects x to z. Successive pairs $(x, y), \ldots$ are *links* in the chain, so a chain of length m has m links. The couple (x, z) formed by the extremities is the *span* of the chain. Since

$$xR^m y \Leftrightarrow (\vee z_0 Rz_1 \ldots Rz_m) \; x = z_0 \wedge y = z_m,$$

elements have the power relation R^m if they are connected one to the other by a chain of length m.

The *chain extension* of R is the relation $\vec{R}$ holding between the extremities of an R-chain, so it is defined by

$$x\vec{R} \equiv (\vee m)xR^m y;$$

that is,

$$\vec{R} = \cup_{m = 1, 2, \ldots} R^m.$$

Thus, $x\vec{R}y$ means that (x, y) is the span of some R-chain. Evidently this relation is such that $R \subset \vec{R}$, and moreover it has the property

$$x\vec{R}y\,\vec{R}z \Rightarrow x\vec{R}z,$$

by which it is *transitive*. We have this because, if there are chains from x to y and from y to z then by joining them together at y we have one from x to z. Put another way,

$$\begin{aligned} x\vec{R}y\,\vec{R} &\Rightarrow (\vee m, n)xR^m yR^n z \\ &\Rightarrow (\vee m + n)xR^{m+n} z \\ &\Rightarrow x\vec{R}z. \end{aligned}$$

In addition to a product, any $R \subset U \times V$ and $S \subset V \times W$ also have a *sum* relation $R + S \subset U \times W$, defined by

$$x(R + S)z \equiv (\wedge y)xRy \vee ySz,$$

so that

$$x(R+S)z \Leftrightarrow xR \cup Sz = V.$$

That is, one point has the sum relation to another if every point in the domain V is R'-related to one or S-related to the other. As with the product the sum operation is associative and not commutative. The two are connected by

$$\overline{RS} = \bar{R} + \bar{S};$$

that is, the complement of the product is the sum of the complements. Unlike the product, we do not have much use for this sum operation.

2.2 CLASSIFICATION OF RELATIONS

Various possible properties, and combinations of properties, for binary relations will be considered, by which they are classified into various types.

A *reflexive* relation R in U is such that xRx for all $x \in U$, and an *irreflexive* relation is such that $xRy \Rightarrow x \neq y$. A particular reflexive relation $D \subset U \times U$, the *diagonal* in $U \times U$, or *identification* relation in U, is defined by $xDy \equiv x = y$. Then a reflexive relation is one that contains the diagonal, $D \subset R$, and an irreflexive relation is any contained in the complement of it, $R \subset \bar{D}$. Any relation R has an *irreflexive part* $R \cap \bar{D}$, which is irreflexive and identical with R if R is irreflexive, and similarly a *reflexive closure* $R \cup D$. Reflexivity of a relation implies the same property for the chain extension, but irreflexivity does not.

For a *symmetric* relation R, if it holds one way between a pair of elements then it also holds the other, $xRy \Rightarrow yRx$; that is, $R \subset R'$. Equivalently, $R = R'$, or it is identical with its converse relation. In any case, $R \cap R'$ and $R \cup R'$ are symmetric relations. They are the largest symmetric relation that is contained in R and the smallest symmetric relation that contains R, and define the *symmetric part* and *symmetric closure* of R. If R is symmetric, then so is the chain extension $\vec{R}$.

A relation R is asymmetric if $xRyRx \Rightarrow x = y$, that is if $R \cap R' \subset D$, which is to say the symmetric part is contained in the diagonal. Also, R is *antisymmetric* if $xRyRx$ is impossible. Equivalently, $xRy \Rightarrow y\bar{R}x$; that is, $R \subset \bar{R}'$, or $R \cap R' = 0$. From these definitions, antisymmetry is equivalent to asymmetry together with irreflexivity, and asymmetry of a relation is equivalent to antisymmetry of its irreflexive part. For any R the relation $P = R \cap \bar{R}'$ is in any case antisymmetric, because

$$P = R \cap \bar{R}' \subset R \cup \bar{R}' = \bar{P}',$$

so $P \subset \bar{P}'$.

THEOREM I For any relation R, the subrelations
$$E = R \cap R', \qquad P = R \cap \bar{R}'$$
are symmetric and antisymmetric and such that
$$E \cap P = 0, \qquad E \cup P = R,$$
so they are a partition of R into symmetric and antisymmetric parts, and moreover they are the unique such partition.

It remains to show the uniqueness. Let E, P be any such relations, so that $E \cap P = 0, E \cup P = R$, and also $E \subset E', P \subset \bar{P}'$. Then from $E \subset E'$ and $E \subset R$ follows $E \subset E \cap R'$. Also, from $R = E \cup P$ and $P' \subset \bar{P}$ we have

$$R \cap R' = (E \cup P) \cap (E' \cup P') \subset (E \cup P) \cap (U \cup \bar{P}) = E,$$

so also $E \supset R \cap R'$, and hence $E = R \cap R'$. Now finally,

$$
\begin{aligned}
R \cap \bar{R}' &= (E \cup P) \cap (\bar{E}' \cap \bar{P}') \\
&= P \cap \bar{P} \cap E &&\because E = E' \\
&= P \cap \bar{E} &&\because P \subset \bar{P}' \\
&= P &&\because E \cap P = 0.
\end{aligned}
$$

A relation R is *transitive* if $xRyRz \Rightarrow xRz$, that is if $R^2 \subset R$. This implies that $R \supset R^2 \supset R^3 \supset \dots$ and hence that $R \supset \vec{R}$; equivalently, $xRy \dots Rz \Rightarrow xRz$. In any case, $R \subset \vec{R}$, so this condition is equivalent to $R = \vec{R}$.

While for any relation antisymmetry implies irreflexivity but not conversely, for a transitive relation irreflexivity also implies antisymmetry. For let R be transitive and irreflexive. Then $xRyRx \Rightarrow xRx$, by transitivity. But xRx is impossible, by irreflexivity. Therefore $xRyRx$ is impossible; that is, R is antisymmetric. Thus we have that, *for a transitive relation, irreflexivity is equivalent to antisymmetry.*

THEOREM II The antisymmetric part of any transitive relation is transitive.

With R transitive it has to be shown that so also is $P = R \cap R'$. Thus, from the definition of P and transitivity of R,

$$xPyPz \;\Rightarrow\; xRyRz\overline{R}y\overline{R}x \;\Rightarrow\; xRy \wedge xRz \wedge z\overline{R}y.$$

But,

$$x\overline{P}z \Leftrightarrow x\overline{R}z \vee zRx,$$

again from the definition of P, so that

$$xRz \;.\Rightarrow.\; x\overline{P}z \Leftrightarrow zRx.$$

Thus we have

$$xPyPz \wedge x\overline{P}z \;\Rightarrow\; xRy \wedge zRx \wedge z\overline{R}y$$
$$\Rightarrow\; zRy \wedge z\overline{R}y,$$

and so, the conclusion otherwise being a contradiction, we have $xPyPz \Rightarrow xPz$. QED

Any intersection of transitive relations is transitive. Also, there exist transitive relations containing any given relation R, the chain extension being one. The intersection of all of them therefore is a transitive relation which contains R and is contained in every transitive relation which contains R. This therefore is the minimal transitive relation which contains R, and it defines the *transitive closure* of R.

THEOREM III The transitive closure of any relation is identical with its chain extension.

For any relation T which contains R we have $R \subset T$, and hence $\vec{R} \subset \vec{T}$. Therefore if T is also transitive, so that $\vec{T} \subset T$, then we have $\vec{R} \subset T$. Thus $\vec{R}$ is contained in every transitive relation that contains R. But in any case $\vec{R}$ is transitive and contains R, so this identifies $\vec{R}$ with the transitive closure of R. QED

A reflexive transitive relation we call an *order*. An order R is *complete* if $xRy \wedge yRx$, *simple* if

$$xRy \wedge yRx \;\Rightarrow\; x = y,$$

and a *total order* if it is simple and complete. Reflexivity and transitivity together with symmetry define an *equivalence* relation. An equivalence relation is therefore the same as a symmetric order.

A relation R is *acyclic* if

$$xRyR\ldots zRx \;\Rightarrow\; x = y\ldots = z,$$

and *anticyclic* if

$$xRy\ldots Rz \;\Rightarrow\; z\overline{R}x.$$

Evidently acyclicity implies asymmetry, and is equivalent to the asymmetry of the chain extension. Also, anticyclicity, which implies antisymmetry, is equivalent to the irreflexivity, and the antisymmetry, of the chain extension. Anticyclicity implies acyclicity, and for an irreflexive relation they are equivalent. For a transitive relation, irreflexivity, antisymmetry and acyclicity are all equivalent.

Any relation is *connected* if

$$x \neq y \Rightarrow xRy \wedge yRx,$$

and for a reflexive relation this is equivalent to completeness. A relation P which is irreflexive and transitive is called a *strict order*. This is not essentially different from a simple order. For its reflexive closure $R = P \cup D$ is then a simple order. Also, given any simple order R, which is to say one for which the symmetric part $E = R \cap R'$ is such that $xEy \Rightarrow x = y$, that is $E \subset D$, its irreflexive part $P = R \cap D$, which in this case coincides with its antisymmetric part $P = R \cap \overline{R'}$, is a strict order. Thus the simple and strict orders are in a one–one correspondence, and either can be dealt with in the form of the other by taking the reflexive part or reflexive closure.

The chain extension of an anticyclic relation is a strict order, and the chain extension of a reflexive acyclic relation is a simple order.

For a reflexive relation the transitivity condition $R^2 \subset R$ is equivalent to $R^2 = R$. But for an irreflexive relation P we do not have that equivalence, and $P^2 = P$ signifies that there exists a further element lying between any two that have the relation. This is as with the rationals, but not the integers, in the relation $<$.

2.3   ORDER AND EQUIVALENCE

An order being any reflexive transitive relation, one example is provided by the inclusion relation $\subset$ between subsets of some set. But this is more than just an example. It is *the* model for an order relation, as the following shows.

THEOREM I   Any binary relation R is an order if and only if

$$xRy \Leftrightarrow Rx \subset Ry.$$

Thus, under the mapping $x \rightarrow Rx$, any order R becomes represented by the inclusion relation $\subset$.

If we have $xRy \Leftrightarrow Rx \subset Ry$, then immediately R is reflexive and transitive, and so an order. For the converse, suppose R is an order. Then, by transitivity,

$$xRy . \Rightarrow . (\wedge z) zRx \Rightarrow zRy . \Rightarrow . Rx \subset Ry,$$

and by reflexivity, $x \in Rx$, so that $Rx \subset Ry \Rightarrow xRy$, and so we have the theorem.

As seen in the last section, any relation R has a unique resolution into a union of disjoint symmetric and antisymmetric parts E and P. Now we can see that if R is an order then E is an equivalence and P a strict order, and one moreover with certain *absorption* properties.

A relation A absorbs a relation B on the right if $AB \subset A$, that is if $xAyBz \Rightarrow xAz$, and on the left if $BA \subset A$, and we say that A *absorbs* B if it does on both sides, which if B is reflexive is equivalent to $BAB = A$.

THEOREM II For any relation R and the symmetric and antisymmetric parts

$$E = R \cap R', P = R \cap \overline{R}'$$

which partition it, so that

$$E \cap P = 0, \quad E \cup P = R,$$

if R is an order, then E is an equivalence and P is a strict order, where E is absorbed by R and P, and R is absorbed by P.

From the form of its definition, E is symmetric, and it is reflexive and transitive because R is, so it is an equivalence relation. Thus the symmetric part of any order R is an equivalence relation, defining the relation of *equivalence in the order*. Also, P is antisymmetric, and so irreflexive, from the way it is defined, and we have its transitivity from that of R, by Theorem 2.2.II. Thus it is irreflexive and transitive, and so a strict order, defining the *strict part* of the order R.

The absorption properties are seen easily on the basis of Theorem I with the observation that $xEy \Leftrightarrow Rx = Ry$. These can be stated $xRyEz \Rightarrow xRz$, $xPyEz \Rightarrow xPz$, $xPyRz \Rightarrow xPz$, and so forth.

A set Π of subsets of a set U is a *partition* of U if any distinct pair is disjoint, i.e. if

$$A, B \in \Pi \wedge A \neq B \Rightarrow A \cap B = 0,$$

and U is their union, $U = \cup \Pi$, or

$$U = \cup [A : A \in \Pi].$$

We call the sets in Π classes or components in the partition. This concept is connected, and virtually identical, with that of an equivalence relation, as is shown by the following.

If E is an equivalence relation in a set U, from the symmetry $E = E'$ we have $xE = E'x = Ex$ and so E_x can without ambiguity denote both Ex and xE. Then from reflexivity we have $x \in E_x$. An equivalence being the same as a symmetric order, now from transitivity, by Theorem I, we have

$$xEy \Leftrightarrow E_x = E_y.$$

Also,

$$z \in E_x \cap E_y \Rightarrow xEzEy \Rightarrow xEy,$$

so that

$$E_x \cap E_y \neq 0 \Rightarrow xEy,$$

or, in the contrapositive form,

$$x\overline{E}y \;\Rightarrow\; E_x \cap E_y = 0.$$

It follows that, for all x and y,

$$E_x = E_y \;\vee\; E_x \cap E_y = 0;$$

in other words, any pair of sets of the form E_x is either identical or disjoint. The distinct sets therefore form a partition of their union. But since $x \in E_x$ for all $x \in U$, their union is U.

We call the sets of the form E_x associated with any equivalence relation E its *equivalence classes*, and so we have the following:

> THEOREM III　For any equivalence relation, the equivalence classes form a partition of its domain.

Every element $x \in U$ belongs to one and only one equivalence class of E, given by E_x; this is the unique class of which it is a *representative*.

Given any partition Π, we can define a relation E to hold between elements that belong to the same class,

$$xEy \;\equiv\; (\vee\, A \in \Pi\,)x,\, y \in A.$$

Obviously, this is an equivalence relation, and the partition formed by its equivalence classes is identical with Π. With this, we now have a complete correspondence between the concepts of equivalence relation and partition, showing them to be just two ways of talking about the same thing.

Given any equivalence relation E in a set U, we use U/E to denote the set of subsets of U which are equivalence classes of E, so that

$$U/E = [A : A = E_x,\, x \in U].$$

This is called the *quotient set* of U by the equivalence E. It is obtained by identifying equivalent elements in U as the same object, these objects now forming the set U/E; and $x \to E_x$ is the *canonical map* of U into U/E.

Now let R be any order in a set U, and let E be the relation of equivalence in R, given by its symmetric part. It will now be seen that the order R determines a unique simple order of U/E, denoted R/E, such that, for all $A, B \in U/E$ and all $x \in A$, $y \in B$:

$$A(R/E)B \;\Leftrightarrow\; xRy.$$

We have this because, by the absorption of E by R in Theorem II,

$$xEx' \;\wedge\; yEy' \;\Rightarrow\; xRy \Leftrightarrow x'Ry'.$$

This relation, induced by R in U/E, has the property

$$xRy \;\Leftrightarrow\; E_x(R/E)E_y.$$

It can be verified that R/E with this property is unique, and is reflexive and transitive, and therefore an order, and also simple; that is,

$$A(R/E)B \;\wedge\; B(R/E)A \;\Rightarrow\; A = B.$$

This property also shows that R can be reconstructed from E and R/E. Consequently, *an order has the structure of a simple order of its equivalence classes.* The sense is that, from any order R in U, one can determine the equivalence E given by its symmetric part, and then the simple order R/E of the quotient set U/E, and can then recover R from these.

THEOREM IV Any order R of U with equivalence E determines a unique simple order R/E of U/E such that

$$xRy \Leftrightarrow E_x(R/E)E_y.$$

2.4 ORDER REFINEMENT

If a relation R is acyclic, that is

$$xRyR\ldots Rz \Rightarrow z\overline{R}x,$$

or, equivalently, the transitive closure $\vec{R}$ is irreflexive, then $\vec{R}$, since this is in any case transitive and contains R, is a partial order that contains R. Conversely, if there exists a partial order S that contains R, so that $R \subset S$ where S is irreflexive and transitive, so that $S = \vec{S}$, then $\vec{R} \subset \vec{S} = S$. Then from $\vec{R} \subset S$ it follows that xSx if xRx. But, with S irreflexive, xSx is impossible, so xRx is impossible; that is, $\vec{R}$ is irreflexive. Therefore we have the following.

THEOREM I A necessary and sufficient condition for any relation to be contained in some partial order is that it be acyclic, equivalently that its transitive closure be irreflexive. Then its transitive closure is one such partial order, and it is contained in any other, and so the smallest.

For two partial orders of a given set, one is a *refinement* of the other if it properly contains it. The set of all partial orders is partially ordered by this relation. A *maximal partial order* is one without refinements.

THEOREM II The maximal partial orders are identical with the total orders.

The total orders have no refinements. For let T be a total order and suppose, if possible, that is has a refinement P. Then, from $T \subset P$ with $T \neq P$, we have xTy and xPy for some x, y. Then, because P is antisymmetric, yPx and $x \neq y$. Then because T is connected, from xTy and $x \neq y$ we have yTx, and from this yPx, again because $T \subset P$. Thus yPx and yPx, making a contradiction, and so giving the required conclusion.

Also, there exists a refinement for any partial order that is not a total order. For if P is not a total order then aPb and bPa for some $a \neq b$. Then $Q = P \cup (a, b)$ is acyclic. For suppose, if possible, that a Q-cycle exists. This cannot be a P-cycle, because P is acyclic. Therefore it must contain a link (a, b) together with a P-chain from b to a, which, by transitivity of P, implies bPa, contrary to hypothesis, so also this is impossible. Because Q is acyclic, and properly contains P, $P^+ = \vec{Q}$ is a partial order which properly contains P, so it is a refinement of P, as required.

THEOREM III For any partial order of a finite set, either it is a total order or it has a total order refinement.

Let L be the set of partial orders of a finite set U. If U is finite then so is L. For any P in L, either it is a total order or it has a refinement, by Theorem II. Let P^+ be a choice from among the refiniments of P, when P is not a total order.

With any initial $P_0 \in L$, consider the sequence $P_i \in L$ ($i = 0, 1, \ldots$) where, for any i, we have $P_{i+1} = P^+$, when this is defined, and otherwise the sequence terminates with P_i. Because any P_i which is not a total order must have a successor, a terminal P_i, should there be one, must be a total order. Since the refinement relation between orders is irreflexive and transitive, all P_i in the sequence must be distinct. Therefore the length of the sequence cannot exceed the finite number of members in L, so it must terminate. This shows the existence of a terminal P_i, which must be a total order which, by transitivity, is a refinement of the initial P_0.

An R-chain, for any order R, reflexive and transitive, is given by a sequence $x, y, \ldots, z$ for which $xRyR\ldots Rz$. Generally the same set of points in another order could form another R-chain. The order of the points is therefore essential in specifying an R-chain. However, with a partial order P, irreflexive and transitive, and so also antisymmetric, if it is given that a set of points forms a P-chain when taken in some order, there is no ambiguity about the order, because it is determined by P. All that is conveyed is that the partial order P becomes a total order when considered as an order of just those points. This leads to the following definitions.

Let $P \subset U \times U$ be a partial order in a set U. Then for any $V \subset U$ the relation $Q \subset V \times V$ given by

$$Q = P \cap (V \times V)$$

is a partial order of V, such that

$$xQy \Leftrightarrow xPy \text{ for all } x, y \in V.$$

This is the partial order which the partial order P of U *induces* in any subset $V \subset U$. A subset V of U is a *chain* for P if P induces a total order in V. Then any chain W is a refinement of V simply if it properly contains V. A *maximal* chain is one without refinements.

Sets are partially ordered by proper inclusion, so these definitions can apply, a chain in a set of sets meaning a chain in this partial order. Thus, a chain in a set S of sets is a set $C \subset S$ such that, for any distinct $A, B \in C$, either $A \subset B$ or $B \subset A$. Then for a maximal chain $M \subset S$, no chain $C \subset S$ exists which is a refinement of it.

Among axioms of axiomatic set theory is the following:

AXIOM Every chain in a set of sets has a maximal refinement.

As well known, this is equivalent to the Axiom of Choice, and to Zorn's Lemma.

THEOREM IV (*Szpilrajn*) Every partial order has a refinement which is a total order.

Let S be the set of partial orders of a set U, this being the set of subsets of $U \times U$ defined by irreflexivity and transitivity. For a given $P_0 \epsilon S$, let

$$S_0 = [P \epsilon S : P_0 \subset P].$$

So this is the set of partial orders of U which refines the given partial order P_0. *The set $C \subset S_0$ whose single element is P_0 is a chain in S_0. Then, by the Axiom, there exists a maximal chain M in S_0 which refines this. The union of the sets in any chain which refines C is a partial order which refines P_0. Hence $T = \cup M$ is a partial order which refines P_0. It must be a total order. For were it not, by Theorem II, there must exist a partial order refinement T^+ of T. Then $M^+ = M \cup \{T^+\}$ would be a chain refinement of M, contradicting that M is a maximal chain. Hence T is a total order refinement of P_0, as required.

I am indebted to C. Davis for pointing out this theorem in 1954, the finite case of which has use in the finite demand theory of Chapters II and III. It is attributed to E. Szpilrajn (1930).

2.5 REPRESENTATION THEOREMS

Let S be a strict order of a topological space U. The transitivity of S is equivalent to

$$xSy \Rightarrow Sx \subset Sy.$$

Consider S with the properties

$$Sx \text{ is open, } xSy \Rightarrow \text{cl } Sx \subset Sy.$$

As with Peleg (1970), cl A denotes the closure of any set $A \subset U$. Such S, following Peleg (1970), can be called a *lower-continuous strict order*, and an *upper-continuous strict order* is defined correspondingly with reference to the sets xS. A *semi-continuous strict order* is one which is both lower and upper-continuous.

An order, reflexive and transitive, can also be characterized as any relation R for which

$$xRy \Leftrightarrow Rx \subset Ry,$$

and, equivalently,

$$xRy \Leftrightarrow xR \supset yR.$$

It is a *semi-continuous order* in U if also the sets xR, Rx are closed.

For any strict order S, the transitivity property $xSySz \Rightarrow xSz$ can also be stated $S^2 \subset S$, and it is a *dense* strict order if also

$$xSy \Rightarrow (\vee z) xSzSy,$$

that is, if $S \subset S^2$, in which case there is the idempotence $S = S^2$. Thus the dense strict orders are those with this idempotence property. For any elements that have such a relation, there exists a further element which is between them in that relation, and by irreflexivity it is different from both. For another statement, a strict order S is dense if

$$xSy \Rightarrow xS \cap Sy \neq 0.$$

A *base* for a strict order S is a denumerable set B such that

$$xSy \Rightarrow xS \cap B \cap Sy \neq 0.$$

Then a *separable strict order* is one, necessarily dense, which has a base.

THEOREM I If S is a strict order in a separable topological space for which the sets xS, Sx are open and $x \in \mathrm{cl}\, xS$, then S is a dense strict order.

For then

$$xSy \Rightarrow x \in \mathrm{cl}\, xS \cap Sy \Rightarrow \mathrm{cl}\, xS \cap Sy \neq 0.$$

Also, with xS and Sx open,

$$\mathrm{cl}\, xS \cap Sy \neq 0 \Rightarrow xS \cap Sy \neq 0.$$

Hence

$$xSy \Rightarrow xS \cap Sy \neq 0,$$

showing that S is dense.

THEOREM II The antisymmetric part of a semi-continuous complete order in a connected topological space is a dense semi-continuous strict order.

For an order R with antisymmetric part $P = R \cap \bar{R}'$, we have

$$xPzPy \Rightarrow xP \supset zR \supset yP.$$

If R is complete, so that $\bar{R}' \subset R$, then $P = \bar{R}'$, so that if xR, Rx are closed then xP, Px are open. Also,

$$yR \cap Rx \neq 0 \; . \Rightarrow . \; yRx \Rightarrow x\bar{P}y,$$

so that

$$xPy \Rightarrow yR \cap Rx = 0.$$

Further, with U connected, closed sets cannot be complements, so that

$$yR \cap Rx = 0 \Rightarrow yR \cup Rx \neq U \Rightarrow Py \cap xP \neq 0.$$

Hence

$$xPy \Rightarrow xP \cap Py \neq 0,$$

showing that P is dense. Then also

$$\begin{aligned}
xPy &\Rightarrow (\vee z)\, xPzPy \\
&\Rightarrow (\vee z)\, xP \supset zR \supset yP \\
&\Rightarrow xP \supset \mathrm{cl}\, yP,
\end{aligned}$$

so P is upper semi-continuous, and similarly lower semi-continuous, and hence semi-continuous.

THEOREM III If S is a dense strict order in a topological space U for which the sets xP, Px are open, any base for U is a base for P, so if U is a separable topological space then P is a strict order.

For if U is separable, let B be a base, that is, a denumerable set which is dense in U, or has U as its closure, so that every non-empty open set of U contains some point of B. If P is dense and xP, Px are open, then xPy implies that $xP \cap Py$ is non-empty and open, and hence that its intersection with B is non-empty, showing that B is a base for P.

LEMMA For a separable strict order S in a topological space U such that the sets xS are open and
$$xSy \Rightarrow xS \supset \text{cl } yS,$$
if aSb, then there exists a continuous function
$$\varrho : U \to <0, 1>$$
such that $\varrho(a) = 0$, $\varrho(b) = 1$ and
$$xSy \Rightarrow \varrho(x) \leq \varrho(y)$$
(Peleg, 1970).

With $I = <0, 1>$, let J denote the binary rationals in I, and J_n those with denominator 2^n, these being
$$r_n^m = m/2^n \; (m = 0, 1, \ldots, 2^n; n = 0, 1, 2, \ldots).$$

Thus, for all n,
$$r_n^0 = 0, \quad r_n^{2^n} = 1; \; r_n^m = r_{n+1}^{2m}.$$

Also,
$$J_0 \subset J_1 \subset \ldots \subset J \text{ and } J = \cup_{n = 1, 2, \ldots} J_n.$$

Consider an order-preserving one-one mapping
$$\sigma_n : J_n \to U,$$
of J_n into a P-chain $C_n = \sigma_n(J_n)$ in B with first and last elements a, b. Thus, with
$$z_n^m = \sigma_n(m/2^n),$$
we have
$$a = z_n^0 P z_n^1 P \ldots P z_n^{2^n} = b,$$
so that
$$1 < m \Leftrightarrow z_n^l P z_n^m.$$

Also let
$$\sigma_n(r_n^m) = \sigma_{n+1}(r_{n+1}^{2m}),$$

so that $z_n^m = z_{n+1}^{2m}$, making the P-chain C_{n+1} a refinement of C_n obtained by the introduction, using some rule, of an element

$$\sigma_{n+1}(r_{n+1}^{2m+1}) = z_{n+1}^{2m+1}$$

of B between every successive pair of elements z_n^m and z_n^{m+1} of C_n, thereby making σ_{n+1} an extension of σ_n.

Given any σ_n, it is possible to do this, because P is dense, and separable with base B. By taking σ_0 with

$$\sigma_0(0) = a, \quad \sigma_0(1) = b,$$

and with any rule for the introduction of intermediate elements, the existence of which is assured by the Axiom of Choice, σ_n is now recursively defined for all n. The mapping $\sigma : J_n \leftrightarrow U$, whose graph is the union of the graphs of the mappings $\sigma_n : J_n \leftrightarrow U$, is such that $\sigma(0) = a$, $\sigma(1) = b$, and

$$r < s \Leftrightarrow \sigma(r)P\sigma(s)(r, s \,\epsilon\, J).$$

For the range $C = \sigma(J)$ we have that, but for the points a, b, it is contained in the set $aP \cap B \cap Pb$, and is a P-chain, that is, a set which is totally ordered by P. Moreover, it is a dense P-chain with a, b as first and last elements.

The inverse mapping of σ is a mapping $\varrho: C \to J$ such that

$$xSy \Leftrightarrow \varrho(x) < \varrho(y).$$

In other words, ϱ represents S in the subset C of U. Now let the domain of ϱ be extended from C to U, thus: for all $x \,\epsilon\, U$, if zSx for some $z \,\epsilon\, C$ let

$$\varrho(x) = \sup\, [\varrho(x) : zSx, z \,\epsilon\, C],$$

and otherwise let $\varrho(x) = 0$. Then

$$0 \le \varrho(x) \le 1\,(x \,\epsilon\, U), \quad \varrho(a) = 0, \quad \varrho(b) = 1,$$

and, by transitivity of S,

$$xSy \Rightarrow Sx \subset Sy \Rightarrow \varrho(x) \le \varrho(y).$$

It remains now to show that $\varrho(x)$ is continuous. For this it is enough to show that the sets

$$[x : \varrho(x) < t], \quad [x : \varrho(x) > t]\,(0 < t < 1)$$

are nonempty and open.

Consider $0 < t < 1$ and any $x \,\epsilon\, U$ such that $t < \varrho(x)$. From the definition of $\varrho(x)$, there exists $z \,\epsilon\, Sx$ such that $t < \varrho(z)$, and also

$$zSy \Rightarrow \varrho(z) \le \varrho(y) \Rightarrow t < \varrho(y).$$

Because zS is open, contains x, and lies in the set $[y : t < \varrho(y)]$, x is an interior point of this set. But x is any point of the set, so the set is open.

Now consider any $x \,\epsilon\, U$ such that $\varrho(x) < t$. There exists $r, s \,\epsilon\, J$ such that $\varrho(x) < r < s < t$, and then $y = \sigma(r)$, $z = \sigma(s)$ in C are such that

$\varrho(y) = r$, $\varrho(z) = s$. Then $y\bar{S}x$, because

$$ySx \Rightarrow r = \varrho(y) \le \varrho(x),$$

and also ySz, and this implies that $yS \supset cl\ zS$. It follows that the complement of cl zS contains x. In any case zS contains this complement. Also,

$$w \in zS \Rightarrow \varrho(w) \le \varrho(z) = s < t.$$

For if $\varrho(w) > \varrho(z)$, then $\varrho(z') > \varrho(z)$ for some $z' \in C \cap Sw$ such that $z'\ Sw$. But then $zSz'\ Sw$, which implies zSz, that is, $w \in zS$. Accordingly, the complement of cl zS is an open neighbourhood of x in the set $[w : \varrho(w) < t]$, showing that this set is open. This proves the continuity of ϱ, and the theorem.

THEOREM IV   If S is a separable strict order in a topological space U such that the sets Sx are open and

$$xSy \Rightarrow cl\ Sx \subset Sy,$$

then there exists a continuous function

$$\sigma : U \to <0, 1>$$

such that

$$xSy \Rightarrow \sigma(x) < \sigma(y)$$

(Peleg, 1970); and if, moreover, S is a total order, then

$$xSy \Leftrightarrow \sigma(x) < \sigma(y).$$

Since S is separable, let B be a base, and let (a_i, b_i) $(i = 1, 2, \ldots)$ be an enumeration of $S \cap (B \times B)$. Then, by Peleg's lemma, for each i there exists a continuous function $\sigma_i : U \to <0, 1>$ such that

$$\sigma_i(a_i) = 0, \sigma_i(b_i) = 1, 0 \le \sigma_i(x) \le 1$$

and

$$xSy \Rightarrow \sigma_i(x) \le \sigma_i(y).$$

Let

$$\sigma(x) = \sum_{i=1}^{\infty} 2^{-i} \sigma_i(x).$$

The series is uniformly convergent and its terms are continuous, so $\sigma(x)$ is defined and continuous for all $x \in U$. Its value is 0 for a minimum element and 1 for a maximum element, if there are any, and generally $0 \le \sigma(x) \le 1$. It remains to show that

$$xSy \Rightarrow \sigma(x) < \sigma(y).$$

Thus, if xSy, then $xSa_i\ Sb_i\ Sy$ for some i. Because

$$\sigma_i(a_i) = 0 < 1 = \sigma_i(b_i)$$

and also

$$\sigma_j(a_i) \le \sigma_j(b_i) \text{ for all } j,$$

it follows that

$$\sigma(a_i) < \sigma(b_i).$$

But also

$$\sigma(x) \leq \sigma(a_i), \ \sigma(b_i) \leq \sigma(y).$$

Hence $\sigma(x) < \sigma(y)$, as required to prove Peleg's theorem.

For the additional remark, the conclusion there is equivalent to

$$\sigma(x) \geq \sigma(y) \Rightarrow x\overline{S}y,$$

so if, moreover, S is connected, to make it a total order, that is, if

$$x\overline{S} \wedge x \neq y \Rightarrow ySx,$$

then this implies

$$\sigma(x) > \sigma(y) \Rightarrow x\overline{S} \wedge x \neq y \Rightarrow ySx,$$

showing that in this case

$$xSy \Leftrightarrow \sigma(x) < \sigma(y),$$

as required.

THEOREM V If R is a complete order in a connected separable topological space such that the sets xR, Rx are closed, then there exists a continuous function $\varrho(x)$ such that

$$xRy \Leftrightarrow \varrho(x) \leq \varrho(y).$$

For such R, $P = \overline{R}'$ satisfies the conditions of Peleg's theorem. Hence there exists a continuous function $\varphi(x)$ such that

$$xRy \Rightarrow \varphi(x) < \varphi(y);$$

equivalently,

$$xRy \Leftarrow \varphi(x) \leq \varphi(y).$$

But Theorem V proposes the existence of a continuous function $\varphi(x)$ such that

$$xRy \Leftrightarrow \varphi(x) \leq \varphi(y).$$

There is a defect here for an immediate view of Theorem V as a consequence of Peleg's theorem. Offering the above together with this remark in a class at the University of Waterloo in April 1972, brought an ingenious response from L. F. Lee (1973), as follows.

Let R satisfy the conditions of Theorem V, and let E, P be its symmetric and antisymmetric parts. Then, as just remarked, P satisfies the conditions of Peleg's theorem. Lee's argument then proceeds as follows. Consider the quotient set $\mathbf{U} = U/E$ and the canonical map $1/E: U \rightarrow \mathbf{U}$, in which any $x \in U$ has as its image the E-equivalence class to which it is a representative, denoted x/E, or E_x. In the quotient topology in the quotient set $\mathbf{U}$, a set $\mathbf{A} \subset \mathbf{U}$ is open if its inverse image in the canonical map, this being $A = \cup \mathbf{A} \subset U$, is open in the topology of U. Thus the quotient topology is defined so as to make the canonical map continuous.

Because R and P absorb E, the quotient relations $\mathbf{R} = R/E$ and $\mathbf{P}$ are defined. Then $\mathbf{R}$ is a complete simple order, and so a total order, of $\mathbf{U}$. Also $\mathbf{P}$ is at once its antisymmetric part, its irreflexive part and its converse complement. Because

$$xPy \Leftrightarrow (x/E)(P/E)(y/E),$$

the separability of $\mathbf{P} = P/E$ follows from that of P. Also,

$$(xP)/E = (x/E)(P/E), \quad (Px)/E = (P/E)(x/E),$$

so the sets $X\mathbf{P}$, $\mathbf{P}X$ are open because the sets xP, Px are open and the canonical map $1/E$ is continuous. Because $\mathbf{P}$ is transitive,

$$XPY \Rightarrow \mathbf{P}X \cup \{X\} \subset \mathbf{P}Y,$$

and because it is irreflexive and connected,

$$X\mathbf{P} = \mathbf{P}X \cup \{X\} \supset \mathbf{P}X.$$

But since $X\mathbf{P}$ is open, $X\bar{\mathbf{P}}$ is closed, and hence

$$X\bar{\mathbf{P}} \supset \text{cl } \mathbf{P}X.$$

It follows that

$$XPY \Rightarrow \text{cl } \mathbf{P}X \subset \mathbf{P}Y.$$

Thus $\mathbf{P}$ satisfies the conditions of Peleg's theorem, so there exists a function $f\colon \mathbf{U} \to I$ such that

$$X\mathbf{P}Y \Rightarrow f(X) < f(Y).$$

But because $\mathbf{P}$ is a total order this is equivalent to

$$X\mathbf{P}Y \Leftrightarrow f(X) < f(Y).$$

But

$$xRy \Leftrightarrow (x/E)(R/E)(y/E),$$

so with $\varphi\colon U \to I$ given by

$$\varphi(x) = f(x/E),$$

it follows that

$$xRy \Leftrightarrow \varphi(x) \le \varphi(y),$$

and so Theorem V is proved.

Consider the lexicographical order L, or the order of first differing elements, on the unit hypercube I^n. This order is complete and simple, and so a total order of the hypercube, but the sets xL, Lx are not closed. It will be shown that, *for $n > 1$, L is incapable of representation by a function $f\colon I^n \to I$ such that $xLy \Leftrightarrow f(x) \le f(y)$*. This well known example is attributed to von Neumann.

Assume such a representation. Then, because L is simple,

$$xLy \wedge x \ne y \Rightarrow f(x) < f(y). \tag{*}$$

With $t \in I$ and $x \in I^{n-1}$, so that $(t, x) \in I^n$, let

$$u(t) = \inf_x f(t, x), \, v(t) = \sup_x f(t, x),$$

so that, by ($*$), assuming $n > 1$, we have $u(t) < v(t)$ for all t. Hence, for all t, it is possible to choose a rational $r(t)$ such that

$$u(t) < r(t) < v(t).$$

We can now see how

$$s \neq t \Rightarrow r(s) \neq r(t).$$

Suppose the contrary, i.e. that

$$r(s) = r = r(t) \text{ where } s \neq t,$$

so that $u(s) < r < v(t)$ and hence, for some $x, y \in I^{n-1}$,

$$f(s, x) < r < f(t, y).$$

Then, from ($*$) and the definition of L, $s\,t$ implies that $s < t$, and similarly $t < s$, so $s \neq t$ is impossible.

It appears from this that the function $r(t)$ establishes a one–one correspondence between an interval of the reals and a subset of the rationals, which is impossible, since the rationals are denumerable and the reals are not. Hence our initial assumption must be false. QED

Intersections and Fixed Points

A mapping $f: S \rightarrow S$ of a set S into itself can be thought of as a movement of the points of S, where any point $x \in S$ goes to another $f(x)$ S, its image under f. Then a *fixed point* of f is a point x which does not move; that is, $f(x) = x$. For example, if S is a circular disc and it is rotated through some angle, then every point moves except the centre, which is a fixed point. Characteristics of the mapping can assure the existence of at least one fixed point. The theorem of L. E. J. Brouwer is an example: if S is a simplex, or equivalent, and f is continuous, then there must be a fixed point. From the 'neighbourhood' nature of this theorem, if it is true for a triangle, and its higher dimensional counterpart is the simplex, then it must also be true for a square, a circle, and other topologically equivalent regions, and their counterparts in any dimension.

Alternatively, this theorem can be represented as an intersection theorem. With

$$F = [(x, y): y = f(x)]$$

as the graph of the mapping f, and

$$D = [(x, y): y = x]$$

as the 'diagonal', Brouwer's theorem asserts that $F \cap D \neq 0$. Von Neumann's intersection theorem is a generalization. Kakutani gave a more satisfactory proof of a special case and deduced the general theorem from it.

Von Neumann used the theorem for the existence question which arises with his economics model. Possibly this was the first application of this type of theorem to economics. He used it also for saddle point existence questions arising with his economic model and games. John Nash brought the fixed point theorem again to economics with his equilibrium concept for an n-person game and the existence proof using Brouwer's theorem. MacKenzie and Arrow-Debreu applied a similar argument to general equilibrium models. Wald had pointed out that the counting of equations and variables used by Walras was

useless. The method used with Brouwer's theorem overcame that difficulty
with substantially more general models. Gale proved another intersection-type
theorem which took a form that exactly suited the general equilibrium application, so condensing the matter greatly, eliminating much discussion.

3.1   SIMPLICES AND DISSECTIONS

Let S be a simplex and V the set of its vertices, these being $n + 1$ in number if S has
dimension n, making it an *n-simplex*. Taking barycentric coordinates with S as
simplex of reference, any point $x \in S$ has coordinates x_i ($i = 0, 1, \ldots, n$) where

$$x_i \geq 0, \ \Sigma x_i = 1.$$

Thus *vertex j* of S has coordinates $x_i = 0$ ($i \neq j$), $x_j = 1$.

A *face* of S is a simplex S' whose vertices are a subset $V' \subset V$ of the vertices of S. The vertices of S are the faces of dimension 0, and S itself is the
only face of dimension n. The 1-faces or *edges* are the line segments joining
pairs of vertices.

A *simplicial dissection* of S is a collection T of simplices covering S, any
pair of which are either disjoint or have a common face for their intersection.
The vertices of T include all the vertices of its simplices, and so also all the
vertices of S. A dissection T of S provides a dissection also of the faces of
S, whose simplices are faces of the simplices of T. By dissecting the simplices
of a dissection T of S we have a further *finer* dissection of S, whose vertices
contain the vertices of T as a subset.

The *barycentric subdivision* of a simplex S is the particular simplicial dissection $B(S)$ whose vertices are the vertices of S together with the bisectors of
the edges. Barycentric subdivision can also apply to any dissection. By n-times
repeated subdivision, we have the nth barycentric subdivision $B(\ldots B(S)\ldots)$
of S, whose simplices have edges which are $1/2^n$ of the edges of S.

The *carrier face* of any point of S is the face of lowest dimension which
contains it. Thus, $V_x = [i : x_i > 0]$ is the set of vertices of the carrier face
S_x of x. The vertices of S are their own carrier faces. Also, any face of a
simplex of a dissection has a carrier face, which is the face of lowest dimension of the base simplex which carries all its vertices.

A *Sperner label* for a point of S can be any vertex of its carrier face. Thus,
L is a Sperner label for x if $L \in V_x$, that is if $x_L > 0$. In particular, the only
possible Sperner label for a vertex of S is the vertex itself. A *Sperner labelling*
for a simplicial dissection T of S is a function L which assigns a Sperner label
$L(x)$ to every vertex x of T. Then a *Sperner simplex* is a simplex of T whose
vertex labels describe all the vertices of S.

3.2   SPERNER'S LEMMA

THEOREM (*Sperner*)   For any simplex S and any simplicial dissection
T of S, and any Sperner labelling of the vertices of T, the number of
Sperner simplices is odd, and consequently there exists at least one.

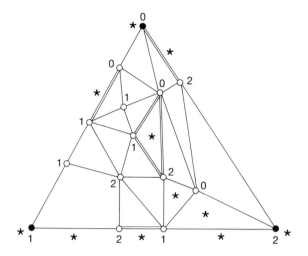

● simplex S
○ simplicial dissection T of S
★ Sperner simplices — odd number in each face

Figure 1   Sperner's lemma

The terms in this theorem are given in the last section. First we will see what it means for a 1-simplex S, with vertices 0, 1. This is a line segment with 0, 1 as end-points, say on the left and right.

1—Simplex S

For a simplicial dissection of T of S the vertices are a set of points of S including 0 and 1. Neighbouring ones join in segments, which are the simplices of the dissection T. These cover S, and any pair either are disjoint or have a face, in this case an end-point, in common.

Dissection T of S

S itself is the carrier face of every vertex of T except its own vertices, which carry themselves. Therefore with a Sperner labelling they carry either 0 or 1 as labels, while the vertices of S label themselves.

Sperner labelling L of T

A Sperner simplex is a segment whose vertex labels include both 0 and 1. It is clear that one must exist in this special case. Scanning the vertices of T from the left, we start with a 0. Succeeding ones carry labels 0 or 1, but the last has the label 1. The first 1 that occurs produces the first Sperner simplex. Since there is a vertex which carries the label 1, the last being a case, so that a 1 must be encountered sooner or later, at least one Sperner simplex exists. The argument of the theorem is that the number of Sperner simplices is odd, so there must be at least one. We can see that in this case. In scanning the vertices from the left, every alternation of labels produces a Sperner simplex. Starting from label 0, any number of alternations that ends with a 1 must be odd, and we do end with a 1 on the right. Therefore the number of Sperner simplices is odd.

For the general proof of the theorem, the method is by induction on the simplex dimension n. The case $n = 0$ is true, vacuously. We have, moreover, just given an independent proof for $n = 1$. Suppose now that the theorem is true for dimension $n - 1$, and consider a simplex S of dimension n. Let T be a simplicial dissection of S, and let L be a Sperner labelling of T. These induce the same on every face of S, to which the inductive hypothesis applies. Therefore every face of S contains a simplex, a face of some simplex of T, whose vertex labels exactly describe its vertices; moreover, there is an odd number of such simplices in any face. The proof of the theorem has two parts and we use this consequence of the inductive hypothesis in the second.

Consider the class C of faces of T with vertex labels $1, \ldots, n$. Any one is a face of a simplex of T whose remaining vertex label is either 0 or different from 0 and so among $1, \ldots, n$. Let N be the number of simplices of T with labels $0, 1, \ldots, n$. These are the Sperner simplices. Also let N' be the number of simplices of T with labels $1, \ldots, n$ and another repeating one of these. Each of the N has one face of class C and each of the N' has two. Thus the number of occurrence of a simplex of class C as a face of some simplex of T is $N + 2N'$.

Now further, each C-simplex is counted once if it is in a face of S, since then it is a face of just one simplex of T, and otherwise twice, since then it is a face of two simplices of T. But a C-simplex in the face $1, \ldots, n$ of S is a Sperner simplex for that face, and by the inductive hypothesis the number of these is odd. Also, a C-simplex cannot lie in any other face, by the Sperner labelling rule. Thus an odd number M of faces of T have been counted once in the total $N + 2N'$ and the remaining ones, say M', have been counted twice. Thus we have $N + 2N' = M + 2M'$, where M is odd. It follows that N is odd. QED

3.3 THE KKM LEMMA

LEMMA If U is compact and closed subsets $F_i \subset U$ are such that $\cap_i F_i = 0$ then there exists $\epsilon > 0$ such that, for any X, if $X \cap F_i \neq 0$ for all i then X has diameter at least ϵ.

The set $X_i F_i$ is compact, and the function

$$f(x) = \min_{ij} |x_i - x_j| \quad (x_i \in F_i)$$

defined on it is continuous and so attains a minimum ϵ, where $\epsilon > 0$ since $\cap_i F_i = 0$. Hence for any a_i, $a_i \epsilon X \cap F_i$ for all i implies that the diameter of X is

$$\sup \, [\, |x - y| \, : x, \, y \, \epsilon \, X \,] \geq f(a) \geq \epsilon \, ,$$

so it is at least ϵ. QED

THEOREM (*Knaster – Kuratowski – Mazurkiewicz*) If S is a simplex, S_v the face on any subset v of vertices, F_i a closed subset associated with any vertex i, and $F_v = \cup_{i \, \epsilon \, v} F_i$, and if $S_v \subset F_v$ for all v, then $\cap_i F_i \neq 0$.

Suppose if possible that $\cap_i F_i = 0$ and let $\epsilon > 0$ be as in the lemma. Consider a simplicial subdivision T of S where the simplices have diameter $< \epsilon$. For any vertex t of T let v be the set of vertices of the carrier face of S, so that $t \, \epsilon \, S_v \subset F_v$ and hence $t \, \epsilon \, F_i$ for some i. Let $L(t) = i$. Then L is a Sperner labelling of the vertices of T. Hence by Sperner's lemma there exists a simplex X of T such that, for all i, $L(t) = i$ for some vertex t of X, so $X \cap F_i \neq 0$ for all i. But by the lemma this is impossible since X has diameter less than ϵ. Hence the hypothesis is impossible. QED

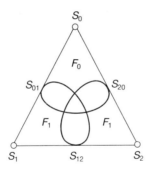

Figure 2

3.4 BROUWER'S FIXED POINT THEOREM

THEOREM (*Brouwer*) If S is a simplex and $f : S \rightarrow S$ is continuous, then $f(x) = x$ for some x.

We can take S to be described by vectors x where $x_i \geq 0$, $\Sigma x_i = 1$, and consider the sets

$$F_i = [\, x : f_i(x) \leq 1 \,] \, .$$

These are closed, by continuity of f. It will be shown that $S_v \subset F_v$, where S_v is the face of S on any set of vertices v and

$$F_v = \cup_{i \, \epsilon \, v} F_i \, ,$$

and hence, by the KKM lemma, that

$$\cap F_i \neq 0.$$

Since $x \in \cap F_i$ is equivalent to $f_i(x) \leq x_i$ and hence to $f(x) = x$, the theorem will then be proved.

Thus, for $x \in S_v$ we have, by definition, $\Sigma_{i \in v} x_i = 1$, so that

$$\Sigma_{i \in v} f_i(x) \leq \Sigma_{i \in v} x_i.$$

This implies that $f_i(x) \leq x_i$ for some i, equivalently, $x \in S_v$. QED

H. W. Kuhn's argument can be put as follows. If we had

$$x_i > 0 \Rightarrow f_i(x) > x_i$$

we would have

$$\Sigma f_i(x) \geq \Sigma_{x_i > 0} f_i(x) > \Sigma_{x_i > 0} x_i = \Sigma x_i = 1,$$

and so $\Sigma f_i(x) > 1$, which is impossible. Therefore the function

$$i(x) = \min [i : f_i(x) \leq x_i, x_i > 0]$$

is defined for all $x \in S$ and is such that

$$x_{i(x)} > 0 \qquad\qquad \text{(i)}$$

$$f_{i(x)}(x) \leq x_{i(x)}. \qquad\qquad \text{(ii)}$$

Because of (i), $i(x)$ provides a Sperner labelling of the vertices of the mth barycentric subdivision $S^{(m)}$ of S, for any m. Hence, by Sperner's lemma, there exists a simplex $E^{(m)}$ of $S^{(m)}$ which is a Sperner simplex with the labelling $i(x)$. That is, for all i, $i(x) = i$ for some vertex x of $E^{(m)}$. For this x, by (ii), $f_i(x) \geq x_i$.

By compactness of S, the sequence $E^{(m)}$ ($m = 1, 2, \ldots$) has a subsequence where the sequences of vertices associated with any label i are all convergent. Since the diameter of the simplices converges to zero, they must have the same limit x. By continuity of f, this x is such that $f_i(x) \leq x_i$ for all i, since for all i this is true for some limit, but the limits coincide in x; equivalently, $f(x) = x$.

3.5 KAKUTANI AND VON NEUMANN

THEOREM (*Kakutani*): If U is a compact convex set in a real finite-dimensional linear space and $R \subset U \times U$ is closed and such that xR is nonempty and convex for all $x \in U$, then xRx for some x.

The proof is first given for the case where U is a p-simplex, and then this is extended. With U as a simplex, let U_n be its nth barycentric subdivision, and for each x_n which is a vertex of this choose $y_n \in x_n R$, so that there is a function f_n defined on these vertices giving $f_n(x_n) = y_n$. Then f_n has a linear continuation on any simplex of U_n determined by its values at the vertices. The continuations on two simplices with a common face give the same values on that face. Thus, f_n is extended as a single-valued and continuous funtion on U. Then by Brouwer's theorem, $f_n(x_n) = x_n$ for some $x_n \in U_n$. Because U is compact, the x_n ($n = 1, 2, \dots$) have a limit point x. It will be seen that xRx.

Each $x_n \in U_n$ belongs to a simplex X_n of U_n, say with vertices x_{ni} ($i = 0, 1, \dots p$), so that

$$x_n = \Sigma_i x_{ni} t_{ni},$$

for unique t_{ni} such that

$$t_{ni} \geq 0, \Sigma_i t_{ni} = 1,$$

and, from the definition of f_n,

$$y_{ni} = f_n(x_{ni}) \in x_{ni} R,$$

that is, $x_{ni} R y_{ni}$, and also

$$f_n(x_n) = \Sigma_i f_n(x_{ni}) t_{ni}.$$

For some subsequence N of $1, 2, \dots$, the sequence x_n ($n \in N$) converges to x, and the correponding sequences t_{ni} and y_{ni} also are convergent, say with limits t_i and y_i. Because the diameter of the simplex X_n, which contains x_n, decreases to zero, the sequences of vertices x_{ni} ($n \in N$), for all i, are convergent to x. Then

$$x = \Sigma_i y_i t_i, t_i \geq 0, \Sigma_i t_i = 1.$$

Because R is closed, xRy_i for all i, and now, because xR is convex, xRx. QED

Now let U be compact convex and S any simplex containing it. There exists a continuous mapping $f: S \to U$ such that $f(x) = x$ for all $x \in U$. For instance, because U is compact convex, $f(x)$ could be the unique point of U which is nearest to x. Now $R \subset U \times U$ has an extension $Q \subset S \times S$ where

$$xQy \Leftrightarrow f(x)Rf(y).$$

By what has been proved, xQx for some $x \in S$, equivalently, $f(x)Rf(x)$ for some $f(x) \in U$.

A case of this theorem has a simple proof:

THEOREM If U and $R \subset U \times U$ are compact convex and $xR \neq 0$ for all $x \in U$, then xRx for some x.

Otherwise R and the diagonal D in $U \times U$, which are compact convex, are disjoint and hence, by the Theorem of the Separating Hyperplane, there exists $(p, q) \neq 0$ and t such that

$$xRy \Rightarrow qy - px < t, xDy \Rightarrow qy - px > t.$$

But xDy means $x, y \in U$ and $x = y$, so we have $(q - p)x > t$ for all $x \in U$. Then

$$s = \min [qz : z \in U] = q\bar{z}$$

for some $\bar{z} \in U$, and then $qy - p\bar{z} \geq t$ for all $y \in U$. It follows that $\bar{z}R = 0$, contrary to hypothesis, and proving the theorem.

THEOREM (*von Neumann*) If U, V are compact convex and R, $S \subset U \times V$ are closed and such that xR, Sy are nonempty convex for all $x \, \epsilon \, U$, $y \, \epsilon \, V$ then $R \cap S \neq 0$.

Kakutani treated the case with $V = U$ and S as the diagonal D, and then deduced the theorem from it. Thus, introduce

$$T \subset (U \times V) \times (U \times V)$$

where

$$(x, y) T(x', y') \equiv xRy' \wedge x'Sy.$$

The hypothesis on R, S immediately gives the conditions on T which assure that $(x, y) T(x, y)$ for some (x, y); that is, xRy and xSy, as required.

3.6 THE NASH EQUILIBRIUM

A particular case of motion is rest, and so if motion requires a cause, rest must occur where this cause is absent. There are typical cases in which the cause is nullified by an equalization, or a balance of opposites—for example the Archimedean fulcrum and lever, the weighing scales in a market place, a playground see-saw, and also Newton's Law, where action and reaction between bodies at rest in contact are equal and opposite. It is so also with the Law of Supply and Demand, and the Budget Allocation Rule.

In mechanics, as frequently though not always in economics, an equilibrium corresponds to some extreme. A football, after erratic travel, finally comes to rest in a ditch where it is in a position of minimum potential energy. How the object finds its equilibrium is an important question. The football could have been in equilibrium also at the top of the hill, but it did not go there. This is because, on its own, it moves only downwards, following the potential gradient. To be in equilibrium at the top of the hill it would have to be *put* there.

The way the market can come into an equilibrium must be different, since there is no one to put it there, or even to know where the equilibrium is, and it has no gradient to follow automatically in order to arrive at an equilibrium when the gradient vanishes. Any movement it has is subject to the Law of Supply and Demand, and if that does not get it there, nothing else will. The forces for change lead to a position in which they are nullified, and, though welfare doctrine about the market maintains otherwise, nothing of outside significance is at an extreme there.

Similarly, one can consider a society of individuals where the state at any time is described by a vector x, the element x_i of which is controlled by individual i who reacts by giving it a new value $x_i^* = F_i(x)$. Any state x therefore has a successor $x^* = f(x)$, f being the vector of individual reaction functions F_i. If $x \neq x^*$ there will be a movement from x to x^*. For a social equilibrium x one must have $x = F(x)$, in other words a fixed point of the mapping F. This is a situation in which no one will do anything else if no one else does. The Nash equilibrium is similar, the reaction functions having a special form where x_i is a function of the x_j ($j \neq i$) which makes a 'payoff function' $f_i(x)$ a maximum, for any given x_j ($j \neq i$).

With an ordinary optimization problem there are variables x that can be chosen by an individual, any other factors being fixed. The situation that results from the action x is a function of the action, since nothing else is variable. Then the value of the outcome situation to the individual is also a function of x, say $f(x)$, and the optimization problem is to choose x that makes the value $f(x)$ as large as possible. Were there other factors in the situation, say some variables y not controlled by the individual and not fixed, the outcome of the action would be determined by these also, and the value that results would be some function $f(x, y)$. The individual would like this to be as large as possible but can only influence x, so in ignorance of y does not have a straightforward optimization problem. Fearing the worst and acting to make the best of it, one would choose x to make $\min_y f(x, y)$ a maximum. With this *max-min strategy*, if the worst happens one would then be as well off as possible in the circumstances.

This is the predicament of players in a game. If any player knows what all the other players are going to do, then the problem of what to do is simple. But the characteristic of a game is that all is not known. The situation of economic agents is typically a game situation, because there are many other agents whose unknown actions will enter into the value of any outcome. Chamberlin's theory gives an illustration. If agent i is a monopolist in control of situation variables x_i, then $x^* = F(x)$ describes the Chamberlin short-run dynamic, and an $\bar{x}$ such that $\bar{x} = F(\bar{x})$ is a 'monopolistic competition equilibrium'. In the Chamberlin model there is also an x that gives all the monopolistic firms maximum profit simultaneously, but under usual conditions it is quite different from the equilibrium $\bar{x}$. To get to it, they would have to cease acting independently as competitors and form a coalition that fixes the price. The idea of the Nash equilibrium is present also in the duopoly theory of Cournot.

In an n-person game the players' actions x_i taken together determine the resulting situation, described therefore by $x = (x_1, \ldots, x_n)$. But each player gives a different value to the result x, as determined by payoff functions $f_i(x)$. Each player i would like his payoff value to be as large as possible but has control only over his own action x_i, that is, over just one of the arguments. That is so at least when no cooperation is involved, as is now assumed. Were all the players in perfect agreement about what is good and bad — that is, were all the payoff functions the same, say $f_i(x) = f(x)$ for all i — the situation would be rather simple. By maximizing $f(x)$, everybody would be as happy as possible. The matter is not so simple when their views about what is desirable differ.

Player i's reaction to actions x_j ($j \neq i$) of the other players would be to choose y_i to make $f_i(x)$ a maximum at $x_i = y_i$; that is,

$$f_i(x_1, \ldots, x_i, \ldots, x_n) \leq f_i(x_1, \ldots, y_i, \ldots, x_n),$$

for all x_i. For a *Nash equilibrium* each player's action already represents its reaction to the actions of all the others. Thus x is a Nash equilibrium if, for all i,

$$f_i(x_1, \ldots, y_i, \ldots, x_n) \le f_i(x_1, \ldots, x_i, \ldots, x_n),$$

for all y_i.

A contrast with the special case where there is a complete harmony of interest between the players, expressed by their payoff functions being identical, is provided by another special case expressing a complete opposition of interests. This is the case of a *zero-sum game*, for which

$$\Sigma_i f_i(x) = 0,$$

identically, so that a gain to one player is a loss to the total for the others, so each player is opposed to the rest. This case will be taken further for two-person games, where the game is described by a single payoff function that determines gains to one player and therefore losses to the other. The Nash equilibrium for this case corresponds to a saddle point of the payoff function.

3.7 SADDLE POINTS

A function $f(x, y)$ has (a, b) as a *saddle point* if

$$f(x, b) \le f(a, b) \le f(a, y) \text{ for all } x, y.$$

More explicitly, this is a max-min saddle point, max for x and min for y, telling us that $f(x, b)$ is max for $x = a$ and $f(a, y)$ is min for $y = b$. Then the function has $S = f(a, b)$ as a *saddle value*. Figure 3 shows $f(x, y)$ with $(0, 0)$ as a max-min saddle point, and saddle value 0 (the rider is astride the x-axis).

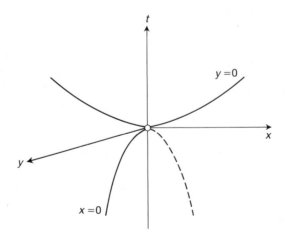

Figure 3

Saddle points can be many, but there can be at most one saddle value. For if t, t' are saddle values let (a, b), (a', b') be corresponding saddle points, so that

$$f(x, b) \leq t \leq f(a, y) \text{ for all } x, y \qquad \text{(i)}$$

and

$$f(x, b') \leq t' \leq f(a', y) \text{ for all } x, y. \qquad \text{(ii)}$$

Then, by taking $y = b'$ in (i) and $x = a$ in (ii), we have

$$t \leq f(a, b') \leq t',$$

so that $t \leq t'$. Similarly, $t' \leq t$, and hence $t = t'$.

Introducing

$$W = \max_x \min_y f(x, y), \, M = \min_y \max_x f(x, y)$$

as the *max-min* and *min-max values* of f, we have the following, which again shows that if a saddle value exists it is unique:

THEOREM In any case $W \leq M$, and f has a saddle value t, if and only if $W = M$, in which case $W = t = M$.

Let

$$W(x) = \min_y f(x, y), \, M(y) = \max_x f(x, y),$$

so that

$$W(x) \leq f(x, y) \leq M(y)$$

for all x, y and let these attain a max and min at $x = a$ and $y = b$, so that

$$W = W(a) \geq W(x), \, M = M(b) \leq M(y)$$

for all x, y. Then we have

$$W(a) \leq f(a, b) \leq M(b)$$

and hence $W \leq M$. Also, $W = M$ is equivalent to

$$W(a) = f(a, b) = M(b),$$

from which, because

$$M(b) \geq f(x, b), \, W(a) \leq f(a, y),$$

we have

$$f(x, b) \leq f(a, b) \leq f(a, y),$$

for all x and y, showing that (a, b) is a saddle point. Conversely, from this it follows that

$$M(b) \leq f(a, b) \leq W(a),$$

from which we have

$$W(a) = f(a, b) = M(b),$$

and so again $W = M$.

Though saddle points can be many, the set S of saddle points has a restricted form, from being given by a Cartesian product. Thus, consider the sets

$$A = [x: W(x) = W], \, B = [y: M(y) = M].$$

Given that $W = M$, we have

$$a \in A, \, b \in B \Leftrightarrow W(a) = M(b) \Leftrightarrow aSb,$$

so that $S = A \times B$.

Now consider relations H, K given by

$$xHy \equiv W(x) = f(x, y), \, xKy \equiv M(y) = f(x, y).$$

We have

$$a(H \cap H)b \Leftrightarrow W(a) = f(a, b) = M(b) \Leftrightarrow aSb$$

and so also $S = H \cap K$. From this, with suitable assumptions about f, von Neumann's Intersection Theorem can be applied to give the conclusion that the intersection $H \cap K$ is non-empty, in other words that a saddle point exists for f. This is the method followed by von Neumann (1945, first published in 1938), and then more generally by Kakutani (1941). Thus, $xH \neq 0, Ky \neq 0$ for all x, y, together with topological assumptions, imply xHy and xKy, that is xSy, for some x, y.

Saddle points have various connections, some of which will now be noted. A well-known application is in game theory, where a solution concept for a zero-sum two person game involves a saddle point of the payoff function. First we will relate this concept to the Nash equilibrium.

For a two-person game with payoff functions f, g, a Nash equilibrium is provided by an (a, b) for which

$$f(x, b) \leq f(a, b) \text{ for all } x,$$
$$g(a, y) \leq g(a, b) \text{ for all } y.$$

If this is a zero-sum game, we have

$$f(x, y) + g(x, y) \equiv 0;$$

in other words, the gain or loss to one player is identical with the loss or gain to the other. In this case the condition for a Nash equilibrium becomes equivalent to the condition on the function f given by

$$f(x, b) \leq f(a, b) \leq f(a, y) \text{ for all } x, y$$

or the equivalent one in terms of the function $g = -f$. This is the condition for (a, b) to be a max-min saddle point of f, and equivalently a min-max saddle of g. The saddle point is a *solution*, and the saddle value is the *value*, of the game. The solutions can be many, but the game value, if it has one, is unique. Now we will consider the special case of a matrix game, and its solubility by linear programming. This is the famous Minimax theorem of von Neumann.

For any matrix a consider the game with payoff function uax, u and x being distribution vectors, and so such that

$$Jx = 1, \, x \geq 0, \, uI = 1, \, u \geq 0.$$

The max-min value is

$$W = \max_x \min_u [uax : uI = 1, u \geq 0, Jx = 1, x \geq 0].$$

But because, by LP duality,

$$\min [uax : uI = 1, u \geq 0] = \max [t : It \leq ax],$$

we have

$$W = \max [t : It \leq ax, Jx = 1, x \geq 0].$$

Similarly, for the min-max value,

$$M = \min [s : sJ \geq ua, uI = 1, u \geq 0].$$

But these formulae for W and M are dual LP formulae, and both are feasible. Therefore both have optimal solutions, and $W = M$, by the LP Duality Theorem, and any x, u which are optimal solutions provide a saddle point, and so a game solution, (x, u).

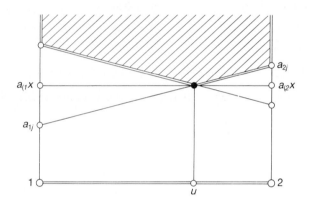

Figure 4

The case where the matrix a is $2 \times n$ can be represented graphically, as in Figure 4. Thus, a has columns a_j) with elements a_{1j}, a_{2j} and rows $a_{(i}$ with elements a_{i1}, $\ldots a_{in}$. The distributions $u = (u_1, u_2)$ describe the horizontal segment joining the two origins 1, 2 through which there are vertical axes. The values a_{ij} determine points on the axis through origin i ($i = 1, 2$). The line joining a_{1j}, a_{2j} determines the value of ua_j) for any u, and there are n such lines. Also, for any distribution x we have a line joining $a_{(1}x$, $a_{(2}x$ similarly determining the value of uax for any u. We identify these as x-lines, and the n j-lines are included among these. For x, u that solve the game, in a typical case, the x-line is horizontal and touching the upper boundary of the region swept out by the x-lines in a point corresponding to u.

A simple saddle point formulation occurs in linear programming. For a standard dual pair of problems

(M)   max px: $ax \le q$, $x \ge 0$,
(W)   min uq: $ua \ge p$, $u \ge 0$,

we have that x is an optimal solution of one problem and u is an optimal solution of the other if and only if (x, u) is a saddle point of the function

$$L(x, u) = px + uq - uax \ (x \ge 0, u \ge 0).$$

Now consider a general optimal programming problem

(M)   max $f(x)$: $g(x) \le q$.

It has limit function

$$V(z) = \sup [f(x): g(x) \le z],$$

and Lagrangean

$$L(x, u) = f(x) - u\{g(x) - q\} (u \ge 0).$$

For an optimal solution x we have the condition

$$M(x) \equiv g(x) \le q, \quad g(y) \le q \Rightarrow f(y) \le f(x),$$

and for a support solution u,

$$D(u) \equiv V(z) - V(q) \le u(z - q) \text{ for all } z.$$

With $S(x, u)$ as the statement that (x, u) is a max-min saddle point of L, we have

$$S(x, u) \Leftrightarrow M(x) \wedge D(u).$$

This holds without any assumptions whatsoever about the functions f, g or even about the domain in which they are defined.

Applied to the LP problem (M), the limit function V is concave conical and so the condition $D(u)$ takes the form shown by

$$D(u) \Leftrightarrow V(q) = uq \wedge V(z) \le uz.$$

Let $W(u)$ state that u is an optimal solution of problem (W), and $C(x)$ that x is a support solution. Then, from a symmetry in the relation of the function L to the two problems, we also have

$$S(x, u) \Leftrightarrow W(u) \wedge C(x),$$

and now consequently

$$M(x) \wedge D(u) \Leftrightarrow W(u) \wedge C(x).$$

Thus optimal solutions of one problem are identical with support solutions of the other.

Von Neumann's economic model provides another case where a main issue can be expressed by the existence of a saddle point. The model is based on a pair of matrices $a, b \geq 0$ which determine the input-output relation across a production period with the definition

$$xRy \equiv (vt) \, x \geq at, \, bt \geq y.$$

An equilibrium is defined by semi-positive activity and price vectors t, p, and a positive factor v, which is simultaneously the maximum grow and minimum interest factor, such that

$$bt \geq atv \, , \, pb \leq vpa.$$

An equivalent statement is that (t, p) is a saddle point of the function pbt/pat, and v is the saddle value.

3.8 BASIC GAMES

During 1949 – 50, Dr S. Vajda was Director of the Mathematics Group, Admiralty Research Laboratory. I learnt about games from him, and about linear programming from Martin Beale, our colleague there. Later, during the four years, 1958–62, in an office next to Oskar Morgenstern's, shadows of the entire world of Game Theory crossed my door at some time or other. Professor Morgenstern frequently remarked good-humouredly on my apparent imperviousness to everything to do with game theory. As for apparent imperviousness, that was true, but still there are limits. This section is dedicated to his memory, recalling his tolerance of eccentric, if well-founded submissions about economics; from which, it might be supposed as in so many other cases, this book reaped a benefit, since much of it is associated with that time.

The following program, MINIMAX.BAS, depends on the observation, proceeding from the last section, that

$$\max_x \min_u uax \, (Jx = 1, \, uI = 1, \, x \geq 0, \, u \geq 0)$$
$$= \max \, [\, t : It - ax \leq 0, \, Jx = 1 \,]$$
$$= \max \, [\, t : I - axt^{-1} \leq 0, \, Jxt^{-1} = t^{-1} \,]$$
$$= 1/\min \, [\, Jy : I - ay \leq 0 \,],$$

with the substitution $y = xt^{-1}$; and similarly for min-max. Thus we have to solve the LP problem

$$\min Jy : ay \geq I, \, y \geq 0,$$

to find $x = y(1/Jy)$, and the dual problem

$$\max vI : va \leq J, \, v \geq 0,$$

to find $u = (1/vI)v$, where, moreover, $Jy = vI$.

Following this program is another one for the graphics of $2 \times N$ games. A part of the data consists of identification of the vertex associated with the solution, from knowing which pure strategies are involved. One may use MINIMAX.BAS to obtain this data, or, in many cases, simply inspect the graphic output from the program itself. The figure at the end of the section is output from a similar program for $3 \times N$ games; being unfinished, this has not been included.

```
MINIMAX.BAS

      Zero-Sum Two-Person
      Matrix Games

      solves
        Min Jy: ay =>I
        Max vI: va<= J
      by the Simplex Algorithm

      to determine strategies
        x = y(1/Jy) for maximin
        u = (1/vI)v for minimax


    <Space> to continue, <CR> to rerun, <Esc> to exit

    output to screen, printer or disk (s, p or d)?


                 Game Directory

    B:\
    VAJDA .PRB
     270336 Bytes free

     Name of Game?
    ? VAJDA

       loading B:VAJDA.PRB ... RUN again, then <CR> at this
point
```

VAJDA.PRB

Vajda, Readings in LP, p.91

Let two players, A and B, both think of a number, 1, 2, or 3,
and write it down, unknown to the other. If they have chosen
the same number, then A pays B that number of pennies.
Otherwise B pays A the number of pennies A has written down.

rows for Max Player, columns for Min Player

Initial tableau:

	X1	X2	X3
0	-1	-1	-1
U1 -1	-1	2	3
U2 -1	1	-2	3
U3 -1	1	2	-3

pivot element 1 in row 2 column 1

	U2	X2	X3
-1	1	-3	2
U1 -2	1	0	6

```
X1 -1            1              -2              3
U3  0           -1               4             -6
```

pivot element 4 in row 3 column 2

```
                  U2            U3            X3
     -1          .25           .75          -2.5
U1 -2           1             0             6
X1 -1           .5            .5            0
X2  0           .25           .25          -1.5
```

pivot element 6 in row 1 column 3

```
                  U2            U3            U1
   -1.833333     .6666666      .75          .4166667
X3 -.3333334     .1666667      0            .1666667
X1 -1           .5            .5            0
X2 -.5           0            .25          .25
```

solution found

Game Value: .5454546

Strategies:

```
                    X3 = .1818182
                    X1 = .5454546
                    X2 = .2727273
                    U2 = .3636364
                    U3 = .4090909
                    U1 = .2272727
```

```
1 DATA 2,16
2 DATA"          MINIMAX.BAS               ",
3 DATA"          Zero-Sum Two-Person
4 DATA"          Matrix Games             ",
5 DATA"          solves
6 DATA"            Min Jy: ay => I
7 DATA"            Max vI: va <= J
8 DATA"          by the Simplex Algorithm",
9 DATA"          to determine strategies
10 DATA"           x = y(1/Jy) for maximin
11 DATA"           u = (1/vI)v for minimax ",,
14 '
15 DATA" <Space> to continue, <CR> to rerun, <Esc> to exit ",,*
16 DATA" output to screen, printer or disk (s, p or d)? ",*
17 DATA" Name of Game? ",*
19 '
50 DEFINT C,D,I-K,M,N,R-T
51 DIM A(20,20),B(20,20),C(20),D(20)
52 GOTO 1000
59 '
90 IF FI THEN FI=0:INPUT K$ ELSE K$=INPUT$(1)
91 IF K$=ESC$ THEN 9999 ELSE IF K$=CR$ THEN RUN ELSE RETURN
92 '
98 '===== simplex algorithm
99 '___ find pivot column S, if optimum then end
100 L=00:FOR J=1 TO N:A=A(0,J)
```

```
110 IF A<0 AND L>A THEN L=A:S=J
120 NEXT:IF L=OO THEN PRINT#1,"solution found -":GOSUB
900:RETURN
199 '___ find pivot row R
200 L=OO:FOR I=1 TO M
210 IF A(I,S)>0 THEN Q=-A(I,0)/A(I,S):IF L>Q THEN L=Q:R=I
220 NEXT:P=A(R,S):PRINT#1,"pivot element";P;"in
row";R;"column";S;CR$
299 '___ pivot on A produces new tableau B
300 FOR I=0 TO M:FOR J=0 TO N
310 B(I,J)=A(I,J)-A(I,S)*A(R,J)/P
320 IF I=R THEN B(I,J)=A(I,J)/P
330 IF J=S THEN B(I,J)=-A(I,J)/P
340 IF I=R AND J=S THEN B(I,J)=1/P
350 NEXT J,I:SWAP D(S),C(R):' register exchange
399 '___ B becomes A for another loop
400 GOSUB 600:FOR I=0 TO M:GOSUB 700:FOR J=0 TO N:A(I,J)=B(I,J)
410 PRINT#1,TAB(4+J*T)A(I,J);:NEXT:PRINT#1,:NEXT:PRINT#1,
420 IF LEN(INKEY$) THEN GOSUB 90
430 GOTO 100
489 '
499 '___ identify variables, basic or non-basic
500 IF FB THEN V=D(J) ELSE V=C(I)
510 IF V>N THEN V$="U":V=V-N ELSE V$="X"
520 V$=V$+MID$(STR$(V),2):RETURN
599 '___ basic labels
600 FB=1:FOR J=1 TO N:GOSUB 500
610 PRINT#1,TAB(6+J*T)V$;:NEXT:PRINT#1,:RETURN
699 '___ non-basic labels
700 IF I THEN GOSUB 500:PRINT#1,V$; ELSE FB=0
710 RETURN
719 '
899 '_____ results
900 Z=-1/A(0,0):PRINT#1,CR$,"Game Value:";Z
910 PRINT#1,CR$,"Strategies:"
920 FB=0:FOR I=1 TO M:GOSUB 500:PRINT#1,,,V$;" =";
930 IF LEFT$(V$,1)="X" THEN PRINT#1,-A(I,0)*Z ELSE PRINT#1,0
940 NEXT:FB=1:FOR J=1 TO N:GOSUB 500:PRINT#1,,,V$;" =";
950 IF LEFT$(V$,1)="U" THEN PRINT#1,A(0,J)*Z ELSE PRINT#1,0
960 NEXT:RETURN
969 '
989 '___ text
990 READ R,C:CLS:LOCATE R
991 READ L$:IF L$<>"*" THEN PRINT#1,TAB(C);L$:GOTO 991
992 GOSUB 90:RETURN
998 '
999 '============ init
1000 ESC$=CHR$(27):CR$=CHR$(13):CRR$=CR$+CR$:T=14:OO=1E+32:'
=Inf
1010 OPEN "SCRN:" FOR OUTPUT AS 1:KEY OFF:GOSUB 990:GOSUB
991:O$=K$
1020 IF O$="p" OR O$="P" THEN O$="LPT1:"
1021 IF O$="S" OR O$="s" THEN O$="SCRN:"
1030 CLS:PRINT CRR$,,"Game Directory";CRR$
1040 FILES"B:*.PRB":PRINT1,:FI=1:C=0:GOSUB 991:IF K$="" THEN
1100
1050 PRB$="B:"+K$+".PRB"
```

```
1060 PRINT CR$;"loading ";PRB$;" ... RUN again, then <CR> at
     this point"
1070 MERGE PRB$
1099 '
1100 RESTORE 2000:READ G$,H$,M,N:PRB$=G$+".PRB":SLN$="B:"+G$+"
     .SLN"
1101 IF O$="D" OR O$="d" THEN O$=SLN$ ELSE IF O$=" " THEN
     O$="SCRN:"
1102 IF O$=SLN$ THEN PRINT"Output written to disk file ";O$
1110 CLOSE#1:OPEN O$ FOR OUTPUT AS #1
1120 PRINT#1,CR$;PRB$;CRR$;H$;CR$
1199 '
1210 FOR I=1 TO M:B(I,0)=-1:FOR J=1 TO N:B(0,J)=-1:READ B(I,J):
     NEXT J,I
1220 FOR J=1 TO N:D(J)=J:NEXT:' basic are 1 to n
1230 FOR I=1 TO M:C(I)=N+I:NEXT:' non-basic are N+1 to N+M
1299 '
1300 C=2:GOSUB 991
1310 PRINT#1,CR$;"columns for Max Player, rows for Min
     Player";CR$
1320 PRINT#1,"Initial tableau:";CR$
1330 GOSUB 400:CLOSE#1:GOSUB 90
1399 '
1999 '_____ payoff matrix
2000 DATA VAJDA,"Vajda, Readings in LP, p.91",  3, 3:' = M, N
2010 DATA      -1,       2,       3
2020 DATA       1,      -2,       3
2030 DATA       1,       2,      -3
2099 '
2110 DATA"Let two players, A and B, both think of a number, 1,
     2, or 3,"
2120 DATA"and write it down, unknown to the other. If they have
     chosen"
2130 DATA"the same number, then A pays B that number of
     pennies."
2140 DATA"Otherwise B pays A the number of pennies A has
     written down.",*
2999 '
9999 CLS:KEY ON:END
```

```
                 MNMX2.BAS

                 zero-sum 2-person games
                 Von Neumann's MINIMAX THEOREM

                 graphics program for
                 2 x N games



         <Space> to continue, <CR> to rerun, <Esc> to exit


             Paint Instructions

                 <Arrow> keys      move cursor
                 <Home>            changes paint colour
```

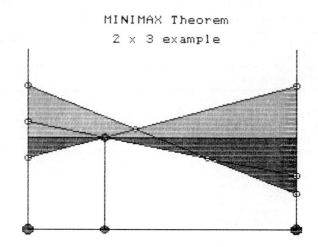

Figure 1

<pre>
              Payoff Matrix
               Min Player
                1   2   3
       Max 1   .4   .6   .8
     Player 2   .8   .3   .2

            Solution Strategies
   Max Player   .285714 .7142858
   Min Player   .4285714   .5714286   0
          Game Value   .5142857
</pre>

Figure 2

```
                    <End>              changes boundary colour
                    <Pg Up>            blanks messages
                    <Pg Dn>            toggles cursor step
        small/large

                    <Ins>  colour    <Del>  removes colour

                    <Esc>              when done
```

```
1 DATA 5,16
2 DATA"            MNMX2.BAS                            ",
3 DATA"            zero-sum 2-person games
4 DATA"            Von Neumann's MINIMAX THEOREM    ",
5 DATA"            graphics program for
6 DATA"            2 x N games                          ",,,,
7 '
8 DATA" <Space> to continue, <CR> to rerun, <Esc> to exit",*
9 '
10 DEFINT I-K:DIM
    Y(9,1),XX(9,9),YY(9,9),P(8),Q(8),C(9),M(9),U(9)
11 GOTO 1000
89 '
90 K$=INPUT$(1)
91 IF K$=ESC$ THEN 9999 ELSE IF K$=CR$ THEN RUN ELSE RETURN
98 '
599 '--- cursor step
600 FC=1-FC:LOCATE 25,36
610 IF FC THEN DX=16:DY=8:PRINT"fast";:ELSE
    DX=4:DY=1:PRINT"slow";
620 RETURN
699 '--- locate
700 PUT(X,Y),P,PSET
710 IF K=5 THEN X=X-DX ELSE IF K=7 THEN X=X+DX
720 IF K=2 THEN Y=Y-DY ELSE IF K=10 THEN Y=Y+DY
730 GET(X,Y)-STEP(S,S),P
740 LOCATE 1,1:PRINT X;Y;:RETURN
749 '--- paint
750 PUT(X,Y),P,PSET
760 IF K=12 THEN PAINT(X,Y),CA,CB ELSE IF K=13 THEN
    PAINT(X,Y),0,CB
770 GET(X,Y)-STEP(S,S),P:RETURN
779 '--- blank
780 PUT(X,Y),P,PSET:LOCATE 25,1:PRINT SP$;:LOCATE,33:PRINT SP$;
785 LOCATE 1,1:PRINT SP$;" ";:GOSUB 90:RETURN
799 '--- colour (by hand)
800 F=1F:IF F THEN PUT(X,Y),P,PSET ELSE PUT(X,Y),Q,PSET
805 K$=INKEY$:IF K$=ESC$ THEN GOSUB 780:RETURN
810 IF LEN(K$)<2 THEN K$="":GOTO 800
820 K=ASC(RIGHT$(K$,1))-70:K$=""
830 IF K=5 OR K=7 OR K=2 OR K=10 THEN GOSUB 700
850 IF K=12 OR K=13 THEN GOSUB 750
860 IF K=3 THEN GOSUB 780 ELSE IF K=11 THEN GOSUB 600
870 IF K=1 THEN CA=(CA+1)MOD 4 ELSE IF K=9 THEN CB=(CB+1)MOD 4
880 LOCATE 25,1:PRINT" a";CA;"b";CB;
890 GOTO 800
899 '--- text
```

```
900 READ R,C:CLS:LOCATE R
910 READ L$:IF L$<>"*" THEN LOCATE,C:PRINT L$:GOTO 910
920 GOSUB 90:RETURN
998 '
999 '======== main
1000 RESTORE 1010
1010 READ A, B, U, V, CA, CB, DX, DY, XO, YO, C, S, FC
1020 DATA 40,28,248,150,1, 3, 16, 8, 24, 24, 3, 0, 1
1030 CR$=CHR$(13):ESC$=CHR$(27):SP$=SPACE$(8):CRR$=CR$+CR$
1039 '
1080 KEY OFF:SCREEN 0:WIDTH 80
1090 RESTORE:GOSUB 900:RESTORE 9100:GOSUB 900:RESTORE 1200
1099 '
1100 READ N, I1, I2:' I1, I2 are pure strategies of the Min
     Player
1200 DATA 3, 1, 2:'          involved in the min-max strategy
1210 DATA  0,0, .4,.8, .6,.3, .8,.2
1999 '
2000 CLS:KEY OFF:SCREEN 1
2010 LINE(0,0)-STEP(S,S),3,BF
2020 GET(0,0)-STEP(S,S),Q:CLS
2030 LOCATE 1,14:PRINT"MINIMAX Theorem";
2040 LOCATE 3,15:PRINT"2 x";N;"example";
2099 '--- strategies
2100 R=5:FOR I=0 TO N:FOR J=0 TO 1:READ Y(I,J):NEXT
2110 LINE(A,B+V-V*Y(I,0))-(A+U,B+V-V*Y(I,1)),C
2120 CIRCLE(A,B+V-V*Y(I,0)),R,C:CIRCLE(A+U,B+V-V*Y(I,1)),R,C
2130 R=3:NEXT:LINE(A,B)-STEP(0,V),C:LINE(A+U,B)-STEP(0,V),C
2199 '--- slope and intercept
2200 FOR I=1 TO N
2210 C(I)=Y(I,0):M(I)=Y(I,1)-C(I)
2220 NEXT
2299 '--- basic solutions
2300 FOR I=2 TO N:FOR J=1 TO I1
2310 XX(I,J)=(C(J)-C(I))/(M(I)-M(J))
2320 YY(I,J)=(M(I)*C(J)-M(J)*C(I))/(M(I)-M(J))
2330 CIRCLE(A+U*XX(I,J),B+V-V*YY(I,J)),2,C
2340 NEXT J,I
2399 '--- saddle point
2400 I=I1:J=I2:IF I<J THEN SWAP I,J
2410 U(I)=Y(J,0)-Y(J,1):U(J)=Y(I,1)-Y(I,0)
2420 Z=U(I)+U(J):U(I)=U(I)/Z:U(J)=U(J)/Z
2499 '
2500 X=XX(I,J):Y=YY(I,J):XE=X:YE=Y
2510 LINE(A+U*X,B+V-V*Y)-STEP(0,V*Y),C
2520 CIRCLE(A+U*X,B+V-V*Y),4,C
2530 CIRCLE(A+U*X,B+V),4,C
2540 LINE(A,B+V-V*Y)-STEP(U,0),C
2599 '--- colour
2600 X=XO:Y=YO:GET(X,Y)-STEP(S,S),P:K$="":GOSUB 800
2699 '
6999 '--- game results
7000 RESTORE 9000:GOSUB 900
7010 LOCATE 9:FOR I=0 TO 1:PRINT CR$
7020 T=13:FOR J=1 TO N:LOCATE,T
7030 PRINT Y(J,I);:T=T+8:NEXT J,I
7040 LOCATE 18,13:PRINT XE;:LOCATE,21:PRINT 1-XE
7060 LOCATE 20,13:FOR I=1 TO N:PRINT U(I);:NEXT
```

```
7070 LOCATE 22,21:PRINT YE
7090 GOSUB 90:GOTO 1080
8998 '
8999 '---
9000 DATA 5,1
9010 DATA"             Payoff Matrix            ",
9020 DATA"                Min Player            ",
9030 DATA"            1        2        3       ",
9040 DATA"    Max  1                           ",
9050 DATA" Player  2                           ",,
9060 DATA"           Solution Strategies       ",
9070 DATA" Max Player                          ",
9080 DATA" Min Player                          ",
9090 DATA"          Game Value                 ",*
9099 '
9100 DATA 5,10
9110 DATA"   Paint Instructions:",
9120 DATA"    <Arrow> keys      move cursor
9130 DATA"    <Home>            changes paint colour
9140 DATA"    <End>             changes boundary colour
9150 DATA"    <Pg Up>           blanks messages
9160 DATA"    <Pg Dn>           toggles cursor step
                                    small/large",
9180 DATA"    <Ins>  colour    <Del>  removes colour",
9190 DATA"    <Esc>             when done",*
9989 '
9999 CLS:SCREEN 0:WIDTH 80:KEY ON
```

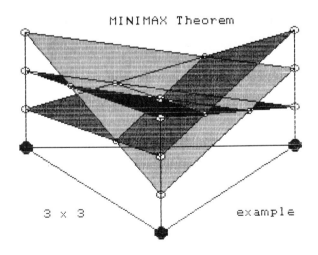

MINIMAX Theorem

3 x 3   example

Bibliography

Abraham-Frois, Gilbert and Edmond Berrebi (1979). *Theory of Value, Prices and Accumulation: A mathematical integration of Marx, von Neumann and Sraffa.* Cambridge University Press. Translation by M. P. Kregel-Javaux of the original: *Théorie de la valeur, des prix et de l'accumulation.* Paris: Editions Economica, 1976.

Aczél, J. and W. Eichhorn (1974). Systems of functional equations determining price and productivity indices. *Utilitas Mathematica,* 5, 213–26.

Afriat, S. N. (1951). The quadratic form positive definite on a linear manifold. *Proceedings of the Cambridge Philosophical Society,* 47(1), 1–6.

_____ (1954a). Symmetric matrices, quadratic forms, and linear constraints. *Publicationes Mathematicae,* 3, 305–8.

_____ (1954b). Budget decentralization (private communication to Robert H. Strotz). Department of Applied Economics, Cambridge.

_____ (1955a). Probabilities of preference and choice (mimeo). Department of Applied Economics, Cambridge.

_____ (1955b). The consistency condition and other concepts in the theory of value and demand (mimeo). Department of Applied Economics, Cambridge.

_____ (1956a). The calculation of index numbers of the standard and cost of living (mimeo). Department of Applied Economics, Cambridge.

_____ (1956b). On index numbers in the theory of value and demand (mimeo). Department of Applied Economics, Cambridge.

_____ (1956c). Theory of economic index numbers (mimeo). Department of Applied Economics, Cambridge.

_____ (1956d). The approach to scalar growth of a vector transformed by an increasing power of a matrix. *Proc. Cambridge Phil. Soc.,* 53, 2, 213–14.

_____ (1957a). Orthogonal and oblique projectors and the characteristics of pairs of vector spaces. *Proceedings of the Cambridge Philosophical Society,* 53(4), 800–16.

_____ (1957b). On value and demand and theory of index-numbers of the standard and cost of living. *Bulletin of the Research Council of Israel,* 7 (Section F: Mathematics and Physics), 1 (December).

_____ (1959). Value and expenditure. *Research memorandum no.* 7 (February), Econometric Research Program, Princeton University.

_____ (1960a). The analysis of preferences. *Research memorandum no.* 11 (January), Econometric Research Program, Princeton University.

_____ (1960b). Preference scales and expenditure systems. *Research memorandum no.* 13 (March), Econometric Research Program, Princeton University; published in *Econometrica,* 30 (1962), 305–23.

_____ (1960c). The system of inequalities $a_{rs} > X_s - X_r$. *Research memorandum no.* 18 (October), Econometric Research Program, Princeton University; published in *Proceedings of the Cambridge Philosophical Society,* 9 (1963), 125–33.

_____ (1960d). Preferences and the theory of consumers' expenditures. Washington meeting of the Econometric Society, December 1959; abstract in *Econometrica*, 28, 3, 693–95.

_____ (1961a). The conceptual problem of a cost of living index. Stanford meeting of the Econometric Society, August 1960; abstract in *Econometrica*, 29, 3, 440.

_____ (1961b). The validity of the expected utility hypothesis. *Proceedings of the Princeton University conference on Recent Advances in Game Theory*, 4–6 October 1961, edited by M. Maschler. Princeton, NJ: The Princeton University Conference; reprinted in *Metroeconomica*, 20(1) (1968), 63–72.

_____ (1961c). Gradient configurations and quadratic functions. *Research memorandum no*. 20 (January), Econometric Research Program, Princeton University; published in *Proceedings of the Cambridge Philosophical Society*, 59(1963), 287–305.

_____ (1961d). Expenditure configurations. *Research memorandum no*. 21 (February), Econometric Research Program, Princeton University.

_____ (1961e). The cost of living index. *Research memoranda* Nos. 24 (March), 27 (April) and 29 (August), Econometric Research Program, Princeton University.

_____ (1962). A formula for ranging the cost of living. In *Recent Advances in Mathematical Programming, Proceedings of the Chicago Symposium, 1962*, edited by R. L. Graves and P. Wolfe. New York: McGraw Hill.

_____ (1963a). An identity concerning the relation between the Paasche and Laspeyres indices. *Metroeconomica*, 15(2–3), 136–40.

_____ (1963b). The method of limits in the theory of index numbers. Joint European Conference of the Institute of Mathematical Statistics and the Econometric Society, Copenhagen, July 1963; published in *Metroeconomica*, 21(2),(1969), 141–65.

_____ (1963c). On Bernoullian utility for goods and money. *Metroeconomica*, 15(1), 38–46.

_____ (1963d). The algebra of revealed preference. Pittsburgh meeting of the Econometric Society, December 1962; abstract in *Econometrica* 31(4), 755.

_____ (1964). The construction of utility functions from expenditure data. *Cowles Foundation Discussion Paper no*. 144 (October), Yale University; presented at the First World Congress of the Econometric Society, Rome, September 1965; published in *International Economic Review*, 8(1) (1967), 67–77

_____ (1965a). The equivalence in two dimensions of the strong and weak axioms of revealed preference. *Metroeconomica*, 17(1–2), 24–8

_____ (1965b). People and Population. *World Politics*, 17(1–2), 431–9. Japanese translation with foreword by Ambassador Edwin Reishauer: *Japan-American Forum* 2(10).

_____ (1966). The production function. Summer School in Mathematical Economics, Frascati, Italy, 1966.

_____ (1967a). Economic transformation. In *Economia Matematica*, edited by Bruno de Finetti. Rome: Edizioni Cremonese, 1–64.

_____ (1967b). The cost of living index. In *Studies in Mathematical Economics in Honor of Oskar Morgenstern*, edited by Martin Shubik. Princeton University Press, 335–65.

_____ (1967c). Principles of choice and preference. *Research Report* no. 160 (February), Economics Department, Purdue University.

_____ (1967d). The construction of cost-efficiencies and approximate utility functions from inconsistent expenditure data. Department of Economics, Purdue University. New York meeting of the Econometric Society, December 1969.

_____ (1969a). Activity constraints in demographic variables. Annual meeting of the Population Association of America, Atlantic City, New Jersey, 1969.

_____ (1969b). The output limit function in general and convex programming and the theory of production. Thirty-sixth National Meeting of the Operations Research Society of America, Miami Beach, Florida, November 1969; published in *Econometrica*, 39 (1971), 309–39.

_____ (1969c). Regression and projection. In *Economic Models, Estimation and Risk Programming: Essays in Honor of Gerhard Tintner*, edited by K. A. Fox, J. K. Sengupta and G. V. L. Narasimham. Berlin-Heidelberg: Springer Verlag, 277–301.

_____ (1969d). The construction of separable utility functions from expenditure data (mimeo). Department of Economics, University of North Carolina at Chapel Hill.

_____ (1969e). The cost and utility of consumption (mimeo). Department of Economics, University of North Carolina at Chapel Hill.

_____ (1969f). Analytical theory of production (mimeo, original version of 1971b). Department of Economics, University of North Carolina at Chapel Hill.

_____ (1970a). The concept of a price index and its extension. Second World Congress of the Econometric Society, Cambridge, August 1970.

_____ (1970b). The progressive support method for convex programming. Seventh Mathematical Programming Symposium, The Hague, 1970; published in *Journal of Numerical Analysis*, 7(3) (1970), 44–57.

_____ (1971a). Theory of maxima and the method of Lagrange. *SIAM Journal on Applied Mathematics*, 20(3), 343–57.

_____ (1971b). Efficiency estimation of production functions. Boulder meetings of the Econometric Society, September 1971; published in *International Economic Review*, 13(3) (1972), 568–98.

_____ (1971c). Review of *Theory of Measurement* by J. Pfanzagle. *Econometrica*, 39(3), 649.

_____ (1971d). Centralized and decentralized programming: an extension of the theory of shadow prices. New Orleans meeting of the Econometric Society, December 1971.

_____ (1972a). The purchasing power of incomes. Meeting of the Canadian Economic Association, Montreal, June 1972.

_____ (1972b). A non-parametric approach to production. Conference on Applications of Duality Theory, Ottawa, 8–9 September 1972.

_____ (1972c). The case of the vanishing Slutsky matrix. *Journal of Economic Theory*, 5(2), 208–23.

_____ (1972d). The theory of international comparisons of real income and prices. In *International Comparisons of Prices and Output*, edited by D. J. Daly (Studies in Income and Wealth no. 37; proceedings of the conference at York University, Toronto, 1970). New York: National Bureau of Economic Research, 13–84.

_____ (1972e). Reservations about market sovereignty: Four notes. In *Policy Formation in an Open Economy*, edited by R. A. Mundell. Proceedings of the Policy Formation: Canada Conference, University of Waterloo, 11–14 November 1972; published by Waterloo Research Institute, 1974.

_____ (1972f). A Theorem on the dual identity of optimal and support solutions in linear programming. *Waterloo Economic Series no*. 56, Department of Economics, University of Waterloo.

_____ (1972g). Revealed preference revealed. *Waterloo Economic Series no*. 60, Department of Economics, University of Waterloo.

_____ (1973a). The maximum hypothesis in demand analysis. *Waterloo Economic Series no*. 79, Department of Economics, University of Waterloo.

_____ (1973b). Demand functions and utility orders. *Waterloo Economic Series no*. 81, Department of Economics, University of Waterloo.

_____ (1973c). Direct and indirect utility. *Waterloo Economic Series no*. 83, Department of Economics, University of Waterloo.

_____ (1973d). Collective decision and optimality. Paper presented at the International Seminar on Public Economics, Certosa di Pontignano, Siena, 3–6 September 1973; proceedings issued as *Theory and Measurement of the Demand for Public Services* (mimeo), edited by R. A. Musgrave, Department of Economics, Harvard University.

_____ (1973e). On a system of inequalities in demand analysis: An extension of the classical Method. *International Economic Review*, 14(2), 460–72.

_____ (1973f). A theorem on shadow prices. *Econometrica*, 41(6), 1197–99.

_____ (1973g). Reciprocity theorems in a von Neumann economy. Winter Meeting of the Econometric Society, New York, December 1973.

_____ (1973h). Adam Smith and Robinson Crusoe (mimeo). A note following the celebrations of the 250th Birthday of Adam Smith at Kirkcaldy, Scotland, 4–5 June 1973.

_____ (1974a). Sum-symmetric matrices. *Linear Algebra and its Applications*, 8, 129–40.

_____ (1974b). Measurement of the purchasing power of incomes with linear expansion data. *Journal of Econometrics*, 2(3), 343–64.

_____ (1974c). On Hansson's democratic neutrality. *Discussion Paper no*. 7407, Department of Economics, University of Ottawa; published in *Atlantic Economic Review*, 3(2) (1975), 18–21.

_____ (1974d). Democratic order functions. *Discussion Paper* no. 7414, Department of Economics, University of Ottawa; published in *Atlantic Economic Review*, 3(2) (1975), 13–18.

_____ (1974e). *Production Duality and the von Neumann Theory of Growth and Interest*. Meisenheim am Glan: Verlag Anton Hain.

_____ (1974f). Production Duality. In *Production Theory*, edited by W. Eichhorn, R. Henn, O. Opitz and R. W. Shephard (International Seminar on Production Theory, Karlsruhe, May–July, 1973). Berlin: Springer-Verlag.

_____ (1974g). Review of *The Effect of Education on Efficiency in Consumption* by Robert T. Michael. *Monthly Labour Review*, 97(1), 86–7.

_____ (1974h). The marginal price index method. *Discussion Paper no*. 7415, Department of Economics, University of Ottawa.

_____ (1975a). Elementary theory of exchange and prices. *Discussion Paper no*. 7506, Department of Economics, University of Ottawa.

_____ (1975b). Ramsey's Rule of Savings. *Discussion Paper no*. 7512, Department of Economics, University of Ottawa.

_____ (1975c). Inflation maps and the total and incremental inflation rates. Third World Congress of the Econometric Society, Toronto, August 1975.

_____ (1975d). Inflation and purchasing power. Quantitative Methods and Forecasting Seminar, Department of Manpower and Immigration, Ottawa, 14 October 1975.

_____ (1975e). The purchasing power of incomes. *Annals of Economic and Social Measurement*, 4(1); special issue on Consumer Demand (Proceedings of the National Bureau of Economic Research Conference, NBER West Coast Center, Palo Alto, California, 2–3 May 1974).

_____ (1975f). The algebra and geometry of statistical correlation. In Afriat, Sastry and Tintner (1975), 7–107.

_____ (1976a). *Combinatorial Theory of Demand*. London: Input-Output Publishing Co.

_____ (1976b). The incremental price index. Economic Theory and Econometrics Seminar, Oxford University, 18 June 1976.

_____ (1976c). The marginal price index in theory and practice. Helsinki meeting of the Econometric Society, August 1976.

_____ (1976d). Consumers' expenditures and inflation. Government of Canada Interdepartmental Project, Economic Council of Canada.

_____ (1977a). Slutsky and Frobenius. Vienna meeting of the Econometric Society, September 1977; published in *Zeitschrift für Nationalökonomie*, 37(3–4), 307–22.

_____ (1977b). *The Price Index*. Cambridge University Press (2nd impression 1978).

_____ (1977c). Linear markets. Economic Theory Workshop, Queen's University, Kingston, Ontario, 28–30 March 1977.

_____ (1977d). Marshallian and Walrasian Markets. Ottawa meeting of the Econometric Society, June 1977.

_____ (1977e). Review of *Mathematical Theory of Expanding and Contracting Economies* by Oskar Morgenstern and Gerald L. Thompson. *KYKLOS*, 30(3), 562–4.

_____ (1977f). The flow-decomposition of a non-negative matrix. *Discussion Paper no.* 7703, Department of Economics, University of Ottawa.

_____ (1977g). On minimum paths and subpotentials in a valuated network. *Discussion Paper no.* 7704, Department of Economics, University of Ottawa.

_____ (1978a). Review of *Index Numbers in Theory and Practice* by R. G. D. Allen. *Canadian Journal of Economics*, 11(2), 367–9.

_____ (1978b). Review of *Theory of the Price Index: Fisher's Test Approach and Generalizations* by Wolfgang Eichhorn and Joachim Voeller. *Journal of Economic Literature*, 16, 129–30.

_____ (1978c). Sraffa's Prices. Geneva meeting of the Econometric Society, September 1978.

_____ (1978d). On Wald's 'New Formula' for the Cost of Living. In *Theory and Application of Economic Indices*, edited by W. Eichhorn, R. Henn, O. Opitz, R. W. Shephard (proceedings of an International Seminar held at the University of Karlsruhe, 23 June–1 July, 1976). Würzburg: Physica-Verlag.

_____ (1979). The power algorithm for generalized Laspeyres and Paasche indices. Athens meeting of the Econometric Society, September 1979.

_____ (1980a). Matrix powers: Classical and variations. Matrix Theory Conference, Auburn, Alabama, 19–22 March 1980.

_____ (1980b). Production functions and efficiency measurement. Conference on Current Issues in Productivity, Columbia University, New York, 16–18 April 1980

_____ (1980c). Sraffa and the theory of value. Sraffa Symposium, Meeting of the Eastern Economics Association, Montreal, 8–10 May 1980.

_____ (1980d). *Demand Functions and the Slutsky Matrix*. Princeton Studies in Mathematical Economics no. 7. Princeton University Press.

_____ (1980e). Microcomputing with the simplex algorithm. *Discussion Paper no.* 8007, Department of Economics, University of Ottawa.

_____ (1981). On the constructibility of consistent price indices between several periods simultaneously. In *Essays in Theory and Measurement of Demand: In Honour of Sir Richard Stone*, edited by Angus Deaton. Cambridge University Press, 133–61.

_____ (1982a). *The Ring of Linked Rings*. London: Duckworth.

_____ (1982b). The power algorithm for minimum paths, and price indices. Eleventh International Symposium on Mathematical Programming, University of Bonn, 23 – 27 August 1982.

_____ (1982c). Models of inefficiency. Conference on Current Issues in Productivity, Cornell University, Ithaca NY, 30 November–2 December 1982.

_____ (1984). The true index. In *Demand, Trade and Equilibrium: Essays in Honor of Ivor Pearce* (proceedings of the Conference at University of Southampton, 5– 7 January 1982), edited by A. Ingham and A. M. Ulph. London: Macmillan.

_____ (1986a). Efficiency in Production and Consumption. Conference on Current Issues in Productivity, Graduate School of Management, Rurgers University, New Jersey, 2–4 December, 1985. In *Modern Production Theory: Efficiency and Productivity*, edited by Ali Dogramaci and Rolf Färe. Boston: Kluwer-Nijhoff, forthcoming.

_____ (1986b). Von Neumann's Economic Model. In *Matrix Theory: Proceedings of the Conference at Auburn University, Alabama, 19–22 March 1986*, edited by Robert Grone and Frank Ulig. New York: Elsevier Scientific Publishing Co., forthcoming.

_____ , M. V. Sastry and G. Tintner (1975). *Studies in Correlation: Multivariate Analysis and Econometrics*. Göttingen: Vandenhoeck & Ruprecht.

Aigner, D. J. and S. F. Chu (1968). On estimating the industry production function. *American Economic Review*, 58 (4), 826–39.

_____ , and P. Schmidt (eds) (1980). Specification and estimation of frontier production functions, profit and cost functions. Supplementary issue, *Journal of Econometrics*, 13, 1–138.

Alchian, A. A. (1953). The meaning of utility measurement. *American Economic Review*, 43, 26–50.

Allen, R. G. D. (1933). On the marginal utility of money and its applications. *Economica*, 40, 186–209.

_____ (1949). The economic theory of index numbers. *Economica*, n.s. 16(3), 197– 203.

_____ (1975). *Index Numbers in Theory and Practice*. London: Macmillan.

Antonelli, G. B. (1886). *Sulla Teoria Matematica della Economia Pura*. Pisa; reprinted in *Giornale degli Economisti*, 10 (1951), 233–63.

Armstrong, W. E. (1951). Utility and the theory of welfare. *Oxford Economic Papers*, 3, 259–71.

_____ (1955). Concerning marginal utility. *Oxford Economic Papers*, 7, 170–76.

_____ (1958). Utility and the ordinalist fallacy. *Review of Economic Studies*, 25, 172 – 81.

Arrow, K. J. (1950a). An extension of the basic theorems of classical welfare economics. In *Proceedings of the Second Berkeley Symposium on Mathematical Statistics and Probability*, edited by J. Neyman. Berkeley: University of California Press, 502–37.

_____ (1950b). A difficulty in the concept of social welfare. *Journal of Political Economy*, 58, 328–46.

_____ (1951). *Social Choice and Individual Values*. New York: John Wiley (2nd edition 1963).

_____ (1958). Utilities, attitudes, choices: A review note. *Econometrica*, 26, 1–23.

_____ (1959). Rational choice functions and orderings. *Economica*, n.s. 26, 121–7.

_____ and G. Debreu (1959). Existence of an equilibrium for a competitive economy. *Econometrica*, 22, 265–90.

_____ , S. Karlin and P. Suppes (eds) (1959). *Mathematical Methods in the Social Sciences*. Stanford University Press.

_____ and F. H. Hahn (1972). *General Competitive Analysis*. Edinburgh: Oliver & Boyd.

Balk, B. M. (1981). Second thoughts on Wald's cost-of-living index and Frisch's double expenditure method. *Econometrica*, 49(6), 1553–8.

Ballesteros, Albert, Paulina Beato, Michael Jerison and Joseph Oliu (1976). The mathematics of Sraffa's model of prices, wage, and rate of profit. *Discussion Paper* no. 76–7, Center for Economic Research, Department of Economics, University of Minnesota.

Banker, R. D., A. Charnes, W. W. Cooper, and A. P. Schinnar (1981). A bi-extremal principle for frontier estimation and efficiency evaluations. *Management Science*, 17(12), 1370–82.

_____ , R. F. Conrad, and R. F. Strauss (1981). An application of data envelopment analysis to the empirical investigation of a hospital production function. *Working Paper*, Carnegie-Mellon University, School of Urban and Public Affairs, Pittsburg.

Bannerjee, D. (1964). Choice and order; or, First things first. *Economica*, 31, 158–67.

Barone, E. (1935). The Ministry of Production in the collectivist state. In *Collectivist Economic Planning*, edited by F. A. von Hayek. London: Routledge & Kegan Paul.

Basmann, R. L. (1956). A comment on some recent criticisms of modern demand theory. *Schweizerische Zeitschrift die Volkswirtschaft und Statistik*, 92(2), 183–90.

Bastiat, Frédéric (1850). *Economic Harmonies*.

Baumol, William (1952). *Welfare Economics and the Theory of the State*. London: Bell.

Beale, E. M. L. and M. Drazin (1956). Sur une note de Farquharson. *Comptes Rendus de l'Académie des Sciences, Paris*. 243, 123–5.

Bell, Daniel and Irving Kristol (eds) (1981). *The Crisis in Economic Theory*. New York: Basic Books.

Bellman, Richard (1960). *Introduction to Matrix Analysis*. New York: McGraw Hill, chapter V.

_____ , Kenneth L. Cooke, and Jo Ann Lockett (1970). *Algorithms, Graphs and Computers*. New York & London: Academic Press, pp. 21, 42, 87, 103.

Berge, C. (1963). *Topological Spaces*. New York: Macmillan.

_____ and A. Ghouila-Houri (1965). *Programming, Games and Transportaion Networks*. London: Methuen; New York: John Wiley.

Bergson, A. (1938). A reformulation of certain aspects of welfare economics. *Quarterly Journal of Economics*, 52, 310–34.

_____ (1954). On the concept of social welfare. *Quarterly Journal of Econonomics*, 68), 233–52.

_____ (1966). *Essays in Normative Economics*. Cambridge, Mass.: Harvard University Press.

Bernadelli, H. (1938). The end of the marginal utility theory? *Economica*, 5, 192–212.
_____ (1954). A rehabilitation of the classical theory of marginal utility. *Economica*, 19, 240–43.
Black, Duncan (1948). On the rationale of group decision-mking. *Journal of Political Economy*, 56, 23–34.
_____ (1958). *The Theory of Committees and Elections*. Cambridge University Press.
_____ (1969). On Arrow's Impossibility Theorem. *Journal of Law and Economics*, 12(2), 229–32.
Black, R. P. (1945). Trinity College, Dublin and the theory of value, 1832–1863. *Economica*, 12, 140–8.
Blair, Douglas H. and Robert A. Pollack (1982). Acyclic collective choice rules. *Econometrica*, 50(4), 931–43.
_____ (1983). Rational Collective Choice. *Scientific American*, 249(2), 88–95.
Blau, J. H. (1957). The existence of social welfare functions. *Econometrica*, 25, 302–13.
Blaug, M. (1962). *Economic Theory in Retrospect*. Homewood, Illinois: Irwin.
Bohnert, H. G. (1954). The logical structure of the utility concept. In *Decision Processes*, edited by R. M. Thrall, C. H. Coombs and R. L. Davis. New York: John Wiley.
Boland, L. A. (1975). The law of demand, weak axiom of revealed preference and price-consumption curves. *Australian Economic Papers*, June, 104–19.
_____ (1977). Testability, time and equilibrium-stability. *Atlantic Economic Journal*, 5(1), 39–47.
Borch, K. H. (1968a). Indifference curves and uncertainty. *Swedish Journal of Economics*, 70, 19–24.
_____ (1968b). *The Economics of Uncertainty*. Princeton University Press.
_____ (1969). A note on uncertainty and indifference curves. *Review of Economic Studies*, 36, 1–4.
Boulding, Kenneth E. (1963). The legitimation of the market (mimeo). Lecture delivered at Rice University, Houston, Texas).
Bowley, A. L. (1923). Review of *The Making of Index Numbers* by Irving Fisher. *Economic Journal*, 33, 90–4.
_____ (1928). Notes on Index Numbers. *Economic Journal*, 38, 216–37.
Bromeck, Tadeusz (1972). Equilibrium levels in decomposable von Neumann models. Symposium on Mathematical Methods in Economics, Warsaw, February–July 1972.
Brown, Donald J. (1975). Aggregation of preferences. *Quarterly Journal of Economics*, 89(3), 456–69.
Buchanan, James M. and Gordon Tullock (1962). *The Calculus of Consent*. Ann Arbor: University of Michigan Press.
Byushgens, S. S. (1925). Ob Odnom klasse giperpoverkhnostey: po povodu 'idealnovo indeksa' Irving Fisher' a pokupatelnoi sili denig. *Mathematischeskii Sbornik*, 32, 625–31. (On a class of hypersurfaces: Concerning the 'ideal index' of Irving Fisher. Citation by Irving Fisher: S. S. Buscheguennce, Sur une classe des hypersurfaces. A propos de 'l'index idéal' de M. Irving Fisher. *Recueil Mathématique* (Moscow) 32(4)).
Champernowne, D. G. (1945). A note on J. von Neumann's article on 'A Model of Economic Equilibrium'. *Review of Economic Studies*, 13(1), 10–8.

Charnes, A., W. W. Cooper and E. Rhodes (1978). Measuring the efficiency of decision making units. *European Journal of Operations Research*, 5(2), 429–44.

Charnes, A., W. W. Cooper, and A. P. Schinnar (1976). A theorem on homogeneous
functions and extended Cobb-Douglas forms. *Proceedings of the National Academy
of Sciences* (USA), 73(10), 3747–48.

Charnes, A., W. W. Cooper, L. Seiford, and J. Stutz (1981). A multiplicative model
for efficiency analysis. *Research Report* CCS 416, Center for Cybernetic Studies,
University of Texas, Austin; published in *Socio-Economic Planning Sciences*, 16
(1982), 223–4.

_____ (1982). Invariant multiplicative efficiency and piecewise Cobb-Douglas
envelopments. *Research Report* CCS 441, Center for Cybernetic Studies, University of Texas, Austin; presented at the Conference on Current Issues in Productivity,
Cornell University, Ithaca NY, 30 November–2 December 1982.

Chase, A. E. (1960). Concepts and uses of price indices. Division of Prices and Cost
of Living, Bureau of Labour Statistics, US Department of Labor, Washington, DC.
Presented at the American Statistical Association Meeting, August 1960.

Cheyney, E. W. and A. A. Goldstein. (1959). Newton's method for convex programming and Tchebycheff approximation. *Numerical Mathematics*, 1, 253–68.

Chipman, John S. (1960). The foundations of utility. *Econometrica*, 28, 193–224.

_____ , L. Hurwicz, M. K. Richter, and H. Sonnenschein (eds) (1971). *Preferences,
Utility and Demand*. New York: Harcourt Brace Jovanovich.

Churchman, C. West. (1961a). Decision and value theory. In *Progress in Operations
Research* (2 volumes), edited by Russell L. Ackoff. New York: Wiley, Volume 1.

Clark, J. M. (1946). Realism and relevance in the theory of demand. *Journal of Political
Economy*, 54, 347–53.

Clarkson, G. P. E. (1963). *The Theory of Consumer Demand: A Critical Appraisal*.
Englewood Cliffs, NJ: Prentice-Hall.

Cody, M. L. (1974). Optimization in Ecology. *Science*, 183, 1156–64.

Coleman, J. S. (1966). The possibility of a social welfare function. *American Economic
Review*, 56, 1105–22.

_____ (1967). The possibility of a social welfare function: reply. *American Economic
Review*, 57, 1311–17.

_____ (1969). Beyond Pareto optimality. In *Philosophy, Science, and Method. Essays
in Honor of Ernest Nagel*, edited by Sidney Morgenbesser, Patrick Suppes and Mor-
ton White. New York: St Martin's Press.

Condorcet, M. (1785). *Essai sur l'application de l'analyse à la probatilité des decisions
rendues a la pluralité des voix*. Paris: l'Imprimerie Royal, 54ff.

Contini, Bruno. (1959). Inconsistency of preferences as a measure of psychological
distance. In *Measurement: Definitions and Theories*, edited by C. West Churchman
and Philburn Ratoosh. New York: John Wiley.

_____ (1966). A note on Arrow's postulates for a social welfare function. *Journal of
Political Economy*, 74, 278–80.

Crapo, Henry (1973). Class notes (mimeo). Department of Pure Mathematics, University of Waterloo.

Dantzig, G. (1963). *Linear Programming and its Extensions*. Princeton University Press.

_____ , B. Curtis Eaves, and U. G. Rothblum (1983). A decomposition and scaling inequality for line-sum-symmetric nonnegative matrices. *Technical Report SOL 83 – 21.* Department of Operations Research, Stanford University.

Datta, Bhabatosh (1953). The state of consumption theory. *Indian Economic Journal*, 1, 113–23.

Davis, J. M. (1958). The transitivity of preferences. *Behavioural Science.* 3, 26–33.

Deane, Phyllis (1978). *The Evolution of Economic Ideas.* Cambridge University Press.

Deaton, A. S. (1972). The estimation and testing of systems of demand equations: A note. *European Economic Review*, 3, 399–411.

_____ (1974). The analysis of consumer demand in the United Kingdom, 1900–1970. *Econometrica*, 42, 341–67.

_____ (1981) (ed). *Essays in Theory and Measurement of Demand: In Honour of Sir Richard Stone.* Cambridge and New York: Cambridge University Press.

_____ and J. Muellbauer. (1980). *Economics and Consumer Behaviour.* Cambridge University Press.

Debreu, G. (1959). *Theory of Value: An Axiomatric Analysis of Economic Equilibrium.* Cowles Foundation Monograph no. 17. New York: John Wiley.

De Finetti, Bruno (1937). Problemi de 'optimum'. *Giornale dell'Instituto italiano egli attuari*, 15, 48–67.

_____ (1952). Sulla preferibilita. *Giornale degli Economiste e Annali di Economia*, 11, 685–709.

Dell, Alice M., R.L. Weyl and G.L. Thompson (1971). Roots of matrix pencils. *Communications of the Association of Computing Machinery*, 14, 113–17.

Dewdney, A. K. (1985). Computer recreations—Yin and Yang: recursion and iteration, the Tower of Hanoi and the Chinese rings. *Scientific American.* 251(5) (November), 19–28.

Divine, T. F. (1943). The derivation of the Marshallian curve from the Paretian indifference curves. *American Economic Review*, 3, 125–9.

Dobb, M. H. (1969). *Welfare Economics and the Economics of Socialism.* Cambridge University Press.

Dodgson, C. L. 1876. *A Method of Taking Votes on More Than Two Issues.* Oxford: Clarendon Press.

Dorfman, Robert (1964). *The Price System.* Englewood Cliffs, NJ: Prentice Hall.

_____ , P. A. Samuelson and R. M. Solow. (1958). *Linear Programming and Economic Analysis.* New York: McGraw Hill.

Downs, Anthony. (1961). In defence of majority voting. *Journal of Political Economy*, 69, 192–9.

Drucker, Peter F. (1981). Toward the next economics. In Bell and Bristol (1981).

Dummett, Michael and Robin Farquharson (1961). Stability in voting. *Econometrica*, 29, 33–43.

Eaves, B. Curtis (1976). A finite algorithm for the linear exchange model. *Journal of Mathematical Economics*, 3, 197–203.

_____ (1984). Finite solution of pure markets with Cobb-Douglas utilities (mimeo). Department of Operations Research, Stanford University.

_____ , U. G. Rothblum and H. Schneider (1983). Line-sum-symmetric scalings of square nonnegative matrices. *Technical Report*, Department of Operations Research, Stanford University.

Edgeworth, F. Y. (1881). *Mathematical Psychics.* London: Routledge & Kegan Paul.

_____ (1896). A defense of index numbers. *Economic Journal*, 6, 132–42.

_____ (1925). *Papers Relating to Political Economy*. London: Macmillan.

Edmunds, Jack (1973). Minimum paths (private communication). Department of Combinatorics and Optimization, University of Waterloo.

Eggleston, H. G. (1963). *Convexity* (2nd edition). Cambridge University Press.

Eichhorn, W. (1972). *Functional Equations in Economics*. Applied Mathematics and Computation Series, no. 11. Reading, Mass.: Addison-Wesley.

_____ and J. Voeller (1976). *Theory of the Price Index: Fisher's Test Approach and Generalizations*. Berlin, Heidelburg and New York: Springer-Verlag.

Eilenberg, S. (1941). Ordered topological spaces. *American Journal of Mathematics*, 63, 39–45.

El-Hodiri, M. A. (1966). Constrained extrema of functions of a finite number of variables: Review and generalizations. *Research Paper* no. 141, Economics Department, Purdue University.

Ellman, M. (1966). Individual preferences and the market. *Economics of Planning*, 3, 240–50.

Ellsberg, Daniel (1954). Classic and current notions of 'measurable utility'. *Economic Journal*, 64, 528–56.

Elster, J. (1975). *Leibnitz et la formation de l'esprit capitaliste*. Paris: Aubier & Montaigne.

_____ (1978a). *Logic and Society: Contradictions and Possible Worlds*. New York: John Wiley.

_____ (1978b). The labor theory of value. *Marxist Perspectives*, 1, 70–101

_____ (1979). *Ulysses and the Sirens*. Cambridge University Press.

Fan, Ky (1956). On systems of linear inequalities. In Kuhn and Tucker (1956), 99–156.

Färe, R., S. Grosskopf and C. A. K. Lovell (1985). *The Measurement of Efficiency of Production*. Boston: Kluwer-Nijhoff.

Farkas, J. (1902). Über die Theorie der einfachen Ungleichungen. *Journal für die Reine Angewandte Mathematik*, 124, 1–24.

Farquharson, Robin (1969). *Theory of Voting*. Yale University Press.

Farrell, M. J. (1957). The measurement of productive efficiency. *Journal of the Royal Statistical Society*, A, 120(3), 253–81.

_____ (1959). The convexity assumption in the theory of competitive markets. *Journal of Political Economy*, 67, 377–91.

_____ and M. Fieldhouse. (1962). Estimating efficient production functions under increasing returns to scale. *Journal of the Royal Statistical Society*, A, 125(2), 252–67.

Fellner, W. (1967). Operational utility: The theoretical background and a measurement. In *Ten Economic Studies in the Tradition of Irving Fisher*. New York: John Wiley.

Fels, Eberhard (1962). Some relations between alternative rational choice criteria for consumer behaviour theories based on weak orderings. *Weltwirtschaftliches Archiv*, 89, 293–300.

Fenchel, W. (1949). On conjugate convex functions. *Canadian Journal of Mathematics*, 1, 73–7.

_____ (1953). *Convex cones, sets and functions*. Notes by D. W. Blackett of lectures delivered in the Department of Mathematics, Princeton University.

Ferejohn, J. A. and D. M. Grether (1977). Weak path Independence. *Journal of Economic Theory*, 14, 19–31.

Ferrar, W. L. (1951). *Finite Matrices*. Oxford: Clarendon Press.

Fiedler, M. and V. Ptak. (1967). Diagonally dominant matrices. *Czechoslovak Mathematical Journal*, 17, 420–33.

Fisher, Irving. 1892. Mathematical investigations in the theory of values and prices. *Transactions of Connecticut Academy of Arts and Sciences*, 9, 1–124.

_____ (1911). *The Purchasing Power of Money*. New York: Macmillan.

_____ (1918). Is 'utility' the most suitable term for the concept it is used to denote? *American Economic Review*, 8, 335–7.

_____ (1922). *The Making of Index Numbers*. Boston & New York: Houghton Mifflin (third edition 1927).

_____ (1923). Professsor Bowley on index numbers. *Economic Journal*, 33, 246–51.

_____ (1927). A statistical method for measuring marginal utility and testing the justice of a progressive income tax. In *Economic Essays, Contributed in Honor of John Bates Clark*, edited by J. H. Hollander. New York: Macmillan.

Fleetwood, William 1707. *Chronicon Preciosum: Or, An Account of English Money, the Price of Corn, and Other Commodities, for the Last 600 Years—in a Letter to a Student in the University of Oxford*. London: T. Osborne in Gray's-Inn (anonymous 1st edition; 2nd edition 1745, in Codrington Library).

Fleming, J. Marcus. (1952). A cardinal concept of welfare. *Quarterly Journal of Economics*, 66, 366–84.

_____ (1957). Cardinal welfare and individualistic ethics: a comment. *Journal of Political Economy*, 65, 355–7.

Ford, L. R. Jr and D. R. Fulkerson (1962). *Flows in Networks*. Princeton University Press.

Foster, W. T. (1922). Prefatory note. In Fisher (1922).

Frisch, R. (1932). *New Methods of Measuring Marginal Utility*. Tübingen: Verlag von J. C. B. Mohr.

_____ (1936). Annual survey of general economic theory: The problem of index numbers. *Econometrica*, 4(1), 1–39.

_____ (1959). A complete scheme for computing all direct and cross demand elasticities in a model with many sectors. *Econometrica*, 27, 177–96.

_____ (1960). *Maxima et minima, théorie et applications économiques*. Paris: Dunod. English translation Chicago: Rand McNally, 1966.

Frobenius, G. (1908). Über Matrizen aus positiven Elementen. *S.-B. Kgl. Preuss. Akad. Wiss.*, 471–6.

Gale, D. (1955). The law of supply and demand. *Mathematica Scandinavica*, 3, 155–69.

_____ (1956). The closed linear model of production. In Kuhn and Tucker (1956), 285–303.

_____ (1960a). A note on revealed preference. *Economica*, n.s. 27, 348–54.

_____ (1960b). *The Theory of Linear Economic Models*. New York: McGraw-Hill.

_____ (1967). Geometric duality theorem with economic applications. *Review of Economic Studies*, 34, 19–24.

Gantmacher, F. R. (1959). *The Theory of Matrices*, Vols. I and II. New York: Chelsea.

Geary, R. C. (1958). A note on the comparison of exchange rates and purchasing power between countries. *Journal of the Royal Statistical Society*, A, 121, 97–9.

Geiss, Charles (1969). Private communication. Department of Economics, University of North Carolina at Chapel Hill.

_____ (1971a). Computations of critical efficiencies and the extension [Afriat 1969f and

1971b] of Farrell's method in production analysis (mimeo). Department of Economics, University of North Carolina at Chapel Hill.

———— (1971b). Program descriptions and operations guide: A set of programs designed to furnish efficiency estimation of production functions using the method described in 'Efficiency Estimation of Production Functions' [Afriat 1971b] (mimeo). Department of Economics, University of North Carolina at Chapel Hill.

Georgescu-Roegen, N. (1950). The theory of choice and the constancy of economic laws. *Quarterly Journal of Economics*, 64, 125–38.

———— (1954a). Choice and revealed preference. *Southern Economic Journal*, 21, 119–30.

———— (1954b). Choice, expectations and measurability. *Quarterly Journal of Economics*, 68, 503–34.

———— (1966). *Analytical Economics: Issues and Problems*. Cambridge, Mass.: Harvard University Press.

———— (1971). *The Entropy Law and the Economic Process*. Cambridge, Mass.: Harvard University Press.

Gibbard, A. (1974). A Pareto-consistent libertarian claim. *Journal of Economic Theory*, 7, 388–410.

Goldman, A. J. and A. W. Tucker (1956). Polyhedral convex cones. In Kuhn and Tucker (1956).

Goldman, S. M. and H. Uzawa (1964). A note on separability in demand analysis. *Econometrica*, 32, 387–98.

Goodman, Leo A. and Harry Markowitz (1952). Social welfare functions based on individual rankings. *Americal Journal of Sociology*, 58, 257–62.

Gorman, W. M. (1953). Community preference fields. *Econometrica*, 21, 63–80.

———— (1955). The intransitivity of certain criteria used in welfare economics. *Oxford Economic Papers*, 7, 25–35.

———— (1957a). Convex indifference curves and diminishing marginal utility. *Journal of Political Economy*, 65, 40–50.

———— (1957b). Intertemporal choice and the slope of indifference maps. *Metroeconomica*, 9, 167–80.

———— (1957c). Some comments on Professor Hicks' revision of demand theory. *Metroeconomica*, 9, 167–80.

———— (1959a). Are social indifference curves convex? *Quarterly Journal of Economics*, 73, 485–96.

———— (1959b). Separable utility and aggregation. *Econometrica*, 27, 469–87.

———— (1961). On a class of preference fields. *Metroeconomica*, 13, 53–6.

———— (1967). Tastes, habits and choices. *International Economic Review*, 8, 218–22.

———— (1968). The structure of utility functions. *Review of Economic Studies*, 35(4), 367–90.

———— (1976). Tricks with utility functions. In *Essays in Economic Analysis*, edited by M. J. Artis and A. R. Nobay. Cambridge University Press.

Gould, F. J. (1967). Extensions of Lagrange multipliers in nonlinear programming. Center for Mathematical Studies in Business and Economics, *Report* no. 6721 (July), University of Chicago; published in *SIAM Journal of Applied Mathematics*, 17, 1969, 1280–97.

Graaff, J. de V. (1957). *Theoretical Welfare Economics*. Cambridge University Press.

Green, H. A. John (1957). Some logical relations in revealed preference theory. *Economica*, 24, 315–23.

Hahn, F. H. (1973). *On the Notion of Equilibrium in Economics*. Cambridge University Press.

Hallden, Soren. (1957). *On the Logic of Better*. Lund: C. W. K. Gleerkup.

_____ (1966). Preference logic and theory of choice. *Synthèse*, 16, 307–20.

Hamburger, M. J., G. L. Thompson and R. L. Weyl (1967). Computation of expansion rates for the generalized von Neumann model of an expanding economy. *Econometrica*, 35, 542–7.

_____ (1969). Computing results from the generalized von Neumann model and using them for planning. *Jahrbuch der Osteuropäischen Wirtschaft*, 1, 107–28.

Hancock, H. (1914). *Theory of Maxima and Minima*. New York: Dover Press (1960).

Hanoch, G. and M. Rothschild (1972). Testing the Assumptions of Production Theory. *Journal of Political Economy*, 256–75.

Hansson, Bengt. (1968a). Fundamental axioms for preference relations. *Synthèse*, 18, 423–42.

_____ (1968b). Choice structures and preference relations. *Synthèse*, 18, 443–58.

_____ (1969a). Group preferences. *Econometrica*, 37, 50–4.

_____ (1969b). Voting and group decision functions. *Synthèse*, 20, 526–37.

Harsanyi, J. (1976). Can the maximum principle serve as a basis for morality? *American Political Science Review*, 69, 594–606.

_____ (1977). *Rational Behaviour and Bargaining Equilibrium in Games and Social Situations*. Cambridge University Press.

Hicks, J. R. (1942). Consumers' surplus and index numbers. *Review of Economic Studies*, 9(2), 126–37.

_____ (1948). *Value and Capital* (2nd edition). Oxford: Clarendon Press.

_____ (1954). Robbins on Robertson on utility. *Economica*, 31, 154–7.

_____ (1956). *A Revision of Demand Theory*. Oxford: Clarendon Press.

_____ (1961). Prices and the turnpike—The story of a mare's nest. *Review of Economic Studies*, 28(1), 77–88.

_____ and R. G. D. Allen. (1934). A reconsideration of the theory of value, I, II. *Economica*, 1, 52–75, 196–219.

Histake, M. (1959). A reconsideration on the concept of utility. *Annals of Hitotsubashi Academy*, 10, 171–80.

Hotelling, H. (1932). Edgeworth's taxation paradox and the nature of demand and supply functions. *Journal of Political Economy*, 40, 577–616.

_____ (1935). Demand functions with limited budgets. *Econometrica*, 3, 66–78.

_____ (1938). The general welfare in relation to problems of taxation and railway and utility rates. *Econometrica*, 6, 242–69.

Houthakker, H. S. (1950). Revealed preference and the utility function. *Economica*, n.s. 17, 159–74.

_____ (1953). La forme des courbes d'Engel. *Cahiers du Seminarie d'Économetrie*, 2, 59–66.

_____ (1957). An international comparison of household expenditure patterns, commemorating the centenary of Engel's law. *Econometrica*, 25, 532–51.

_____ (1961). The present state of consumption theory. *Econometrica*, 29, 704–40.

_____ (1962). The econometrics of family budgets. *Journal of the Royal Statistical Society*, A, 115, Part 1, 1–21.

_____ (1963). Some problems in the international comparison of consumption patterns. In *L'Évaluation et le role des besoins de consommation dans les divers regimes economiques*. Paris: Centre National de la Recherche Scientifique, 89–102.

_____ and L. D. Taylor (1970). *Consumer Demand in the United States, 1929–1970* (2nd edition). Cambridge Mass.: Harvard University Press.

Hu, T. C. (1969). *Integer Programming and Network Flows*. Reading, Mass.: Addison Wesley.

International Labour Office (1932). A contribution to the study of international comparisons of costs of living. *Studies and Reports*, Series N, 17, Geneva.

Janis, I. (1972). *Victims of Group-Think*. Boston Mass.: Houghton Mifflin.

Jazairi, N. T. (1971). An empirical study of the conventional and statistical theories of index numbers. *Bulletin of the Oxford University Institute of Economics and Statistics*, 33, 181–95.

_____ (1972a). Fisher's Ideal Index reformulated. *International Statistical Review*, 40, 47–51.

_____ (1972b). Note on Fisher's Ideal Index. *Journal of the Royal Statistical Society*, C, 21, 89–92.

_____ (1979). The functional form of the relation between alternative real income comparisons. *Economic Journal*, 89, 127–30.

_____ (1983a). The present state of the theory and practice of index numbers. *Bulletin of the International Statistical Institute*, 50, 122–47.

_____ (1983b). Index numbers. *Encyclopedia of Statistical Sciences*, 4. Edited by Samuel Kotz and Norman L. Johnson. New York: John Wiley.

_____ (1984a). Marshall-Edgeworth-Bowley index. *Encyclopedia of Statistical Sciences*, 5. Edited by Samuel Kotz and Norman L. Johnson. New York: John Wiley.

_____ and Alan Abouchar (1984). Paasche-Laspeyres indexes. *Encyclopedia of Statistical Sciences*, 6. Edited by Samuel Kotz and Norman L. Johnson. New York: John Wiley.

_____ and Louis Lefeber (1984). Productivity measurement. *Encyclopedia of Statistical Sciences*, 6. Edited by Samuel Kotz and Norman L. Johnson, New York: John Wiley.

_____ and Rasesh Thakker (1984). Purchasing power parity. *Encyclopedia of Statistical Sciences*, 6. Edited by Samuel Kotz and Norman L. Johnson, New York: John Wiley.

Jevons, W. Stanley. (1871). *The Theory of Political Economy (5th edition). New York: Kelley and Millman (1957).*

Johnson, Harry G. (1975). *On Economics and Society*. Chicago & London: University of Chicago Press.

Kakutani, S. (1941). A generalization of Brouwer' fixed point theorem. *Duke Mathematical Journal*, 8, 457–9.

Kaldor, Nicholas (1939). Welfare propositions of economics and interpersonal comparisons of utility. *Economic Journal* 49, 549–52.

Karlin, S. (1959). *Mathematical Methods and Theory in Games, Programming and Economics*. Reading, Mass.: Addison-Wesley.

Kauder, Emil (1953a). Genesis of the maginal utility theory: From Aristotle to the end of the eighteenth century. *Economic Journal*, 63, 638–50,

———— (1953b). The retarded acceptance of the maginal utility theory. *Quarterly Journal of Economics*, 67, 564–75.

———— (1965). *A History of Marginal Utility Theory*. Princeton University Press.

Keeney, R. L. and H. Raiffa. (1976). *Decisions with Multiple Objectives*. New York: John Wiley.

Kelley, J. E. (1960). The cutting plane method for solving convex programs. *SIAM Journal of Applied Mathematics*, 8, 703–12.

Kemeny, J. G. (1956). Game theoretic solution of an economic problem. *Progress Report* No. 2, The Dartmouth Mathematics Project.

Kemeny, John G., Hazleton Mirkil, J. Laurie Snell and G. L. Thompson. (1959). *Finite Mathematical Structures*. Englewood Cliffs, NJ: Prentice-Hall.

————, O. Morgenstern and G. L. Thompson. (1956). A generalization of the von Neumann model of an expanding economy. *Econometrica*, 24, 115–35.

————, J. Laurie Snell and G. L. Thompson. (1957). *Finite Mathematics*. Englewood Cliffs NJ: Prentice Hall.

————, and J. Laurie Snell. (1962). *Mathematical Models in the Social Sciences*. New York, Toronto and London: Blaisdell.

Kendall, M. G. (1969). The early history of index numbers. *Review of the International Statistical Institute*, 37(1), 1–12.

Kenen, P. B. (1957). On the geometry of welfare economics. *Quarterly Journal of Economics*, 71, 426–47.

Kennedy, Charles. (1950). The common sense of indifference curves. *Oxford Economic Papers*, 2, 123–31.

Keynes, J. M. (1930). *A Treatise on Money*. Vol. I, *The Pure Theory of Money*. New York: Harcourt, Brace.

Klein, L. R. and H. Rubin (1947). A constant utility index of the cost of living. *Review of Economic Studies*, 15(38), 84–7.

Knaster, B., K. Kuratowski and S. Mazurkiewiez (1931). Ein Beweis des Fixpunktsatzes für n-dimensionale Simplexe. *Fundamenta Mathematica* 14, 132–7.

Knight, Frank H. (1935). Marginal utility economics. In *Encyclopedia of the Social Sciences*, 5. New York and London: Macmillan.

———— (1944). Realism and relevance in the theory of demand. *Journal of Political Economy*, 52, 289–318.

Könus, A. A. (1924). The problem of the true index of the cost of living. *Economic Bulletin of the Institute of Economic Conjuncture* (Moscow), 9–10, 36–7 and 64–71.

Koopmans, T. C. (ed) (1951a). *Activity Analysis of Production and Allocation*. Cowles Commission Monograph no. 13. New York: John Wiley.

———— (1951b). Analysis of production as an efficient combination of activities. In Koopmans (1951a), 33–97.

———— (1957). *Three Essays on the State of Economic Science*. New York: McGraw-Hill.

———— (1961). Convexity assumptions, allocative efficiency, and competitive equilibrium. *Journal of Political Economy*, 69, 478–9.

———— and A. F. Bausch (1959). Selected topics in economics involving mathematical reasoning. *SIAM Review*, 1(2).

Kuhn, H. W. (1956a). A note on the law of supply and demand. *Mathematica Scandinavica*, 4, 143–6.

———— (1956b). On a theorem of Wald. In Kuhn and Tucker (1956), 265–74.

_____ and A. W. Tucker (1950). Nonlinear programming. In Neyman (1950), 481–92.

_____ and A. W. Tucker (eds) (1956). *Linear Inequalities and Related Systems*. Annals of Mathematics Studies no. 38. Princeton University Press.

_____ and A. W. Tucker (1958). John von Neumann's work in the Theory of Games and Mathematical Economics. *Bulletin of the American Mathematical Society*, 64, 100–22.

Kusumoto, Sho-Ichiro (1977). Global characterization of the weak Le Chatelier-Samuelson principles and in application to economic behaviour, preferences, and utility-embedding theorems. *Econometrica*, 45, 1925–55.

Kuttner, Robert (1985). The poverty of economics: A report on a discipline riven with epistemological doubt on the one hand and rigid formalism on the other. *Atlantic Monthly* (February), 74–84.

Lagrange, J. L. (1762). Essai sur une nouvelle mthode pour determiner les maxima et minima des formules integrales indefinies. *Miscellanea Taurinensia*, 2, 173–95 (also *Théorie des fonctions analytiques*, 1797).

Lancaseter, Peter (1969). *Theory of Matrices*. Academic Press.

Lange, O. (1934). The determinateness of the utility function. *Review of Economic Studies*, 1, 218–24.

_____ (1942). The foundations of welfare economics. *Econometrica*, 10, 215–28.

Laspeyres, E. (1871). Die Berechnung einer mittleran Waarenpreissteigerung. *Jahrbücher für nationalökonomie und Statistik*, 16, 296–314.

Lee, Lung-Fei (1973). The theorems of Debreu and Peleg for ordered topological spaces. *Econometrica*, 40, 1151–3.

Leontief, W. W. (1936). Composite commodities and the problem of index numbers. *Econometrica*, 4(1), 39–59.

_____ (1951). *The Structure of American Economy: 1919–1939* (2nd edition). New York: Oxford University Press.

_____ (1953). *Studies in the Structure of the American Economy*. New York: Oxford University Press.

_____ (1957). Introduction to a theory of the internal structure of functional relationships. *Econometrica*, 15, 361–73.

_____ (1966). *Input-Output Economics*. New York: Oxford University Press.

Lerner, A. P. (1935). A note on the theory of price index numbers. *Review of Economic Studies*, 50–6.

_____ (1962). The analysis of demand. *American Economic Review*, 52, 783–97.

Liebhafsky, H. H. (1961). Marshall and Slutsky on the theory of demand. *Canadian Journal of Economics and Political Science*, 27, 176–91.

Little, I. M. D. (1949a). A reformulation of the theory of consumer's behaviour. *Oxford Economic Papers*, 1, 90–9.

_____ (1949b). The foundations of welfare economics. *Oxford Economic Papers*, 1, 227–46.

_____ (1950). Recent developments in welfare economics. *Zeitschrift für Ökonometrie*, 1, 47–62.

_____ (1952). Social choice and individual values. *Journal of Political Economy*, 60, 422–32.

_____ (1957). *A Critique of Welfare Economics* (2nd edition). Oxford University Press.

Lloyd, W. F. (1833). A lecture on the notion of value as distinguishable not only from utility, but also from value in exchange. Oxford.

_____ (1837). *Lecture on population, value, poor-laws, and rent.* New York: Kelley (1968).

Lorch, E. R. (1951). Differentiable inequalities and the theory of convex bodies. *Transactions of the American Mathematical Society*, 71(2), 243–66.

Los, J. (1971). A simple proof of the existence of equilibria in von Neumann models. *Bulletin de l'Academie Polonaise des Sciences.* Ser. Math. October.

_____ (1972). Equilibria in a generalized von Neumann model. Symposium on Mathematical Methods in Economics, Warsaw, February–July 1972.

Machlup, Fritz. (1957). Professor Hicks' revision of demand theory. *American Economic Review*, 47, 119–35.

_____ (1967). *Essays in Economic Semantics.* New York: W. W. Norton.

Majumdar, Tapas (1958). *The Measurement of Utility.* London: Macmillan.

Malinvaud, E. (1972). *Lectures on Microeconomic Theory.* Amsterdam and London: North-Holland Publishing Company.

Malthus, T. R. (1823). *The Measure of Value Stated and Illustrated with an Application of it to the Alteration in the Value of English Currency since 1790.*

_____ (1827a). *Definitions in Political Economy.* London.

_____ (1827b). *On the Meaning which is Most Usually and Most Correctly Attached to the Term Value of Commodities.*

Mann, H. B. (1943). Quadratic forms with linear constraints. *American Mathematical Monthly*, 50, 430–3.

Marris, R. L. (1957). Professor Hicks' index number theorem. *Review of Economic Studies*, 25(66), 25–40.

Marshall, Alfred (1876). On Mill's theory of value. *Fortnightly Review*, 591–602.

Matsumoto, Yasumi (1982). *Choice Functions: Preferences, Consistency and Neutrality.* Thesis submitted for the degree of Doctor of Philosophy in the University of Oxford.

May, Kenneth O. (1954). Intransitivity, utility, and aggregation in preference patterns. *Econometrica*, 22, 1–13.

McKenzie, Lionel W. (1954). On Equilibrium in Graham's Model of World Trade and Other Competitive Systems. *Econometrica*, 22, 147–61.

_____ (1957). An elementary analysis of the Leontief system. *Econometrica*, 25, 456–62.

_____ (1959). On the existence of general equilibrium for a competitive market. *Econometrica*, 27, 54–71.

_____ (1960). Stability of equilibrium and the value of positive excess demand. *Econometrica*, 28, 606–17.

_____ (1967). Maximal paths in the von Neumann model. Chapter 2 in *Activity Analysis in the Theory of Growth and Planning*, edited by M. O. L. Bacharach and E. Malinvaud. London.

_____ (1971). Capital accumulation optimal in the final state. *Zeitschrift für Nationalökonomie*, Suppl. 1, 107–20.

Meeusen, Wim and Julien van den Broeck (1977). Efficiency estimation from Cobb-Douglas production functions with composed error. *International Economic Review*, 18(2), 435–44.

Minas, J. Sayer and Russell I. Ackoff (1964). Individual and collective value judgments. In *Human Judgments and Optimality*, edited by Maynad W. Shelly II and Glenn L. Bryan. New York: John Wiley.

Mises, Ludvig von (1949). *Human Action*. New Haven, Conn.:Yale University Press.

Mishan, E. J. (1957). An investigation into some alleged contradictions in welfare economics. *Economic Journal*, 68, 445–54.

_____ (1961). Theories of consumer's behaviour: a cynical view. *Economica*, 28, 1–11.

Moore, James C. (1973). Revealed preference and observed demand behaviour (mimeo). Department of Economics, Purdue University.

Morgenstern, Oskar (1931a). Die drei Grundtypen der Theorie des subjektiven Wertes. *Schriften des Vereins für Sozialpolitik* 183, 1–43.

_____ (1931b). Mathematical Economics. *Encyclopedia of the Social Sciences*, 5. New York: Macmillan.

_____ (1934). Das Zeitmoment in der Wertlehre. *Zeitschrift für Nationalökonomie*, 5, 433–58.

_____ (1941). Professor Hicks on value and capital. *Journal of Political Economy*, 51, 361–93.

_____ (1948). Demand theory reconsidered. *Quarterly Journal of Economics*, 2, 165–201.

_____ (1954) (editor). *Economic Activity Analysis*. New York: Wiley.

_____ (1963). *On the Accuracy of Economic Observations*. Princeton University Press.

_____ (1964). Pareto optimum and economic organization. *Systeme und Methoden in den Wirtschafts und Sozialwissenschaften, Festschrift für Erwin von Beckerath* Tübingen: J. C. B. Mohr.

_____ (1968). John von Neumann. *International Encyclopedia of the Social Sciences*, 16. New York: Macmillan.

_____ (1972). Thirteen critical points in contemporary economic theory: An interpretation. *The Journal of Economic Literature*, 10, 1163–89.

_____ (1976). Some reflections on utility. In *Selected Economic Writings of Oskar Morgenstern*, edited by Andrew Schotter, New York University Press.

_____ and G. L. Thompson (1976). *Mathematical Theory of Expanding and Contracting Economies*. Lexington Mass.: D. H. Heath.

Morishima, M. (1960). Economic expansion and the interest rate in generalized von Neumann models. *Econometrica*, 28, 362–3.

_____ (1964). *Equilibrium, Stability and Growth*. Oxford: Clarendon Press.

_____ and F. Seton (1961). Aggregation in Leontief matrices and the labour theory of value. *Econometrica*, 29, 203–20.

Morowitz, Harold (1981). Review of Entropy, a New World View by Jeremy Rivkin and Ted Howard. *Discover*, January, 83–5.

Mudgett, B. D. (1951). *Index Numbers*. New York: John Wiley.

Mueller, Dennis C. (1967). The possibility of a social welfare function: comment. *American Economic Review*, 57, 1303–11.

_____ (1979). *Public Choice*. Cambridge University Press.

Nataf, André (1964). *Théorie des choix et fonctions de demande*. Monograph du Centre d'Économetrie, Paris: Centre National de la Recherche Scientifique.

Negishi, Takashi. (1962). The stability of a competitive economy: A survey article. *Econometrica*, 30, 635–69.

Newman, Peter K. (1961a). Basic assumptions in preference theory. *Economic Journal*, 71, 535–8.

―― (1961b). Representation problems for preference orderings. *Journal of Economic Behaviour*, 1, 149–69.

―― (1965). *The Theory of Exchange*. Englewood Cliffs, NJ: Prentice Hall.

Neyman, J. (ed.) (1950). *Proceedings of the Second Berkeley Symposium on Mathematical Statistics and Probability*. Berkeley: California University Press.

Nicholson, Michael (1965). Conditions for the 'voting paradox' in committee decisions. *Metroeconomica*, 17, 29–44.

Nikaido, H. (1956). On the classical multilateral exchange problem. *Metroeconomica*, 8, 135–45.

―― (1957). A supplementary note to 'On the classical multilateral exchange problem'. *Metroeconomica*, 9, 209–10.

Olsen, M. (1965). *The Logic of Collective Action*. Harvard University Press.

Paasche, H. (1874). Über die Priesentwickelung der letzen Jahre, nach den Hamburger Börsennotierungen. *Jahrbücher für Nationalökonimie und Statistik*, 23, 168–78.

Page, Alfred N. (1968). *Utility Theory: A Book of Readings*. New York: John Wiley.

Pareto, V. (1892–1893). Considerazioni sui principii fondamentali dell' economia politica pura. *Giornale degli Economisti*, 2(4), 389–420, 486–512; (5), 119–57; (6), 1–37; (7), 279–321.

―― (1894). Il massimo di utilità dato dalla libera concorrenza. *Giornale degli Economisti*, 2(9), 48–66.

―― (1913). Il massimo di utilità per una colletività in Sociologia. *Giornale degli Economisti*, 46, 337–41.

Pasinetti, L. L. (1960). A mathematical formulation of the Ricardian system. *Review of Economic Studies*, 27(1), 78–98.

Peleg, Bezalel (1970). Utility functions for partially ordered topological spaces. *Econometrica*, 38, 93–6.

Persons, C. E. (1913). Marginal utility and marginal disutility as ultimate standards of value. *Quarterly Journal of Economics*, 27, 545–78.

Preston, Maurice H. (1967). Changing utility functions. In *Essays in Mathematical Economics in Honor of Oskar Morgenstern*, edited by Martin Shubik. Princeton University Press.

Pfouts, Ralph W. (ed.) (1960). *Essays in Economics and Econometrics: A Volume in Honor of Harold Hotelling*. Chapel Hill, NC: University of North Carolina Press.

Pigou, A. C. (1903). Some remarks on utility. *Economic Journal*, 13, 58–68.

Plott, C. R. (1973). Path independence, rationality and social choice. *Econometrica*, 41, 1075–91.

Quesnay, François (1758). *Tableau économique*, Versailles.

Rader, T. Trout (1963). The existence of a utility function to represent preferences. *Review of Economic Studies*, 30, 229–32.

Rajoaja, V. (1958). A study in the theory of demand functions and price indexes. *Commentationes physico-mathematicae*, Societas Scientiarum Fennica (Finska vetenskaps-societen, Helsingfors), 21, 1–96.

Ramsey, F. R. (1928). A mathematical theory of savings. *Economic Journal*, 38(152), 543–59.

Reder, M. W. (1961). Production of Commodities by Means of Commodities: A review article. *American Economic Review*, 51, 688–95.

Richmond, J. (1974). Estimating the efficiency of production. *International Economic Review*, 15, 515–21.

Robinson, Joan and John Eatwell (1973). *An Introduction to Modern Economics*. Maidenhead, Berks.: McGraw-Hill.

Rockafellar, R. T. (1967a). Duality in non-linear programming. Presented at the Symposium on Recent Advances in Mathematical Programming, Princeton University.

_____ (1967b). Monotone processes of convex and concave type. *Memoirs of the American Mathematical Society* No. 77.

_____ (1967c). A monotone convex analog of linear algebra. *Proceedings of the Colloquium on Convexity, Copenhagen, 1965*. Kobenhavns Universitets Matematiske Institut, 1967.

_____ (1970). *Convex Analysis*. Princeton University Press.

Rose, H. (1958). Consistency of preference: The two-commodity case. *Review of Economic Studies*, 25, 124–5.

Roy, R. (1947). La distribution du revenu entre les divers biens. *Econometrica*, 15, 205–25.

Rubin, H. (1967). Private communication. Department of Mathematics, Purdue University.

Ruggles, R. (1967). Price indices and international price comparisons. In *Ten Economic Studies in the Tradition of Irving Fisher*. New York: John Wiley.

Samuelson, P. A. (1938). Note on the pure theory of consumer's behaviour. *Economica*, n.s. 5, 67–71.

_____ (1938). Note on the pure theory of consumer's behaviour: An addendum. *Economica*, n.s. 5, 353–4.

_____ (1947). *Foundations of Economic Analysis*. Cambridge, Mass.: Harvard University Press.

_____ (1948). Consumption theory in terms of revealed preference. *Economica*, n.s. 15, 243–53.

_____ (1950a). Evaluation of real national income. *Oxford Economic Papers*, n.s. 2(1), 1–29.

_____ (1950b). The problem of integrability in utility theory. *Economica*, 17(68), 355–85.

_____ (1960). Structure of a minimum equilibrium system. In Pfouts (1960), 1–33.

_____ (1966). *The Collected Scientific Papers of Paul A. Samuelson*, edited by J. E. Stiglitz, 2 Vols. Cambridge, Mass.: MIT Press.

_____ (1970). Maximum principles in analytical economics. Lecture delivered in Stockholm, Sweden, 11 December 1970; included in *Les Prix Nobel en 1970*, Amsterdam and New York: Elsevier; reprinted in *Science*, 10 September 1971, and *American Economic Review*, 1972, 249–62.

_____ (1971). Understanding the Marxian notion of exploitation: A summary of the transformation problem between Marxian values and competitive price. *Journal of Economic Literature*, 9, 399–431.

_____ and S. Swamy (1974). Invariant economic index numbers and canonical duality: Survey and synthesis. *American Economic Review*, 64, 566–93.

Scarf, Herbert (1973). *The Computation of Economic Equilibria*. New Haven, Conn.: Yale University Press.

Schefold, Bertram (1978). On counting equations. *Zeitschrift für Nationalökonomie*, 3–4, 250–74.

_____ (1979). Von Neumann and Sraffa, mathematical equivalence and conceptual difference. Institut für Merkt und Plan, University of Frankfurt.

Schmidt, Christian (1974). J. von Neumann et P. Sraffa: Deux contributions differentes à la critique de l'analyse traditionelle des prix et de la production. *Revue d'Économie Politique*, 6, 872–90.

Schultz, H. (1939). A misunderstanding in index number theory: The true Könus condition on cost of living index numbers and its limitations. *Econometrica*, 7, 1–9.

Schumpeter, J. A. (1954). *History of Economic Analysis*. New York: Oxford University Press.

Schwartz, Thomas. (1970). On the possibility of rational policy evaluations. *Theory and Decision*, 1, 89–106.

_____ (1972). Rationality and the Myth of the Maximum. *Noûs*, 6, 97–117.

_____ (1972b). *Freedom and Authority*. Belmont, Mass.: Dickinson.

Sen, Amartya K. (1970a). *Collective Choice and Social Welfare*. San Francisco: Holden Day.

_____ (1970b). The impossibility of a Paretian liberal. *Journal of Political Economy*, 78, 152–7.

_____ (1971). Choice functions and revealed preference. *Review of Economic Studies*, 38, 307–17.

_____ (1974). Choice, orderings and morality. In *Practical Reason*, edited by S. Korner. Oxford: Basil Blackwell.

_____ (1977). Rational fools: A critique of the behavioural foundations of economic theory. *Philosophy and Public Affairs*, 6, 317–44.

_____ (1979a). The welfare basis of real income comparisons: A survey. *Journal of Economic Literature*, 17, 1–45.

_____ (1979b). Personal utilities and public judgements: or What's wrong with welfare economics. *Economic Journal*, 89, 537–59.

_____ (1982). *Choice, Welfare and Measurement*. Cambridge, Mass.: MIT Press.

_____ and Bernard Williams (1982). *Utilitarianism and Beyond*. Cambridge University Press.

Shephard, R. W. (1953). *Cost and Production Functions*. Princeton University Press.

Shore, M. L. (1980). Shortest paths. *Creative Computing*, 6(11), 108–113.

Simon, H. (1954). A behavioral theory of rational choice. *Quarterly Journal of Economics*, 69, 99–118.

Slater, M. (1950). Lagrange multipliers revisited: A contribution to non-linear programming. *Cowles Commission Discussion Paper*, Math 403 (November).

Slutsky, E. E. (1915). Sulla teoria del bilancio del consumatore. *Giornale degli Economisti*, 51, 1–26. Translated by O. Ragusa: On the theory of the budget of the consumer. In G. J. Stigler and K. E. Boulding (eds), *Readings in Price Theory*. Chicago: Richard D. Irwin, 1952. 27–56.

Sraffa, Piero (1960). *Production of Commodities by Means of Commodities: Prelude to a Critique of Economic Theory.* Cambridge University Press.

Staehle, H. (1935). A development of the economic theory of price index numbers. *Review of Economic Studies*, 2, 163–88.

―――― (1950). A general method for the comparison of the price of living. *Review of Economic Papers*, New Series, 2(1), 1–29.

Stiemke, E. (1915). Über positive Lösungen homogener linearer Gleichungen. *Mathematische Annalen*, 76, 340–2.

Stigler, George J. (1950). The development of utility theory. *Journal of Political Economy*, 58, 307–27, 373–96; reprinted in Page (1968), 55–119.

―――― (1966). *The Theory of Price* (3rd edition). New York: Macmillan.

Stone, J. R. N. (1951). *The Role of Measurement in Economics.* Cambridge University Press.

―――― (1954). Linear expenditure systems and demand analysis: An application to the pattern of British demand. *Economic Journal*, 64, 511–27.

―――― (1966). Assisted by D. A. Rowe, W. J. Corlett, R. Hurstfield, and M. Potter. *The Measurement of Consumers' Expenditure and Behaviour in the United Kingdom, 1920–1938.* Cambridge University Press.

Strotz, Robert H. (1957). The empirical implications of a utility tree. *Econometrica*, 25, 269–80.

Stuval, G. (1957). A new index number formula. *Econometrica*, 26(1), 123–31.

Suzumura, Kotaro. (1974). General possibility theorems for path-independent social choice. *Discussion Paper* no. 077, Kyoto Institute of Economic Research.

―――― (1977). Houthakker's axiom in the theory of rational choice. *Journal of Economic Theory*, 14(2), 284–90.

Szpilrajn, E. (1930). Sur l'extension de l'ordre partiel. *Fundamenta Mathematica*, 16, 386–9.

Theil, H. (1975–6). *Theory and Measurement of Consumer Demand*, 2 volumes. Amsterdam: North-Holland Publishing Co.

Thompson, G. L. (1956). On the solutions of a game-theoretic problem. In Kuhn and Tucker (1956), 275–84.

―――― (1974). Computing the natural factors of a closed expanding economy model. *Zeitschrift für Nationalökonomie*, 34, 57–68.

―――― (1975a). Extensions of the Perron-Frobenius theorem to generalized eigensystems. *Working Paper*, Carnegie-Mellon University.

―――― (1975b). Solutions of von Neumann-Leontief expanding economy models and a generalization of the Perron-Frobenius theorem. *Working Paper*, Carnegie-Mellon University.

―――― and R.L. Weyl (1969). Further relations between game theory and eigensystems. *SIAM Review*, 11, 597–660.

―――― (1970). Reducing the rank of $(A - \lambda B)$. *Proc. American Math. Soc.*, 26, 381–94.

―――― (1971). Von Neumann model solutions are generalized eigensystems. In *Contributions to the von Neumann Growth Model*, edited by G. Bruckmann and W. Weber. *Zeitschrift für Nationalökonomie*, Suppl. 1, 139–44.

―――― (1972). The roots of matrix pencils $(A - \lambda B)$: existence, calculations, and relations to game theory. *Linear Algebra and its Applications*, 5, 207–26.

Tompkins, C. B. (1964). Sperner's Lemma and some extensions. In E. F. Beckenbach (ed), *Applied Combinatorial Mathematics*. New York: John Wiley, 416–27.

Tucker, A. W. (1950). Dual systems of homogeneous linear relations. In Kuhn and Tucker (1950), 3–18.

Tullock, Gordon (1967). The general irrelevance of the general impossibility theorem. *Quarterly Journal of Economics*, 81, 256–70.

Ulmer, M. J. (1949). *The Economic Theory of Cost of Living Index Numbers*. New York: Columbia University Press.

Uzawa, H. (1959). Preference and rational choice in the theory of consumption. In Arrow, Karlin, and Suppes (1959), 129–48.

Varian, Hal (1981). Non-parametric methods in demand analysis. *Economic Letters*, 9, 23–9.

_____ (1982). The non-parametric approach to demand analysis. *Econometrica*, 50(4), 945–73.

_____ (1984). The non-parametric approach to production analysis. *Econometrica*, 52(3), 579–98.

Viner, J. (1925). The utility concept in value theory and its critics. *Journal of Political Economy*, 33, 369–87 and 638–59.

Volterra, V. (1906). L'economia matematica. Review of *Manuale di Economia Politica* by V. Pareto. *Giornale degli Economisti*, 32, 296–301.

Von Neumann, J. (1945). A model of general economic equilibrium. *Review of Economic Studies*, 13, 1 – 9. Translation by O. Morgenstern of the original: Über ein ökonomisches gleischungssystem und eine Verallgemeinerung des Brouwerschen Fixpunktsatzes. In *Ergebenisse eines Mathematischen Seminars*, edited by K. Menger, Vienna, 1938.

_____ and O. Morgenstern. (1953). *Theory of Games and Economic Behaviour* (3rd edition). Princeton University Press.

Von Wright, G. H. (1963). *The Logic of Preference*. Edinburgh University Press.

Wald, A. (1936). Über einige Gleichungssysteme der mathematischen ökonomie. *Zeitschrift für Nationalökonomie*, 7, 637–70. Translation published in *Econometrica*, 19 (1951), 368–403.

_____ (1939). A new formula for the index of the cost of living. *Econometrica*, 7(4), 319–35.

_____ (1940). The approximate determination of indifference surfaces by means of Engel curves. *Econometrica*, 8, 144–75.

_____ (1952). On a relation between changes in demand and price changes. *Econometrica*, 20, 304–5.

Walsh, C. M. (1901). *The Measurement of General Exchange-Value*. New York: Macmillan.

Walters, A. A. (1963). Production and cost functions: An econometric survey. *Econometrica*, 31, 1–66.

Weyl, R.L. (1964). An algorithm for the von Neumann economy. *Zeitschrift für Nationalökonomie*, 24, 371–84.

_____ (1968). Game theory and eigensystems. *SIAM Review*, 10, 360–7.

_____ (1970). Solutions to the decomposable von Neumann model. *Econometrica*, 38, 278–82.

Wiener, P. P. (1973). *The Roots of Scientific Thought*. New York: Basic Books.

Williams, A. C. (1963). Marginal values in linear programming. *SIAM Journal on Applied Mathematics*, 11, 82–94.

———— (1974). (Review of Afriat, 1969b.) *Mathematical Reviews*, 2267.

Wold, H. O. A. (1943–4). A synthesis of pure demand analysis, I-III. *Skandinavisk Aktuarietidskrift*, 26(1943), 85–118, 221–263; 27(1944), 69–120.

Yen, J. Y. (1975). *Shortest Path Network Problems*. Meisenheim am Glan: Verlag Anton Hain.

Yokoyama, T. (1953). A logical foundation of the theory of consumer's demand. *Osaka Economic Papers*, 2, 71–9.

Young, H. Peyton. (1975). Social choice and scoring functions. *SIAM Journal on Applied Mathematics*, 28(4), 824–38.

Index